AA

CAMPING AND CARAVANNING IN BRITAIN

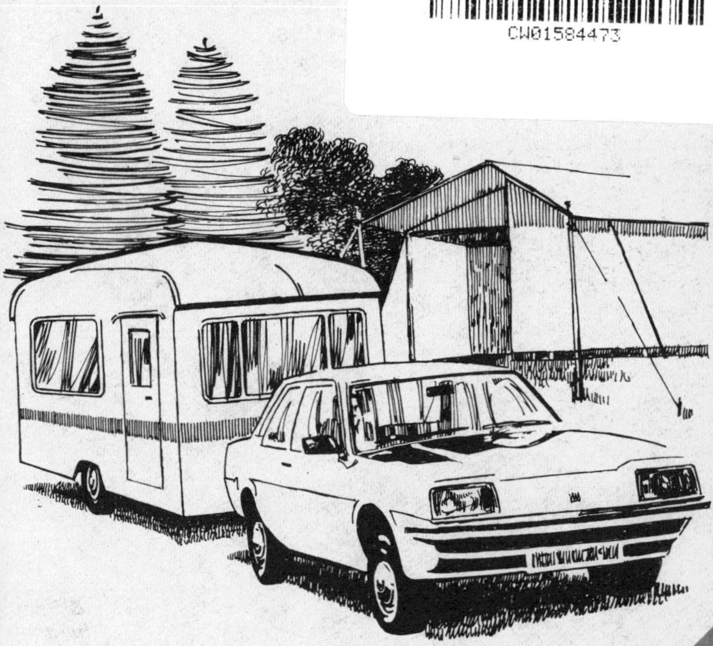

Editor: Joan Fensome
Designer: Turnergraphic
Gazetteer compiled by
the Publications Research Unit
Maps by Cartographic Department
Advertising: Peter Whitworth.
Tel Basingstoke 20123

WARNING

VAT: The majority of prices quoted include VAT at the rate in operation prior to the Budget of 12 June 1979 and are liable to adjustment

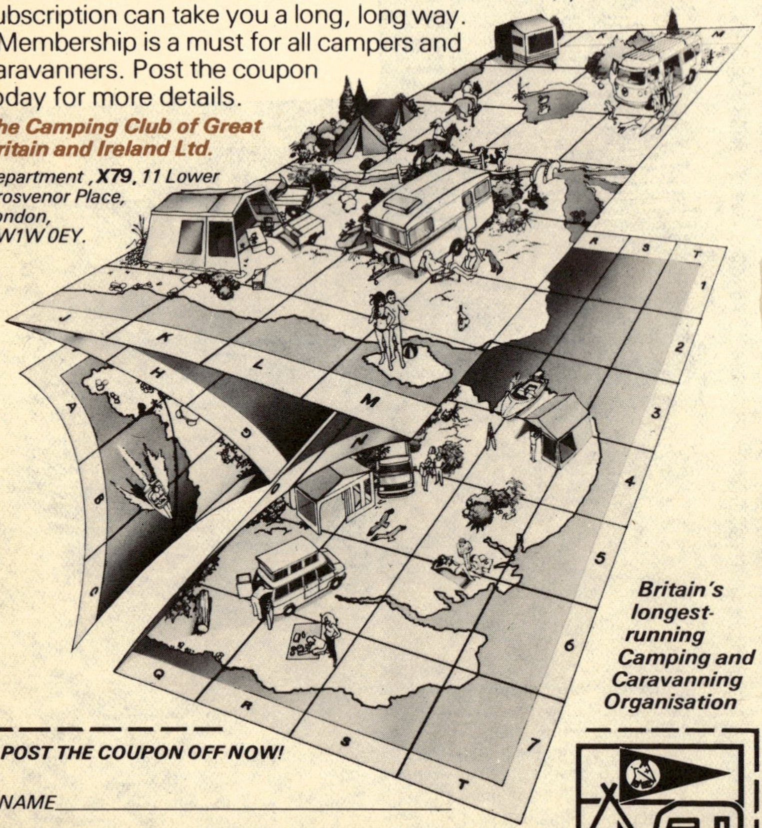

Contents

Produced by the Publications Division of the Automobile Association, Fanum House, Basingstoke, Hampshire RG21 2EA

Photographic sources: John Disley, AA photo library
Town plans in this book are based on the Ordnance Survey Map with the sanction of the Controller, HMSO

Printed by Purnell & Sons Ltd, Paulton
Photo-typeset by Petty & Son Ltd, Leeds
Colour printing by Camgate Litho Ltd., London

ISBN 0 86145 007 8

Abbreviations and symbols

ABBREVIATIONS AND SYMBOLS

acres	total area available for *touring* pitches
all year	site open all year
C	century
cdp	chemical closet disposal point
central hot water	hot water from a central source (*ie* geyser installation)
CTV	colour television
dry	facilities for drying clothes
E	east
Etr	Easter
fr	from
hc	hot and cold water
hrs	hours
iron	iron(s) and ironing board(s)
ltr	long term rates
m	mile
mdnt	midnight
N	north
nc	no children (with age limit)
OS	Ordnance Survey
pub	public house with garden or facilities for children
rs	restricted service
S	south
signposted	officially prescribed sign to site
spin	spin dryer
stables	horse-riding stables
static	static/residential pitches
TV	black and white television
W	west
warden	warden in attendance on site
wc	toilet
wash	washing machine
1 ❷ ⚠	AA qualitative assessment symbol (see page 75)
▶	AA pennant classification (see pages 75 & 80)
☎	public telephone available
☎	site telephone number
[caravan]	touring caravans
[motor caravan]	motor caravans
▲	tents
Ⓐ	separate tent enclosure
[hook-up]	electrical hook-up
[bath]	bath(s)
[shower]	shower(s)
⊙	electric razor point(s)
[shop]	shop on site or within 200yd
mobile [shop]	mobile shop calls at the site at least 5 days a week
[indoor pool]	indoor swimming pool
[outdoor pool]	outdoor swimming pool
[tennis]	tennis court
[no dogs]	no dogs
[tap]	drinking water stand-pipes
⊞	first aid facilities
⊖	amenities within three miles of site
[fish]	fishing
[boat]	boats for hire
[golf]	golf course
()	chargeable facilities

ABREVIATIONS ET SYMBOLES

acres	surface totale disponible pour camping *touristique*
all year	emplacement ouvert toute l'année
C	siècle
cdp	lieu d'évacuation pour W-C chimiques
central hot water	eau chaude d'une source centrale
CTV	TV en couleurs
dry	facilités de séchage de linge
E	Est
Etr	Pâques
fr	à partir de
hc	eau chaude et froide
hrs	heures
iron	fer(s) et planche(s) à repasser
ltr	tarif pour séjours prolongés
m	mille
mdnt	minuit
N	Nord
nc	pas d'enfants (avec limite d'âge)
OS	Etat-Major
pub	Public-house avec jardin ou facilités pour enfants
rs	service limité
S	Sud
signposted	indicateur officiellement recommandé vers le site
spin	essoreuse
stables	écuries pour l'équitation
static	emplacements stationnaires/ d'habitation
TV	TV en noir et blanc
W	Ouest
warden	gardien en service au site
wc	W-C
wash	machine à laver
1 ❷ ⚠	symbole AA d'évaluation qualitative (voir page 75)
▶	classification drapeau AA (voir pages 75 & 80)
☎	téléphone public
☎	numéro de téléphone du site
[caravan]	caravanes tourisme
[motor caravan]	caravanes à moteur
▲	tentes
Ⓐ	enclos séparé pour tentes
[hook-up]	Price de courant
[bath]	bain(s)
[shower]	douche(s)
⊙	prise(s) pour rasoirs électriques
[shop]	magasin au site oú endéans de 180m
mobile [shop]	magasin ambulant visitant le site au moins 5 jours par semaine
[indoor pool]	piscine couverte
[outdoor pool]	piscine extérieure
[tennis]	court de tennis
[no dogs]	chiens non permis
[tap]	robinets d'eau potable
⊞	facilités de premiers secours
⊖	agréments endéans de 5km d site
[fish]	pêche
[boat]	bateaux en location
[golf]	terrain de golf
()	facilités facturées

ERKLARING DER TEKENS

acres	totale grondoppervlakte aan kampeerplaatsen beschikbaar voor overnachtingen
all year	gehele jaar open
C	eeuw
cdp	afvalpunt voor chemisch toilet
ntral hot water	warm water van een centrale bron
CTV	kleurentelevisie
dry	drooggelegenheid
E	oost
Etr	Pasen
fr	van
hc	warm en koud water
hrs	uren
iron	strijkijzer(s) en strijkplank(en)
ltr	kortingen voor vakantiegangers
m	mijl (1.6km)
mdnt	middernacht
N	noord
nc	geen kinderen (met leeftijdsgrens)
OS	Topografische Dienstkaart
pub	pub met tuin of voorzieningen voor kinderen
rs	beperkte service
S	zuid
nposted	wettelijk voorgeschreven wegwijzer naar terrein
spin	centrifuge
stables	manege
static	terrein voor stacaravans
TV	zwart/wit televisie
W	west
warden	terreinbewaker aanwezig
wc	toilet
wash	wasmachine
1 ❷ △	AA kwaliteit symbool (zie pagina 75)
►	AA classificatie wimpel (zie pagina 75 & 80)
☎	openbare telefooncel aanwezig
☎	telefoonnummber terrein
	trekcaravan
	kampeerwagen
▲	tenten
	gescheiden standplaats voor tenten
	Aansluiting op electrisch net
	bad(en)
	douche(s)
	kontaktpunt voor scheerapparaat
	Winkel op terrein of binnen een afstand van 180m
nobile	tenminste 5 dagen per week een rijdende winkel op terrein
	overdekt zwembad
	openlucht zwembad
	tennisbaan
	geen honden
	drinkwater fonteintjes
⊞	EHBO-post
	recreatie mogelijkheden binnen 5km van terrein
	visplaats
	bootverhuur
	golfbaan
()	betaalbare voorzieningen

ZEICHENERKLÄRUNG

acres	Gesamtfläche des für Übernachtungseinheiten benutzbaren Campingplatzes
all year	Ganzjährig geöffnet
C	Jahrhundert
cdp	Ausguss für Chemikaltoiletten
central hot water	Warmwasser von einem Zentralanschluss
CTV	Farbfernsehen
dry	Trockengelegenheit
E	Ost
Etr	Ostern
fr	Von
hc	Warm- und Kaltwasser
hrs	Stunden
iron	Bügeleisen und Bügelbrett
ltr	Ermässigungen für Feriengästen
m	Meile
mdnt	Mitternacht
N	Nord
nc	Kinder nicht gestattet (mit Altersgrenze)
OS	Landesvermessung
pub	Gasthaus mit Garten oder Kinderraum
rs	Beschränkte Dienstleistungen
S	Sud
signposted	Amtlicher Strassenschild zum Platz
spin	Trockner
stables	Reitstall
static	Dauereinheiten
TV	Schwarzweissfernsehen
W	West
warden	Aufseher am Platz anwesend
wc	Toilette
wash	Waschmaschine
1 ❷ △	AA Kategorisierung der Qualität (siehe Seite 75)
►	AA Fähnchenklassifizierung (siehe Seiten 75 und 80)
☎	Öffentliche Telefonzelle vorhanden
☎	Telefonnummer des Campingplatzes
	Reisewohnwagen
	Campingwagen
▲	Zelt
	abgetrennter Zeltplatz
	Stromanschluss
	Bad(e)
	Dusche(n)
	Stromanschlüsse für Rasierapparate
	Lebensmittelgeschäft direkt am Platz oder nicht weiter entfernt als 180m
mobile	Autoladen besucht den Platz wenigstens fünfmal in der Woche
	Hallenbad
	Freibad
	Tennisplatz
	Hundeverbot
	Trinkwasserstandröhre
⊞	Unfallstation
	Freizeitmöglichkeiten nicht weiter entfernt als 5km
	fischen
	Bootverleih
	Golfplatz
()	Gebührenpflichtige Einrichtungen

Time for an Act

What has the Housing of the Working Classes Act of 1885 got to do with holidays in 1980? Not a great deal, one would think.

A hundred years ago 'van towns' – overcrowded, insanitary, breeding grounds for disease and crime – were causing problems. They were, in the main, occupied by the very poor, the dregs of humanity. The 1885 Act (1897 in Scotland) empowered local authorities to make bye-laws to control these 'towns', and the provisions of the Public Health Act of 1936 in respect of camping were based on the earlier law. Caravans are further controlled by post-war planning and development legislation.

With this historical background it is not surprising that caravans and tents are treated completely separately in law. But from the amenity and health angles, what is the difference between a frame tent and a collapsible caravan? The frame tent may house a family while the caravan is suitable for two, yet regulations in respect of the latter are far the more stringent.

On the other hand, while it is necessary to keep tight control of static caravan sites, there is a case for relaxing the requirements regarding touring vans (most of which have their own sanitary arrangements these days); apart from other considerations, imposing the same rules for both encourages site owners to use a large proportion of their land for static caravans, the income from which is secure, instead of providing much-needed accommodation for touring vans.

We are particularly concerned about the so-called '28-day rule' which permits three caravans at a time to occupy a site of five or more acres for up to 28 days in a 12-month period. This, like so many good ideas, had led to difficulties unforeseen by those who thought it up. It was intended to enable landowners to take a few caravans during the holiday period without the need to obtain a licence, but with the great increase in the numbers of people using trailer or motorised caravans, and the consequent pressure on site operators, the 28-day exemption has been exploited in ways not originally intended. Not only can a site operator use any 5-acre field which he may have available, but he can rent land from neighbouring farmers, so providing a number of 'annexe' sites which need have no sanitary provisions let alone the other amenities advertised.

Tents, which are in any case subject to less stringent controls, are exempt entirely for a similar 28-day period, and there is nothing to say that they cannot be in the same field as the three caravans. So your one 5-acre field may contain an unlimited number of tents, three caravans, and no toilets.

If you've been going from site to site looking for somewhere to rest your caravan you will be only too glad to find a place to park and won't mind having to make your way to the main site to find the ablution block. But suppose you've booked up months ahead (as we advised in last year's edition of this book)? Few sites will reserve a particular pitch – it's a case of first come, first served. So if you arrive late you may be directed to a pitch in a rough field with none of the amenities which you are entitled to expect.

Local authorities, urged on by tourist boards, are eager to attract holiday-makers but encounter many headaches in ensuring that sufficient accommodation for touring vans is available. We suggest that they could help site-owners by providing temporary facilities such as mobile toilets for overspill sites. At the same time we feel that booked pitches should be reserved on the main site, possibly with a 'latest time of arrival' proviso.

It is some years since the Camping Working Party, set up by the Minister of Housing and Local Government in 1969, published its report; since then the numbers of people taking this type of holiday has increased considerably and the problems have become proportionately more acute. There is certainly a case for treating static and touring caravans separately, while bringing tents into line with the latter. Existing exemptions for organisations such as Scouts, and for backpackers camping 'in the wild' should not be affected. At the same time provision needs to be made for peak-season overspills, and it is not easy to work out a good way of balancing this requirement with the maintenance of health standards. However, it is to be hoped that new legislation, relevant to today's (and tomorrow's) needs, will be enacted without further delay.

In the meantime it is too often the late bird that has to eat worms, however early he stakes his claim.

The forest can resemble the nave of a great cathedral with the canopy of leaves filtering the light that falls on the bracken floor. *Photo: John Cleare*

Orienteering ~ the thought sport

by John Disley

'The forest was as quiet as a cathedral, not a twig snapped in the lofty nave of coniferous trees. There was now little doubt that I was lost – not totally lost but certainly firmly mislaid. Nothing fitted no matter which way I faced or how I twisted my small map or adjusted my magnetic compass. I tried to stay calm and settle my beating heart.

'The forest had become alien and I was becoming increasingly insecure. Every minute I wasted standing still meant that another pursuer was

John Disley C.B.E.

An Olympic medalist in the 3,000 metres steeplechase in Helsinki 1952, John Disley turned his attention to getting orienteering established in England when he gave up athletics in the sixties.

He is a former chairman of the British Orienteering Federation, and is now a member of the International Council for the sport.

He is a Vice-chairman of the British Sports Council and Chairman of the National Jogging Association. He is married to former Olympic sprinter Sylvia Cheeseman and has two very active teenage daughters.

starting after me and those already following my route would be catching me up. I'd blown any chance of success that I might have had when I started that morning.'

No, you haven't started reading about an escape from a Siberian labour camp, but just my experience in a recent orienteering race in a benign Hampshire woodland. On this occasion it was not the intervention of some ubiquitous CIA agent disguised as a wood-cutter that saved me, but a lucky meeting with a bouncy twelve year old girl who condescendingly pointed out that if I ran eastwards for 250 metres I must be collected by a forestry road and then even a blind-man would be able to work out where he was.

She was, bless her pig-tails, absolutely right. I had been trying to bend the terrain to fit the map, on which I had stupidly confused the contour pattern of parallel ridges and valleys. Given correct instructions, I was able to relocate myself and progress to the next control flag.

The absorbing sport of orienteering is beautifully simple. Someone hangs a dozen or so coloured flags in the forest, marking their positions on a map. Then we go out and find the flags aided by the map and a compass. By starting at intervals and timing ourselves around the circuit of flags we make a competition out of the navigational exercise.

However, this description is rather like describing the game of soccer as 'just to kick a ball through a goal thirty feet wide' and forgetting to mention that there are eleven men trying to stop you. In orienteering there are no physical conflicts with opposing players, but rather, as in mountaineering and chess, it is up to the individual to cope with those problems produced by nature or posed by the siting of the controls.

It is the intricate, beautiful, perplexingly-shaded environment of the forest that provides the challenge and the fun. In orienteering we have an exciting mixture of a treasure hunt and a hare and hounds chase. The red and white marker flags are the rewards to be found every few hundred metres, and the chase is provided by the minute-interval start arrangement. We start at intervals so that we can solve the problems of navigation on our own. It never fails to amaze me how easily a forest can swallow up the competitor in front of me in one minute. Even a small forest just a mile across can absorb into its complexities several hundred orienteers who can complete the course without seeing more than a handful of fellow navigators.

When I was temporarily lost in my Hampshire forest it was fortunate that it was a fellow orienteer who gave me instructions on how to proceed. Orienteers, even myself, on a good day, are totally at home with maps, scale, direction and distance. Give them a topographical Ordnance Survey map, a sea chart, a city street plan, an Underground guide, or an architect's drawing, and they can instantly abstract the relevant information. Orienteering teaches map-reading in a practical fun way.

A sense of direction and the ability to relate to the main compass points are not strong assets in the average British repertoire of practical geographical skills.

If you feel that your GCE geography course at school left you a little short on way-finding skills, why not try orienteering and learn the 'play-way'?

Games involving the use of maps and compass have probably been used by various groups to teach map reading since the early part of this century. An annual sports programme of the 34th Army Brigade held in Baghdad in 1917 lists a 'Chart and Compass' race for British officers only. But it is generally agreed that the use of maps and compasses to make a sport was first developed in Scandinavia. In 1918, a Major Killander, a youth leader, organised running events in the forest near Stockholm in an attempt to popularize distance running. To make his races more attractive he set up check points in the forest and issued maps and instructions to his runners. These prototype events proved so popular that Ernst Killander soon found that he had a new sport on his hands. The sport spread across Scandinavia, down into central Europe and reached Britain in 1962.

After a few false starts – the Swedish missionaries spent a year looking for the Sherwood Forest – the sport suddenly took off in the mid-sixties when fell runners and ex-athletes like Chris Brasher, Roger Bannister and Gordon Pirie found that orienteering was a far more attractive form of running than revolving around a track.

The sport now has world championships (Britain held them in 1976) with several dozen countries competing, and provides everyone from junior to grandad with an active challenge in the great outdoors.

How an orienteering event is organised

The venue:

The races take place in mature forested terrain, usually in areas with a few small hills. This means that the visibility is reduced – hills and valleys get in the way – and that there are lots of potential problems regarding navigation and route choice. Surprisingly enough, there are hundreds of suitable forests in Britain and many of them are quite close to our cities and towns. The North Downs, the Chilterns, Cannock Chase and the Forest of Dean all provide wonderful opportunities for orienteering, while the Lake District, West of Scotland and Wales offer harder terrain for championship events.

Who competes?:

In the 1979 British JK Championships at Chagford in Devon there were over 3,000 competitors ranging from 8 to 73 years old, most of them in family groups. Orienteering is great for families. Father can grapple with a tough course while his children run in their age class groups in easier areas of the forest, and Mother can walk around a way-faring course of a couple of kilometres, which will enable her to enjoy following the paths through the most beautiful parts of the forest, if she does not feel up to a competitive course, or has babies in tow. Orienteering has been carefully developed to make sure that all ages and abilities can gain enjoyment and satisfaction in solving problems – at an acceptable level of physical exertion.

The whole family can enjoy the fascination of finding their way around a Wayfaring Trail in the forest. Controls are placed on tracks and paths so that difficult terrain can be avoided.
Photo: J. Gillett

The Course:

Orienteering has been likened to 'trying to do a cross-word puzzle while hurrying to catch a train', while addicts to the sport have car stickers which proclaim that orienteering is 'The Thought Sport' or 'Cunning Running'.

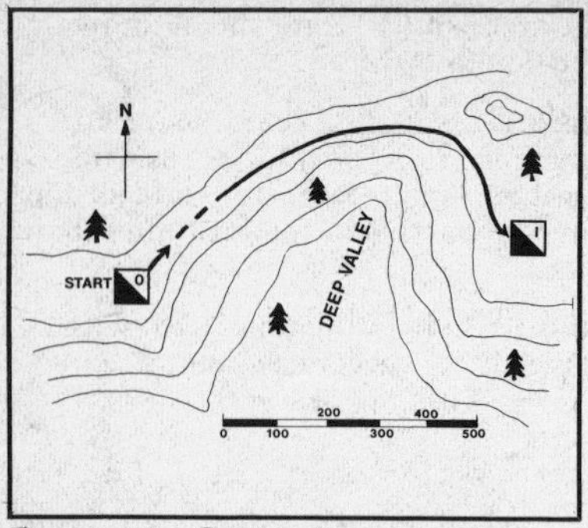

Diagram A **Contouring**
The bee-line route from the Start to Control 1 is about 800 metres, but there is a valley 100 ft. deep in between. Therefore, the clever orienteer will probably decide to contour around the head of the valley, running an extra 200 metres but avoiding any energy-sapping climb.

The course-setter devises a shape of course that will present a series of problems to the orienteer. He puts out the flags so that between each control there is a problem of navigation or route choice. Sometimes there is a steep hill or an area of thick forest between controls, or he uses an area of forest which is featureless and has to be crossed accurately if the next flag is to be found first time. The length of course is similar to that of an appropriate cross-country race – for the keen and fit about 10 kilometres and for the young teenage girl no more than 2 kilometres. Obviously speeds in the forest are much slower than on the track or park-land, so the winning times are usually between 90 and 25 minutes over the range of classes.

Control points are indicated by red and white prism-shaped markers just 30cms square. These are hung up openly at body height, but usually so positioned that they cannot be seen until you are about 20 metres away. A small pin-punch hangs from each flag and the orienteer marks his control card in small numbered boxes with this punch as he progresses around the course. There are usually between 8 and 20 of these controls in a race. Sometimes they are only 100 metres apart but most courses would include some longer legs of up to 1000 metres from flag to flag.

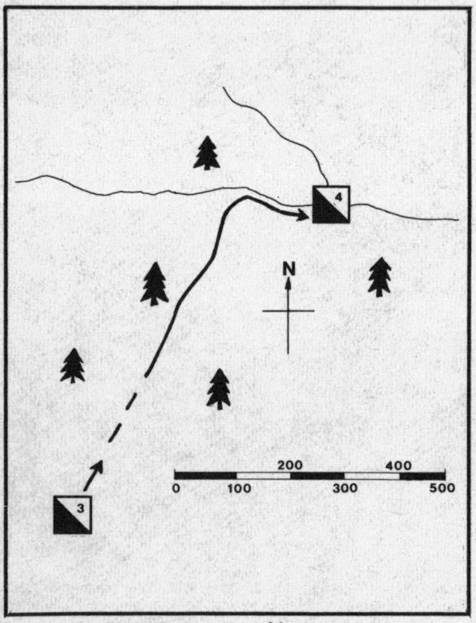

Diagram B **Aiming-off**
A direct compass bearing from Control 3 to 4 may be difficult to follow through the featureless forest on this section of the course. The experienced navigator knows that it is safer to 'aim-off' to one side of the control and then when he hits the stream he can turn eastwards with confidence. This is a well-used technique in orienteering.

The competition:

Competitors usually start at one minute intervals in each class. At the word 'go' they race, run, jog or walk to the master-map area. There they copy down on their own large scale map, supplied by the organiser, the little red circles that denote the shape of their particular course. In large events the organisers supply maps with the courses already over-printed. The map is a large-scale map especially made for orienteering. It is often 1:15,000 or 1:20,000 ($3\frac{1}{2}''$ or $3''$ to the mile) four- or five-colour map showing every small detail of the landscape. Orienteering has its own system of conventional signs which are easy to understand and designed to show all the useful navigational features and highlight all the hazards which would slow down progress through the forest. Open forest, boggy ground, felled-areas, young plantations of spruce, brambles and briar patches are all easily recognisable on a modern orienteering map.

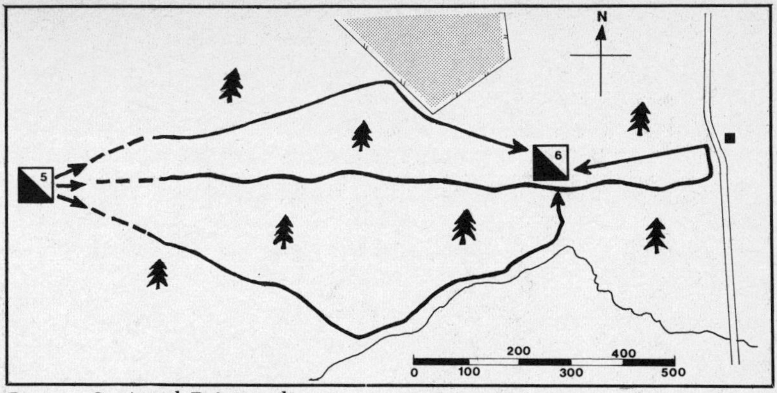

Diagram C **Attack Points and Collecting Features**
Orienteers are always looking for routes that will maximise their chances of finding the flag quickly. If they can run on a rough bearing knowing they will be collected by a long feature such as a field-fence, road or stream, then they will do so.

Then they will look for an 'attack-point' as near to the flag as possible. In Diagram C, the northern route relies upon the field and its corner to collect and give the orienteer an accurate start for the last careful 200 metres to the control. In the southern route, the stream collects the runner and the prominent bend gives the attack point. In the middle route the runner has decided to aim at the control in the hope of staying on line for the whole section; however, he knows that if he misses the flag he will be caught by the road and can use the small building to retrace his way to the control.

It is this variety of route choice that makes orienteering so fascinating.

Once the course is marked on the map, the orienteer has to select a route to the first control. His legs may be raring to go but his head must work out a plan. Seldom is a straight line the best route. Most experienced orienteers like to play themselves in carefully at the start of a race. If there is a path system that can be used to get near the first control they use it, noting carefully how the map relates to the terrain. Perhaps there is a valley between the start and the control, so is it better to contour around the valley head to the other side or go up and down? *(See Dia. A.)*

He can be confronted by a blank area of map with no details to help navigation. Out comes his Silva protractor-type compass and a bearing quickly found to the flag. But can he rely on hitting the control on the 'button' after 750 metres of travel? Perhaps it would be safer to traverse to the west and hit that fence corner and get a more secure approach for the last 100 metres? *(See Dias. B and C.)*

Having made a route choice the orienteer is off and running (or jogging or walking), jumping over fallen trees, leaping across streams, bounding down bracken covered slopes, struggling through marshes, and pushing aside leafy branches. And all the time his eyes are seeking out ditches and dykes, tracks and paths, knolls and pits, making sure that for all his haste he checks off on the map each feature as he passes. *(See Dia. D.)*

These and dozens of other similar stimuli will ensure that the orienteer will be totally absorbed for the next hour or so, while his legs, lungs and heart revel in the best exercises of all – running, jogging or walking.

How did I go? The results are displayed and always produce a focus of attention and comment.

Diagram D **Map Memory**
Constant stopping to look at the map wastes time. The keen orienteer tries to memorize the next few hundred metres as shown on the map, (a) and then mentally ticks the key features off as he passes them. (b).

How to get started:

Every region of Britain has its own lively orienteering association and selection of local clubs. Small and friendly events, usually on Sundays, are regularly held by these clubs, who are enthusiastic to make new converts to the sport and hopefully gather new members too. So you are sure to be welcomed and shown how to get started.

You won't need any special clothes for your first few events. An old track suit or even a pair of jeans and a jersey will do just fine. On the feet a pair of jogging shoes, basket-ball or hockey boots will give you all the grip you need. Remember that whatever you wear it is sure to get muddy and perhaps torn, so don't go all dressed-up.

A compass will be very useful but not essential for your first try. Most orienteers use a protractor-type compass that can measure bearings as well as indicate direction. The most popular make is SILVA and types 1, 2, 4 or 7 are very suitable for orienteering, but ask advice at your first event before paying out between £3 and £10 for your compass. You *must* take a whistle (to be blown only if you get in real difficulties.)

Failing a local contact with the sport, drop a line to:
British Orienteering Federation Office, Lea Green Centre, nr Matlock, Derbyshire DE4 5GJ.

and ask for details of addresses and telephone numbers of clubs in your area and a list of scheduled events. Enclose a stamped addressed 8″ x 4″ envelope for the reply.

An Avon Inflatable gets you further away from it all

With an Avon inflatable as part of your camping/caravanning equipment, an outdoor holiday develops a new dimension on the water.

Unpack your dinghy or sportboat from its compact kit bag and in minutes the portable Avoncraft is inflated, fitted out and ready to launch in shallow water over the rockiest beach.

Now you are free to explore the pleasures of fishing, diving, water skiing or simply escaping from the crowds to a quiet inaccessible cove.

Back ashore your Avon boat is soon deflated and economically stowed in your car boot or caravan.

Apart from their versatile nature, Avon craft are tough, being constructed from the highest quality materials using proven manufacturing methods.

AVON

The World's Toughest Inflatables!

Avon Inflatables Ltd., Hendy, Pontardulais, Dyfed, S. Wales.
Telephone: (0792) 883838

CAMPING

AA

1st category (Automobile Association five pennants)

WINDERMERE

IN THE HEART OF THE ENGLISH LAKELAND

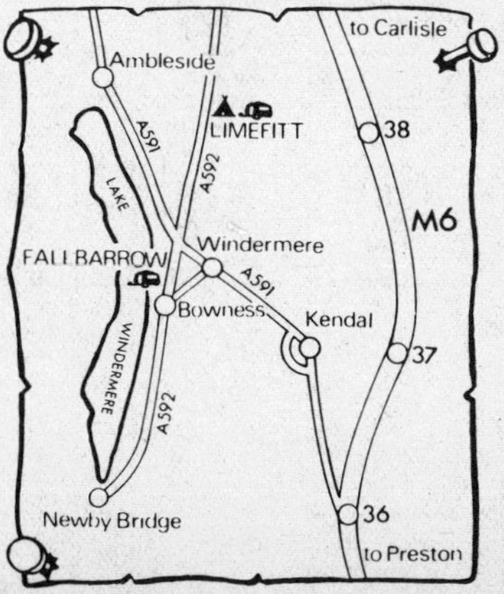

LIMEFITT PARK

In a beautiful valley in the Lake District National Park. Originally a Lakeland Sheep Farm, the 18th Century Barns now accommodate first-class camping facilities. Café, Bar, Shop, Laundrette, under cover Cooking and Dining, Showers and TV. Also on the Site, Pony Trekking, Children's Play Area, etc.

Limefitt Park, Camping Windermere England ☎ Ambleside (096 63) 2300

FALLBARROW PARK

In wooded parkland on the shore of Lake Windermere. Facilities include: Shop, Restaurant, Bar, Laundrette, Showers and TV. Electricity for all Sites, Children's Play Area, Water Sports facilities, etc.

Fallbarrow Park, Camping Windermere England ☎ Windermere (096 62) 4421

The National Grid

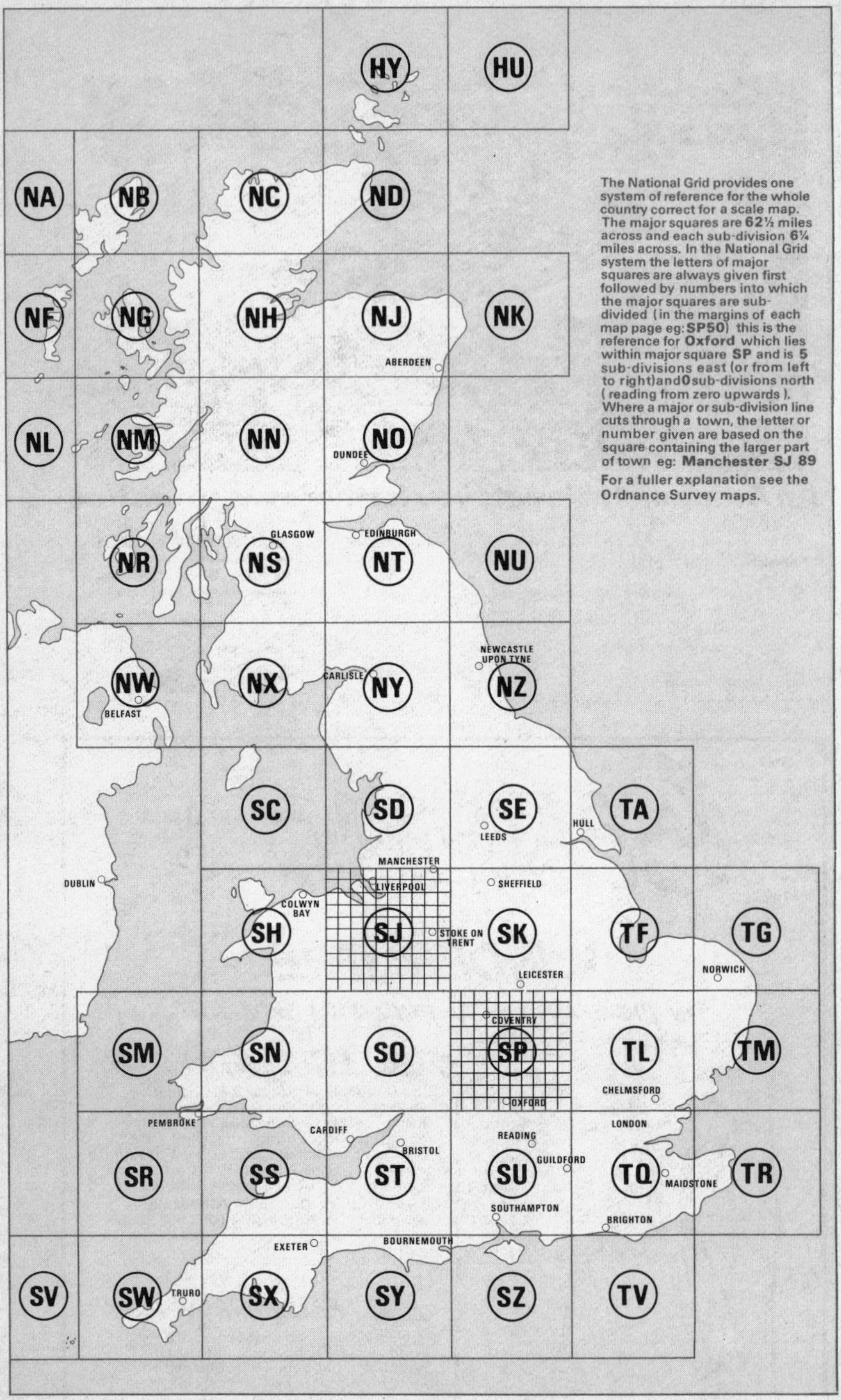

The National Grid provides one system of reference for the whole country correct for a scale map. The major squares are **62½** miles across and each sub-division **6¼** miles across. In the National Grid system the letters of major squares are always given first followed by numbers into which the major squares are sub-divided (in the margins of each map page eg: **SP50**) this is the reference for **Oxford** which lies within major square **SP** and is **5** sub-divisions east (or from left to right) and **0** sub-divisions north (reading from zero upwards). Where a major or sub-division line cuts through a town, the letter or number given are based on the square containing the larger part of town eg: **Manchester SJ 89**

For a fuller explanation see the Ordnance Survey maps.

Key to Atlas

Use the AA Caravanning Map of Great Britain for planning your route. The maps which follow show site locations only.

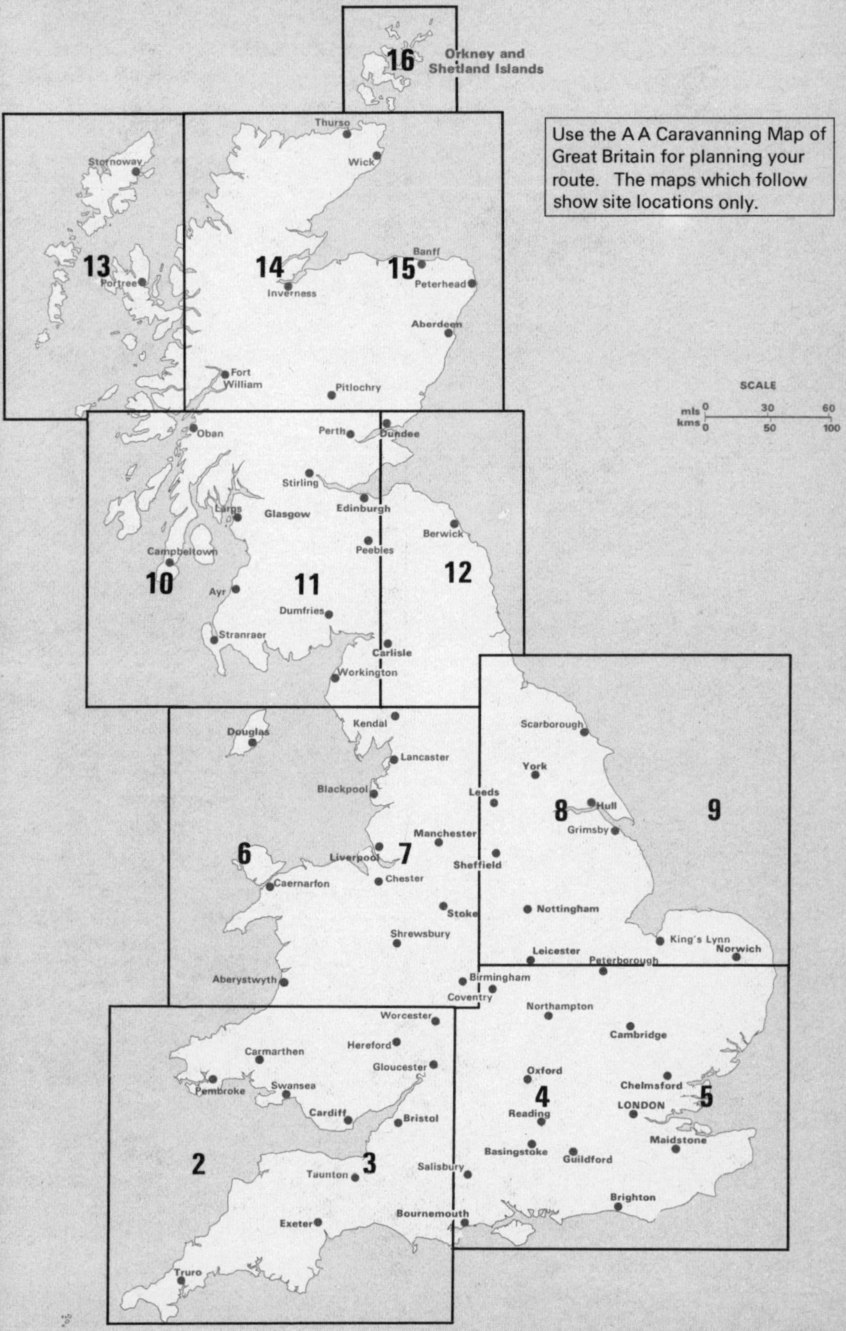

This atlas is for location purposes Only: see Member's Handbook for current road and AA road services information

Maps produced by

The AA Cartographic Department (Publications Division), Fanum House, Basingstoke, Hampshire RG21 2EA

Based on the Ordnance Survey Map with the Sanction of the Controller H.M.S.O.

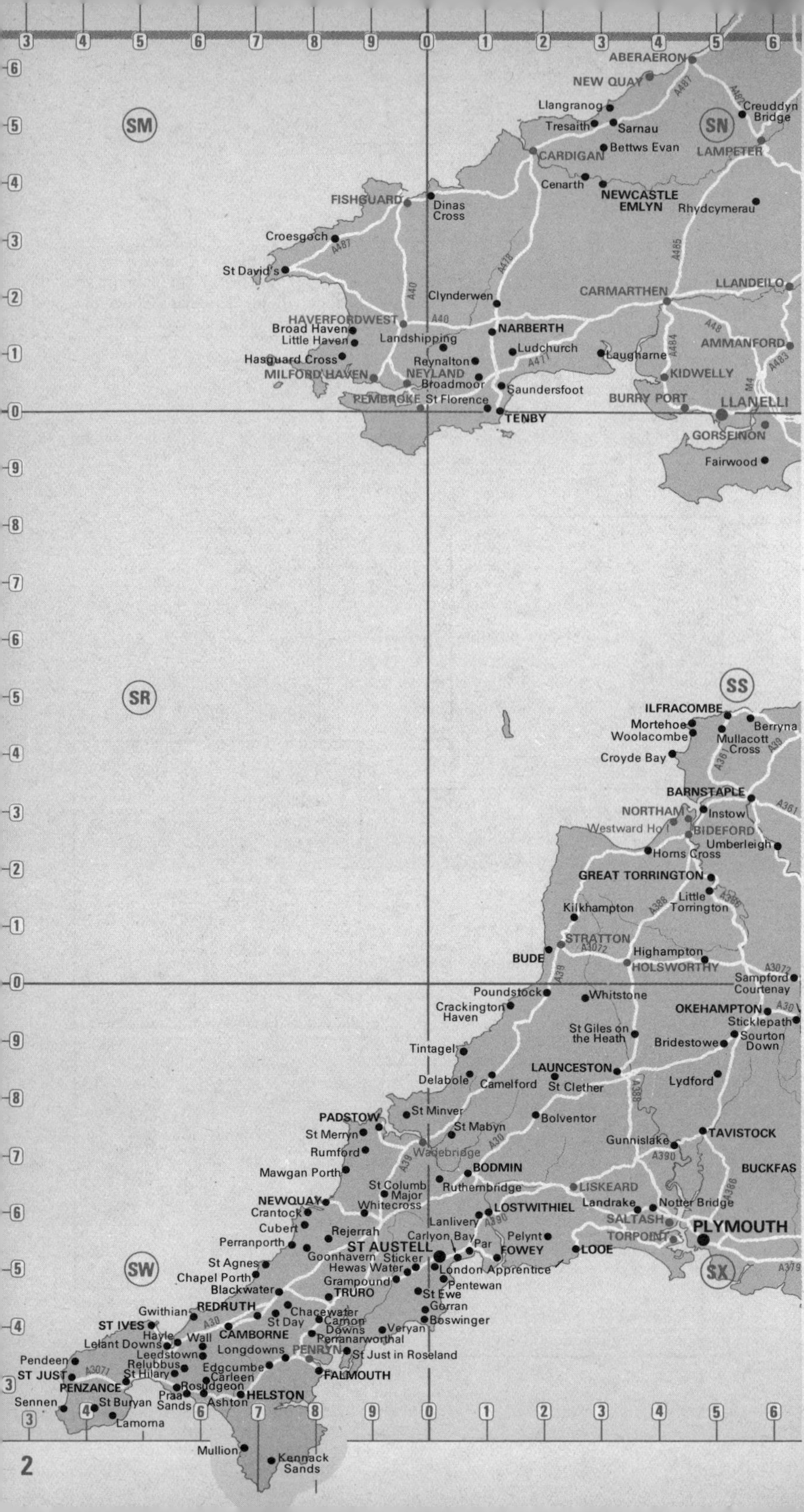
SM
SN
SR
SS
SW
SX
ABERAERON
NEW QUAY
Llangranog
Tresaith
Sarnau
Creuddyn Bridge
Bettws Evan
CARDIGAN
LAMPETER
Cenarth
NEWCASTLE EMLYN
Rhydcymerau
FISHGUARD
Dinas Cross
Croesgoch
St David's
Clynderwen
CARMARTHEN
LLANDEILO
HAVERFORDWEST
Broad Haven
Little Haven
Landshipping
NARBERTH
Ludchurch
Laugharne
AMMANFORD
Hasguard Cross
MILFORD HAVEN
Reynalton
NEYLAND
Broadmoor
KIDWELLY
Saundersfoot
PEMBROKE
St Florence
BURRY PORT
LLANELLI
TENBY
GORSEINON
Fairwood
A487
A482
A40
A478
A485
A48
A484
A477
A483
M4
ILFRACOMBE
Mortehoe
Woolacombe
Berryna
Mullacott Cross
Croyde Bay
BARNSTAPLE
NORTHAM
Instow
Westward Ho!
BIDEFORD
Umberleigh
Horns Cross
GREAT TORRINGTON
Little Torrington
Kilkhampton
STRATTON
BUDE
Highampton
HOLSWORTHY
Sampford Courtenay
Poundstock
Whitstone
Crackington Haven
OKEHAMPTON
Sticklepath
St Giles on the Heath
Bridestowe
Sourton Down
Tintagel
LAUNCESTON
Delabole
Camelford
St Clether
Lydford
PADSTOW
St Minver
Bolventor
St Merryn
St Mabyn
TAVISTOCK
Gunnislake
Rumford
Wadebridge
BODMIN
BUCKFAS
Mawgan Porth
St Columb Major
Ruthernbridge
LISKEARD
NEWQUAY
Whitecross
Landrake
Notter Bridge
Crantock
LOSTWITHIEL
SALTASH
Cubert
Lanlivery
Rejerrah
Carlyon Bay
Pelynt
PLYMOUTH
Perranporth
ST AUSTELL
Par
TORPOINT
St Agnes
Goonhavern
Sticker
FOWEY
LOOE
Chapel Porth
Hewas Water
London Apprentice
Blackwater
Grampound
Pentewan
TRURO
St Ewe
Gwithian
REDRUTH
Chacewater
Gorran
ST IVES
St Day
Carnon Downs
Veryan
Boswinger
Hayle
Wall
CAMBORNE
Perranarworthal
Lelant Downs
Leedstown
Longdowns
PENRYN
St Just in Roseland
Pendeen
Relubbus
Edgcumbe
ST JUST
St Hilary
Carleen
FALMOUTH
PENZANCE
Rosudgeon
HELSTON
Praa Sands
Ashton
Sennen
St Buryan
Lamorna
Mullion
Kennack Sands
A361
A39
A386
A388
A3072
A30
A390
A3071
A379

● Campsite
● Other Towns for Location only

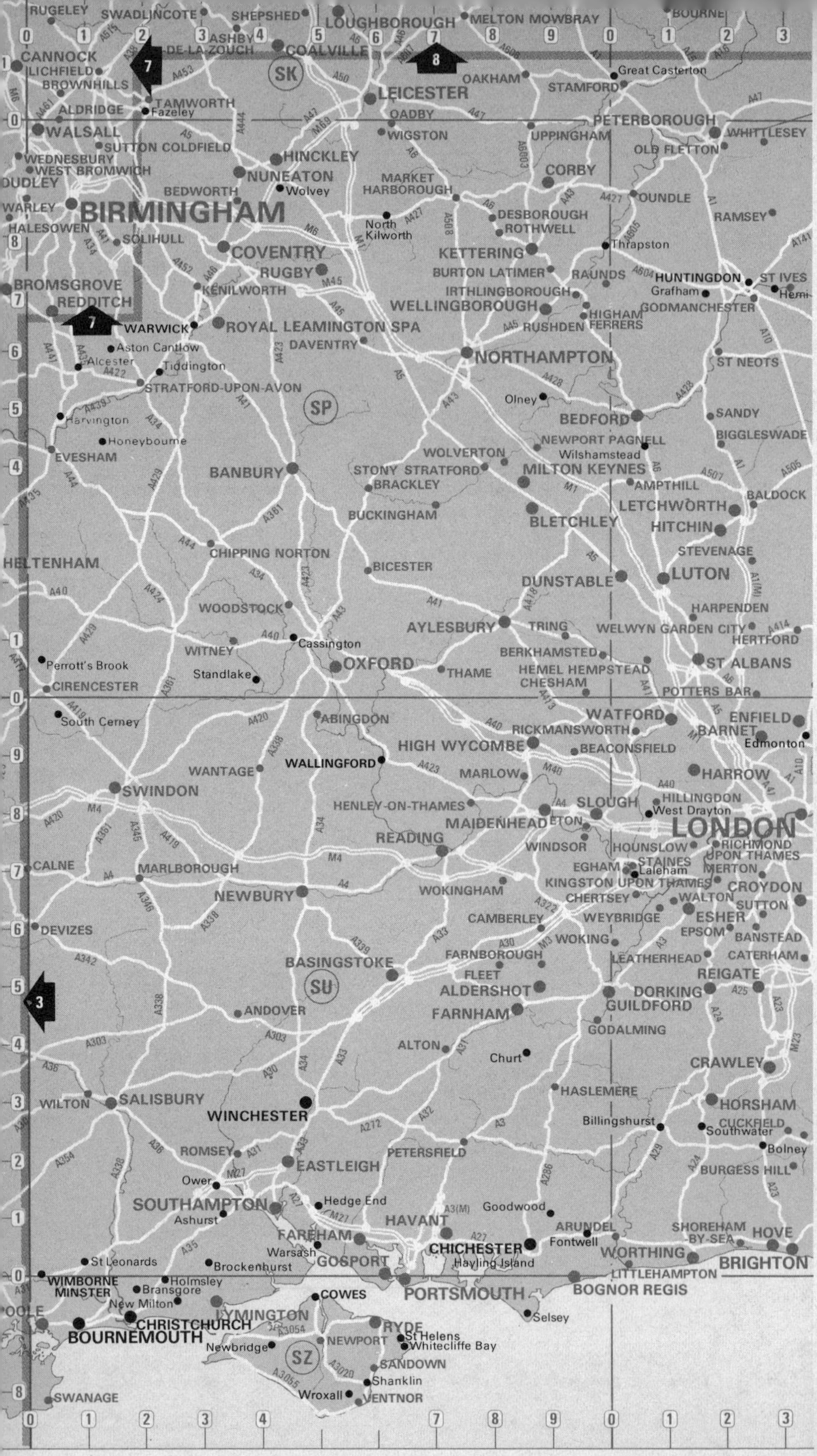
RUGELEY
SWADLINCOTE
SHEPSHED
LOUGHBOROUGH
MELTON MOWBRAY
BOURNE
ASHBY DE-LA-ZOUCH
COALVILLE
CANNOCK
LICHFIELD
BROWNHILLS
SK
OAKHAM
Great Casterton
STAMFORD
LEICESTER
ALDRIDGE
TAMWORTH
Fazeley
OADBY
PETERBOROUGH
WALSALL
WIGSTON
UPPINGHAM
WHITTLESEY
SUTTON COLDFIELD
OLD FLETTON
WEDNESBURY
HINCKLEY
WEST BROMWICH
CORBY
DUDLEY
NUNEATON
MARKET HARBOROUGH
BEDWORTH
Wolvey
OUNDLE
WARLEY
BIRMINGHAM
DESBOROUGH
RAMSEY
HALESOWEN
North Kilworth
ROTHWELL
SOLIHULL
Thrapston
COVENTRY
KETTERING
RUGBY
BURTON LATIMER
RAUNDS
HUNTINGDON
ST IVES
BROMSGROVE
KENILWORTH
IRTHLINGBOROUGH
Grafham
Hemi
REDDITCH
WELLINGBOROUGH
HIGHAM FERRERS
GODMANCHESTER
WARWICK
ROYAL LEAMINGTON SPA
RUSHDEN
DAVENTRY
Aston Cantlow
NORTHAMPTON
Alcester
Tiddington
ST NEOTS
STRATFORD-UPON-AVON
SP
Olney
Harvington
BEDFORD
SANDY
Honeybourne
NEWPORT PAGNELL
BIGGLESWADE
Wilshamstead
EVESHAM
WOLVERTON
BANBURY
STONY STRATFORD
MILTON KEYNES
AMPTHILL
BRACKLEY
BALDOCK
LETCHWORTH
BUCKINGHAM
BLETCHLEY
HITCHIN
CHIPPING NORTON
STEVENAGE
CHELTENHAM
BICESTER
LUTON
DUNSTABLE
HARPENDEN
WOODSTOCK
AYLESBURY
TRING
WELWYN GARDEN CITY
HERTFORD
WITNEY
Cassington
BERKHAMSTED
Perrott's Brook
OXFORD
ST ALBANS
Standlake
THAME
HEMEL HEMPSTEAD
CIRENCESTER
CHESHAM
POTTERS BAR
WATFORD
South Cerney
ABINGDON
ENFIELD
RICKMANSWORTH
BARNET
Edmonton
HIGH WYCOMBE
BEACONSFIELD
WANTAGE
WALLINGFORD
MARLOW
HARROW
SWINDON
HILLINGDON
HENLEY-ON-THAMES
SLOUGH
West Drayton
MAIDENHEAD
ETON
LONDON
READING
WINDSOR
HOUNSLOW
RICHMOND UPON THAMES
CALNE
STAINES
MERTON
Laleham
EGHAM
MARLBOROUGH
KINGSTON UPON THAMES
CROYDON
NEWBURY
WOKINGHAM
CHERTSEY
WALTON
SUTTON
DEVIZES
CAMBERLEY
WEYBRIDGE
ESHER
EPSOM
BANSTEAD
WOKING
FARNBOROUGH
LEATHERHEAD
CATERHAM
BASINGSTOKE
FLEET
REIGATE
SU
ALDERSHOT
DORKING
GUILDFORD
ANDOVER
FARNHAM
GODALMING
ALTON
Churt
CRAWLEY
HASLEMERE
WILTON
SALISBURY
HORSHAM
WINCHESTER
Billingshurst
CUCKFIELD
Southwater
ROMSEY
PETERSFIELD
Bolney
EASTLEIGH
BURGESS HILL
Ower
SOUTHAMPTON
Hedge End
Goodwood
Ashurst
HAVANT
ARUNDEL
SHOREHAM-BY-SEA
FAREHAM
Fontwell
HOVE
St Leonards
Warsash
CHICHESTER
WORTHING
Brockenhurst
GOSPORT
Hayling Island
BRIGHTON
WIMBORNE MINSTER
Holmsley
LITTLEHAMPTON
Bransgore
COWES
PORTSMOUTH
BOGNOR REGIS
POOLE
New Milton
LYMINGTON
Selsey
CHRISTCHURCH
RYDE
BOURNEMOUTH
NEWPORT
St Helens
Whitecliffe Bay
Newbridge
SZ
SANDOWN
Shanklin
SWANAGE
Wroxall
VENTNOR

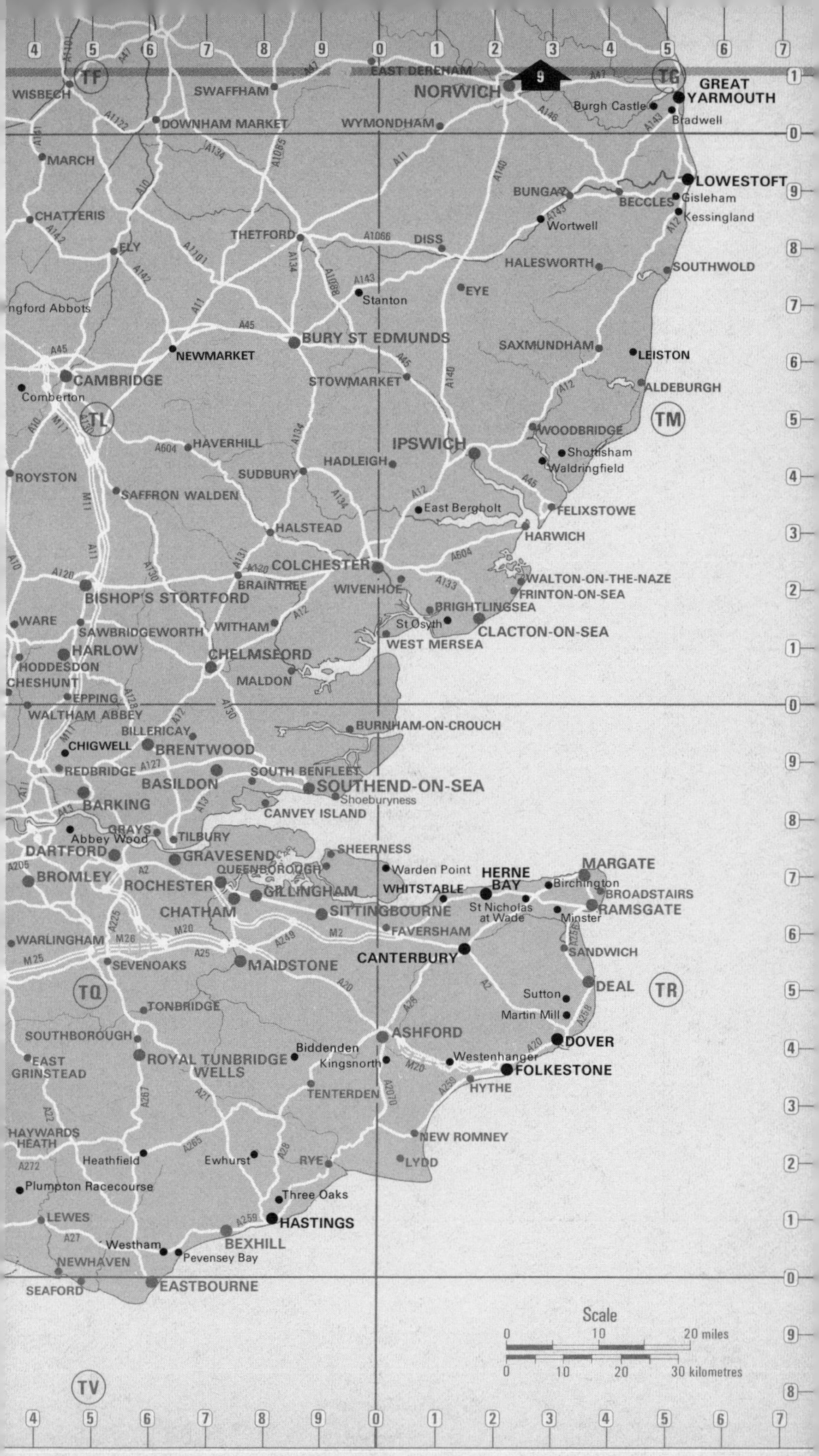

● Campsite

● Other Towns for Location only

RAMSEY
Laxey
PEEL
Hillberry
DOUGLAS
CASTLETOWN
Ravenglass
Silecroft
DALTON-IN-FUR
BARROW-IN-FURNE
SC
PO
BL
LYTHA
IRISH SEA
AMLWCH
HOLYHEAD
Brynteg
LLANFAIRFECHAN
PENMAENMAWR
LLANDUDNO
COLWYN BAY
PRESTATYN
RHYL
CONWY
Llysfaen
BEAUMARIS
Pentraeth
Llandudno Junction
ABERGELE
Rhosneigr
LLANGEFNI
MENAI BRIDGE
BANGOR
Brynsiencyn
BETHESDA
DENBIGH
Llanrug
CAERNARFON
Pont-Rug
Trefriw
LLANRWST
RUTHIN
Betws Garmon
BETWS-Y-COED
Llandwrog
SH
Beddgelert
BLAENAU FFESTINIOG
FFESTINIOG
Glan-yr-Afon
CRICCIETH
Penrhyndeudraeth
Llandderfel
Morfa Bychan
PORTHMADOG
BALA
Llandrillo
PWLLHELI
Llanbedrog
Llanuwchllyn
Abersoch
Penybontfawr
Tal-y-Bont
DOLGELLAU
LLANFYLLIN
BARMOUTH
Pentrebeir
Llangyniew
CARDIGAN BAY
Llwyngwril
TYWYN
MACHYNLLETH
Abermule
NEWTOWN
Llandre
LLANIDLOES
ABERYSTWYTH
SN
Llanrhystud
Llanon
ABERAERON
LLANDRINDOD WELLS
Scale
0 10 20 miles
0 10 20 30 kilometres
11
2

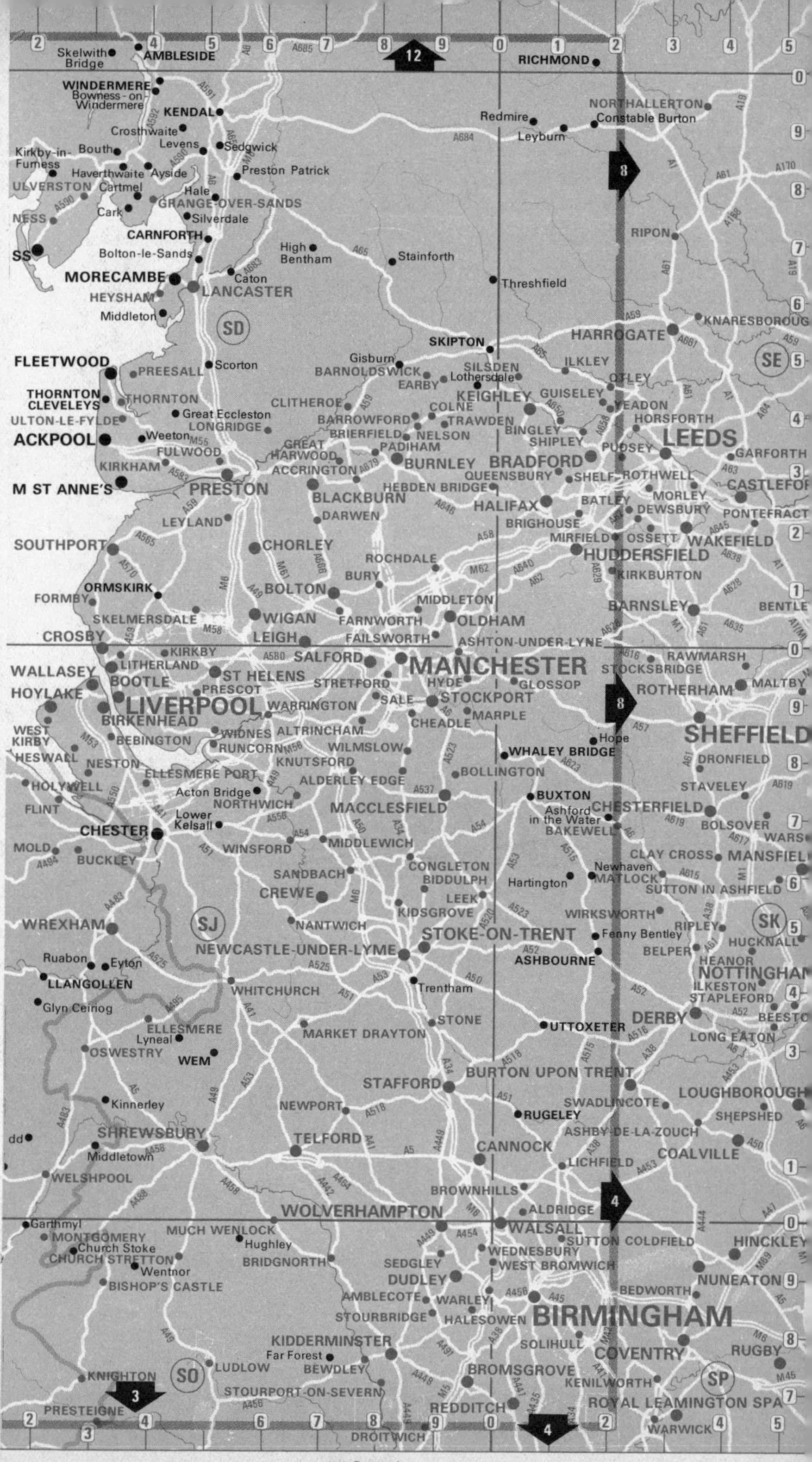

● Campsite
● Other Towns for location only

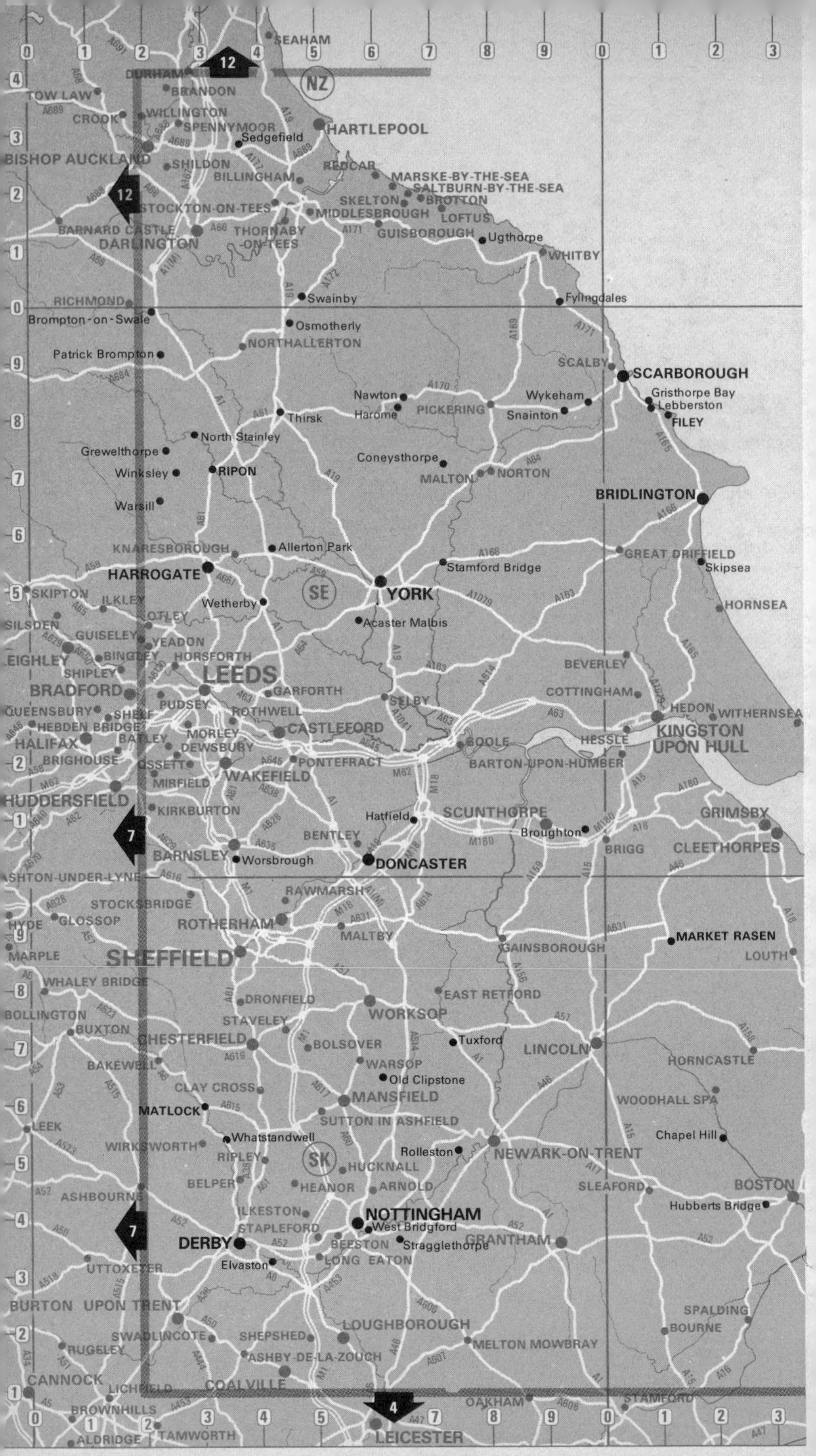

SEAHAM
NZ
DURHAM
12
TOW LAW
BRANDON
CROOK
WILLINGTON
SPENNYMOOR
HARTLEPOOL
Sedgefield
BISHOP AUCKLAND
SHILDON
REDCAR
BILLINGHAM
MARSKE-BY-THE-SEA
SALTBURN-BY-THE-SEA
SKELTON
BROTTON
STOCKTON-ON-TEES
MIDDLESBROUGH
LOFTUS
BARNARD CASTLE
DARLINGTON
THORNABY -ON-TEES
GUISBOROUGH
Ugthorpe
WHITBY
RICHMOND
Swainby
Fylingdales
Brompton-on-Swale
Osmotherly
NORTHALLERTON
Patrick Brompton
SCALBY
SCARBOROUGH
Nawton
Wykeham
Gristhorpe Bay
Lebberston
Harome
PICKERING
Snainton
FILEY
Thirsk
North Stainley
Grewelthorpe
Coneysthorpe
Winksley
RIPON
MALTON
NORTON
BRIDLINGTON
Warsill
KNARESBOROUGH
Allerton Park
GREAT DRIFFIELD
HARROGATE
Stamford Bridge
Skipsea
SKIPTON
ILKLEY
SE
YORK
Wetherby
HORNSEA
OTLEY
SILSDEN
Acaster Malbis
GUISELEY
YEADON
KEIGHLEY
BINGLEY
HORSFORTH
SHIPLEY
BEVERLEY
LEEDS
BRADFORD
GARFORTH
COTTINGHAM
PUDSEY
QUEENSBURY
SHELF
ROTHWELL
SELBY
HEDON
WITHERNSEA
HEBDEN BRIDGE
MORLEY
CASTLEFORD
KINGSTON UPON HULL
HALIFAX
BATLEY
DEWSBURY
GOOLE
HESSLE
BRIGHOUSE
OSSETT
PONTEFRACT
BARTON-UPON-HUMBER
MIRFIELD
WAKEFIELD
HUDDERSFIELD
KIRKBURTON
SCUNTHORPE
GRIMSBY
Hatfield
7
BENTLEY
Broughton
BRIGG
CLEETHORPES
BARNSLEY
Worsbrough
DONCASTER
ASHTON-UNDER-LYNE
RAWMARSH
STOCKSBRIDGE
HYDE
GLOSSOP
ROTHERHAM
MALTBY
MARKET RASEN
MARPLE
SHEFFIELD
GAINSBOROUGH
LOUTH
WHALEY BRIDGE
DRONFIELD
EAST RETFORD
BOLLINGTON
WORKSOP
STAVELEY
BUXTON
CHESTERFIELD
BOLSOVER
Tuxford
LINCOLN
HORNCASTLE
BAKEWELL
WARSOP
Old Clipstone
CLAY CROSS
MANSFIELD
WOODHALL SPA
MATLOCK
LEEK
SUTTON IN ASHFIELD
Chapel Hill
WIRKSWORTH
Whatstandwell
SK
Rolleston
NEWARK-ON-TRENT
RIPLEY
HUCKNALL
BELPER
HEANOR
ARNOLD
SLEAFORD
BOSTON
ASHBOURNE
ILKESTON
NOTTINGHAM
Hubberts Bridge
West Bridgford
STAPLEFORD
DERBY
BEESTON
Stragglethorpe
GRANTHAM
LONG EATON
Elvaston
UTTOXETER
BURTON UPON TRENT
SPALDING
LOUGHBOROUGH
BOURNE
SWADLINCOTE
SHEPSHED
MELTON MOWBRAY
RUGELEY
ASHBY-DE-LA-ZOUCH
CANNOCK
LICHFIELD
COALVILLE
4
OAKHAM
STAMFORD
BROWNHILLS
ALDRIDGE
TAMWORTH
LEICESTER

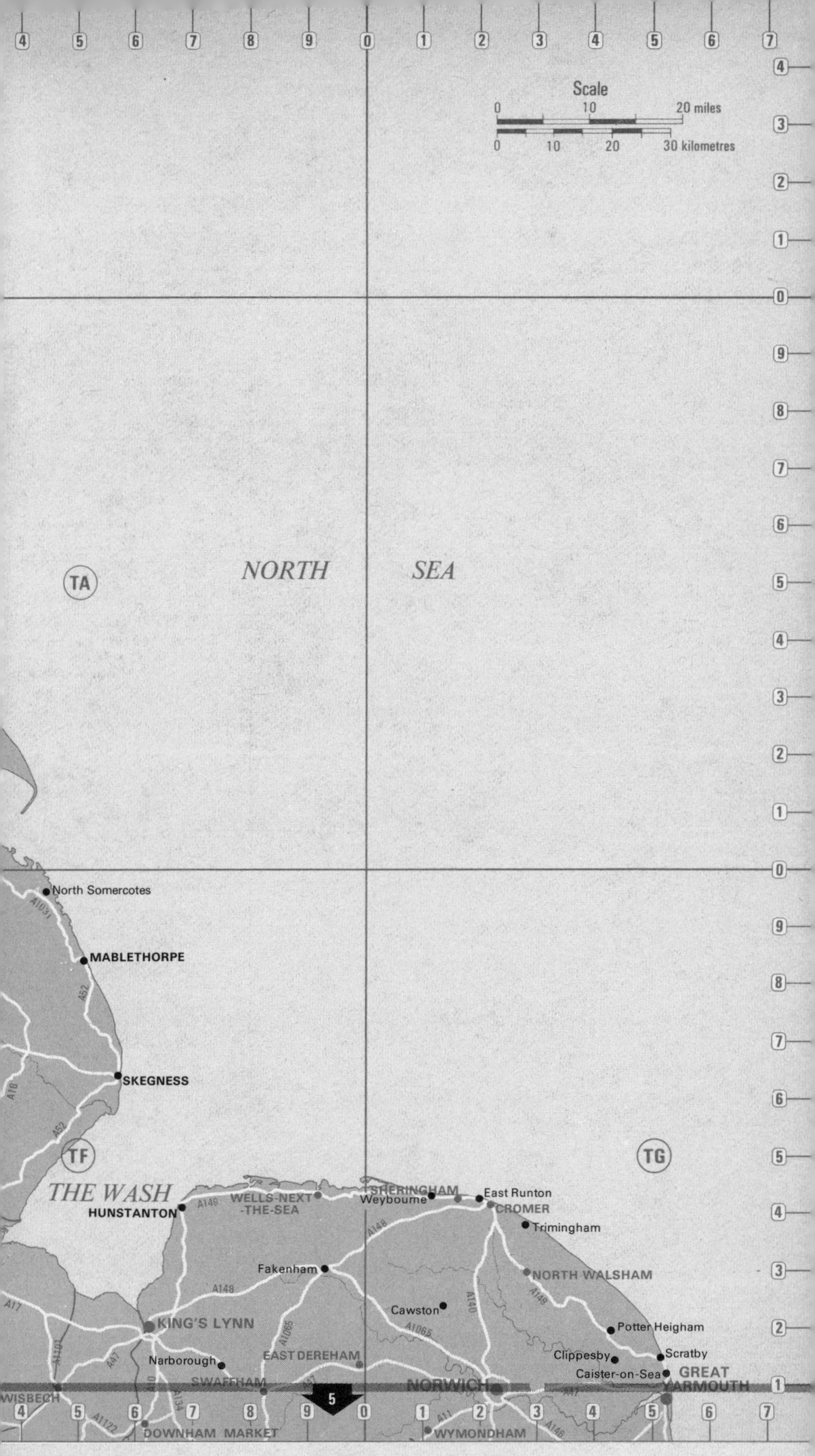

● Campsite
● Other Towns for Location only

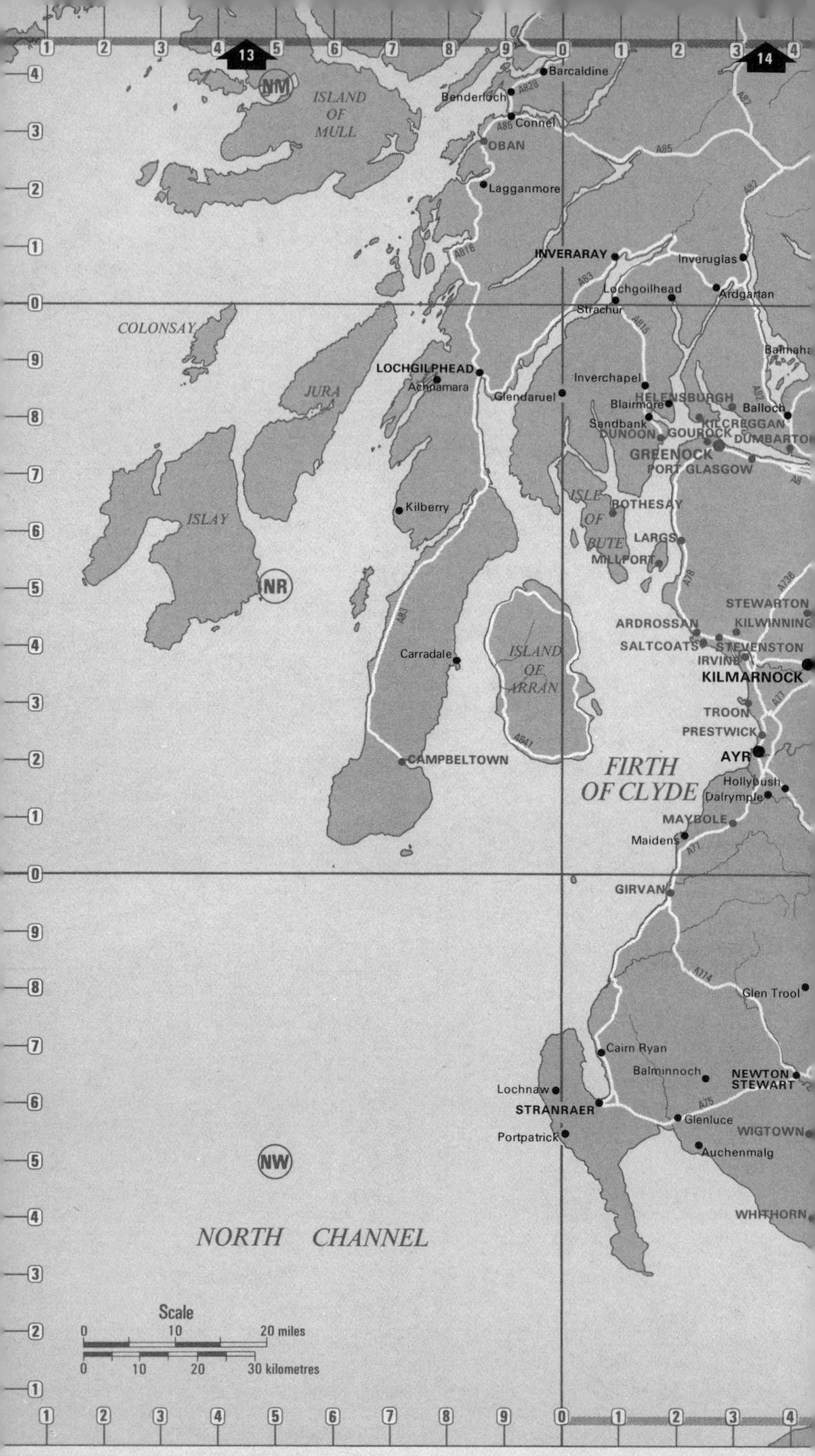
13
14
NM
ISLAND OF MULL
Barcaldine
Benderloch
A828
A85
Connel
OBAN
A85
A82
Lagganmore
A816
INVERARAY
Inveruglas
A83
Lochgoilhead
Ardgartan
Strachur
A815
COLONSAY
Balmaha
LOCHGILPHEAD
Achnamara
JURA
Inverchapel
Glendaruel
HELENSBURGH
A82
Blairmore
Balloch
Sandbank
KILCREGGAN
DUNOON
GOUROCK
DUMBARTON
GREENOCK
PORT GLASGOW
A8
ISLAY
Kilberry
ISLE OF BUTE
ROTHESAY
LARGS
MILLPORT
NR
A78
A736
STEWARTON
A83
ARDROSSAN
KILWINNING
SALTCOATS
STEVENSTON
Carradale
ISLAND OF ARRAN
IRVINE
KILMARNOCK
A77
TROON
PRESTWICK
A841
AYR
CAMPBELTOWN
FIRTH OF CLYDE
Hollybush
Dalrymple
MAYBOLE
Maidens
A77
GIRVAN
A714
Glen Trool
Cairn Ryan
Balminnoch
NEWTON STEWART
Lochnaw
A75
STRANRAER
Glenluce
WIGTOWN
Portpatrick
Auchenmalg
NW
WHITHORN
NORTH CHANNEL
Scale
0
10
20 miles
0
10
20
30 kilometres

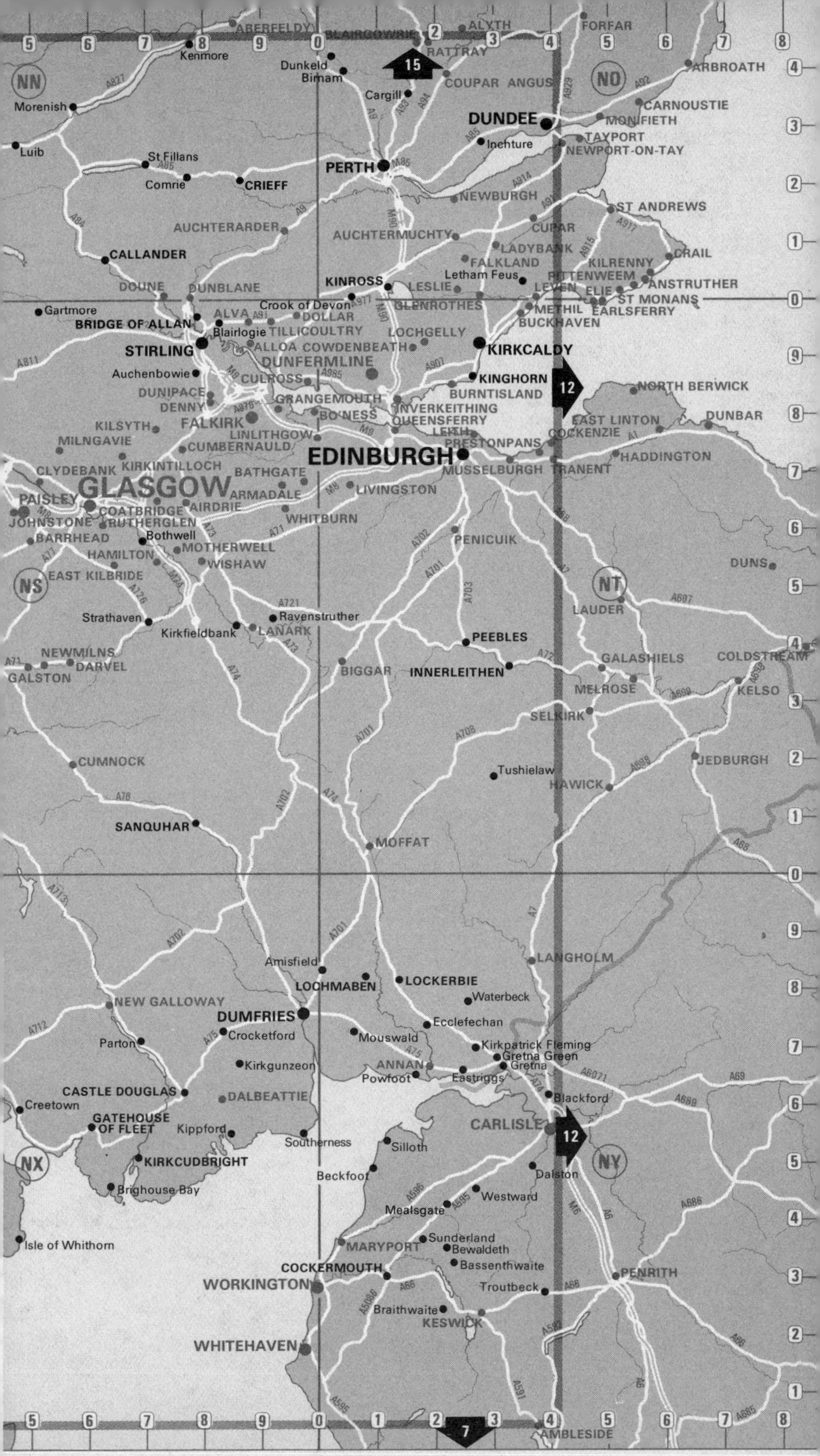

Campsite
Other Towns for Location only

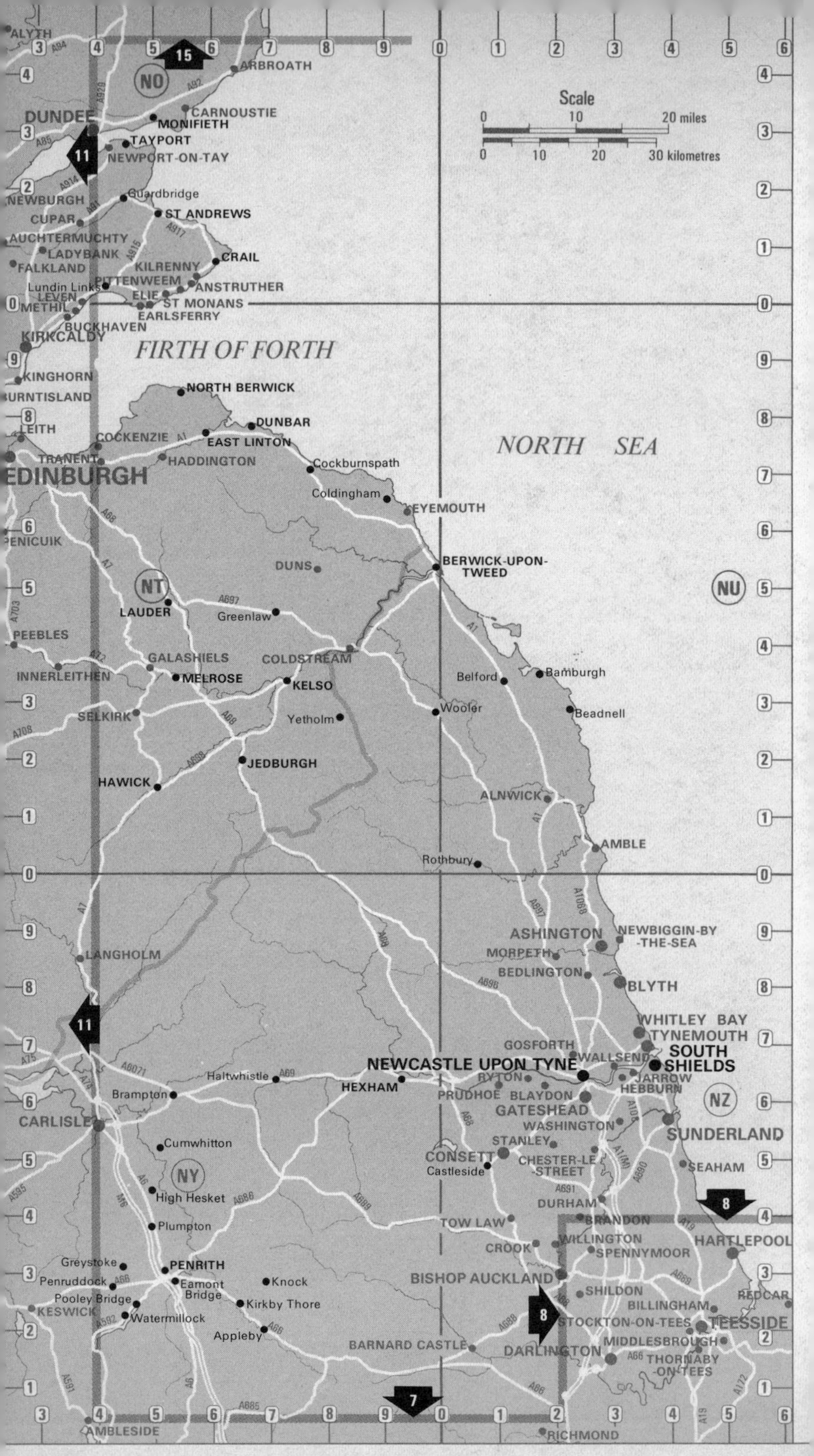

ALYTH
15
ARBROATH
NO
Scale
0 10 20 miles
0 10 20 30 kilometres
DUNDEE
CARNOUSTIE
MONIFIETH
TAYPORT
11
NEWPORT-ON-TAY
NEWBURGH
Guardbridge
ST ANDREWS
CUPAR
AUCHTERMUCHTY
LADYBANK
CRAIL
FALKLAND
KILRENNY
PITTENWEEM
Lundin Links
ANSTRUTHER
LEVEN
ELIE
METHIL
ST MONANS
EARLSFERRY
BUCKHAVEN
KIRKCALDY
FIRTH OF FORTH
KINGHORN
BURNTISLAND
NORTH BERWICK
DUNBAR
LEITH
COCKENZIE
EAST LINTON
NORTH SEA
TRANENT
HADDINGTON
EDINBURGH
Cockburnspath
Coldingham
EYEMOUTH
PENICUIK
BERWICK-UPON-TWEED
DUNS
NT
NU
LAUDER
Greenlaw
PEEBLES
GALASHIELS
COLDSTREAM
INNERLEITHEN
MELROSE
KELSO
Belford
Bamburgh
SELKIRK
Yetholm
Wooler
Beadnell
JEDBURGH
HAWICK
ALNWICK
AMBLE
Rothbury
ASHINGTON
NEWBIGGIN-BY-THE-SEA
LANGHOLM
MORPETH
BEDLINGTON
BLYTH
WHITLEY BAY
TYNEMOUTH
SOUTH SHIELDS
GOSFORTH
NEWCASTLE UPON TYNE
WALLSEND
Haltwhistle
HEXHAM
RYTON
JARROW
HEBBURN
Brampton
PRUDHOE
BLAYDON
NZ
GATESHEAD
CARLISLE
WASHINGTON
SUNDERLAND
Cumwhitton
STANLEY
CONSETT
CHESTER-LE-STREET
NY
Castleside
SEAHAM
High Hesket
DURHAM
8
Plumpton
TOW LAW
BRANDON
WILLINGTON
HARTLEPOOL
CROOK
SPENNYMOOR
Greystoke
PENRITH
Penruddock
Eamont Bridge
Knock
BISHOP AUCKLAND
Pooley Bridge
SHILDON
REDCAR
KESWICK
Kirkby Thore
BILLINGHAM
Watermillock
STOCKTON-ON-TEES
TEESSIDE
Appleby
BARNARD CASTLE
MIDDLESBROUGH
DARLINGTON
THORNABY-ON-TEES
7
AMBLESIDE
RICHMOND

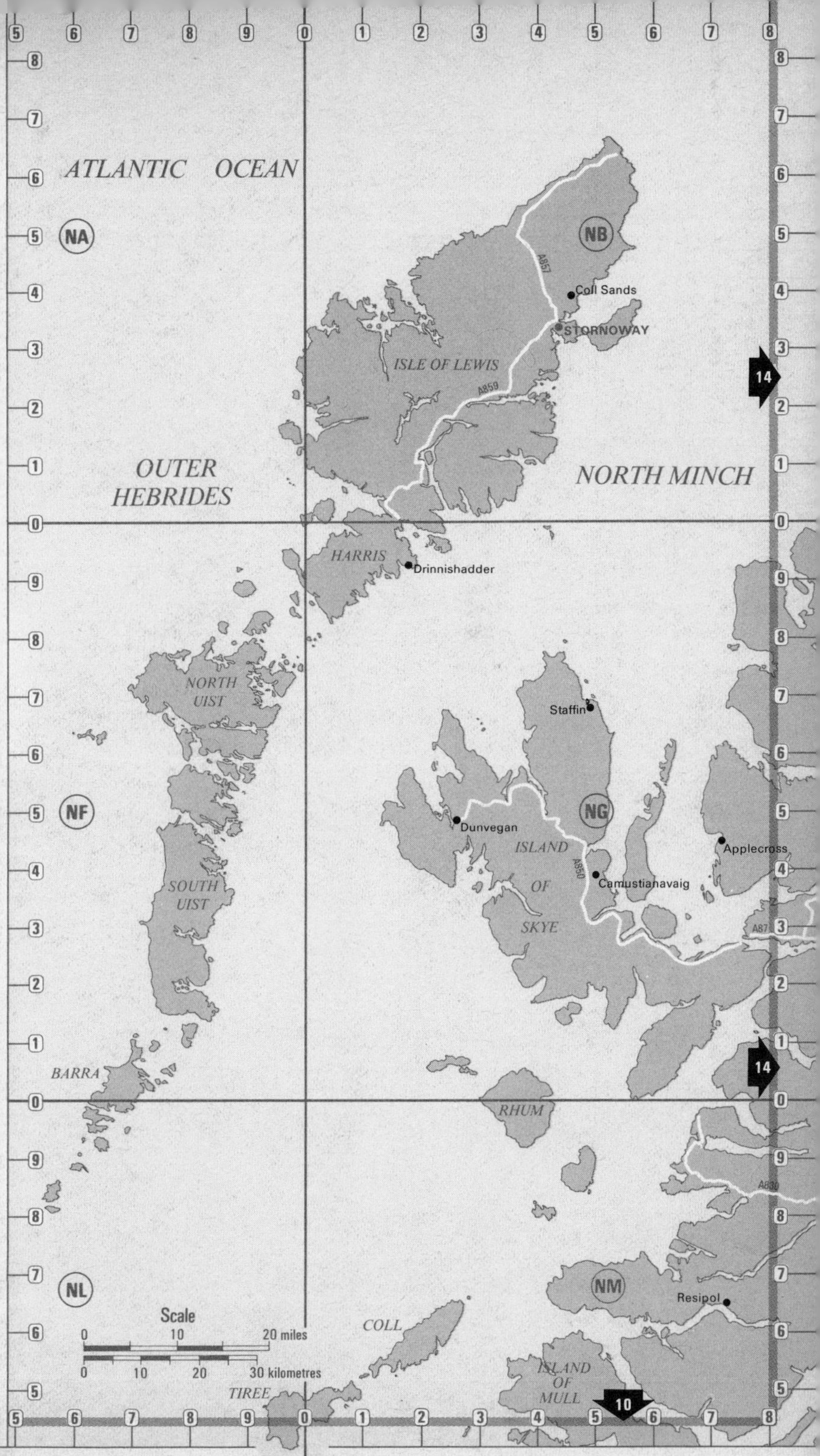

● Campsite
● Other Towns for location only

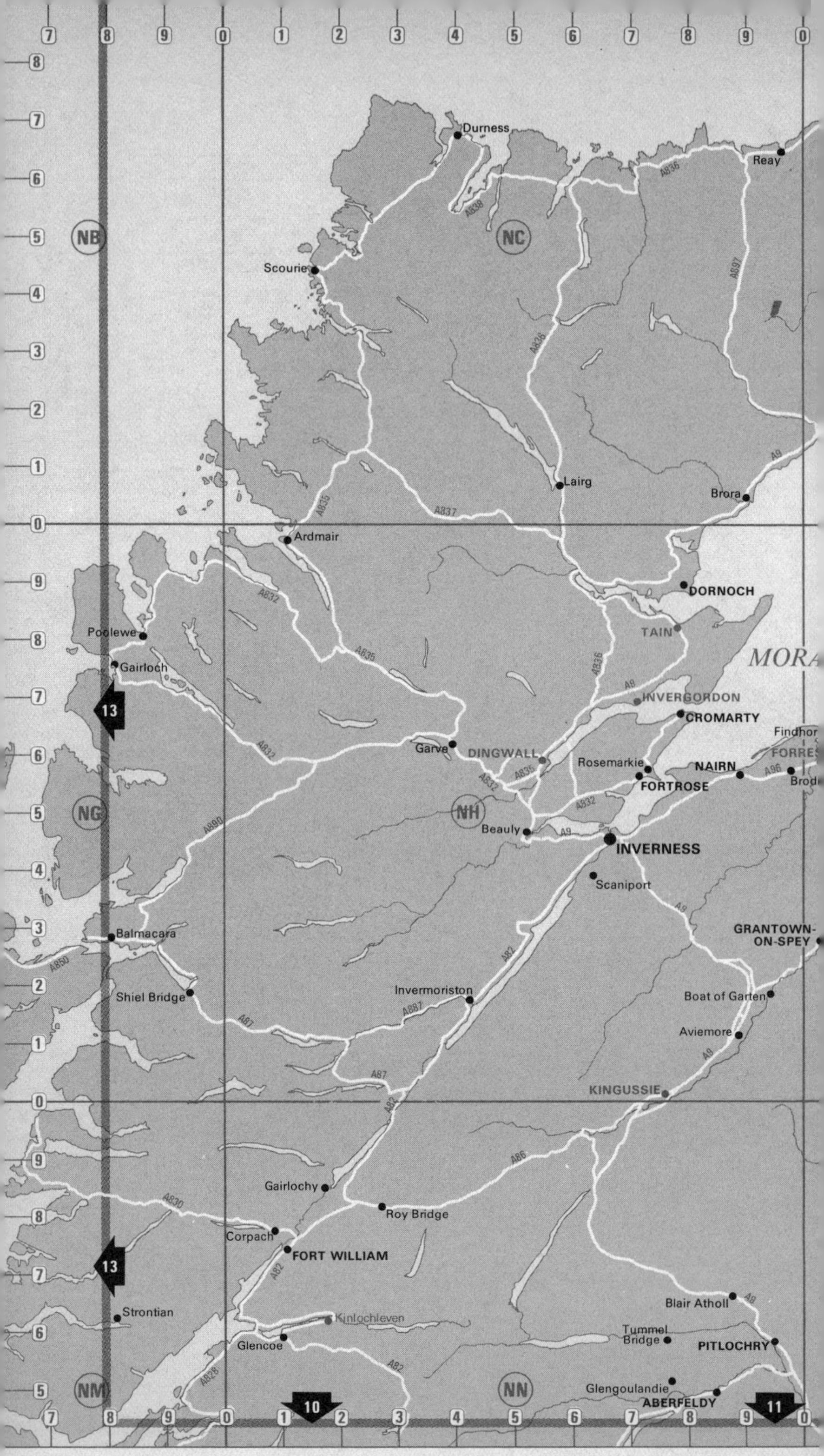
Durness
Reay
A836
A838
NB
NC
Scourie
A897
A836
A9
Lairg
Brora
A835
A837
Ardmair
DORNOCH
A832
Poolewe
TAIN
A835
MORA
Gairloch
A836
A9
INVERGORDON
13
CROMARTY
Findhor
Garve
DINGWALL
Rosemarkie
FORRES
A832
A835
NAIRN
A96
Brod
FORTROSE
NG
A832
NH
A890
Beauly
A9
INVERNESS
Scaniport
A9
Balmacara
GRANTOWN-
ON-SPEY
A850
A82
Shiel Bridge
Invermoriston
Boat of Garten
A887
A87
Aviemore
A9
A87
KINGUSSIE
A82
A86
Gairlochy
A830
Roy Bridge
Corpach
FORT WILLIAM
13
A82
Blair Atholl
A9
Strontian
Kinlochleven
Tummel
Bridge
Glencoe
PITLOCHRY
A82
A828
NN
Glengoulandie
NM
10
ABERFELDY
11

● Campsite
● Other Towns for Location only

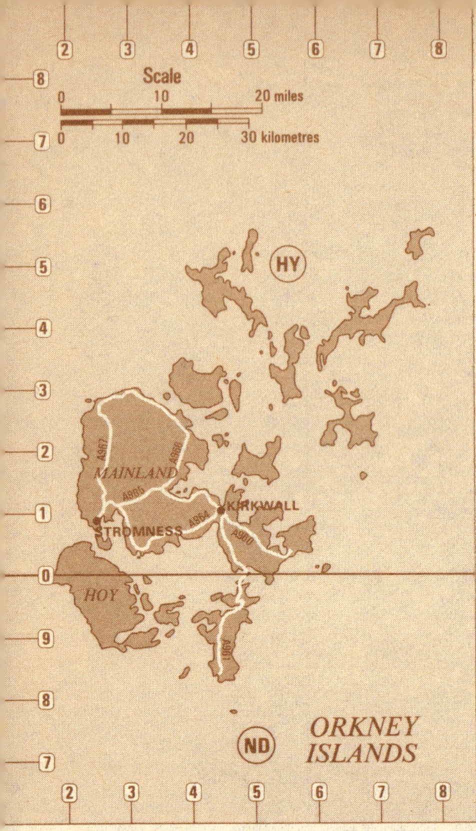

- Campsite
- Other Towns for Location only

Two for the price of one?

Motorised caravans are, in theory, the answer to many people's problems. They offer more comfort than tenting, with less time spent in pitching camp and packing up next morning when touring; and the bogy of trailing a caravan in heavy traffic, or negotiating narrow roads and awkward corners, disappears.

But – there always is a 'but' – you can't just unhitch the living part and use the traction bit as daily transport. Which usually means running two vehicles – the motorised van and a car – and with a motorised van costing far more than a trailer van, the expense puts the one-piece holiday vehicle out of the financial reach of many people.

Having seen the Suntor Marina at the Camping and Caravanning Exhibition, we wondered whether the problem could be solved by a small-vehicle conversion. Torcars of Torrington, North Devon, kindly agreed to put the Marina at our disposal for a week, and we also tried out their more-spacious (but slightly-more-expensive) Sherpa conversion. Chris and Sue Taylor took the Marina round Devon and Cornwall, the Sherpa around Wales. Their report aims to give an idea of what a holiday in a converted small van is like, without going into technical details; and to present their own opinions on the practicality of such a vehicle in the dual roles of everyday run-about and holiday home.

Chris and Sue Taylor tried out two vehicles for us – the Suntor Marina and Suntor Sherpa. Here they are, with the two vans, at Torcars' Torrington headquarters.

Two for the price of one?

Chris and Sue Taylor report

When we were asked to try out a couple of motorised caravans we were naturally delighted by the idea of two extra holidays.

Then we found that the first week was to be spent in a converted Marina van. A Marina? For a week? Do you know just how small they are? We couldn't imagine two people travelling, cooking, eating, washing, dressing, sleeping, in a Marina.

We picked up the Suntor Marina from Torrington on a squally March day and were immediately impressed by the ingenuity of the conversion. For travelling around it is little different from an estate car, with four forward-facing seats, but it sleeps two – three at a pinch – and has its own cooker, washing-up bowl with faucett over, wardrobe and storage cupboards, with three under-floor lockers for spare tyre, tools, and anything else you want to stow away.

Our first job was to install, in the many small cupboards, door-racks and lockers, all the things we had taken with us; some shelves were too shallow to take a 15oz tin and not deep enough for a sauce bottle, while the wardrobe was too short to take a dress, but in the end we found homes for everything other than our sleeping bags and pillows, which we dumped on the back seats – which was fine in our case but not so good had we been carrying passengers. When the roof was raised – and we'll come

Clever use of space includes racks on the doors.

to that later – there was plenty of room for bedding in the space over the cab, but then we had a bit of trouble with condensation, especially while we were cooking.

There was rain on the wind and we were glad when we were ready to leave. We set off in good spirits, our only immediate criticism being the time taken to fill the petrol tank. The trouble was something to do with the breather valve – a fault surely not beyond the ingenuity of man to rectify. A plus mark here was the fact that the 1300 engine runs on two-star petrol – not only cheaper but emitting less lead than higher-octane fuels. Petrol consumption proved to be very good considering the extra weight being carried, averaging out around 30 mpg.

The first real test came when we arrived at Crantock, just south of Newquay, where we planned to spend our first night. It was about 7pm, with dusk creeping over a deserted campsite, and we had to knock up the site proprietor to light the Ascot and open up the loos for us. It was a bit eerie, with the wind whistling off the Atlantic and ghosts of holidaymakers past and future drifting between the empty static vans. We rather wished we had stopped well before dark that first night, when we had to work out just how the Marina switched from a car to living quarters. But not many sites are open at that time of year and we had had little choice.

After the four clips holding the roof in position were released the roof went up with a single push, giving 6′ 2″ headroom for an area of 5″ x 3″. This opens up a third possible bunk space (the bunk is an optional extra) which would accommodate a child or, perhaps, a flat-race jockey. A preferable alternative if more than two people are using the vehicle would, we feel, be to invest in the optional annexe tent. This would be useful as an extension lounge for prolonged stays, too.

Barbican, the old quarter of Plymouth which survived Hitler's bombs, is a colourful hive of small ships and fishing boats.

Up – up – up . . . Raising the roof gave us no trouble, but you still need to be agile to get in and out via the rear doors.

The storage space over the cab takes the dismantled rear seats as well as accommodating the bedding. Reverting to the condensation problem, we realized it would have been a good idea to put our bedding in big plastic bags. This would have enabled us to deposit it on the floor of the van while we were travelling and would have kept moisture away when we were stationary. But at the time we did not have plastic bags because we had anticipated that lockers would be provided for bedding.

The front seats reverse to provide comfortable chairs for eating and leisure, with individual tables formed by lifting the top-hinged doors of the forward lockers. We had quite a struggle to perform the seat-reversing operation that first night, even with the clear instruction sheet supplied by Torcars; but having once achieved the seemingly-impossible, the task became easier and eventually we were able to do the complete 'home conversion' within fifteen minutes.

The cooker, sited at the offside rear of the van, was easy to set up. It swings up from its normal vertical storage position and has adequate shields to protect surrounding surfaces. A hinged flap underneath forms a useful shelf for items needed close to hand whilst cooking. One word here, though, about possible dangers.

The van has no stabilizers and it is essential to park on flat ground – preferably on a hard standing – if pans are to be safe; and care is needed if using the rear doors while cooking is in progress, both because of the danger of catching against a pan handle and because the sudden transfer of weight may cause cooking utensils to rock.

The wash basin is fixed on the opposite side of the van, mounted on the wardrobe door, and it is virtually impossible to use the rear doors when both this and the cooker are positioned. If the front seats and tables are arranged for eating it is a scramble to use the side doors too, so that one is fairly trapped.

As the wash basin is only 10″ x 9″ we found it most convenient – and safest – to use site facilities for washing dishes, but it had its uses all the same. Fed from a 5-gallon under-floor tank, with an electric pump (the switch comes easily to hand and a warning light shows when the tank is getting low) and drainage, it can be used for vegetable preparation, hand washing, etc. A minor criticism is that the water pump is noisy – noisy enough, in fact, to attract comment from other site-users. We discovered that a long-spouted water can or a length of hose was a necessary piece of equipment for filling the tank (via a plugged hole in the central door pillar), as sites do not reckon to provide more than just a tap. As a general point, we thought that many site taps could have been more sensibly positioned.

For preparing a meal on a warm summer's day the cooker, with its two burners and small grill, would be adequate for two or three people. Heat up a tin of soup, follow with cold meat, salad and new potatoes, a cold sweet and coffee – what could be nicer? But on a wintry evening we felt we needed a good cooked meal and a larger grill pan would have suited our needs better.

The driver's seat reverses and the top-hinged locker door lifts to form an individual table; there is a similar arrangement on the passenger side. The seat is comfortable and the table will take a dinner plate and cutlery, but it's not a very sociable seating plan.

A floor-level view of cooker and wash-basin with handy shelves below. We found it unwise to have both in use at one time as the rear doors were then inaccessible.

However we realized this requirement was a bit unreasonable in such a small home and managed to fare pretty well in spite of the limited cooking facilities.

The small tables on which our plates were balanced were not very sociable, but we enjoyed that first meal – which we both needed after our struggles with the equipment. Now we were able to take further stock of our surroundings. The van's standard colour scheme is basically cream and soft brown, with carpeted floor, tweedy upholstery and good quality curtains with plenty of fullness. The curtains run on rails at the side windows, are attached by press-studs at the rear door and around the cab, and by velcro in the roof-lights. The curtains are fastened together with velcro too, ensuring privacy for the occupants. The carpet is comforting to walk on, but not very practical at the kitchen end where occasional spills are inevitable.

The cap of the roof extension is lined with foam-backed vinyl which, apart from providing padding to protect the heads of giants, is supposed to deter condensation. We had already discovered that condensation was going to be a problem, in spite of an easily-operated push-up air vent, and two gauze inserts in the roof, covered by flaps which can be lifted when additional ventilation is needed. Standing at the cooker one was wreathed in steam even with these roof vents open; but in less chilly weather the doors could be left open – provided one was careful to park with them to the lea side of the van – and this difficulty would not arise to such a degree as we experienced.

Looking down the narrow inlet of the River Valency towards Boscastle Harbour where small fishing boats can shelter from the Atlantic Gales.

The interior finish is of high quality, with fittings clad in good quality plastic laminate and the natural wood surfaces coated with clear polyurethane. For such a tiny home-on-wheels it has a surprisingly spacious feel about it, which must have something to do with the clever design.

We relied on site and public toilet facilities. A Porta Potti is an optional extra and can be stored in the lower section of the wardrobe cupboard, but this would further reduce the already-limited storage space. For anyone not carrying a chemical toilet of this sort a good battery lamp is essential, for even if site toilets are lit there are hazards in picking one's way through caravans and guy-lines in the dark. In case you do trip over, or have any other mishap, a first-aid kit is a standard accessory in Torcars' vehicles.

The Marina, with its white roof interior and many windows, is bright and airy (though we thought a second roof light would make it better still), while after dark the artificial lighting, provided by three well-positioned strip lights, is excellent.

The omissions – no mirror, no rubbish receptacle, for instance – can mostly be put down to lack of space; and one needs to be careful, as well as agile, to get at some of the storage areas. But Torcars could not have done more in their efforts to make the most of the space available.

There is not a great deal one can do in the Marina during a dark evening except read or, perhaps, sit on the floor and play cards (or some other indoor game), so a portable TV set might be an asset on isolated sites which do not provide entertainment facilities.

Turning our kitchen/dining room into a bedroom was an easy operation. Folding the cooker and sink away presented no problems, and the seat frames fold flat to the floor with the seat cushions arranged on top to make a bed at floor level. Obviously sleeping bags are the best form of bedding in these circumstances. Brochure pictures show sleepers lying with their heads at the front of the van – which no doubt makes a better photograph with the camera positioned at the rear doors – but we found it best to lie the other way round as it was easier to keep feet clear of the steering wheel and gear lever than to have these essential pieces of equipment within flailing distance of arms and bumping distance of heads. We found the bed a bit narrow but were rocked to sleep by a force five gale and slept reasonably well considering the buffeting we were getting.

At least the high winds blew some of the clouds away and the next day dawned bright and sunny. Keen to set off while the good weather lasted, we found dressing (one at a time because of limited space), breakfasting, repacking, turning the Marina back into a motor vehicle by replacing the seats and lowering the roof (a slightly more complicated process than raising it because we had to wipe off condensation and make sure that the walls 'collapsed' evenly and were not trapped outside the roofcap) took quite a long time. The windows were liable to be misted over by morning, too, and we found an anti-condensation cloth helpful. Even with practice it took us at least an hour to get ready to continue our travels.

The seating cushions, laid on the floor, formed a comfortable bed. We chose to lie with our feet in the cab as the steering wheel and gear lever were not very cuddly, but this decreased elbow-room by the width of the side cupboards. Well-made curtains ensure privacy.

The next few days, touring around Cornwall and Devon – Penzance, Land's End, Mousehole (pronounced 'Mouzel' locally), Helston where they dance the Floral Dance, the old port of Falmouth, Truro (Cornwall's county town), Lostwithiel, Looe, Plymouth, Torbay, Dartmoor, Exeter – gave us ample opportunity to judge the Marina's performance and to adjust our first impressions of the van as living quarters.

It proved easily manoeuvrable, even down the narrow streets of St Ives and through Devon's winding lanes with their infrequent 'passing places' which we could not have tackled with a trailer caravan, and as its newness began to wear off (it had only fourteen miles on the clock when it was collected) the gearbox became much less 'lumpy'. It was inclined to be under-powered on the hills but one cannot have the fuel economy of a 1300 engine and expect high-powered performance too. A blind spot on the rear nearside, caused by the wardrobe compartment, is unfortunate but unavoidable; the large and well-positioned wing mirrors help to overcome this difficulty.

The vehicle attracted a good deal of attention both on site and when we stopped in towns. On several occasions we stopped while it was studied and commented upon, doing our best to answer queries and to explain the intricacies of its interior design.

At the end of our week we were quite sorry to part with the Marina. We had had time to find out the disadvantages of such a small 'home' as well as to enjoy the pleasures of being truly mobile. We had travelled 648 miles, sometimes on quite difficult roads, without encountering any significant snags, and the weather had been very kind to us.

A few weeks later we were again at Torrington, this time collecting a Sherpa conversion. Although this vehicle may be said to come in the small-van category – its kerbside weight is approximately 30cwt compared with the approximate 20cwt of the Marina – it seemed roomy out of all proportion after experiencing the limited, even though well-arranged, living space of the latter vehicle.

For travelling it has four forward-facing seats, or the rear seats can be turned sideways and extended to take four people, making adequate seating for a total of six adults. Two single beds or one double can be made from the standard cushions, with bunks available as extras – one across the cab and one each side of the roof space – accommodating, say Torcars, a maximum four adults and one child. The basic single beds were a bit narrow and we settled for pushing them together to make a double bed, leaving a bit of space either side for 'overhang'. As roof bunks were fitted we decided to try them out. Getting into bed was quite a performance as we both had to get on one bunk while the other was lowered into position – the space between them was then just a few inches. Once in, we found them quite comfortable but a bit small for an adult. As with the Marina, we felt that a tent annexe might be better than trying to sleep too many people within the confines of the van itself. There is space on the cab roof for stowing an awning or items such as picnic chairs.

When used as transport, the Sherpa has four forward-facing seats, or the rear seats can be rearranged, as shown here, to increase the total number of seats to six.

Pulled together, the seating was transformed into a good-sized double bed. As two singles, we found the beds rather narrow. Soft furnishings are the same as in the Marina.

For eating and leisure, the Sherpa, with its central table, was pleasant and comparatively spacious.

Food preparation is a pleasure in the Sherpa.

Under-bed compartments give plenty of room for bedding, while cupboards and good-sized wardrobes provide ample storage space for clothing. Space is allocated for a 1 cu ft refrigerator and a Porta Potti 33 (available as extras). Cupboards and racks for kitchen stores are more commodious than those in the Marina, and welcome additions to equipment are a mirror and a waste bin.

Other points on which the Sherpa scores are the ease with which seats are repositioned (the driver's seat and front passenger seat are left *in situ*); the more-sociable table (stored above the cab seats when not in use) which is positioned centrally between the seats; the cooker, which has an oven as well as grill and top burners, from which Sue produced some appetising meals without the frustrations experienced in the Marina; and the stainless-steel sink (served by a 12-gallon tank) and draining board.

The roof is raised from inside, the operation being power-assisted, but we found the roof vents less easy to operate than those in the Marina. However we did not have the same trouble with condensation although we had more wet weather than on our earlier trip. Interior trim and soft furnishings are very similar to the Marina with equal attention to detail.

All in all our initial impression of the Sherpa was that it overcame most of the problems we had encountered in the Marina. However, driving it – and I must add here that we had little experience of driving a vehicle as big as this – presented problems. Visibility and elbow-room were excellent, and it was nice to be able to see over the hedges, but the steering was heavy and it took a while to get used to allowing for the additional width and height.

The Sherpa on site at Mitchel Troy. The roof can be elevated from inside, the operation being power-assisted.

We drove along the rugged North Devon coast into Avon, crossing the Severn into Wales at Chepstow. Thence we zig-zagged our way up through Wales, touching Monmouth with its great castle, then Pembroke and the west coast north to the Mawddach valley, Dolgellau and Snowdonia, with an obligatory visit to the little Festiniog railway (Chris could not let that opportunity pass), returning through central Wales.

The sites at which we stayed were a little more awake than those we encountered in the south-west, a number having opened up at Easter; but we could not complain that either they, or the roads, were crowded. Some of the Welsh roads, with a cliff on one side and a precipice on the other, are not at all suitable for towing caravans. In general they are not as narrow as the Devon lanes, but some corners are difficult to negotiate and need to be taken slowly, with consequent annoyance to other road users. In many cases there are no alternative routes between main centres and resorts, whereas in the south-west peninsula there is a good network of trunk roads as alternatives to the awkward-to-negotiate lanes.

The Sherpa, once we got used to driving it, presented us with no such problems in getting around the country, but we did experience some difficulties when it came to parking, the van's over-all 7′ 2″ being well in excess of the usual height limit in private-vehicle parks. We were not, of course, at a disadvantage in comparison with a caravan (though a caravan can be left on site and the unhitched car be used for sight-seeing), but for touring-cum-living the Sherpa was not, in this respect, as convenient as the Marina.

We were able to take the Sherpa on narrow roads without danger of obstructing other road users. Here we are at St David's.

We found plenty of interest on our journey round Wales. This water wheel was at Felin Geri Mill.

A pleasant day at Porthmadog, but it was still jeans and jersey weather.

As dual-purpose vehicles both the Marina and the Sherpa have something to offer. Obviously as an everyday run-about the Marina is more economical, more manoeuverable, easier to park, and will fit into the sort of garage which most householders have at their disposal. On the other hand you must be pretty agile to live in such a limited space and you have to be well-organized too, or you will find the things you need are in inaccessible places just when you've succeeded in rearranging the equipment ready to do some particular chore. Even for people who are pretty nippy we feel that this vehicle is really only suitable for weekend trips and an occasional holiday of not much more than a week (unless one had a tent annexe, which would make it fine for a longer holiday). The makers tell us that it is popular with retired couples, who can use it for shopping and short trips, and go away for a few days whenever they take it into their heads that they would like to do so. Of course many retired people are still quite fit and supple and for them the Marina could meet all their needs. In particular those who still take part in sports, like the veteran Orienteers mentioned in John Disley's article, would find it the ideal solution to the problem of overnight accommodation before an event or during a championship meeting, while providing them with economical transport.

The sites were not crowded . . . Land-meets-sea-meets-sky at Hasguard Cross, in the Pembrokeshire National Park.

Daffodils at St Fagan's Castle.

But it is not suitable for people of any age who have back trouble, or difficulty in getting up and down steps, or in stooping; nor is it suitable for very big people since those much over 6ft would be continually bending; and heavyweights would find the beds too small even if they managed to squeeze behind the table flap and avoided knocking the pans off the cooker.

The Sherpa, because it is more spacious, is preferable as a mobile holiday home. Less time need be spent in rearranging everything to convert the vehicle from transport to living space; equipment is less basic; eating is more civilized; cooking and other chores are less frustrating; and storage space is adequate. But you might not want to use it as normal transport if you travel a long way daily to and from work, or to take the kids to school, because of the high running costs, and for shopping the difficulty in finding parking space would prove a drawback.

The truth is that if your funds are limited you have to compromise somewhere. If you want to be able to get away from home without too much prior planning – whether you intend to stay on recognized sites, visit friends or relations who have no spare bedrooms, or ask permission to park in a field somewhere – and at the same time to be able to get off the main roads, turn up an inviting lane which may, for all you know, peter out into a farm track, or drive into the quaint, narrow streets of some of our old towns and villages, then you may decide that a small vehicle in which you can cook, wash and sleep is just the job. If so we can recommend Torcars for the ingenuity of their conversions and the thought and skill which goes into detail. Other firms have found other solutions, perhaps using vehicles other than those manufactured by British Leyland and with different priorities in tackling design; they may cost quite a bit more than Torcars, they are unlikely to cost much less. Look around until you find the vehicle that most nearly meets *your* requirements, remembering that you are unlikely to find a small conversion that does not have quite a few drawbacks.

In the end you may decide that a trailer caravan suits you best after all. It just depends on your priorities.

Anyway we enjoyed our extra holidays. Thank you, Torcars.

Have one for the road.
St Ivel
five pints
INSTANT SPRAY
DRIED SKIMMED MILK
WITH NON MILK FAT
IDEAL FOR COOKING, DRINKS & PICNICS
gaz
globe trotter

ZZZZZZZ..

Good^safe^night.

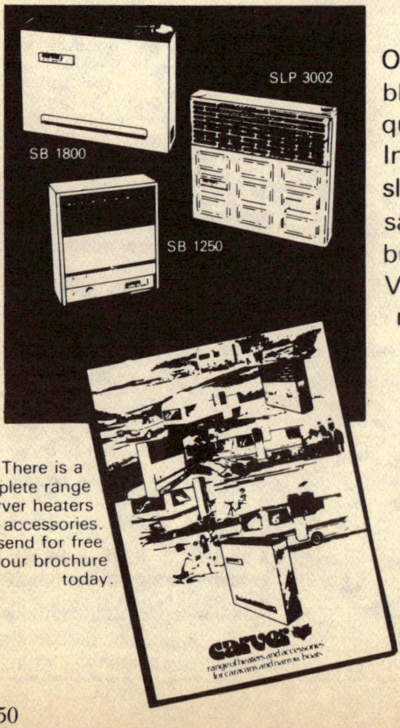

On the coldest night, in the bleakest spot, your Carver heater quietly warms and comforts you. In your snug caravan you will sleep through the night in absolute safety, protected by the quality built into every Carver heater. Very easy to install and completely room sealed. We can say with safety . . . sleep on.

There is a complete range of Carver heaters and accessories. Please send for free colour brochure today.

carver

Caravan Heating

Carver and Co. (Engineers) Ltd., Coppice Side, Brownhills, Walsall WS8 7ES. Telephone: 054-33 4521.

Know your vehicle

Car and driver alike have a considerable weight of caravan or trailer to contend with. There will be increased strain on both. Much of the art of towing safely comes with experience – but by being aware of some of the problems before setting off, many dangers can be eliminated.

Driving

Remember the three 'C's.

Care, Courtesy, Consideration

1 Know your car and how to drive it well – *before* attempting to tow.
2 Stop *before* you get tired.
3 Check that car, caravan, and towing gear are in top mechanical condition before setting off.
4 Plan the journey in advance, checking that the roads are suitable for towing.
5 Have the right mirrors and use them. Remember *Mirror, Signal, Manoeuvre.*
6 Keep well to the left of the road so that faster vehicles can overtake. If traffic builds up behind you, pull up in a safe place and let it pass.
7 Keep a safe stopping distance behind the vehicle in front.
8 *See and be seen* – Switch on lights whenever visibility gets poor.
9 Keep to the speed limit and make good use of the gears, especially on hills.
10 Allow plenty of time when overtaking or pulling across a main road.
11 Never stop on narrow roads, bends, crests of hills, or anywhere that could be dangerous to yourself and other road users.
12 In case of breakdown or accident, use hazard flashers or advance warning triangles.

Automatic gearboxes

The fluid in an automatic gearbox does more work when it has to cope with the extra weight of a caravan. It becomes hotter and thinner, so there is more slip and more heat generated in the gearbox. The oil temperature should not rise above 120°C. Many manufacturers recommend the fitting of a gearbox oil cooler, or the cheaper and less satisfactory alternative of an oil temperature gauge. Check with the manufacturer what is suitable for your car.

Cars which incorporate the 1, 2, and D gear shift positions offer advantages over the earlier models which do not; these gear positions should be used to reduce the work required of the torque convertor. It is beneficial also to downshift (D-2) when descending a long or steep hill thus reducing the work required of the car braking system.

Brakes

Both car and caravan brakes must always be in peak condition. Check especially fluid levels in the brake cylinder and the thickness of the brake lining material on both van and car (see Know the Law, page 65).

It is of the utmost importance on a car which is frequently used to tow a caravan for the brake fluid to be completely changed in accordance with the manufacturer's instructions or at intervals of not more than 18 months or 18000 miles. For the relative expense, it is good advice to change the brake fluid regardless of the above prior to departing on a Continental holiday, particularly if the journey includes a hilly or mountainous area.

Ensure that the caravan braking mechanism is adjusted to suit the car brakes. If a breakaway safety mechanism is used, the cable between car and caravan must be firmly anchored so that the trailer brakes are pulled on immediately if the two part. These brakes must be put out of action before reversing.

If you stop on a down slope and the safety latch is difficult to engage, chock the caravan wheels, and ease the car forward. Alternatively an electrically controlled system, which cancels the brake automatically as soon as reverse gear is selected, can be used.

Bracket and Couplings (see Towing brackets and their fitting).

Clutch and Cooling system

These will be under more strain, particularly in hilly country. Both should be well serviced, the clutch adjustment checked, and cooling system examined for blockage, leaks, faulty thermostat, and worn fanbelt. Ensure also that the radiator cap is in good condition.

Get any clutch slip (*ie* when the engine speed increases but the car speed does not) rectified immediately, as continued driving will burn out the linings.

Flashers

All six direction indicators should be working at between 60–120 flashes per minute. Most standard car flasher units will be overloaded by the two extra lamps, and a special heavy duty unit or a relay device should be fitted (see Know the Law, page 65).

Headlamps

The vertical setting of the car headlamps is raised when the caravan is attached, so the lamps should be reset when car and caravan are fully laden.

Level

The caravan should be level, or very slightly nose down when linked to the car and fully laden. A nose-up attitude can be corrected by a hitch height adjuster. These are available in various heights from the caravan manufacturer or dealer. An adaptor plate can be used to lower the two ball mounting, but it does put extra bending stresses on the bracket.

Mirrors

It is essential to fit mirror accessories for better rear vision. The accessories available include: extensions that clip on existing wing mirrors; arms to extend wing mirrors; long-arm wing or door mirrors; and periscopes which are fitted on the car roof and reflect the rear view through the caravan window. A periscope and wing mirrors used together should eliminate all blind spots.

The longer the mirror arm is, the more rigid its mounting has to be. Some mirrors have supporting legs or extra brackets to minimise vibration. A mirror mounted on the door pillar gives a wider field of vision because it is close to the driver. However, it has the disadvantage that it is at a greater angle to his forward line of sight. Convex mirrors give an even wider field of vision, but practice is needed before distances can be judged accurately, due to the diminished image.

Nose weight

The front of the trailer should be heavier than the rear by about 25–50kg (approx 60–100lb), depending on the manufacturer's recommendations. Check the nose weight when the caravan is laden, using bathroom scales or a spring balance (see Weighing). A twin axle trailer must be weighed when the coupling is at the exact towing height. Too much weight can result in excessive pitching, and too little can lead to instability.

Overhang

Cars with more length at the rear, and therefore greater distance between the back axle and the towing ball, tend to be more difficult to handle than cars with less overhang. The design and weight distribution of the trailer would, however, tend to have the greatest effect on overall performance.

Pitching

If the caravan starts to pitch, stability and control are reduced. If the nose weight is right, and the heavier movable items are stored as near as practicable to the axle of the caravan (see Weight Distribution), pitching can be prevented by stiffening the towing car's rear suspension. To do this, a supplementary rubber or air spring unit can be fitted to the rear springs, or heavier duty shock absorbers can be used, although the latter are more expensive. Before any alterations are made check that the car's front and rear shock absorbers are in good working condition.

Excessive pitching can lead to snaking, as the vertical movement starts to sway the caravan sideways.

Rear Fog Lights

Since October 1979 it has been a legal requirement that all new cars and trailers are fitted with at least one working rear fog light. Because of this there has also been a change in the seven-pin plug and socket wiring necessary when towing a new trailer. Pin 2/52 (blue wire), which was used to supply trailer accessories such as the interior lights, radio, water pump, etc, is now used to supply current for the trailer rear fog lights. Where a trailer requires an accessory supply, a separate plug and socket will be required. Caravan manufacturers are using a second seven-pin plug which looks the same as the plug providing the trailer's lights but which has a different pin arrangement. The trailer manufacturer or hirer should be able to give advance information on the number and type of sockets which will be required on the towing vehicle.

Snaking

This can be caused by heavy pitching or bad weight distribution. Snaking can be particularly dangerous as it is tempting for the driver to steer against the movement, and make matters worse. It is best to steer straight and decelerate gently. Stabilisers are available, but it is better to cure the cause than to rely on preventative methods.

Stabilisers

If snaking still occurs at a reasonable speed although weight distribution, nose weight, and the car suspension are right, a stabiliser can provide some damping between car and trailer. The damping force helps prevent a small sway (such as caused by a sudden crosswind) developing into a snake, by introducing a controlled amount of friction between car and trailer. The stabiliser can be with a special coupling or tow ball mounting, or as a separate linkage.

Security chains

These are to keep the trailer attached if the coupling parts. Some towing brackets have hooks on either side of the mounting plate for the chains. Both chains and attachments must be very strong to cope with any sudden impact. Generally it is unlikely that a well-maintained and fitted coupling will become detached.

Soft ground

Avoid low sites liable to be waterlogged, sand that will not take the force of a driving wheel, and stones and shingle that may take the weight but not provide any grip.

If you have to drive over difficult ground, keep moving slowly with a very light throttle. If you stop, do not accelerate hard or the wheels will spin and dig in. Move gently backwards and forwards to get out of a dip. If the driving wheels do dig in, dig out a gradient in front of the wheels and put brushwood or sacks in front and behind the wheels. To move the trailer manually, pull sideways on the drawbar and work it forwards by chocking alternate wheels.

Stop lights

As the extra pair of stop lights may overload the car stop light switch, a combined stop light flasher relay unit should be fitted.

Towing car

Almost any car can be used for towing. A large engine gives better low speed pulling power, and for further ease of towing the gear ratio of the back axle can be changed. Independent rear suspension is likely to need some stiffening to help prevent pitching (see Pitching). A long wheelbase gives good stability, but the amount of overhang must be taken into consideration (see Overhang).

For more detailed information on how to choose a good tow car see page 56.

Tyres

See Know the Law, page 69. Find out the recommended tyre pressures suitable for the extra load from the manufacturer. They will vary according to the type, size, and ply rating of the tyres. If a lot of high speed driving is to be done, check that the ply rating is adequate. The rear tyre pressures, for example, may have to be increased by 2–3lb per square inch. Pressures can only be checked accurately when the tyres are cold.

If the caravan tyres are not going to be used for a long period, they should be properly inflated, and have the weight taken off them by jacking the axle on to wood blocks. Leave in an airy place where they will not be exposed to the sun.

Weight

Caravan literature usually refers to weights as Ex-works or Delivered but they can be misleading due to the fact that it normally is based on a standard model and need not necessarily take into account any extras fitted. If the weight is referred to as above and the manufacturer cannot be contacted it is recommended that the as-delivered weight be obtained by having it weighed at the nearest Public Weighbridge. This weight subtracted from the manufacturer's recommended maximum gross weight will give you the weight that can be utilised for personal effects and equipment. The kerbside weight of the tow car is defined as, the weight of the vehicle (inclusive of any towing bracket with which it is normally equipped) when it carries, no person, a full supply of fuel, a supply of other liquids incidental to its propulsion, eg, water, oil, brake fluid etc, and no load other than the loose tools and equipment with which the vehicle is normally equipped.

Weight distribution

General stability will be improved by keeping as much weight as possible near the trailer axle. Heavier equipment should be stored on or near the caravan floor, to cut down the possibility of pitching (see Nose Weight, page 52).

TOWING BRACKETS AND THEIR FITTING

There are a large number of different towing brackets available from manufacturers, approved accessory shops, car manufacturers and franchise agents. There is often little difference between them in their ability to do the job, but some towing brackets tend to be more cumbersome than is necessary.

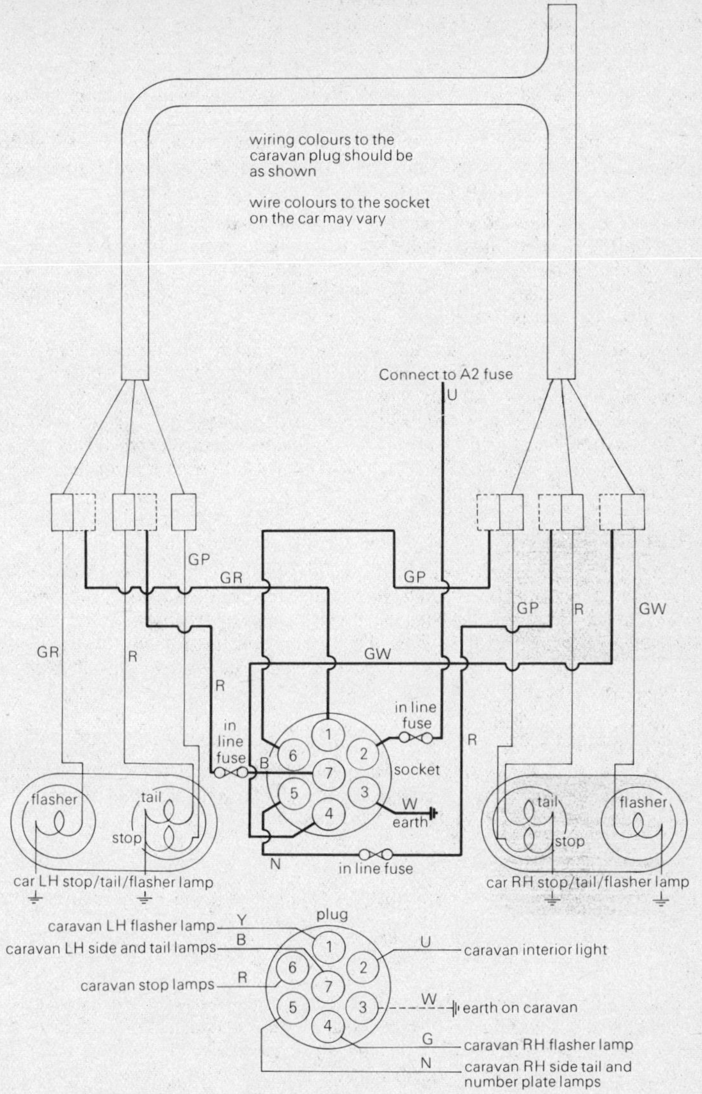

NB: Where the trailer is fitted with rear fog lights Pin 2 in the diagram (blue wire) is used for their supply – trailer accessories will require a second plug and socket.

Plug and socket Reference		
International Pin Number	Alternative Number	
1	L	L54
2	54G	52
3	31	
4	R	R54
5	58R	58S
6	54	
7	58L	58C

W White	P Purple	R Red	Y Yellow
G Green	N Brown	B Black	U Blue
——— existing wiring			
- - - - - - additional wiring			
existing single snap connector			
existing single snap connector replaced with double snap connector			

The cost varies considerably and it is advisable to shop around before coming to a final decision. Continental car manufacturers' brackets can be rather more expensive in this country: it is therefore much better to buy from one of the specialist manufacturers in this country. Before buying a towing bracket check with the manufacturer the height of the towing ball from the ground. If this height does not match up with the caravan coupling, adjusters may be necessary in order to achieve a level ride. When passengers and luggage are aboard and the car and caravan are connected, the ball height will drop by possibly 50mm (2in) or more.

Some towing brackets now being imported into this country have an integral ball which means that the towing height cannot be adjusted. The type of towing attachment that ends in the standard two-holed faceplate is preferred in most cases. Couplings usually conform to British Standards although the design is not defined by any law.

The diameter of the ball is defined by a British Standard as 50mm with a tolerance of + nil to − 0.25mm and another British Standard defines the coupling bolt holes as of 15mm ($\frac{5}{8}$in) clearance at 90mm ($3\frac{1}{2}$in) centres and the distance vertically between bolt hole centres and the centre of the ball as 70mm ($2\frac{3}{4}$in). The height to the bolt hole centres above ground is defined as 405mm (16in) + 50mm (2in) with towing vehicle in kerb weight condition.

Fitting

On the majority of cars, towing bars are fairly easy to fit and within the capabilities of a competent DIY type with a reasonable tool kit, elementary mechanical knowledge, and the use of pit, ramps or strong axle stands. Perhaps most important of all is confidence in one's ability to do the job well. The consequences of an incorrectly fitted bracket breaking loose could be very serious indeed.

If the job cannot be done at home there are plenty of competent garages capable of carrying out a first class job. However, where possible it is usually better to have the bracket fitted by a garage that specialises in this kind of work. The local dealer for your particular caravan will often be able to advise you on where to get a towing bracket fitted.

Electrical

An internationally agreed 7-pin plug and socket, wired in accordance with ISO standards, is the standard electrical connection between car and caravan, and allows interchangeability of caravan and/or car, should the necessity arise.

In order to allow the flashing indicators to operate simultaneously on car and caravan at the legal rate of between 60 and 120 flashes per minute, a heavy-duty flasher unit or relay device is necessary. Wiring of the electrical connections involved in this modification is best left to a garage or auto electrical specialist.

See also under *Rear Fog Lights*.

HOW TO CHOOSE A GOOD TOW CAR

We're back to the old chicken and egg story when it comes to towing car and caravan buying. Do you buy your caravan to suit the car or vice versa? In either case, the most influential criteria are personal preference and price range. If you do already have a caravan and are thinking of changing your car, it will be worth taking a look at some of the points we suggest, that will help you get the best performance out of both vehicles.

The car must have enough power in reserve to cope with the extra load of a caravan. Basically, the heavier the car the better, but certainly, the car's kerbside weight (for definition see page 54) must at least equal the maximum gross weight of the caravan to be towed. As an extra precaution

Anyone can add a towing bracket to a car.

But at Special Tuning, we know there's more involved.

Working together with BL engineers, we've prepared a wide range of kits for most BL cars.

We make a range of oil cooler kits for both engines and transmissions, to ease the strains of towing.

We also offer progressive rear bump stop kits. These stop the rear of the car sagging when towing, in return for only a slightly firmer ride during normal use.

Then there's our Pluspac 'A' tuning kit that improves pulling power for better road performance. Yet it does so without affecting the car's warranty or Supercover.

Send for more details, plus the address of your nearest Special Tuning dealer.

And we'll keep your car ahead of your caravan.

Special Tuning, Abingdon-on-Thames, Oxon OX14 1AU.
Please send me details of ☐ towing aids ☐ spoilers ☐ Pluspacs.

Name ______________________

Address ______________________

____

Model of car ______________ Year ______________

SPECIAL TUNING
Gives you more car

check with the car manufacturer the maximum recommended weight the car can comfortably tow. The idea is to achieve maximum stability under all conditions. If you have a penchant for long trips over hilly mountainous roads, the car/caravan combination chosen should be a weight-to-weight ratio lower than the formula – *ie*, the car should be about 50kg (1cwt) heavier than the maximum gross weight of the caravan.

The distance from the centre of the car's rear wheels to the point where the coupling is attached, should be as short as possible. A long tail acts as a lever and allows the car's springs to be compressed unduly by the caravan nose-weight, and may well lead to pitching, especially if the springs are soft. The rear springing of a car can greatly affect the stability of a complete outfit, and although there is nothing wrong with independent rear suspension systems for towing, they do have a tendency to be softer than the conventional springing.

Soft systems may produce poor towing performances and should be avoided if possible. However, soft suspensions can be used if supplemented by the use of spring assisters or heavy duty shock absorbers.

Maximum brake horse power alone is not sufficient to make a good tow car engine. What is needed is good torque at fairly low revs, something between 1,800–2,000rpm, which will enable a well-matched outfit to pull away on a reasonable gradient. High gearing admittedly is conducive to fuel economy and easy engine performance at high road speeds, but the caravanner will find that a high-geared car would necessitate a lot of gear-changing. It is therefore worth considering estate cars, for example, which sometimes have lower overall gearing.

Automatic transmissions incorporating a torque converter – which is of course able to deliver full torque to the road wheels at zero miles per hour – are ideal for starting away on a gradient with a caravan attached. However, the car manufacturer should be consulted as to whether the car is suitable for towing and whether an oil cooler is necessary, if one is not fitted as standard.

WINTER STORAGE AND SPRING OVERHAUL

It is a misguided and sometimes dangerous belief, that a caravan, being a relatively simple structure in comparison with the car which tows it, and because it spends most of the time stationary, requires little or no maintenance other than to keep it clean. This, as inferred, is far from true, and in order to keep the caravan in prime condition it is recommended that it is given a thorough examination twice a year, in addition to the periodic checks which should become routine while the caravan is in relatively frequent use.

The two major inspections and maintenance programmes should be conducted prior to, and at the end of, the season of use and the notes which follow are intended to provide guidance. A number of the recommendations apply also to those owners who use their caravan all the year round who should also plan for a periodic inspection of the underside.

Let us start then with the things to do and look for when taking it out of its winter 'mothballs' on the first sunny and warm day in early spring.

SPRING

Chassis and Underside

While the caravan is still up on its corner legs with, preferably, blocks under the axle to take the weight off the tyres, thoroughly examine the main chassis members throughout the length together with any steel crossmembers or outriggers. Almost invariably you will find some evidence of rust which is inevitable and need not cause too much concern. Where more serious corrosion exists, evidenced by flaking of the material, a simple assessment can be made by use of a small hammer ($\frac{1}{4}$–$\frac{1}{2}$lb) or similar tool. Using the hammer gently, tap the area of corrosion and if the hammer bounces off the metal and the noise is a relatively sharp clear knock or ding the corrosion is not too serious. If, however, the hammer does not bounce and the noise is subdued and hollow sounding it would be as well to obtain the opinion of your local dealer, car body repairer or garage.

A further tip – do not lie immediately under where you are tapping or you may get an eye full of dirt or rust, either of which can be painful. You will soon become aware of any significant difference in the sound if you tap all the way along so do not worry too much about these definitions. While under the caravan look also at the wooden bearers – these are the wooden beams which rest on the chassis members and onto which the caravan body is built.

Look also at any wiring that may be visible and make sure it is not chafing against anything which could in time bare the conductor, and ensure also that the cable has not been nibbled and does not show any deterioration of the outer insulation. It is good practice to secure the cables to prevent them from chafing.

The gas pipes should be closely examined for cracks or chafing and similar to the wiring it is important for them to be secured to eliminate any possibility of the pipes flexing which could result in fracture. In some cases the water pipes run beneath the floor and this provides an opportunity, if the pipes are of clear plastic, to see that they are clean inside.

Wheels and Tyres

As previously suggested, it is preferable for the caravan to winter with the weight off the tyres. Or better still if you have sufficient space, remove the wheels and store them under cover. However, whichever method is employed the tyres must be carefully examined before being put into use.

Firstly, inflate them to the correct pressure and make sure that valve caps are in place. Check the tread depth which, as with the car, must not be less than 1mm. Preferably, however, 2mm should be your lower limit.

Generally, caravan tyre tread wear does not occur at the same rate as on the car and therefore the tyres are often taken for granted. This can be dangerous as, because of the time the caravan stands, cracking of the tyre side walls can occur which could result in tyre failure. Therefore, carry out a close and careful examination of the tyre side walls and should you find any evidence of cracking consult your nearest tyre dealer, for his advice.

Parking brake

Apply the parking brake and ensure that it holds on the ratchet. Then check each brake drum in turn to see that you are unable to turn either drum. If one drum can be turned while the other cannot there is a braking fault which must be investigated before the caravan is used.

Having carried out the above check, release the parking brake and again check the drums. On this occasion they should turn quite freely. If one or both brake drums is still held, or turns with some difficulty accompanied by a rubbing or binding noise, a fault exists which must be rectified.

Providing the brakes function correctly, check and adjust the brakes in accordance with the manufacturer's instructions shown in the Handbook.

Wheel bearings

Much will depend on one's DIY ability whether to tackle dismantling the wheel bearings for cleaning, inspection and subsequent lubrication. If in doubt ask your caravan dealer or local garage to do it for you. However, it is a simple matter to check the bearing adjustment. Hold the wheel, or if removed, the brake drum at the top and the bottom – 12 o'clock and six o'clock – and rock the drum. Barely perceptible movement should be felt.

No movement, or relatively free movement, indicates that adjustment is necessary.

Before adjusting the bearings spin the drum which should revolve quite easily and quietly. If a rumbling noise is evident, or if when turning the drum it feels notchy, either or both the bearings in that hub require attention.

Suspension

While the wheels are off examine the various suspension components.

Examine the springs for broken coils or collapse due perhaps to overloading.

Look also at the shock absorbers which should not show any sign of oil seepage down the main body. Check also that the rubber mountings top and bottom are intact. Finally examine the main axle beam or arms, depending on the type of suspension employed, together with its mountings and pivots.

Corner legs

Finally oil or grease the threads of the corner legs. Ensure they operate freely when you let the caravan down and check that the main components have not become bent or distorted while the caravan has rested upon them during the winter.

That concludes the dirty underneath work except for the coupling which we will come to later.

Exterior

Thoroughly wash the van using a car shampoo or mild detergent and remove whatever stains have appeared during the winter storage period. A good car polish will help to remove some of the more stubborn blemishes and serve also to protect the paintwork.

While proceeding around the caravan cleaning and polishing, take the opportunity to examine the various panel seams to see that the sealer appears intact. Check also the roof seams, particularly in the area of the roof guttering; if using a ladder, take care not to damage the moulding into which the awning fits.

Interior

Now one's attention can be turned to the interior which in general terms can be treated the same as domestic spring cleaning. Special attention should be paid to the interior panels around windows and doors for evidence of dampness caused perhaps by ineffective seals. Look in corners and under carpets for evidence of dampness, not forgetting the inside of lockers under seats.

Finally check that all ventilators are free and not obstructed by anything.

While on the subject of ventilators have you added any gas-burning equipment since you bought the caravan? If you have, the chances are that you now have insufficient ventilation, which could prove extremely dangerous. **Calor Gas consider this to be the most serious single failing of caravan users in connection with the use of gas.**

The caravan should now be ready for the road except for checking the coupling and the lighting. There is presently no ruling on the internal dimension of the coupling socket and therefore the most practical method is to clean all grease from the ball and socket – connect the caravan to the car and feel for movement between the two. Although there is no legal dimensional tolerance for the ball it is considered that no more than 1mm of wear is acceptable.

With regard to the lighting, couple the 7-pin connector. First switch on the sidelamps and check that the front and rear lights on the caravan illuminate, not forgetting the rear number plate lamp. Follow this by checking the flashing indicators, first one side, then the other, and finally check the stop lamps. The law requires the indicators on the front and rear of the car to illuminate as well as those on the rear of the caravan.

It my be necessary for you to obtain assistance from somebody who can check the lamps while you apply the foot brake or vice versa. Alternatively you may be able to keep the brake pedal depressed with a piece of wood or a brick. **Do not forget** to switch the ignition on for this check, and, equally important, off when you have finished.

Subject to the foregoing your caravanning should be as enjoyable as you hoped and cause no reason for concern over the caravan's condition. Depending on the amount of mileage covered, you will only need to make a periodic check of tyre pressures and condition and obligatory lamps.

WINTER

Laying up

To preserve the condition of the caravan during the winter it is important to carry out a number of tasks whether the caravan has to stand out completely exposed or is stored in a barn. Obviously it would be of considerable benefit if a space could be found which would afford the caravan some protection from the weather.

There could be some advantage in working in the reverse order to what has been previously written and therefore we will deal with the interior first.

Interior

Thoroughly clean the interior and ensure that all lockers and cupboards are clean and not harbouring old papers or any material which could be edible to insects or mice or provide nesting material.

Ensure that all fixed ventilators are free and where these open into a cupboard or similar, leave the doors open. In fact it is good policy to leave all doors and lids open in order to permit as free a circulation of air as possible. If stored under cover leave also the roof ventilator fractionally open to assist with interior ventilation. Wherever possible, store cushions and mattresses in the house or enclose them in plastic bags and stand them in the caravan in a way that permits maximum air circulation.

Much will depend on the type of caravan but if the water pipes from the water container to the pump and pump to tap are reasonably to hand remove them for thorough cleaning.

Exterior

Thoroughly clean the paintwork, as at the start of the season, and apply a good coating of wax polish. Make a note of any dents or scars that may have been collected during the season as it could be good sense to arrange for the repairs to be carried out during the off-season. Similarly, to combat corrosion it will be necessary to make good any damaged paintwork.

Final Checks

Use washing soda and hot water to clear collected grease from the sink waste pipe, and make sure the sink plug is installed. If possible tie up the outside end of the waste pipe and blank off with a cork or similar to prevent the pipe from becoming a temporary home for insects or others.

The gas bottles require no special treatment for the winter other than in terms of ensuring their security. If they are normally housed in a lockable locker they may be left, making sure that they are fully turned off. Otherwise remove and store them in a shed or garage in a well-ventilated position just in case there might be a slow leak from the shut-off valve.

Chassis and Underside

Although this part of the treatment is dirty and by far the most unpleasant aspect, it must not be overlooked in the interests of the useful life of the caravan and road safety.

Jack up one side of the caravan until the tyre is clear of the ground and place blocks or some solid support beneath the chassis member as close to the wheel as possible, lower the corner legs merely to steady the caravan. Do the same the other side, and gently shake the caravan to ensure it is safe and unlikely to be blown off its supports by a strong wind.

Coil the 7-pin plug and cable and put in a plastic bag off the ground. Grease the brake actuating shaft using the nipples provided and thoroughly grease the inside of the coupling. This can be covered or enclosed in a plastic bag if desired. Oil the coupling release lever.

Oil or grease the threads of the jacking type jockey wheel and smear grease on the outer sleeve. Oil the locking screw threads.

Now examine the chassis and underside and check for damage and corrosion and test any corrosion you may find in the manner previously explained. Where only surface rust is evident use a wire brush and remove all the loose material and any dirt which may exist.

The next step depends largely on the individual as the chassis frame could be painted, using first a good zinc based primer. Otherwise the metalwork could be covered in an undersealing material which can be purchased in most accessory shops.

Failing either of these methods a liberal coating of waste engine oil can be painted on which serves as an excellent and cheap preservative. The same can be used on the corner legs and has the combined advantage of protection and lubrication; also oil the brake rods and attachments.

Generally examine the axle and or main suspension components for damage or worn parts. Remove the wheels and examine the suspension components; protect with whichever method decided on, those parts of the understructure thus exposed.

Either store the wheels and tyres under cover or replace on caravan; either method however inflate the tyres 2–3lb over recommendation. **Make sure the parking brake is left off.**

Motor caravan

It is assumed that these vehicles are in general use or relatively so and therefore no special precautions are required over and above the servicing and maintenance instructions of the manufacturer.

Painting

The paint finish of a modern caravan is very similar to that of a car and should be treated in the same way. Any reinstatement of a sizeable area should be carried out by spraying. Small chips or small scratches however can be successfully touched in by using a small brush and matching colour.

In general terms, brush painting an area of touring caravan could result in a reduction of the caravan's value at the time of sale.

The Caravan Club

Tel : East Grinstead (Code 0342) 26944

The Caravan Club is the biggest organisation of its kind in the world and administers the largest private network of sites in the U.K. Its service to its 200,000 member families is unrivalled, and is backed by some sixty years experience. Whatever your interests, you'll find they are catered for ; and motor and trailer caravanners are equally welcome. The coupon will bring you full membership details.

TO : THE CARAVAN CLUB · EAST GRINSTEAD HOUSE · EAST GRINSTEAD WEST SUSSEX RH19 1UA

Please send me full·details of membership

NAME..

ADDRESS ....

.... **AAyb**

SITES DIRECTORY AND HANDBOOK LISTING 128 CLUB SITES AND SOME 3,500 CERTIFICATED LOCATIONS (5-VAN FARM SITES EXCLUSIVE TO MEMBERS), AND ABOUT 900 SPECIALLY SELECTED OTHER SITES * COLOUR MAGAZINE, 'EN ROUTE' * RED PENNANT FOREIGN TOURING SERVICE * INFORMATION SERVICE * RESCUE REIMBURSEMENT SCHEME * PUBLIC RELATIONS FOR TOURING CARAVANNERS * LEGAL AID * RALLIES AND SOCIAL EVENTS * COMPREHENSIVE '5 C'S' CARAVAN INSURANCE SCHEME * MEMBERS' FINANCE PLAN * SPECIAL CAR AND MOTOR CARAVAN INSURANCE * PRACTICAL CARAVANNING COURSES.

4665

Know the law

This section, produced by AA Legal Services, provides a synopsis of some of the more important provisions applicable in Great Britain which affect the ordinary car user when towing one trailer. The contents are believed correct as at 17 May 1979, but the position may be checked through your AA Regional Office.

The measurements quoted have been extracted from the relevant authorities and this accounts for the fact that some are metric and others imperial.

Brakes

Generally, every trailer exceeding 102kg unladen weight must be equipped with an efficient braking system, the requirements of which differ according to the date of the trailer's manufacture.

Trailers over 102kg, manufactured on or after 1 January 1968, must have brakes that can be applied to all wheels whilst being drawn. If the brakes of either car or trailer fail, the driver or attendant must still be able to apply brakes to two wheels of the trailer (or one wheel in the case of a two wheeled trailer). This does not apply if the trailer has brakes which operate automatically on the overrun. Parking brakes must be sufficient to hold the trailer on a gradient of 1 in 6.25, and operable by a person standing on the ground.

Every part of the braking system and its means of operation must at all times while the trailer is used on a road be maintained to prescribed standards, be in good and efficient working order and properly adjusted.

NB Special rules apply to certain categories of modern trailers meeting European Economic Community technical braking standards and in respect of which the appropriate certificate has been issued.

Dimensions

The maximum permitted overall length for a trailer is 7 metres excluding the drawbar and drawbar fittings. If the trailer has at least four wheels and the distance between the front and rear wheels on the same side is not less than 3/5ths of its overall length and the drawing vehicle weighs more than 2030kg, the maximum length of the trailer allowed is 12 metres.

The maximum permitted width is generally 2.3 metres, but may be 2.5 metres if prescribed conditions are met.

Direction indicators

All trailers manufactured after 1 July 1955 and before 1 January 1974 must be fitted with automatic direction indicators. This does not apply when the trailer (laden or unladen) is squarely behind the drawing vehicle and both rear or side direction indicators on the drawing vehicle can be seen 6 metres from the rear of the trailer. All trailers manufactured on or after 1 January 1974 must be fitted with amber-coloured flashing indicators optically separate from any other lights on the vehicle. They must be marked with the prescribed E approval mark and a specified number. The indicators may be of single or dual intensity but it is worth checking up on the wiring conditions which apply to the latter.

Any trailer may meet alternative requirements introduced recently instead of the above.

Fire extinguishers

There is no legal requirement for a fire extinguisher to be carried in a private saloon car, or trailer towed by such a car.

Front side lights

A trailer exceeding 1600 millimetres in width must carry two front side lamps meeting certain positional and technical requirements, if more than

5ft from the drawing vehicle. If any load carried on a trailer projects sideways by more than 12in additional front lamps must be carried in order to indicate the limit of the projection.

Insurance

Any trailer drawn by a vehicle on a road must be covered by effective road traffic insurance, generally by an extension of the towing vehicle's policy cover. There is no legal requirement for a trailer to be separately covered, but it is recommended that it be insured against loss or damage, and legal liability, even when it is not being towed.

Roads within holiday sites may not necessarily be public highways in law and consequently motorists are advised to check with their insurers that their policies cover the use of vehicles on such private sites.

Lay-bys

Lay-bys may not be used for overnight stops except where provided for by authorised traffic signs. See Obstruction, Rest Areas.

Learner drivers

It is illegal for provisional licence holders to drive a car towing a trailer.

Lights (general)

If the distance between drawing vehicle and trailer is more than 5ft both must be lit as if they were separate vehicles. The distance is that between the nearest point of the two vehicles disregarding the drawbar or any fitting or attachment. A trailer, not exceeding 1600mm in width, is exempt from the requirement for showing lights to the front.

Mirrors

Regulations provide that, subject to exceptions, every motor vehicle shall be equipped either internally or externally with a mirror so constructed and fitted to the motor vehicle as to assist the driver, if he so desires, to become aware of traffic to the rear of the vehicle.

The majority of motor vehicles (including motor cars, dual-purpose vehicles and goods vehicles) made after November 1977 and first used after May 1978 must be equipped with both an interior rear view mirror and an exterior rear view mirror fitted to the off-side of the vehicle. If the interior mirror does not provide an adequate view of the road to the rear of the vehicle an additional exterior mirror must be fitted on the near-side of the vehicle. When the vehicle is drawing a trailer, the mirrors must assist the driver to become aware of traffic to the rear of the trailer. In addition it should be noted that there are regulations governing the type of mirror fitted, its specifications and its position.

The lack of adequate rear vision may help to substantiate a charge of negligence in a claim for damages, or a charge of driving without due care and attention.

Motorways

Vehicles drawing a trailer must not use the right outside lane of a three lane carriageway when all three lanes are open for use by traffic going in the same direction, unless the vehicle being passed is of such exceptional width that it can only be passed by using the outside lane.

Number plates

A duplicate number plate must be fitted to the rear of the trailer and illuminated at night. Reflecting number plates are compulsory on cars registered on or after 1 January 1973, but not on trailers, where they are merely discretionary.

Obstruction

It is an offence to cause unnecessary obstruction on the highway. Vehicles must not be left for an unreasonable or unnecessary time, or in a dangerous position. The Police can remove vehicles that are causing obstruction or parked contrary to waiting restrictions and charge for that removal and subsequent storage. With few exceptions, the roadside verge is a part of the highway. A build-up of traffic behind a vehicle towing a caravan may constitute the basis of an offence.

Parking

Drivers have no automatic right to park on a public highway except at an authorised parking place. Parking at picnic sites and rest areas is subject to local by-laws.

Generally speaking, the use of common land, town or village greens is limited to right of access and for recreational purposes only. By-laws generally prohibit the parking of caravans on such land and the Local Authority concerned should be consulted before doing so. It is an offence to drive any vehicle on all other land subject to statutory control, or to camp, or light a fire. It is not an offence to park a vehicle on open land within 15 yards of the road (subject to local by-laws). See *Trespassing, Rest Areas.*

Parking lights

Although certain vehicles may park during the hours of darkness without lights, a vehicle with trailer attached must display standing lights.

Passengers

All passengers travelling in a motor vehicle must be covered by insurance. It is an offence to use a caravan for the carriage of passengers.

Radio and television

A radio fitted in a car or a caravan does not require a licence. A separate television licence is needed if the set is fitted permanently in a motor vehicle. A television screen must not be visible to the driver either wholly, partly or by reflection.

Rear lamps

A trailer must be fitted with two rear lamps in prescribed positions. On a trailer manufactured on or after 1 August 1973, and supplied on or after 1 January 1974, the lamps must be marked with a prescribed E approval mark and specified number. If the load projects more than 3ft 6in beyond the vehicle's tail lights, there must be an additional red rear lamp attached to within 3ft 6in of the rear of the load. If the load overhangs laterally by more than 12in an additional rear lamp is required to be hung, at most, 12in from the load's outer edge, on the same side as the overhang.

Rear fog lamps

All trailers, subject to specified exceptions, manufactured on or after 1 October 1979 and first used on or after 1 April 1980, must be equipped with not more than two fog lamps meeting prescribed requirements. Such lamps must be maintained in clean and efficient working order. In addition, on and after 1 October 1979, every trailer fitted with rear fog lamps must meet prescribed conditions. The regulations provide that such lamps may only be used if visibility conditions are poor.

Reflectors

Trailers should be fitted with two triangular red reflectors marked with a prescribed E approval mark and a specified number, or a British Standard specification number and markings.

Trailers not exceeding 1600mm in width, not fitted with front lights, must be fitted in prescribed positions with two white reflectors meeting specified requirements.

Trailers over 5 metres long must during the hours of darkness carry two side-facing amber coloured reflectors marked with an E approval mark and a specified number.

Certain trailers over 1 ton unladen weight must be fitted with red and yellow reflective rear markings, but living-van trailers not exceeding 2 tons unladen weight and trailers being drawn as a result of a breakdown are exempt from this rule.

Rest areas and picnic sites

These sites are controlled by local by-laws and are provided as a means of temporary relief from driving; they should not be used for overnight parking unless signposted to this effect.

Road tax

No additional excise duty is payable when a trailer is towed by a privately licensed vehicle.

Speed limits

General Purpose roads:

The maximum speed limit at which a trailer may be drawn on such roads is 50mph, subject to specified conditions being observed. If these are not complied with, the limit is reduced to 40mph. The conditions referred to above are:

1 The kerbside weight of the drawing vehicle must be marked on the outside of the vehicle on its nearside, or inside the vehicle.

2 The maximum gross weight of a living van trailer or non-goods trailer must be marked on its nearside.

3 The weights in 1 and 2 may be expressed in either imperial or metric units but the same units should be used for both.

4 A '50' plate of prescribed form must be fitted to the rear of a trailer.

5 The following weight ratios must be observed:

a the maximum gross weight of a living van trailer, the laden weight of a braked goods trailer and the maximum gross weight of any other kind of braked trailer must not exceed the kerbside weight of the drawing vehicle:

b the laden weight of an unbraked goods trailer and the maximum gross weight of any other unbraked trailer (not being a living van) must not exceed 60% of the kerbside weight of the drawing vehicle.

Motorways:
Trailers with less than four wheels, or close-coupled four-wheeled trailers, are restricted to a maximum speed of 50mph when drawn on a motorway. ('Close coupled' means that the wheels on the same side of the trailer are so fitted that at all times while it is in motion they remain parallel to the longitudinal axis of the trailer, and that the distance between the centres of the respective areas of contact with the road surface does not exceed 33in.) This is reduced to 40mph when the drawing vehicle has an unladen weight not exceeding 30cwt and the trailer is two-wheeled or a close-coupled four-wheeled trailer, in circumstances where the speed limit for the vehicle on ordinary roads is 40mph or less.

Springs

All trailers must be equipped with suitable springs between each wheel and the frame of the vehicle.

Stop lamps

Normally, all trailers manufactured before 1 January 1971 must be fitted with one rear red stop lamp fitted on or to the right of the centre line.

Trailers manufactured on or after that date must have two red stop lamps meeting specified requirements and in the prescribed position. They must also be marked with the E approval mark and a specified number and can be of single or dual intensity as long as the particular wiring conditions are observed in the latter type.

Storing

Before storing the caravan at home, check whether doing so would contravene local by-laws or any clauses in the title documents relating to the property. As long as the use of the caravan is incidental to the enjoyment of the house, and it is parked behind the building line, there should be no contravention of the Town and Country Planning Acts.

Trespassing

Anyone camping outside a licensed campsite must be sure that they are not either breaking the law or trespassing.

In England and Wales a member of the public should not enter land unless

a he is given permission to do so by the owner or

b he is authorised by Act of Parliament or

c he is using a right of way.

A trespasser can be sued by the owner or occupier of the land even if no damage has been caused and can be ordered to leave or be ejected from the land by the shortest possible route. A trespasser cannot be prosecuted unless he has committed or attempts to commit a crime.

In Scotland, camping without permission on private land, or lighting a fire on or near a private road or cultivated land constitutes a criminal offence. Only if actual damage occurs can compensation be obtained, but a Court Order to prevent repetition may be sought. Trespassing in pursuit of game animals or fish is illegal and is usually dealt with as poaching.

Tyres

The minimum legal tread is 1mm but in addition to this the regulations prohibit the use of tyres with cuts, breaks, bumps, bulges, exposed ply cords, and worn-down tread patterns. Tyres of different size, road carrying capability or method of construction must not be fitted on the same axle. It is similarly an offence for radial ply tyres to be fitted to the front axle and cross ply tyres to the rear of the drawing vehicle. Each faulty tyre can constitute a separate offence. It is an endorsable offence to drive a car, or for a car to tow a trailer, with defective tyres. Apart from this a person convicted of a tyre offence might invalidate his insurance policy. Subjecting tyres to loads above their recommended maximum can be dangerous and would certainly be classified as an offence; the caravan or tyre manufacturers should be consulted before any change is made to the size or type of tyre used.

Warning triangles

These are voluntarily used (in the UK) to warn traffic that a vehicle has stopped or broken down ahead. The triangle should be placed at least 50 yards (150 yards on the hard shoulder of motorways) away from the obstruction and in such a position that it will warn traffic approaching on the same side of the carriageway. It must be of reflective material and conform to prescribed conditions. You use them at your own risk.

Weight

Generally, the total weight transmitted to the road surface by any two wheels of a trailer in line transversely must not exceed 9150kg. The total laden weight of a trailer with less than 6 wheels (not forming part of an articulated vehicle) must not exceed 14230kg.

The total laden weight of a trailer manufactured before 27 February 1977 which has no other brake than a parking brake and brakes which automatically come into operation on the overrun of the trailer, must not exceed 3560kg. The total laden weight of a trailer manufactured on or after 27 Febraury 1977 and fitted with brakes which automatically come into operation on the overrun of the trailer, whether or not any other brake is fitted, must not exceed 3500kg.

Generally speaking, the total laden weight of a trailer plus that of the drawing vehicle must not exceed 22360kg.

Wild plants

Subject to the provisions of The Conservation of Wild Creatures and Wild Plants Act 1975, it is not an offence to pick mushrooms growing wild on any land, or to pick flowers, fruit, or foliage from a plant growing wild, unless done for sale, reward or any other commercial purpose. In the case of mushrooms, the entire plant may be picked, but in all other cases one may only pick from a plant. Picking cultivated plants is an offence. However, the rules relating to trespass on private land apply.

Wings

Unless adequate protection is afforded by the body of the trailer, the rear wheels of every trailer and both wheels of a two wheeled trailer must be fitted with mud wings or similar fittings.

Using this guide

Finding a campsite

Gazetteer

The gazetteer is divided into three main sections – England, Wales, and Scotland, with the Channel Islands and the Isle of Man following on immediately after England. Sites on other off-shore islands, *eg* Isle of Wight and the Scottish Islands, are listed under individual place names; refer to the location atlas in the first instance. Place names appear in alphabetical order and the sites are listed in order of pennant status (starting with five pennants), and then alphabetically.

Location maps

The **location maps** at the beginning of the book make a good first reference point, especially since sites can be situated at places with unfamiliar names. The maps will also show you if there are any other sites in the area you have chosen. Refer to the **key on page 17** to find the right page in the atlas. *Only the place names printed in black have sites listed in the gazetteer.*

Map reference Example: 7 SO29

If you use the gazetteer to find a site, the place can be identified on the location maps by using the **map reference** alongside the entry. The first figure is the map page number, then follows the National Grid reference. An explanation of how to use this is given on page 16 (immediately preceding the atlas section). In addition six-figure references are given after the campsite name. These can be used in conjunction with larger scale Ordnance Survey maps to pinpoint the position.

Planning your route

The atlas preceding the gazetteer is not a road map and does not show roads suitable for caravans. The *AA Camping & Caravanning Map of Great Britain* on a scale of 10 miles to one inch shows suitable roads, gradients, direction of slopes, sites listed in this guide, etc.

District maps

District maps on a larger scale, covering the more popular areas, appear in the campsite gazetteer near the main place in the area they cover. Beneath the maps other place names under which sites are listed in the gazetteer are indicated; these are keyed by numbers to the district map.

Signposted

This does not refer to AA signs but indicates that the site is signposted on the nearest main road by an officially prescribed sign.

Telephone

It is most important that the following note on telephone numbers is read and understood. Much confusion has arisen in the past by members not reading it and consequently misinterpreting numbers in the gazetteer entries.

IMPORTANT – *unless otherwise stated, the exchange is that of the place under which the entry is listed.* For instance, if an establishment is listed under Bath and the telephone number is given as (☎12345), the exchange to dial is Bath. In a case such as Moor End Farm, Acaster Malbis, however, which is listed under Acaster Malbis, the number is given as (☎York 706727), and the exchange to dial is York. During the currency of this guide the Post Office are liable to change some telephone numbers. If you have any difficulty in contacting a site, check with the telephone operator.

Static van pitches

Information on static/residential pitches is limited to the number available in order to give a clearer picture of the nature of the site. Our system is geared to touring campers and caravanners; the inspectors do not vet the fixed types of accommodation. Static van pitches are not included in the pennant rating, and we cannot take responsibilitv for the condition of the caravans or chalets concerned. See p237 for list of sites which have static caravans.

Some site operators ask that cars be put in a parking area separate from the pitches, others will not allow more than one car on site for each caravan or tent.

At some sites motor caravans are only accepted if they remain static throughout the stay.

Individual pitches

Sites offering this facility have marked out individual pitches for tourists.

WC lit all night

Because the general standard of lighting on sites at night varies so much, we specify only whether the toilet blocks are lit.

Chemical closet disposal point

A point is usually a requirement for sites rated above one pennant, except those catering only for tents or motor caravans. They may consist of a specially constructed unit, or a wc permanently set aside for this purpose with adjacent rinsing and soak away facilities. However, some local authorities are concerned about the effect of chemicals on bacteria in cesspools, etc, and the provision of cdp's in these areas may be limited or non-existent.

This means that direct electrical hook up for caravans is available. There may be only a few of these available so check when booking.

Warden

If this word appears in a gazetteer entry it means that a warden is in attendance 24hrs a day. Other sites may have less comprehensive cover.

Cold storage

This takes the form of a fridge and/or freezer for the use of the campers and caravanners.

Shop

The range of food and equipment in site shops is usually in proportion to the size of the site. As far as our pennant requirements are concerned a general store within 200yd of the site entrance is acceptable for a three-pennant rating, but four- or five-pennant sites should have a site shop. Where a mobile shop calls at least five days a week, this is shown in the text.

Apply to

This wording appears after the campsite name if, for booking purposes, application must be made to a place other than the campsite. The booking address follows.

Information

Establishment names shown in *italics* indicate that particulars have not been confirmed by the management.

Site rules

No dogs and other rules Most sites display a set of rules and it is worthwhile to read these on your arrival. Sites where all dogs

are banned are indicated in the gazetteer by the appropriate symbol. On other sites, dogs are allowed as long as they are kept on a lead. Some proprietors will not admit larger breeds. Sleeping in cars is not encouraged by most proprietors. Some sites accept neither single sex groups nor groups of unsupervised youngsters unless they are members of a recognised camping club. Young people should ask proprietors in advance whether any conditions govern their acceptance.

Restricted service rsOct–Mar

Restricted service means that full site services are not available during the period stated. The facilities withdrawn during these periods vary from one site to another, so check with the site before setting off.

Book

Booking It is advisable to book in advance during the peak holiday season – from June to August inclusive and at public holidays. Any other recommended booking period specified by the site is noted in the gazetteer. Where individual sites always require advance booking, 'must book' appears in the entry. It is also wise to check whether a reservation entitles you to a particular pitch or not. It does not necessarily follow that an early booking will get you the best pitch on site; you may just have the choice of what is available at the time you check in at the site.

Some sites will not accept overnight bookings unless payment for a full minimum period (*eg* two or three days) is made. If you are not sure whether your type of equipment will be acceptable at a site, check with the proprietor beforehand.

The AA cannot undertake to find accommodation or make reservations.

Last arrival

Unless otherwise stated, sites will usually accept arrivals at any time of the day or night. Some sites have a special 'late-arrivals' enclosure where you can pitch temporarily to avoid disturbing everyone else late at night.

Last departure

At many sites the overnight charge covers a specified period of time, *eg* noon of one day to noon of the next. If you overstay the departure time you could be charged for an extra day. It is therefore advisable to check this point on arrival at the site.

Pitches and charges
10[caravan]£2
10[motor caravan]£2
10▲£1

The **number of pitches** available for each type of outfit allowed on a site is indicated immediately before the relevant symbol. If the entry reads 10 [caravan] £2 or 10 [motor caravan] £2 or 10 ▲ 50p, it means that the site has a maximum number of 10 pitches that can be used by caravans, motor caravans or tents. The **site charges** given immediately after the appropriate symbol apply to the overnight cost for:

one tent or caravan, one car, two adults, one child over 12yrs, one child under 12yrs.

or one motor caravan, two adults, one child over 12yrs, one child under 12yrs.

They are intended to indicate what an average family can expect to pay. If your group contains more or less people than the 'norm' you can expect to pay correspondingly more or less for your pitch. The set figure also makes comparison between site charges easier. But remember that some site facilities may have a charge over and above the pitch fee, if so they are bracketed (1[symbol]) in the gazetteer entry. Prices are the current charges when this book went to press (July 1979).

Complaints

Inform the site proprietor or warden immediately if you have any complaints, so that the matter can be dealt with promptly. If a personal approach fails, inform the AA as soon as possible – at least within a week – so that we can make an early investigation. Use the report forms on pages 253/6.

Explanation of a gazetteer entry

The example is fictitious

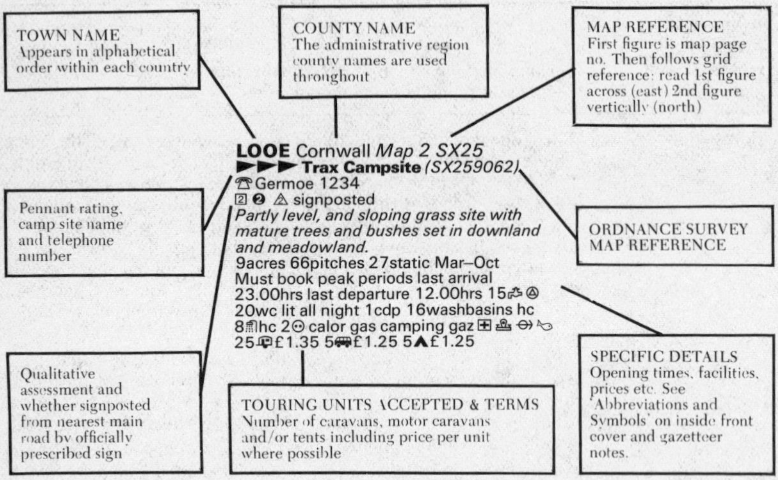

How we classify

Campsites in this book have one thing in common. All are of a consistently high standard within their own categories, and have been approved by our inspectors and graded accordingly.

A one-pennant site should be just as good in its own particular way as a five-pennant site. But usually, the higher the pennant rating, the better the equipment. The pennants give a good outline as to the type of amenities to expect, though sites reflect the character and personality of individual site proprietors, irrespective of pennant ratings. Some, for example, may have a separate area for campers with children, some may be able to provide lots of information about nearby entertainments, others may have a bar and clubhouse, while others may pride themselves on being small and quiet. Whatever the site, though, we find that visitors tend to return year after year, coming from all over Europe and even farther afield.

All the sites listed are visited by an inspector every year. In addition, our inspectors visit sites which have just applied for inclusion in next year's guide. Sites undergo a thorough examination, the inspectors working from a directive which details requirements. Recommendations on classification are then submitted to a special Classification Committee at the AA headquarters in Basingstoke for a final decision to be taken. Even though a site may offer all the facilities specified for AA recommendation, it will not necessarily qualify for pennant rating if it does not maintain a reasonable standard of cleanliness and tidiness.

If all goes well, however, and a site is approved, it may lease a yellow and black sign showing the pennant rating awarded. Since we only provide signs to sites that request them (the display of which is subject to local planning regulations) it does not automatically follow that a site not showing a sign has not been recommended.

We only consider a site for classification if the proprietor asks for it to be listed. In this way, we can be sure of getting the fullest co-operation from proprietors, particularly in regard to solving any problems which may arise.

All inspections are carried out based on the same criteria, whether sites cater for tents, or caravans, or both. Existing and proposed Government regulations, including recommendations of the Department of the Environment's Camping Working Party, have been given consideration, but are quite independent of our classification system.

All the time we aim to keep our system of classification in line with changes in public demand. As camping and caravanning become increasingly popular, emphasis on existing requirements may alter, and further facilities and services may well be included in classification categories in the future.

Since the book is primarily intended for touring campers or caravanners, a site must have at least six touring pitches, or, if there are between 60 and 600 pitches overall, at least 10 per cent must be reserved for tourers. If a site has more than 600 pitches, at least 60 of them must be reserved for touring purposes. Some of our sites may, in fact, not take 10 per cent at present, since a period of time is being allowed for making the necessary amendments to licences, etc. The omission of sites which are predominantly static or residential does not reflect adversely on their standard and facilities.

Qualitative assessment

🄸 ❸ ⚠

Our qualitative assessment scheme is concerned with quality, rather than quantity. In other words, by using our symbols as a guide you can judge far more accurately than before the standards to be expected. The qualitative assessment symbols should not be confused with pennants. Pennants show the range and number of facilities available, whereas the symbols refer to the actual marks awarded, even though facilities may be limited within the scope of the rating. On the other hand, a top-ranking five-pennant site may have all the amenities one would expect, but our opinion of the amenities may be only 'good' rather than 'exceptional'.

🄸 environment ❸ sanitary installations
⚠ equipment and facilities
1 means adequate 2 means good 3 means excellent

All the sites in this edition have qualitative assessment ratings as well as pennant gradings. Please note that our assessment does not cover facilities which are not actually on the site itself (i.e. anything listed after the symbol ⊖ which indicates amenities within three miles of the site.

►

* site licence (unless specially exempted)
* site density not more than thirty (reasonably spaced) per acre of land suitable for camping
* at least 10% of pitches allocated to touring units
* separate toilets with 2 WCs (ladies) and 1 WC and 1 urinal (men) for 30 pitches. Chemical closets allowed if provided at double the ratio
* tap water supply of good quality and quantity
* waste water disposal facilities within 50yd of any touring pitch
* adequate collection, storage, and disposal of refuse, so that the site is always clean and tidy
* regular cleaning of ablution block
* fire precautions that meet local authority regulations
* well-drained ground

* entrance and exit roads wide and well-surfaced enough to eliminate possibilities of damage to towed vehicles
* first aid facilities signposted and emergency telephone numbers displayed

►►

* all one-pennant facilities *plus*
* flush toilets
* separate washrooms, with 2 washbasins each sex per 30 pitches, each with hot and cold water
* unless the site only caters for tents and motor caravans, a properly designed point for disposing of chemical closet contents (as some local authorities will not allow such contents to mix with cesspools, there are exceptions to this rule)
* warden available at certain times of the day

►►►

* all the aforementioned facilities, *plus*
* one shower or bath each sex per 30 pitches with hot and cold water
* deep sinks for washing clothes
* electric shaver points and mirrors in washrooms
* all-night lighting of toilet blocks; push button time switches acceptable if time duration clearly displayed after dark
* facilities for buying milk, bread, and basic camping requisites available regularly on site or within 200yd of site entrance (a formal shop is not necessary, and there is no need for the facility to be provided throughout the day)
* if the size warrants it, there should be internal roads with satisfactory and well-maintained surfaces
* warden in attendance during day; on call at night

►►►►

* a higher degree of organisation than on lower graded sites
* attention paid to landscaping
* signposted reception office
* signposted late-arrivals enclosure as near to the entrance as possible
* first aid hut
* properly equipped shop offering a wide range of food and other camping requisites, open at least six days a week
* access routes to essential facilities lit after dark
* children's playground, fenced or in a safe area
* shelter for campers in case of bad weather
* hard standings for touring vans
* warden in attendance all day; on call at night

►►►►►

* a comprehensive range of services and equipment
* careful landscaping especially in relation to individual pitches
* 24hr supervision by warden on site
* automated laundry, including a selection of washing and drying machines, spin dryers, drying cabinets, irons and ironing boards
* public telephone
* indoor recreational facilities for children
* extra facilities for indoor and outdoor recreation
* must achieve a rating of good ❷ in all areas of qualitative assessment

In case you don't know

Forestry Commission caravan and campsites

Only those Forestry Commission sites which come within the scope of the Automobile Association's Caravan and Campsite classification scheme are listed in this guide. There are others which are deliberately maintained as minimum-facility sites and are suitable for the camper or caravanner who prefers to be completely self-sufficient and carries his own chemical toilet.

Free pamphlets – The following give details of all recreational facilities in forests:
See Your Forests – Northern England
See Your Forests – Southern England
See Your Forests – Wales

See Your Forests – Scotland
Forestry Commission Cabins and Holiday Houses
Single copies will be sent on application to the Forestry Commission, 231 Corstorphine Road, Edinburgh EH12 7AT.

Guernsey

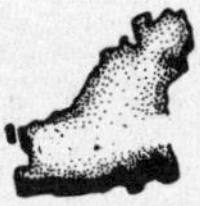

Towed caravans are only allowed temporarily on to the island in exceptional circumstances. Apply in advance to the Island Development Committee, Longstore House, St Peter Port, Guernsey. Motorised caravans may be temporarily imported provided the following are complied with:

1 The vehicle is used as a means of transport only and not as sleeping or habitable accommodation.
2 Previous arrangements have been made with a campsite owner for the motorised caravan to be put under cover when not being used as a means of transport.

Jersey

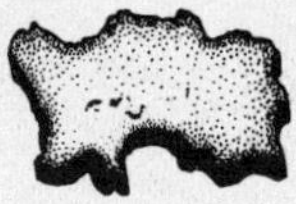

Importation of domestic caravans is not permitted other than for residents, and this is subject to the vehicles not being used for habitation while on the island, and to other conditions. Camping is permitted only at recognised sites. Trailer tents may be imported and used, but only on recognised campsites. With the introduction of roll on/roll off ferries, the authorities have banned motor caravans completely.

Isle of Man

Trailer caravans are not permitted on the island for holiday purposes unless they are to be used in connection with trade, at shows and exhibitions, or for demonstration purposes; they must not be used for living accommodation.

Isles of Scilly

No sites on the Isles of Scilly hold AA classification. Caravans and motor caravans are not allowed on the islands; tents only are permitted. **Note** – Strict control is kept on the landing of animals in the islands. Booking is essential on all sites. For details about the licensed site on St Mary's write: Mr E A F Davison, Garrison, St Mary's. For details about sites on Bryher, St Agnes, and St Martin's write: The Town Hall, St Mary's.

Bridges, Tunnels and Ferries

Information regarding bridges, tunnels and ferries, including regulations regarding the carriage of gas cylinders, can be found on p234.

Caravan and Campsite Advisory Services

In most areas Tourist Boards and Local Authorities provide services, varying from maps and lists of sites to day-by-day information on vacancies and booking services. The AA is preparing a leaflet (HH69) giving details of such local services and this will be available free to members from late Spring 1980.

In The Country-

Kill nothing but time

Take nothing but photographs

Leave nothing but footprints

Season of mists and mellow fruitfulness

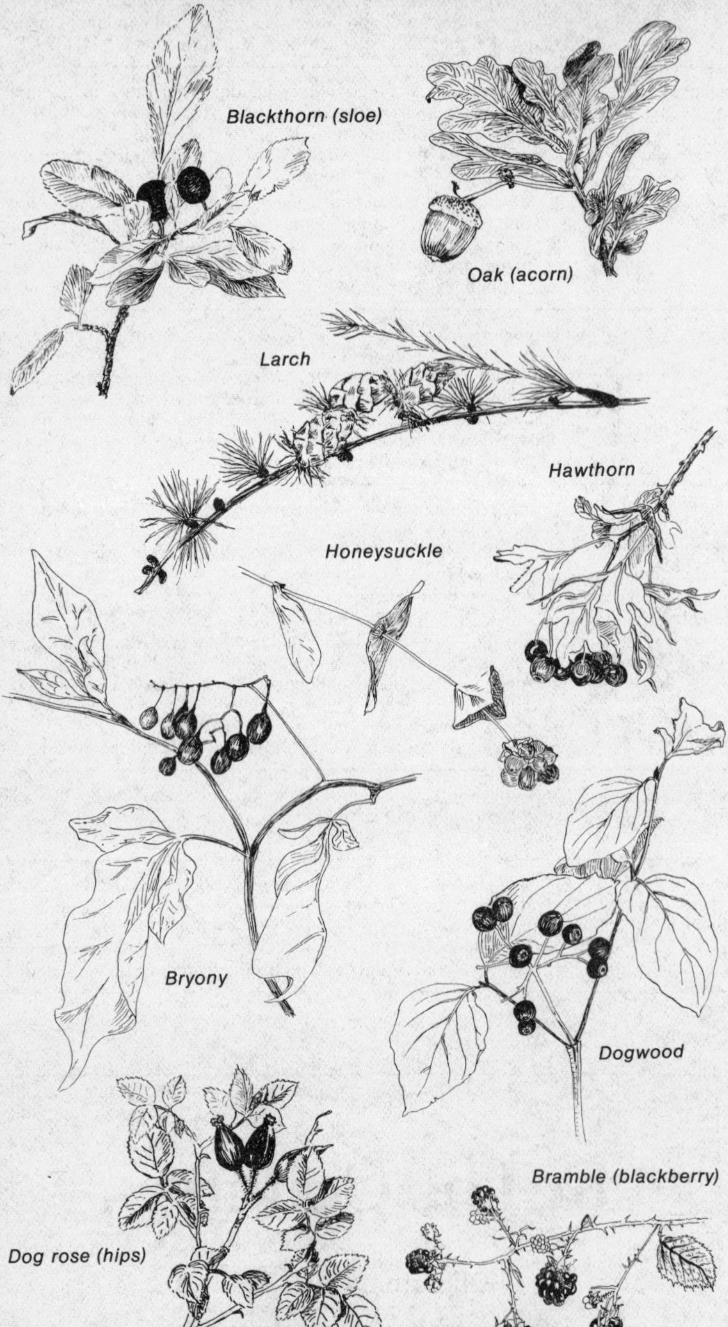

Autumn
a good time for your holiday

ENGLAND

ACASTER MALBIS North Yorkshire
Map 8 SE54
►►► **Chestnut Farm Caravans** *(SE589456)*
☎York 706371
2 ❷ ⚠ signposted
Level, grassy site with assorted trees, saplings and shrubs, lying adjacent to river. 3acres 25pitches 45static
Apr–Oct must book public hols last arrival 23.59hrs last departure 12.00hrs 5 individual pitches 14wc lit all night 1cdp 12washbasins hc (1central hot water) (6hc) 3 iron games room (cold storage) calor gas camping gaz toilet fluid stables launderette pub
20£2 5£2 (awnings) ltr
►►► **Mount Pleasant Caravan Village** *(SE583445)* ☎ York 707078
2 ❸ ⚠ signposted
This site is secluded but not remote and is close to the River Ouse, with trees and gardens. 6acres 120pitches 200static
Apr–Oct no bookings last departure 16.00hrs 16 late arrivals enclosure wc lit all night 4cdp washbasins hc central hot water (hc) warden (wash spin dry) calor gas camping gaz toilet fluid ☎ children's playground stables launderette pub
120£2.50 or 120£2.50 or 120▲£2.50 (awnings) ltr
►► **Moor End Farm** *(SE589457)* ☎York 706727
1 ❶ ⚠ signposted
Level, grassy site with hedges. Set in meadowland adjacent to road. ⅓acre 10pitches 5static
Apr–Oct must book peak periods last arrival 22.00hrs last departure 14.00hrs 2 individual pitches 4wc lit all night 1cdp 4washbasins hc (2hc) 1 (cold storage) children's playground launderette pub
10£1.90 or 10£1.90 or 10▲£1.90 (awnings) ltr

ACTON BRIDGE Cheshire Map 7 SJ57
► **Woodbine Cottage** *(SJ603755)*
☎Weaverham 852319
1 ❶ ⚠
A basic site situated by the banks of the River Weaver in open countryside on the A49. 1acre 17pitches 30static
Mar–Oct must book public hols 3 individual pitches 8wc lit all night 1cdp washbasins hc (hc) 2 (1wash) (1dry) (1iron) cold storage calor gas camping gaz children's playground take away food stables launderette pub
17£2.25 or 17£2.25 17▲£2.25

ALCESTER Warwickshire Map 4 SP05
► ***Hoo Mill*** *(SP108579)* ☎2515
2 ❶ ⚠
Level and grassy site with mature trees. 3acres 40pitches 60static
Mar–Oct rsNov–Feb must book peak periods last arrival 22.00hrs last departure 12.00hrs 5 individual pitches 10wc 1cdp warden calor gas mobile shop launderette pub
40 or 40 or 40▲ (awnings)

ALLERTON PARK North Yorkshire
Map 8 SE45
►►► ***Allerton Park Caravan Site*** *(SE417576)* ☎Green Hammerton 30569
1 ❶ ⚠
Gently sloping, grass site with varied types of trees in sylvan surroundings, adjacent to main road. 3acres 30pitches 80static
Apr–Oct must book Bank Hols last arrival 20.00hrs last departure 14.00hrs 5 20wc lit all night 1cdp washbasins hc central hot water (hc) calor gas children's playground ☎ pub
30 or 30 (awnings)

AMBLESIDE Cumbria Map 7 NY30
See Windermere sketch map
►► **Low Wray National Trust Campsite** *(SD372013)* Low Wray
2 ❷ ⚠
Delightful site set on western shore of Lake Windermere. The site is divided into three camping fields; one set aside especially for families, with direct access to the lake; one with an open aspect and the third amongst trees and bushes. 3m SW via A583 to Clappersgate then B5286 and unclassified road. 20acres 206pitches
Etr–Oct no bookings 8 no cars by tents 18wc lit all night 2cdp 22washbasins hc central hot water 4hc calor gas camping gaz ☎ private beach & boat launching stables cinema launderette pub
6£1.75 200▲£1.75 no awnings ltr

APPLEBY Cumbria Map 12 NY62
►►►► **Wild Rose Park** *(NY698165)*
Ormside ☎51077
1 ❷ ⚠ signposted
The site is set in peaceful surroundings on rising ground overlooking the Eden Valley in the midst of a good touring area. 12acres 234pitches 184static
May–Sep rsApr & Oct last departure 12.00hrs (peak periods only) 100 individual pitches late arrivals enclosure 36wc lit all night 3cdp 36washbasins hc (6central hot water) 12hc 14 warden (1wash) (1spin) (1dry) 2iron 2CTV cold storage calor gas camping gaz toilet fluid ☎ children's playground & teenagers' room stables launderette pub
184£2.85–£3.30 or 184£2.85–£3.30 50▲£2.85–£3.30 (awnings)

ASHBOURNE Derbyshire Map 7 SK14
►►►► **Sandybrook Hall Holiday Centre** *(SK179481)* ☎2679
1 ❶ ⚠ signposted
Grassy site with a slight gradient set in downland and meadowland, adjacent to road. 1m N of Ashbourne on A515. 5acres 80pitches
Etr–5 Nov must book public hols individual pitches wc lit all night 1cdp washbasins hc hc (dry) games room TV calor gas camping gaz toilet fluid licensed club & children's playground stables launderette
80£2–£2.50 or 80£2–£2.50 or 80▲£2–£2.50 awnings

ASHBURTON Devon Map 3 SX77
►►► River Dart Country Park
(SX734700) Holne Park ☎52511
3 ❷ ⚠ signposted
Mainly level site in Holne Country Park just off B3357. Adjacent to river. 140pitches
Etr & Jun–Sep rs mid Apr–May must book peak periods last departure 22.30hrs 6[ ] individual pitches 30wc lit all night 1cdp washbasins hc central hot water [ ]hc ⊙ (wash spin) iron [ ] [ ] CTV calor gas camping gaz toilet fluid cafe restaurant ☎ ⊞ licensed club & children's playground [ ] ⊖ stables cinema [ ] launderette pub
140[ ]£4.20 or 140[ ]£4.20 or 140▲£4.20 awnings

►► Ashburton Caravan Park Waterleat
☎Moretonhampstead 543
2 ❶ ⚠
Mainly level grass site with trees and bushes on partly level ground. Set in hilly meadowland with some woodland; adjacent to a rocky stream. 4acres 30pitches 40static
All year 2[ ] [ ] 10wc washbasins hc central hot water [ ]hc ⊙ warden cold storage calor gas camping gaz ☎ ⊞ children's playground [ ] ⊖ stables [ ] launderette pub
30[ ] or 30▲

ASHFORD IN THE WATER Derbyshire Map 7 SK16
►►► Greenhills Caravan Park *(SK195697)*
Crow Hill Ln ☎Bakewell 3467
2 ❸ ⚠ signposted
Grass site with assorted trees and bushes on partly level ground. Set in hilly meadowland with some woodland. 4acres 40pitches 60static
Etr–Oct rsMar must book peak periods 16[ ] 25wc lit all night 1cdp 14washbasins hc 1central hot water 6[ ]hc 2⊙ warden (1wash) 1spin calor gas ⊞ licensed club & battery charger ⊖ stables [ ] launderette [ ] pub
40[ ]£2 or 40[ ]£1.80 or 40▲£2 (awnings)

ASHTON Cornwall Map 2 SW62
►► Boscreage Caravan Park *(SW591303)*
☎Germoe 2231
2 ❷ ⚠
Level, grass site with varied trees and bushes. Set in mixed woodland and meadowland adjacent to the sea. Good sandy beach and main road nearby. 1acre 15pitches 23static
Apr–Oct last arrival 21.00hrs last departure 12.00hrs 3[ ] 6wc lit all night 1cdp washbasins hc central hot water ([ ]hc) ⊙ warden spin iron games room CTV TV cold storage ☎ ⊞ children's playground mobile shop ⊖ stables [ ] [ ] [ ] launderette [ ] pub
15[ ]£2.16 or 15[ ]£2.16 or 15▲£2.16 (awnings)

ASHURST Hants Map 4 SU31
►► Ashurst Camp *(SU332102)*
2 ❸ ⚠ signposted
Situated just off the A31 Southampton to Bournemouth road, this quiet, secluded Forestry Commission site is set amongst woodlands and heathland on the fringe of the New Forest. See page 124 for further information.
18.5acres 280pitches
7[ ] late arrivals enclosure 29wc lit all night 4cdp 45washbasins hc 8[ ]hc 8⊙ calor gas camping gaz paraffin toilet fluid ☎ ⊞ ⊖ stables [ ] [ ] cinema [ ] launderette pub
280[ ] or 280[ ] or 280▲ (awnings)

ASTON CANTLOW Warwickshire Map 4 SP15
► Island Meadow Caravan Park *(SP078981)*
The Mill House ☎ Great Alne 273
2 ❶ ⚠
Meadowland bordered by the River Alne and its mill stream. Mature willows line the banks. ¼m W of Aston Cantlow on the road to Alcester.
7acres 15pitches 55static
Mar–Oct must book peak periods 5[ ] 16wc lit all night 1cdp (7washbasins hc, 10[ ]hc) ⊙ warden (cold storage) ⊞ ⊖ stables [ ] [ ] pub
15[ ]£1.60 or 15[ ]£1.60 (awnings)

AYSIDE Cumbria Map 7 SD38
See sketch map of Cartmel.
► **Oak Head Caravan Park** *(SD389839)*
☎ Newby Bridge 475 (to be prefixed by 31)
1 ❶ ⚠ signposted
Level and sloping site, set in hilly country with woodland, close to A590. No open fires
3acres 60pitches 71static
Mar–Oct must book public hols
last departure 12.00hrs 8 individual pitches
22wc lit all night 1cdp washbasins hc
central hot water (hc) ⊙ warden (spin)
calor gas camping gaz toilet fluid ☎ ⊞
stables pub
30 £2 or 30 £2 or 30▲£2 awnings ltr

BAMBURGH Northumberland Map 12 NU13
►► **Glororum Caravan Park** *(NU166334)*
Glororum Farm ☎205
1 ❶ ⚠ signposted
A pleasantly situated site off B1341 1m W of Bamburgh. The open countryside setting gives views of Bamburgh Castle and surrounding farmland. 6acres 100pitches 125static
Apr–Oct must book peak periods
last departure 12.00hrs 6 late arrivals
enclosure 35wc lit all night 3cdp
washbasins hc central hot water hc ⊙
warden iron (cold storage) calor gas toilet fluid
☎ ⊞ childrens' playground & off licence
stables launderette pub
100 £1.50–£2 or 100 £1.30–£1.80 (awnings)

BARNSTAPLE Devon Map 2 SS53
►►► **Midland Caravan Park**
Braunton Rd ☎3691
2 ❷ ⚠ signposted
Level, grassy site with trees and bushes. Set in hilly country near to river about $1\frac{1}{4}$m W of Barnstaple on A361. 5acres 63static
Mid May–mid Sep rsMar–mid May & mid Sep–Oct must book peak periods last arrival 23.00hrs last departure 12.00hrs 14
25wc lit all night 1cdp 16washbasins hc
2central hot water (8hc) 3⊙ warden
(2wash, 2spin, 1dry, 3iron) CTV (1cold storage)
calor gas camping gaz toilet fluid cafe
restaurant licensed bar ☎ ⊞ stables
cinema launderette pub
20 fr£1.50 or 20 fr£1.50 200▲fr£1.50 (awnings)

BARROW-IN-FURNESS Cumbria
Map 7 SD16
►►► ***South End Caravan Site*** *(SD205630)*
Walney Island ☎42823
1 ❶ ⚠ signposted
Mainly level grass site adjacent to sea. On Walney Island 1m SE. 3acres 20pitches
Mar–Oct must book Bank Hols 2 6wc
lit all night 1cdp 14washbasins hc central hot
water 8hc ⊙ warden (dry) cold storage
calor gas camping gaz licensed bar ☎ ⊞
cinema launderette pub
20 or 20 or 20▲

BASSENTHWAITE Keswick, Cumbria
Map 11 NY23
►►► ***Traffords Caravan Site*** *(NY223318)*
Lowood ☎ Bassenthwaite Lake 298
2 ❶ ⚠
A level, grassy site surrounded by bushes and hedges, with pleasant views to the distant hills. Situated on A591. 5acres 50pitches
Mar–Oct 8 11wc 1cdp 6washbasins hc
4hc 2⊙ calor gas toilet fluid ⊞
20 50▲ (awnings)

BATH Avon Map 3 ST76
►►►► **Newbridge Caravan Park**
☎28778
2 ❸ ⚠ signposted
This small site is level and some touring pitches are on a concrete hardstanding.
2acres 72pitches
All year must book peak periods last departure 12.00hrs 5 individual pitches late arrivals enclosure 12wc lit all night 4cdp
washbasins hc hc ⊙ (wash) (spin) (iron)
calor gas camping gaz ☎ ⊞ children's playground stables cinema
72 £2.30 or 72 £2.30 (awnings)

BEADNELL Northumberland Map 12 NU22
▶▶▶ **Beadnell Links** *(NU229299)*
The Chimes ☎ Chathill 241
1 ❶ ⚠ signposted
Level site lying in farmland, with grass, gravel and sand surface. Beadnell Bay and beach nearby. 1acre 10pitches 140static
Apr–Oct must book peak periods
last departure 12.00hrs 5 32wc lit all night
5cdp 14washbasins hc 6central hot water
16 hc 12⊙ calor gas ☎ ⊞ stables
launderette pub
10 £2.50 or 10 £2.50 (awnings) ltr

▶ ***Beadnell Camping Site*** *(NU229298)*
Annstead ☎ Seahouses 720586
1 ❶ ⚠
Level, grassy site set in coastal area with access to sea, beach and main road. 36acres
160pitches
Etr–mid Sep last arrival 21.00hrs last departure
12.00hrs 4 19wc 6 hc 4⊙ ☎ ⊞
stables launderette
160 or 160▲ ltr

BECKFOOT Cumbria Map 11 NY04
▶▶ **Abbey Holme Caravan Park**
(NY095498) ☎ Silloth 31653
2 ❷ ⚠
Level site, with grass and gravel surface overlooking Solway Firth. Adjacent to B5300 Silloth-Maryport road. Ideal position for touring the northern Lake District.
2½acres 25pitches 25static
Mar–Sep must book peak periods last arrival
22.00hrs 9 11wc lit all night cdp
13washbasins hc 2central hot water 6 hc ⊙
warden (1spin) (1iron) cold storage calor gas
☎ ⊞ children's playground stables
launderette pub
25 £2 or 25 £2 or 25▲£2 (awnings) ltr

BELFORD Northumberland Map 12 NU13
▶▶▶ **Waren Caravan Site** *(NU155343)*
Waren Mill ☎ Bamburgh 366
2 ❷ ⚠ signposted
Seaside site within walking distance of beach; surrounded by a slight grassy embankment affording shelter for caravans. All pitches are numbered and situated around a central green. 2m E of town on B1342 Bamburgh road.
5acres 105pitches 240static
May–Oct rsEtr–Apr 4 Ⓐ 16wc lit all night
1cdp 14washbasins hc central hot water
8 hc 3⊙ (1wash, 1dry) iron calor gas
camping gaz toilet fluid ☎ ⊞ stables
launderette pub
90 £1.50–£2.30 or 90 £1.50–£2.30
15▲£1.50–£2.30 (awnings)

BERROW Somerset Map 3 ST35
▶ **Unity Farm** Coast Rd ☎ Brean Down 235
1 ❶ ⚠ signposted
Mainly level site with bushes set in meadowland overlooking the Bristol Channel. 1m N of Berrow on the Brean road, 4m from M5.
30acres 450pitches 180static
Etr–Sep rsMar & Oct must book peak periods
last arrival 22.00hrs last departure 12.00hrs
40 individual pitches Ⓐ 80wc lit all night
12cdp 60washbasins hc (5central hot water,
3 hc, 27 hc) 12⊙ (4wash, 1spin, 3dry, 5iron)
( ) (games room) (3cold storage) calor gas
camping gaz paraffin toilet fluid cafe restaurant
☎ ⊞ (children's playground) licensed clubs
skatepark amusements hairdryers
stables cinema launderette pub
450 £1.75 or 450 £1.50 or 450▲£1.50
(awnings)

BERRYNARBOR Devon Map 2 SS54
See Ilfracombe sketch map.
▶▶▶▶ **Sandaway Holiday Park**
(SS568474) ☎ Combe Martin 3555
2 ❷ ⚠ signposted
Well designed site, carefully screened and well laid out, overlooking the sea. Situated on A399 ½m from Combe Martin on coast side of road.
1¼acres 42pitches 69static
May–Oct rs15 Mar–Apr & 16–31 Oct
Booking advisable peak periods last departure
10.30hrs 10 individual pitches Ⓐ
late arrivals enclosure wc lit all night 1cdp
15washbasins hc (3central hot water, 12 hc)
3⊙ (3wash, 2dry, 2iron) games room CTV
(cold storage) calor gas camping gaz toilet fluid
☎ ⊞ children's playground licensed club
private beach launderette pub
12 fr£2 or 12 fr£2 30▲fr£1.50 awnings

▶▶▶▶ **Watermouth Cove** *(SS558477)*
☎ Ilfracombe 62504
3 ❸ ⚠ signposted
Mainly level, grass site amidst trees and bushes, set in meadowland with access to sea, beach and main road. 5.2acres 90pitches
Etr & Spring Bank Hol–Sep rsmid Apr–mid May
last arrival 22.00hrs last departure 11.00hrs
14 individual pitches 26wc lit all night 1cdp
19 washbasins hc central hot water hc ⊙
warden (wash, spin, dry) iron games room
(cold storage) calor gas camping gaz cafe
restaurant ☎ ⊞ licensed club private beach
children's playground fishing stables
cinema launderette pub
90 £2.50–£5 or 90 £2.50–£5 awnings

▶ ***Berrynarbor Trailer Caravan Park & Camping Site*** *(SS564466)* Storridge Valley
☎ Combe Martin 2631
3 ❶ ⚠
Part level and part sloping grassy site with bushes. Set in hilly moorland country.
2acres 40pitches 51static
Etr–Sep 19 Ⓐ 13wc 2cdp (4washbasins hc)
(4 hc) 3⊙ warden calor gas stables
cinema launderette
15 25 (awnings)

▶ **Napps Camping Site** *(SS565476)*
Old Coast Rd ☎ Ilfracombe 64103
1 ❶ ⚠ signposted
Site is situated on cliff top adjacent to Combe Martin where seclusion is guaranteed.
3½acres 75pitches
Spring Bank Hol–Sep rsEtr–mid May 5
late arrivals enclosure 15wc lit all night 1cdp
(8 hc) 2⊙ (spin, dry, iron) (cold storage)
calor gas camping gaz toilet fluid ☎ ⊞ hairdryer
stables cinema launderette pub
75 £1.40–£1.60 or 75 £1.25–£1.40
or 75▲£1.25–£1.40 (awnings)

BERWICK-UPON-TWEED Northumberland Map 12 NT95
►►► ***Ord House Caravan Park*** *(NT982515)* East Ord ☎5288
1 ❶ ⚠ signposted
Situated on the A698, 1m from Berwick; the site is set in pleasant sylvan surroundings with mature trees and bushes. 5acres 40pitches 206static
May–Sep rsMar–Apr & Oct must book Bank Hols last departure 12.00hrs 7 individual pitches 45wc lit all night 3cdp washbasins hc central hot water (hc) hc ⊙ warden (2wash, 1spin, 1dry, 1iron) cold storage calor gas camping gaz toilet fluid licensed bar ☎ ⊞ stables cinema launderette pub
40 or 40 (awnings) ltr

BEWALDETH Cumbria Map 11 NY23
►►► **North Lakes Caravan & Camping Park** *(NY205356)* ☎Bassenthwaite Lake 510
2 ❷ ⚠ signposted
A tranquil rural site set in wooded hilly countryside. A small beck meanders through the site and small bridges have been placed across it to facilitate short walks in the surrounding wooded area. Adjacent to A591 Keswick–Carlisle road. 15acres 162pitches
Mar–14 Nov must book public hols last arrival 22.00hrs last departure 12.00hrs 10 individual pitches late arrivals enclosure wc lit all night washbasins hc (hc) ⊙ warden (wash, dry, iron) (games room) (cold storage) calor gas camping gaz toilet fluid ☎ ⊞ children's playground, indoor washup sinks, licensed club & fishing stables
112£3 or 112£2.50 50▲£2 (awnings) ltr

BICKINGTON Devon Map 3 SX87
►►► **Lemonford Holidays** *(SX793722)* ☎242
2 ❷ ⚠ signposted
Small, secluded and well maintained site approached on old A38 from Drumbridge or from A383 Newton Abbot road. peak periods 4acres 55pitches 20static
Mid Mar–Oct last departure 12.00hrs 3 individual pitches 11wc lit all night 1cdp (washbasins hc) (central hot water) (hc) ⊙ warden wash spin dry iron cold storage calor gas camping gaz paraffin toilet fluid ⊞ stables cinema launderette pub
37£2 or 40£2 or 40▲£2 (awnings)

BIDDENDEN Kent Map 5 TQ83
►► **Woodlands Park** *(TQ857372)* Tenterden Rd ☎291216
2 ❷ ⚠ signposted
Ten acre site of level grassland with hedges and trees surrounding. 1½m S of Biddenden on northern side of A262. 10acres 100pitches 205static
Mar–Oct rsNov–Feb booking advisable peak periods last arrival 21.00hrs last departure 09.00hrs 7 30wc lit all night 1cdp 8washbasins hc (4hc) 4⊙ warden iron calor gas camping gaz paraffin toilet fluid cafe restaurant ☎ ⊞ children's playground & licensed club stables launderette pub
100£2.60 or 100£2.30 50▲£2.60 (awnings) ltr

BILLINGSHURST West Sussex Map 4 TQ02
► **Limeburner's Arms** *(TQ073254)* Newbridge ☎2311
1 ❶ signposted
Essentially a touring site, set in a quiet and secluded field surrounded by trees, alongside the attractive Limeburner's Arms. A short distance from the village of Billingshurst and the peaceful course of the River Arun. 2¾acres 40pitches
Mid Apr–Sep last arrival 22.00hrs last departure 12.00hrs 3 individual pitches 4wc lit all night washbasins ⊙ cold storage calor gas camping gaz ☎ ⊞ licensed club, children's playground stables launderette pub
30£1.30 10£1.30 or 10▲£1.30 awnings

BIRCHINGTON Kent Map 5 TR26
► **Quex Caravan & Camping Park** *(TR321685)* Park Rd. Apply to: Keat Farm Caravans Ltd, Reculver Rd, Herne Bay, Kent CT6 6SR ☎Thanet 41273
1 ❶ ⚠ signposted
A small site surrounded by tall hedges and mature trees, with a wooded tent area in a quiet secluded field. 6acres 150pitches 58static
Mar–Oct last arrival 20.00hrs last departure 10.00hrs 8 24wc lit all night 4cdp washbasins hc central hot water (hc) ⊙ (wash, spin) (iron) calor gas camping gaz toilet fluid ⊞ children's playground & wash up sinks stables cinema launderette
150£2.16 or 150£2.16 or 150▲£2.16 (awnings)

BLACKFORD Cumbria Map 11 NY36
►► **Dandy Dinmont Caravan Site** *(NY399620)* ☎Rockcliffe 611
2 ❷ ⚠ signposted
A level sheltered site, screened on two sides by hedgerows. Situated alongside A7 about 1m N of junction 44 of M6. 4acres 47pitches 15static
Mar–Oct must book peak periods last departure 16.00hrs 6 14wc lit all night 1cdp (washbasins hc) (4hc) 3⊙ cold storage calor gas ⊞ stables launderette
27£1.60 or 27£1.60 20▲fr£1.20 (awnings)

BLACKPOOL Lancashire Map 7 SD33
►►►► ***Marton Mere Leisure Centre*** *(SD348348)* Mythop Rd ☎64280
2 ❷ ⚠ signposted
A large site built on gently sloping land around the natural Marton Mere. Pleasantly situated on edge of town. 50acres 650pitches 800static
Mar–Apr individual pitches late arrivals enclosure wc lit all night washbasins hc central hot water hc ⊙ (wash, spin, iron) calor gas camping gaz toilet fluid cafe restaurant licensed bar ☎ ⊞ stables cinema launderette
650 or 650 no awnings ltr

►► **Cropper Caravan Park** *(NY345334)* Cropper Rd, Marton ☎62051
1 ❶ ⚠ signposted
Situated on flat open countryside near to M55 terminus. Site is well signposted on approaches. 7acres 121pitches
Mar–Oct must book last departure 12.00hrs 6 late arrivals enclosure wc lit all night 3cdp washbasins hc (hc) ⊙ warden (wash, spin, dry) calor gas ☎ ⊞ children's playground stables cinema launderette pub
121£2.50 or 121£2.50 (awnings)

BLACKWATER Cornwall Map 2 SW74
►►► **Trewarth Farm Caravan Site**
☎Truro 560266
1 ❶ ⚠ signposted
A farm site. 4m E of Redruth on A30.
4acres 30pitches 61static
Etr–Oct must book peak periods 5 ⓐ
late arrivals enclosure 14wc lit all night 1cdp
14washbasins hc central hot water hc hc
2⊙ 1wash 1spin 1dry 1iron games room
cold storage calor gas camping gaz paraffin
toilet fluid ☎ ⊞ children's playground &
hairdrying room stables cinema
launderette pub
30£2 or 30£1.75 or 30▲£2 (awnings) ltr

BLEADON Avon Map 3 ST35
►► ***Purn Farm Caravan Park*** ☎812203
1 ❶ ⚠ signposted
Purpose-built site situated on flat, open land alongside main road. 6acres 145pitches
80static
Mar–Oct 10 ⓐ 40wc lit all night 1cdp
30washbasins hc (5hc) 2⊙ warden (1wash,
1spin, 1dry, 1iron) cold storage calor gas
camping gaz ☎ ⊞ children's play area
stables launderette pub
100 or 100 45▲ (awnings)

BLUE ANCHOR Somerset Map 3 ST04
See Watchet sketch map.
►►► ***Beeches Holiday Site***
☎Washford 391
2 ❷ ⚠
Set amidst trees and bushes with extensive views of Welsh Coast. ½m E of village on the Old Cleeve road. 3acres 35pitches 130static
Etr–Oct last arrival 21.00hrs last departure
10.30hrs 8 21wc lit all night 1cdp
8washbasins hc (4hc) (2hc) 2⊙ warden
(3wash, dry, iron) calor gas camping gaz ☎ ⊞
stables launderette
35 or 35 or 35▲ (awnings) ltr

► ***Blue Anchor Bay Caravan Park***
☎Dunster 360
1 ❶ ⚠
Large, coastal site; partly wooded and individual acres screened. On flat ground overlooking bay. ½m E of West Somerset Railway station on B3191. 75pitches 475static
Etr–Oct rsMar–Etr last arrival 22.00hrs
last departure 12.00hrs 60 45wc lit all night
1cdp (hc) ⊙ iron (cold storage) calor gas ☎
⊞ stables launderette pub
75 or 75 (awnings)

BODMIN Cornwall Map 2 SX06
► **Camping Club Site** *(SX079675)*
Old Callywith Rd ☎3834
2 ❶ ⚠ signposted
Undulating grassy site with saplings and bushes set in meadowland within urban area, close to main road and river. 10½acres
200pitches
28 Mar–Sep must book peak periods
last arrival 22.00hrs last departure 12.00hrs
24 individual pitches 18wc lit all night
3cdp (21central hot water) (6hc) 3⊙ warden
(1spin) (1iron) calor gas camping gaz ☎ ⊞
children's playground wash up sinks (hairdryers)
cinema launderette pub
200£2.28 or 200£2.28 or 200▲£2.28
awnings

BOLNEY West Sussex Map 4 TQ22
►►► ***Alder House Tent, Dormobile & Caravan Site*** *(TQ268238)* Broxmead Ln ☎378
2 ❶ signposted
Pleasant, secluded site a short distance from A23 London to Brighton road at Bolney. Attractively terraced layout with good access roads. 4acres 50pitches 50static
Open all year no bookings accepted last
departure 12.00hrs 20 ⓐ 13wc lit all night
4cdp washbasins hc central hot water (hc)
(hc) ⊙ (wash, spin, dry) calor gas
camping gaz toilet fluid cafe licensed bar ☎ ⊞
50 or 50 or 50▲ (awnings)

BOLTON-LE-SANDS Lancashire
Map 7 SD46
See Morecambe sketch map.
►►► **Sandside Caravan & Camping Site** *(SD472680)* St Michael's Ln
☎Hest Bank 822311
2 ❷ ⚠ signposted
A well-maintained site pleasantly situated on sloping ground overlooking Morecambe Bay; distant views of the Lake District. 6acres
100pitches 35static
Mar–Oct must book peak periods last arrival
21.00hrs last departure 12.00hrs 7 12wc
lit all night 2cdp 17washbasins hc (4hc) ⊙
(1wash, 1dry) iron calor gas camping gaz ☎ ⊞
children's playground stables
launderette pub
10£1.60 10£1.25 80▲£1.25 (awnings)

►► **Bolton Holmes Farm** *(SD481693)*
☎Carnforth 2854
1 ❶ ⚠
A gently sloping site forming part of a farm complex, offering good views across Morecambe Bay and to the hills of the Lake District. 5acres 25pitches 40static
Apr–Oct must book peak periods 3 ⓐ
late arrivals enclosure 16wc lit all night 1cdp
(10washbasins hc, 2hc, 2hc) 2⊙ warden
(cold storage) calor gas stables
launderette pub
25£1.10 or 25£1.10 or 25▲£1.10
(awnings)

►► **Detron Gate Farm** *(SD486695)*
☎Carnforth 2842
1 ❶ ⚠ signposted
Conveniently positioned to A6. A popular site on sloping ground with a small farm adjacent. Views across Morecambe Bay. 7acres
200pitches 52static
May–Oct rsMar & Apr must book peak periods
last arrival 22.30hrs last departure 16.30hrs
8 ⓐ 20wc lit all night 1cdp 20washbasins hc
4central hot water (4hc) 2⊙ warden (wash)
(spin) games room CTV TV cold storage
calor gas camping gaz ☎ ⊞ children's
playground stables cinema
launderette pub
100£1.10 or 100£1.10 100▲90p
(awnings)

BOLVENTOR Cornwall Map 2 SX17
►►► Lords Waste Country Club & Camping & Caravan Site ☎Cardinham 335
[2] ❷ ⚠ signposted
The site is on Bodmin Moor not far from the A30 at Bolventor and is well situated for moorland walks. 3½acres 40pitches
Spring Bank Hol–Sep rsEtr–mid May must book last departure 23.00hrs 2⛟ individual pitches late arrivals enclosure 9wc lit all night 1cdp washbasins hc central hot water (⛆hc) ⊙ warden (wash, spin) (games room) (cold storage) calor gas camping gaz toilet fluid cafe restaurant ☎ ⊞ (licensed club), children's playground ⛟ ⊖ ⛟ launderette pub
40⛟ or 40⛟ or 40▲ (awnings)

BOSWINGER Cornwall Map 2 SW94
►►►► Seaview International Caravan & Camping Park *(SW990408)*
☎Mevagissey 3425
[3] ❸ ⚠ signposted
Grass site, set in hilly country overlooking the English Channel at Dodman Point. Access to sea and beach. 14acres 172pitches 59static
Etr–Oct must book peak periods last arrival 21.00hrs last departure 12.00hrs 12⛟ individual pitches Ⓐ late arrivals enclosure 35wc lit all night washbasins hc (⛟hc, ⛆hc) ⊙ warden (3wash, 3spin, 2dry, 3iron) (2⛟) games room (cold storage) calor gas camping gaz toilet fluid ☎ ⊞ children's playground, hairdryers & TV hire ⛟ ⊖ ⛟ ⛟ launderette pub
172⛟£2.92 or 172⛟£2.92 or 172▲£3.13 (awnings)

BOURNEMOUTH Dorset Map 4 SZ09
See Christchurch sketch map.
►►► Cara Caravan Park *(SZ138935)*
Old Bridge Rd, Iford
☎Christchurch 482121
[2] ❷ ⚠ signposted
Picturesque site on level ground with grass and gravel surface; varied trees and bushes. Direct access to river and A35. no animals 1½acres 40pitches 90static
All year must book peak periods last arrival 21.00hrs last departure 10.00hrs 8⛟ individual pitches late arrivals enclosure 32wc lit all night 1cdp ⛟ washbasins hc central hot water ⛆hc ⊙ warden iron calor gas toilet fluid ☎ ⊞ fishing ⛟ ⊖ stables ♁ ⛟ cinema launderette pub
30⛟£2–£3 10⛟£1.50–£2.25 (awnings)

►►► Chesildene Touring Caravan Park
55 Chesildene Av, Throop ☎513238
[2] ❷ ⚠ signposted
A grassy site situated 3 miles from the sea-front and town centre in pleasant rural surroundings. The approach road is unmade so care is required. From Ringwood take the Bournemouth Spur road and at roundabout turn right onto A3060 then in one mile, opposite Bournemouth School for Girls, turn right. 3½acres 70pitches
Apr–Oct must book peak periods last departure 12.00hrs 6⛟ individual pitches late arrivals enclosure 16wc lit all night 1cdp 10⛟ 12washbasins hc central hot water (6⛆hc) 2⊙ warden 1spin 1iron games room calor gas toilet fluid ☎ ⊞ children's playground ⛟ ⊖ stables ♁ ⛟ cinema ⛟ launderette pub
70⛟£2.60 or 70⛟£2.60 (awnings)

BOUTH Cumbria Map 7 SD38
See Cartmel sketch map.
► Black Beck Caravan Park *(SD334855)*
☎Greenodd 274
[1] ❶ ⚠ signposted
A secluded site situated in woodland, with a stream (from which the site's name is derived) running through the middle. N of A590. 2acres 45pitches 220static
Mar–Oct must book last arrival 22.00hrs last departure 13.00hrs 10⛟ individual pitches Ⓐ late arrivals enclosure wc lit all night 2cdp (washbasins hc) (⛆hc) ⊙ (wash, spin, iron) TV calor gas camping gaz paraffin toilet fluid ☎ ⊞ children's playground ⛟ ⊖ stables ⛟ ⛟ launderette pub
45⛟£2 or 45⛟£2 20▲£2 (awnings)

BOWNESS-ON-WINDERMERE Cumbria Map 7 SD49
Sites are listed under Windermere.

BRADWELL Norfolk Map 5 TG50
See Yarmouth (Great) sketch map.
►►►► Blue Sky Caravan Park *(TG507052)*
Burgh Rd ☎Great Yarmouth 780571
[1] ❸ ⚠ signposted
Level, grassy site close to Gt. Yarmouth, set in mixed woodland and meadowland, adjacent to A143 and Burgh Castle. 7acres 80pitches 133static
Spring Bank Hol–Sep rsEtr–mid May & Oct last departure 12.00hrs 17⛟ Ⓐ late arrivals enclosure wc lit all night 3cdp washbasins hc central hot water ⛆hc ⊙ warden wash spin iron CTV calor gas camping gaz ☎ ⊞ licensed club, children's playground, take-away food & amusement arcade ⛟ ⊖ stables ♁ ⛟ cinema ⛟ launderette pub
80⛟£2 or 80⛟£2 or 80▲£2 (awnings) ltr

BRAITHWAITE Cumbria Map 11 NY22
► Scotgate Caravan Site *(NY235235)* ☎343
[1] ❶ ⚠ signposted
Two large fields in a pleasant rural setting with views of the distant hills. Situated at junction of A66 and B5292. 5acres 135pitches 35static
Mar–Oct no bookings 4⛟ Ⓐ 28wc lit all night 1cdp (central hot water, ⛆hc) ⊙ (spin, dry, iron) calor gas camping gaz ⊞ ⛟ ⊖ stables ⛟ cinema ⛟ launderette pub
15⛟£2.10 or 15⛟£2 120▲£2.20 (awnings)

BRAMPTON Cumbria Map 12 NY56
►► Irthing Vale Caravan Park *(NY522613)*
Old Church Ln ☎2237
[2] ❷ ⚠ signposted
Situated in a quiet area just off the A6071 on the edge of the town. 4acres 40pitches 20static
Mar–Oct must book last arrival 22.00hrs last departure 12.00hrs 5⛟ individual pitches Ⓐ 8wc lit all night 1cdp washbasins hc central hot water (⛆hc) ⊙ warden (1wash) calor gas toilet fluid ☎ ⊞ children's play area ⊖ stables ♁ ⛟ ⛟ launderette ⛟ pub
30⛟£1.50 or 30⛟£1.50 10▲£1.20 (awnings) ltr

BRANSGORE Hampshire Map 4 SZ19
See Christchurch sketch map.
►►► Heathfield Caravan Park *(SZ209985)*
☎72397
[2] ❷ ⚠ signposted
A well laid-out site situated amongst open rural countryside, set away from main road and on fringe of New Forest. Within easy reach of sea. 14acres 200pitches
5 Mar–Oct must book peak periods last arrival 21.00hrs last departure 11.00hrs 36⛟ individual pitches late arrivals enclosure 39wc lit all night 2cdp washbasins hc central hot water ⛆hc ⊙ calor gas camping gaz toilet fluid ⊞ ⛟ ⊖ pub
200⛟£1.40–£1.80 or 200⛟£1.40–£1.80 (awnings)

BREAN Somerset Map 3 ST35
►►► Northam Farm Caravan & Camping Site ☎Brean Down 244
[1] ❶ ⚠
The site is situated by the coast in a farmyard setting, screened by hedges. North of Burnham-on-Sea on the Brean road. 10acres 90static
Etr–Sep 6⛟ 26wc lit all night 2cdp washbasins hc (⛆hc) ⊙ (cold storage) calor gas camping gaz toilet fluid ☎ ⊞ children's playground ⛟ ⊖ stables ♁ ⛟ ⛟ launderette pub
7⛟£1.50 ▲£1.25 awnings

BRIDESTOWE Devon Map 2 SX58
► Bridestowe Caravan Park ☎261
[1] ❶ ⚠ signposted
Site enjoys a secluded position in close proximity to the A30. Pitches are level and of grass. Situated ½m SE of Bridestowe; approach road is unclassified and leaves B3278 in Bridestowe village near the inn. Good situation for night stops or long stays for lovers of Dartmoor. ½acre 10pitches 12static

Etr–Oct must book Jul–Aug last arrival 22.00hrs last departure 12.00hrs 2♣ 12wc lit all night 1cdp 4washbasins hc central hot water 5⋔hc 2⊙ (spin, iron) (cold storage) camping gaz paraffin toilet fluid ☎ ⊞ ♨ ⊖ stables ♘ ✈ cinema ⤻ launderette pub
10⊏ or 10🚐 or 10▲ ltr

BRIDLINGTON Humberside Map 8 TA16
► The Poplars Caravan Site *(TA194701)*
45 Jewison Ln, Sewerby ☎77251
① ❶ ⚠ signposted
A part level, part sloping grassy site with mature trees, set in an urban area adjacent to a main road. From Bridlington follow the Flamborough road B1255 then t lt into Jewison Lane, signed Bempton, for the site entrance on lt. No motorcycles 1⅓acres 30pitches
Mar–Nov rsDec–Feb 5 vans only must book peak periods last arrival 23.00hrs last departure 12.00hrs 3♣ individual pitches 6wc 1cdp 4washbasins hc (2⋔hc) 1⊙ warden (cold storage) calor gas camping gaz ⊞ battery charger ♨ ⊖ ♘ ✈ cinema ⤻ launderette pub
30⊏£2 or 30🚐£2 (awnings)

BRIXHAM Devon Map 3 SX95
►►► Hillhead Camp *(SX903534)*
☎ Churston 842336
② ❷ ⚠ signposted
The site overlooks the sea and is situated on the B3205. Pitches are level and grassy; low banks afford protection. 12½acres 400pitches
Jun–Aug rsEtr–May & Sep–Oct must book peak periods last arrival 22.00hrs last departure 11.00hrs 8♣ Ⓐ late arrivals enclosure 36wc lit all night 1cdp washbasins hc ⋔hc 4⊙ (wash, spin, dry, iron) ⩯ games room CTV calor gas camping gaz toilet fluid cafe restaurant ☎ ⊞ licensed club children's playground & entertainment ♨ ⊖ stables ♘ ✈ cinema ⤻ launderette pub
400🚐£3.20 or 400▲£3.20 awnings

►► Upton Manor Farm Camping Park
(SX922560) St Mary's Rd ☎2384
② ❷ ⚠ signposted
Gently sloping, grass site with trees and bushes set in meadowland, about ¼ mile from the sea and beach and close to the town centre.
⚘ 7acres 175pitches
Etr & Spring Bank Hol–Sep rsmid Apr–mid May last arrival 21.00hrs last departure 11.00hrs 6♣ wc 25washbasins hc 16⋔hc 8⊙ iron (cold storage) calor gas camping gaz ⊞ ♨ ⊖ stables ♘ ✈ cinema ⤻ launderette pub
175🚐 or 175▲

BROCKENHURST Hampshire Map 4 SU30
►► Hollands Wood Camp Site
(SU303038)
② ❶ ⚠ signposted
A fairly secluded site within the New Forest. See page 124 for further information.
136acres 700pitches
9♣ 51wc lit all night 3cdp 55washbasins hc 12⋔hc 15⊙ calor gas camping gaz paraffin toilet fluid cafe ☎ ⊞ ⊖ stables ♘ ✈ cinema ⤻ launderette ♨ pub
700⊏ or 700🚐 or 700▲ (awnings)

BROMPTON-ON-SWALE North Yorkshire Map 8 SE29
►► Brompton-on-Swale Caravan Site
(NZ201003) ☎ Richmond 4629
② ❶ ⚠ signposted
A mainly level grass and gravel site set in meadowland adjacent to main road on the banks of the River Swale. 5½acres 60pitches
Mar–Oct must book peak periods last arrival 22.00hrs last departure 13.00hrs 5♣ Ⓐ late arrivals enclosure 12wc lit all night 2cdp washbasins hc central hot water ⋔hc ⊙ calor gas camping gaz toilet fluid ☎ ⊞ fishing ♨ ⊖ stables ♘ cinema launderette pub
60⊏£2.20 or 60🚐£2.20 or 60▲£2.20 (awnings) ltr

BROMYARD Hereford and Worcester
Map 3 SO65
►►► Bromyard Caravan Park *(SO661543)*
Bishell House, Petty Bridge ☎2267
③ ❶ ⚠ signposted
Undulating grassy site with trees and bushes, set in downland and adjacent to main road.
6½acres 15pitches 140static
Mid Mar–23 Oct must book peak periods 5♣ 18wc lit all night 1cdp washbasins hc central hot water (⋔hc) ⊙ cold storage calor gas camping gaz toilet fluid ⊞ children's playground ♨ ⊖ stables ⤻ launderette pub
15⊏£1.50 or 15🚐£1.50 (awnings)

►►► Saltmarshe Castle *(SO671579)*
☎3207
② ❷ ⚠
Level grassy site in wooded downland.
2acres 30pitches
15 Mar–Oct last arrival 23.59hrs last departure 16.00hrs 4♣ 14wc 4cdp central hot water (⋔hc) ⊙ warden calor gas ☎ ⊞ licensed club with facilities for children ♨ ⊖ stables pub
30⊏£1.50 or 30🚐£1.50 (awnings) ltr

BROUGHTON Humberside Map 8 SE90
►► *Briggate Lodge Caravan & Picnic Site*
(SE955068) ☎ Brigg 54275
② ❷ ⚠ signposted
Level, grassy site with gravel paths, trees and bushes. Set in woodland adjacent to main road, and Junc 4 of M180 (Scunthorpe bypass).
2½acres 45pitches All year last arrival 22.30hrs last departure 12.00hrs 2♣ Ⓐ late arrivals enclosure 3wc lit all night 1cdp 4washbasins hc 1⋔hc 2⊙ ⊖ stables ♘ ♨ pub
25⊏ 10🚐 10▲ (awnings)

BUCKFASTLEIGH Devon Map 3 SX76
►► Buckfast Caravan Park *(SX742670)*
☎2479
② ❷ ⚠ signposted
Level, grassy site with numbered pitches. Well-screened by young saplings and within walking distance of the Abbey. The River Dart borders eastern side of site. Entrance is by Municipal Car Park on the Abbey Road just NW of A38. 2½acres 80pitches
Apr–Oct must book peak periods last arrival 22.00hrs last departure 12.00hrs 3♣ individual pitches late arrivals enclosure 12wc lit all night 1cdp 19washbasins hc 6⋔hc ⊙ (2wash, 3dry, 1iron) cold storage calor gas camping gaz cafe ☎ ⊞ battery charger ♨ ⊖ stables ⤻ launderette pub
80⊏£2–£2.30 or 80🚐£2 (awnings) ltr

BUDE Cornwall Map 2 SS20
►►► Bude Holiday Park Maer Ln ☎2472
② ❸ ⚠ signposted
Site is situated on gently sloping land. Nearby are the cliffs and Atlantic Ocean. 1m from town; approach by way of town centre.
11acres 250pitches 150static
Jun–Sep last arrival 23.59hrs 12♣ 36wc lit all night 1cdp washbasins hc central hot

water (hc) ⊙ warden (wash, spin, dry) iron (cold storage) calor gas camping gaz cafe ☎ ⊞ licensed bar children's playground stables cinema launderette pub 300 £2.50 or 300 £2.50 or 300▲£2.50 awnings ltr

▶▶▶ Wooda Farm Camping & Caravanning Park Poughill (2m E) ☎2069
2 ❷ ⚠ signposted
There are sea views as the site stands on raised ground overlooking Bude Bay; from the A39 at the edge of Stratton follow the unclassified Coombe Valley road.
9acres 200pitches 25static
Spring Bank Hol–Aug rsApr, May, Sep & Oct last arrival 20.00hrs last departure 10.30hrs 16 late arrivals enclosure 29wc lit all night 2cdp (28washbasins hc) (14 hc) 4⊙ (1wash) (2dry, 1iron) (1cold storage) calor gas camping gaz toilet fluid ☎ ⊞ children's playground hairdryers & wash up sinks stables cinema launderette pub 200 £1.50 or 200 £1.50 or 200▲£1.50 (awnings)

BURGH CASTLE Norfolk Map 5 TG40
See Yarmouth (Great) sketch map.
▶▶▶ Cherry Farm Caravan & Chalet Park *(TG490044)* Mill Rd ☎ Great Yarmouth 780229
1 ❶ ⚠ signposted
Flat, grassed site, with many fruit trees. In rural surroundings 4m from sea; off A143 Beccles-Yarmouth road. 6acres 105pitches 212static
25 May–13 Sep rsApr–24 May & 14 Sep–Oct (no shop) must book last arrival 00.30hrs last departure 11.00hrs 20 52wc lit all night 1cdp washbasins hc hc ⊙ (wash, spin, dry, iron, games room) calor gas camping gaz cafe ☎ ⊞ licensed club children's playground putting table tennis cinema launderette pub 35 £2.35 70 £2.35 or 70▲£2.35 (awnings)

BUXTON Derbyshire Map 7 SK07
▶ Dukes Drive Caravan Site *(SK068725)* ☎2777
1 ❶ ⚠ signposted
Simple site situated in a long valley on gently sloping ground with some trees and bushes. An impressive railway viaduct lies at one end of the valley. 3acres 25pitches 25static
Mar–Oct 7 wc lit all night washbasins hc central hot water hc hc ⊙ calor gas camping gaz paraffin toilet fluid cafe restaurant licensed bar ☎ ⊞ stables cinema launderette pub 25 or 25 & ▲ (awnings)

CAISTER-ON-SEA Norfolk Map 9 TG51
See Yarmouth (Great) sketch map.
▶▶▶ Grasmere Caravan Park *(TG521115)* 7 Bultitudes Lake, Yarmouth Rd ☎ Great Yarmouth 720382
1 ❸ ⚠ signposted
Mainly level grass and gravel site with mature trees. Set in meadowland in an urban area with direct access to A149. 2acres 49pitches 74static
Apr–mid Oct must book peak periods last arrival 23.00hrs last departure 10.00hrs 6 individual pitches 24wc lit all night 1cdp washbasins hc (hc) ⊙ calor gas toilet fluid ☎ ⊞ children's playground stables cinema launderette pub 49 £1.40 or 49 £1.40 (awnings)

CAMBORNE Cornwall Map 2 SW64
▶▶ *Magor Farm Caravan Site* Tehidy ☎713367
2 ❶ ⚠ signposted
Surrounded by trees, very sheltered easy access. Short drive from beaches, leisure centre and town. 7½acres 48pitches
Mar–Sep 4 10wc lit all night 1cdp (washbasins hc) (central hot water) (hc) (⊙) cold storage calor gas camping gaz ⊞ stables launderette pub 48 or 48 or 48▲ rates on application (awnings)

CAMELFORD Cornwall Map 2 SX18
▶▶▶ Juliot's Well Holiday Park ☎3302
2 ⚠ signposted
Sloping, grassy site with woodlands. 1m SW of Camelford off the A39. 30pitches 32static
Apr–Oct must book last arrival 22.00hrs last departure 10.00hrs 4 individual pitches late arrivals enclosure 16wc lit all night 1cdp washbasins hc 10 hc 3⊙ warden (1wash, 1spin, 1dry, 1iron) 2games rooms TV (cold storage) calor gas camping gaz ☎ ⊞ licensed clubs, children's playground & bicycles for hire stables launderette pub 30 or 30 or 30▲rates on application (awnings)

▶▶▶ Valley Truckle Touring Caravan Park ☎2206
2 ⚠ signposted
Part level, part sloping grass site, set in typical Cornish downland. 5acres 80pitches
Etr–Oct booking advisable peak periods last departure 12.00hrs 5 individual pitches late arrivals enclosure 12wc lit all night 1cdp 14washbasins hc central hot water 6 hc 4⊙ warden (2wash, 1spin, 1dry, 2iron) (, cold storage) calor gas camping gaz toilet fluid ☎ ⊞ children's playground, hairdryers & wash up sinks stables launderette pub 80 £2.10 or 80 £2.10 or 80▲£2.10 (awnings) ltr

CANTERBURY Kent Map 5 TR15
▶▶ St Martins Touring & Camping Site *(TR173575)* Bekesbourne Ln ☎63216
2 ❷ ⚠ signposted
An attractive tree-screened site in pleasant rural surroundings. Off A257 Canterbury–Sandwich road. 12acres 100pitches
Etr–Sep no bookings last arrival 23.00hrs last departure 12.00hrs 4 23wc lit all night 1cdp washbasins hc hc ⊙ warden (wash) ☎ ⊞ stables cinema launderette pub 100 £2.25 or 100 £2.25 or 100▲£2.25 (awnings)

CARK-IN-CARTMEL Cumbria Map 7 SD37
See Cartmel sketch map.
▶▶ Old Park Wood Caravan Site *(SD335785)* Apply to: Holker Estates Co, Cark-in-Cartmel ☎Flookburgh 266
2 ❶ ⚠ signposted
A delightfully secluded site surrounded by woodland and overlooking part of Ulverston Sands. Hill and mountain views form the background. The spacious grass fields are divided by neatly constructed stone walls. 4½m W of Grange-over-Sands off B5277.
4acres 80pitches 292static
Mar–Oct must book last arrival 23.00hrs 10 individual pitches 30wc lit all night 6cdp washbasins hc central hot water (8 hc) ⊙ (wash, spin, dry) calor gas toilet fluid ☎ ⊞ children's playground stables pub 80 £2.50 or 80 £2.50 awnings ltr

CARLEEN Cornwall Map 2 SW63
▶▶▶ *Lower Polladras Farm* ☎Germoe 2220
2 ❷ ⚠ signposted
Situated in secluded valley at Polladras on A394, this site provides an ideal base from which to tour the Lands End peninsula. 4acres 60pitches
Apr–Oct must book Jul & Aug last arrival 21.00hrs last departure 12.00hrs 6 12wc lit all night 1cdp 8washbasins hc 1central hot water 2 hc 1⊙ (1wash, 1spin) 1iron (cold storage) calor gas camping gaz toilet fluid ⊞ stables cinema launderette pub 60 or 60 or 60▲

▶ Poldown Caravan Park *(SW634293)* Poldown ☎Helston 4560
1 ❷ ⚠
A small, quiet site set in attractive countryside. From the A394 turn off onto the B3302, Hayle road, at Hilltop Garage then take second left to Carleen for site is ¾ mile on right.
¾acre 10pitches 5static
Apr–Oct must book peak periods last arrival

22.00hrs last departure 11.00hrs 1♨ individual pitches 4wc lit all night 4central hot water (2♨hc) 1⊙ (1iron) cold storage calor gas camping gaz ⊞ children's playground & laundry room ⊖ stables ♘ ✈ cinema ⊱ launderette ♨ pub 10₽£2.05 or 10₽£2.05 or 10▲£2.05 (awnings)

CARLYON BAY Cornwall Map 2 SX05
See St Austell sketch map.
►**Bethesda Camping Site** *(SX052527)*
Cypress Av ☎Par 2735
1 ❶ ⚠
Situated in urban area, this sloping, grass site with trees and bushes is set in meadowland, with access to sea, beach and A390. 12acres 200pitches 2static
Apr–Sep must book peak periods 6♨ ⊗ 20wc lit all night 1cdp 8washbasins hc (1central hot water) (6♨hc) 1⊙ warden (1dry, 1iron) games room CTV (cold storage) calor gas camping gaz toilet fluid ⊞ children's playground & fish and chip delivery ♨ ⊖ stables ♘ ✈ cinema ⊱ launderette pub 50₽£1.25 150₽£1 or 150▲£1.25 (awnings)

CARNFORTH Lancashire Map 7 SD47
See Morecambe & District sketch map.
►►**Netherbeck Caravan Site** *(SD509711)*
North Rd, Netherbeck ☎3218
2 ❶ ⚠
A sloping site with mature trees and bushes. Situated 1 mile northeast of town on an unclassified road. 2acres 6pitches 32static
Mar–Oct must book 2♨ 5wc lit all night 1cdp ⊕ 4washbasins hc central hot water (2♨hc) ⊙ cold storage calor gas ⊞ children's playground ⊖ stables ✈ ⊱ launderette ♨ pub
6₽£1.25 or 6₽£1.25 or 6▲£1.25 (awnings) ltr

CARNON DOWNS near Truro, Cornwall Map 2 SW84
►►**Carnon Downs Caravan & Camping Park** *(SW804408)* ☎Devoran 862283
2 ❶ ⚠ signposted
A level, grassy site with mature trees, set in meadowland and woodland just outside the urban area, adjacent to A39 Falmouth–Truro road. 8acres 100pitches
Apr–Oct must book peak periods 5♨ 7wc lit all night 1cdp 7washbasins hc 2central hot water (4♨hc) 2⊙ (spin) games room TV cold storage calor gas camping gaz toilet fluid ⊞ ♨ ⊖ stables ♘ ✈ cinema ⊱ launderette pub
100₽£3 or 100₽£3 or 100▲£3 awnings

►►**Ringwell Holiday Park** *(SW794417)*
Bissoe Rd ☎Devoran 862194
2 ❷ ⚠ signposted
A level grassy site with mature trees, set in hilly country and woodland just outside the urban area, adjacent to A39 Falmouth–Truro road. 1½acres 20pitches 25static
Apr–Oct must book peak periods last arrival 23.00hrs last departure 12.00hrs 8♨ 9wc lit all night washbasins hc ♨hc ⊙ (wash, spin) iron calor gas camping gaz ☎ ⊞ ⊖ ♨ pub
20₽£2.38 or 20₽£2.38 or 20▲£2.38 (awnings)

CARTMEL Cumbria Map 7 SD37
See sketch map.
►**Wells House Farm** *(SD378784)*
2 ❶ ⚠
Pleasantly situated in village, the site offers secluded camping in unspoilt rural surroundings. The River Eea runs close to the site and the priory gatehouse and the 15th–17th C church can be visited at one's leisure. 3acres 40pitches
Mar–Oct no bookings last arrival 20.00hrs last departure 18.00hrs 3♨ ⊗ 13wc (3washbasins hc, 1central hot water) (3♨hc) 2⊙ calor gas camping gaz ⊞ ♨ ⊖ stables ♘ launderette pub
40▲ (awnings)

CASSINGTON Oxfordshire Map 4 SP41
►►**Cassington Mill Caravan Park** *(SP450103)* Eynsham Rd ☎Oxford 881490 (may change to 881081 during the currency of this guide)
2 ❷ signposted
Site surrounded by fields, hills and woods, and the River Everdale runs through the centre of the park. Left onto B4449 5m W of Oxford. 3½acres 83pitches 50static
Apr–Oct no bookings Jul & Aug last departure 14.00hrs 14♨ 16wc lit all night 1cdp 12washbasins hc 3central hot water 4♨hc 2⊙ calor gas camping gaz toilet fluid ⊞ ⊖ launderette ♨ pub
83₽fr£1.60 or 83₽fr£1.60 or 83▲fr£1.60 (awnings)

CASTERTON (GREAT) Leicestershire Map 4 TF00
►►►***Casterton Filling Station & Motel*** *(TF002088)* Old North Rd ☎Stamford 54376
1 ❷ ►
A level grass site with grass and mixed vegetation set in downland and meadowland, just outside the urban area. Adjacent to main road. 1½acres 45pitches 12static
All year must book peak periods last arrival 22.00hrs last departure 12.00hrs 3♨ late arrivals enclosure 8wc lit all night 1cdp washbasins hc central hot water (⇨hc) (♨hc) ⊙ warden (wash, spin) (cold storage) calor gas camping gaz paraffin toilet fluid cafe restaurant licensed bar ☎ ⊞ ♨ ⊖ stables ♘ ✈ cinema ⊱ launderette pub
24₽ 6₽ 15▲ (awnings)

CASTLESIDE Co Durham Map 12 NZ04
►►►**Allensford Park Caravan Site** *(NZ083505)* Apply to: Derwentside District Council, Council Offices, Consett, Co Durham. ☎Consett 509522
2 ❶ ⚠ signposted
Gently sloping parkland with mature trees. Set in hilly moorland and woodland country near the urban area adjacent to River Derwent and A68. 14acres 50pitches 48static
Apr–Oct 4♨ 13wc lit all night 1cdp washbasins hc central hot water ♨hc ⊙ warden (wash, spin, iron) cold storage calor gas camping gaz toilet fluid cafe restaurant ☎ ⊞ children's playground ♨ ⊖ stables ♘ cinema ⊱ launderette pub
25₽£1.90 or 25₽£1.90 25▲£1.50 (awnings)

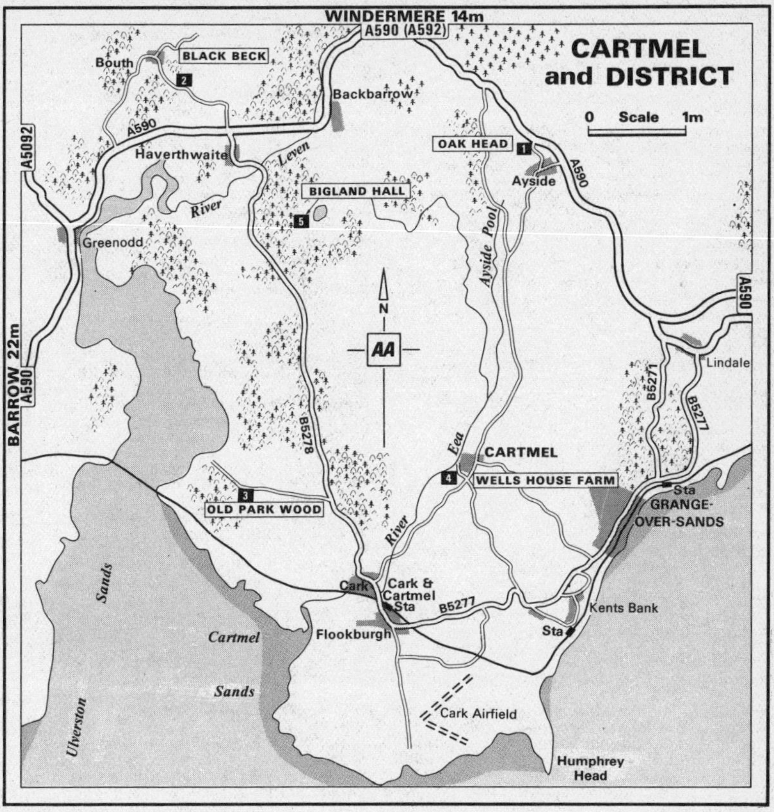

Sites listed under: **1** Ayside **2** Bouth **3** Cark-in-Cartmel **4** Cartmel **5** Haverthwaite

CATON Lancashire Map 7 SD56
See Morecambe sketch map.
►► ***Crook O'Lune Caravan Park***
(SD519643) ☎770216
[2] ❶ △
Set in hilly woodland, adjacent to river, main road and exit 34 of M6. 1acre 15pitches 138static
Mar–Oct must book peak periods last arrival 19.00hrs last departure 17.00hrs 7 individual pitches late arrivals enclosure no cars by caravans 24wc lit all night 1cdp 12washbasins hc (12hc) 3⊙ calor gas toilet fluid licensed bar ☎ stables
15 or 15 (awnings) ltr

CAWSTON Norfolk Map 9 TG12
► **Haveringland Hall Caravan Park**
(TG153213) Haveringland Hall Farm ☎302
[3] ❶ △ signposted
A level, grassy site with mature trees set in woodland and meadowland with direct access to lake. 10m N of Norwich on Cawston road, turn right at Stump Cross. 8acres 50pitches 65static
Mar–Oct must book peak periods last arrival 20.00hrs last departure 12.00hrs 8 individual pitches for caravans 18wc lit all night 1cdp 15washbasins hc hc ⊙ calor gas camping gaz toilet fluid ☎ ⊞ fishing stables pub
50£2.32 or 50£2.32 or 50▲£2.32 (awnings) ltr

CERNE ABBAS Dorset Map 3 ST60
► **Giant's Head Caravan Park**
Giant's Head Farm, Old Sherborne Rd ☎242
[1] ❶ △ signposted
Part level, part sloping, grassy site set in Dorset downland near Cerne Giant (a figure cut into the chalk). Adjacent to main road, 2m NE from Cerne Abbas. 4acres 12pitches
Etr–Oct must book peak periods last departure 13.00hrs 2 3wc lit all night 1cdp washbasins hc central hot water (hc) ⊙ TV ⊞ stables pub
12£1.70–£2.05 or 12£1.50–£1.80 or 12▲£1.70–£2.05 (awnings)

CHACEWATER Cornwall Map 2 SW74
►►► ***Chacewater Caravan Park***
(SW740438) Coxhill ☎ St Day 820762
[1] ❷ △ signposted
A level grassy site with young trees set in meadowland. 5acres 75pitches 15static
Etr–Oct last departure 14.00hrs 4 16wc lit all night 1cdp 12washbasins hc 8hc 2⊙ (1iron) games room TV calor gas camping gaz toilet fluid ⊞ car repairs, mechanic on call & battery charger launderette pub
75£1.60–£2 or 75£1.60–£2 or 75▲£1.60–£2 (awnings)

CHANNEL ISLANDS
Details follow England.

CHAPEL HILL Lincolnshire Map 8 TF25
►►► **Orchards Caravans** *(TF208543)*
☎ Coningsby 42414
1 ❷ ⚠ signposted
Level, grassy site with assorted trees and bushes set in meadowland with direct access to River Witham and near to A153. 1½ acres 33pitches 48static
Jun–Oct rsNov, Dec & Feb–May must book peak periods 4 10wc lit all night cdp washbasins hc (hc, hc) ⊙ (wash, iron) CTV calor gas camping gaz ☎ ⊞ children's playground & licensed club stables cinema launderette pub
33£1.90 or 33£1.90 or 33▲£1.90 (awnings)

CHAPEL PORTH Cornwall Map 2 SW64
See Perranporth sketch map.
►►► ***Chapel Porth Caravan Park*** *(SW699496)* ☎ St Agnes 2720
2 ❷ ⚠ signposted
Undulating, grassy site with young trees and bushes situated in hilly moorland country, and adjacent to the sea and beach. 1m SW of St Agnes off B3277. ½acre 10pitches 16static
Etr–Sep must book peak periods last arrival 18.30hrs last departure 12.00hrs 2 individual pitches 6wc lit all night 1cdp 5washbasins hc 2hc 1⊙ iron calor gas camping gaz ☎ ⊞ stables launderette
6 6 6▲ (awnings)

CHARMOUTH Dorset Map 3 SY39
►►► **Newlands Caravan & Camping Park** *(SY374935)* 2 Camping Site ☎60259
2 ❷ ⚠ signposted
Gently sloping, grass and gravel site in hilly country near the sea. 4m W of Bridport on A35. 14acres 206pitches 220static
Jun–16 Oct rs16 Mar–May must book peak periods last arrival 22.00hrs last departure 22.00hrs 20 individual pitches late arrivals enclosure 39wc lit all night 1cdp washbasins hc (hc) ⊙ wash spin dry games room calor gas camping gaz toilet fluid cafe ☎ ⊞ licensed club & children's playground stables cinema launderette pub
70£2–£3 20£1.50–£2.50 110▲£1.50–£2.50 awnings

CHEDDAR Somerset Map 3 ST45
See sketch map.
►►►► **Broadway House Caravan & Camping Park** ☎742610
2 ❸ ⚠
Level, grassy site with varied trees and bushes set in hilly woodland country with direct access to main road. 10acres 200pitches 38static
25 May–Sep rsMar–24 May & Oct last departure 12.00hrs 28 late arrivals enclosure 47wc lit all night 2cdp 35washbasins hc (6central hot water) (4hc) (21hc) 16⊙ warden (4wash, 1spin, 2dry) (2iron) CTV cold storage calor gas camping gaz toilet fluid cafe licensed bar ☎ ⊞ children's playground amusement arcade ladies' hairdryers invalid facilities & wash up sinks stables launderette pub
200£2.50 or 200£2 or 200▲£2.50 (awnings)

►► **Froglands Farm** ☎742058
2 ❷ signposted
Farmland site set on undulating ground. Trees and shrubs abound. 4½acres 60pitches 60static
Spring Bank Hol–mid Sep rsEtr–mid May & mid Sep–Oct last arrival 22.00hrs last departure 12.00hrs 4 individual pitches 16wc 1cdp 8washbasins hc (6hc) 2⊙ warden (cold storage) calor gas camping gaz toilet fluid ⊞ children's playground stables launderette pub
18 or 18 42▲ rates on application awnings

► **Church Farm Camping Site** Church St
1 ❶
Field behind farmyard, for both camping and touring vans, has flat surface and hedge-screening. 4½acres
Etr–Oct no bookings last arrival 22.30hrs last departure 12.00hrs 6 10wc lit all night 1cdp (6washbasins hc) (6hc) 2⊙ calor gas camping gaz ⊞ hairdryers stables launderette pub
£1.50 £1.25 ▲£1.25 (awnings)

► **Round Oak Farm** ☎742561
1 ❶ signposted
Camping field behind farmyard with trees and hedge-screening. Adjacent to B3151 Wells-Bristol road. 4½acres 92pitches
Spring Bank Hol–Sep no bookings

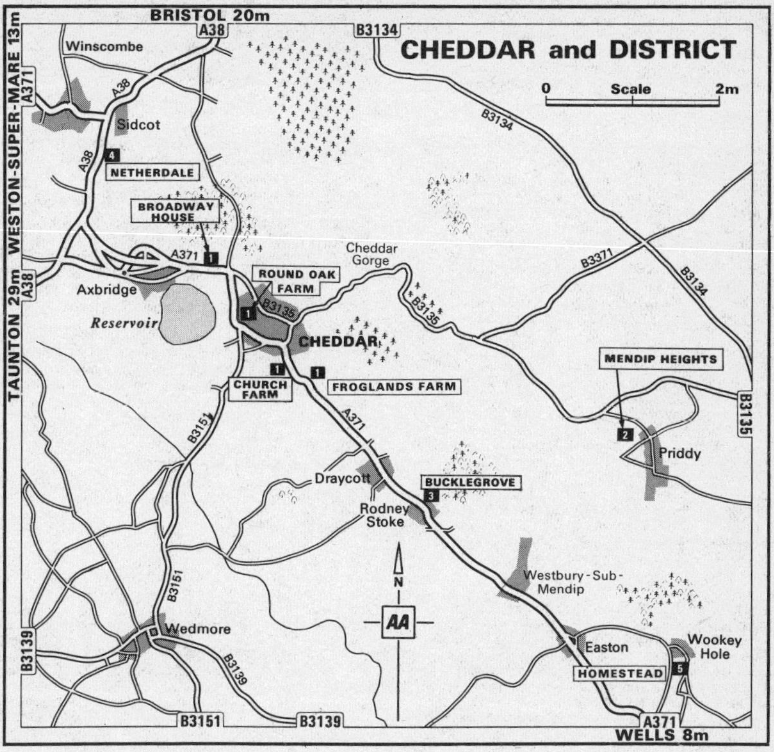

Sites listed under: **1** Cheddar **2** Priddy **3** Rodney Stoke **4** Sidcot **5** Wookey Hole

last arrival 22.00hrs last departure 12.00hrs 2⛺ individual pitches Ⓐ 9wc lit all night cdp ⊙ cold storage calor gas camping gaz ⊞ 🏪 ⊖ stables ↬ launderette pub 12🚐£1.50 3🚙£1.50 75▲£1.25 (awnings)

CHELTENHAM Gloucestershire Map 3 SO92
▶▶**Trax Campsite** Prestbury Park (Racecourse)
2 ❶ △ signposted
A mainly level site in hilly country with nearby downland. 1½m N of town on A435 Evesham road. 5¼acres 84pitches
2 May–4 Oct no bookings last arrival 22.30hrs last departure 15.00hrs 2⛺ 20wc lit all night 1cdp 16washbasins hc 2central hot water 4🚿hc 2⊙ warden (1wash, 1spin, 1dry) 1iron CTV calor gas camping gaz toilet fluid ☎ ⊞ children's playground 🏪 ⊖ ♂ ↞ cinema launderette pub
84🚐£2–£2.35 or 84🚙£2–£2.35 awnings

CHESTER Cheshire Map 7 SJ46
▶▶***Racecourse Caravan Park** (SJ399662)*
1 ❷ △ signposted
Well-equipped site adjacent to Roodee (Chester Racecourse) and close to city centre. 2¼acres 45pitches
Etr–Oct closed Race meetings no booking last arrival 21.00hrs last departure 12.00hrs 2⛺ individual pitches 8wc lit all night 1cdp 8washbasins hc central hot water (4🚿hc) 2⊙ cold storage calor gas camping gaz paraffin toilet fluid ☎ ⊞ 🏪 ⊖ stables ♂ ↞ cinema ↬ launderette pub
45🚐 or 45🚙 ltr

CHICHESTER West Sussex Map 4 SU80
▶▶▶▶***Southern Leisure Centre***
(SU878039) Vinnetrow Ln ☎787715
2 ❷ △
Well-constructed Leisure Park close to Chichester and the Goodwood Estate, within easy reach of the sea. The park is surrounded by twelve lakes which provide good coarse and trout fishing. 7acres
Mar–Oct 4⛺ late arrivals enclosure 20wc lit all night 1cdp 16washbasins hc 🛁hc 16🚿hc 8⊙ warden ⊞ 🏪 ⊖ ♂ ↞ ↬
141🚐 or 141🚙

CHIGWELL Essex Map 5 TQ49
▶▶▶▶▶**Grange Farm Leisure Centre**
(TQ439947) High St
2 ❷ ▶ signposted
Although the site is only 14m from London and has direct access to A113 and M11, it is well laid out in attractive rural surroundings and consists of natural parkland overlooking Roding Valley and Epping Forest. 600pitches
May–Aug rsMar–Apr & Sep–Nov no bookings last departure 12.00hrs 24⛺ Ⓐ late arrivals enclosure wc lit all night cdp 36🚐 washbasins hc 🚿hc ⊙ (wash, spin) iron ⛵ ⛳ games room CTV calor gas camping gaz toilet fluid ☎ ⊞ children's playground licensed club mini golf & take away food 🏪 ⊖ stables ♂ cinema ↬ launderette pub
200🚐£2.60–£3.80 100🚙£2.60–£3.80 300▲£2.60–£3.80 (awnings)

CHILLINGTON Devon Map 3 SX74
►► ***Union Inn Caravan Site*** *(SX793427)*
☎ Torcross 241
[2] ❷ ►
Level, grass and gravel site with mature trees, saplings and bushes. Set in woodland and meadowland adjacent to beach and A379 Kingsbridge road. ¾acre 10pitches 4static Mid Mar–Oct must book peak periods last departure 10.00hrs 2🐕 individual pitches late arrivals enclosure 3wc lit all night 1cdp 3washbasins hc (1central hot water) (🚿hc) ⊙ (spin) iron (cold storage) calor gas camping gaz paraffin cafe restaurant licensed bar ☎ ⊞ ⛱ ⊖ stables ♘ ⇜ ⛳ launderette pub
10🚐 or 10🚗 wkly terms only (awnings)

CHRISTCHURCH Dorset Map 4 SZ19
See Christchurch sketch map.
►►►► **Grove Farm Meadow Holiday Caravan Park** *(SZ136946)* Stour Way
☎483597
[2] ❸ ⚠ signposted
A level, grassy site with mature trees and near the River Stour. ✤ 2acres 50pitches 200static Mar–Oct no bookings last arrival 22.00hrs last departure 12.00hrs 17🐕 individual pitches late arrivals enclosure wc lit all night cdp (12washbasins hc) (2🛁hc, 8🚿hc) 3⊙ warden (2wash, 2spin, 1dry, 4iron) calor gas camping gaz toilet fluid ☎ ⊞ children's playground fishing & off license ⛱ ⊖ stables ♘ ⇜ cinema launderette pub
55🚐£2–£2.80 or 55🚗£2–£2.80 (awnings)

►►►► **Hoburne Farm Caravan Park** *(SZ194937)* Highcliffe Rd ☎ Highcliffe 3379
[2] ❶ ⚠ signposted
Level, grassy site with gravel paths, mature trees, saplings and bushes, set in meadowland and adjacent to sea, beach and main road.
16acres 285pitches 298static
Mar–Oct rsNov–Feb, wknds only must book peak periods last arrival 22.00hrs last departure 10.00hrs 50🐕 individual pitches late arrivals enclosure no cars by caravans wc lit all night 5cdp 🚐 24washbasins hc 16central hot water 1🛁hc (24🚿hc) 6⊙ warden (7wash, 5spin) (5iron) ⛵ (🎱 games room) CTV cold storage calor gas cafe restaurant ☎ ⊞ (licensed club) children's playground ⛱ ⊖ stables ♘ ⇜ ⛳ launderette pub
285🚐£2.55 or 285🚗£2.55 awnings ltr

►► **Haven Caravan Park** *(SZ185920)*
Bure Ln, Mudeford ☎ Highcliffe 4662
[2] ❷ ⚠ signposted
Level, grassy site with varied trees and bushes. Set in woodland within the urban area with direct access to sea, beach and main road.
26pitches 58static
Mar–Oct no bookings 12🐕 individual pitches wc washbasins hc 🚿hc ⊙ (wash, spin, iron) calor gas camping gaz paraffin toilet fluid ☎ ⊞ children's playground ⛱ ⊖ stables ♘ ⇜ cinema ⛳ launderette pub
26🚐£3.24 or 26🚗£2.16 awnings

CHUDLEIGH KNIGHTON Devon Map 3 SX87
► **Ford Farm** ☎ Chudleigh (Devon) 853253
[2] ❷ ⚠
Small grassy secluded site with varied trees and bushes. From A38 Exeter-Plymouth road take B3344 for Chudleigh Knighton. 2½acres 48pitches 2static
Mar–Oct rsNov–Feb must book for caravans last departure 12.00hrs 2🐕 ⊗ 6wc lit all night 1cdp (central hot water, 🚿hc) ⊙ (wash, spin, iron) calor gas camping gaz paraffin ⊞ ⛱ ⊖ stables ⛳ launderette pub
12🚐£1 6🚗£1 30▲£1 (awnings)

CHURT Surrey Map 4 SU83
► **Symondstone Farm** *(SU845381)*
[1] ❶
Secluded site surrounded by woodlands on the Surrey/Hampshire border, close to the village of Churt; once the home of Lloyd George. For sailing enthusiasts, close by are the famous Frensham Ponds. 8acres 70pitches
Apr–Oct must book public hols last arrival 23.59hrs 4🐕 5wc 2cdp calor gas ☎ ⊞ ⊖ stables ♘ ⇜ launderette
70🚐80p or 70🚗80p or 70▲80p awnings ltr

CLEVEDON Avon Map 3 ST47
► **Colehouse Farm Camp Site** ☎872680
[1] ❶
Level, grassy site with mature trees, saplings and bushes, set in meadowland. 1m S of Clevedon off B3133. 2½acres 39pitches 41static
Apr–Sep must book peak periods 12🐕 wc lit all night 1cdp washbasins hc (4🚿hc) 1⊙ calor gas camping gaz ☎ mobile shop ⊖ stables ♘ ⇜ cinema ⛳ launderette pub
39🚐£1 or 39🚗£1 or 39▲£1 awnings ltr

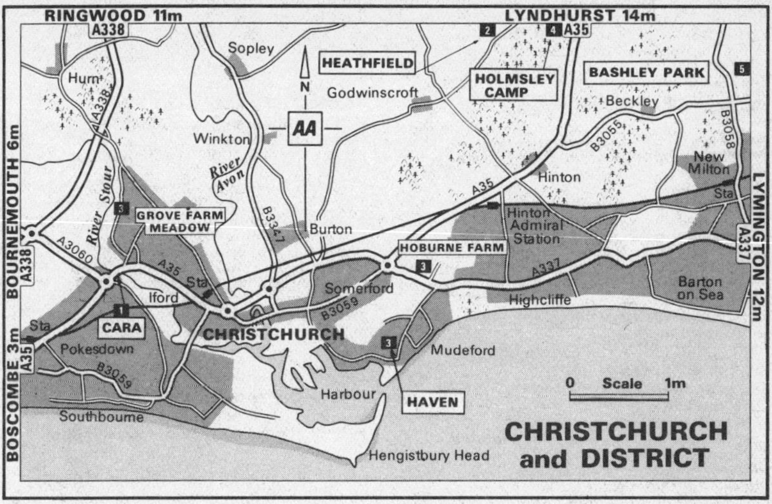

Sites listed under: **1** Bournemouth **2** Bransgore **3** Christchurch **4** Holmsley **5** New Milton

CLIFFORD BRIDGE Devon Map 3 SX78
►►► ***Clifford Bridge Caravan Park***
☎ Cheriton Bishop 226
3 ❶ ⚠ signposted
A level, grassy site with mature trees and bushes. Situated in moorland and woodland country not too far from River Teign 2m W of Dunsford off B3212. 5acres 20pitches 10static 18 Mar–25 Oct must book peak periods last arrival 20.00hrs last departure 12.00hrs 3 individual pitches Ⓐ 8wc lit all night (4 hc) 2⊙ warden (1wash) dry (iron) ( ) games room cold storage calor gas toilet fluid cafe restaurant licensed bar ☎ ⊞ stables launderette
15 5 (awnings)

CLIPPESBY Norfolk Map 9 TG41
►►► **Clippesby Holiday Caravan Park**
(TG423147) ☎ Fleggburgh 367
3 ❷ ⚠ signposted
A mainly level site with slight gradients and grass surface with trees and bushes and situated amidst woodland. no toilet tents 10acres 60pitches Mid May–Sep must book peak periods last arrival 17.00hrs last departure 17.00hrs 6 individual pitches late arrivals enclosure 20wc lit all night 2cdp 14washbasins hc (2central hot water, 4 hc) 6⊙ (1wash, 1dry, 2iron) games room calor gas camping gaz cafe licensed bar ☎ ⊞ licensed club children's playground & putting green stables launderette pub
60 £3.78 or 60 £3.78 or 60▲£3.78 (awnings) ltr

COCKERMOUTH Cumbria Map 11 NY13
►►► **Violet Bank Caravan Site**
(NY126295) off Lorton Rd ☎822169
2 ❷ ⚠ signposted
Well maintained mainly level, some slight gradient, grassy site in pleasant rural setting affording excellent views to the Buttermere hills. Approach by way of A5292 Lorton Rd, via town centre. 3½acres 40pitches 40static Apr–Oct last arrival 23.59hrs last departure 12.00hrs 6 individual pitches 9wc lit all night 1cdp 6 8washbasins hc (1central hot water) (4 hc) 2⊙ (1wash, 1spin) (1iron) (cold storage) calor gas camping gaz ⊞ children's playground stables cinema launderette pub
40 £2.70 or 40 £2.70 or 40▲£2.70 awnings

►►► **Wyndham Hall Caravan Park**
(NY133309) St Helen's Rd ☎822571
1 ❶ ⚠ signposted
A partly level and sloping grass site with mature trees and bushes, near to river. Lake District National Park nearby. 8½acres 52pitches 80static Mar–15 Nov must book peak periods last departure 12.00hrs 8 Ⓐ late arrivals enclosure wc lit all night 1cdp 14washbasins hc hc ⊙ warden (wash, spin) iron games room CTV cold storage calor gas paraffin toilet fluid cafe ☎ ⊞ licensed club & children's playground stables launderette pub
40 £2.50 or 40 £2.50 15▲£2.50 (awnings)

COMBERTON Cambridgeshire Map 5 TL35
► **Highfield Farm Camping Site**
(TL388573) Long Rd ☎2308
2 ❷ ⚠ signposted
A level and grassy site. 3m W of Cambridge between A45 and A603. 4acres 60pitches Apr–Sep must book peak periods last arrival 22.00hrs last departure 14.00hrs 4 individual pitches Ⓐ late arrivals enclosure 11wc lit all night 1cdp 11washbasins hc (central hot water, 4 hc) 2⊙ (cold storage) calor gas camping gaz paraffin toilet fluid ☎ ⊞ children's playground stables launderette pub
40 £1.70 or 40 £1.55 20▲£1.70 (awnings)

COMBE MARTIN Devon
See under Berrynarbor.

CONEYSTHORPE near Malton, North Yorkshire Map 8 SE77
►►► ***Castle Howard Caravan & Camping Site*** *(SE705710)* Apply to: Castle Howard Estate Ltd, Estate Offices, Castle Howard, York YO6 7DA. ☎366
2 ❶ ⚠ signposted
An attractive rural site adjacent to the lake on the Castle Howard Estate. The site is ideally positioned for visiting Castle Howard, York and the North York Moors National Park.
9acres 150pitches
Mar–Oct must book last arrival 19.00hrs last departure 10.00hrs 6 individual pitches Ⓐ late arrivals enclosure 26wc lit all night 3cdp 24washbasins hc 6 hc (6⊙) (wash, spin) calor gas camping gaz ☎ ⊞
120 or 120 30▲ (awnings) ltr

CONSTABLE BURTON North Yorkshire Map 7 SE19
►► **Constable Burton Hall Caravan Park**
(SE158907) ☎428
1 ❷ ⚠ signposted
Situated within the parkland of Constable Burton Hall, it lies in unspoilt farmland at the entrance to Wensleydale. Located off the A684,

but screened behind the old deer park wall.
10acres 100pitches
Apr–Oct must book public hols last arrival 23.00hrs 5 individual pitches late arrivals enclosure 14wc lit all night 3cdp washbasins hc (hc) ⊙ warden (wash, dry) calor gas camping gaz ☎ ⊞ wash up sinks launderette pub
100£2–£2.20 or 100£2–£2.20 (awnings)

CORFE CASTLE Dorset Map 3 SY98
►► **Woodland Camping Park** Glebe Farm, Bucknowle
2 ❶ ⚠ signposted
Undulating grass site with trees and bushes. Set in woodland adjacent to main A351 road to Swanage. 6½acres 80pitches
Spring Bank Hol–mid Sep rs mid Sep–30 Sep no bookings last arrival 21.00hrs last departure 11.00hrs 3 10wc lit all night washbasins hc (hc) ⊙ cold storage camping gaz ⊞ laundry sinks stables cinema launderette pub
80£2.75 or 80▲£2.75 (awnings)

CORSTON Avon Map 3 ST66
► **Bury View Farm** Corston Fields
☎ Saltford 3672
1 ❶ signposted
Level site with grass, gravel and sand surface. Set in meadowland with trees and bushes and adjacent to A39, Bath-Wells road.
1acre 12pitches 6static
Apr–Sep no bookings Aug last arrival 20.00hrs last departure 13.00hrs 3 3wc lit all night 1cdp ⊙ warden calor gas camping gaz ⊞ cinema launderette pub
6£1.30 or 6£1.30 or 6▲£1.30 (awnings) ltr

COVE Devon Map 3 SS91
► **Orchard Caravan Park** ☎ Bampton 563
1 ❶ ⚠
This site is adjacent to the A396 Tiverton-Bampton road, and overlooking the River Exe, with pitches well-spaced between apple trees.
¾acre 13pitches 2static
Etr–Oct must book 2 4wc 1cdp (hc) ⊙ calor gas camping gaz ⊞ stables pub
13 or 13 or 13▲ (awnings)

COWES Isle of Wight Map 4 SZ49
►►► **Thorness Bay Holiday Village**
(SZ465959) Thorness Bay
☎ Newport (Isle of Wight) 523109/522723
2 ❷ ⚠
5m W of Cowes on rising ground with views of Thorness Bay and the Solent. Situated in the centre of a holiday complex of chalets and static caravans on level grassy ground.
10acres 200pitches 327static
Etr–Oct last arrival 22.00hrs 7 24wc lit all night cdp 18washbasins hc 8hc 7⊙ 6wash 1spin (6iron) TV cold storage calor gas camping gaz cafe licensed bar ☎ ⊞ children's playground
200 or 200

CRACKINGTON HAVEN Cornwall Map 2 SX19
►►► **Hentervene Farm Caravan Site**
☎ St Gennys 365
2 ❷ ⚠ signposted
Gently sloping grass site with young trees and bushes set in hilly meadow country 2m from the sea and beach on A39. 1½acres 35pitches 21static
Apr–Oct must book peak periods last arrival 20.00hrs last departure 12.00hrs 4 individual pitches 6wc lit all night 1cdp washbasins hc (hc) ⊙ warden (spin, iron) cold storage calor gas camping gaz toilet fluid ⊞ children's playground stables launderette pub
35£1.30–£1.50 or 35£1.30–£1.50 or 35▲£1.30–£1.50 (awnings)

CRANTOCK Newquay, Cornwall Map 2 SW75
See Newquay sketch map.
►►►►► *Trevella Caravan Park*
(SW801599) ☎308
[2] ❷ ⚠ signposted
A pleasant touring caravan and camping site, surrounded by trees and hedgerow, situated in rural area close to Newquay between Crantock and A3075. 15acres 350pitches
Etr–Oct must book peak periods 18⛟ individual pitches late arrivals enclosure 53wc lit all night 1cdp 53washbasins hc 8central hot water (18🚿hc) 10⊙ warden (2wash, 2spin, 2dry, 5iron) ⛬ CTV calor gas camping gaz toilet fluid cafe ☎ ⊞ ⛼ ⊖ stables ♘ ✈ cinema ⤿ launderette
350🚐 or 350🚙 or 350▲

►►► Treago Farm Caravan Site
(SW782601) ☎277
[2] ❷ ⚠ signposted
Grass site set in open farmland in a south-facing sheltered valley: direct access to Crantock and Polly Joke beaches, National Trust land and many natural beauty spots. 4acres 100pitches 7static
Etr–Oct must book last arrival 23.00hrs last departure 11.00hrs 9⛟ individual pitches Ⓐ 13wc lit all night 1cdp 20washbasins hc central hot water (10🚿hc) 5⊙ warden (1wash, 1spin, 1dry) 1iron games room cold storage calor gas camping gaz paraffin toilet fluid ☎ ⊞ ⛼ ⊖ stables ♘ ✈ cinema ⤿ launderette pub
8🚐£3.24 or 8🚙£3.24 92▲£3.24 awnings

►► Quarryfield Caravan Park *(SW793608)*
☎Newquay 2792
[1] ❶ ⚠ signposted
Mainly level grassy site with young trees and bushes set in meadowland. Adjacent to sea and beach, NE of the village. 5acres 125pitches 31static
May–Oct must book for caravans last arrival 23.00hrs last departure 12.00hrs 7⛟ Ⓐ 20wc lit all night 1cdp washbasins hc (🚿hc) ⊙ warden (wash, spin, dry, iron) (⛬) CTV calor gas camping gaz ☎ ⊞ licensed club & hairdresser ⛼ ⊖ stables ♘ ✈ cinema ⤿ launderette pub
22🚐£2.05–£3 125▲£2.05–£3 no awnings

CROSSWAYS Dorset Map 3 SY78
►►► Heathfield Caravan Site
☎Warmwell 852357
[2] ❸ ⚠ signposted
Gently sloping site with grass, sand and gravel surfaces. Set in meadowland with an abundance of trees and bushes. Very pleasant rural setting with gardens around pool. No skateboards. 7acres 150pitches
16 Mar–Oct must book peak periods last arrival 23.00hrs last departure 11.00hrs 13⛟ individual pitches late arrivals enclosure 21wc lit all night 1cdp 15washbasins hc 2central hot water 10🚿hc 3⊙ (1wash, 1spin, 1dry) (2iron) ⛬ games room TV (1cold storage) calor gas camping gaz toilet fluid ☎ ⊞ children's playground ⛼
100🚐£2 or 100🚙£1.90 50▲£2 (awnings)

CROSTHWAITE Cumbria Map 7 SD49
See Windermere sketch map.
► Lambhowe Caravan Park *(SD422914)*
☎483
[2] ❶ ⚠
An attractive site, on rising ground, set amidst a Lakeland wood. ½acre 10pitches 110static
Apr–Oct rsMar must book peak periods last departure 12.00hrs 2⛟ 16wc lit all night 1cdp (1washbasins hc) (1central hot water) (4🚿hc) 1⊙ warden (1spin) games room calor gas toilet fluid ⊞ licensed club ⊖ ♘ ✈ cinema ⤿ ⛼ pub
10🚐£2.25 or 10🚙£2.25

CROYDE BAY Devon Map 2 SS43
See Ilfracombe sketch map.
►►►► Ruda Holiday Park *(SS438397)*
☎*Croyde 890671*
[2] ❷ ⚠ signposted
Gently rolling grassland set in downland adjacent to the beach at Croyde Bay and the

B3231. 16acres 400pitches 200static Etr–Oct must book peak periods last arrival 22.00hrs last departure 10.00hrs 25 individual pitches 80wc lit all night 2cdp washbasins hc central hot water hc hc (wash, spin, dry) iron games room (cold storage) calor gas camping gaz toilet fluid cafe restaurant licesned bar live entertainment in bar & children's entertainment in children's room stables cinema launderette pub
80£1.90–£3.70 400£1.70–£2.90 or 400▲£1.70–£2.90 (awnings)

CUBERT Cornwall Map 2 SW75
See Newquay sketch map.
►► Treworgans Farm *(SW782590)*
Crantock 200
2 1 signposted
Site is situated off Cubert–Crantock road, SW of Newquay, and offers level grassy pitches.
1acre 20pitches 20static
Etr–Sep must book peak periods last departure 12.00hrs 2 wc lit all night cdp (washbasins hc) 1central hot water (2hc) stables launderette pub
20£1 or 20£1 or 20▲£1 (awnings)

CUMWHITTON Cumbria Map 12 NY55
► Cairndale Caravan Park *(NY518523)*
Croglin 280
2 2
Mainly level grass site set in tranquil Eden Valley.
1acre 14pitches 10static
Mar–Oct must book peak periods last arrival 22.00hrs 7 individual pitches 5wc lit all night 1cdp 5washbasins hc central hot water (2hc) 1 (1wash, 1iron) cold storage calor gas stables pub
6£1.50–£1.75 or 6£1.50–£1.75
8▲£1.10–£1.25 awnings ltr

DALSTON Cumbria Map 11 NY34
►► Dalston Hall Caravan Site *(NY378519)*
Dalston Hall Estate Carlisle 24145
2 2 signposted
An exceptionally well-maintained site, on level grassy ground, situated in the grounds of the estate which is located between Carlisle and Dalston on the B5299. Ideal position for touring the northern Lake District, Carlisle and the surrounding country. 4acres 60pitches Apr–Oct last arrival 21.00hrs last departure 13.00hrs 6 individual pitches 17wc lit all night 1cdp 10washbasins hc central hot water 4hc 5 (cold storage) calor gas camping gaz children's playground cinema launderette pub
60£1.65 or 60£1.65 or 60▲£1.65 awnings

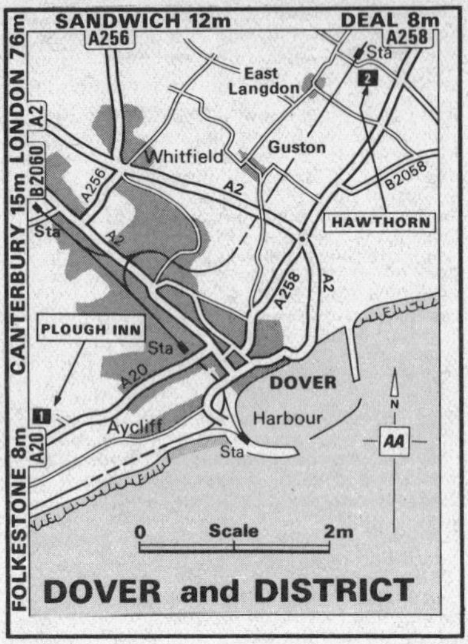

Sites listed under:
1 Dover **2** Martin Mill

DALWOOD Devon Map 3 ST20
►►► Andrewshayes Caravan Park
Wilmington 225
2 2
Slightly sloping site, within easy reach of Lyme Regis, Seaton, Branscombe and Sidmouth. Adjacent to A35. 6acres 100pitches 80static May–Sep rs15 Mar–Apr & Oct must book peak periods last arrival 23.00hrs last departure 12.00hrs 10 individual pitches 24wc lit all night 2cdp 15washbasins hc 2central hot water 18hc 5 warden (2wash, 1spin, 1dry, 2iron) (cold storage) calor gas camping gaz toilet fluid children's playground launderette pub
50£1.80 or 50£1.60 50▲£1.80 (awnings) ltr

DAWLISH Devon Map 3 SX97
▶▶▶ ***Lady's Mile Farm*** ☎863411
2 3 △
This site is fairly central for the surrounding beaches. The good level pitches are surrounded by hedges and trees. 1m N of Dawlish on A379.
10acres 185pitches
Etr–Sep must book peak periods last departure 13.00hrs 7 30wc lit all night 1cdp washbasins hc 12 hc 6 (3wash, dry, iron) games room TV calor gas camping gaz toilet fluid ☎ launderette
185 or 185 or 185▲ (awnings) ltr

DELABOLE Cornwall Map 2 SX08
▶▶▶ **Planet Park** ☎ Camelford 3361
2 2 △ signposted
This site, which has panoramic views, is situated in the valley of Delabole.
3acres 81pitches 40static
Apr–Oct must book peak periods last arrival sunset last departure 12.00hrs 5 10wc lit all night 1cdp 8washbasins hc (2 hc) 2 (1wash) (1spin) (1iron) (1cold storage) calor gas camping gaz stables launderette pub
81 £1.35–£2.16 or 81 £1.35–£2.16 or 81▲£1.35–£2.16 awnings

DERBY Derbyshire Map 8 SK33
▶▶▶ ***Alvaston Mobile Home Park*** *(SK381342)* Meadow Ln ☎72204
1 2 △
Mainly level grass site, 3m SW of Derby off A6.
9pitches 137static
Apr–Oct rsNov–Mar 1 5wc lit all night 1cdp washbasins hc 4 hc wash, dry toilet fluid ☎ cinema
9 or 9

DONCASTER South Yorkshire Map 8 SE50
▶▶ **Trax Campsite** *(SE601028)*
Doncaster Racecourse
2 1 △ signposted
Level and grassy site. On Ledger Way off A18 Scunthorpe road. 2acres 60pitches
23 May–6 Sep no bookings last arrival 22.30hrs last departure 15.00hrs 2 9wc lit all night 2cdp 8washbasins hc 2central hot water 2 hc 3 warden (1spin) CTV ☎ games area free racing for campers 27 & 28 Jun, 30 & 31 Jul stables cinema launderette pub
60 £2–£2.35 or 60 £2–£2.35 or 60▲£2–£2.35 awnings

DOVER Kent Map 5 TR34
See Dover sketch map.
Also see entry Martin Mill.
▶ **Plough Inn** *(TR283397)* Folkestone Rd ☎206166
1 1 △
A partly level and sloping site set in sylvan surroundings off the A20 Folkestone–Dover road.
2½acres 20pitches 20static
Mid Apr–Nov rsMar–mid Apr must book Jul 4 no cars by tents 12wc 1cdp washbasins hc hc toilet fluid ☎ stables cinema launderette pub
20 £1.65 or 20 £1.65 or 20▲£1.50 (awnings) ltr

DUNKESWELL Devon Map 3 ST10
▶ **Fishponds House Campsite** *(ST154074)* ☎ Luppitt 698
2 1 △
Site is set in wildlife sanctuary, surrounded by trees. 1¼acres 15pitches
Mar–Oct last arrival 20.00hrs last departure 12.00hrs 2 individual pitches 4wc cdp 4washbasins hc 1 hc warden pub
15▲£2.50

Eamont Bridge

EAMONT BRIDGE Cumbria Map 12 NY52
►►► Lowther Caravan Park *(NY517239)*
☎ Penrith 3631
2 ❷ ⚠ signposted
A partly level and sloping grass site with mature trees and bushes. River and lake nearby. Good centre for touring Lake District. 3m S of Penrith off A6. 10acres 196pitches 375static
16 Mar–27 Oct must book public hols
last arrival 22.00hrs last departure 16.00hrs
39 late arrivals enclosure 114wc
lit all night 5cdp washbasins hc central hot water (hc) ⊙ (wash, spin) iron (cold storage) calor gas camping gaz toilet fluid ☎ ⊞ children's playground & fishing stables cinema launderette pub
146£2.50 or 146£2.50 50▲£2.50
awnings ltr

EAST ANSTEY Devon Map 3 SS82
►►► Zeacombe Caravan & Camping Park
Blackerton Cross ☎ Anstey Mills 279
2 ❸ ⚠ signposted
Site has good panoramic views of surrounding countryside and is situated within 100 yds of A361 Taunton–Barnstaple road. 3acres 40pitches
15 Mar–15 Nov booking advisable peak periods
last arrival 22.00hrs 5 9wc lit all night
1cdp 10washbasins hc central hot water (4hc) 2⊙ iron stables pub
40£1–£1.50 or 40£1–£1.50 or 40▲£1–£1.50 (awnings)

EAST BERGHOLT Suffolk Map 5 TM03
►►► Grange Caravan Park *(TM098353)*
The Grange ☎567
2 ❸ ⚠ signposted
A level, grassy site with mature trees and bushes situated in hilly woodland with some moorland nearby. 3m off A12 between Colchester and Ipswich. 7acres 148pitches 52static
Apr–Sep no bookings last arrival 23.00hrs last departure 18.00hrs 16 47wc
lit all night 3cdp wasbasins hc central hot water (hc) ⊙ warden (wash, spin, dry) iron () games room (cold storage) calor gas camping gaz toilet fluid cafe restaurant ☎ ⊞ licensed club & children's playground stables launderette pub
80£2.50 20£2.50 48▲£2.50 (awnings)

EAST RUNTON Norfolk Map 9 TG14
►►► Woodhill Camping Site *(TG195428)*
Laburnum Farm ☎ West Runton 473
2 ❶ ⚠ signposted
Gently sloping, grass site with bushes set in meadowland adjacent to sea, beach and the coast road (A149). 13acres 360pitches
Spring Bank Hol—Sep rsEtr–mid May
no bookings 11 50wc lit all night 1cdp (38washbasins hc) (2central hot water) (14hc) ⊙ calor gas camping gaz ☎ ⊞ children's playground stables cinema launderette pub
60£1.60 300▲£1.60 (awnings)

► Woodhill Caravan Park
☎ West Runton 473
2 ❶ ⚠ signposted
Gently sloping grass site set in meadowland and ¼m from East Runton, adjacent to the sea and beach. 1acre 20pitches 115static
Etr–Sep no bookings 6 individual pitches
24wc lit all night 1cdp (12washbasins hc, central hot water, 12hc) ⊙ spin iron calor gas camping gaz ☎ ⊞ children's playground stables cinema launderette pub
20£2 or 20£2 (awnings)

EAST WORLINGTON Devon Map 3 SS71
►►► Yeatheridge Farm Caravan Park
☎ Witheridge 330
2 ❸ ⚠
Gently sloping, grass site with young trees set in meadowland in rural Devon. On B3042 ¼m W of Thelbridge Arms Inn. Site is ***NOT*** *in East Worlington village.* 7acres 50pitches 5static

Spring Bank Hol–Aug rsEtr–mid May must book peak periods last arrival 22.00hrs last departure 12.00hrs 7⛐ individual pitches Ⓐ late arrivals enclosure 8wc lit all night 1cdp (10washbasins hc, central hot water, 4⛆hc) 2⊙ (wash, spin, dry, iron) ▭ games room TV (cold storage) calor gas camping gaz toilet fluid ☎ ⊞ children's playground ⛟ ⊖ stables ⇝ pub
50⛟£2.40 or 50⛟£2.40 or 50▲£2.40 (awnings)

ECCLESTON (GREAT) Lancashire Map 7 SD43
▶ ***Meadowcroft Caravan Park*** *(SD405403)*
Garstang Rd ☎70266
1 ❶ ⚠ signposted
A mainly residential site located on A586 in pleasant open countryside. ½acre 6pitches 40static
Etr–Oct must book peak periods last arrival 22.00hrs 2⛐ 9wc lit all night (washbasins hc) (central hot water) (⛆hc) ⊙ warden (spin, dry) calor gas camping gaz toilet fluid ⊞ ⊖ stables ♿ ⇝ launderette ⛟ pub
6⛟ or 6⛟ no awnings

EDGCUMBE Cornwall Map 2 SW73
▶▶▶▶ **Retanna Country Park** *(SW720331)* ☎ Constantine 40643
2 ❷ ⚠ signposted
This well kept site is situated on the A394 4m E of Helston. 5acres 44pitches 26static
Apr–Oct must book peak periods last arrival 22.00hrs last departure 22.00hrs 6⛐ individual pitches Ⓐ late arrivals enclosure 10wc lit all night 1cdp 12washbasins hc 2central hot water 8⛆hc 4⊙ 2spin 2iron 1cold storage calor gas camping gaz toilet fluid ☎ ⊞ children's playground ⛟ ⊖ stables ♿ ✈ cinema ⇝ launderette pub
44⛟£2.35 or 44⛟£2.35 40▲£2.35 (awnings)

ELVASTON Derbyshire Map 8 SK43
▶▶ **Elvaston Castle Park Site** *(SK413332)*
Borrowdale Rd (before 28 Mar apply to: The Caravan Club, East Grinstead House, East Grinstead, W Sussex RH19 1UA)
☎ Derby 73735
2 ❸ ⚠ signposted
Situated within country park; site is run by Caravan and Camping Club. The thoughtful layout and range of amenities make this a very attractive site. Off B5010, which runs between the A6, 2m W of Shardlow and Borrowash on A6005. 3acres 45pitches
fr28 Mar must book last arrival 21.00hrs last departure 12.00hrs 5⛐ individual pitches late arrivals enclosure 6wc lit all night 2cdp washbasins hc central hot water ⛆hc ⊙ warden calor gas camping gaz toilet fluid ☎ ⊞ ⊖ stables ♿ ⇝ ⛟

55⛟fr£1.65 or 55⛟fr£1.65 or 55▲£2.15 (awnings)

EMBOROUGH Somerset Map 3 ST65
▶▶ ***Old Down House Camping Site***
☎ Stratton-on-the-Fosse 232355
1 ❶
An open, level site with hedges screening it from the main road. Site entrance opposite Old Down Inn adjacent to crossroads A37/B3139. 3acres 25pitches 20static
15 Mar–1 Nov must book peak periods last arrival 20.00hrs last departure 12.00hrs 3⛐ wc lit all night 1cdp (4washbasins hc) (2⛆hc) 1⊙ cold storage calor gas camping gaz ⊞ ⊖ ⇝
5⛟ or 5⛟ 20▲

EVERSHOT Dorset Map 3 ST50
▶ **Clay Pigeon Caravan Park**
☎ Dorchester 3613
2 ❷ ⚠ signposted
A level grassy site overlooking the Blackmore Vale. 3acres 60pitches
16 Mar–Oct must book peak periods 4⛐ individual pitches 6wc lit all night 1cdp (8washbasins hc, 2central hot water, 2⛆hc, 1⊙) (dry) calor gas camping gaz cafe restaurant licensed bar ☎ ⊞ children's playground ⛟ ⊖ ⛟ pub
60⛟£1.50 or 60⛟£1.50 or 60▲£1.50 (awnings) ltr

EWHURST East Sussex Map 5 TQ72
▶ **Lordine Court Caravan Park** *(TQ799228)*
☎ Staplecross 209
2 ❶ ⚠ signposted
Remote site away from villages and main roads in the heart of the Sussex countryside. From A229 Hastings road follow B2165 Staplecross road, for 3m. ✗ 4¼acres 120pitches 150static
Etr–Oct rsMar & Oct must book public hols last arrival 18.00hrs last departure 12.00hrs 6⛐ 37wc (washbasins hc central hot water ⛆hc ⛆hc ⊙) warden (iron, ⛟) calor gas camping gaz paraffin ☎ ⊞ children's playground & licensed club ⛟ ⊖ stables ♿ ⇝ pub
120▲£1.50

EXFORD Somerset Map 3 SS83
▶ **Westermill** ☎238
2 ❶ ⚠
Camping site situated alongside river with partial wooded areas; stands in sheltered valley in the heart of Exmoor. Leave Exford on the Porlock road. After ¼m fork left. Continue for 2¼m along valley until 'Westermill' sign seen on tree, then fork left. 6acres 60pitches 3static
27 May–Oct rs1–26 May must book peak periods 4⛐ 14wc (central hot water) (⛆hc) ⊙ (spin) iron (cold storage) calor gas camping gaz ☎ ⊞ ⛟ ⊖ stables ⇝ pub
60⛟£2.60 or 60▲£2.60

EYPE Dorset Map 3 SY49
►►► Highlands End Farm Caravan Park
(SY454913) ☎ Bridport 22139
2 ❸ △
Part level, part sloping grass site set in hilly country and meadowland within the urban area. Adjacent to sea and beach. nc 12yrs 6acres 60pitches 160static
Apr–Sep must book peak periods last arrival sunset last departure 12.00hrs 22 individual pitches 36wc lit all night 1cdp washbasins hc central hot water (hc) warden cold storage calor gas camping gaz toilet fluid ☎ stables cinema launderette pub
20 £3.24 40 £2.16 or 40▲£2.16 (awnings)

FAKENHAM Norfolk Map 9 TF92
►►► Crossways Caravan Park *(TF973328)*
Holt Rd, Little Snoring ☎ Thursford 335
2 ❷ △ signposted
A level site with mature trees and bushes set in woodlands and near the sea. 3m E of Fakenham on A148. 1½acres 25pitches
21 Mar–Oct booking advisable last arrival 21.00hrs last departure 12.00hrs 1 individual pitches late arrivals enclosure 7wc lit all night 1cdp (washbasins hc, hc) iron calor gas camping gaz paraffin toilet fluid launderette pub
25 £1.45 or 20 £1.45 (awnings)

►► Trax Campsite *(TF926288)*
Fakenham Racecourse
2 ❶ △ signposted
A level grassy site with mature trees. ¾m SE of town off A1065 Swaffham road. 8acres 150pitches
May–Sep no bookings last arrival 22.30hrs last departure 15.00hrs 8 32wc lit all night 3cdp 21washbasins hc 4central hot water 6hc 3 warden (1wash, 1spin, 2iron) CTV calor gas camping gaz ☎ games area free racing for campers 26 May & 26 Sep launderette
100 £2–£2.75 or 100 £2–£2.75 or 100▲£2–£2.75 awnings

FALMOUTH Cornwall Map 2 SW83
See sketch map.
►►►► *Maen Valley Caravan Park*
(SW798312) ☎312190
2 ❷ △ signposted
This site is situated in rural surroundings in a beautiful valley with a picturesque stream running through. 1½m S of Falmouth, but within walking distance of Swanpool beach. 4acres 116pitches 138static
End May–Sep rsEtr must book Jul–Aug last arrival 22.00hrs last departure 12.00hrs 20 late arrivals enclosure 30wc 3cdp 26washbasins hc (12hc) 6 warden (wash, spin) iron cold storage calor gas camping gaz paraffin toilet fluid children's play area licensed bar ☎ stables cinema launderette pub
136 or 136 or 136▲ (awnings)

►►► Golden Bank Caravans *(SW794313)*
(No 1 site) Swanpool Rd ☎312103
2 ❶ △ signposted
Gently sloping, grass site with mature trees and bushes. Set in meadowland, the site is adjacent to the main road. ½acre 6pitches 72static
Etr–Oct must book for caravans last arrival 22.00hrs last departure 10.00hrs 3 individual pitches 8wc lit all night 1cdp 8washbasins 2central hot water (hc) 2 warden (1wash, 1spin) 1iron cold storage calor gas camping gaz ☎ ladies hair drier stables cinema launderette pub
6 £1.30–£3.50 or 6 £1.30–£3.50 awnings ltr

►►► Tremorvah *(SW798313)*
Swanpool ☎312103
2 ❷ △ signposted
Pleasant site situated near the Swanpool; trees and bushes predominate in this meadowland setting. Adjacent to beach and sea.
3½acres 75pitches
Mid May–Oct rsEtr–mid May must book peak periods last arrival 22.00hrs last departure 10.00hrs 6 late arrivals enclosure 14wc lit all night 1cdp washbasins hc central hot water 13hc (4hc) 2 warden (1spin, 1dry) 1iron cold storage calor gas camping gaz ☎ hair drier & wash up sinks stables cinema launderette pub
75 £1.30–£3.50 or 75▲£1.30–£3.50 ltr

FAR FOREST Worcestershire Map 7 SO77
► Acre Farm Caravan Park *(SO720748)*
☎ Rock (Kidderminster) 266458
2 ❷ △
Part level, part sloping, grass site with varied trees, set in hilly woodland country with direct access to A4117. ½acre 8pitches 85static
Apr–Oct must book last arrival 20.00hrs

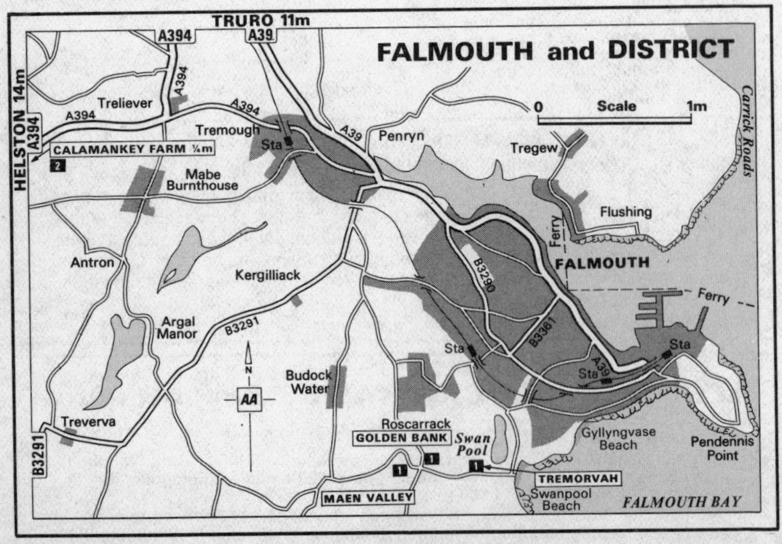

Sites listed under: **1** Falmouth **2** Long Downs

last departure 10.00hrs 12⛹ 14wc lit all night (6⛹hc) 2⊙ calor gas ⊞ children's playground ⊖ stables ✈ ⛵ launderette ⛵ pub
8⛟£2.16 or 8⛟£2.16

FAZELEY Staffordshire Map 4 SK20
► Drayton Manor Park *(SK195014)*
1 ❶ ⚠ signposted
Gently sloping, grass site with wooded parkland and lakes. Adjacent to A5 and A4091. 4acres 75pitches 75static
Etr–Oct no bookings 4⛹ 20wc lit all night 2cdp washbasins hc ⛹hc ⊙ cafe restaurant licensed bar ☎ ⊞ zoo ⊖ stables ♿ ✈ cinema launderette ⛵ pub
75⛟£1.50 or 75⛟£1.50 or 75▲£1.50 (awnings) ltr

FENNY BENTLEY Derbyshire Map 7 SK14
► Bank Top Farm *(SK181498)*
☎ Thorpe Cloud 250
2 ❶ ⚠
Sloping grass site set in hilly meadowland country and adjacent to main road.
5acres 80pitches
Etr–Sep 1⛹ 9wc 1cdp washbasins hc (⛹hc) ⊙ (cold storage) calor gas ⛵ ⊖ stables ♿ launderette
80⛟£1.20 or 80⛟£1.20 or 80▲£1.20 (awnings)

FILEY North Yorkshire Map 8 TA18
See Scarborough sketch map.
►►► North Cliff Touring Caravan Site *(TA121811)* Arndale. Apply to: Scarborough Borough Council, Tourist & Amenities Dept, Normanton Rise, Holbeck Hill, Scarborough YO11 2XD ☎ Scarborough 66212
1 ❷ ⚠ signposted
A level, grass site with mature trees near the sea and beach. 5acres 122pitches
End Mar–Sep must book last arrival 21.00hrs last departure 12.00hrs 4⛹ late arrivals enclosure 16wc lit all night 1cdp washbasins hc (⛹hc) ⊙ (wash, dry) (cold storage) calor gas camping gaz paraffin toilet fluid ☎ ⊞ children's playground ⛵ ⊖ stables ♿ ✈ cinema ⛵ launderette pub
122⛟£1.20–£2.20 or 122⛟£1.20–£2.20 (awnings)

FLEET Dorset Map 3 SY68
►►► Sea Barn Farm Camping Site
☎ Weymouth 786304 (Weymouth 782218 out of season)
2 ❶ ⚠ signposted
Spacious level site with panoramic views of sea and country; overlooking Lyme Bay and the Chesil Beach. 11acres 150pitches
15 May–Sep rs16 Mar–14 May & Oct must book peak periods 8⛹ Ⓐ 16wc lit all night 1cdp 22washbasins hc 1central hot water (12⛹hc) 6⊙ (1wash, 1spin, 1dry) 2iron games room CTV cold storage calor gas camping gaz ☎ ⊞ children's playground ⛵ ⊖ ⛵
150▲

►►► West Fleet Farm
☎ Weymouth 786242
2 ❷ ⚠ signposted
Partly level, partly sloping, grass site with young trees and bushes, set in meadowland. Adjacent to lake and sea. 12acres 250pitches
Etr–Sep must book peak periods last arrival 22.00hrs last departure 12.00hrs 7⛹ Ⓐ 26wc lit all night 6cdp (38washbasins hc, 16central hot water, 10⛹hc) 3⊙ (1wash, 2spin, 1dry, 2iron) TV (cold storage) calor gas camping gaz toilet fluid cafe ☎ ⊞ children's playground ⛵
250▲£1–£1.60 ltr

FLEETWOOD Lancashire Map 7 SD34
► Broadwater Holiday Centre *(SD325455)*
Fleetwood Rd ☎2796
1 ❶ ⚠
A large, busy commercial site with all attendant facilities, situated on the main road between Thornton and Fleetwood, A587. ⛟ 45pitches 405static
Spring Bank Hol–Sep rsMar–mid May & Oct no bookings last arrival 23.59hrs last departure 10.00hrs 22⛹ 63wc lit all night 4cdp washbasins hc central hot water 18⛹hc ⊙ warden wash spin TV calor gas paraffin toilet fluid ☎ ⊞ children's playground hire service & licensed club ⛵ ⊖ stables ♿ ✈ cinema ⛵ launderette pub
45⛟£1.50 or 45⛟£1.50 (awnings) ltr

Folkestone

FOLKESTONE Kent Map 5 TR23
See sketch map.
►►► Warren Camping Site *(TR247377)*
☎55093
[3] ❶ ⚠ signposted
This site is situated at the foot of the world famous 'white cliffs' and immediately adjacent to a sandy beach. The pitches are on different levels some of which are secluded and sheltered.
3½acres 100pitches
Apr–25 Sep must book peak periods last arrival 21.00hrs last departure 12.00hrs 4⛲ 20wc lit all night washbasins hc central hot water ⇝hc (⛲hc) ⊙ warden camping gaz ☎ ⊞ ♨ ⊖ ♿ cinema ⚲ pub
100▲£2.48
►► Little Switzerland Camping & Caravanning Site *(TR247377)* The Warren
☎52168
[2] ❶ ⚠ signposted
The site is situated on high ground overlooking the sea. Set amidst mature trees and well sheltered from the west winds by steep hills.
25pitches 24static
Mar–Oct must book peak periods last departure 12.00hrs 5⛲ Ⓐ no cars by tents 13wc lit all night 1cdp washbasins hc central hot water (⛲hc) ⊙ 1warden calor gas restaurant licensed bar ⊞ ⊖ stables ♿ ✈ cinema ⚲ launderette ♨ pub
9🚐£2.25 or 9🚗£2.25 16▲£2.10 or £2.40 (awnings)

FONTWELL West Sussex Map 4 SU90
►► Trax-Fontwell Park Racecourse *(SU948066)*
[1] ❶ ⚠
Mainly level, partly grassy site with trees situated in meadowland near main road.
2acres 60pitches
6 Jun–20 Sep except 12, 13, 26 & 27 Aug, 9 & 10 Sep no bookings last arrival 22.30hrs last departure 15.00hrs 2⛲ 10wc lit all night 1cdp 10washbasins hc 6⛲hc 4⊙ warden ☎ ⊞ games area ⊖ stables ♿ ✈ cinema ⚲ launderette
60🚐£2–£2.35 or 60🚗£2–£2.35 or 60▲£2–£2.35 awnings

FOWEY Cornwall Map 2 SX15
► Penhale Camping & Caravanning Park *(SX103527)* ☎3425
[1] ❶ ⚠
Part level, part sloping, mainly grassy site with trees and bushes set in meadowland adjacent to sea and beach. 2m W of Fowey on A3082.
7acres 56pitches
Apr–Oct must book 12⛲ wc lit all night 2cdp (4washbasins hc, 9⛲hc) 7⊙ warden iron calor gas camping gaz toilet fluid ☎ ⊞ ♨ ⊖ stables ♿ ✈ ⚲ launderette pub
56🚐£2–£2.75 or 56🚗£1.50–£2.00 or 56▲£2–£2.75 (awnings)

FYLINGDALES ('FLASK' INN) North Yorkshire Map 8 NZ90
►►► Grouse Hill Caravan Park *(NZ930009)* Flask Bungalow Farm
☎Robin Hood's Bay 543 (to be changed to Whitby 880543)
[2] ❷ ⚠ signposted
Situated in the North York Moors National Park adjacent to A171 Whitby–Scarborough road. Site overlooks a wooded valley and heather-clad moorland. 300pitches
Apr–Oct must book peak periods last departure 12.00hrs 9⛲ Ⓐ wc lit all night 3cdp 60washbasins hc 24⛲hc 12⊙ warden (1cold storage) calor gas toilet fluid ☎ ⊞ ♨ ⊖ stables pub
300🚐£1.20–£2 or 300🚗£1.20–£2 or 300▲£1.20–£2 (awnings)

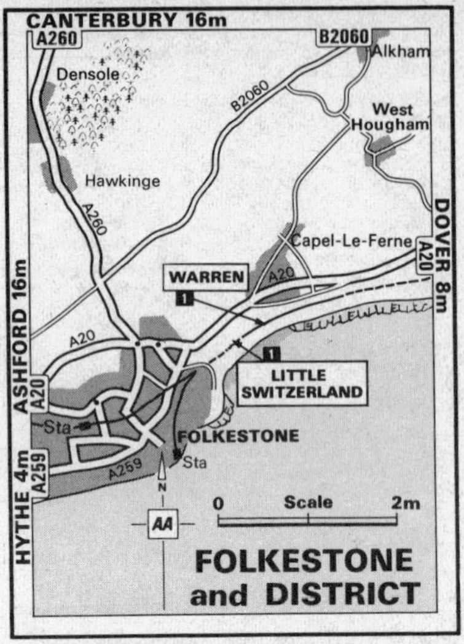

All sites listed under: Folkestone

GISBURN Lancashire Map 7 SD84
►►► Todber Caravan Park *(SD833466)*
☎322
[2] ❶ ⚠
A rural site on a sloping ground with good views all round. An interesting steam museum is located on the site. 5acres 70pitches 200static
Apr–Sep rsMar & Oct booking advisable public hols last arrival 22.00hrs last departure 16.00hrs 20⛲ individual pitches late arrivals enclosure 48wc lit all night 1cdp washbasins hc ⛲hc ⊙ calor gas camping gaz toilet fluid ⊞ children's playground & putting green ♨ ⊖ pub
70🚐£1.50 or 70🚗£1.50 or 70▲£1.50 awnings ltr
►► Commercial Hotel & Cafeteria Caravan Site *(SD833488)* ☎235
[1] ❶ ⚠
Partly sloping grass and gravel site with trees, saplings and bushes situated in meadowland

FORESTRY COMMISSION CARAVAN AND CAMPSITES

Only those Forestry Commission sites which come within the scope of the Automobile Association's Caravan and Campsite classification scheme are listed in this guide. Others are deliberately maintained as minimum-facility sites and are suitable for the camper or caravanner who prefers to be completely self-sufficient and carries his own chemical toilet.
Free pamphlets *See Your Forests* are available from *Forestry Commission, 231 Corstorphine Road, Edinburgh EH12 7AT.* State whether you are interested in Northern England, Southern England, Wales or Scotland. A leaflet *Forestry Commission Cabins and Holiday Houses* is also available.

just off the A59. Extensive views of Ribble Valley. 2acres 15pitches
Mar–Oct booking advisable last arrival 20.00hrs last departure 12.00hrs 1 individual pitches 18wc lit all night 1cdp (washbasins hc) (hc) dry cold storage calor gas cafe restaurant licensed bar licensed club & children's playground stables cinema pub
15£1.45 or 15£1.45 5£1.45 awnings ltr

GISLEHAM Suffolk Map 5 TM58
Chestnut Farm Touring Park *(TG510866)*
Lowestoft 740227
2 signposted
Level, grass site with trees and bushes. Set in meadowland, close to sea, beach, river and main road. In Kessingland follow signs for Mutford/Rushmere at S end of village. 3acres 20pitches
Apr–Oct must book public hols last departure 16.00hrs 3 4wc lit all night 1cdp (central hot water, hc) warden cold storage calor gas children's playground & fishing stables launderette pub
20£1.50 or 20£1.50 or 20£1.50 awnings

GOODWOOD West Sussex Map 4 SU91
Trax Campsite *(SU884109)*
Goodwood Racecourse
2 signposted
Level and grassy site with mature trees set in South Downs. 5m N of Chichester. 2½acres 66pitches
3 Apr–27 Sep except 28 Jul–2 Aug, 21–23 Aug, 11–15 Sept no bookings last arrival 22.30hrs last departure 15.00hrs 3 30wc lit all night 1cdp 12washbasins hc 1central hot water 2hc 2 warden (spin) iron CTV calor gas camping gaz children's playground & games area stables
66£2–£2.75 or 66£2–£2.75 or 66£2–£2.75 awnings

GOONHAVERN Cornwall Map 2 SW75
See Perranporth sketch map.
Silverbow Park *(SW782531)*
Perranwell Perranporth 2347
3 signposted
Small, spacious and sheltered site with a gently sloping surface. Hard roads and paths serve the grassed area, which is set in meadowland. Site lies adjacent to the A3075 road, ½m N of village. 2½acres 52pitches 13static
Spring Bank Hol–Oct rsEtr–mid May must book last arrival 22.00hrs last departure 12.00hrs 8 individual pitches late arrivals enclosure 11wc lit all night 1cdp 20washbasins hc (2hc) (6hc) 7 (1wash, 1spin, 2dry, 2iron) games room 1cold storage calor gas camping gaz toilet fluid children's playground, badminton courts & wash up sinks stables launderette pub
52£1.40–£4 or 52£1.40–£4 or 52£1.40–£4 awnings

Rosehill Farm Tourist Park
Perranporth 2448
2 signposted
Part level and part sloping, grass site with young trees and bushes set in hilly meadowland, ½m W of village on B3285. 6½acres 65pitches
May–Sep. rsApr & Oct must book 4 late arrivals enclosure 10wc lit all night 1cdp (washbasins hc, central hot water, hc) warden (iron) cold storage calor gas camping gaz toilet fluid cafe children's playground stables launderette pub
65£2.20 or 65£2.20 or 65£2.20 (awnings)

GORRAN Cornwall Map 2 SW94
Tregarton Farm Caravan & Camping Park *(SW984437)* Mevagissey 3666
2
Spacious site set in undulating meadowland with mature trees and bushes. The site lies 2m from the sea and adjacent to a minor road to Gorran Haven. 10acres 150pitches
Apr–Oct must book peak periods last arrival 22.00hrs last departure 12.00hrs 5 15wc lit all night 1cdp 20washbasins hc 6hc 4 (1spin, 2iron) (cold storage) calor gas camping gaz paraffin toilet fluid children's playground, babysitter & take away food launderette pub
150£2.21–£3.24 or 150£2.21–£3.24 or 150£2.21–£3.24 (awnings)

GRAFHAM Cambridgeshire Map 4 SP16
Old Manor Caravan Park *(TL157695)*
Church Ln Huntingdon 810264
3 signposted
A well kept site situated in quiet, picturesque countryside. 6½acres 66pitches 4static
All year must book last arrival 21.00hrs last departure 12.00hrs 10 individual pitches 7wc lit all night 1cdp 12 8washbasins hc 8central hot water 6hc 2 warden (1wash) 2iron cold storage calor gas camping gaz toilet fluid children's playground, washing up room & hairdryers launderette pub
66£3 or 66£3 or 66£3 awnings ltr

GRAMPOUND Cornwall Map 2 SW94
See St Austell sketch map.
Lynwood Camping & Caravan Park *(SW936487)* Mill Ln St Austell 882458
2 signposted
Quiet, level site in the sheltered Fal valley; grassed surface with trees and bushes, set in highland meadow country. 1¼acres 28pitches 3static
May–Oct rsApr must book peak periods last arrival 23.00hrs last departure 11.00hrs 5 individual pitches 7wc lit all night 1cdp 6washbasins hc 3central hot water (2hc) 1 (cold storage) calor gas camping gaz toilet fluid
15£1.50–£1.70 3£1.50–£1.70 10£1.50–£1.70 (awnings)

GREAT
Placenames incorporating the word 'Great', such as Gt Malvern and Gt Yarmouth, will be found under the actual placename, *ie* Yarmouth.

GREWELTHORPE North Yorkshire
Map 8 SE27
►► **Newholme Caravan Site** *(SE232758)*
☎Kirkby Malzeard 225
[2] ❷ ⚠ signposted
A small, peaceful farm site in rural setting and surrounded by neat hedgerows and stone walls.
nc12 yrs 1½acres 10pitches 20static Etr–Sep must book 4 individual pitches 6wc 1cdp washbasins hc ⊙ calor gas ⊞ stables pub
6 £1.80–£2 4 £1.80–£2 (awnings)

GREYSTOKE Cumbria Map 12 NY43
►►► **Whit Barrow Hall Caravan Park** *(NY405289)* ☎456
[2] ❷ ⚠ signposted
Level site with a grass and gravel surface, set in mountainous country with trees and shrubs. The site lies 500yds from the A66 and has a good approach road. 10acres 100pitches 140static Mar–Oct must book peak periods last departure 12.00hrs 4 individual pitches wc lit all night 1cdp washbasins hc hc ⊙ (wash, spin) iron calor gas camping gaz paraffin toilet fluid ☎ ⊞ children's playground, licensed club & sauna/solarium stables launderette pub
100 £2.40 or 100 £2.40 or 100▲£2.40 (awnings)

GRISTHORPE BAY North Yorkshire
Map 8 TA08
See Scarborough sketch map.
►►► **Blue Dolphin Holiday Park** *(TA090830)* ☎Scarborough 512219
[1] ❷ ⚠ signposted
Undulating grass site set in meadowland, on the coast and lying adjacent to A165 Scarborough road. 30acres 520pitches 307static May–22 Sep rsEtr booking advisable last arrival 19.00hrs last departure 11.00hrs 12 late arrivals enclosure 103wc lit all night 3cdp 70washbasins hc 6central hot water (28hc) 16⊙ (5wash, 3spin, 5dry, 12iron) calor gas camping gaz cafe ☎ ⊞ licensed club, children's playground & children's theatre cinema launderette pub
420 fr£2.75 or 420 fr£2.75 100▲fr£2.75 (awnings) ltr

GUERNSEY Details for Channel Islands follow England.

GUNNISLAKE Cornwall Map 2 SX47
►►► **Honicombe Holiday Centre**
Callington ☎832583
[2] ❶ ⚠ signposted
A level, grassy site set amongst sylvan surroundings. From Tavistock follow A390, turn right at top of Gunnislake Hill.
4acres 50pitches 100static
Apr–Oct 6 9wc lit all night 1cdp 6washbasins hc central hot water 9hc 2⊙ (1iron) games room CTV cold storage calor gas camping gaz toilet fluid cafe restaurant ☎ children's entertainment, disco & licensed club stables launderette pub
50 £2.16 or 50 £2.15 or 50▲£1.94 awnings ltr

GWITHIAN Cornwall Map 2 SW54
See Hayle sketch map.
►►► **Godrevy** 54 Upton Towans
☎ Hayle 753100 (out of season Hayle 753546.
[2] ❷ ⚠ signposted
Level, grassy site set in meadowland lying adjacent to St Ives Bay, sands and B3301.
6acres 115pitches
May–Sep rsApr must book last arrival 20.00hrs last departure 11.00hrs 15 28wc lit all night 1cdp 16washbasins hc (central hot water) (10hc) 4⊙ (2iron) calor gas camping gaz ☎ ⊞ hot snacks available cinema launderette pub
115 fr£2.20 or 115 fr£2.20 or 115▲fr£2.20 (awnings) ltr

HALDON RACECOURSE Devon Map 3 SX98
►►► **Trax Campsite** *(SX898836)*
[1] ❸ ⚠ signposted
Level grassy site in Devonshire countryside. Adjacent to A38 Exeter–Plymouth road.

Convenient overnight stop for travellers to and from Cornwall. 10acres 100pitches 2 May–20 Sep no bookings last arrival 22.30hrs last departure 15.00hrs 5 30wc lit all night 1cdp 22washbasins hc 4central hot water 6hc 5 warden (1wash) dry 2iron TV calor gas camping gaz games area free racing for campers 26 May, 6, 7, 20, 21, 27 & 28 Aug 100£2–£2.75 or 100£2–£2.75 or 100▲£2–£2.75 awnings

HALE Cumbria Map 7 SD57

►►► Fell End Caravan Park *(SD505780)* Slackhead Rd Milnthorpe 2122 2 1 signposted *Pleasantly situated, partly level and sloping gravel site with mature trees, saplings and bushes. Within easy access of the lakes and south Cumbria. 4¾m from junction 35 of M6.* 10acres 70pitches 215static Mar–Oct must book public hols 8 late arrivals enclosure 38wc lit all night 3cdp 8washbasins hc central hot water (6hc) 6 iron TV (cold storage) calor gas camping gaz paraffin toilet fluid children's playground & facilities for the disabled pub 50£2–£2.50 or 50£1.20–£1.50 20▲£2–£2.50 (awnings)

►► Hallmore Farm Caravan Park *(SD503786)* Milnthorpe 2375 1 1 signposted *A mainly level grassy site set in meadowland. Adjacent to main road.* 8acres 80pitches 56static Mar–Oct must book Bank Hols last arrival 23.59hrs last departure 13.00hrs 5 11wc 3cdp washbasins hc (hc) warden cold storage calor gas camping gaz stables launderette 40 or 40 40▲ ltr

HALTWHISTLE Northumberland Map 12 NY76

► Yont The Cleugh *(NY699588)* Coanwood 20274 1 1 signposted *This remote rural site has a small wood and stream adjoining, and offers distant views of the Cheviots and Hadrian's Wall. The approach is by a rather narrow and hilly road and is located 4½m S of Haltwhistle. Signposted from the A69; also from the A689 at Lambley.* 2acres 12pitches 40static Mar–Oct must book last arrival 21.00hrs 3 6wc lit all night cdp washbasins hc central hot water hc (1wash, 1spin, 1dry) calor gas putting green, children's playground & licensed club 12£3 or 12£3 or 12▲£3 (awnings) ltr

HAROME North Yorkshire Map 8 SE68

►►► Foxholme Caravan Park *(SE660830)* Helmsley 416/Scarborough 61668 3 3 *1m S of Beadlam. Level site in open countryside of North Ryedale, within 4m of North York Moors National Park.* 4½acres 30pitches Etr–Oct 6 late arrivals enclosure 12wc lit all night cdp 8washbasins hc 4hc 2 1wash 1spin 1iron calor gas camping gaz stables 30£1.50–£2 or 30£1.50–£2 awnings

HARROGATE North Yorkshire Map 8 SE35

►►► High Moor Farm Park *(SE244566)* High Moor Farm, Skipton Rd 63637 2 2 signposted *Situated beside a small wood and surrounded by thorn hedges. On the A59, Harrogate to Skipton road, 4m from Harrogate.* 6¾acres 138pitches Apr–Oct must book last departure 12.00hrs 10 individual pitches late arrivals enclosure 28wc lit all night 1cdp 20washbasins hc central hot water (12hc) 5 warden (wash, spin, dry, iron) calor gas camping gaz toilet fluid licensed club & children's playground 138£2.40 or 138£2.40 or 138▲£2.40 (awnings) ltr

►►► Rudding Touring Caravan Park *(SE870439)* Rudding Park, Follifoot 870439 2 2 signposted *Site set amidst gardens of Rudding Park and is screened by walls and hedges. Situated 3m SE of Harrogate off the A661.* 90pitches 16 Mar–17 Oct must book public hols 8 individual pitches late arrivals enclosure 21wc lit all night 1cdp 14washbasins hc central hot water (14hc) 2 calor gas camping gaz toilet fluid stables cinema launderette pub 90£2–£2.50 or 90£2–£2.50 awnings ltr

►► Shaws Trailer Park *(SE325557)* Knaresborough Rd 884432 1 1 *A level, grassy site with mature trees. On A59 Harrogate–Knaresborough road.* 65pitches 146static All year must book Bank Hols last arrival 21.00hrs last departure 14.00hrs 25 25wc lit all night 1cdp washbasins hc (central hot water) (hc) (hc) calor gas cafe restaurant licensed bar stables cinema launderette pub 65 or 65 or 65▲ (awnings)

HARTINGTON Derbyshire Map 7 SK16

► Barracks Farm Caravan Site *(SK127585)* Beresford Dale 261 1 1 *A level, grassy site with mature trees. From A515 (Ashbourne–Buxton) turn left onto B5054, then left again for Alstonfield and Beresford Dale.* 5acres 50pitches Etr–Oct 2 5wc 1cdp calor gas 20 30▲ (awnings)

HARVINGTON Hereford and Worcester Map 4 SP04

►►► Carr's Caravans Ltd *(SP061488)* Small Moors Caravan Park, Anchor Ln 446 2 2 *A level, grassy site with mature trees and bushes, near the river and set among hilly, woodland country. On A439 4m N of Evesham.* 2acres 100static 15 Mar–31 Oct must book peak periods last arrival 23.00hrs last departure 19.00hrs 2 individual pitches 18wc lit all night 1cdp 14washbasins hc (4hc) 2 warden calor gas toilet fluid stables cinema launderette 30 or 30 ltr

HASTINGS & ST LEONARDS E Sussex
Map 5 TQ80
▶ ***Holiday Homes Trailer Park*** *(TQ792124)*
Battle Rd ☎51671
[1] ❷ ⚠ signposted
A level site off A2100 N of Hastings. 2acres 8pitches 44static
Mar–Oct last arrival 22.00hrs last departure 11.00hrs 5♣ nor cars by caravans 8wc lit all night 11washbasins hc (2⚲hc) 1⊙ warden (iron) calor gas ⊞ ♨ ⊖ stables ♂ ✈ cinema ↬ launderette
8🚐 or 8🚙

HATFIELD South Yorkshire Map 8 SE60
▶▶▶ **Hatfield Marina Caravan & Camp Site** *(SE668101)* ☎ Doncaster 841572
[2] ❷ ⚠ signposted
A local council site with specialised facilities for water sports. 400yds from A18 and adjacent to marina. 10acres 60pitches
All year last arrival 21.00hrs last departure 12.00hrs 4♣ Ⓐ late arrivals enclosure 10wc lit all night 2cdp 12washbasins hc 3central hot water 4⚲hc 2⊙ warden iron ☎ ⊞ children's playground sailing & canoeing fishing ♨ ⊖ stables ✈ cinema launderette pub
60🚐£1.25 or 60🚙£1 20▲£1 (awnings)

HAVERTHWAITE Cumbria Map 7 SD38
See Cartmel sketch map.
▶▶▶ **Bigland Hall Caravan Park** *(SD350829)* ☎ Newby Bridge 702 (to be prefixed by 31)
[1] ❷ ⚠ signposted
A well-wooded site in part of the Bigland Estate within the Lake District National Park. 3m from the southern end of Lake Windermere, also near to the Lakeside and Haverthwaite Steam Railway. 15acres 86pitches 39static
Mar–Oct must book peak periods last arrival 21.00hrs last departure 13.00hrs 3♣ individual pitches late arrivals enclosure 24wc lit all night 3cdp washbasins hc central hot water (⚲hc) ⊙ warden (wash, dry, iron) CTV calor gas paraffin toilet fluid ☎ ⊞ ♨ ⊖ stables ✈ ↬ launderette pub
86🚐£2.20 or 86🚙£2.20 (awnings)

HAWFORD Hereford and Worcester
Map 3 SO85
▶ ***Mill House*** *(SO845605)*
[2] ❶ ⚠ signposted
Level, grassy site with trees, set in meadowland, adjacent to river. 7½acres 150pitches
Etr–Oct no booking last arrival 22.30hrs 4♣ Ⓐ late arrivals enclosure 10wc lit all night 3cdp 10washbasins hc 2central hot water 2⚲hc 2⊙ warden cold storage calor gas camping gaz toilet fluid ☎ ⊞ ♨ ⊖ stables ♂ ✈ cinema ↬ launderette pub
80🚐 15🚙 55▲ (awnings)

HAWKCHURCH Devon Map 3 ST30
▶ **Scouse Farm Caravan Park** *(SY345988)*

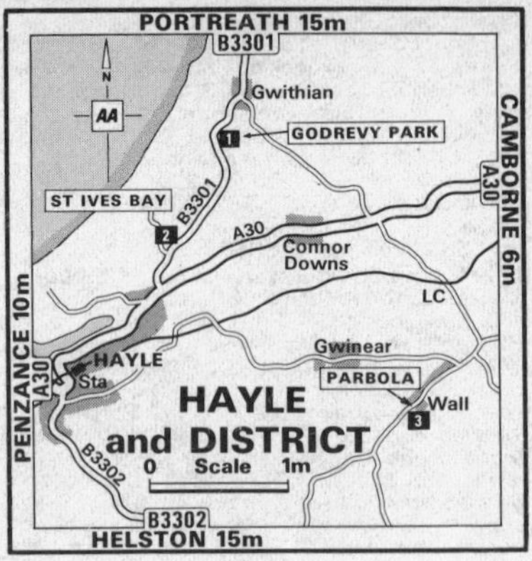

Sites listed under:
1 Gwithian **2** Hayle **3** Wall

Scouse Farm ☎402
[2] ❷ ⚠
Level site surrounded by trees; good views. On B3165 between Blackpool Corner and Marshwood. 8acres 170pitches
Apr–15 Nov must book peak periods last departure 12.00hrs 28♣ 38wc lit all night 1cdp (17⚲hc) 3⊙ warden (spin, dry, iron) games room (cold storage) calor gas camping gaz toilet fluid restaurant licensed bar ☎ ⊞ (licensed club) children's playground battery charger & hairdryer ♨ ⊖ stables ♂ cinema ↬ launderette pub
170🚐£2.68 or 170🚙£2.10 (awnings)

HAYLE Cornwall Map 2 SW53
See sketch map.
▶ **St Ives Bay Chalet & Caravan Park** *(SW577398)* The Holiday Centre, Upton Towans ☎752274
[2] ❶ ⚠ signposted
The site is set amidst undulating grassland and sand dunes, adjoining the beach. 1m N of Hayle off B3301. 20acres 250pitches 200static
24 May–27 Sep rs3 May–23 May no bookings last arrival 23.00hrs last departure 09.00hrs 25♣ Ⓐ wc lit all night 7cdp (⚲hc) 12⊙ warden (2wash, 1spin, 2dry, 6iron, games room, cold storage) calor gas camping gaz paraffin cafe licensed bar ☎ ⊞ (licensed club) children's playground private beach & battery charger ♨ ⊖ stables ♂ cinema ↬ launderette pub
250🚐£2.40 or 250🚙£2.40 or 250▲£2.40 (awnings)

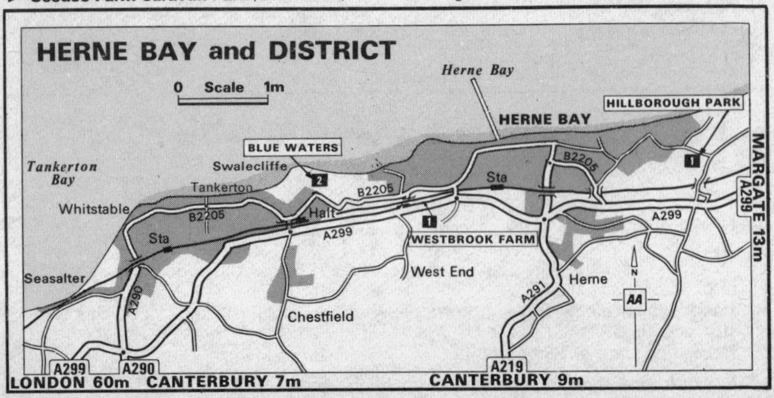

Sites listed under: **1** Herne Bay **2** Whitstable

HAYLING ISLAND Hampshire Map 4 SU70
►► **Lower Tye Farm** *(SZ722995)*
Copse Ln ☎2479
2 ❷ ⚠ signposted
A level grass site, ¼m E of A3023. 5½acres 135pitches 72static
Etr & Spring Bank Hol–Sep rs mid Apr–mid May & Oct must book peak periods last departure 12.00hrs 10 individual pitches ⊗ 16wc lit all night 1cdp 18washbasins hc 1central hot water 12 hc 3⊙ (3wash, 3dry, 4iron) (cold storage) calor gas camping gaz toilet fluid cafe ☎ ⊞ children's playground & car wash ⊖ stables cinema launderette pub
61 £1.60–£2.50 or 61 £1.60–£2.50 74▲£1.60–£2.50 (awnings)
► **Oven Camping Site** *(SZ714993)* Manor Rd ☎3244 (office and enquiries)
2 ❶ ⚠ signposted
Level grassy sheltered site, set in meadowland lying 1m from sandy beach, the site has direct access to the A3023. no motorcycles
10acres 330pitches
Mar–Oct must book public hols last arrival 22.00hrs last departure 22.00hrs 4 ⊗ late arrivals enclosure 21wc lit all night 1cdp washbasins hc hc ⊙ wash cold storage calor gas camping gaz children's playground ⊖ stables cinema launderette pub
110 £1.50 or 110 £1.50 220▲£1.50 awnings

HEATHFIELD East Sussex Map 5 TQ52
►►► **Greenview Caravan Fields** *(TQ605223)* Broad Oak ☎3531
2 ❸ ⚠
Small, attractive site adjoining main A265 in village of Broad Oak 1m E of Heathfield.
½acre 6pitches 51static
Apr–Oct must book public hols last departure 10.30hrs 2 7wc lit all night 1cdp 2 washbasins hc (hc, hc) ⊙ warden (wash, spin) iron TV calor gas camping gaz toilet fluid ☎ ⊞ children's play area & (licensed club) ⊖ stables launderette pub
6 £1.75 or 6 £1.75 or 6▲£1.25–£1.75 (awnings) ltr

HEDGE END Hampshire Map 4 SU41
►► **Grange Caravan Park** *(SU492144)*
Shamblehurst Ln ☎ Botley 3895
2 ❶ ⚠ signposted
A level grassy site, 6m N of Southampton off B3035. ⅓acre 26pitches 155static
All year no bookings 1 individual pitches 2wc lit all night 1cdp (washbasins hc) (hc) ⊙ calor gas camping gaz ☎ ⊞ ⊖ stables cinema launderette pub
26 £1.50 or 26 £1.50 awnings

HELSTON Cornwall Map 2 SW62
►► **Glenhaven Touring Park** *(SW665274)*
Clodgey Ln ☎2734
1 ❷ ⚠ signposted
Well-laid out touring site adjacent to outskirts of Helston. S of town on A3083 Helston–Lizard road near to RAF Culdrose. 4½acre 70pitches
All year booking advisable peak periods last departure 12.00hrs 6 12wc lit all night 1cdp 14washbasins hc 2central hot water (10 hc) 3⊙ warden (1wash, 1spin) 1iron cold storage calor gas camping gaz ☎ ⊞ children's playground mobile shop ⊖ stables cinema launderette pub
70 £3 or 70 £2.75 or 70▲£3 (awnings)

HEMINGFORD ABBOTS Cambridgeshire Map 4 TL27
►►► **Heming Abbots Caravan Park** *(TL283712)*
1 ❶ ⚠ signposted
Level grassy site in a River Ouse village. Set in meadowland adjacent to A604. ¾acre 20pitches 40static
Apr–Oct rsNov–Mar no bookings last arrival 22.00hrs last departure 12.00hrs 2 11wc lit all night 2cdp (washbasins hc) (hc) ⊙ warden iron calor gas camping gaz paraffin toilet fluid ⊞ boating & angling ⊖ stables cinema launderette pub
 £2 £1.50 ▲fr£1.50 (awnings)

HEREFORD Hereford and Worcester Map 3 SO54
►► **Trax Campsite** *(SO501420)*
Hereford Racecourse
1 ❷ ⚠ signposted
Quiet, grass and gravel site within easy reach of town centre. Adjacent to A49 Leominster road and A4103. 5acres 60pitches
30 May–4 Sep except 22 & 23 Aug no bookings last arrival 22.30hrs last departure 15.00hrs 2 21wc lit all night 2cdp 9washbasins hc 3central hot water 2 hc 3⊙ warden TV calor gas camping gaz ☎ ⊞ children's playground & games area ⊖ stables cinema launderette
60 £2–£2.75 or 60 £2–£2.75 or 60▲£2–£2.75 awnings

HERNE BAY Kent Map 5 TR16
See sketch map.
► ***Hillborough Park*** *(TR209679)*
Reculver Rd ☎4618
2 ❹ ⚠
Set on high ground, amidst well-kept lawns, the site is situated a few minutes' from the sea, and ten minutes' walk from shopping centre.
1acre 10pitches 395static
Apr–mid Oct must book peak periods last arrival 22.00hrs last departure 22.00hrs 10 12wc lit all night (2central hot water) (4 hc) 2⊙ (2wash, dry, iron) calor gas camping gaz toilet fluid licensed bar ☎ ⊞ ⊖ stables cinema launderette
10 or 10 (awnings)
► **Westbrook Farm Caravan Park** *(TR158673)* Sea St ☎5586
1 ❶ ⚠
Small site within easy reach of the Thanet Way and Herne Bay. The club house is in an attractive 17th-C farmhouse surrounded by fields.
5acres 150pitches
Apr–15 Oct no bookings 5 individual pitches ⊗ wc lit all night 1cdp (central hot water, hc) ⊙ calor gas camping gaz toilet fluid (licensed club) children's playground ⊞ ⊖ stables cinema launderette pub
150 £1.50 or 150 £1.50 or 150▲£1.50 (awnings)

Hewas Water

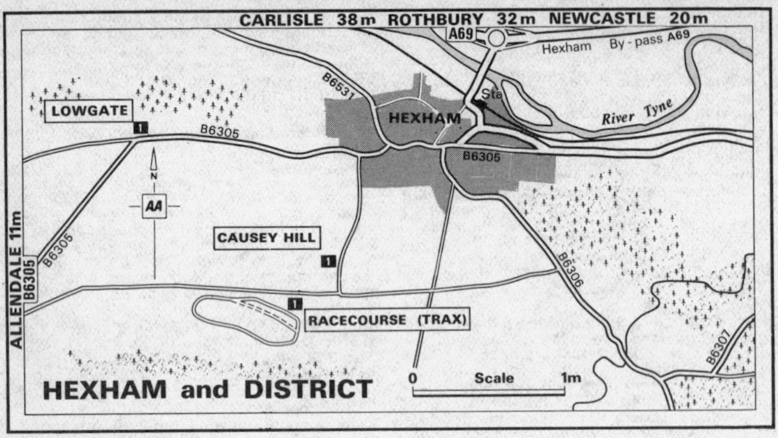

All sites listed under: 1 Hexham

HEWAS WATER Cornwall Map 2 SW94
See St Austell sketch map.
►►► **Trencreek Farm Caravan Park** *(SW966485)* ☎ Grampound Road 882540
2 ❷ △ signposted
Part level, part sloping grass site with mature trees and bushes close to river and lake. Off B3287, 1m from junction with A390. 5acres 32pitches 37static
Etr–Oct must book peak periods last arrival 22.00hrs last departure 10.00hrs 4 individual pitches 10wc lit all night 1cdp 8washbasins hc (2 hc) 2⊙ (1wash, 1dry) 1iron games room CTV calor gas camping gaz cafe restaurant ☎ ⊞ fishing & take-away meals stables launderette
50 fr£2 or 50 fr£2 or 50▲fr£2 (awnings)

HEXHAM Northumberland Map 12 NY96
See sketch map
►►► ***Causey Hill Caravan Park*** *(NY925625)* Benson's Fell Farm ☎2834
2 ❶ △
On sloping ground attractively screened by trees. 50pitches 75static
Apr–Sep rsMar & Oct must book Apr–Sep last arrival 19.30hrs last departure 11.30hrs 5 late arrivals enclosure 24wc lit all night 2cdp washbasins hc hc ⊙ (wash, spin, dry) (cold storage) calor gas ☎ ⊞ stables launderette pub
40 10 (awnings) ltr

►► **Trax Campsite** *(NY919623)*
Hexham Racecourse
2 ❶ △
A partly level and partly sloping grassy site with mature trees surrounded by moorland. 4acres 60pitches
30 May–6 Sep no bookings last arrival 22.30hrs last departure 15.00hrs 2 16wc lit all night 1cdp 9washbasins hc 1central hot water 2 hc 2⊙ warden TV ☎ ⊞ games area stables launderette
60 £2–£2.35 or 60 £2–£2.35 or 60▲£2–£2.35 awnings

►► **Lowgate Caravan Site** *(NY903642)*
☎2827
2 ❷ △ signposted
Level, grass site with mature trees and bushes set in hilly wooded and moorland country. Adjacent to B6305 Hexham–Allendale road.
10pitches 65static
21 Mar–Oct must book public hols last arrival 21.00hrs last departure 12.00hrs 2 14wc lit all night 1cdp washbasins hc central hot water hc ⊙ warden calor gas toilet fluid ☎ ⊞ stables launderette pub
10 £2 or 10 £2 (awnings) ltr

HIGHAMPTON Devon Map 2 SS40
►►► ***South Trew Farm***
☎Black Torrington 277
2 ❸ △
Level, grass site with mature trees and bushes, set in meadowland and near to River Torridge. 4m W of Hatherleigh on A3072. 3acres 15pitches 6static
Etr–Oct booking advisable peak periods last arrival 22.00hrs 4 11wc lit all night 1cdp 7washbasins hc central hot water 6 hc 2⊙ (cold storage) indoor drying room ⊞ stables
7 or 7 8▲ ltr

HIGH BENTHAM North Yorkshire Map 7 SD66
►► **Riverside Caravan Park** *(SD665688)*
Wenning Av ☎ Bentham 61272
2 ❷ △ signposted
Situated on edge of the town, the site is in a quiet location screened by trees. 2acres 30pitches 150static
7 Mar–Oct must book last arrival 21.00hrs last departure 12.00hrs 3 8wc lit all night 1cdp 8washbasins hc (hc) ⊙ warden (dry) games room TV calor gas toilet fluid ☎ ⊞ children's playground fishing launderette pub
30 £1.75 or 30 £1.75 (awnings) ltr

HIGHBRIDGE Somerset Map 3 ST34
►►► **Edithmead Dairy Trailer Park**
☎ Burnham-on-Sea 783475
1 ❶ △ signposted
Level, compact site adjacent to the M5. 10acres 30pitches
Mar–Oct no bookings last arrival 23.59hrs last departure 12.00hrs 8 individual pitches late arrivals enclosure 12wc lit all night 1cdp washbasins hc central hot water (hc) ⊙ warden wash spin iron cold storage calor gas children's playground stables cinema pub
30 £2 or 30 £2 or 30▲£2 (awnings)

HIGH HESKET Cumbria Map 12 NY44
►►► **Astra Caravan Site** *(NY430433)*
The Astra ☎ Southwaite 541
1 ❷ △ signposted
Lies off the A6 with easy access to M6 motorway. A mainly level site with grass and gravel surface. Scenic views of Lake District. 2acres 45pitches
Apr–Oct booking advisable peak periods last departure 12.00hrs 7 individual pitches 9wc lit all night 1cdp washbasins hc (central hot water) (hc) ⊙ warden toilet fluid cafe restaurant licensed bar ☎ ⊞ children's playground pub
45 £2 or 45 £2 awnings ltr

HOLMSLEY Hampshire Map 4 SZ29
See Christchurch sketch map.
►►► **Holmsley Camp** *(SZ218992)*
Holmsley Old Aerodrome, Hinton
2 △ signposted
A large Forestry Commission site, set in rural surroundings on the fringe of the New Forest. See page 124 for further information.

25acres 700pitches
Apr–Sep must book Spring Bank Hol
last departure 12.00hrs 30 individual pitches
wc lit all night washbasins hc central hot water
hc ⊙ calor gas camping gaz toilet fluid cafe
☎ ⊞ stables pub
700 or 700 250▲ awnings

HOLTON HEATH Dorset Map 3 SY99
►►►► Sandford Park Caravans Ltd
☎ Lytchett Minster 622513
[2] ⚠ signposted
Level, grassy and gravel site with mature trees set in wooded meadowland with direct access to A351 Poole–Wareham road. (Jun–Aug)
10acres 250pitches 150static
Mar–Oct no bookings last arrival 23.59hrs
last departure 12.00hrs 14 individual pitches
late arrivals enclosure 108wc lit all night
4cdp 73washbasins hc (36hc) 15⊙
(4wash, 2spin, 2dry) iron (1games room) 3CTV
(cold storage) calor gas camping gaz paraffin
toilet fluid cafe restaurant ☎ (licensed club)
& children's playground stables
cinema launderette pub
250£2.30–£2.80 or 250£2.30–£2.80 or
250▲£2.30–£2.80 (awnings)

HONEYBOURNE Hereford and Worcester Map 4 SP14
►►► Ranch Caravan Park *(SP113444)*
☎ Evesham 830744
[2] ❶ ⚠ signposted
Level grassy site with trees and bushes set in farmland in the Vale of Evesham 2m from B4035.
6acres 100pitches 160static
Spring Bank Hol–Oct rs25 Mar–mid May
must book last arrival 20.00hrs last departure
16.00hrs 32wc lit all night 2cdp
32washbasins hc (1central hot water, 7hc)
4⊙ warden (1dry, 1iron) (1) games room
TV (cold storage) calor gas camping gaz
toilet fluid ☎ ⊞ (licensed club) & children's
playground stables launderette
pub
100£2.20 or 100£2.20 (awnings) ltr

HONITON Devon Map 3 ST10
► *Northcote Caravan Park* Lower Northcote
☎2917
[1] ❶ ⚠ signposted
A mainly level, grassy site with some slopes with trees, saplings and bushes. Situated in the urban area with direct access to main road (A30).
8½acres 167pitches
16 Mar–16 Nov must book peak periods
last departure 11.00hrs 9wc lit all night
3cdp washbasins hc central hot water (hc)
⊙ (wash, dry, iron) calor gas camping gaz ☎
⊞ launderette pub
152 or 152 15▲

HOPE Derbyshire Map 7 SK18
►►► *Losehill Hall Caravan Site*
(SK156834) ☎ Hope Valley 20636
[2] ❷ ⚠
A pleasantly situated site in the Hope Valley. Well secluded with mature trees and bushes on the west side of Hope village. Near Castleton and the famous Peak Caverns and Peverill Castle. 6acres 95pitches
22 Mar–15 Oct must book wknds & Bank Hols
last departure 12.00hrs 4 late arrivals enclosure
10wc lit all night 1cdp (2hc) 1⊙ warden
calor gas ☎ ⊞ stables launderette
75 or 75 20▲ (awnings)

►► Laneside Caravan Park *(SK178832)*
Laneside Farm ☎ Hope Valley 20215
[2] ❶ ⚠
A pleasantly situated rural site on east side of Hope Village. Surrounded by wooded hills.
4acres 50pitches 22static
Etr–Oct must book peak periods & all wknds
last departure 14.00hrs 7 17wc lit all night
2cdp 17washbasins hc 4central hot water
(4hc) 3⊙ (1spin, 1dry) (cold storage)
calor gas camping gaz toilet fluid stables
launderette pub
50£1.30–£1.65 or 50£1.30–£1.65 or
50▲£1.30–£1.65 (awnings) ltr

HORNS CROSS Devon Map 2 SS32
►►► *Steart Farm* ☎Clovelly 239
[2] ❷ ⚠ signposted
Undulating grass and gravel site with mature trees, set in meadowland in rural area with access to A39 to Bideford and Barnstaple Bay.
4acres 60pitches 9static
Etr–Oct last arrival 22.00hrs last departure
12.00hrs 5 12wc lit all night 2cdp
6washbasins hc 1central hot water (2hc) 2⊙
(1spin) (cold storage) calor gas camping gaz
☎ stables pub
20 10 40▲ (awnings)

HUBBERTS BRIDGE Lincolnshire Map 8 TF24
►► *Orchards Caravan Park* *(TF273433)*
☎328
[2] ❷ ⚠
A level, grassy site with mature trees and bushes, not far from the canal. 3½m W of Boston on B1192. 2acres 30pitches 100static
Apr–Oct last arrival 22.00hrs last departure
14.00hrs 7 20wc lit all night 1cdp
12washbasins hc (central hot water) (4hc)
2⊙ iron cold storage calor gas ☎ ⊞
30 or 30 (awnings) ltr

HUGHLEY Salp Map 7 SO59
►►► Mill Farm Caravan Site *(SO564979)*
☎ Brockton 208
[2] ❷ ⚠ signposted
Level grass and gravel site with mature trees and bushes, set in meadowland adjacent to river.
2acres 25pitches 49static
Mar–Oct must book public hols last arrival
22.00hrs last departure 10.00hrs 7
late arrivals enclosure wc lit all night 2cdp
(washbasins hc) (hc) ⊙ warden calor gas
camping gaz toilet fluid ⊞ horse riding &
fishing launderette pub
25 or 25 or 25▲ (awnings)

HUNSTANTON Norfolk Map 9 TF64
► Searles Camping Ground *(TF671400)*
South Beach ☎2342
[1] ❶ ⚠ signposted
A level, grassy site with bushes adjacent to sea and beach. On B1161, in South Hunstanton, off A149 King's Lynn road. 9acres 135pitches
575static
Apr–Sep rsMar & Oct must book peak periods
last arrival 22.00hrs last departure 12.00hrs
5 individual pitches late arrivals enclosure
wc lit all night washbasins hc hc ⊙ warden
(wash, spin, iron,) TV calor gas camping gaz
toilet fluid cafe restaurant ☎ ⊞ (licensed
club) & children's playground stables
launderette pub
50 10 75▲ rates on application
(awnings) ltr

HUNTINGDON Cambridgeshire Map 4 TL27
►► Anchor Cottage Riverside Caravan & Camping Site *(TL253725)* Church Ln,
Hartford ☎ Huntingdon 55642
[3] ❶ ⚠ signposted
A level grassy site with mature trees and bushes set in woodland with river nearby. 1m NE of Huntingdon on A141. nc16 2acres
29pitches 15static
All year must book peak periods last arrival
21.00hrs last departure 12.00hrs 8
individual pitches 5wc 1cdp (2washbasins hc)
(2hc) 1⊙ ⊞ fishing & moorings
stables cinema launderette pub
29fr£1.60 or 29fr£1.60 or 29▲fr£1.60
(awnings)

ILFRACOMBE Devon Map 2 SS54
See sketch map.
► Big Meadow Camping Site *(SS546484)*
Lydford Farm ☎62282
[2] ❶ ⚠ signposted
Level grassy site with a variety of trees and shrubs set in wooded meadowland with access to sea, beach, river and A399. Opposite Watermouth Castle. 9acres 150pitches
20 May–Oct no bookings 3 16wc lit all
night washbasins hc central hot water (hc)
⊙ warden calor gas camping gaz paraffin
toilet fluid ☎ ⊞ children's playground
stables cinema launderette pub
150£1.80 or 150▲£1.80 ltr

INSTOW Devon Map 2 SS43
► *Lagoon View Caravan Park* ☎860423
[2] ❷ signposted
This site is situated on A39 overlooking estuary where the rivers Taw and Torridge meet and the

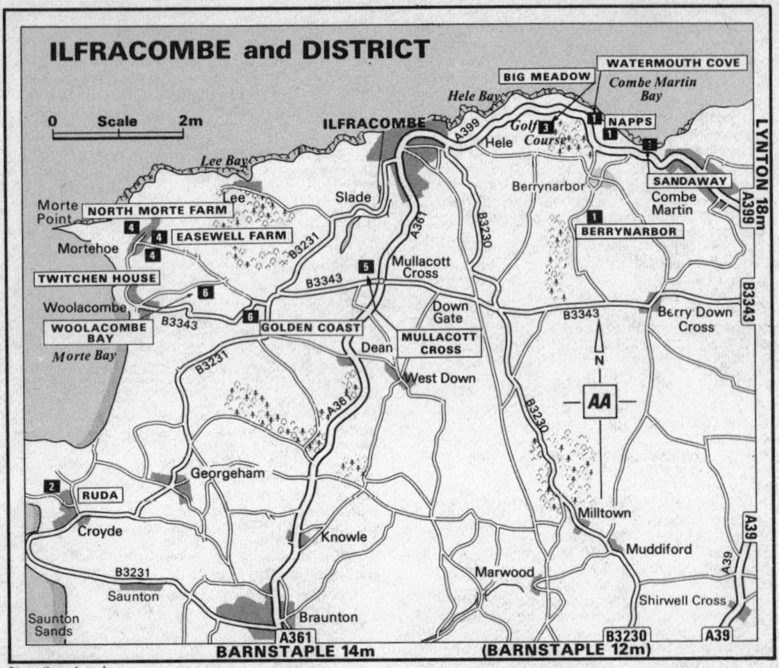

Sites listed under:
1 Berrynarbor **2** Croyde Bay **3** Ilfracombe **4** Mortehoe **5** Mullacott Cross **6** Woolacombe

sand dunes of Saunton and Crow. The site slopes slightly northwards with tarmac roads and well-maintained pitches. 1¼acres 28pitches 200static
Etr–Sep rsOct must book school hols last arrival 22.00hrs last departure 10.30hrs individual pitches late arrivals enclosure wc lit all night 2cdp washbasins hc (hc) ⊙ wash, spin, iron calor gas camping gaz toilet fluid licensed bar ☎ ⊞ ⊖ stables pub 28 or 28 (awnings)

ISLE OF MAN
Details follow England.

ISLE OF WIGHT
Places with AA-classified caravan and campsites are indicated on the location map on page 4 of the atlas section. Full details of these will be found under individual placenames within the England gazetteer section.

JERSEY
Details for Channel Islands follow England.

KEMPSEY Hereford and Worcester
Map 3 SO84
► **Court Meadow Caravan Park** *(SO848492)*
☎ Worcester 820295
1 3 ⚠ signposted
Mainly level, grass site amidst a variety of trees and bushes. Set in meadowland adjacent to main road and River Severn. 8acres 20pitches
All year 7 23wc lit all night washbasins hc (hc) ⊙ (wash, spin) cold storage calor gas toilet fluid ⊞ boat hire & moorings ⊖ stables cinema launderette pub 20£1.85 or 20£1.85 awnings ltr

KENDAL Cumbria Map 7 SD59
►► **Millcrest Caravan Park** *(SD525949)*
☎21075
2 1 ⚠ signposted
Sloping, grass site set in hilly woodland and meadowland. Exit 36 off M6 from S then A65 or exit 37 off M6 from N then A684. 1½m N of Kendal. 2acres 36pitches
mid Mar–Oct must book peak periods last arrival 21.00hrs last departure 12.00hrs 2 individual pitches 6wc lit all night 1cdp 6washbasins hc central hot water (4hc) 2⊙ 1spin 1iron calor gas ☎ ⊞ ⊖ stables cinema launderette
36£1.60 or 36£1.60 (awnings) ltr

KENNACK SANDS Cornwall Map 2 SW71
See sketch map.
►►► **Sea Acres Caravan Park** *(SW731163)*
☎The Lizard 665
2 ❶ ⚠
Mainly level site with some bushes, set in meadowland. Adjacent to sea and beach 10m SE of Helston. dogs charged for 3acres 50pitches 94static
Mid May–Sep rsEtr–mid May must book peak periods last arrival 22.00hrs last departure 10.00hrs 10 late arrivals enclosure 27wc lit all night 1cdp (13washbasins hc, 1 hc, 13 hc) 5⊙ (2wash, 2dry, 2iron) TV calor gas camping gaz toilet fluid ☎ ⊞ (licensed club) stables launderette
50 £3 or 50 £3 or 50▲£3 (awnings)
►► **Silver Sands Holiday Park** *(SW732171)*
☎ The Lizard 631
2 ❷ ⚠ signposted
Level, grass site with young trees and bushes, set in moorland and meadowland with access to sea and beach at Kennack Sands. dogs charged for 1acre 20pitches 30static
15 May—Sep must book peak periods last departure 12.00hrs 5 10wc lit all night 1cdp (6washbasins hc, 6central hot water) hc 2⊙ warden (1spin, 1iron) calor gas camping gaz cafe restaurant ☎ ⊞ stables pub
20 £1.50–£2 or 20 £1.50–£2 or 20▲£1.50–£2 (awnings)
► ***Kennack Sands Caravan Park*** *(SW732163)* ☎ The Lizard 533
1 ❶ ⚠
Slightly sloping grass site with shrubbery and hedges set in meadowland. The site is adjacent to sea and beach and 9m S of Helston off B3293. ⅓acre 6pitches 46static
Etr–Sep must book all times last arrival 18.00hrs last departure 10.00hrs 12 13wc lit all night 1cdp washbasins hc central hot water hc ⊙ warden iron calor gas paraffin ⊞ stables launderette
3 3

KENNFORD Devon Map 3 SX98
►►► **Kennford International Caravan Park** *(SX912857)* ☎833046
2 ❷ ⚠ signposted
Situated to the S of Exeter in a central position for touring South Devon. 4acres 82pitches
16 Mar–13 Jan must book peak periods last departure 13.00hrs 10 24wc lit all night 3cdp 12washbasins hc central hot water (8 hc) 7⊙ warden (wash, spin, dry) iron (cold storage) calor gas camping gaz paraffin toilet fluid ☎ ⊞ children's playground & hairdryers stables cinema launderette pub
82 £2.50 or 82 £2.50 or 82▲£2.50 (awnings) ltr

KESSINGLAND Suffolk Map 5 TM58
►►► **Kessingland Beach Caravan Camp** *(TM530860)* Beach Rd ☎Lowestoft 740368
1 ❸ ⚠ signposted
Level, grass site with bushes set in meadowland on coast, adjacent to Kessingland beach and cliffs. Direct access to A12 London road via B1437. 3acres 68pitches 100static
Etr–last Sat in Sep must book peak periods last arrival 23.59hrs last departure 12.00hrs 4 22wc lit all night 1cdp 24 14washbasins hc 12 hc 4⊙ warden (2wash, 2spin, 1dry, 2iron) calor gas camping gaz toilet fluid cafe ☎ ⊞ licensed club stables cinema launderette pub
68 £2.50 or 68 £2.50 awnings
►► **Denes Holiday Village** *(TM539861)*
☎Lowestoft 740636
1 ❶ ⚠ signposted
Level, grass and gravel site set in meadowland with direct access to sea and beach. 4acres 90pitches 200static
10 May–20 Sep rsApr–9 May & 21–30 Sep must book last arrival 22.00hrs last departure 10.00hrs 3 16wc lit all night 1cdp

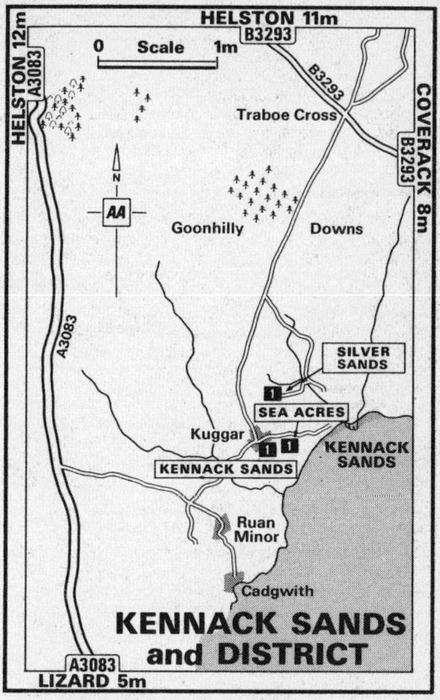

All sites listed under: Kennack Sands

washbasins hc hc hc ⊙ (wash, spin, dry) iron games room CTV calor gas camping gaz toilet fluid cafe restaurant licensed bar ☎ ⊞ licensed club children's playground (hairdressing) (sauna) & clock golf
90 £2–£2.80 or 90 £2–£2.80 or 90▲£2–£2.80 awnings
►► **Heathland Caravan Park** *(TM530873)*
London Rd ☎Lowestoft 740337
3 ❷ ⚠ signposted
Level, grass site with mature trees and bushes set in meadowland with direct access to sea and beach. Direct access to A12, Lowestoft road via B1437. 1acre 20pitches 180static
Apr–Oct must book peak periods last arrival 22.00hrs 10 late arrivals enclosure 37wc lit all night 1cdp washbasins hc central hot water hc ⊙ warden spin iron cold storage calor gas paraffin toilet fluid ☎ ⊞ children's playground & private beach stables cinema launderette pub
20 £2.50 or 20 £2.50 (awnings)

KILKHAMPTON Cornwall Map 2 SS21
►► **Easthorn Caravan & Camping Park** *(SS260110)* ☎235
1 ❷ ⚠
Small rural campsite situated adjacent to non-working farm. Ideally positioned for touring Devon and Cornwall. In village centre follow B3254 Launceston road for approx. ¾m. 2acres 19pitches
Apr–Oct must book last arrival 21.00hrs last departure 10.00hrs 4 individual pitches late arrivals enclosure 5wc lit all night 1cdp (6washbasins hc, central hot water) 2 hc 4⊙ warden (dry) games room (cold storage) calor gas, camping gaz, toilet fluid ⊞ children's playground, take-away meals, badminton & volley ball stables launderette pub
19 £1.75–£2.50 or 19 £1.75–£2.50 or 19▲£1.75–£2.50 (awnings)

KINGSNORTH Kent Map 5 TR03
►►► **Broad Hembury Farm** *(TR009387)*
Steeds Ln ☎Ashford (Kent) 20859
1 ❶ ⚠ signposted
This is a small farm site surrounded by sheep grazing land and high hedges. It is well secluded from the B2070 and approx. 4m from

centre of Ashford. 5acres 55pitches 25static Apr–Oct rsMar must book peak periods 7⛟ individual pitches 16wc lit all night ⛟ 8washbasins hc ⛆hc 3⊙ warden iron games room TV (cold storage) calor gas camping gaz ⊞ children's playground ⛟ ⊖ stables ♘ cinema ⛟ launderette pub 55⛟£2.40 or 55⛟£2.40 or 55▲£2.40 awnings

KINNERLEY Salop Map 7 SJ32
▶▶▶ Cranberry Moss Camping & Caravan Park *(SJ361214)* ☎Nesscliffe 444
2 ❸ ⚠ signposted
Part level, part sloping site with a variety of trees. Direct access to A5 Shrewsbury–Llangollen road. 4acres 60pitches Apr–Sep rsOct must book peak periods last departure 12.00hrs 3⛟ late arrivals enclosure 8wc lit all night 1cdp (6washbasins hc, ⛆hc) 2⊙ (1spin, iron) cold storage calor gas camping gaz toilet fluid ☎ ⊞ children's playground ⛟ ⊖ pub
60⛟£1.65 or 60⛟£1.65 or 60▲£1.45 awnings ltr

KIRKBY-IN-FURNESS Cumbria Map 7 SD28
▶▶▶ *Longlands Caravan Park* *(SD239836)* ☎342
1 ❶ ⚠ signposted
Part level, part sloping site with bushes. Overlooks Duddon Sands: 1m NE of village off A595. 2acres 30pitches Mar–Oct last arrival 23.00hrs last departure 12.00hrs 2⛟ wc lit all night 1cdp washbasins hc central hot water ⛆hc ⊙ calor gas toilet fluid ⊞ ⛟ ⊖ ♘ cinema ⛟ pub
30⛟ or 30⛟ or 30▲

KIRKBY THORE Cumbria Map 12 NY62
▶ *Low Moor Caravan Site* *(NY624259)* ☎231
1 ❶ ⚠
Part level, part sloping, grass site, 7m SE of Penrith on A66. 1½acres 25static Apr–Oct 3⛟ ⊛ 6wc 2cdp 5washbasins hc 2central hot water (2⛆hc) 2⊙ warden dry, iron cold storage calor gas camping gaz ⛟
10⛟ 5⛟ ▲ (awnings) ltr

KNOCK Cumbria Map 12 NY62
▶ Silver Band Caravan Park *(NY681269)* ☎Kirkby Thore 218
2 ❶ ⚠ signposted
Small, unspoilt site beneath hillside under Cross Fell, overlooking Eden Valley. Site is situated 5m N of Appleby off A66 Appleby–Penrith road, near Kirkby Thore. ½acre 11pitches 1static Mar–Sep rs Nov–Feb must book peak periods last arrival 22.00hrs last departure 12.00hrs 1⛟ individual pitches 4wc lit all night 1cdp washbasins hc (⛆hc) ⊙ calor gas camping gaz paraffin toilet fluid ⊞ off licence & garage facilities ⛟ ⊖ stables ♘ ⛟ launderette pub
11⛟£1.50 or 11⛟£1.50 (awnings)

LADRAM BAY Devon Map 3 SY08
▶ Ladram Bay Caravan Site ☎Colaton Raleigh 68398
2 ❶ ⚠
A large caravan site with many static vans. A separate camping area is set on terraced grounds in wooded surroundings. The site overlooks a rocky shingle beach. 9acres 272pitches 398static May–Sep rsApr no bookings last arrival 20.00hrs last departure 10.00hrs ⊛ wc (washbasins hc, ⛆hc, ⊙) (wash, spin, dry, iron) calor gas camping gaz cafe restaurant licensed bar ☎ ⊞ pub private beach ⛟ ⊖ ⛟ ⛟ launderette
22⛟fr£2.50 or 22⛟fr£2 250▲fr£1.75 (awnings)

LALEHAM Surrey Map 4 TQ06
►► **Laleham Park Camping Site**
(TQ052684) Apply to: Alannah, Abbey Dr, Laleham, Staines, Middx ☎Staines 54162
[1] ❶
Quiet camping site set in a field among trees beside a peaceful stretch of the River Thames.
5acres 150pitches
Apr–Sep must book for caravans & motor vans must book peak periods for tents last arrival dusk 3♨ Ⓐ 15wc lit all night 1cdp washbasins hc (⋒hc) ⊙ warden ⊞ children's playground ⇔ ♘ ⇝ cinema ⊱ launderette ♔ pub
15⊕£1.20 or 15⊜£1.20 135▲80–90p no awnings

LAMORNA Cornwall Map 2 SW42
See St Buryan sketch map.
► **Boleigh Farm Camp Site** *(SW435249)*
☎St Buryan 305
[1] ❶ △
4m S of Penzance on B3315. 1½acres 30pitches
Mar–Oct must book last arrival 22.00hrs last departure 10.00hrs 3♨ 3wc lit all night 1cdp 4washbasins hc (1central hot water) 1⋒hc 1⊙ cold storage calor gas camping gaz ⊞ mobile shop
15⊕£2 or 15⊜£2 15▲£2 (awnings) ltr

LANDRAKE Cornwall Map 2 SX36
►►► ***Dolbeare Caravan Park*** *(SX364616)*
St Ive Rd ☎332
[2] ❷ △ signposted
A mainly level grass site with trees and bushes set in meadowland. 4acres 50pitches
1 wk before Etr–Oct must book peak periods last departure 12.00hrs 3♨ individual pitches late arrivals enclosure 6wc lit all night 1cdp (8washbasins hc) (4⋒hc) 2⊙ cold storage calor gas camping gaz toilet fluid ⊞ ♔ ⇔ stables pub
50⊕ or 50⊜ or 50▲ (awnings)

LANLIVERY Cornwall Map 2 SX05
►►► **Powderham Castle Caravan & Tourist Park** *(SX083593)*
☎ Lostwithiel 872277
[2] ❷ △ signposted
Set amongst woodland in hilly country, this level and grassy site has mature trees and bushes. 8acres 70pitches 34static
Etr–Oct must book peak periods last arrival 21.30hrs 14♨ individual pitches Ⓐ late arrivals enclosure 15wc lit all night 1cdp ⊕ 13washbasins hc (central hot water, ⋒hc) ⊙ warden (1wash, 1spin, 1dry, 1iron) cold storage calor gas camping gaz ⊞ children's playground, battery charging & boat mooring mobile shop ⇔ stables ♘ ⇝ ⊱ launderette pub
70⊕£2 or 70⊜£2 or 70▲£2 (awnings)

LAUNCESTON Cornwall Map 2 SX38
► **Travadlock Hall Holiday Park**
☎ Coads Green 392
[2] ❷ △ signposted
A mainly level grassy site with trees and saplings situated amidst woodland and meadowland. 6m SW on A30 thence B3257 and unclassified road. ½acre 18pitches 28static
Mar–Oct must book peak periods last departure 15.00hrs 2♨ individual pitches Ⓐ 3wc lit all night 1cdp ⊕ washbasins hc central hot water (⋒hc) ⊙ warden (wash, dry, iron) ⌓ (⊛) games room (cold storage) restaurant ☎ ⊞ licensed club & children's playground ♔ ⇔ stables ♘ ⊱ launderette pub
10⊕£2–£3.50 or 10⊜£2–£3.50 8▲£2–£3.50 (awnings)

LEBBERSTON North Yorkshire Map 8 TA08
See Scarborough sketch map.
►►► **Lebberston Caravan Park**
(TA080821) ☎ Scarborough 582254
[2] ❷ △
A part level and part sloping grass site with saplings and bushes set in meadowland. Off A165 Filey–Scarborough road. 7½acres 125pitches
6 May–Sep rsMay day–Spring Bank Hol must book peak periods last arrival 22.00hrs last departure 12.00hrs 6♨ individual pitches 24wc lit all night 2cdp washbasins hc ⋒hc ⊙ calor gas ⊞ children's playground mobile shop ⇔ stables ⇝ cinema ⊱ launderette pub
125⊕£1.50 or 125⊜£1.50 (awnings)

LEEDSTOWN near Hayle, Cornwall
Map 2 SW63
See Praa Sands sketch map.
►►► **Calloose Farm Caravan Park**
(SW597352) ☎431
[2] ❶ △ signposted
A level and grassy site with bushes, set in hilly country not far from river. Follow B3302 from 'Duke of Leeds' public house in Leedstown centre for approx. ½m. 5acres 78pitches 12static
Etr–Oct must book peak periods last arrival 21.00hrs last departure 11.00hrs 9♨ individual pitches 15wc lit all night 1cdp 14washbasins hc 2central hot water (4⋒hc) 4⊙ warden iron cold storage calor gas camping gaz toilet fluid ☎ ⊞ baby sitting ♔ ⇔ stables ♘ cinema ⊱ launderette pub
78⊕£2.11 or 78⊜£2.11 or 78▲£2.11 (awnings)

LEISTON Suffolk Map 5 TM46
►► ***King George's Caravan Park***
(TG454621) King George's Av ☎830129
[2] ❸ △ signposted
A level, grass and gravel site with mature trees and bushes set in the urban area with access to main road. 3acres 18pitches 24static
Apr–Oct must book Bank Hols last arrival 21.00hrs last departure 17.00hrs 1♨ individual pitches 45wc 1cdp 4washbasins hc central hot water (8⋒hc) calor gas ☎ ⊞ ♔ ⇔ stables ♘ ⇝ cinema ⊱ launderette
18⊕

LELANT DOWNS Cornwall Map 2 SW53
See St Ives sketch map.
►► **Sunny Meadow Caravan Park**
(SW519368) ☎ Hayle 752243
[2] ❷ △
Level, grass site with varied trees and bushes, set in wood and meadowland, 1½m from nearest beach, adjacent to river and near A3074 St Ives road. ¼acre 6pitches 6static
Apr–Oct must book last arrival 21.00hrs last departure 11.00hrs 1♨ individual pitches 4wc lit all night 1cdp 4washbasins hc (2⋒hc) 1⊙ (1wash, 1spin, 1dry, 1iron) cold storage calor gas camping gaz ⊞ ♔ ⇔ stables ♘ ⇝ cinema ⊱ launderette pub
6⊕£2.75 or 6⊜£2.75 (awnings)

LEVENS Cumbria Map 7 SD48
►► ***Sampool Caravan Site*** *(SD478843)*
☎ Witherslack 265
[1] ❶ △
This level and open site is located off A590, ½m from its junction with the A6. 1½acres 30pitches 195static
May–Sep rsMar & Apr must book Bank Hols 9♨ 40wc lit all night 4cdp washbasins hc central hot water ⋒hc ⊙ cold storage calor gas ☎ ⊞ ♔
30⊕ or 30⊜ ltr

LEYBURN North Yorkshire Map 7 SE19
See sketch map.
►► **Yorkshire Dales Caravan Park**
(SE125904) Harmby ☎ Wensleydale 23511
[1] ❶ △ signposted
A level, stony site with mature trees and bushes situated in hill and moorland country. 1m E of Leyburn on A684. 1acre 10pitches 140static
Mar–Oct must book last arrival 22.00hrs last departure 12.00hrs 10♨ 28wc lit all night 3cdp washbasins hc central hot water (⋒hc) ⊙ iron calor gas ☎ ⊞ ⇔ ⊱ launderette pub
10⊕£2 or 10⊜£2 (awnings) ltr

LITTLE TORRINGTON Devon Map 2 SS41
►►► **Smytham Caravan & Campsite**
(SS493168) ☎Torrington 2110
[2] ❶ △ signposted
A small site situated in a secluded wooded area in the grounds of an old manor house adjacent to A386. Access is by a good approach road with ramps. 2acres 25pitches 25static
15 Mar–Oct must book Jul & Aug 6♨ Ⓐ 9wc

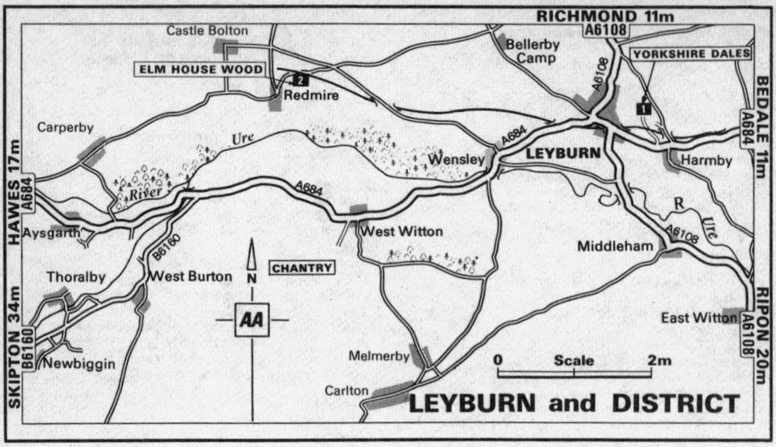

Sites listed under: **1** Leyburn **2** Redmire

1cdp washbasins hc (⛆hc) ⊙ iron ⛴ games room (cold storage) calor gas camping gaz paraffin ☎ ⊞ children's playground ⛱ ⊖ stables ♪ cinema ⛵ launderette pub
25🚐£1.75 or 25🚗£1.75 or 25▲£1.75 (awnings)

LOCKING Avon Map 3 ST35
► Oak Tree & West End Caravan Park
☎Banwell 822529
2 ❶ ⚠ signposted
A secluded site with views of Weston-Super-Mare and surrounding countryside. Off A371 Wells road. 10acres 80pitches
Mar–Oct must book peak periods
last arrival 22.30hrs last departure 12.00hrs
7✿ individual pitches ⊗ 15wc lit all night 1cdp (10washbasins hc) (4⛆hc) 2⊙ (wash, dry) iron (cold storage) calor gas camping gaz toilet fluid ☎ ⊞ children's playground battery charger ⛱ ⊖ stables ♪ ⛵ cinema ⛵ launderette pub
80🚐£1.85 or 80🚗£1.85 or 80▲£1.85 (awnings)

LONDON (GREATER)
For details of other sites in the vicinity of London, see also Chigwell (14m), Laleham (19m), West Drayton (15m).

Abbey Wood SE2 Map 5 TQ47
►►► Co-operative Woods Camping & Caravan Site *(TQ473784)* Federation Rd
☎01-310 2233
2 ❶ ⚠ signposted
Well secluded and pleasantly wooded site, situated in quiet residential area on the outskirts of London. Easy access to the city from the British Rail (Southern Region) station at Abbey Wood. 9acres 300pitches
All year must book for tents last arrival 22.00hrs last departure 12.00hrs 8✿ ⊗ late arrivals enclosure no cars by tents 30wc lit all night 3cdp (⊜) 42washbasins hc 14⛆hc 12⊙ warden (1spin, 1dry, 2iron) (cold storage) calor gas camping gaz toilet fluid ☎ ⊞ off licence ⛱ ⊖ stables ♪ cinema launderette pub
150🚐£3.89 50🚗£3.78 100▲£4.42 (awnings)

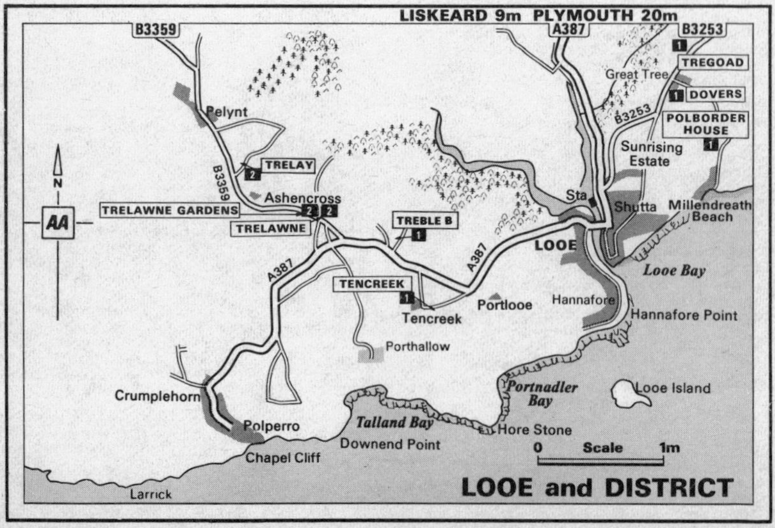

Sites listed under: **1** Looe **2** Pelynt

Edmonton N9 Map 4 TQ39
►► **Picketts Lock Centre** *(TQ360945)*
☎01-803 4756
1 3 ⚠ signposted
Level, grass site with young trees set in meadowland in London, with direct access to the River Lee and the main road. All year rsSep–May 5acres 200pitches
Must book peak periods last arrival 22.00hrs last departure 12.00hrs 4 12wc lit all night 1cdp washbasins hc (central hot water) (hc) warden (, , games room)
calor gas camping gaz cafe restaurant ☎ ⊞ licensed club & children's playground
cinema launderette pub
75£2.50 or 75£2.50 125▲£2.50 awnings

LONDON APPRENTICE Cornwall Map 2 SX05
See St Austell sketch map.
► ***Molingey Campsite*** *(SX009502)*
☎St Austell 3533
2 2 ⚠ signposted
A small, well-secluded, level site located on B3273 S of St Austell. Ideal situation for visiting Fowey, Mevagissey, Pentewan and surrounding district. 2½acres 40static
Apr–Oct 7 12wc lit all night (8washbasins hc) (6hc) 1 (wash, iron)
calor gas camping gaz ⊞ stables launderette
60 or 60 or 60▲

LONG DOWNS Cornwall Map 2 SW73
See Falmouth sketch map.
► **Calamankey Farm** *(SW745342)*
☎Stithians 860314
1 1 ⚠
This is a farm situated on A394. Falmouth and Helston are in close proximity and the whole of the Land's End Peninsula can be explored from this site. 2½acres 26pitches
Apr–Oct last arrival 21.00hrs last departure 12.00hrs 9 7wc (1hc) calor gas camping gaz ⊞ stables
26£1.20 or 26£1.40 or 26▲£1.40 awnings

LOOE Cornwall Map 2 SX25
See sketch map.
►►►► **'Treble B' Holiday Centre** Polperro Rd ☎2425
3 2 ⚠ signposted
A site situated on undulating high ground with pleasant country views. Comprises three fields on mainly level ground and has tarmac internal roads. 20acres 450pitches 30static
Mid May–Sep rsEtr–mid May must book last departure 12.00hrs 35 late arrivals enclosure 95wc lit all night 4cdp washbasins hc central hot water (hc) warden (wash, spin, dry, iron) games room TV cold storage calor gas camping gaz toilet fluid cafe restaurant ☎ ⊞ licensed club & children's playground battery charger stables cinema launderette pub
450£1.50–£4 or 450£1.50–£4
450▲£1.50–£4 (awnings)

►►► **Polborder House** ☎Widegates 265
3 3 ⚠ signposted
Mainly level, grass site with mixed trees and bushes, set in meadowland, 2½m E of Looe, with access to the sea, beach, river and main road. 3acres 34pitches 3static
Apr–Oct must book peak periods last arrival 23.00hrs last departure 11.00hrs 3 individual pitches 14wc lit all night 1cdp 12washbasins hc (central hot water) (8hc) (1wash, 1dry, 1iron) (cold storage) calor gas camping gaz ⊞ stables launderette pub
34£2.20–£2.80 or 34£2.20–£2.80
▲£2.20–£2.80 (awnings)

►►► ***Tencreek Caravan and Camping Park***
☎ St Austell 61897
2 2 ⚠ signposted
Gently sloping, grass site set in meadowland adjacent to sea, sandy beach and A387 Looe road. 20acres 250pitches 42static
Mid May–mid Sep rsEtr–mid May & mid Sep–30 Sep must book mid May–mid Sep last arrival 18.00hrs last departure 10.00hrs

individual pitches Ⓐ wc lit all night 2cdp washbasins hc central hot water (🚿hc) ⊙ (wash, spin, iron) games room (11TV) calor gas camping gaz crazy golf children's playground live entertainment nightly cafe licensed bar ☎ ⊞ ⛳ ⊖ stables ♂ ✈ cinema ⛵ launderette pub
🚐 🚌 ▲ rates on application ltr
▶▶ Dovers Camping Camp ☎2757
② ❷ △ signposted
Partly level and partly sloping, grass site with mixed trees, set in hilly meadowland adjacent to B3253. 1½m E of Looe. 15acres 285pitches
Apr–Oct must book last arrival 22.00hrs last departure 11.00hrs 17⛺ individual pitches 50wc lit all night (washbasins hc, central hot water, 🚿hc) ⊙ (wash, spin, dry, iron, cold storage) calor gas camping gaz toilet fluid ☎ ⊞ children's playground ⛳ ⊖ stables ♂ ✈ ⛵ launderette pub
100🚐£2 or 100🚌£2 185▲£2 awnings
▶ Tregoad Caravan & Camping Park *(SX279573)* St Martin ☎2718
① ❶ △ signposted
The site has fine sea and rural views and is a good base for touring Cornwall. 1m NE of Looe on B3253. 7acres 150pitches 2static
Spring Bank Hol–Oct rs Apr no bookings last departure 10.30hrs 15⛺ Ⓐ 20wc lit all night 1cdp 10washbasins hc (2central hot water, 5🚿hc) 3⊙ (1wash, 1spin, 1dry, 2iron) games room (cold storage) calor gas camping gaz ☎ ⊞ (licensed club) children's playground ⛳ ⊖ stables ♂ ✈ ⛵ launderette pub
65🚐 10🚌 75▲ rates on application awnings

LOSTWITHIEL Cornwall Map 2 SX15
***▶ Downend Camp Site** (SX117598)*
☎872363
② ❶ △
Level, grass site with young trees and bushes, set in hilly meadowland, adjacent to A390. 2acres 26pitches 3static
May–Sep rsOct–Apr must book Aug 2⛺ 6wc lit all night (3washbasins hc) (2🚿hc) ⊙ cold storage calor gas camping gaz paraffin toilet fluid ⊞ ⛳ ⊖ stables ⛵
10🚐 10🚌 6▲

LOTHERSDALE North Yorkshire Map 7 SD94
▶▶ Springs Caravan Park *(SD944451)*
Springs Farm ☎ Cross Hills 32533
① ❷ △ signposted
Set on rising ground in rural setting overlooking a small lake. Well signposted from A6068 at Cross Hills. 3acres 30pitches 7static
Mar–Oct last departure 18.00hrs 2⛺ 5wc 1cdp 6washbasins hc 2🚿hc 1⊙ warden calor gas wash up sinks ⊖ stables ⛵ launderette ⛳ pub
20🚐£1.70 5🚌£1.45 5▲£1.70 (awnings) ltr

LOWER KELSALL Cheshire Map 7 SJ56
▶▶ Northwood Hall Camping Site *(SJ516685)* ☎ Kelsall 51305
② ❶ △ signposted
Pleasantly situated in countryside with trees and shrubs, on gently sloping ground. Short distance from village. 2½acres 20pitches
Mar–Oct must book last arrival 21.00hrs last departure 12.00hrs 2⛺ individual pitches 6wc lit all night 1cdp 4washbasins hc 1central hot water (2🚿hc) ⊙ calor gas camping gaz toilet fluid ⊞ ⊖ ⛳
20🚐£1.70 or 20🚌£1.70 awnings ltr

LOWESTOFT Suffolk Map 5 TM59
▶ North Denes Caravan Site *(TM553946)*
North Denes ☎3197
① ❶ △
A level, sandy and grassy site near the sea. A12 between Lowestoft and Gt Yarmouth turn right into Whapload Road. 20acres 625pitches
Apr–mid Oct must book for caravans no booking for motorvans or tents 46⛺ individual pitches for caravans Ⓐ 64wc lit all night 4cdp 42washbasins hc 26🚿hc 12⊙ (2wash, 2spin, 2dry) 3iron ✂ calor gas camping gaz cafe restaurant licensed bar ☎ ⊞ ⛳ ⊖ stables ✈ cinema ⛵ launderette pub
25🚐£2 300🚌£1.75 or 300▲£2 (awnings) ltr

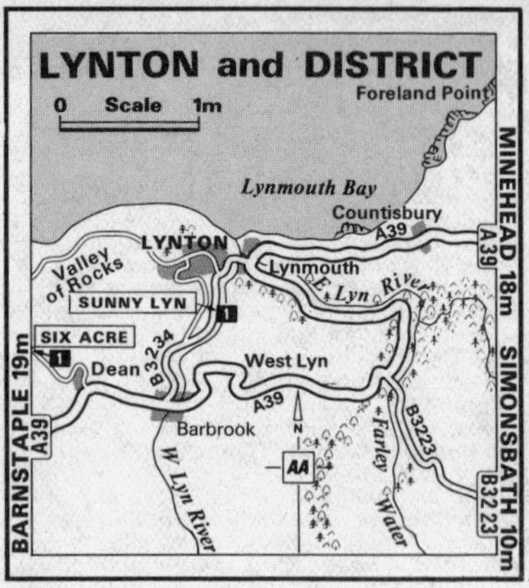

All sites lusted under: Lynton

LYDFORD Devon Map 2 SX58
▶▶ Pulborough Farm Caravan & Camping Park *(SX512853)* The Croft ☎275
② ❸ △ signposted
Site on nearly level ground, looking towards the western slopes of Dartmoor at the edge of the village. 4acres 70pitches
Etr–Sep must book mid Jun–Aug last arrival 23.00hrs 9⛺ individual pitches Ⓐ 18wc lit all night 1cdp 12washbasins hc 1central hot water 8🚿hc 2⊙ (2wash, 2spin, 1dry, 1iron) (1cold storage) calor gas camping gaz paraffin toilet fluid ⊞ children's playground & wash up sinks ⊖ stables ⛵ ⛳ pub
70🚐£2.30 or 70🚌£2.30 or 70▲£2.30 awnings ltr

LYNEAL near Ellesmere Salop Map 7 SJ43
▶▶▶ Fernwood Caravan Park *(SJ445346)*
☎ Bettisfield 221
② ❷ △ signposted
Set in wooded country, this partly level and sloping grassy site with mature trees is not far from canal, 4m SE of Ellesmere off B5063. 50pitches 150static
Apr–Oct must book public hols 14⛺ 27wc lit all night 1cdp washbasins hc (🚿hc) ⊙ warden (spin, iron) calor gas camping gaz toilet fluid ☎ ⊞ children's playground ⛳ ⊖ stables ⛵ pub
50🚐£1.70 or 50🚌£1.70 (awnings) ltr

LYNTON Devon Map 3 SS74
See sketch map.
▶▶▶ Sunny Lyn Caravan Site *(SS719486)*
Lynbridge ☎3384
② ❷ △ signposted
Part level, part sloping site in wooded combe; sea less than a mile away. 1½acres 32pitches 31static
Spring Bank Hol–Sep rsEtr–mid May no bookings last arrival 20.00hrs last departure 12.00hrs 8⛺ Ⓐ wc lit all night 1cdp 🚐 washbasins hc central hot water 🚿hc ⊙ wash spin iron games room CTV cold storage calor gas camping gaz paraffin ☎ ⊞ fishing ⛳ ⊖ stables ✈ cinema launderette pub
7🚐£3.36 or 7🚌£2.85 25▲£3.18 (awnings)
▶▶ Six Acre Caravan Park *(SS701483)*
Six Acre Farm ☎3224
② ❷ △ signposted
A level grassy site, with bushes set below hill. The countryside around is well-wooded. 2m SW of Lynton off A39 Barnstaple–Minehead road. 4½acres 105pitches
15 Mar–15 Nov must book peak periods last arrival 23.00hrs last departure 12.00hrs 7⛺ individual pitches 21wc lit all night 1cdp 14washbasins hc (2central hot water, 10🚿hc) 4⊙ (cold storage) calor gas ☎ ⊞ wash up sinks ⊖ stables ⛵ launderette ⛳ pub
105🚐£1.90 or 105🚌£1.90 or 105▲£1.90 awnings

LYTCHETT MINSTER Dorset Map 3 SY99
►►►South Lytchett Manor Caravan Park
☎622577
2 ❶ ⚠
A partly level and sloping site set in meadowland, adjacent to A35. 10acres 92pitches
Apr–15 Oct must book peak periods last arrival 22.00hrs last departure 11.00hrs 17⛟ individual pitches ⊛ 23wc lit all night 1cdp washbasins hc central hot water ⛆hc ⊙ warden (wash, spin, iron) CTV (cold storage) calor gas camping gaz toilet fluid ⊞ children's playground & take away food ⛼ ⊖ stables ⛳ ✈ cinema ⛵ launderette pub
60⛟£2.15 or 60⛟£2.15 32▲£2.15 (awnings) ltr

LYTHAM ST ANNES Lancashire Map 7 SD32
►►►►Eastham Hall Caravan Site
(SD379291) Saltcotes Rd ☎ Lytham 737907
2 ❷ ⚠ signposted
A level secluded site, trees and hedgerows, standing in rural surroundings 2m NE of Lytham. 18acres 250pitches 175static
Mar–Oct must book peak periods last arrival 22.00hrs last departure 15.00hrs 20⛟ individual pitches late arrivals enclosure 62wc lit all night 8cdp 48washbasins hc 6central hot water (24⛆hc) 14⊙ warden cold storage calor gas camping gaz toilet fiuid ☎ ⊞ children's playground ⛼ ⊖ stables ⛳ ✈ cinema ⛵ launderette pub
230⛟£2.50 20⛟£2.50 ltr

MABLETHORPE Lincolnshire Map 9 TF58
►►►►Golden Sands Estates *(TF501861)*
Quebec Rd ☎2671
1 ❷ ⚠
A level, grassy site near the sea and beach. 1m W of town off A1031 Cleethorpes road. 10acres 200pitches 1750static
26 May–17 Sep rsEtr–25 May & 18 Sep–1 Oct no bookings last departure 12.00hrs 20⛟ 40wc lit all night 3cdp washbasins hc ⛆hc ⊙ warden (6wash, 6dry, ⊡, ⛴, games room) TV calor gas toilet fluid cafe restaurant licensed bar ☎ ⊞ (licensed club & children's playground) ⛼ ⊖ stables ⛳ ✈ cinema ⛵ launderette pub
200⛟£2.50 (awnings) ltr
►►Mermaid Caravan & Tenting Site
(TF505843) Seaholme Rd
1 ❶ ⚠ signposted
A level and grassy site, ½m SW of Mablethorpe. 2acres 268pitches
15 Mar–20 Oct no bookings last departure 10.00hrs 4⛟ ⊛ 40wc lit all night 2cdp washbasins hc central hot water ⛆hc ⊙ calor gas camping gaz toilet fluid cafe licensed bar ⛼ ⊖ stables ⛳ ⛵ launderette pub
28⛟£2 or 28⛟£1.25 240▲£1.50
►Highfield Camping & Caravan Site
(TF497846) 120 Church Ln ☎2374
2 ❷ ⚠
Level, mainly grassy site situated off main road about one mile from sea. 6acres 120pitches
Mar–Sep must book peak periods last departure 14.00hrs 1⛟ ⊛ 12wc lit all night 1cdp 8washbasins hc 2central hot water (2⛆hc) 2⊙ calor gas camping gaz toilet fluid ⊞ ⛼ ⊖ stables ⛳ ✈ ⛵ launderette pub
40⛟£1.50 or 40⛟£1.20 80▲£1.20 (awnings) ltr

MALBOROUGH Devon Map 3 SX74
►►►Alston Farm Camping & Caravanning Site *(SX720409)* ☎ Galmpton 260
2 ❶ ⚠ signposted
Partly level and sloping grass site with mixed vegetation, set in hilly wood and meadowland adjacent to river estuary with cliff scenery to the south. Near to A381 Kingsbridge—Salcombe road. ⛒ 9½acres 210pitches 40static
Etr–Sep rsOct no bookings last departure 12.00hrs 18⛟ individual pitches caravans only ⊛ 30wc lit all night 1cdp (42washbasins hc) central hot water (14⛆hc) 4⊙ (iron) cold storage calor gas camping gaz toilet fluid ⊞ ⛼ ⊖ stables ⛳ ✈ ⛵ launderette
75⛟fr£1.50 5⛟£1.30 130▲£1.30 (awnings)

MARKET RASEN Lincolnshire Map 8 TF18
►►Trax Campsite *(TF123883)*
Market Rasen Racecourse, Legsby Rd
2 ❷ ⚠ signposted
Mainly level, grass site set in meadowland. 1m SE; from town centre leave by A631 Louth road and turn right into Legsby road. 3acres 60pitches
23 May–13 Sep except 2–4 Aug no bookings last arrival 22.30hrs last departure 15.00hrs 1⛟ 18wc lit all night 1cdp 10washbasins hc 1central hot water 4⛆hc 1⊙ warden TV ☎ ⊞ children's playground games area free racing for campers 16 & 23 Aug ⛼ ⊖ stables ⛳ launderette
60⛟£2–£2.35 or 60⛟£2–£2.35 or 60▲£2–£2.35 awnings

MARTIN MILL Kent Map 5 TR34
See Dover sketch map.
►►►Hawthorn Caravan & Camping Site
(TR342464) ☎ Dover 852658
2 ❷ ⚠ signposted
This pleasant rural site is screened by young trees and hedgerows. Included within its grounds are a rose garden and woods. 11acres 160pitches 130static
Mar–Oct no bookings 25⛟ ⊛ late arrivals enclosure 32wc lit all night 2cdp ⛟ 42washbasins hc 3central hot water 20⛆hc 12⊙ warden (cold storage) calor gas camping gaz toilet fluid ☎ ⊞ ⛼ ⊖ stables ⛳ ✈ ⛵ launderette pub
53⛟£2.60 or 53⛟£2.60 107▲£2.60 awnings

MATLOCK Derbyshire Map 8 SK36
►►Packhorse Farm *(SK323617)*
Matlock Moor ☎2781
2 ❷ ⚠
A level, grassy site set amidst hills and moorland. 2acres 15pitches
Mar–Oct must book public hols 2⛟ individual pitches ⊛ 3wc lit all night 1cdp washbasins hc central hot water ⊙ ⊞ ⊖ stables ⛳ cinema ⛵ launderette ⛼ pub
15⛟£1.25 or 15⛟£1.25 6▲£1.25 (awnings)

MAWGAN PORTH Cornwall Map 2 SW86
See Newquay sketch map.
►►►Gluvian Caravan & Camping Site
☎ St Mawgan 373
2 ❷ ⚠ signposted
Part level, part sloping, sheltered grass site with mature trees set in meadowland, near the sea and sandy beach. Stream adjacent to camping field. 4½acres 96pitches 36static
Apr–Oct bookings advisable last arrival 21.30hrs last departure 12.00hrs 9⛟ individual pitches 20wc lit all night 4cdp 30washbasins hc 10⛆hc 5⊙ warden (wash, spin, dry, iron, cold storage) calor gas camping gaz toilet fluid ☎ ⊞ children's playground hairdryers ⛼ ⊖ stables ⛳ ⛵ launderette pub
38⛟£1.40–£3.50 or 38⛟£1.40–£3.50 58▲£1.40–£3.50 awnings
►►Trevarrian Holiday Park
☎ St Mawgan 381
2 ❶ ⚠ signposted
Level, grassy site set amongst Cornish Downland. Adjacent to sea and river. 5acres 120pitches
Etr–Oct must book last arrival 19.00hrs last departure 10.00hrs 8⛟ individual pitches 30wc lit all night 1cdp (23washbasins hc, 3central hot water, 1⛴hc, 12⛆hc) 3⊙ warden (1wash, 1spin, 1dry, 1iron) ⊡ calor gas camping gaz paraffin toilet fluid ☎ ⊞ children's playground ⛼ ⊖ stables ⛳ ✈ ⛵ launderette pub
120⛟£2.10 or 120⛟£1.94 or 120▲£2.10 (awnings)

MEALSGATE Cumbria Map 11 NY24
►►►Larches Caravan Park *(NY205415)*
☎ Low Ireby 379
2 ❷ ⚠ signposted
Set in wooded rural surroundings on the fringe of the Lake District National Park. Situated on the A595 Carlisle–Cockermouth road. 4acres 73pitches 177static

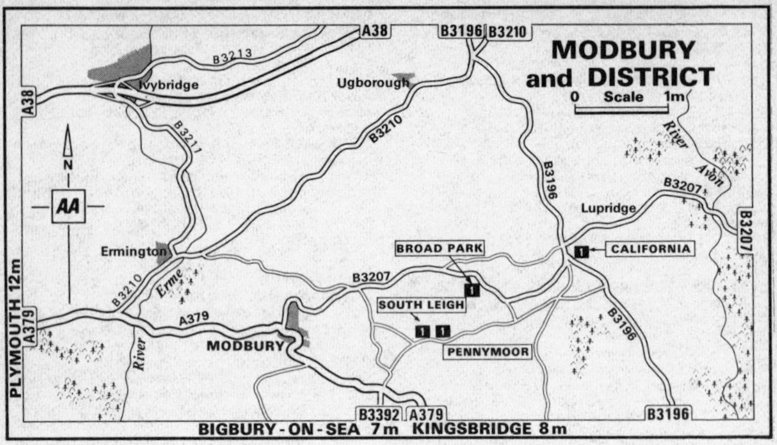

All sites listed under: Modbury

Mar–Oct must book peak periods last arrival 23.50hrs last departure 12.00hrs 6⛲ Ⓐ late arrivals enclosure 18wc lit all night 1cdp 12washbasins hc 8♨hc 4⊙ (1wash, 1spin, 1dry) ⛵ (games room) (cold storage) calor gas camping gaz toilet fluid ☎ ⊞ licensed club & children's playground ⛫ ⊖ ♿ ⊳ pub 73⊡£2 or 73⊟£1.50 or 73▲£2 (awnings) ltr

MIDDLETON Morecambe, Lancashire Map 7 SD45
See Morecambe sketch map.

►►► Hawthorn Camping Site *(SD415575)*
Carr Ln ☎ Heysham 52074
[2] ❶ △
Level grass site with trees and bushes set in woodland. Access to sea and beach at Middleton Sands. 6acres 70pitches
Etr–Sep must book 3⛲ 11wc lit all night 9washbasins hc 3♨hc 4⊙ calor gas camping gaz children's playground ⛫ ⊖ stables ♿ ⊷ ⊳ launderette pub
20⊟£1.40 50▲£1.40 awnings

► Melbreak Camp Site *(SD415584)*
Carr Ln ☎ Heysham 52430
[1] ❶ △
Small, simple site set in open countryside to the south of Morecambe. 1½acres
Apr–Sep booking advisable peak periods last arrival 22.00hrs last departure 12.00hrs 2⛲ Ⓐ 7wc lit all night 9washbasins hc (4♨hc) 2⊙ calor gas camping gaz ⊞ ⛫ ⊖ stables ♿ ⊳ launderette pub
50⊟£1.20 or 50▲£1.20 awnings

MINSTER (Thanet) Kent Map 5 TR36

►► Wayside Caravan Park *(TR319651)*
Foxborough Ln ☎ Thanet 821272
[3] ❶ △
Small, secluded site overlooking open farmland. Situated ½m from Minster and 2m from Pegwell Bay. ⊘ nc12 except overnight 10pitches 54static
Mar–Oct no bookings last arrival 21.00hrs last departure 12.00hrs 4⛲ individual pitches 7wc lit all night 1cdp ⊡ 6washbasins hc (3♨hc) 1⊙ warden (1iron) calor gas camping gaz ⊞ drying area ⊖ stables ♿ launderette ⛫ pub
10⊡£1.90 or 10⊟£1.90

MODBURY Devon Map 3 SX65
See sketch map.

►►► Broad Park Caravan Site *(SX690523)*
Higher East Leigh Farm ☎830256
[2] ❸ △ signposted
This site is in the heart of the South Hams in a rural setting, within striking distance of Salcombe, Thurlescombe and Bigbury Bay.
5acres 105pitches
Apr–1st Mon in Oct must book peak periods last arrival 22.00hrs last departure 11.00hrs 12⛲ individual pitches Ⓐ late arrivals enclosure 15wc 1cdp ⊡ washbasins hc central hot water (4♨hc) 2⊙ (spin, dry, iron) (cold storage) calor gas camping gaz toilet fluid ☎ ⊞ badminton & children's playground battery charger ⛫ ⊖ stables pub
75⊡£1.80–£2.20 or 75⊟£1.80–£2.20 30▲£1.80–£2.20 (awnings)

►►► California Caravan Park *(SX705530)* ☎ Gara Bridge 281
[2] ❷ △
This site slopes gently eastwards and is protected by high hedges around perimeter.
2acres 49pitches 1static
15 Mar–14 Nov must book peak periods last arrival 23.00hrs last departure 12.00hrs 7⛲ 12wc lit all night 2cdp 8washbasins hc 6♨hc 2⊙ (cold storage) calor gas camping gaz paraffin toilet fluid ⊞ children's playground ⛫ ⊖ stables ⊳ pub
49⊡£2 or 49⊟£2 (awnings)

►►► Pennymoor Camping & Caravan Park *(SX885516)* ☎542
[2] ❶ △ signposted
A grassy site with some bushes and hedges, situated in hilly woodland with moorland, nearby. 10m SE of Plymouth off A379. one dog per unit
7acres 155pitches 70static
15 Mar–14 Nov must book 8⛲ Ⓐ late arrivals enclosure 24wc lit all night 2cdp ⊡

19washbasins hc central hot water (14 hc)
4⊙ 1spin (1dry, 1iron) (cold storage) calor gas camping gaz toilet fluid ☎ ⊞ children's playground & take away meals stables pub
119 £1.20–£1.80 or 119 £1.10–£1.60
35▲£1.10–£1.60 (awnings)

►►► South Leigh Caravan Park *(SX682515)* ☎346
2 ❷ ⚠
Situated in the heart of the South Hams in rural surroundings. This site offers seclusion and protection provided by high hedges around perimeter. 4½acres 15pitches 67static
Spring Bank Hol–Sep rsEtr must book peak periods last departure 12.00hrs 10 26wc lit all night 1cdp (washbasins hc, central hot water, hc) ⊙ (wash, spin, dry, iron) (cold storage) calor gas camping gaz toilet fluid ☎ ⊞ licensed club & children's playground stables launderette pub
15 fr£1.80 or 15 fr£1.80 or 15▲fr£1.50 (awnings) ltr

MOLLAND Devon Map 3 SS82

►► Molland Caravan Park *(SS787264)*
Black Cock Hotel ☎ Bishops Nympton 297
2 ❷ ⚠ signposted
Mainly level site in hilly countryside within sight of Exmoor ¾m N of A361 Taunton–Barnstaple road at Coombsland New Cross. 7acres 65pitches
15 Mar–14 Nov must book peak periods last arrival 23.59hrs last departure 12.00hrs 4 15wc lit all night 1cdp washbasins hc central hot water hc ⊙ warden (wash, spin, dry, iron) games room cold storage calor gas cafe restaurant ☎ ⊞ licensed club, children's playground & sauna stables cinema launderette pub
45 £2.50 10 £2.25 10▲£2.50 (awnings)

MORECAMBE Lancashire Map 7 SD46
See sketch map.

►►►► Municipal Caravan Park
(SD436633) Westgate ☎412986
1 ❶ ⚠ signposted
This level, grassy site is situated in the urban area off the A589. 1½acres 45pitches 300static
Mar–Oct rsNov–Feb must book peak periods last arrival 22.00hrs. last departure 12.00hrs 23 individual pitches 48wc lit all night 2cdp 38washbasins hc 27 hc 12⊙ warden (2wash, 2dry, 2iron) calor gas ☎ ⊞ children's playground, wash up sinks, & points for hairdryers stables cinema launderette pub
45 £1.75–£2.50 or 45 £1.75–£2.50 no awnings

►►►► *Regent Caravan Park* *(SD438630)*
Westgate ☎413940
1 ❶ ⚠
A level, grass site with mature trees, set in urban area with direct access to main road.
2acres 36pitches 324static
Mid Mar–mid Oct must book peak periods last arrival 20.00hrs last departure 12.00hrs 25 individual pitches late arrivals enclosure 62wc lit all night 3cdp 40washbasins hc 36 hc 12⊙ warden (2wash, 1spin, 2dry) calor gas camping gaz toilet fluid cafe restaurant licensed bar ☎ ⊞ children's play area amusement arcade stables cinema launderette pub
36 £3 or 36 £3 no awnings

► Encee Caravan Park *(SD448633)*
Westgate ☎ Lancaster 68764
1 ❶ ⚠
Situated within urban area. ¾acre 20pitches 16static
All year must book last arrival 23.59hrs last departure 11.00hrs 4 8wc lit all night 1cdp washbasins hc hc ⊙ (wash, dry) cafe restaurant ⊞ children's playground stables cinema launderette pub
20 £2 or 20 £2 no awnings

MORTEHOE Devon Map 2 SS44
See Ilfracombe sketch map.

►►► Twitchen House & Mortehoe Caravan Park *(SS465448)* ☎ Woolacombe 476
2 ❶ ⚠ signposted
Part level, part sloping grass site with trees and bushes. Set in downland and wooded meadowland. 130pitches 295static
19 May–29 Sep rsEtr–18 May & 30 Sep–Oct must book peak periods last departure 10.00hrs 7 individual pitches (caravans) wc lit all night 1cdp 35washbasins hc (central hot water) 2 hc (32 hc) ⊙ (4wash, 6dry, 2iron) (games room) CTV calor gas camping gaz toilet fluid cafe restaurant ☎ ⊞ (licensed club) & children's playground stables cinema launderette pub
42 £2–£3.25 80 £1.50–£2.75 or 80▲£1.50–£2.75 (awnings)

► Easewell Farm *(SS465455)*
☎ Woolacombe 225
2 ❶ ⚠
A level, grassy site set in hilly country, adjacent to sea and shingle/rocky beach and rock viewpoint. last 2 wks July & Aug 18acres 250pitches
20 May–Sep rsApr–19 May & Oct must book peak periods last arrival 23.00hrs last departure 12.00hrs 6 24wc lit all night 1cdp 29washbasins hc (10 hc) 2⊙ (1spin, 1dry) 1iron games room TV calor gas camping gaz ⊞ children's playground stables cinema launderette pub
20 £2 230▲£2 awnings

► North Morte Farm Caravan & Camping Site *(SS461457)* North Morte
☎ Woolacombe 381
2 ❶ ⚠ signposted
Set amid moorland and downs, this level and grassy site is near the sea and beach. 15acres 200pitches 73static
Etr–Oct must book for caravans last arrival 23.00hrs last departure 10.00hrs 19 individual pitches 21wc lit all night 1cdp (9washbasins hc, 8 hc) ⊙ warden (1spin, 2dry) 2iron calor gas camping gaz ⊞ children's playground stables cinema launderette pub
9 200▲ awnings

MULLACOTT CROSS Devon Map 2 SS54
See Ilfracombe sketch map.

►►► *Mullacott Cross Caravan Park*
(SS511446) ☎ Ilfracombe 62212
2 ❶ ⚠
Sited on gentle grass slopes with views over the Atlantic coastline, the park is set in meadowland 2m S of Ilfracombe and 3m E of the sandy beach at Woolacombe. Located adjacent to A361 Braunton–Ilfracombe road. 10acres 125pitches 150static
Etr–Oct must book Jul & Aug last arrival

Mullion

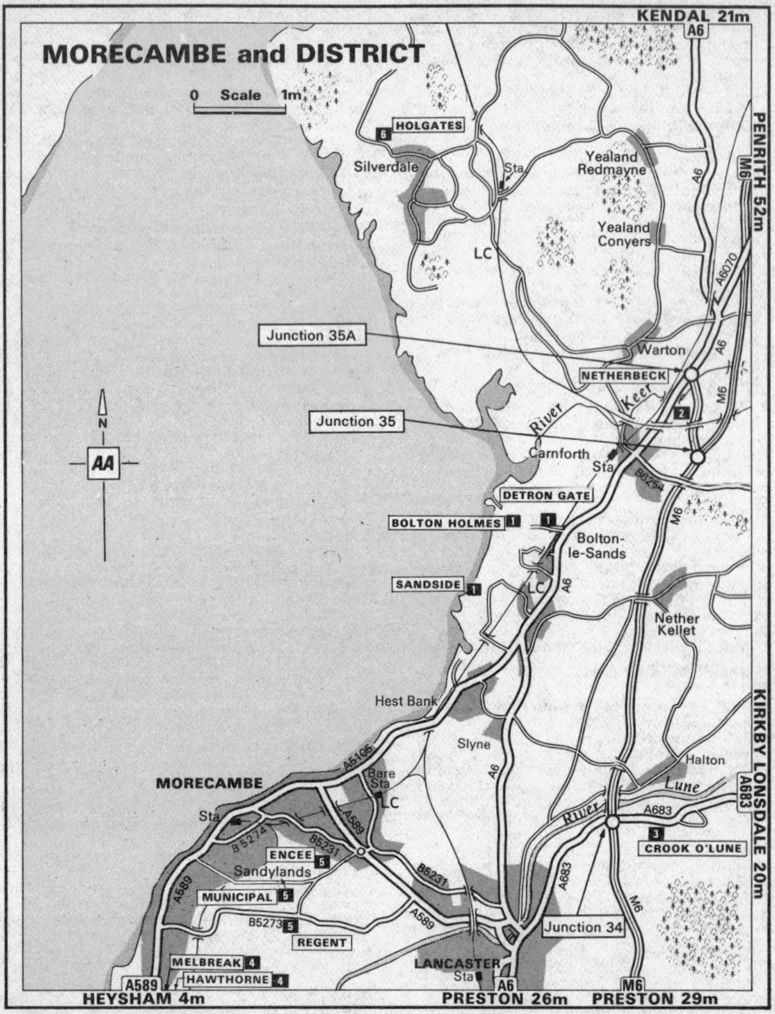

Sites listed under:
1 Bolton-le-Sands **2** Carnforth **3** Caton **4** Middleton **5** Morecambe **6** Silverdale

22.00hrs last departure 12.00hrs 17 showers ⊗ 42wc lit all night 1cdp (9washbasins hc) (central hot water) (18 hc) 4⊙ (3wash, spin, iron) calor gas camping gaz toilet fluid ☎ ⊞ ⊖ stables cinema launderette 65 60 or 60▲ (awnings) ltr

MULLION Cornwall Map 2 SW61
See sketch map.

►►► Mullion Cove Holiday Park *(SW699182)* (formerly Red Triangle Caravan Park) Penhale Cross ☎240428
2 ❷ △
A level, grass site with bushes set in rugged moorland adjacent to A3083 Helston road.
12acres 250pitches 245static
26 May–Sep rsApr–25 May booking advisable peak periods last arrival 19.00hrs last departure 10.00hrs 12 ⊗ 48wc lit all night (20washbasins hc, 16 hc) 6⊙ (3wash, 1dry, 4iron) 2 games room calor gas camping gaz toilet fluid cafe restaurant ☎ ⊞ licensed club & children's playground ⊖ stables launderette pub
105 £2.16–£2.81 or 105 £2.16–£2.81
145▲£2.16–£2.81 (awnings)

►► Criggan Mill Caravans *(SW670179)*
Mullion Cove ☎240496
2 ❷ △
A secluded site with level pitches set in a combe near to Porth Mellin. From the A3083 Helston road take B3296 for Mullion.
½acre 12pitches 33static
Apr–Oct booking advisable last departure 10.30hrs 6 individual pitches ⊗ 6wc lit all night 1cdp (4washbasins hc, 6central hot water, 1 hc, 3 hc) 1⊙ (1wash, 1spin, 1dry, 1iron) calor gas ⊞ ⊖ stables launderette pub
12 £1.90 or 12 £1.90 or 12▲£1.90 (awnings)

► *Franchis* *(SW698203)* Cury Cross Lanes ☎240301
2 ❷ △
This site is surrounded by hedges and coppice,

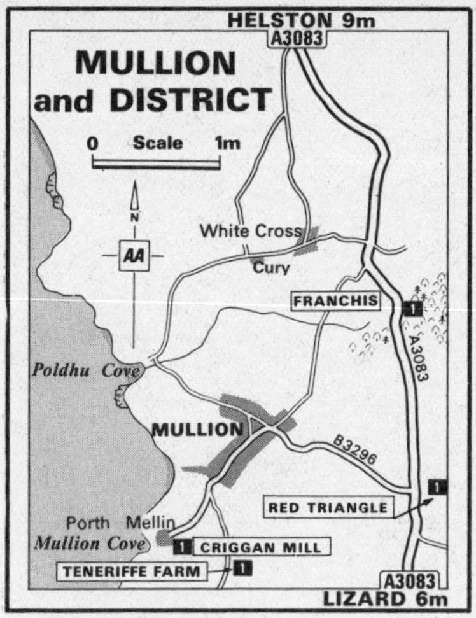

All sites listed under: Mullion

situated on the A3083 between Helston and The Lizard. Ideal position for exploring The Lizard peninsula. 4acres 70pitches
Apr–Oct must book peak periods last arrival 22.00hrs last departure 12.00hrs 5 6wc 1cdp ⊙ calor gas camping gaz paraffin toilet fluid ☎ ⊞ stables cinema launderette
30 10 30▲ (awnings)

▶Teneriffe Farm Caravan Site *(SW674166)*
☎240293
1 ❶ ⚠
Part level, part sloping grass site set in meadowland adjacent to sandy beach and rocky scenery. 3acres 15pitches 5static
Etr–Oct must book 15 Jul–15 Aug 6 3wc lit all night 1cdp washbasins hc (2hc) 1⊙ calor gas ⊞ stables launderette pub
15£1.75 or 15£1.75 or 15▲£1.75 (awnings) ltr

NARBOROUGH Norfolk Map 9 TF71
▶▶▶Pentney Park *(TF742141)*
Gayton Rd ☎337479
3 ❸ ⚠ signposted
Level, grass site with mature trees and bushes. Set in woodland and meadowland adjacent to A47 Swaffham–King's Lynn road. 16acres 120pitches
Mar–Oct last arrival 20.00hrs last departure 12.00hrs 6 24wc lit all night washbasins hc (central hot water) hc ⊙ (wash, spin, dry, iron) (cold storage) calor gas camping gaz toilet fluid ☎ ⊞ fishing, off licence & children's playground stables launderette pub
120£2.20 or 120£2.20 40▲£2.20 (awnings) ltr

NAWTON North Yorkshire Map 8 SE68
▶Wrens of Ryedale Caravan Site
(SE656839) ☎ Kirkdale 260
2 ❶ ⚠ signposted
A level and grassy site with mature trees and bushes set in the Rye Valley. ½m S of A170.
3½acres 30pitches 15static
Etr–mid Oct must book peak periods 3 individual pitches wc lit all night 1cdp washbasins hc (hc) ⊙ (cold storage) calor gas camping gaz ⊞ stables pub
30 or 30 or 30▲ rates on application (awnings) ltr

NEWBRIDGE Isle of Wight Map 4 SZ48
▶▶▶▶Orchards Holiday Caravan Park
(SZ637899) ☎ Calbourne 331
2 ❷ ⚠ signposted
Gently sloping grass site with mature trees and bushes, set in downland and meadowland adjacent to B3401 and near the sea. 8acres 175pitches 60static
May–Sep rsMar, Apr & Oct must book peak periods last arrival 22.00hrs last departure 11.00hrs 10 individual pitches 33wc lit all night 1cdp 10 37washbasins hc (2hc, 11hc) 8⊙ (3wash) 4spin 5iron 1 TV cold storage calor gas camping gaz toilet fluid ☎ ⊞ battery charger launderette
175 or 175 or 175▲ awnings

NEWCASTLE UPON TYNE Tyne and Wear Map 12 NZ26
▶▶▶Trax Campsite *(NZ251711)*
Gosforth Park Racecourse
1 ❶ ⚠ signposted

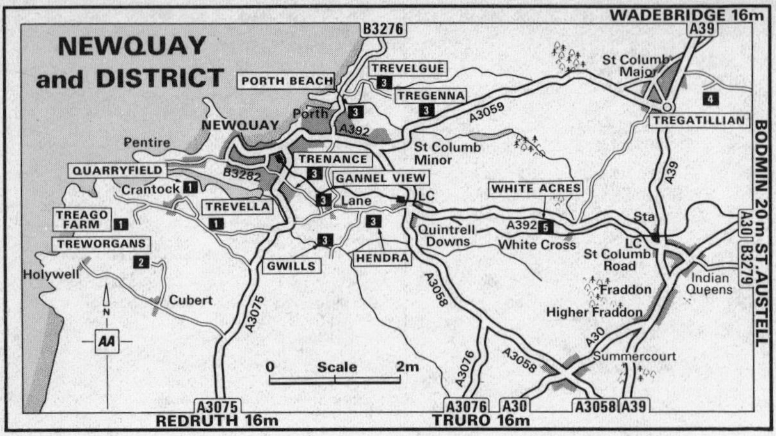

Sites listed under: **1** Crantock **2** Cubert **3** Newquay **4** St Columb Major **5** Whitecross

Level and grassy site, set in meadowland off B1318 Morpeth road. 10acres 90pitches 23 May–20 Sep no bookings last arrival 22.30hrs last departure 15.00hrs 2 11wc lit all night 3cdp 11washbasins hc 3central hot water 4hc 3⊙ warden (1wash, 1spin) 1iron TV calor gas camping gaz paraffin licensed bar ☎ ⊞ children's playground & golf course stables launderette pub 90£2–£2.75 or 90£2–£2.75 or 90▲£2–£2.75 awnings

NEW FOREST

The New Forest covers 144 square miles and is composed of broadleaf and coniferous woodland, open commonland and heath. This unique area was originally a royal hunting forest and there are long-established rights of access. It is not a 'Forest Park' but similar facilities for visitors are maintained by the Forestry Commission; these include caravan and camp sites, picnic sites, car parks, way-marked walks and ornamental drives.

The forest is always popular but advance booking at caravan sites is not possible except for the Spring Bank Holiday period, when access to Forestry Commission sites is strictly limited to holders of campsite access tickets. Details of this scheme may be found in a leaflet, published by the Forestry Commission, entitled *Camping 1980*: this also lists sites in the New Forest and explains the regulations which control camping and caravanning in this protected area. It is available from the Deputy Surveyor of the New Forest, Queen's House, Lyndhurst, Hants.

See Ashurst, Brockenhurst and Holmsley for AA listed sites.

NEWHAVEN Derbyshire Map 7 SK16
►►►► Newhaven Holiday Camping & Caravan Park *(SK167602)* ☎ Hartington 300
2 ❶ ⚠ signposted
A pleasantly situated site within the Peak District National Park. 4acres 100pitches 70static
Mar–Oct must book 7 individual pitches Ⓐ late arrivals enclosure wc lit all night 1cdp 16washbasins hc 8hc 6⊙ warden (1wash, 1spin, 1iron) games room (cold storage) calor gas camping gaz toilet fluid ☎ ⊞ children's playground stables pub 100£1.50–£2 or 100£1.50–£2 or 100▲£1.50–£2 (awnings) ltr

NEWMARKET Suffolk Map 5 TL66
►►► Trax Campsite *(TL619628)*
Rowley Mile Racecourse
2 ❸ ⚠ signposted
A level and grassy site 1m W of town centre. Off A1304. 8acres 120pitches
23 May–20 Sep no bookings last arrival 22.30hrs last departure 15.00hrs 5 individual pitches 43wc lit all night 4cdp 39washbasins hc 2central hot water 8hc 5⊙ warden CTV calor gas camping gaz paraffin toilet fluid licensed bar ☎ ⊞ children's playground launderette 120£2–£2.75 or 120£2–£2.75 or 120▲£2–£2.75 awnings

NEW MILTON Hampshire Map 4 SZ29
See Christchurch sketch map.
►►►►► Bashley Park *(SZ252968)*
Sway Rd ☎612340
3 ❸ ⚠ signposted
This site is located in reasonably flat open fields with hard gravel standings, and is bordered by woodland and shrubbery. 20acres 420pitches 380static
May–Oct rsMar & Apr must book peak periods last arrival 20.00hrs last departure 10.00hrs 58 individual pitches late arrivals enclosure wc lit all night 4cdp 169 washbasins hc (hc) ⊙ warden (wash, spin, dry, iron) () games room TV calor gas camping gaz paraffin toilet fluid cafe restaurant ☎ ⊞ licensed club, children's playground, bicycle & portable TV hire stables launderette pub 420£2–£3.75 or 420£2–£3.75 (awnings) ltr

NEWQUAY Cornwall Map 2 SW86
See sketch map.
►►►►► Hendra Tourist Park
(SW833601) Lane (2m SE) ☎5778
2 ❷ ⚠ signposted
A partly level and sloping site with mature trees and bushes set in downland. 2m SE of Newquay, off Lane–Quintrel Down road. 36acres 1004pitches
25 May–Oct rsApr–24 May must book peak periods last departure 10.00hrs 29 individual pitches Ⓐ late arrivals enclosure 130wc lit all night 4cdp washbasins hc central hot water (hc) ⊙ warden (wash, spin, iron) (games room) CTV (cold storage) calor gas camping gaz paraffin toilet fluid cafe restaurant licensed bar ☎ ⊞ licensed club (children's playground) & hairdresser

stables ♂ ✈ cinema ⛴ launderette 1004🚐£1.50–£4.50 or 1004🚙£1.50–£4.50 or 1004▲£1.50–£4.50 (awnings)

►►►► Newquay Tourist Park *(SW853626)* St Columb Minor (3m E off A3059) ☎3257
2 ❶ ⚠ signposted
A pleasant informal touring and holiday site situated on rising ground affording country views.
21acres 312pitches 47static
25 May–Sep rs1–24 May must book peak periods 10 individual pitches late arrivals enclosure 47wc lit all night 2cdp 64washbasins hc (21hc) 6 warden (3wash, 1spin, 2dry) 2iron CTV calor gas camping gaz cafe ☎ ⊞ licensed club children's playground crazy golf pitch & putt stables cinema launderette pub 312🚐 or 312🚙 or 312▲ awnings

►►► Gannel View Holiday Park *(SW828606)* Lane (2m SE) ☎4634
2 ❷ ⚠ signposted
Gently sloping and level grass surfaced site close to A392. 2acres 28pitches 45static
Apr–Aug must book last 2 wks Jul & 1st 2 wks Aug last arrival 20.00hrs last departure 18.00hrs 6 12wc lit all night 1cdp washbasins hc (central hot water, hc) (wash, spin, iron) TV (cold storage) calor gas camping gaz ⊞ (licensed club) & children's playground stables cinema launderette pub 28🚐£1–£3.50 or 28🚙£1–£3.50 or 28▲£1–£3.50 awnings

►►► Gwills Caravan Park *(SW829592)* Lane (2m SE) ☎3617
2 ❸ ⚠ signposted
This part level and part sloping site situated near the river has clumps of trees. From A30 turn right at Indian Queens to A392 then follow

unclassified road between Lane and Newlyn East. 8acres 60pitches
May–Sep must book Jul & Aug last arrival 22.00hrs last departure 10.00hrs 7 ⊗ 12wc 2cdp 15washbasins hc 2central hot water 7hc 4⊙ (1wash, 1dry, 1iron) calor gas camping gaz toilet fluid ☎ ⊞ stables cinema launderette
50 10 or 50▲

▶▶▶ Porth Beach Tourist Park
Porth (1m NE) ☎6531
3 ❸ ⚠
Mainly level, grass site with saplings and bushes, set in meadowland adjacent to sea, beach and main road. 6¾acres 201pitches
Apr–Oct booking advisable peak periods last departure 12.00hrs 9 individual pitches late arrivals enclosure 24wc lit all night 1cdp washbasins hc (hc) ⊙ warden (iron) (cold storage) calor gas camping gaz ☎ ⊞ drying room stables cinema launderette pub
201 £1.50–£5 or 201 £1.50–£5 or 201▲£1.50–£6 (awnings)

▶▶▶ Trenance Caravan & Chalet Park
(SW818612) Edgcumbe Av ☎3447
1 ❶ ⚠
A partly level and sloping grassy site 1m S of Newquay on A3075. 10acres 80pitches 214static
Apr–Oct must book last arrival 20.00hrs last departure 10.00hrs 7 individual pitches 52wc lit all night 4cdp 19washbasins hc (2central hot water, 25hc) 8⊙ (3wash, 1spin, 2dry, 2iron) (games room, cold storage) calor gas camping gaz ☎ ⊞ stables cinema launderette pub
80 £2.30 or 80 £2.10 (awnings)

▶▶▶ *Trevelgue Caravan Park*
(SW839633) Porth (1m NE) ☎3475
2 ❶ ⚠ signposted
Level grass site set in meadowland with direct access to Porth and Whipsiderry beaches. Off B3276 Porth–Padstow road. 4½acres 100pitches 132static
Apr–Oct rsNov–Mar last departure 12.00hrs wc lit all night washbasins hc (hc) ⊙ (wash, dry) iron ( ) games room CTV (cold storage) calor gas camping gaz licensed bar ☎ ⊞ stables cinema launderette
100 or 100 or 100▲

NEWTON ABBOT Devon Map 3 SX87

▶▶▶ Country Touring Caravan Centre
(SX847679) Two Mile Oak. Apply to: P & C Holiday Homes Ltd, Leisure House, Dendy Rd, Paignton, Devon TQ4 5DB
☎ Paignton 553581
2 ❸ ⚠ signposted
Mainly level, gravel site with mature trees, set in meadowland and adjacent to main road,

This year come to Trevella

the A.A. 5 pennant Cornish centre for caravans and camping

Trevella is a secluded parkland Caravan and Camping Park $2\frac{1}{2}$ miles from Newquay with its seven golden beaches. Nearby is Crantock Village and its mile-long sandy beach which is ideal for surfing. Bring your own Tent, Caravan or Dormobile or, if you prefer, we have Holiday Caravans for hire to accommodate up to 8 people. Site facilities include :–

✱ Free heated swimming pool with large sunbathing area.
✱ Modern hygienic toilets, hot and cold showers, wash basins, razor-points, dishwashing sinks and FREE hot water.
✱ Launderette with fully-automatic machines, tumble driers, free spin-driers, airing cupboards, irons and ironing boards.
✱ Free hairdressing facilities.
✱ Well stocked self-service shop.
✱ Microwave kitchen for selection of tasty food at a sensible price, cooked in only 2 minutes.
✱ Children's playgrounds with lots of swings and amusements for the young, including a full-size tractor for the budding farmer.
✱ Teenager's Room.
✱ T.V. Room
✱ Cleanliness and personal service.

Because of amenities such as these, the A.A. awarded us 5 pennants, their highest rating. Why not come and enjoy them for yourself. Send for our free brochure now. (S.A.E. much appreciated).

Approved by: A.A., British Tourist Association, The Caravan Club, The Camping Club, The Motor Caravanners Club, The Camper, Cornwall Tourist Board.

AA TREVELLA PARK

DEPT. AA TREVELLA PARK, CRANTOCK, NEWQUAY, CORNWALL.
TELEPHONE CRANTOCK (063 77) 308

A381 Newton Abbot—Totnes. ¾acre 11pitches Mid Apr–mid Oct last arrival 23.00hrs last departure 12.00hrs 2 individual pitches late arrivals enclosure wc lit all night 1cdp (4washbasins hc, 2hc) 1 warden (1spin, 1dry, 1iron) calor gas toilet fluid children's playground stables cinema launderette pub 11£1.25–£3.06 or 11£1.25–£3.06 (awnings)

NORTH KILWORTH Leicestershire Map 4 SP68
Kilworth Caravan Park *(SP605838)*
Market Harborough 880385
1 1 signposted
Gently sloping, grass and gravel site with mixed vegetation. Set in hilly woodland and meadowland with access to A427 Market Harborough road, and near the canal. 3acres 50pitches 50static Apr–Dec rsJan–Mar (toilets closed) no bookings last arrival 20.00hrs last departure 12.00hrs 2 late arrivals enclosure 6wc lit all night 1cdp (hc) calor gas camping gaz toilet fluid stables pub
50£1.30 or 50£1.30 (awnings) ltr

NORTH SOMERCOTES Lincolnshire Map 9 TF49
Lakeside Lido Holiday Centre *(TF436955)* 315
1 2 signposted
A large coastal site with pine trees scattered throughout the site. Located on the A1031 Cleethorpes–Skegness road just south of the village. 150pitches
15 Mar–Oct no bookings last arrival 23.59hrs 8 25wc lit all night 1cdp 10washbasins hc central hot water (6hc) 4 warden (2wash, 2spin, 6iron) cold storage calor gas camping gaz toilet fluid cafe restaurant licensed club & children's playground stables cinema launderette pub
150£1.75 or 150£1.75 or 150£1.75 awnings ltr

NORTH STAINLEY North Yorkshire Map 8 SE27
Sleningford Water Mill *(SE280783)*
Ripon 85201
2 2 signposted
Level, grassy site with mature trees set in wood and meadowland adjacent to River Ure, and A6108. 12acres 65pitches 25static
23 May–Oct rs4 Apr–22 May – caravans only booking advisable last arrival 22.00hrs last departure 12.00hrs 22 individual pitches for caravans late arrivals enclosure 14wc lit all night 6cdp 17washbasins hc central hot water 9hc 4 warden (1wash, 1spin, 1dry, 1iron) games room calor gas camping gaz toilet fluid children's playground off licence & fishing
25£1.60–£2.20 40£2.20 or 40£2.20 (awnings) ltr

NOTTER BRIDGE Cornwall Map 2 SX36
Notter Bridge Caravan & Camping Park Saltash 2318
3 3 signposted
Level, grass site with mature trees and bushes set in hilly wooded meadowland country adjacent to river and A38; 3m W of Saltash.
3½acres 50pitches 17static
Apr–Sep rsOct–Mar must book peak periods last arrival 23.59hrs last departure 11.00hrs 4 late arrivals enclosure 11wc lit all night 2cdp 12washbasins hc (4hc) 4 warden (1wash, 1spin, 1dry, 1iron) calor gas camping gaz children's playground & fishing stables launderette pub
50£1.74–£2.16 or 50£1.74–£2.16 or 50£1.74–£2.16 (awnings)

NOTTINGHAM Nottinghamshire Map 8 SK53
See sketch map.
Surprise View Trailer Park *(SK503535)* Bestwood Park 204695
2 2 signposted
Site is level and sloping in parts with grass and mixed vegetation, set in hilly woodland and meadowland. Off A60 between Nottingham and Mansfield on a private road. nc16 4acres 50pitches 225static
Apr–Sep rsOct–Mar no bookings 20 late arrivals enclosure wc lit all night 6cdp 20washbasins hc central hot water 10hc 6 warden (2wash, 1spin, 1dry, 2iron,) games room TV (cold storage) calor gas camping gaz cafe restaurant (licensed club) children's playground & mini golf stables cinema launderette pub
50£2.20 or 50£2.20 or 50£2.20 (awnings)

Trax Campsite – Nottingham Racecourse *(SK598395)* Colwick Park (2m E off B686)
1 2 signposted
Level, well drained campsite with hardstanding for 12 pitches. On the outskirts of the city adjacent to River Trent. 3acres 69pitches
23 May–20 Sep except 5, 19 & 28 Aug no bookings last arrival 22.30hrs last departure 15.00hrs 2 13wc lit all night 1cdp 12washbasins hc 2central hot water 4hc 2 warden TV calor gas camping gaz children's playground games area free racing for campers 16 & 30 Jun, 11, 12 Aug & 1 Sep
69£2–£2.35 or 69£2–£2.35 or 69£2–£2.35 awnings

OKEHAMPTON Devon Map 2 SX59
Okehampton Motel Caravan Harbour *(SX684927)* 2879
2 3 signposted
Small site with hedges that offer seclusion and protection from prevailing winds. Good views of Dartmoor. 1m E of Okehampton on A30.
1½acres 25pitches
May–Sep must book 3 individual pitches 7wc lit all night 1cdp 6washbasins hc central hot water (1hc) 4hc 2 warden 1spin 1iron cold storage cafe restaurant

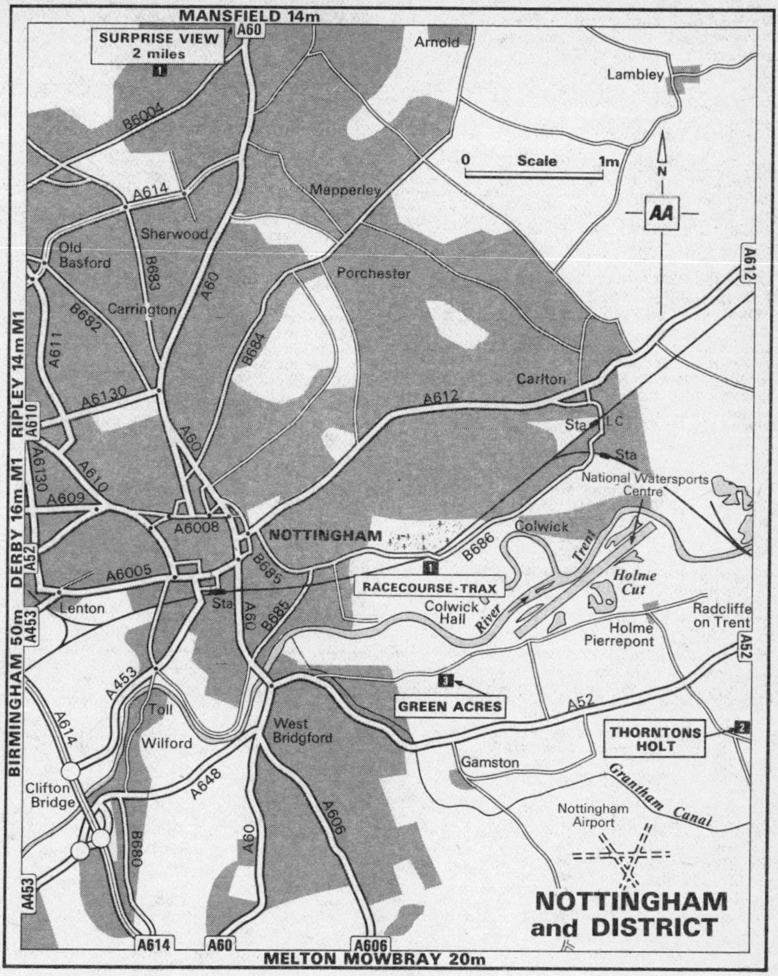

Sites listed under. **1** Nottingham **2** Stragglethorpe **3** West Bridgford

☎ ⊞ licensed club & children's playground mobile shop ⊖ stables ♁ cinema ⟲ launderette ⌂ pub
25 £3 or 25 £3 or 25▲£3 (awnings)

OLD CLIPSTONE Nottinghamshire Map 8 SK66
►►► Sherwood Forest Caravan Site *(SK590651)* ☎Mansfield 823132
3 ❷ ⚠ signposted
Level, grass site with mature trees, saplings and bushes, set in wooded meadowland, adjacent to River Maun and lake. 3m SW of Edwinstowe. 12acres 100pitches 4static Apr–Sep rsOct must book Bank Hols last arrival 21.00hrs last departure 18.00hrs 11 individual pitches 10wc lit all night 4cdp washbasins hc (hc) ⊙ calor gas camping gaz toilet fluid licensed bar ☎ ⊞ ⌂ ⊖ stables ♁ launderette
100 or 100 or 100▲ (awnings) ltr

OLNEY Buckinghamshire Map 4 SP85
►►► *Emberton Park* *(SP886500)*
☎Bedford 711575
2 ❶ ⚠ signposted
This site is situated 1m outside Olney and set in pleasant surroundings in the Ouse Valley adjacent to the river. There are four main areas of water for sailing. 56pitches 114static Apr–Oct rsNov–Mar must book peak periods 10 individual pitches 3wc lit all night 3cdp washbasins hc hc ⊙ calor gas camping gaz cafe ⊞ ⊖ stables ⌂ pub
†56 or 56 or 56▲ †no caravans Nov–Mar

ORGANFORD Dorset Map 3 SY99
►►► Pear Tree Farm Caravans & Camping
☎Lytchett Minster 622434
2 ❷ ⚠
Level, grass site with mature trees and bushes set in wooded meadowland. 6m W of Poole off A351 at Holton Heath. 7½acres 105pitches Etr–15 Oct no bookings last arrival 22.00hrs last departure 12.00hrs 7 individual pitches for caravans ⊗ 21wc lit all night 2cdp 20washbasins hc (10hc) 4⊙ (1spin, 1iron) (cold storage) calor gas camping gaz ⊞ ⌂ ⊖ stables ♁ ↔ cinema ⟲ launderette pub
105£1.80 or 105£1.80 or 105▲£1.80 (awnings)

ORMSKIRK Lancashire Map 7 SD40
►►► **Abbey Farm Caravan Site**
(SD434098) Blyth Ln ☎72686
2 ❶ ⚠
Screened by trees and bushes this site is in the ground of Burscough Abbey. 1½acres 39pitches 40static
All year must book peak periods last arrival 22.00hrs last departure 13.00hrs 8 individual pitches 12wc lit all night 1cdp 12washbasins hc (central hot water) (4hc) 2 (1spin, 1dry, 1iron) calor gas ☎ cinema launderette
14 £1.50 25 £1.50 or 25▲£1.50 (awnings)

OSMINGTON MILLS Dorset Map 3 SY78
►► **Osmington Mills Holidays**
☎Preston (Dorset) 832311
2 ❶ ⚠ signposted
Undulating, grass site with mature trees, saplings and bushes – set in hilly woodland and meadowland with direct access to the sea, beach, lake and main road. The area is classed as one of outstanding natural beauty. 4m E of Weymouth off A353. 14acres 175pitches 100static
Etr, Spring Bank Hol–Oct rsApr & May must book for tents peak periods must book for caravans and motor caravans last arrival 21.00hrs last departure 10.00hrs 14 wc lit all night 2cdp 40washbasins hc central hot water 16hc 10 (3wash, 3spin, 2dry, 3iron) games room CTV (cold storage) calor gas camping gaz cafe restaurant ☎ ⊞ licensed club & children's playground stables pub
25 150▲ (awnings)

OSMOTHERLEY North Yorkshire Map 8 SE49
► **Cote Ghyll Caravan Park** *(SE461983)*
☎425
1 ❶ ⚠ signposted
Grass site with mixed trees and bushes, set beneath the Cleveland Hills. Situated off A19. 8acres 77pitches 18static
Apr–Oct must book public hols last arrival 21.00hrs last departure 12.30hrs 10 9wc lit all night 1cdp washbasins hc 1 warden calor gas ⊞ pub
57 £1.60 or 57 £1.40 20▲£1.60 (awnings)

OWER Hampshire Map 4 SU31
► **Green Pastures Farm** *(SU321158)* ☎444
2 ❶ ⚠ signposted
Open level grassy field on farm in rural surroundings. 45pitches 2static
15 Mar–Oct no bookings 3 individual pitches 7wc lit all night 1cdp 7washbasins hc (4hc) 2 calor gas camping gaz ⊞ stables launderette pub
45 £1.50 or 45 £1.50 (awnings)

OWERMOIGNE Dorset Map 3 SY78
►►► **Sandy Holme Caravan Park**
(SY768863) Moreton Rd
☎Warmwell 852677
2 ❷ ⚠ signposted
Level, grass site with trees and bushes set in woodland and near the coast at Lulworth Cove. 1m N of A352. 12acres 270pitches 35static
16 Mar–Oct must book peak periods last arrival 21.30hrs last departure 10.30hrs 8 individual pitches late arrivals enclosure 20wc lit all night 1cdp washbasins hc (central hot water) (hc) warden (wash, spin, dry, iron) (cold storage)

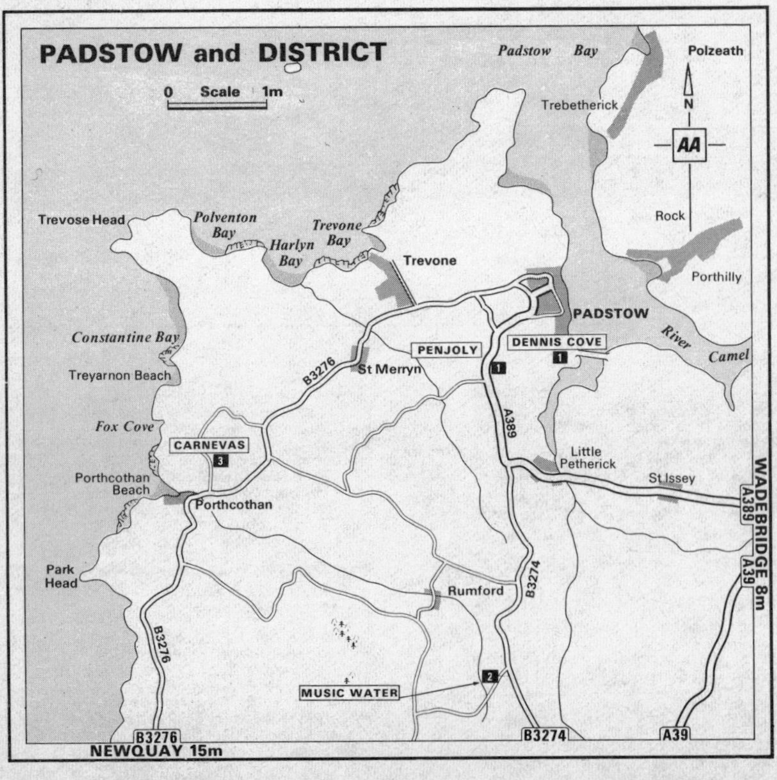

Sites listed under: **1** Padstow **2** Rumford **3** St Merryn

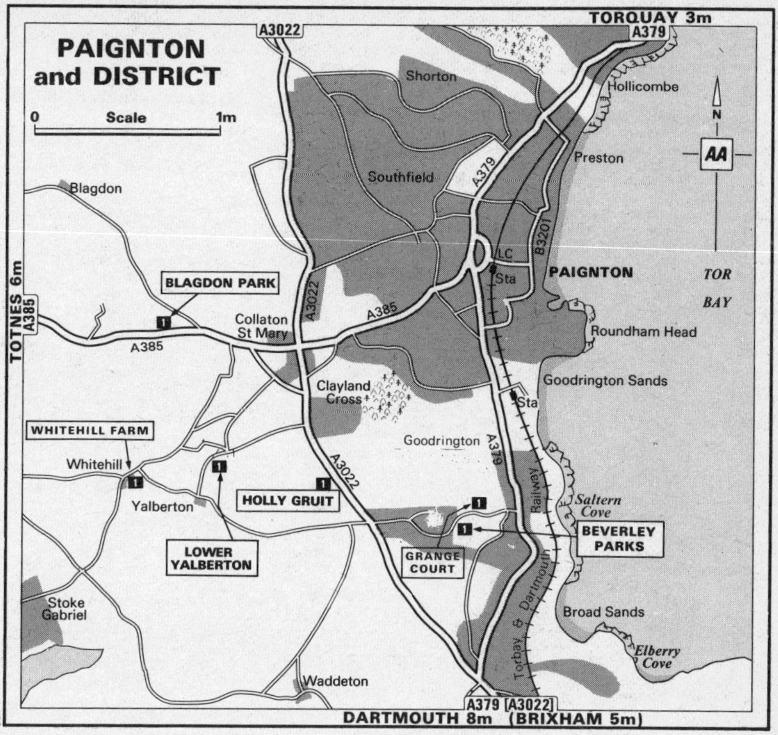

All sites listed under: Paignton

calor gas camping gaz toilet fluid ☎ ⊞
off licence, fishing, children's playground & bicycles for hire ⛺ ⊖ stables ♁ launderette pub
70 £2.20 or 70 £2.20 200▲£2.20 (awnings)

PADSTOW Cornwall Map 2 SW97
See sketch map.
►► Penjoly Caravan Park ☎532289
2 ❷ ⚠
Level, grass site with trees and bushes set in meadowland with access to sea, at Dennis Cove, and Padstow. ½m S of Padstow off A389. 1acre 25pitches 70static
Etr–Sep must book peak periods
last arrival 21.00hrs last departure 12.00hrs
4 18wc 1cdp (10washbasins hc) (4 hc)
2⊙ (1iron) (cold storage) calor gas ⊞ ⊖
stables ♁ cinema launderette pub
10 10 5▲ rates on application
(awnings) ltr
► Dennis Cove Site ☎532349
2 ❷ ⚠
Level and slightly sloping site with grass and mature trees set in meadowland with access to River Camel estuary and Padstow Bay beach. Approaching Padstow from Wadebridge, turn right into Sarahs Lane. 3acres 75pitches
7 May–25 Sep booking advisable peak periods
last arrival 21.00hrs last departure 12.00hrs
4 Ⓐ 19wc lit all night 1cdp 15washbasins hc
(3central hot water) (4 hc) 3⊙ ()
calor gas camping gaz cafe ⊞
private beach, canoeing, fishing, stables & slipway to R. Camel mobile shop ⊖ ♁
cinema launderette pub
75 £1.75–£2.75 or 75▲£1.75–£2.75
(awnings)

PAIGNTON Devon Map 3 SX86
See sketch map.
►►►►► Beverley Parks Caravan & Camping Site *(SX886582)* Goodrington Rd
☎Churston 843887
2 ❶ ⚠ signposted
A large commercial site on raised ground adjacent to residential area south of the town; with pleasant sea views. 22acres 240pitches 300static
Mid May–Sep rsEtr–mid May must book for caravans & motor caravans last arrival 22.00hrs
last departure 10.00hrs 20 individual pitches for caravans Ⓐ late arrivals enclosure 56wc
lit all night 2cdp washbasins hc
central hot water (hc, hc) ⊙ (wash, spin, dry, iron) games room CTV (cold storage)
calor gas camping gaz toilet fluid cafe
restaurant licensed bar ☎ ⊞ licensed club & children's playground ⊖ stables ♁
cinema launderette pub
60 £3.80 or 60 £3.80 180▲£3.30
(awnings)
►►►►► Grange Court Holiday Centre *(SX888588)* Grange Rd ☎558010
2 ❸ ⚠ signposted
Large grassy site situated amidst woodland near to the sea. 1½m from Paignton on Brixham road. no pets 4½acres 81pitches 589static
Mar–Oct must book last arrival 19.00hrs
last departure 12.00hrs 8 individual pitches
late arrivals enclosure 18wc lit all night
2cdp (16washbasins hc) (central hot water)
(8 hc) 4⊙ warden (6wash, 4dry, 4iron)
games room TV cold storage calor gas
camping gaz toilet fluid cafe restaurant
☎ ⊞ licensed bar, children's playground & pitch & putt ⊖ stables ♁ cinema

launderette pub
81£2.25–£3.75 or 81£2.25–£3.75
awnings

►►► **Holly Gruit Camp** *(SX875588)*
Brixham Rd ☎550763
[2] ❷ △
A grass site with mixed trees and bushes, set in hilly meadowland, within the urban area. Off A3022 Brixham road. 3acres 70pitches
May–Sep must book peak periods
last arrival 22.30hrs last departure 11.00hrs
2 11wc lit all night 12washbasins hc
2⊙ warden (1iron) games room TV (cold storage) calor gas camping gaz ⊞ licensed club & children's playground stables cinema launderette pub
70▲ rates on application

►►► **Lower Yalberton Caravan Park & Camping Site** *(SX869584)* Long Rd
☎558127
[2] ❶ △ signposted
A partly level and sloping, grassy site with mature trees. Off Paignton Ring Road.
25acres 545pitches 8static
Jun–Aug rsMar–May & Sep–Oct must book peak periods last departure 10.00hrs 14 wc lit all night 2cdp 30washbasins hc
12hc 6⊙ 5wash 1spin 4dry 2iron 1
CTV cold storage calor gas camping gaz
toilet fluid ☎ ⊞ licensed club & children's playground stables cinema launderette pub
242£3 303£3 or 303▲£2.50 (awnings)

►►► **Whitehill Farm Caravan & Camping Site** *(SX857588)* Stoke Gabriel Rd
☎Stoke Gabriel 338
[2] ❸ △ signposted
This site is situated in rural surroundings approximately 1m from Paignton. Within striking distance of the Dartmoor National Park and Torquay. Ideal for those who like the seaside and country lovers. 30acres
411pitches 66static
May–Sep must book peak periods
last departure 12.00hrs 12 42wc lit all night 1cdp 35washbasins hc 4central hot water 30hc 4⊙ (wash, spin, dry) iron
games room TV calor gas camping gaz
toilet fluid licensed bar ☎ ⊞ children's playground, take-away meals, hairdryers stables cinema
50fr£2.80 361fr£2.80 or 361▲fr£2.40
awnings

► ***Blagdon Park Camping Site*** *(SX853601)*
☎521684
[2] ❷ △
Gently sloping grass site with mixed vegetation, set in meadowland within the urban area, near river and with access to beach at Torbay. Situated on A385 between Totnes and Paignton. 10½acres 247pitches
Etr–Sep rsOct–Etr must book peak periods
last departure 10.30hrs 10 36wc
lit all night 1cdp (4washbasins hc)
(2central hot water) (12hc) ⊙ warden
(3wash, spin) iron games room (cold storage)
calor gas camping gaz paraffin cafe ☎ ⊞
children's play area stables cinema launderette
3 50 or 247▲ (awnings)

PAR Cornwall Map 2 SX05
See St Austell sketch map.

►►► ***Mount Holiday Park*** *(SX070529)*
The Mount ☎2616
[2] ❷ △
Gently sloping, grass site with mature trees and bushes set in hilly, meadowland country adjacent to sea, sandy beach and lake.
20acres 11pitches 60static
21 May–Sep must book peak periods
last arrival 19.00hrs last departure 12.00hrs
6 14wc (8washbasins hc) (2hc)
(4hc) 2⊙ warden (2wash, 1dry, 2iron)
calor gas camping gaz toilet fluid licensed bar
☎ ⊞ stables cinema
launderette pub
11 or 11 or 11▲ (awnings)

►Par Beach Caravan & Camp Park
(SX083533) ☎2868
1 ❶ ⚠ signposted
Level, grass and sand site with various trees and bushes. Situated on the coast on the A3082, Fowey–St Austell road, close to river, lake, beach and sea. 15acres 220pitches 215static Apr–Sep last departure 12.00hrs 24 75wc lit all night 1cdp washbasins hc central hot water (hc) ⊙ warden (2wash, spin, dry, iron) () (games room) TV calor gas cafe restaurant licensed bar ☎ ⊞ ⊖ stables cinema launderette
220 or 220▲ (awnings)

PATHFINDER VILLAGE Devon Map 3 SX89
►►►►►Pathfinder Touring Caravan Park ☎Tedburn St Mary 239
3 ❸ ⚠ signposted
A partly level and sloping grass and gravel site set in meadowland. 5m W of Exeter off A30.
2acres 30pitches
All year must book peak periods
last departure 12.00hrs 3 individual pitches late arrivals enclosure 6wc lit all night 1cdp 6 6washbasins hc (1central hot water) 2hc 2⊙ warden (1wash, 1spin) calor gas camping gaz paraffin toilet fluid cafe restaurant ☎ ⊞ (licensed club) children's playground, take away meals ⊖ launderette pub
30£2.50 or 30£2.50 (awnings)

PATRICK BROMPTON North Yorkshire Map 8 SE29
►►►Akebar Park *(SE193905)*
☎Constable Burton 201 (to be changed to Bedale 50201)
2 ❷ ⚠ signposted
Part level, part sloping all grass site with some trees. The golf course is directly adjacent to the site. Off A684 2m W of village.
23acres 110pitches 80static
Etr–Oct rsMar must book peak periods
last departure 18.00hrs 9 late arrivals enclosure 32wc lit all night 4cdp washbasins hc (hc) ⊙ warden (wash, spin, dry) iron (cold storage) calor gas camping gaz toilet fluid ☎ ⊞ children's playground, fishing, sauna, solarium & golf course ⊖ stables launderette
60£2.50 or 60£2.50 50▲£2.50 (awnings) ltr

PELYNT Cornwall Map 2 SX25
See Looe sketch map.
►►►Trelawne Gardens Caravan Park
Trelawne ☎Polperro 72388
3 ❶ ⚠
Mainly level, grassy site with trees and bushes set in meadowland and woodland.
3½acres 85pitches
Jun–Aug rsMay, Sep & Oct must book
last arrival 23.00hrs last departure 11.30hrs
3 individual pitches late arrivals enclosure 12wc lit all night (washbasins hc, central hot water, hc) ⊙ warden iron CTV cold storage calor gas camping gaz toilet fluid ☎ ⊞ licensed club ⊖ stables launderette pub
85£1.50–£4.20 or 85£1.50–£4.20 or 85▲£1.50–£4.20 94 or 94 or 94▲ in season (awnings) ltr

►►►Trelawne Holiday Estate
☎Polperro 72370
2 ❷ ⚠
This site is situated in a wooded area off the B3359, midway between Looe and Pelynt offering good seclusion on level touring pitches.
no pets 1½acres 30pitches 200static
3 May–27 Sep rsEtr must book peak periods
last departure 10.00hrs 2 individual pitches 8wc lit all night 1cdp 6washbasins hc (15hc) 6⊙ (3wash, 1spin, 2dry) 3iron games room CTV cafe restaurant ☎ ⊞ licensed club, children's playground ⊖ stables cinema launderette pub
75£3–£4.50 or 75£3–£4.50 awnings ltr

►►► **Trelay Farm** ☎Lanreath 256
1 ❶ ⚠ signposted
A sloping, grass site with bushes, ½m from Pelynt village off B3359. 3acres 30pitches 20static
May–Sep must book peak periods 6 8wc (4washbasins hc, central hot water) (2hc) 1 calor gas ⊞ stables cinema launderette pub
5£1.94 5£1.72 20▲£1.72 (awnings)

PENDEEN Cornwall Map 2 SW33
►►► **Levant House** Levant Rd
☎St Just 788795
1 ❷ ⚠ signposted
Partly level, partly sloping, grass site set in moorland and meadowland, adjacent to sea 3m N of St Just on B3306. 2acres 43pitches 1static
Apr–Oct must book peak periods
last departure 12.30hrs 8 11wc lit all night 11 8washbasins hc central hot water (8hc) (1iron) games room TV cold storage ☎ ⊞ stables launderette pub
43£1.70 or 43£1.70 or 43▲£1.70 awnings

PENRITH Cumbria Map 12 NY53
►►► **Thacka Lea Caravan Site** *(NY509388)* Thacka Ln ☎3319 (may be prefixed by 6)
1 ❷ ⚠
A mainly level, grassy site in urban area at northern end of town. 2¼acres 25pitches
Mar–Oct must book public hols last departure 12.00hrs 4 individual pitches 7wc lit all night 1cdp washbasins hc (hc) warden (cold storage) calor gas ⊞ cinema launderette pub
25£1.50 or 25£1.50 (awnings)

PENRUDDOCK Cumbria Map 12 NY42
► ***Beckses Caravan Site*** *(NY419278)*
☎Greystoke 224
1 ❶ ⚠ signposted
A small site on sloping ground with some bushes and trees. Views of distant fells. 3acres 21pitches 18static
Etr–Oct must book peak periods 2 individual pitches 10wc lit all night 1cdp 6washbasins hc 6hc 1 warden spin (cold storage) calor gas camping gaz toilet fluid ⊞ children's playground stables launderette
16 or 16 5▲

PENTEWAN Cornwall Map 2 SX04
See St Austell sketch map.
►►► **Penhaven Tourist Park** *(SX007482)*
☎Mevagissey 3687
1 ❷ ⚠ signposted
Level landscaped site in wooded valley. 1m from sandy beach at Pentewan. 6acres 105pitches
Etr–Oct must book peak periods 7 individual pitches late arrivals enclosure 12wc lit all night 1cdp 20 washbasins hc central hot water (hc) warden (wash, dry, iron) calor gas camping gaz toilet fluid ☎ ⊞ children's playground stables launderette pub
105£2.75–£3.75 or 105£2.25–£3.25 or 105▲£2–£3.75 (awnings)

►►► **Pentewan Sands Caravan & Camping Ground** ☎Mevagissey 3485
2 ❶ ⚠
Located adjacent to the beach, this site has well-spaced grass pitches. 24acres 547pitches 53static
17 May–13 Sep rsApr–16 May & 14 Sep–Oct booking advisable peak periods last departure 10.30hrs 26 individual pitches late arrivals enclosure 71wc lit all night 2cdp 16 70washbasins hc (28hc) 19 (3wash, 2spin, 3dry, 5iron) cold storage calor gas camping gaz toilet fluid cafe ☎ ⊞ children's playground, private beach & battery charger launderette pub
547£1.89–£3.24 or 547£1.89–£3.24 or 547▲£1.89–£3.24 awnings

►►► **Sun Valley Caravan Park**
Nansladron House ☎Mevagissey 3266
2 ❸ ⚠ signposted
Mainly level, grass site with mature trees and bushes set in wood and meadowland and within 1m of sea, beach, river and main road. 5acres 30pitches 60static
Apr–Oct must book peak periods
last arrival 22.00hrs last departure 10.30hrs 8 26wc lit all night 18washbasins hc (10hc) 4 (2wash, 2spin, 2dry, 2iron) TV calor gas camping gaz ☎ ⊞ (licensed club) & children's playground stables cinema launderette pub
30£2.25–£3.25 or 30£2.25–£3.25 or 30▲£2.25–£3.25 (awnings)

PENZANCE Cornwall Map 2 SW43
►►► ***Mount's Bay Holiday Centre***
(SW483312) Eastern Green Caravan Park
☎4160
1 ❷ ⚠ signposted
Level, grass site with mature trees and bushes. ½m E of Penzance near junction A30/B3311. 180pitches 150static
31 Mar–30 Oct rsNov–Mar last departure 10.30hrs 8 45wc lit all night 1cdp 38washbasins hc central hot water 14hc 7 warden iron TV camping gaz toilet fluid cafe licensed bar ⊞ stables cinema launderette
30 20 130▲ (awnings)

PERRANARWORTHAL Cornwall Map 2 SW73
►►► **Cosawes Caravan Park** *(SW768376)*
☎Devoran 863724
2 ❶ ⚠ signposted
Level site with a slight gradient on grass and gravel with mixed vegetation. Set in hilly woodland country and meadowland; close to sea 6m W of Truro on A39. 2acres 40pitches 85static
All year must book peak periods 6 6wc lit all night 1cdp 6washbasins hc 2hc 1 warden wash spin dry iron games room CTV TV cold storage calor gas camping gaz paraffin toilet fluid ☎ squash court licensed club, children's playground & private beach stables launderette
20£2.40 or 20£1.80 20▲£2.40 (awnings)

PERRANPORTH Cornwall Map 2 SW75
See sketch map.
►►►►► **Perran Beach Camping & Touring Park** *(SW766566)* ☎3551
1 ❶ ⚠
Mainly level, grass site set in typical Cornish downland. Adjacent to beach, sea and off B3285 Goonhavern–Perranporth road. 40acres 625pitches 307static

17 May–25 Sep rs3–16 May must book peak periods last arrival 21.00hrs last departure 10.00hrs 30 individual pitches late arrivals enclosure wc lit all night 2cdp 58washbasins hc central hot water (20hc) 24 warden (8wash, 2spin, 4dry) games room TV calor gas camping gaz cafe restaurant (licensed club) children's playground, private beach stables launderette pub 625£1.35–£4.54 or 625£1.35–£4.54 or 625▲£1.35–£4.54 (awnings)

►►►► **Perranporth Camping & Touring Site** *(SW768542)* Budnick Rd 2174
1 signposted
Part level, part sloping, grass site with bushes set in meadowland with direct access to sandy beach and sea. ½m E off B3285. 6acres 190pitches 10static
Spring Bank Hol–mid Sep rsEtr–mid May & last 2 wks Sep must book peak periods last arrival 21.00hrs 8 late arrivals enclosure 24wc lit all night 1cdp (33washbasins hc, 1central hot water, 1hc, 10hc) 8 warden (1wash, 1spin, 2iron) CTV (cold storage) calor gas camping gaz toilet fluid (hairdryers) children's playground & licensed club mobile shop stables launderette pub 30£2.60–£3.30 20£2.50–£3.20 140▲£2.50–£3.20 (awnings)

PERROTT'S BROOK Gloucestershire
Map 4 SP00
►► **Mayfield Park** Mayfield North Cerney 301
2
Part level, part sloping grass site, set in hilly meadowland in the Cotswolds – an area of outstanding natural beauty. Lying off A435, 2m from Cirencester, 12m from Cheltenham. 1acre 20pitches 44static
Etr–Oct must book peak periods last arrival sunset last departure 10.00hrs 2 5wc lit all night (1central hot water) (2hc) 1 launderette pub 20£1.60 or 20£1.60 or 20▲£1.60 (awnings)

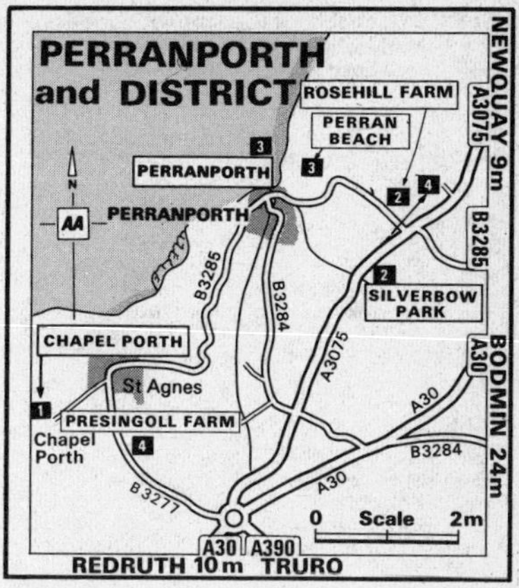

Sites listed under:
1 Chapel Porth **2** Goonhaven **3** Perranporth **4** St Agnes

PETERCHURCH Hereford and Worcester
Map 3 SO33
►► **Poston Caravan & Camping Park** *(SO355373)* 225
2
A level, grassy site with mature trees in hilly country near river. 11m W of Hereford on B4348. 5acres 40pitches 13static
Etr–Oct must book public hols last arrival 23.00hrs 6 10wc lit all night 1cdp 12washbasins hc (4hc) 2 warden (1wash, 1spin, 1iron,) games room (cold storage) calor gas camping gaz off licence stables pub 40£1.67 or 40£1.67 35▲£1.67 (awnings)

PEVENSEY BAY East Sussex Map 5 TQ60
►►►► Castle View Caravan Site
(TQ647033) Eastbourne Rd ☎Eastbourne 763038 (763438 winter)
2 ❸ ⚠
Situated ½m from the beach, this is a particularly well-kept site. Although close to the main road, fencing and bushes ensure privacy. 5acres 100pitches 37static
Apr–Oct must book peak periods
last arrival 20.00hrs last departure 12.00hrs
16 individual pitches Ⓐ 25wc lit all night
1cdp 27washbasins hc 8hc 8hc 14⊙
1iron (cold storage) calor gas camping gaz paraffin toilet fluid ☎ ⊞ children's playground stables cinema launderette pub
26£2.80–£3.60 12£2.10–£2.70
100▲£2.30–£3.10 (awnings) ltr

PLUMPTON Cumbria Map 12 NY43
►►► Greenacres Caravan Park
(NY501371) ☎206
2 ❶ ⚠ signposted
A small, level, grassy site, situated 200yds E of A6. Approach via B6413 from village centre.
1acre 20pitches 30static
Etr–Oct rsmid Mar must book peak periods
6 individual pitches wc 1cdp washbasins hc (1hc) 2hc 2⊙ (cold storage) calor gas ⊞ licensed club
20£2 or 20£2 or 20▲£2 (awnings) ltr

PLUMPTON RACECOURSE East Sussex Map 5 TQ31
►► Trax-Camping Site *(TQ364156)*
Plumpton Green
2 ❶ ⚠
Narrow strips of grass situated in the middle of this pretty racecourse at Plumpton Green set in peaceful and scenic countryside.
3acres 60pitches
2 May–20 Sep except 14, 15, 24 & 25 Aug & 1 Sep no bookings last arrival 22.30hrs last departure 15.00hrs 3 11wc lit all night 1cdp 10washbasins hc 3central hot water 4hc warden TV ☎ ⊞ games area
60£2–£2.35 or 60▲£2–£2.35 awnings

PLYMOUTH Devon Map 2 SX45
►►► Riverside Caravan Park *(SX515575)*
Longbridge Rd, Marsh Mills, Plympton (3m E off A38) ☎334122
3 ❷ ⚠ signposted
Level, with central tarmac road with spurs. The site is bordered on one side by the River Plym and the other by woods. Approach by way of Longbridge Road, which is east of Marsh Mills Roundabout. 4½acres 100pitches
All year must book peak periods 4 individual pitches Ⓐ late arrivals enclosure wc lit all night 1cdp washbasins hc (central hot water) (hc) ⊙ (wash, spin, dry) (cold storage) calor gas camping gaz ☎ ⊞ children's playground stables cinema launderette pub
80£2.16 or 80£2.16 20▲£2.16 (awnings)

POOLEY BRIDGE Cumbria Map 12 NY42
► Hillcroft Caravan & Camping Site
(NY478241) ☎363
1 ❶ ⚠ signposted
The site stands on a hillside overlooking a valley close to Ullswater, but offers only a glimpse of the lake. 10acres 125pitches 200static
Mar–Oct must book peak periods for caravans last departure 12.00hrs 10 Ⓐ 45wc lit all night 1cdp washbasins hc hc ⊙ warden (1wash, 1spin) calor gas camping gaz ⊞ pony trekking stables pub
25£2 10£1.70 90▲£1.80 (awnings)

PORLOCK Somerset Map 3 SS84
►►► Porlock Caravan Park ☎862269
2 ❷ ⚠
A well planned site, in valley, with shrubs and trees. 5acres 40pitches 56static
13 Mar–Oct must book peak periods last

departure 12.00hrs 14 18wc lit all night 1cdp 6washbasins hc (1central hot water) (6hc) (1wash) (1spin) (1dry, 2iron) calor gas camping gaz toilet fluid ladies hairdryer points stables launderette pub 40 or 40 (awnings)

POTTER HEIGHAM Norfolk Map 9 TG41
Homestead Site *(TG415189)*
Bridge Rd 461
Level, grass and gravel site with mature trees and bushes, set in meadowland, near River Thurne. Off A149, 400yds N of Potter Heigham new bridge. ½acre 10pitches 81static
20 Mar–Oct must book peak periods last departure 12.00hrs 6 individual pitches 23wc lit all night 1cdp 14washbasins hc (8hc) 2 (1spin) cold storage calor gas children's playground stables launderette pub
10£2.50 or 10£2.50 awnings

POTTERNE Wiltshire Map 3 ST95
Potterne Wick Touring Caravan Park
Potterne Wick Devizes 3277
signposted
Part level, part sloping, grass site with mature trees and bushes. ½m S of Potterne off A360 Devizes–Salisbury road, near to Kennet and Avon Canal. 1½acres 30pitches
Apr–Oct must book peak periods last arrival 22.00hrs last departure 12.00hrs 1 4wc lit all night 1cdp washbasins hc central hot water hc 1wash 1spin 1iron calor gas toilet fluid stables cinema launderette pub
30£1.60–£2 or 30£1.60–£2 or 30£1.60–£2 (awnings)

POUNDSTOCK Cornwall Map 2 SX29
Middle Penlean Caravan Site
Widemouth Bay 380
Part level, part sloping, grass site with trees and bushes. Situated in hilly woodland, moorland and down. 5m S on A39. 7acres 65pitches 3static
Apr–Oct must book peak periods last arrival 23.59hrs last departure 11.00hrs 5 6wc 1cdp (washbasins hc, central hot water, hc) (spin, dry, iron) cold storage calor gas camping gaz paraffin toilet fluid stables launderette pub
65fr 86p or 65fr75p or 65fr75p awnings

PRAA SANDS Cornwall Map 2 SW52
See sketch map.
Pengersick Caravan & Camping Site *(SW580284)* Germoe 2201
Part level, part sloping, grass site set in meadowland, adjacent to sea and beach at Hoe Point and Rinsey Head. Off A394 Helston–Penzance road. 6acres 200pitches 86static

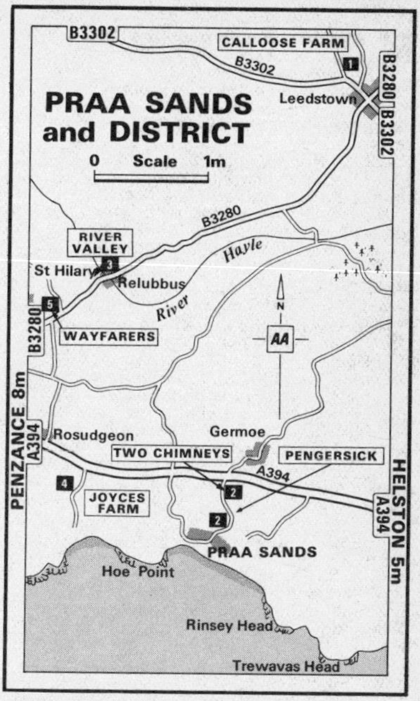

Sites listed under:
1 Leedstown **2** Praa Sands **3** Relubbus
4 Rosudgeon **5** St Hilary

All year no bookings last arrival 21.00hrs last departure 10.00hrs 21 wc lit all night washbasins hc central hot water (hc, hc) (wash, spin, iron) (cold storage) calor gas camping gaz pub
50£1.50 or 50£1.50 150fr£1.50 (awnings)

Two Chimneys Park *(SW580288)*
Germoe 3215
Partly level, partly sloping, grass site with bushes, set in meadowland with access to beach and sea at Praa Sands. 4m SE Marazion on the A394 Helston road. 12acres 70pitches 30static
21 May–24 Sep rsEtr–20 May & 25 Sep–30 Sep booking advisable last arrival 20.00hrs last departure 10.00hrs no pets wc lit all night 3cdp washbasins hc central hot water (hc) (wash, spin, iron) games room TV calor gas toilet fluid cafe licensed bar stables cinema launderette
70 or 70 or 70 ltr

PRESTON PATRICK Cumbria Map 7 SD58
►► Milness Hill Camping Site *(SD533838)*
☎Crooklands 306
[1] ❶ ⚠ signposted
This level and stony site is surrounded by hedges, bushes and trees. Located ½m from exit 36 on M6, this site is in an excellent position for touring the Lake District and Yorkshire Dales National Park. 25pitches 17static
Mar–Oct must book peak periods
last departure 12.00hrs 2 ⊛ 7wc
lit all night 1cdp washbasins hc central hot water (hc) ⊙ ⊖ stables pub
13£1.70 or 13£1.50 12▲£1.40
(awnings)

PRIDDY Somerset Map 3 ST55
See Cheddar sketch map.
► Mendip Heights Caravan & Camping Park Townsend ☎241
[1] ❶ signposted
Situated in an open field in an elevated position overlooking the Mendip Hills.
2½acres 45pitches 2static
Mid Mar–Oct must book peak periods
last arrival 22.00hrs last departure 12.00hrs
3 ⊛ 6wc lit all night 1cdp 6washbasins hc (hc) ⊙ warden (cold storage) calor gas camping gaz cafe ⊞ off licence ⊖ stables pub
45£2.10 or 45£1.90 or 45▲£2.10
(awnings)

RATTERY Devon Map 3 SX76
►►► Edeswell Caravan Site *(SX731606)*
Edeswell Farm ☎South Brent 2177
[2] ❶ ⚠ signposted
Gently sloping, grass site with mature trees, in hilly country and near river. Off A385.
¾acre 10pitches 27static
15 Mar–Oct must book peak periods
last arrival 22.00hrs last departure 12.00hrs
6 ⊛ late arrivals enclosure 5wc
lit all night 1cdp (washbasins hc) (hc) ⊙ spin (iron) cold storage calor gas camping gaz ⊞ ⊖ stables launderette pub
10£1.08 or 10£1.08 or 10▲£1.08
(awnings)

RAVENGLASS Cumbria Map 6 SD09
►► Walls Caravan Park *(SD103966)*
☎250
[2] ❷ ⚠ signposted
This site is set in a woodland park and is part level, and part sloping with a mainly grass surface. 4acres 40pitches
Mar–Oct must book public hols 4
individual pitches late arrivals enclosure wc
lit all night 1cdp washbasins hc central hot water hc ⊙ warden calor gas ⊞ ⊖
pub
40£2 or 40£2 awnings ltr

REDHILL Avon Map 3 ST46
►► *Brook Lodge Caravan Park*
☎Wrington 862311
[1] ❶ ⚠
Farm site is in slightly sloping meadowland with small orchard and walled garden. Off A38.
2acres
Mar–Nov must book Jul & Aug last departure 14.00hrs 6 8wc lit all night 8washbasins hc central hot water (4hc) 3⊙ warden calor gas camping gaz toilet fluid ☎ ⊞ ⊖ stables launderette
29 or 29 or 29▲ (awnings)

REDMIRE North Yorkshire Map 7 SE09
See Leyburn sketch map.
►► Elm House Wood Caravan Site
(SE051914) Elm House ☎Wensleydale 22313
[2] ❷ ⚠ signposted
Site is situated 4½m W of Leyburn on the N side of Wensleydale. On a hillside commanding a superb view looking S to Penn Hill.
1¼acres 20pitches
Etr–Oct booking advisable peak periods
last arrival 20.00hrs last departure 12.00hrs
2 individual pitches 5wc 1cdp
4washbasins hc central hot water 2hc 1⊙
calor gas toilet fluid ⊞ children's playground ⊖ stables launderette pub
20£2 or 20£2 (awnings) ltr

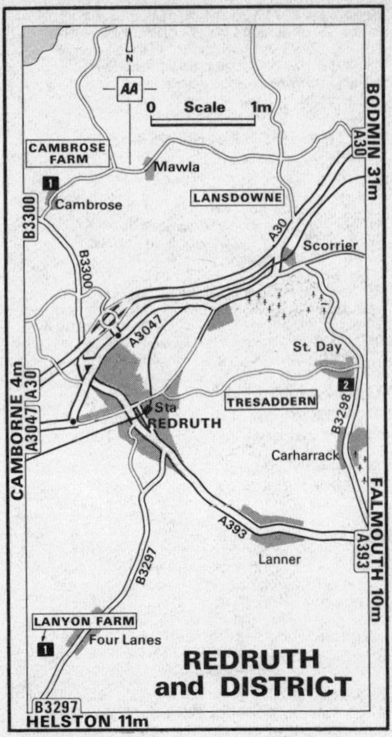

Sites listed under:
1 Redruth **2** St Day

REDRUTH Cornwall Map 2 SW64
See sketch map.
►►► Cambrose Farm Camp Site
(SW684453) Portreath Rd
☎Porthtowan 890747 (out of season Helston 2301)
[2] ❷ ⚠ signposted
A level, grassy site with mature trees and bushes. 2m from Redruth off B3300 by-pass.
3acres 50pitches
Etr–Oct must book peak periods
last arrival 23.00hrs last departure 12.00hrs
4 12wc lit all night 1cdp 11washbasins hc central hot water 5hc 1⊙ warden (1wash, 1spin, 1dry, 1iron) cold storage calor gas camping gaz paraffin toilet fluid ☎ ⊞ children's playground off licence ⊖ stables cinema launderette pub
50£3 or 50£2.50 or 50▲£3 (awnings)

►►► Lanyon Farm Caravan Park
(SW685389) Four Lanes ☎216447
[2] ❷ ⚠ signposted
Part level, part sloping, grass site with young trees and bushes. Situated in meadowland within the urban area, 2m S of Redruth off B3297. 2½acres 25pitches 49static
Spring Bank Hol–Sep rsOct & Etr–mid May
last arrival 22.00hrs last departure 22.00hrs
4 individual pitches late arrivals enclosure
6wc lit all night 1cdp 4washbasins hc
4hc 2⊙ (1wash, 1dry, 1iron) (cold storage)
calor gas camping gaz toilet fluid ⊞
children's playground ⊖ cinema
launderette pub
25£1.89 or 25£1.89 or 25▲£1.89
awnings ltr

REJERRAH Cornwall Map 2 SW85
►►►► Monkey Tree Tourist Park
☎Perranporth 2032
[2] ❷ ⚠ signposted
Situated amidst downland and meadowland.

Access from Rejerrah–Zelah road off A3075. 12acres 185pitches Spring Bank Hol–Oct rsApril must book peak periods last arrival 22.00hrs last departure 13.00hrs 11 individual pitches late arrivals enclosure 29wc lit all night 1cdp washbasins hc 4central hot water 15hc 4 warden (1wash) 1spin (1dry) 2iron games room TV cold storage calor gas camping gaz toilet fluid children's playground off licence stables launderette pub 185£1.10–£3.20 or 185£1.10–£3.20 or 185£1.10–£3.20 awnings

Newperran Tourist Site *(SW803554)* Hendra Croft Perranporth 2407
2 1 signposted
A level, grassy site with well-dispersed bushes. 4m SE of Newquay and 1m S of Rejerrah on A3075. 24acres 350pitches Mid May–mid Sep must book Jul & Aug last arrival 21.00hrs last departure 01.00hrs 21 individual pitches late arrivals enclosure 35wc lit all night 1cdp 35washbasins hc 3central hot water (16hc) 8 warden (2wash) 2spin (2dry) 4iron games room CTV 2cold storage calor gas camping gaz toilet fluid stables cinema 100 50 200

New Braefel Tourist Park *(SW792546)* Perranporth 2561
2 3 signposted
Level, grass site with young trees and bushes, set in meadowland, with access to the sea, Holywell beach and A3075 Newquay road, W of Rejerrah village off unclassified road. 5acres 135pitches 2static Etr–Oct must book peak periods last arrival 21.00hrs last departure 12.00hrs 6 individual pitches late arrivals enclosure wc lit all night cdp 20washbasins hc (10hc) (1spin) 1iron (cold storage) calor gas camping gaz paraffin toilet fluid off licence & children's playground stables launderette pub 135£2.10 or 135£2.10 or 135£2.10 awnings

RELUBBUS Cornwall Map 2 SW53
See Praa Sands sketch map.
River Valley Caravan Park *(SW565320)* Germoe 3398
3 3 signposted
Level, grass and gravel site with mature trees and bushes, set in woodland and meadowland with direct access to shallow trout stream. Situated in a picturesque valley 4m from N and S coast sandy beaches. Site is partly wooded, well-drained and sheltered by gently sloping hills. 3m from Marazion on B3280. 18acres 90pitches Mar–Oct must book 20 Jul–20 Aug last arrival 21.00hrs last departure 12.00hrs 20 individual pitches late arrivals enclosure 20wc lit all night 1cdp 16washbasins hc 4central hot water 8hc 2 (cold storage) calor gas camping gaz trout fishing (battery charging) pub 70fr£2 10fr£2 10fr£2.30 (awnings)

RICHMOND North Yorkshire Map 7 NZ10
Swale View Caravan Site *(NZ134013)* Reeth Rd 3106
1 1
A level, grassy site shaded by trees, lying on the banks of the River Swale in picturesque Swaledale country. 3m W of Richmond on A6108. 10acres 75pitches 100static Mar–Oct must book peak periods last arrival 22.00hrs last departure 12.00hrs 12 individual pitches 24wc lit all night 1cdp washbasins hc hc (spin, dry, iron) calor gas camping gaz toilet fluid children's playground cinema launderette pub 20£1.80 or 5£1.30 or 50£1.70 (awnings)

RIPON North Yorkshire Map 8 SE37
Ure Bank Tourist Caravan Site *(SE317726)* Ure Bank 2964
2 1 signposted
Near the town centre, this pleasant and well-maintained site stands on high ground overlooking the River Ure. 8acres 199pitches Mar–Oct must book peak periods last arrival 22.00hrs last departure 10.00hrs individual pitches 65wc lit all night 4cdp 32washbasins hc 24hc 5 warden games room calor gas camping gaz paraffin toilet fluid children's playground stables launderette pub 175£1.80 or 175£1.80 24£2.10 (awnings)

ROCKBEARE Devon Map 3 SY09
Bidgood Arms Caravan Site Whimple 822262
2 2 signposted
A convenient night stop on the A30, the site is on level ground with grass pitches. 2acres 30pitches 16 Mar–Oct must book peak periods last arrival 23.59hrs last departure 12.00hrs 2 9wc lit all night 1cdp 4washbasins hc (2hc) 2 cold storage calor gas camping gaz cafe restaurant licensed club, children's playground mobile shop stables pub 20£1.50 or 20£1.20 10£1.20 awnings

RODBOROUGH Near Stroud, Gloucestershire Map 3 SO80
Rodborough Fort Holiday Camping & Caravanning Centre Stroud 3478
2 2 signposted
Level and sloping, grass site with saplings and bushes set in hilly country. ¾m E of Stroud from A46. 7acres 53pitches 27static Apr–6 Oct must book peak periods last departure 12.00hrs 4 individual pitches late arrivals enclosure 11wc lit all night 1cdp 10washbasins hc (6hc) 3 (1iron) cold storage) calor gas camping gaz toilet fluid children's play area stables pub 33£1.90–£2.20 or 33£1.90–£2.20 20£2.20–£2.60 (awnings)

RODNEY STOKE Somerset Map 3 ST44
See Cheddar sketch map.
Bucklegrove Caravan & Camping Park Priddy 261
3 2 signposted
Slightly elevated site screened by trees and shrubs but still offering good open rural views. 6acres 98pitches 123static Mar–Oct must book peak periods last arrival 22.00hrs last departure 13.00hrs 11 late arrivals enclosure 18wc lit all night 1cdp (washbasins hc, central hot water, hc hc) (wash, spin, dry, iron) calor gas camping gaz toilet fluid off licence & children's playground stables cinema launderette pub 78£1.80–£2.30 or 78£1.80–£2.30 20£1.80–£2.30 (awnings) ltr

ROLLESTON Nottinghamshire Map 8 SK75
Trax Campsite *(SK735526)* Southwell Racecourse
2 2 signposted
Mainly level, grass site set in meadowland. Approach is via Southwell on A612. 4acres 60pitches 2 May–13 Sep no bookings last arrival 22.30hrs last departure 15.00hrs 3 15wc lit all night 1cdp 10washbasins hc 2central hot water 2hc 2 warden TV calor gas camping gaz children's playground games area free racing for campers 5, 12 & 24 May, 25 & 26 Aug stables cinema launderette 60£2–£2.35 or 60£2–£2.35 or 60£2–£2.35 awnings

ROSS-ON-WYE Hereford and Worcester Map 3 SO52
Cottage Caravan Park *(SO603252)* Ledbury Rd 2362
2 2
Partly level and sloping, grass site with mature

trees and bushes, set in downland and meadowland within the urban area; views overlooking Chase Hill and woods. ½m NE of Ross-on-Wye on A4149. 2acres 50pitches 32static
Mar–Oct must book peak periods last arrival 21.30hrs last departure 12.00hrs 4 individual pitches 6wc lit all night 1cdp 6washbasins hc central hot water (4 hc) 2 warden 1spin (iron) calor gas camping gaz stables cinema launderette
25 £2.50 or 25 £2 25▲£2.50 (awnings)

ROSUDGEON Cornwall Map 2 SW52
See Praa Sands sketch map.
►► Joyces Farm Caravan & Camp Site *(SW562287)* Higher Kenneggy ☎ Germoe 3453
1 ❶ ⚠ signposted
A level, grassy site with bushes, near the sea and beach. Set in hilly woodland country near moorland and downs. 6½m W of Helston off A394, overlooking Mounts Bay. 4½acres 60pitches 9static
Mar–Oct must book peak periods last departure 12.00hrs 12 12wc lit all night 1cdp washbasins hc (central hot water, hc) (wash, spin, dry, iron) (cold storage) calor gas camping gaz ☎ mobile shop stables launderette pub
30 £1.60 or 30 £1.60 30▲£1.60 (awnings)

ROTHBURY Northumberland Map 12 NU00
►► Coquetdale Caravan Park *(NU055007)* Whitton ☎20549
2 ❷ ⚠ signposted
Partly level, and sloping, grass site with mixed vegetation set in hilly country adjacent to River Coquet overlooked by Simonside Hills and moorland, ½m SW of Rothbury on the Newtown road. 1⅓acres 50pitches 154static
Etr–Oct booking advisable peak periods 16 26wc 2cdp washbasins hc (hc) warden (iron) calor gas camping gaz stables launderette pub
50 £2 or 50 £2 or 50▲£2 awnings

ROUSDON Devon Map 3 SY29
►►► West Hayes Caravan Park Sidmouth Rd ☎ Colyton 52502
3 ❷ ⚠
Level, grass site set in downland. On A3052 between Sidmouth and Lyme Regis. 7acres 150pitches
Etr–15 Nov must book peak periods last arrival 23.00hrs 6 individual pitches late arrivals enclosure 16wc lit all night 1cdp (20washbasins hc, 8 hc) 8 warden (2wash, 1dry) (cold storage) calor gas camping gaz toilet fluid cafe ☎ licensed club & children's playground stables cinema launderette pub
150 £2.60 or 150 £2.50 (awnings)

►► Shrubbery Caravan Park ☎ Lyme Regis 2227
2 ❷ ⚠ signposted
Mainly level, grass site adjacent to main road. 11½acres 87pitches
15 Mar–15 Nov must book last arrival 21.30hrs last departure 11.00hrs 28 individual pitches late arrivals enclosure 28wc lit all night 1cdp washbasins hc (hc) (wash, 1spin, 1dry, 1iron) (cold storage) calor gas camping gaz paraffin toilet fluid ☎ children's playground launderette pub
77 £2.43 or 77 £2.06 10▲£2.43 (awnings)

ROWDE Wiltshire Map 3 ST96
►►► Lakeside ☎ Devizes 2767
2 ❷ ⚠ signposted
A level, grass and gravel site with saplings and bushes set in meadowland near lake, and within the urban area. 3acres 30pitches 3static
Apr–Oct must book last arrival 22.00hrs last departure 12.00hrs 4 10wc lit all night 12washbasins hc (1central hot water, 4 hc) 3 warden (cold storage) calor gas camping gaz fishing stables cinema launderette pub
30 £2.20 or 30 £2.20 or 30▲£2.20 (awnings)

RUGELEY Staffordshire Map 7 SK01
► Silver Trees Caravan & Chalet Park *(SK014173)* ☎2185
2 ❶ ⚠
Situated on rising ground on Cannock Chase amidst attractive woodland. 4acres 10pitches 57static
Apr–Oct booking advisable last arrival 20.00hrs last departure 11.30hrs 8 individual pitches 17wc lit all night 2cdp (central hot water, hc, hc) spin (dry, iron) games room TV calor gas children's playground cinema launderette pub
10 £1.50 or 10 £1.50 (awnings) ltr

RUMFORD Cornwall Map 2 SW87
See Padstow sketch map.
►►► Music Water Touring Site ☎257
3 ❷ ⚠ signposted
Quiet park in rural surroundings near sandy beaches. Slightly sloping, level grass and gravel site in moorland and meadowland, 4m S of Padstow on B3274. 7½acres 140pitches 3static
Etr–Oct must book 21 Jul–Aug last departure 10.00hrs 11 late arrivals enclosure 23wc lit all night 2cdp 24washbasins hc central hot water (hc) 4 (1wash, 1spin) (cold storage) calor gas. camping gaz toilet fluid ☎ licensed club children's playground battery charging stables cinema launderette pub
140 £2.10–£3 or 140 £2.10–£3 or 140▲£2.10–£3 (awnings)

RUTHERNBRIDGE Cornwall Map 2 SX06
►►► Ruthern Valley Holidays *(SX014665)* ☎ Lanivet 395
3 ❷ ⚠ signposted
Gently sloping, grass site with mature trees, set in hilly woodland country, adjacent to River Ruthern. Hard standing and well drained grass pitches – 40 minutes from coast. 2m SW of Bodmin off A30. Jul & Aug 2acres 30pitches

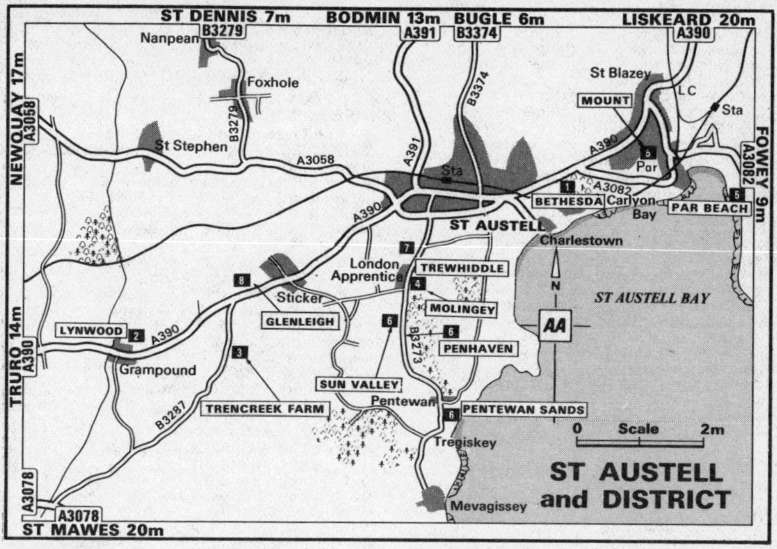

Sites listed under:
1 Carlyon Bay **2** Grampound **3** Hewas Water **4** London Apprentice **5** Par
6 Pentewan **7** St Austell **8** Sticker

18static
May–Sep rsApr & Oct must book last arrival 20.00hrs last departure 11.00hrs 2 individual pitches 4wc lit all night 1cdp 5washbasins hc 2 hc 2 cold storage calor gas camping gaz ⊞ children's playground & wash up sinks stables pub
30 £2.20–£2.90 or 30 £2–£2.70 or 30▲£2.20–£2.90 (awnings)

ST AGNES Cornwall Map 2 SW75
See Perranporth sketch map.
►► Presingoll Farm ☎2333
1 ❶ ⚠
Level, grassy site set in meadowland within the urban area, with cliff scenery close to sand/shingle beach, 1½ m off A30 on B3277. 3½acres 80pitches 2static
Apr–Oct must book peak periods last departure 12.00hrs 3 7wc lit all night 1cdp (9washbasins hc, 3 hc) 2 warden (1spin, 1dry, 2iron) cold storage ☎ ⊞ children's playground stables launderette pub
80 £1.50 or 80 £1.50 or 80▲£1.50 awnings

ST AUSTELL Cornwall Map 2 SX05
See sketch map.
►►► Trewhiddle Caravan & Camping Park *(SX006511)* ☎2659
2 ❷ ⚠ signposted
Secluded wooded site with well kept gardens, lawns and flower beds. 7½acres 125pitches 109static
27 May–30 Sep rsOct–26 May must book peak periods last arrival 22.00hrs last departure 11.00hrs 11 late arrivals enclosure 37wc lit all night 4cdp (4central hot water) (9 hc) 6 warden (2wash, spin, dry, iron) (cold storage) calor gas camping gaz paraffin licensed bar ☎ ⊞ stables cinema launderette
25 100 or 100▲ (awnings)

ST BURYAN Cornwall Map 2 SW42
See sketch map.
►► Lower Treave Caravan Park

Sites listed under: **1** Lamorna **2** St Buryan **3** St Just **4** Sennen

(SW388272) ☎559
2 ❷ ⚠ signposted
Terraced, grass site with saplings and bushes, set in meadowland. 4m NE of Land's End off A30.
4acres 79pitches 5static
Etr–Oct must book peak periods last arrival 22.00hrs last departure 12.00hrs 17 individual pitches 12wc lit all night 1cdp 15washbasins hc (4 hc) 2⊙ warden calor gas camping gaz ⊞ mobile ⊖ launderette
80 or 80 or 80▲ (awnings)

►►Tower Farm Caravan & Camping Park
(SW406263) ☎286
2 ❸ ⚠ signposted
This is a farm site situated near Land's End.
6acres 172pitches 6static
Etr–Oct must book peak periods last arrival 22.00hrs last departure 11.00hrs 14 Ⓐ 22wc lit all night 3cdp washbasins hc central hot water (hc) ⊙ warden (wash, spin, dry, iron) TV (cold storage) calor gas camping gaz paraffin ☎ ⊞ children's playground ⊖ launderette
60fr£2.20 172fr£2.20 or 172▲fr£2.20 (awnings)

►►Treverven Camping & Touring Site
(SW410237) Treverven Farm ☎546
2 ❸ ⚠ signposted
A well maintained campsite with panoramic views. 6acres 80pitches
Etr–Oct no bookings last departure 12.00hrs 10 individual pitches 12wc lit all night 1cdp 14washbasins hc 7 hc 2⊙ (1wash, 1dry) 1cold storage camping gaz ☎ ⊞ mobile shop ⊖ pub
80£2.30 or 80£2.30 or 80▲£2.30 awnings

ST CLETHER Cornwall Map 2 SX28
►Ta-Mill *(SX187848)* ☎ Otterham Station 381
2 ❶ ⚠
Situated in an open valley with stream running through. 8acres 20pitches 3static
Etr–Oct booking advisable peak periods last arrival 22.00hrs last departure 12.00hrs 5 Ⓐ late arrivals enclosure 5wc lit all night 1cdp 7washbasins hc 1central hot water (2 hc) ⊙ warden 1iron games room CTV (2cold storage) toilet fluid cafe licensed bar ☎ ⊞ children's playground fishing lake ⊖ stables
20£2.50 or 20£2 or 20▲£1.50 (awnings)

ST COLUMB MAJOR Cornwall Map 2 SW96
See Newquay sketch map.
►►►Tregatillian Caravan Park
(SW923630) Tregatillian ☎ St Columb 880482
3 ❷ ⚠ signposted
A level site set in hilly woodland country with access to sea and beach. 1½m E of town. Approach from the town is only via the by-pass (A39). 8acres 117pitches 85static
24 May–12 Sep rs10–23 May & 13–30 Sep must book peak periods last departure 13.00hrs 15 Ⓐ 17wc lit all night 1cdp 20washbasins hc 10 hc 6⊙ (2wash, 1spin, 2iron) games room TV cold storage calor gas camping gaz toilet fluid ☎ ⊞ licensed club & children's playground ⊖ stables launderette pub
17£1.50–£2.60 or 17£1.50–£2.60 100▲£1.50–£2.60 (awnings)

ST DAY Cornwall Map 2 SW74
See Redruth sketch map.
►►►Tresaddern Caravan Park
(SW733422) ☎820459
2 ❷ ⚠ signposted
Sloping, grass site with trees and bushes set in meadowland and downland. 2m NE of Redruth on B3298. 2acres 25pitches 12static
Etr–Oct must book peak periods last arrival 22.00hrs last departure 14.00hrs 3 individual pitches 8wc lit all night 1cdp 8washbasins hc central hot water (hc) 4⊙ iron cold storage calor gas camping gaz ☎ ⊞ ⊖ cinema launderette pub
25£1.75–£2 or 25£1.75–£2 or 25▲£1.75–£2 awnings

ST EWE Cornwall Map 2 SW94
►►Pengrugla Caravan & Campsite
(SX001469) ☎ Mevagissey 3485
3 ❶ ⚠
Part level, part sloping, grassy site with trees and

bushes situated amidst woodland and meadowland near main road, off B3273. 6acres 120pitches 17 May–20 Sep booking advisable peak periods last departure 10.30hrs 6 individual pitches 12wc lit all night 1cdp 4 16washbasins hc (6hc) 6⊙ (1wash, 1spin, 1dry, 2iron) cold storage calor gas camping gaz toilet fluid ☎ ⊞ stables launderette pub 60£1.89–£2.70 60£1.89–£2.70 or 60▲£1.89–£2.70 awnings

ST GILES ON THE HEATH Devon Map 2 SX39

►►► Chapmanswell Caravan Park
☎ Ashwater 382
2 ❷ ⚠ signposted
This site is situated on A388 in open country with panoramic views. 3½acres 61pitches 20static Mar–Oct must book peak periods 5 late arrivals enclosure 15wc lit all night 1cdp 15washbasins hc central hot water (hc) ⊙ warden (wash, spin, iron) TV (cold storage) calor gas camping gaz paraffin toilet fluid ☎ ⊞ children's playground stables pub 61£1.80–£2.40 or 61£1.80–£2.40 or 61▲£1.80–£2.40 (awnings)

ST HELENS Isle of Wight Map 4 SZ68
See Shanklin sketch map.

►►► Nodes Point Holiday Village *(SZ637899)* Nodes Rd ☎ Bembridge 2401
2 ❷ ⚠ signposted
Part of large holiday complex. Site on slight gradient with grass surface. Near beach. The campsite entrance is off Duver Road. No pets 10acres 270pitches 243static 19 May–29 Sep must book Jul & Aug last departure 10.00hrs 10 late arrivals enclosure wc lit all night 30washbasins hc 9hc 4⊙ (2wash, 2spin, 1dry) 2iron 2games rooms camping gaz children's playroom cafe entertainment licensed bar ☎ ⊞ stables launderette pub 270▲

ST HILARY Cornwall Map 2 SW53
See Praa Sands sketch map.

►► Wayfarers Camping Site *(SW554311)*
☎ Germoe 3326
2 ❷ ⚠ signposted
A level, grass site with trees, saplings and bushes, adjacent to B3280 1m past Relubbus village, on right. 3½acres 60pitches 6static All year must book peak periods last arrival 23.59hrs last departure 12.00hrs 5 late arrivals enclosure 8wc lit all night 1cdp 10washbasins hc (hc) ⊙ warden (1wash, 1spin, 1dry, 1iron) (cold storage) calor gas camping gaz ☎ ⊞ children's playground, battery charging & hairdryer stables launderette pub 60£1.75–£2.65 or 60£1.75–£2.65 60▲£1.75–£2.65 (awnings)

ST IVES Cornwall Map 2 SW54
See sketch map.

►►► Ayr Holiday Park *(SW509408)*
☎ Penzance 795855
2 ❷ ⚠ signposted
Part level, part sloping, grass site set in meadowland, adjacent to sea and sandy beach. ½m W of B3306. 2acres 40pitches 60static Apr–Oct must book peak periods last arrival 20.30hrs 11 16wc lit all night 1cdp (14washbasins hc) (central hot water) (6hc) ⊙ (1wash, 1dry, 1iron) (cold storage) calor gas camping gaz ☎ ⊞ stables cinema launderette pub 40 or 40 or 40▲ (awnings)

► Higher Penderleith Site *(SW492383)*
Towedrash ☎ Penzance 796576
1 ❶ ⚠ signposted
A level and sloping, grass site 1m SW of Halsetown on B3311. 4acres 50pitches Etr–Oct last departure 11.00hrs 5 11wc lit all night 1cdp stables cinema launderette pub 50 or 50 or 50▲ (awnings)

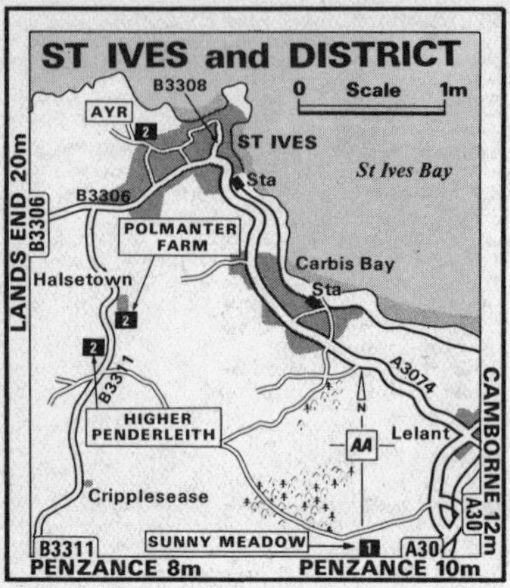

Sites listed under:
1 Lelant Downs **2** St Ives

► **Polmanter Farm Campsite** *(SW510388)*
Halsetown ☎ Penzance 795640
2 ❷ ⚠ signposted
Level grass site set in meadowland with access to sea, beach, hills and St Ives Bay. On B3311.
8¾acres 150pitches
29 May–Sep rsEtr–28 May must book last departure 10.00hrs 10 ⓐ 1wc 1cdp 8washbasins hc 6central hot water (14 hc) 5 warden (2wash, 1spin, 2dry, 1iron) (cold storage) calor gas camping gaz toilet fluid ☎ ⊞ children's playground stables cinema launderette pub
25 £2.35 or 25 £2.20 125▲£2.20 (awnings)

ST JUST Cornwall Map 2 SW33
See St Buryan sketch map.
►► **Kelynack Caravan Park** *(SW374301)*
☎ St Buryan 465
2 ❷ ⚠
Level, grass and gravel site with mature trees and bushes set in moorland and meadowland close to sea, ¾m S of St Just on B3306.
1acre 10pitches 10static
Apr–Oct booking advisable peak periods last arrival 22.00hrs last departure 10.00hrs 6 individual pitches ⓐ 6wc lit all night 1cdp (washbasins hc, central hot water, hc) (iron) calor gas ☎ ⊞ children's playground stables launderette pub
10 £2 or 10 £2 or 10▲£2 awnings

ST JUST-IN-ROSELAND Cornwall Map 2 SW83
►►► **Trethem Mill Caravan Site** *(SW860365)* ☎ Portscatho 504
2 ❷ ⚠ signposted
Part level, part sloping, grass site with young trees and bushes. Set in hilly meadowland country close to sea and main road. 3¾acres 84pitches
Apr–Oct must book last arrival 21.00hrs last departure 11.00hrs 5 individual pitches ⓐ 16wc lit all night 1cdp 12washbasins hc (central hot water, hc,) warden (1wash, 1iron) cold storage calor gas camping gaz paraffin toilet fluid cafe ☎ ⊞ children's playground stables launderette pub
84 £2.82 or 84 £2.82 or 84▲£2.82 (awnings) ltr

ST LEONARDS Dorset Map 4 SU00
►►►► **Camping International** *(SU104024)* Athol Lodge ☎ Ferndown 872817
2 ❷ ⚠ signposted
Small, well-equipped, level camping site surrounded by trees. Adjacent to main A31.
2½acres 60pitches
Etr–Oct rsMar must book peak periods last arrival 22.00hrs last departure 11.00hrs 4 individual pitches ⓐ late arrivals enclosure 10wc lit all night 1cdp 9washbasins hc 9central hot water (4 hc) 4 warden (1spin, 1dry, 1iron) games room CTV cold storage calor gas camping gaz toilet fluid cafe restaurant ☎ ⊞ licensed club, children's playground, cycle hire & take away food stables launderette pub
60 £2.30–£3 or 60▲£2.30–£3 awnings

►►►► **Shamba Camping Park** *(SU105029)* ☎ Ferndown 873302
2 ❸ ⚠ signposted
Level grassy site with mixed vegetation. Set in

hilly woodland country. 3m W of Ringwood on A31. ⊗ Jul & Aug 5½acres 150pitches May–20 Sep rsApr must book peak periods last arrival 22.00hrs last departure 12.00hrs 5🚿 individual pitches 18wc lit all night 1cdp 21washbasins hc central hot water (6🚿hc) 2⊙ 2spin (2dry) 2iron games room TV calor gas camping gaz cafe restaurant ☎ ⊞ licensed club, children's playground, take away food, freezer pack hire ♨ ⊖ stables ♂ ✈ ⚓ launderette pub
150🚐£2.45 or 150▲£2.45 awnings

▶▶▶ *Oakdene Holiday Park* *(SU095014)*
☎ Ferndown 875422
2 ❷ ⚠ signposted
Level, grass site set in commonland. 3m W of Ringwood on A31. 10acres 260pitches 200static
Mar–Oct last departure 12.00hrs 30🚿 individual pitches Ⓐ 36wc lit all night 3cdp 36washbasins hc 18🚿hc 12⊙ warden (games room) calor gas camping gaz paraffin toilet fluid cafe licensed bar ☎ ⊞ paddling pool children's play area ♨ ⊖ stables ♂ ⚓ launderette
260🚗 or 260🚐 or 200▲ (awnings) ltr

ST MABYN Cornwall Map 2 SX07
▶▶▶▶ Glenmorris Caravan & Camping Park ☎236
1 ❶ ⚠ signposted
Site divided into three enclosures on level and well drained land. Situated in delightful rural area between moors and sea. 12acres 150pitches 22static
Apr–Oct must book peak periods last departure 12.00hrs 6🚿 Ⓐ late arrivals enclosure 21wc lit all night 2cdp ⊕ 26washbasins hc 4central hot water (10🚿hc) 4⊙ (1wash, 1spin, 1dry, 1iron) CTV calor gas camping gaz cafe restaurant ☎ ⊞ children's playground, wash up sinks & hairdryers ♨ ⊖ stables pub
150🚗£2.16 or 150🚐£2.16 or 150▲£2.16 (awnings) ltr

ST MERRYN Padstow, Cornwall Map 2 SW87
See Padstow sketch map.
▶ *Carnevas Caravan & Camping Site*
Carnevas Farm ☎520230
2 ❷ ⚠ signposted
Level, grass site set in meadowland. Off B3276 Padstow–Newquay road 2m SW of village. 8acres 198pitches
Apr–Oct must book school hols last arrival 22.00hrs last departure 10.00hrs 10🚿 wc lit all night 2cdp washbasins hc 🚿hc ⊙ spin iron cold storage calor gas camping gaz ☎ ⊞ ♨ ⊖ stables ♂ ✈ cinema ⚓ launderette pub
100🚗 or 100🚐 98▲ rates on application (awnings)

ST MINVER Cornwall Map 2 SW97
▶▶▶ *St Minver House Holiday Estate*
☎ Trebetherick 2305
2 ❶ ⚠ signposted
A level site amongst sylvan surroundings. ⊗ 15acres 233pitches 130static
Mid May–mid Sep rsEtr–mid May must book peak periods last arrival 18.00hrs last departure 10.00hrs 🚿 Ⓐ wc lit all night washbasins hc central hot water (🚿hc) ⊙ (wash, spin, iron) ⛵ games room CTV calor gas camping gaz crazy golf children's playground licensed bar ☎ ⊞ ♨ ⊖ stables ♂ ✈ cinema ⚓ launderette pub
83🚗 150▲ prices on application ltr

ST NICHOLAS AT WADE Kent Map 5 TR26
▶ St Nicholas-at-Wade Camping Site
(TR254672) Court Rd ☎ Thanet 81245
1 ❶ ⚠
A small site near an attractive farmhouse and well secluded by tall hedges; situated in a pleasant country village. 3acres 75pitches
Etr–Oct must book peak periods last arrival 22.00hrs 3🚿 Ⓐ 8wc lit all night 8washbasins hc 4🚿hc 2⊙ (cold storage) calor gas camping gaz ⊞ children's playground ♨ ⊖ stables ♂ ✈ ⚓ launderette pub
5🚐£1.50 70▲£1.80 (awnings)

ST OSYTH Essex Map 5 TM11
▶▶ Hutleys Caravan Park *(TM128128)*
St Osyth Beach ☎ Clacton-on-Sea 820712
2 ❶ ⚠
Situated on St Osyth Marshes, a flat area overlooking the sea. The present owners purchased about 1m of beach in 1920 which is now a sea shore car park and picnic area.
⊗ 1½acres 25pitches 740static
Etr–Oct rsMar must book for caravans last departure 20.00hrs 3🚿 individual pitches late arrivals enclosure wc lit all night 1cdp ⊕ washbasins hc central hot water 🚿hc ⊙ (wash, spin, iron) games room CTV (cold storage) calor gas toilet fluid cafe restaurant ☎ ⊞ licensed club, children's playground, (private beach) & chemist ♨ ⊖ stables ♂ ✈ cinema ⚓ launderette pub
25🚗£1.60 or 25🚐£1.30 (awnings)

SALCOMBE REGIS Devon Map 3 SY18
▶▶ *Salcombe Regis Caravan & Camping Site* ☎ Sidmouth 4303
2 ❷ ⚠
Pleasant hilltop site bordered by hedgerows; situated about 2m from Sidmouth. 16½acres 100pitches 10static
27 May–30 Sep rsEtr must book peak periods last arrival 20.00hrs last departure 10.00hrs 10🚿 individual pitches Ⓐ 15wc 1cdp 14washbasins hc (6🚿hc) 4⊙ (iron) calor gas camping gaz ☎ ⊞ ⊖ stables ♂ cinema ⚓ launderette
40🚗 or 40🚐 60▲ (awnings)

▶ Kings Down Tail Caravan & Camping Site
(SY173907) Kings Down Tail Farm
☎ Branscombe 313
2 ❶ ⚠ signposted
Situated on level ground on east side of Sid Valley in tree sheltered position. Opposite Branscombe water tower on A3052 2½m E of Sidford and 1m W of junction A3052/B3174.
5acres 100pitches
15 Mar–14 Nov must book peak periods

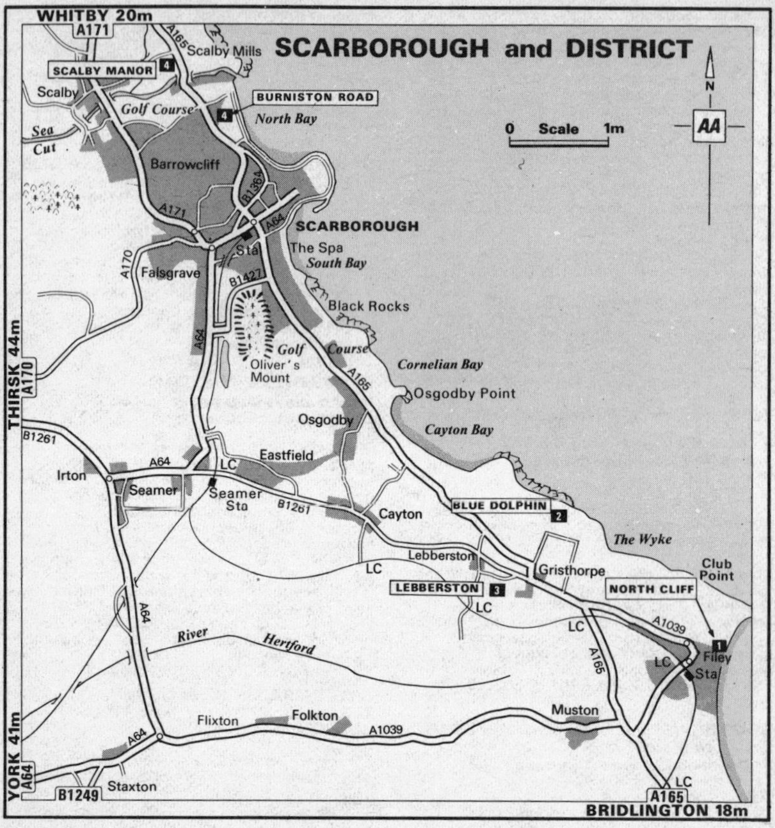

Sites listed under: **1** Filey **2** Gristhorpe Bay **3** Lebberston **4** Scarborough

last arrival 22.30hrs last departure 13.00hrs 7♣ late arrivals enclosure 13wc lit all night 1cdp 9washbasins hc 10⛆hc 4⊖ warden (cold storage) calor gas camping gaz toilet fluid ⊞ ♨ ⊖ stables ⌒ launderette pub 100⊕£2.50–£2.70 or 100⊖£2.40 or 100▲£2.50–£2.70 (awnings)

SAMPFORD COURTENAY Devon
Map 2 SS60

► Culverhayes Campsite *(SS631019)*
☎ North Tawton 431
1 ❶ ⚠ signposted
Part level, part sloping, grass site set in meadowland and close to main road. On A3072. $3\frac{1}{2}$acres 45pitches
15 Mar–Oct must book peak periods last arrival 23.59hrs 6♣ individual pitches 13wc lit all night 1cdp ⊕ 15washbasins hc 6⛆hc 4⊖ warden (1wash, 1dry, 1iron) ▭ games room cold storage calor gas toilet fluid ☎ ⊞ children's play area ♨ ⊖ stables ♪ cinema ⌒ launderette pub
45⊕£2.50 or 45⊖£2.50 or 45▲£2.50 awnings ltr

SCARBOROUGH North Yorkshire Map 8 TA08
See sketch map.

►►►► Scalby Manor Caravan & Camping Site *(TA025912)* Apply to: Scarborough Borough Council Tourist & Amenities Dept, Caravan Booking Office, Normanton Rise, Holbeck Hill, Scarborough YO11 2XD ☎66212
2 ❸ ⚠
Level, grass site with mature trees. On A165 Whitby Coast road. 15acres 345pitches
End Mar–Oct must book peak periods last arrival 21.00hrs last departure 12.00hrs 24♣ Ⓐ late arrivals enclosure 52wc lit all night 1cdp washbasins hc (⛆hc) ⊖ (wash, dry) (cold storage) calor gas camping gaz paraffin toilet fluid ☎ ⊞ children's playground ♨ ⊖ ♪ ↔ cinema ⌒ launderette pub

270🚐£1.20–£2.20 or 270🚙£1.20–£2.20 75▲£1.20–£2.20 (awnings)

►►► **Burniston Road Caravan Site** *(TA034901)* Apply to: Scarborough Borough Council Tourist & Amenities Dept, Caravan Booking Office, Normanton Rise, Holbeck Hill, Scarborough YO11 2XD ☎66212
[2] ❷ ⚠ signposted
Level, grass site with mature trees. 3m N of town near Burniston village. 4acres 85pitches
End Mar–Sep must book last arrival 21.00hrs last departure 12.00hrs 6⚐ 14wc lit all night 1cdp washbasins hc (🚿hc) ⊙ (wash, dry) cold storage calor gas camping gaz paraffin ☎ ⊞ children's playground ⛹ ⊖ ⚲ ✈ cinema ⚬ launderette pub
85🚐£1.20–£2.20 or 85🚙£1.20–£2.20 (awnings)

SCORTON Lancashire Map 7 SD54
►► **Six Arches Caravan Site** *(SD495494)*
☎ Forton 791683
[1] ❶ ⚠
A modern site on mainly level ground with mature trees and bushes. It gains its name from the six railway arches at the entrance crossing the River Wyre. 1acre 20pitches 290static
Spring Bank Hol–Aug Bank Hol rsMar, Apr, Sep & Oct must book last arrival 21.00hrs last departure 14.00hrs ⚐ wc washbasins hc central hot water (🚿hc) ⊙ (wash, 1spin, dry, iron) ⛵ games room TV calor gas ☎ ⊞ (licensed club) children's playground & fishing ⛹ ⊖ stables launderette pub
20🚐£2 or 20🚙£2 no awnings

SCRATBY Norfolk Map 9 TG51
See Yarmouth (Great) sketch map.
►►► **Scratby Hall Caravan Park** *(TG509144)* ☎ Great Yarmouth 730283
[2] ❷ ⚠ signposted
Site at rear of secluded private school. Suitable for quiet rural holidays. 4½acres 108pitches
Spring Bank Hol–Oct rs21 Mar–mid May must book peak periods last arrival 22.30hrs last departure 12.00hrs 4⚐ individual pitches 18wc lit all night 1cdp 14washbasins hc 12🚿hc 3⊙ (1wash, 1dry, 2iron) (games room) (cold storage) calor gas camping gaz toilet fluid ⊞ ⛹ ⊖ ⚬ launderette pub
108🚐£1.90 or 108🚙£1.90 or 108▲£1.90 (awnings)

SEDGEFIELD Co Durham Map 8 NZ32
►► **Trax Campsite** *(NZ348280)*
Sedgefield Racecourse
[1] ❶ ⚠ signposted
Mainly level site with mature trees set in meadowland. Adjacent to rbt A177/A689 SW of town. 2acres 60pitches
13 Jun–13 Sep no bookings last arrival 22.30hrs last departure 15.00hrs 1⚐ 15wc lit all night 1cdp 9washbasins hc 2central hot water 3🚿hc 2⊙ warden TV games area ⊖ launderette
60🚐£2–£2.35 or 60🚙£2–£2.35 or 60▲£2–£2.35 awnings

SEDGWICK Cumbria Map 7 SD58
►►► **Low Park Wood Caravan Site** *(SD509876)* ☎60186
[2] ❷ ⚠ signposted
This site, owned and run by the National Trust, was opened in 1977 on the site of an old gunpowder works. Situated on the banks of the River Kent in woodland area, rich in wildlife. Signposted from junction of A6/A591 at Sedgwick. no swimming or boating in river 18acres 200pitches
Apr–Oct must book peak periods last arrival 23.00hrs last departure 12.00hrs 11⚐ individual pitches late arrivals enclosure 32wc lit all night 3cdp 40washbasins hc 14🚿hc 6⊙ (2wash, 2dry, 2iron) cold storage calor gas ☎ ⊞ fishing ⛹ ⊖ stables ⚲ cinema launderette pub
200🚐£2 or 200🚙£2 (awnings)

SELSEY West Sussex Map 4 SZ89
►►►►► **West Sands Caravan Park** *(SZ846928)* Mill Ln ☎2996
[1] ❷ ⚠ signposted
Level, grass and gravel site with mature trees

and bushes, set in meadowland close to sandy beach, sea and urban area. 8m S of Chichester on B2145. 10acres 150pitches 1400static
Jun–Sep rsMar–May & Oct must book peak periods last arrival 17.30hrs last departure 12.00hrs 50 late arrivals enclosure 250wc lit all night washbasins hc central hot water (hc) warden (wash, spin, dry, iron) (, , , games room) TV (cold storage) calor gas cafe restaurant ☎ ⊞ (licensed clubs) children's playground & private beach stables cinema launderette pub
150£2.38–£3.56 or 150£2.38–£3.56 awnings ltr

SENNEN Cornwall Map 2 SW32
See St Buryan sketch map.
►►► ***Sea View Caravan Park*** *(SW358252)*
☎266
1 2 ⚠ signposted
Part level, part sloping, grass site with bushes, set in meadowland close to sea and beach. ¾m from Land's End on A30. 6acres 75static
Etr–Oct last departure 13.00hrs 12 23wc lit all night 2cdp 2washbasins hc (12hc) 4 warden (1wash, spin, dry) iron calor gas camping gaz toilet fluid ☎ ⊞
20 or 20 60▲

SEVERN BEACH Avon Map 3 ST58
►►► **Villa Caravan Park** ☎Pilning 2540
1 1 ⚠
A conveniently located level, grassy site set within 5m of motorways, with the cities of Bristol and Bath to the E and the Severn Road Bridge to the NW. Exit 21 (M4) from NE and Wales, Exit 18 (M5) from SW. 3acres 25pitches 75static
Mar–Oct last arrival 22.00hrs last departure 12.00hrs 5 late arrivals enclosure 19wc 1cdp (8washbasins hc, central hot water, 6hc) warden (1wash, 1dry) cold storage calor gas camping gaz ⊞ children's playground launderette pub
10£1.50 10£1.40 5▲£1.50 (awnings)

► **Salthouse Farm Caravan Site**
☎Pilning 2274
1 1 ⚠ signposted
Level, grass site with trees and bushes set in meadowland close to beach, river and estuary of Severn at Avonmouth. Close to B4054. 1acre 15pitches 90static
26 May–Sep rsApr–25 May last arrival 23.59hrs last departure 12.00hrs 8 14wc 1cdp 10washbasins hc (4hc) 2 warden cold storage calor gas camping gaz paraffin ☎ ⊞ children's playground pub
15£1.50 or 15£1.50 or 15▲£1.50 (awnings) ltr

SHANKLIN Isle of Wight Map 4 SZ58
See sketch map.
►► **Ninham Farm Camping Site** *(SZ578824)*
☎2049
1 1 ⚠ signposted

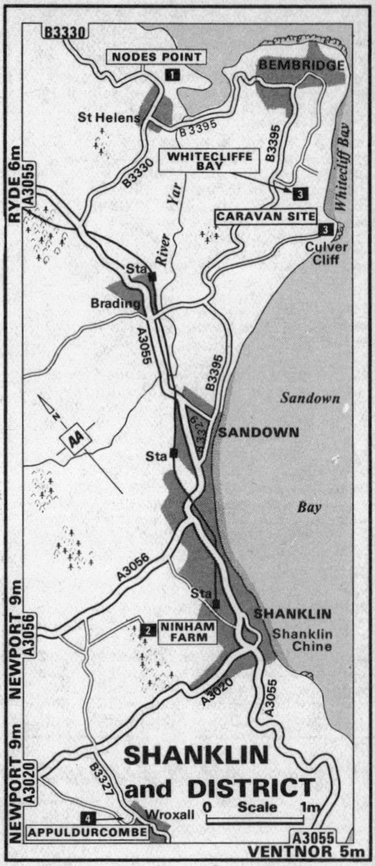

Sites listed under:
1 St Helens **2** Shanklin **3** Whitecliffe Bay
4 Wroxall

Level, grass site with young trees and bushes set in downland and meadowland. 1m from the sea, beach and lake. 1m SE of Apse Heath on A3056, reached by ½m of unmade gravel track. no pets 3½acres 150pitches
Spring Bank Hol–15 Sep rsEtr–mid May must book peak periods last arrival 22.00hrs last departure 22.00hrs 12 20wc lit all night 2cdp 20washbasins hc (16hc) 6 warden

(wash) spin (dry) iron (cold storage) calor gas camping gaz toilet fluid ☎ ⊞ children's playground ⛲ ⊖ stables ♁ ✈ cinema ⛳ launderette pub
150⊡£2 or 150⊟£2 or 150▲£2 awnings

SHEPTON MALLET Somerset Map 3 ST64
►**Manleaze Caravan Park** Cannards Grave
☎3671
[1] ❶
A level, grass site 1m S of Shepton Mallet on A371. ¾acre 15pitches 6static
All year must book peak periods 2⛭ 2wc lit all night 1cdp (1⊓hc) ⊙ calor gas camping gaz toilet fluid ☎ ⊞ ⛲ ⊖ stables ♁ cinema launderette pub
15⊡£1.20 or 15⊟£1.20 or 15▲£1.20 (awnings)

SHOTTISHAM Suffolk Map 5 TM34
►**St Margaret's Guest House** *(TM323447)*
☎247
[2] ❷
Level, grass and sand site with trees and bushes set in wood, moor and meadowland, adjacent to River Deben estuary with sea and beach to west. Turn right on to B1083 from A1152 at Wilford Bridge. 1½acres 25pitches
Apr–Oct must book peak periods last departure 12.00hrs 2⛭ individual pitches ⊗ 4wc lit all night 1cdp 4washbasins hc (2⊓hc) 1⊙ cold storage calor gas camping gaz ⊞ ⛲ ⊖ ⛳ pub
25⊡£1.15 or 25⊟£1.15 or 25▲£1.15 (awnings)

SHRAWLEY Hereford & Worcester Map 3 SO86
►►**Lenchford Hotel** *(SO812638)*
☎Worcester 620229
[2] ❷ ⚠
Level, grass site with trees and bushes, set in meadowland close to River Severn. 7m N of Worcester on B4196 Stourport road. 1m S of Shrawley village. 2acres 12pitches 60static
Mar–Oct rsNov–Feb must book 3⛭ 9wc 6washbasins hc 1central hot water 4⊓hc 2⊙ warden (1wash, 1spin) ⛴ cold storage calor gas restaurant ☎ ⊞ licensed club mobile shop in season ⊖ stables ✈ ⛳ launderette pub
12⊡£2 or 12⊟£2 3▲£2 awnings ltr

SIDCOT Avon Map 3 ST45
See Cheddar sketch map.
►**Netherdale Camping Ground**
Bridgwater Rd ☎Churchill 852340
[2] ❶ ⚠
An elevated and wooded site alongside main road. 1½acres 25pitches 37static
Mar–Oct must book public hols last arrival 22.00hrs last departure 12.00hrs 9⛭ ⊗ 12wc 1cdp washbasins (central hot water) (4⊓hc) 2⊙ calor gas ⊞ children's playground ⊖ stables ⛳ ⛲ pub
25⊡£2.05 or 25⊟£2.05 or 25▲£2.05 (awnings)

SILECROFT Cumbria Map 6 SD18
►**Silecroft Caravan Site** *(SD124811)*
☎Millom 2659
[1] ❷ ⚠
A quietly situated site close to the shore and near small village of Silecroft. 6acres 52pitches 128static
Mar–Oct must book peak periods last arrival 22.00hrs last departure 12.00hrs 12⛭ individual pitches ⊗ 36wc lit all night 1cdp 36washbasins hc central hot water 12⊓hc 7⊙ 1dry ☎ ⊞ ⛲ ⊖ cinema ⛳ launderette pub
52⊡£2.30 or 52⊟£2.30 or 52▲£1.60 (awnings) ltr

SILLOTH Cumbria Map 11 NY15
►►**Tanglewood Caravan Park** *(NY131534)*
Causewayhead ☎31253
[2] ❷ ⚠ signposted
Mainly level, grass site sheltered by a variety of trees and bushes; set in meadowland adjacent to B5302 Wigton–Silloth road. 1½acres 19pitches 41static
Etr–Oct must book peak periods last arrival 23.00hrs last departure 12.00hrs 4⛭ ⊗ 12wc 1cdp 16washbasins hc 1central hot water (4⊓hc) 6⊙ warden 1spin 1iron (cold storage) calor gas camping gaz ☎ ⊞ ⛲ ⊖ stables ♁ ⛳ launderette pub
10⊡£1.70 or 10⊟£1.70 9▲£1.70 (awnings)

SILVERDALE Lancashire Map7 SD47
See Morecambe sketch map.
►►►**Holgate's Caravan Park** *(SD455762)*
Cove Rd ☎701508
[2] ❶ ⚠ signposted
Partly level, partly sloping, grass and gravel site with mature trees and bushes. Set in woodland country overlooking Morecambe Bay, adjacent to sea and beach. 5m NW of Carnforth on A6. 7acres 70pitches 350static
Spring Bank Hol–mid Sep rsMar & mid Sep–14 Nov must book peak periods last arrival 22.30hrs last departure 12.00hrs 6⛭ 76wc lit all night 3cdp washbasins hc (⊓hc) ⊙ (wash, dry, iron) ⛴ calor gas camping gaz toilet fluid cafe ☎ ⊞ children's playground ⛲ ⊖ stables ♁ ⛳ launderette pub
50⊡ or 50⊟ 20▲ (awnings) ltr

SKEGNESS Lincolnshire Map 9 TF56
►►►**Richmond Drive Carapark** *(TF559625)* ☎2097
[1] ❷ ⚠
Level, grass site with young trees, set in meadowland, near to sandy beach and dunes. Off A52. 5acres 100pitches 740static
Spring Bank Hol–Sep rs15 Mar–mid May & Oct must book peak periods last arrival 22.00hrs last departure 18.00hrs 20⛭ 136wc lit all night 2cdp 12⊡ 20washbasins hc 80central hot water (10⊓hc) 10⊙ iron calor gas camping gaz toilet fluid cafe ☎ ⊞ licensed club, children's playground, hire shop & amusement arcade ⛲ ⊖ ♁ cinema ⛳ launderette pub
100⊡£1.50–£1.80 or 100⊟£1.50–£1.80 (awnings)

SKELWITH BRIDGE Ambleside, Cumbria Map 7 NY30
See Windermere sketch map.
►►►***Neaum Crag Camping & Caravan Site*** *(NY342039)* ☎Ambleside 3221
[2] ❶ ⚠ signposted
An extensive, open fell and woodland site. ⚘ 18acres 26pitches 38static
Mar–Oct must book peak periods no bookings for tents last arrival dusk last departure 10.00hrs 6⛭ individual pitches for caravans ⊗ no cars by tents 24wc lit all night 2cdp washbasins hc 8⊓hc 8⊙ 2dry calor gas camping gaz ☎ ⊞ ⛲ ⊖ stables ♁ ✈ cinema ⛳ launderette pub
26⊡ or 26⊟ or 75▲

SKIPSEA Humberside Map 8 TA15
▶▶▶ *Low Skirlington Caravan Site*
(TA188528) ☎213
[2] ❷ ⚠ signposted
Part level, part sloping, grass site with young trees and bushes, set in meadowland adjacent to sea and beach. 3m N of Hornsea on B1242.
15acres 225pitches 386static
Mar–Oct must book peak periods ⛟ wc 1cdp washbasins hc ⇨hc ⋔hc ⊙ wash, spin, dry games room TV calor gas camping gaz toilet fluid amusement arcade licensed bar ☎ ⊞ ⛀ ⊖ stables ♘ ✈ ⛵ launderette pub
225🚐 or 225🚙 or 225▲ (awnings) ltr

▶ Skipsea Sands Caravan Park *(TA177553)*
Mill Ln
[1] ❶ ⚠ signposted
Level, grassy site near sea and beach.
$2\frac{3}{4}$acres 70pitches 748static
Mar–Oct no bookings last departure 16.00hrs 2⛟ individual pitches 10wc 2cdp 2⊙ calor gas camping gaz paraffin toilet fluid ☎ ⊞ licensed club & children's paddling pool ⛀ ⊖ ⛵ launderette
70🚐£1.50 or 70🚙£1.50 (awnings) ltr

SKIPTON North Yorkshire Map 7 SD95
▶▶ Overdale Trailer Park *(SD997526)*
Harrogate Rd ☎3480
[1] ❶ ⚠
Mainly level site; caravans parked on a tarmac area. Surrounded by trees and bushes, the site lies off A59 Harrogate road. 1acre 20pitches 174static
All year must book last arrival 21.00hrs last departure 10.30hrs 14⛟ individual pitches 48wc lit all night 3cdp 25washbasins hc (1⇨hc, 12⋔hc) 4⊙ games room TV calor gas ☎ ⊞ ⊖ stables ♘ ✈ cinema ⛵ launderette ⛀ pub
20🚐£2.10 or 20🚙£2.10 awnings

SLEDGE GREEN Hereford and Worcester Map 3 SO83
▶▶▶ Three Counties Caravan Park
(SO811343) ☎ Birtsmorton 439
[2] ❷ ⚠ signposted
A level, grassy site with trees and bushes 6m from Tewkesbury on A438. 6acres 30pitches 92static
18 Mar–Oct must book peak periods 6⛟ 12wc lit all night washbasins hc central hot water ⋔hc ⊙ iron cold storage calor gas camping gaz toilet fluid ☎ ⊞ children's playground ⛀ ⊖ stables ⛵ pub
30🚐£1.50 or 30🚙£1.50 (awnings)

SLIMBRIDGE Gloucestershire Map 3 SO70
▶▶▶ Tudor Arms Caravan Site
Shepherds Patch ☎ Cambridge (Glos) 483
[1] ❶ ⚠ signposted
Level, grass and gravel site with trees and bushes, set in meadowland, adjacent to canal. Nearby is the Wildfowl Trust. Off A38. $7\frac{1}{2}$acres 60pitches
All year must book peak periods last arrival 23.00hrs last departure 12.00hrs 5⛟ late arrivals enclosure 12wc lit all night 30⚇ (washbasins hc, central hot water, ⋔hc) ⊙ iron cold storage calor gas camping gaz toilet fluid restaurant licensed bar ☎ ⊞ ⛀ ⊖ ⛵ launderette pub
35🚐£2.35 or 35🚙£2 25▲£2 (awnings) ltr

SNAINTON North Yorkshire Map 8 SE98
▶▶ Jasmin Site *(SE928813)* Low Rd
☎ Scarborough 85240
[2] ❷ ⚠ signposted
Level, grass site with mature trees and bushes, in rural area. 1m off A170 Pickering–Scarborough road; turn off by school opposite into Barker Lane. 4acres 60pitches
Apr–Oct must book peak periods last arrival 23.00hrs 6⛟ Ⓐ 14wc lit all night 1cdp (washbasins hc, central hot water) (⋔hc) ⊙ spin calor gas ⊞ ⊖ stables ⛵ ⛀ pub
40🚐£1.40 20🚙£1.40 or 20▲£1.40 (awnings) ltr

SOURTON DOWN Devon Map 2 SX59
▶▶▶ Griggs Prewley Caravan Site
☎ Bridestowe 349
[2] ❷ ⚠ signposted
This site is situated adjacent to junction A30/A386. Fine views of Dartmoor. 4acres 49pitches
15 Mar–Oct last arrival 22.30hrs last departure 10.30hrs 8⛟ individual pitches Ⓐ late arrivals enclosure 14wc lit all night 1cdp ⚇ 8washbasins hc (1central hot water) (4⋔hc) 2⊙ (1wash, 1spin, 1dry, 1iron) ⛴ (cold storage) calor gas camping gaz paraffin toilet fluid ☎ ⊞ children's playground & battery charging ⛀ ⊖ stables ♘ cinema ⛵ launderette pub
49🚐£2.25 or 49🚙£2 or 49▲£1.50–£2.25 (awnings) ltr

SOUTH CERNEY Gloucestershire Map 4 SU09
▶▶ Cotswold Marina Leisure Centre
Broadway Ln ☎216
[1] ❶ ⚠ signposted
Level, grass and gravel site, with young trees and bushes set in meadowland and adjacent to lake. Off A419 Cirencester–Swindon road.
10acres 60pitches 79static
Apr–Oct must book public hols last arrival 23.00hrs ⛟ individual pitches Ⓐ 24wc lit all night 2cdp washbasins hc central hot water (⋔hc) ⊙ warden ⛴ calor gas camping gaz toilet fluid cafe restaurant ⊞ children's playground & private beach ⛀ ⊖ stables ✈ ⛵ pub
60🚐£2 or 60🚙£2 or 60▲£2 awnings ltr

SOUTH SHIELDS Tyne and Wear Map 12 NZ36
▶ Lizard Lane Caravan & Camping Site
(NZ401647) ☎557411 (568841 winter)
[1] ❶ ⚠ signposted
Sloping, grass site near sea and beach. 2m S of town centre on A183 Sunderland road.
30acres 70pitches 65static
Etr–Oct last arrival 22.00hrs last departure 10.00hrs 15⛟ Ⓐ 10wc lit all night 1cdp 10washbasins hc 6central hot water 4⋔hc 3⊙ warden dry calor gas camping gaz ☎ ⊞ wash up sinks ⛀ ⊖ stables ♘ ✈ cinema ⛵

launderette pub
55⊡£1.62 or 55🚐£1.62 15▲£1.62 (awnings) ltr

SOUTHWATER West Sussex Map 4 TQ12
▶▶ *Raylands Park* *(TQ165277)*
Jackrell's Ln ☎730202
2 ❷ signposted
Attractive, natural site, pleasantly landscaped with grass play area for children; peacefully situated off A24 Worthing–Horsham road.
4acres 65pitches 3static
Mar–Oct rsNov–Feb must book Bank Hols last arrival 23.00hrs 9♨ some individual pitches 12wc lit all night 2cdp 4washbasins hc 4⛆hc 1⊙ calor gas ☎ ⊞ ⊖ pub
65⊡ or 65🚐

STAINFORTH North Yorkshire Map 7 SD86
▶▶ Knight Stainforth Hall Caravan & Campsite *(SD816672)* ☎ Settle 2200
2 ❶ ⚠ signposted
Site is located in the Yorkshire Dales National Park in a rural setting. 6acres 75pitches 60static
Mar–Oct must book last arrival 22.00hrs last departure 14.00hrs 11♨ 24wc lit all night 2cdp 18washbasins hc 2⛆hc 2⊙ warden calor gas camping gaz toilet fluid ⊞ fishing ⛹ ⊖ ♁ pub
25⊡£1.35 or 25🚐£1.10 50▲£1.10 awnings ltr

STAMFORD BRIDGE Humberside Map 8 SE75
▶▶▶ Weir Caravan Park *(SE713557)*
☎71377
2 ❷ ⚠
Slightly sloping grass site with trees and bushes set in meadowland near urban area and River Derwent. 50yds off A166 on entering village from York. 2acres 60pitches 98static
Apr–Oct last arrival 22.30hrs last departure 12.00hrs 5♨ 9wc lit all night 2cdp washbasins hc central hot water (2⛀hc, 8⛆hc) 5⊙ (2wash, 2spin, 2dry, 2iron) games room calor gas camping gaz toilet fluid ☎ ⊞ children's playground boats for hire & fishing ⛹ ⊖ launderette
60⊡£2.35–£2.85 or 60🚐£2.35–£2.85 or 60▲£2.35–£2.85 awnings

STANDLAKE Oxfordshire Map 4 SP30
▶▶ Standlake Caravans *(SP395028)*
Lincoln Farm, High St ☎239
1 ❶ signposted
This level grass site is situated in a quite Oxfordshire village. Pleasant unspoilt countryside surrounds the site; on A415 Witney–Abingdon road. 4acres 50pitches 2static
Apr–Oct must book peak periods last arrival 22.00hrs last departure 12.00hrs 2♨ Ⓐ late arrivals enclosure 10wc lit all night 1cdp 2⊡ washbasins hc central hot water ⛆hc ⊙ cold storage calor gas toilet fluid ⊞ children's playground ⛹ ⊖ stables ✈ ⚲ launderette pub
40⊡£1.90 10🚐£1.90 or 10▲£1.50 (awnings) ltr

STANTON Suffolk Map 5 TL97
▶▶ *Shepherds Grove Park* *(TL974733)*
☎388
1 ❷ ⚠ signposted
Part level site with mature trees. Off A143 Ixworth–Diss road. 4acres 60pitches 120static
All year must book peak periods last arrival 22.00hrs 10♨ Ⓐ 14wc lit all night 1cdp 10washbasins hc 4⛆hc 10⊙ warden calor gas camping gaz paraffin toilet fluid ☎ ⊞ children's play area ⛹ ⊖ stables ♁ ✈ ⚲ launderette
60⊡ or 60🚐 or 60▲

STARCROSS Devon Map 3 SX98
▶▶▶ *Cofton Farm Caravan Park*
(SX965805) ☎358
3 ❷ ⚠ signposted
Partly level and sloping grass site. 1m S of Starcross on A379. 16acres 355pitches 60static

15 Mar–Oct must book Jul & Aug last arrival 22.00hrs last departure 12.00hrs 17 36wc lit all night 2cdp 26washbasins hc (10hc) 4 (2wash, dry) iron calor gas camping gaz toilet fluid ☎ stables cinema launderette 355 or 355 or 355▲ (awnings) ltr

STICKER Cornwall Map 2 SW95
See St Austell sketch map.
► **Glenleigh Caravan Park** *(SW975501)* Grampound Rd ☎ St Austell 65633
2 1 signposted
Level grass site with mature trees and bushes. On A390 3m W of St Austell. 3acres 40pitches 40static
Apr–Oct must book peak periods last arrival 22.00hrs last departure 10.00hrs 6 12wc lit all night 1cdp washbasins hc central hot water (hc) iron cold storage calor gas ☎ children's playground stables pub £1.20–£2.50 £1.20–£2.50 ▲£1.20–£2.50 (awnings)

STICKLEPATH Devon Map 2 SX69
►►► **Coombe Head Farm** ☎323
2 2 signposted
Level grass site with bushes set in moorland and meadowland 2m from Okehampton on A30.
7½acres 40pitches 20static
15 Mar–Oct 6 individual pitches late arrivals enclosure 9wc lit all night 1cdp 8washbasins hc (4hc) 4 (1wash, 1dry) 1iron cold storage calor gas camping gaz ☎ (licensed club) children's playground stables cinema launderette pub
40£1.75 or 40£1.75 or 40▲£1.75 ltr

►► ***Olditch Farm Caravan Park*** ☎459
2 2
Partly level and partly sloping site with trees and bushes set in Dartmoor. 400yd E of village on A30. 2½acres 45pitches 6static
15 Mar–15 Nov must book peak periods last departure 12.00hrs 3 late arrivals enclosure 12wc lit all night 1cdp washbasins hc central hot water hc (cold storage) calor gas camping gaz restaurant licensed bar ☎ stables pub
45 or 45 or 45▲ (awnings)

STOKE FLEMING Devon Map 3 SX84
►►► **Deer Park Holiday Estate** *(SX864493)* ☎253
2 2 signposted
Level, grass and gravel site with young trees, set in hilly meadowland, adjacent to sea, beach, river and Stort Bay. 5acres 140pitches 32static
25 May–Oct rs15 Mar–24 May must book last arrival 20.00hrs last departure 10.00hrs 4 individual pitches 17wc lit all night 1cdp 21washbasins hc (6hc) 2 (2wash, 2dry, 1iron) games room (cold storage) calor gas camping gaz licensed bar ☎ children's playground, take away food, aqualung compressor, diving equipment shop & amusement arcade cinema launderette pub
20£2.43 120£2.43 or 120▲£2.43 (awnings)

STRAGGLETHORPE Nottinghamshire Map 8 SK63
See Nottingham sketch map.
►►► **Thornton's Holt Camping Site** *(SK638377)* ☎ Radcliffe-on-Trent 2125
2 2 signposted
A level grass site with young trees and bushes, set in meadowland ½m S of A52 and 2m N of A46. Nearby (2m) is the National Water Sports Centre at Holme Pierrepont. 4acres 69pitches 1static
Apr–Oct must book public hols last arrival 22.00hrs 4 individual pitches 9wc lit all night 1cdp washbasins hc central hot water (hc) (iron) (cold storage) calor gas camping gaz toilet fluid ☎ children's playground stables launderette pub
40£2 or 40£2 30▲£2 (awnings) ltr

SUNDERLAND Cumbria Map 11 NY13
►► **Skiddaw View Caravan Park** *(NY179368)* ☎ Aspatria 20404
1 1 signposted
Level site near hills, moors and mountains of the Lake District. Approach by way of A591 road 1½m S of Bothel. 3acres 40pitches 60static
Apr–Oct must book peak periods last arrival 21.00hrs last departure 12.00hrs 7 wc lit all night 2cdp (washbasins hc, central hot water, hc) calor gas camping gaz toilet fluid ☎ stables cinema launderette pub
40£1.50 or 40£1.50 30▲£1 (awnings) ltr

SUTTON Kent Map 5 TR34
►►► ***Sutton Vale Caravan Park*** *(TR339498)* ☎01-837 1093 (Mon–Fri)
2 2
Small and well-sited park offering well-equipped caravans for hire with limited space for tourers. 6acres 28pitches 114static
Apr–Sep rsMar & Oct must book peak periods last arrival 23.59hrs last departure 12.00hrs 20 individual pitches 20wc lit all night 1cdp (washbasins hc) (central hot water) (hc) warden spin iron games room TV (cold storage) calor gas toilet fluid cafe restaurant licensed bar ☎ stables cinema launderette pub
14 14 rates on application (awnings) ltr

SWAINBY North Yorkshire Map 8 NZ40
► **Blacksmith's Arms** *(NZ475023)* ☎ Hutton Rudby 700303
1 1
Level grass site near river, hills, moorland and woodland. Off A172. ¾acre 12pitches
Apr–Oct must book 1 late arrivals enclosure 3wc lit all night 1cdp washbasins hc central hot water cold storage calor gas camping gaz cafe restaurant ☎ licensed club & children's playground stables pub
12£1.62 or 12£1.62 (awnings)

TAUNTON Somerset Map 3 ST22
►►► **St Quintin Hotel Caravan & Camping Park** Bridgwater Rd, Bathpool ☎73016

2 ❷ △ signposted
Level and grassy site set in meadowland adjacent to the Taunton–Bridgwater Canal. 1m from exit 25 of M5; on A38 behind the Bathpool Inn. 5acres 125pitches 24static
All year must book peak periods last arrival 22.30hrs last departure 12.00hrs 6 wc lit all night 1cdp (8washbasins hc) 4 hc 3⊙ (1wash, 1spin, 1dry) 2iron games room CTV calor gas camping gaz toilet fluid restaurant ☎ ⊞ children's playground stables cinema launderette pub
125 £3.45–£5 or 125 £3.45–£5 or 125▲£3.45–£5 (awnings) ltr

TAVISTOCK Devon Map 2 SX47
►►► *Harford Bridge Park* ☎Mary Tavy 349
2 ❷ △ signposted
Level grassy site with mature trees, set in moorland country near river. 2m N of Tavistock on A386. 10acres 130pitches 60static
27 May–30 Sep rsEtr–26 May must book peak periods last arrival 23.59hrs last departure 12.00hrs 12 individual pitches late arrivals enclosure 11wc lit all night 1cdp (8washbasins hc) (2central hot water) (4 hc) warden (iron) cold storage calor gas camping gaz toilet fluid ⊞ stables launderette
100 or 100 30▲ (awnings) ltr

►►► Higher Longford Farm Caravan Site
☎3360
2 ❷ △
Site is adjacent to B3357 between Ashburton and Tavistock in the Dartmoor National Park 1½acres 30pitches 24static
Spring Bank Hol–Sep rsOct–mid May must book peak periods 2 6wc lit all night 2cdp (washbasins hc, hc) ⊙ games room TV cold storage calor gas camping gaz toilet fluid cafe ☎ ⊞ licensed club & children's playground stables launderette pub
30 £2 or 30 £1.50 or 30▲£2 (awnings) ltr

► Langstone Manor Country Club & Caravan Park Moortown ☎3371
2 ❷ △ signposted
Part level, part sloping, grass site with mature trees and bushes set in hilly moorland. Off B3357 in Dartmoor National Park.
18pitches 20static
Apr–Oct must book 5 no cars by tents 8wc lit all night 1cdp (hc) ⊙ warden camping gaz toilet fluid ☎ ⊞ licensed club & children's playground stables launderette pub
6 £2.25 or 6 £2.25 12▲£2.25 (awnings)

TEDBURN ST MARY Devon Map 3 SX89
► Woodlands Park *(SX831936)* ☎245
2 ❷ △ signposted
Well situated site for Exeter and Dartmoor. E of Tedburn St Mary on old A30. ¼acre 12pitches 20static
Etr–Oct must book peak periods last arrival 22.00hrs last departure 12.00hrs 2 late arrivals enclosure wc lit all night 1cdp washbasins hc central hot water hc ⊙ calor gas camping gaz paraffin toilet fluid ⊞ stables pub
12 £2.42 or 12 £2.42 or 12▲£2.42 (awnings) ltr

THIRSK North Yorkshire Map 8 SE48
►► Trax Campsite *(SE425820)*
Thirsk Racecourse
2 ❷ △ signposted
Mainly level grass site set in meadowland. 1m E of town off A61 Ripon road. 6acres 60pitches
20 May–20 Sep except 30 & 31 May, 1 & 2 Aug & 6 Sep no bookings last arrival 22.30hrs last departure 15.00hrs 3 8wc lit all night 1cdp 8washbasins hc 2central hot water 6 hc 2⊙ warden CTV calor gas camping gaz ☎ ⊞ games area stables launderette
60 £2–£2.35 or 60 £2–£2.35 or 60▲£2–£2.35 awnings

THORN FALCON Somerset Map 3 ST22
► Ashe Caravan & Camp Site
☎Henlade 442567
1 ❶ signposted
Grass site set in sylvan surroundings. 4m SE of Taunton, off A358 Taunton–Ilminster road. Turn by 'Nags Head' public house. 3acres 22pitches 8static
Apr–Oct 3 6wc lit all night (2central hot water) (4 hc) 3⊙ calor gas camping gaz paraffin ⊞ cinema launderette pub
22 £1.60 or 22 £1.60 or 22▲£1.60 awnings ltr

THORNTON CLEVELEYS Lancashire Map 7 SD34
►►► Kneps Farm *(SD353429)* River Rd
☎Cleveleys 823632
1 ❷ △
A level, stony and grassy site with mature trees near a river. 5m N of Blackpool on A587 Thornton Cleveleys road. 3acres 65pitches 100static
Mar–Oct must book last arrival 22.00hrs last departure 12.00hrs 8 individual pitches late arrivals enclosure 33wc lit all night 2cdp 57 22washbasins hc 16 hc 8⊙ warden (2wash) (3games room) cold storage calor gas camping gaz toilet fluid ☎ ⊞ children's playground & off licence stables launderette pub
65 £2.16–£2.70 or 65 £2.16–£2.70 (awnings)

THRAPSTON Northamptonshire Map 4 SP97
► Mill Marina Caravan & Boat Park *(SP994781)* ☎2850
2 ❶ △
Level grass site with mature trees, saplings and bushes, set in urban area with access to River Nene and disused railway line. ½m S of town on A605. 7acres 41pitches 5static
Apr–Sep must book public hols last arrival dusk 3 individual pitches late arrivals enclosure 8wc lit all night 1cdp 6washbasins hc (2 hc) 1⊙ warden iron

calor gas camping gaz ⊞ licensed club children's playground fishing & boating ⊖ launderette pub
23£1.60 6£1.60 12▲£1.60 (awnings)

THREE OAKS East Sussex Map 5 TQ81
►►► Old Coghurst Farm Caravan & Camping Park *(TQ832138)* Rock Ln
☎Hastings 753622
② ❸ △ signposted
Part level, part sloping, grassy site with trees and bushes. Set in hilly country amidst woodland and meadowland. Off unclassified road – formerly A259 and A28 – 4m NE of Hastings.
4acres 60pitches
Mar–Oct must book peak periods last arrival 23.00hrs last departure 12.00hrs 3 individual pitches late arrivals enclosure 7wc lit all night 1cdp 4 8washbasins hc 3central hot water 4hc 3⊙ warden (1wash, 1spin, 1dry, 1iron) () (cold storage) calor gas camping gaz toilet fluid ☎ ⊞ ⊖ stables cinema launderette
60£2.20 or 60£2 or 60▲£2.20 (awnings) ltr

THRESHFIELD North Yorkshire Map 7 SD96
►►► Long Ashes Caravan Park *(SD984645)* ☎Grassington 752261
② ❷ △
Level grass site with trees and bushes set in wooded hills and meadowland adjacent to River Wharfe. 9m N of Skipton on B6265. 1m from Grassington town centre on Skipton road.
100acres 120pitches 300static
15 Mar–Oct must book peak periods last arrival 21.00hrs last departure 18.00hrs 50 individual pitches last arrivals enclosure 52wc 4cdp 50washbasins hc (10hc) ⊙ games room TV calor gas toilet fluid cafe restaurant licensed bar ☎ ⊞ children's playground ⊖ pub
120 (awnings) ltr

TIDDINGTON Warwickshire Map 4 SP25
►► Elms *(SP213558)*
☎Stratford-on-Avon 292312
② ❷ △
Level grass site with mature trees and bushes; not far from the river and 1m from Stratford on B4086. 6acres 50pitches
Apr–Oct must book last departure 12.00hrs 8 wc washbasins hc central hot water hc ⊙ (iron) calor gas camping gaz children's playground & slipway ⊖ stables cinema launderette pub
50£1.75 or 50£1.75 or 50▲£1.75 (awnings)

TINTAGEL Cornwall Map 2 SX08
►►► *Ocean Cove Caravan Park* ☎325
② ❷ △
Partly level, partly sloping, grass site in meadowland; adjacent to sea, beach and downs. 18m W of Launceston on B3263. ½acre 12pitches 159static
May–Sep rsApr no bookings last arrival 23.00hrs last departure 10.00hrs 12 31wc lit all night 1cdp washbasins hc (hc) ⊙ (wash, dry, iron) calor gas licensed bar ⊞ ⊖ stables launderette
12 or 12 (awnings)

► *Headland Caravan & Camping Site*
☎239
② ❶ △
Undulating grass site set in meadowland adjacent to sea and sandy beach. 4½acres 100pitches 25static
Apr–Sep rsMar no bookings Jun–Aug last arrival 22.00hrs last departure 10.00hrs 6 13wc lit all night 3cdp 16washbasins hc (5hc) 4⊙ (wash, spin) calor gas ⊖ stables launderette pub
30 20 50▲ (awnings)

TORRINGTON (GREAT) Devon Map 2 SS41
►►► Greenways Valley Holiday Park *(SS511192)* ☎2153
② ❷ △ signposted
Level, grassed site with mixed trees and bushes set in hilly woodland. 2m SE of town off B3227 South Molton road. ½acre 10pitches 18static
20 May–Oct rs15 Mar–19 May last arrival 22.00hrs last departure 12.00hrs 2 5wc lit all night 1cdp 5washbasins hc 1central hot water 2hc 1⊙ warden (1iron) cold storage calor gas ⊞ children's playground ⊖ stables cinema launderette pub
10£1.50–£2.30 or 10£1.50–£2.30 (awnings)

TRENTHAM Staffordshire Map 7 SJ84
►► Trentham Gardens *(SJ864419)*
Trentham Estate ☎Stoke-on-Trent 657341
② ❷ △
Level woodland, grass and meadowland site lying adjacent to River Trent and Trentham Lakes. Access to A34 and exit 15 of M6.
150acres 250pitches
Mar–Nov last departure 18.00hrs 11 56wc lit all night 5cdp (central hot water) hc ⊙ warden () cold storage calor gas camping gaz toilet fluid cafe restaurant ☎ ⊞ licensed club, fishing & boating children's playground ⊖ stables cinema launderette pub
250£3 or 250£3 100▲£3 awnings

TRIMINGHAM Norfolk Map 9 TG23
►►► Woodlands Caravan Park *(TG284388)*
☎Southrepps 301
③ ❸ △
Level grass site with mature trees, set in woodland and meadowland; adjacent to cliffs overlooking North Sea. 15acres 100pitches
Apr–Sep must book public hols last arrival 23.00hrs last departure 11.00hrs 4 individual pitches 33wc lit all night 2cdp washbasins hc central hot water (hc) ⊙ spin games room calor gas ☎ ⊞ ⊖ stables cinema launderette pub
100£2 or 100£1.50 awnings

TROUTBECK near Penrith, Cumbria Map 11 NY32
► *Hutton Moor End* *(NY365269)*
☎Threlkeld 615
① ❶ △ signposted
Level and slightly sloping grass site with bushes and mature trees, set in hilly wooded countryside. 7m E of Keswick and 4m W of

Penrith on A66. Ideal position for touring Lake District. 3acres 35pitches 15static
Etr–Oct must book peak periods
last arrival 22.00hrs last departure 12.00hrs
3 individual pitches 11wc lit all night
1cdp washbasins hc central hot water (hc)
(iron) (cold storage) calor gas
stables pub
20 or 20 15

TRURO Cornwall Map 2 SW84
Leverton Place *(SW774453)*
Greenbottom, Chacewater 560462
2 3 signposted
This attractive site is situated close to Truro yet in pleasant rural area. 3½m W of city off A390 at Greenbottom. 9acres 190pitches 30static
May–Sep last arrival 22.00hrs last departure 10.00hrs (Jul & Aug only) 12 individual pitches late arrivals enclosure 33wc lit all night
3cdp washbasins hc central hot water (hc)
(wash, dry, iron) games room TV
calor gas camping gaz toilet fluid cafe
restaurant children's playground
licensed club wash up sinks & hairdrying room
stables cinema launderette
190£2.20–£3 or 190£2.20–£3 or
190£2.20–£3 (awnings)

TUXFORD Nottinghamshire Map 8 SK77
Greenacres *(SK751719)* Lincoln Rd
870264
2 1 signposted
Level and slightly sloping grass site with trees, set in rural area outside Tuxford. ¾m E of A1 on A6075 near railway line. 2½acres 75pitches 9static
Apr–Oct must book public hols last arrival 23.00hrs 3 individual pitches
late arrivals enclosure 7wc lit all night 1cdp
8washbasins hc (3hc) 2 warden
(1wash, 1spin, 1iron) cold storage calor gas
camping gaz toilet fluid stables
launderette pub
75£1.70 or 75£1.70 or 75£1.70
(awnings) ltr

UGTHORPE North Yorkshire Map 8 NZ71
Burnt House Caravan Park
(NZ784112) Whitby 840448
2 2 signposted
Level grass site with trees and bushes, set in moorland, 4½m from sea and beach. 9m W of Whitby off A171 Teesside road. 7½acres 86pitches
Mar–Oct must book peak periods last departure 12.00hrs 7 individual pitches 20wc
lit all night 1cdp 12washbasins hc
3central hot water 12hc 5 warden
calor gas toilet fluid children's
playground pub
86£1.78 or 86£1.78 awnings

UMBERLEIGH Devon Map 2 SS62
Overweir Caravan & Camping Site
(SS603239) Overweir High Bickington 387
2 2 signposted
A gently sloping site adjacent to wooded area and offering panoramic views. Approached by metalled road and has wide entrance.
Situated on the B3227, 200yds from the A377 at Umberleigh. 3½acres 70pitches
15 Mar–14 Nov must book peak periods
2 11wc lit all night 1cdp 11washbasins hc
2central hot water 6hc 2 games room
TV calor gas camping gaz children's
playground pony rides & fishing stables
pub
70£1.35 or 70£1.35 or 70£1.08 (awnings)

UPLYME Devon Map 3 SY39
Hook Farm Camping & Caravan Park Lyme Regis 2801
2 2 signposted
This site is situated adjacent to the village of Uplyme, in a wooded valley. 1½m NW of Lyme Regis. 5acres 100pitches 15static
15 Mar–1 Nov rsNov–14 Mar
must book peak periods last arrival 23.00hrs
last departure 12.00hrs 9 15wc lit all night
2cdp 17washbasins hc (4hc) 2
(1wash, spin) calor gas camping gaz
stables cinema launderette
100

UTTOXETER Staffordshire Map 7 SK03
▶▶ Trax Campsite *(SK099334)*
Uttoxeter Racecourse
1 ❷ ⚠ signposted
Situated on SE edge of small market town, mainly level site in hilly country. Off B5017.
3acres 60pitches
30 May–13 Sep no bookings last arrival 22.30hrs last departure 15.00hrs 5 32wc lit all night 1cdp 19washbasins hc 2central hot water 2 hc 2⊙ warden (1iron) TV ☎ ⊞ games area & golf course stables cinema launderette
60 £2–£2.35 or 60 £2–£2.35 or 60▲£2–£2.35 awnings

VERYAN Cornwall Map 2 SW93
▶▶▶ Tretheake Manor Tourist Site *(SW935415)* ☎213
2 ❶ ⚠ signposted
A quiet site situated on slightly undulating land with pleasant country views. The site is well screened with hedgerows and trees.
8acres 220pitches
Etr–mid Oct must book peak periods last arrival 20.00hrs last departure 11.00hrs 5 individual pitches 20wc lit all night 1cdp washbasins hc (hc) ⊙ warden (1wash, 1spin, 1dry, 1iron) games room (CTV) (cold storage) calor gas camping gaz toilet fluid ☎ ⊞ children's playgrounds fishing off licence wash up sinks (& hairdryers) stables launderette pub
220 £2.95 or 220 £2.95 or 220▲£2.95 awnings

WALDRINGFIELD Suffolk Map 5 TM24
▶▶▶ Moon & Sixpence *(TM263454)* ☎650
3 ❸ ⚠ signposted
Level sand and grass site with bushes and mature trees set in sylvan surroundings. 8m E of Ipswich turn right off A12 at Martlesham. Camp site is geared to cater for people using Felixstowe car ferries. 10acres 100pitches 160static
Spring Bank Hol–mid Sep rs15–31 Mar & mid Sep–Oct must book peak periods 8 late arrivals enclosure 40wc lit all night 1cdp 24washbasins hc 4central hot water 12 hc 5⊙ warden (2wash, 1dry, 3iron) (games room) TV cold storage calor gas camping gaz toilet fluid cafe ☎ ⊞ children's playground licensed club & private beach stables cinema launderette pub
100 £2.70–£5.40 or 100 £2.70–£5.40 or 100▲£2.70–£5.40 awnings ltr

WALL Cornwall Map 2 SW63
See Hayle sketch map.
▶▶▶ Parbola Caravan Park *(SW612366)*
☎Praze 503
3 ❷ ⚠
A level grassy site in Cornish downland.
4acres 58pitches 12static
Etr–Sep must book last departure 10.00hrs 8 10wc 1cdp 12washbasins hc 2central hot water (4 hc) 2⊙ iron CTV (cold storage) calor gas camping gaz ☎ ⊞ children's playground
18 £1.50–£2.55 or 18 £1.50–£2.55 40▲£1.50–£2 (awnings)

WALLINGFORD Oxfordshire Map 4 SU68
▶▶ Riverside Caravan & Camping Site *(SP609895)* Apply to: South Oxfordshire District Council, Stone Hall, High St, Wallingford, Oxon OX10 0DF ☎36969
1 ❷
Level grassy meadow surrounded by trees. For caravans approach from the east via Henley and A423. 1acre 28pitches
Mid May–mid Sep must book 3 individual pitches no cars by caravans/tents 8wc lit all night washbasins hc central hot water hc ⊙ ( ) ☎ ⊞ stables launderette pub
28 £2 or 28 £2 or 28▲£2 awnings ltr

WARDEN POINT Kent Map 5 TR07
► **Warden Spring Caravan Park** *(TR017726)*
☎ Eastchurch 216
2 ❶ △
This site is in country surroundings on a well wooded private estate in valley overlooking sea. After crossing Kingsferry Bridge turn right at roundabout on to A250; in 3m at Eastchurch church turn left and follow signs for 'Warden', then 'Warden Point'. 4acres 30pitches 250static
Mar–Oct no bookings 25⛲ 25wc lit all night 20cdp washbasins hc 🚿hc ⊙ warden (wash, spin, dry) iron CTV cold storage calor gas toilet fluid cafe ☎ ⊞ children's playground licensed club & private beach ⛱ ⊖ stables ↬ launderette pub
30🚐£2 or 30🚗£2 (awnings) ltr

WARSASH Hampshire Map 4 SU40
►► **Dibles Park** *(SU505060)* Dibles Rd
☎ Locksheath 5232
2 ❸ △ signposted
Level, grass site with young trees and bushes, set in wood and meadowland. Near River Hamble and The Solent. At Parkgate on A27 turn opposite Lloyds Bank into Locks Rd then Fleet End Rd. no ball games 1acre 22pitches 41static
Etr–Oct must book peak periods last arrival 20.30hrs last departure 13.00hrs 1⛲ individual pitches late arrivals enclosure 7wc lit all night 1cdp 8washbasins hc (4🚿hc) 4⊙ warden calor gas ⊞ ⛱ ⊖ stables ↬ launderette pub
22🚐£2.16 or 22🚗£21.6 awnings

► **Solent Breezes Holiday Estate** *(SU504041)* ☎ Locksheath 2084
1 ❶ △ signposted
Situated in a secluded rural area overlooking Southampton Water. 40pitches
29 Jun–9 Sep rsEtr–28 Jun & 10 Sep–1 Nov must book peak periods last arrival 22.00hrs 6⛲ individual pitches 12wc lit all night 1cdp 6washbasins hc (1central hot water, 2🛁hc, 6🚿hc) 2⊙ (2wash, 1spin, 1dry) 🏓 calor gas toilet fluid cafe ☎ ⊞ children's playground licensed club private beach & slipway ⛱ ⊖ stables ✈ ↬ launderette pub
40🚐£1.60–£2.75 or 40🚗£1.60–£2.75 awnings

WARSILL North Yorkshire Map 8 SE26
►►► **Warren House Caravan Site** *(SE225653)* ☎ Sawley 683
2 ❷ △
Part level, part sloping grass site with trees and bushes set amongst hills, moor and woodland. 2acres 30pitches 70static
Apr–Oct must book public hols 7⛲ individual pitches ⊗ late arrivals enclosure 18wc lit all night 2cdp ⊕ (12washbasins hc, 2central hot water, 6🚿hc) 3⊙ cold storage calor gas camping gaz toilet fluid children's playground ⛱ ⊖ pub
30🚐£1.73 or 30🚗£1.15 10▲£1.50 awnings ltr

WARWICK Warwickshire Map 4 SP26
►►► **Trax Campsite** *(SP278647)*
Warwick Racecourse
1 ❷ △
A level stony site W of town. Off A429 Stratford-upon-Avon road. 3acres 40pitches
2 May–13 Sep no bookings last arrival 22.30hrs last departure 15.00hrs 2⛲ 6wc lit all night 1cdp 8washbasins hc 2central hot water 4🚿hc 2⊙ warden (1wash, 1spin) calor gas ☎ ⊞ children's playground games area free racing for campers 5, 17 & 24 May, 7 & 21 Jun, 1 & 26 Jul & 25 Aug ⛱ ⊖ stables ⛳ ✈ cinema ↬ launderette
40🚐£2–£2.75 or 40🚗£2–£2.75 awnings

WATCHET Somerset Map 3 ST04
See sketch map.
►►►► **Doniford Holiday Village** *(ST095423)* ☎ Williton 32423
2 ❸ △ signposted
A level site with some hard standing pitches for caravans and surfaced internal roadways. E of Watchet off A39 and overlooking the sea (Minehead Bay). no pets 11acres 120pitches 240static
Mid May–mid Sep rsEtr–mid May & end Sep booking advisable last arrival 20.00hrs last departure 10.00hrs 20⛲ individual pitches ⊗ late arrivals enclosure 22wc lit all night 2cdp 12washbasins hc central hot water 8🚿hc ⊙ warden (3wash, 2spin) 1dry (iron) 🏊 🏓 games room (cold storage) calor gas camping gaz toilet fluid cafe restaurant ☎ ⊞ (licensed club) children's playground evening entertainment & TV hire ⛱ ⊖ stables ✈ cinema ↬ launderette pub
100🚐 or 100🚗 20▲ rates on application awnings ltr

►►► **Warren Bay Caravan Park** ☎31460
1 ❶ △
Undulating grass site with mixed trees and bushes, set in hilly downland and wooded country. Adjacent to sea and beach with rocky foreshore and sandy bays. 1m W of town on B3191. 7acres 155pitches 155static
Etr–Oct no bookings last arrival 22.00hrs 25⛲ ⊗ 34wc lit all night 1cdp washbasins hc (🛁hc, 🚿hc) ⊙ warden (wash, spin, dry, iron) cold storage calor gas camping gaz toilet fluid ☎ ⊞ private beach ⛱ ⊖ ✈ ↬ launderette

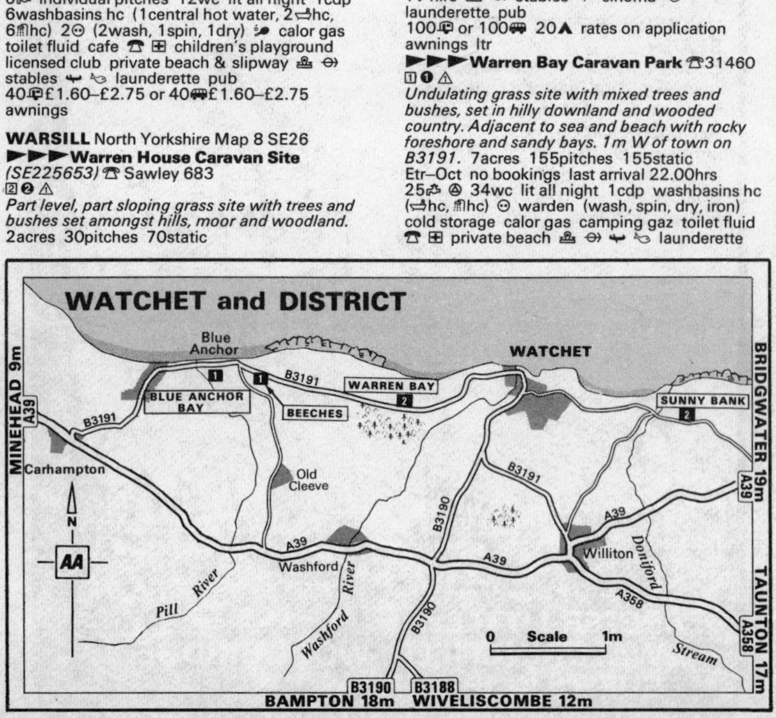

Sites listed under: **1** Blue Anchor **2** Watchet

pub
75⊡£1.85 or 75⊟£1.40 80▲£1.85
(awnings) ltr

►**Sunny Bank Camp** Doniford
☎ Williton 32237
[2] ❶ ⚠ signposted
Coastal site in elevated position developed to accommodate holiday caravans with a good area set aside for tourers. 1¾m E of town on the Doniford rd. 1acre 16pitches 30static
Etr–Oct no bookings last arrival 22.00hrs last departure 12.00hrs 6⛆ 8wc lit all night (3washbasins hc, 2⇐hc, 2⛆hc) 2⊙ warden 1wash (2iron) ⛁ calor gas camping gaz ⊞ ⛁ ⊖ ⛁ launderette pub
6⊡£3 6⊟£3 4▲£3 (awnings)

WATERLOO CROSS Devon Map 3 ST01
►►►**Waterloo Cross Camping & Caravan Park** ☎ Craddock 40317
[2] ❷ ⚠ signposted
A level grassy site with bushes and mature trees. On junction A373 and A38 between Taunton and Cullompton. Adjacent to M5 and junction 27. 4acres 50pitches
May–Sep rs15 Mar–Apr, Oct–15 Nov booking advisable peak periods last arrival 23.00hrs last departure 20.00hrs 5⛆ Ⓐ late arrivals enclosure 7wc lit all night 1cdp ⛁ 13washbasins hc central hot water (2⛆hc) 2⊙ (cold storage) calor gas camping gaz toilet fluid restaurant licensed bar ☎ ⊞ take away food ⊖ stables ⛁ pub
50⊡£1.60 or 50⊟£1.50 or 50▲£1.60 (awnings)

WATERMILLOCK Cumbria Map 12 NY42
►►►**Ullswater Caravan & Camping Site** *(NY437231)* Pooley Bridge 330 (Penrith 3092 winter)
[2] ❷ ⚠ signposted
Level site surrounded by trees next to farm. 4m SW of Penrith off A592 Ambleside rd.
7acres 115pitches 55static
Etr–14 Nov rsMar must book peak periods last arrival 22.00hrs last departure 12.00hrs 10⛆ Ⓐ 28wc lit all night 1cdp ⛁ 20washbasins hc 16⛆hc 3⊙ (1wash, 1dry) (cold storage) calor gas camping gaz paraffin toilet fluid cafe restaurant ☎ ⊞ children's playground ⛁ ⊖ stables ✈ ⛁ pub
40⊡£1.50–£3 10⊟£1–£2 65▲£1–£2 awnings ltr

WEETON Lancashire Map 7 SD33
►**High Moor Farm Caravan Park** *(SD388365)* ☎273
[1] ❶ ⚠ signposted
A small site set in open farmland about 6m from Blackpool. Situated north of M55 (exit 3) off A585 Fleetwood road on B5260. 4acres 60pitches
Mar–Oct must book public hols last arrival 24.00hrs last departure 24.00hrs 3⛆ individual pitches 12wc lit all night 1cdp (washbasins hc, central hot water, ⛆hc) ⊙ calor gas ⊞ children's playground ⛁ ⊖ stables pub
60⊡£1.50 or 60⊟£1.50 or 60▲£1.50 (awnings)

WEM Salop Map 7 SJ52
►►►**Lower Lacon Caravan Park** *(SJ534304)* ☎32376
[2] ❷ ⚠ signposted
Level grass site, set in meadowland. 1½m E of town centre on B5065. 31acres 80pitches
Apr–Oct last departure 19.00hrs 10⛆ Ⓐ late arrivals enclosure 12wc lit all night 1cdp ⛁ washbasins hc (central hot water, ⛆hc) ⊙ warden (iron) (cold storage) calor gas camping gaz toilet fluid ☎ ⊞ children's playground ⛁ ⊖ ♿ launderette pub
40⊡£1.75 20⊟£1.75 20▲£1.75 (awnings) ltr

WENTNOR Salop Map 7 SO39
►►**The Green Camping & Caravanning Site** *(SO379928)* The Green ☎ Linley 256
[1] ❶ ⚠ signposted
Level grass site set in meadowland. 15m SW of Shrewsbury. N of A489 Craven Arms–Newtown road. 10acres 50pitches 12static
Mar–Dec last departure 12.00hrs 3⛆ 8wc lit all night washbasins hc (⛆hc) ⊙ calor gas camping gaz ⊖ stables ⛁ pub
50⊡£2.25 or 50⊟£2.25 or 50▲£1.50 awnings

WEST BRIDGFORD Nottinghamshire Map 8 SK53
See Nottingham sketch map.
►►**Green Acres** *(SK605385)*
☎ Nottingham 864892
[1] ❸ ⚠
Partly level and gently sloping grass and gravel site with trees and bushes, near River Trent in wooded part of urban area. Turn N from A52 at signpost, site ½m on right. 8pitches 85static
All year must book last arrival 22.00hrs last departure 18.00hrs 1⛆ wc lit all night 1cdp washbasins hc central hot water ⇐hc ⊙ calor gas toilet fluid cafe restaurant ☎ ⊞ ⊖ stables ♿ ✈ cinema ⛁ launderette ⛁ pub
8⊡£2.16 or 8⊟£2.16 no awnings

WEST COKER Somerset Map 3 ST51
►**Partway Lane Caravan Park** *(ST505134)* ☎2871
[2] ❶ ⚠ signposted
Well-run and well-maintained site although facilities are basic. Good views over surrounding countryside. W of village adjacent to A30.
½acre 15pitches 11static
Apr–Oct booking advisable peak periods last arrival 22.30hrs last departure 12.30hrs 2⛆ 4wc lit all night 1cdp 4washbasins hc 1central hot water (2⛆hc) 2⊙ dry cold storage calor gas camping gaz ⊞ children's playground ⊖ stables ♿ cinema ⛁ launderette ⛁ pub
5⊡£1.30 5⊟£1.30 5▲£1.30 (awnings) ltr

WEST DRAYTON Gt London Map 4 TQ07
►**Riverside Caravans** *(TQ052791)*
Thorney Mill Rd ☎46520
[1] ❶ ⚠
Level site with sand and gravel surface; bushes are in abundance. Set adjacent to river in the urban area. Access from M4 (exit 4) then via A408 to West Drayton. 33pitches

All year must book last arrival 18.30hrs last departure 11.30hrs 5 9wc lit all night 3cdp (washbasins hc, central hot water, hc,) (wash, spin) games room TV calor gas camping gaz paraffin toilet fluid club room stables cinema launderette pub 33 33 rates on application

WESTENHANGER Kent Map 5 TR13
►► Trax Campsite *(TR125371)*
Folkestone Racecourse
2 ❶ ⚠ signposted
Situated in rural surroundings 7m W of Folkestone and 3m from the nearest beach at Hythe (Kent). Conveniently positioned for the Channel ports. 4acres 60pitches
16 May–13 Sep no bookings last arrival 22.30hrs last departure 15.00hrs 4 9wc lit all night 2cdp 11washbasins hc 2hc 2 warden CTV children's playground games area free racing for campers 2 Jun, 1, 15 & 22 Jul, 4, 12 & 19 Aug & 9 Sep pub 60£2–£2.35 or 60£2–£2.35 or 60▲£2–£2.35 awnings

WESTHAM East Sussex Map 5 TQ60
►► Fairfields Farm Caravan & Camping Site *(TQ639039)* Eastbourne Rd
☎ Eastbourne 763165
1 ❸ ⚠ signposted
A pleasant quiet country touring site on the B2191, signposted out the East side of Eastbourne and off the A27 in the village of Westham. 2m from the sea. 3acres 60pitches
Etr–Oct no bookings 6 12wc lit all night 1cdp 12washbasins hc 2central hot water 6hc 2 calor gas camping gaz toilet fluid stables cinema launderette pub 60£2 or 60£2 or 60▲£2 awnings

WESTON Devon Map 3 SY18
►►► Oakdown Touring Caravan Park
☎ Branscombe 387
3 ❷ ⚠ signposted
This is a level site with short approach road from A3052 between Seaton and Sidmouth. 4acres 52pitches
15 Mar–Nov must book peak periods last arrival 22.00hrs last departure 12.00hrs 5 individual pitches 8wc lit all night 1cdp washbasins hc hc warden (wash, dry) iron calor gas camping gaz ☎ children's playground stables cinema launderette pub
46fr£2.75 or 46fr£2.75 6▲fr£2.75 sae essential for enquiries (awnings)

WESTON-SUPER-MARE Avon Map 3 ST36
►►► Weston Gateway Caravan Site
West Wick ☎33201
1 ❶ ⚠ signposted
A mainly level grassy site with trees and bushes. Near main road (3m E A370, close to M5 junction 21). 9acres 175pitches
Jun–Sep rsOct–May last departure 14.00hrs 40 individual pitches 62wc lit all night 1cdp 40washbasins hc central hot water (18hc) 4 warden (2wash, 1spin) 4dry (2iron) (cold storage) calor gas camping gaz toilet fluid restaurant ☎ licensed club & children's playground stables cinema launderette pub
175£2 or 175£2 or 175▲£2 (awnings)

►► Manor Farm Caravan Park Grange Rd, Uphill ☎29731
2 ❷ signposted
Farm site with separate touring field in open country near Uphill woods. Turn off A370 into Grange Road for site on left. 1acre 30pitches 35static
Apr–Sep must book last arrival 22.00hrs last departure 11.00hrs 8 15wc 1cdp (12washbasins hc, 6hc) 2 calor gas camping gaz stables cinema launderette pub
30£1.80 or 30£1.70 no awnings

► Ardnave Caravan & Chalet Park
Crooks Ln, Kewstoke ☎22319
1 ❶ ⚠
A level grassy site with mature trees set in the country close to Sandy Bay beach. ¾acre 12pitches 105static

Mar–Oct must book peak periods last departure 10.00hrs 13 22wc lit all night 14washbasins hc central hot water (6hc) 2 (iron) calor gas children's playground, TV hire stables cinema launderette pub 12£2–£2.50 or 12£2–£2.50 (awnings)

WESTWARD Cumbria Map 11 NY24
Clea Hall Holiday Park *(NY279425)*
Wigton 2880
2 1 signposted
Level grassy site with bushes and mature trees in hilly country, with surrounding woodland, moorland and mountains. 3½m S of A595. 5acres 50pitches 85static
Mar–mid Nov must book peak periods last arrival 23.00hrs 6 18wc lit all night 1cdp washbasins hc (hc, hc) (wash, spin, dry, iron) games room calor gas camping gaz cafe licensed club & children's playground stables launderette pub 50£2.20 or 50£2.20 (awnings) ltr

WETHERBY West Yorkshire Map 8 SE44
Trax Campsite *(SE423488)*
Wetherby Racecourse
1 2 signposted
Level grassy site, situated on edge of Yorkshire Dales National Park. From Wetherby by-pass (A1) take B1224 York road. 5acres 125pitches
3 May–13 Sep no bookings last arrival 22.30hrs last departure 15.00hrs 3 32wc lit all night 1cdp 22washbasins hc 6central hot water 5hc 3 warden TV calor gas camping gaz paraffin children's playground & games area launderette 125£2–£2.75 or 125£2–£2.75 or 125£2–£2.75 awnings

WEYBOURNE Norfolk Map 9 TG14
Kelling Heath Caravan & Camping Site *(TG117418)* 224
2 1 signposted
Level grassy site set amid pine trees and sandy open spaces. Follow 'Kelling' sign from village centre on A149 Cromer road. 20acres 285pitches 385static
Spring Bank Hol–Sep rsEtr–May & Oct must book peak periods last departure 12.00hrs 30 individual pitches for caravans 100wc lit all night 12cdp washbasins hc central hot water hc (wash, spin, dry, iron) games room TV (cold storage) calor gas camping gaz toilet fluid cafe restaurant (licensed club), children's playground & TV hire stables launderette pub 100£2.05 or 100£2.05 185£2.05 awnings ltr

WEYMOUTH Dorset Map 3 SY67
See also Fleet, Dorset.
Gloucester Farm Caravan Park
Chickerell Rd, Chickerell Epsom (Surrey) 40071
1 1
Level grass site with trees and bushes in urban area. 2½m W of Weymouth near Chickerell on B3157. 1acre 30pitches 44static
15 Mar–Oct must book for caravans, Jul & Aug for motor caravans last arrival 20.00hrs last departure 10.00hrs 5 individual pitches 12wc lit all night washbasins hc (central hot water, hc) warden 1wash 1spin 1dry (2iron) calor gas camping gaz children's playground stables cinema launderette pub 30£2–£3 or 30£2–£3 (awnings)

Littlesea Holiday Park Lynch Ln
74414
1 2
Level, grass site set in meadowland adjacent to sea. 1½m W of Weymouth on B3157 Chickerell road. 17acres 265pitches 680static
23 May–28 Sep rsApr–22 May no bookings last arrival 22.00hrs last departure 10.00hrs 15 wc lit all night 1cdp 64washbasins hc 20hc 12 (5wash, 3dry, 12iron) calor gas camping gaz cafe restaurant licensed club & children's playground stables cinema launderette pub 140£3.50 or 140£3 125£3 (awnings)

WHALEY BRIDGE Derbyshire Map 7 SK08
► **Happy Vans Caravan Site** *(SK025802)*
Tunstead Milton ☎061-483 8888
2 ❶ ⚠
Grass and gravel site with trees and bushes set in meadowland near River Goyt. On A6 1½m W of junction A6/A624 at Chapel-en-le-Frith and 1½m E of junction A6/A5002 at Whaley Bridge. Site entrance opposite Rose & Crown P.H. ¼acre 6pitches 14static
All year must book peak periods last arrival 22.00hrs last departure 11.00hrs 2 4wc lit all night 1cdp (4washbasins hc, 2hc) 1 (1wash) calor gas camping gaz toilet fluid ⊞ stables launderette pub
6fr£1.50 or 6fr£1.50 (awnings)

► ***Ringstones Caravan Park*** *(SK005824)*
Yeardsley Ln ☎2152
1 ❶ ⚠
A secluded site on sloping ground surrounded by hills, with trees and bushes. 1m W of A6 at Furness Vale. 6acres 32pitches 36static
Mar–Oct must book Bank Holidays 4 8wc (2hc) calor gas camping gaz toilet fluid ⊞ stables launderette
12 or 12 20▲ (awnings)

WHATSTANDWELL Derbyshire Map 8 SK35
►►► **Haytop Farm Caravanserai**
(SK330538) ☎ Ambergate 2063
1 ❶ ⚠ signposted
A sloping, stony and grassy site with mature trees set in sylvan surroundings. Off A6 between Belper and Matlock. 60pitches
All year must book peak periods last arrival 21.00hrs 6 9wc washbasins hc central hot water hc iron calor gas camping gaz ☎ ⊞ stables launderette pub
60£2.80 or 60£2.20 or 60▲£2.80 (awnings) ltr

► **Mere Brook Caravan & Camping Park**
(SK333545) ☎ Ambergate 2154
2 ❶ ⚠ signposted
A partly level and sloping, grass site in hilly woodland and moorland country with river and canal nearby. 5m S of Matlock on A6. ¾acre 74pitches 116static
All year must book peak periods last arrival 23.59hrs last departure 15.00hrs 8 28wc lit all night 1cdp washbasins hc (hc) warden cold storage calor gas camping gaz ⊞ fishing & canoeing mobile shop stables pub
14£1.70 or 14£1.40 60▲£1.70 (awnings) ltr

WHIDDON DOWN Devon Map 3 SX69
► **Martin Farm Caravan & Camping Site**
(SX684927) ☎202
2 ❷ ⚠ signposted
Level site off A30 on edge of Dartmoor National Park. 4acres 40pitches
Etr–Sep must book peak periods last arrival 23.00hrs last departure 12.00hrs 2 9wc lit all night 1cdp 6washbasins hc 4hc 2 (cold storage) calor gas camping gaz paraffin ⊞ stables launderette pub
40£1.80 or 40£1.80 or 40▲£1.80 (awnings) ltr

WHITECLIFFE BAY Isle of Wight Map 4 SZ68
See Shanklin sketch map.
►►►► ***Whitecliffe Bay Holiday Park***
(SZ636865) ☎ Bembridge 2671
2 ❷ ⚠ signposted
A partly level and sloping site with mature trees and bushes; situated 20 minutes walk from sea, the centre is divided into two. The caravan site is situated in the main Holiday Park with the camping area the other side of the road, overlooking Bembridge Airport. 14acres
May–Sep rsEtr & Oct must book peak periods 17 54wc lit all night 56washbasins hc central hot water 1hc 26hc 9 warden (wash) iron games room CTV cold storage calor gas camping gaz paraffin toilet fluid cafe restaurant licensed bar ☎ ⊞ stables cinema launderette
80 (awnings)

►►► ***Caravan Site*** *(SZ638861)*
☎ Bembridge 3051 (out of season 2715)

2 ❷ ⚠ signposted
Part level, part sloping site overlooking bay with path down to shingle and sand beach. Along B3395 turn right at airfield. No pets 30pitches 300static
Mid May–mid Sep bookings only 12 66wc lit all night 1cdp (washbasins hc) (central hot water) (hc) ⊙ warden calor gas off-licence ☎ ⊞ stables cinema launderette pub
30 rates on application (awnings)

WHITECROSS Cornwall Map 2 SW86
See Newquay sketch map.
►►► White Acres Holiday Park
(SW895598) ☎ Fraddon 860220
2 ⚠ signposted
Part level, part sloping grass site with mixed trees and bushes set in typical Cornish downland scenery. 2m off A30 on A392 Newquay road. 5acres 248pitches 81static
May–Aug rsEtr–Apr & Sep must book peak periods last arrival 23.00hrs last departure 10.00hrs 20 individual pitches Ⓐ 39wc lit all night 2cdp washbasins hc central hot water (hc) ⊙ warden (spin, dry, iron) games room CTV calor gas camping gaz toilet fluid (licensed club) ☎ ⊞ stables launderette pub
54£3.55 or 54£3.55 194▲£3.55 (awnings)

WHITSTABLE Kent Map 5 TR16
See Herne Bay sketch map.
►►► Blue Waters Touring Harbour
St John's Rd *(TR145675)*
2 ❶ ⚠ signposted
Level, grass site with trees and bushes near to sand/shingle beach. 3m from town on A299.
3acres 45pitches 452static
Apr–16 Oct no bookings 4 individual pitches 11wc lit all night 2cdp (2central hot water, 4hc) 3⊙ (2wash, 1dry, 2iron) calor gas camping gaz toilet fluid ☎ ⊞ children's playground stables cinema launderette pub
45£1.50 or 45£1.50 (awnings) ltr

WHITSTONE Cornwall Map 2 SX29
►►► Keywood Caravan Park
☎ Week St Mary 338
2 ❶ ⚠ signposted
Level and slightly sloping site. On Launceston–Bude road B3254. 1acre 25pitches 50static
Etr–Oct must book peak periods last departure 10.00hrs 7 12wc lit all night 1cdp (10 washbasins hc, 4central hot water, 6hc) 2⊙ (1wash, 1spin, 1iron) cold storage calor gas camping gaz restaurant ☎ ⊞ (licensed club) children's playground & bar snacks
25£1.62 or 25£1.62 or 25▲£1.62 awnings

WILSHAMSTEAD (Wilstead) Bedfordshire Map 4 TL04
►►►► Briar Bank Park *(TL062439)*
☎ Bedford 740236
2 ❶ ⚠ signposted
Situated 4m S of Bedford and conveniently situated for places of interest. The site itself offers some seclusion and is surrounded by fields, woods and hills. 15acres 100pitches 150static
All year must book public hols last arrival 23.00hrs 18 Ⓐ late arrivals enclosure wc lit all night 2cdp washbasins hc central hot water (hc, hc) ⊙ (wash, spin, dry, iron) (games room) TV cold storage calor gas camping gaz paraffin toilet fluid ☎ ⊞ (licensed club) & children's playground stables launderette pub
120£1.95 or 120£1.95 or 120▲£1.95 (awnings) ltr

WIMBORNE MINSTER Dorset Map 4 SZ09
►►► Wilksworth Farm Caravan Park
(SU004018) Cranborne Rd ☎ 885467
2 ❸ ⚠ signposted
Level, grass and gravel site, set in farmland. 1m N on B3078. 8acres 85pitches 60static
Mar–Oct must book peak periods last arrival 22.30hrs last departure 14.00hrs 11 Ⓐ 18wc lit all night 1cdp 25washbasins hc (1central hot water) 10hc 3⊙ (1wash, 1spin, 1dry, 1iron) (games room) cold storage calor gas camping gaz toilet fluid ☎ ⊞ children's playground stables cinema launderette pub
60£1.80–£2.20 or 60£1.80–£2.20 25▲£1.80–£2.20 awnings

WINCANTON Somerset Map 3 ST72
►► Trax Campsite Wincanton Racecourse
1 ❶ ⚠ signposted
Level, grassy site, ½m N of town off B3081 off the Bruton road. 2acres 50pitches
2 May–13 Sep no bookings last arrival 22.30hrs last departure 15.00hrs 1 10wc lit all night 1cdp 10washbasins hc 2central hot water 2hc 3⊙ warden TV calor gas camping gaz ☎ ⊞ games area stables launderette
50£2–£2.75 or 50£2–£2.75 50▲£2–£2.75

WINCHESTER Hampshire Map 4 SU42
►► Mornhill Caravan Site *(SU523295)*
Mornhill ☎ 69877
2 ❷ signposted
A well laid out site in secluded spot surrounded by trees. 6acres 80pitches
28 Mar–Oct must book peak periods individual pitches late arrivals enclosure 8wc lit all night 2cdp washbasins hc hc ⊙ warden calor gas camping gaz toilet fluid ☎ ⊞ cinema launderette pub
80£2.91–£3.16 or 80£2.91–£3.16 or 80▲£2.91–£3.16 (awnings)

► *Winchester Recreation Centre*
(SU486299) Gordon Rd ☎ 69525
1 ❶ ⚠ signposted
Mainly level, grassy site with trees and bushes. Near main road. 150pitches
May–Sep last departure 12.00hrs 2 individual pitches Ⓐ late arrivals enclosure 12wc lit all night 10cdp washbasins hc central hot water hc ⊙ cafe restaurant ☎ ⊞ cinema launderette
150▲ ltr

WINDERMERE Cumbria Map 7 SD49
See sketch map.
►►►►► Fallbarrow Caravan Park
(SD401974) ☎ 4428
2 ❷ ⚠ signposted
Level grass and gravel site with mature trees set in the heart of the Lake District. Adjacent to Lake Windermere. 4acres 80pitches 267static
15 Mar–14 Nov booking advisable peak periods last arrival 23.00hrs last departure 13.00hrs 50 individual pitches 35wc lit all night 3cdp 26washbasins hc 14hc 6⊙ warden (4wash, 2spin, 8dry) 3iron (games room) CTV cold storage calor gas cafe restaurant ☎ ⊞ children's playground licensed club & private beach stables cinema launderette pub
80£2–£5.25 or 80£2–£5.25 (awnings)

►►►►► Limefitt Park *(NY417033)*
☎ Ambleside 2300
2 ❷ ⚠ signposted
Partly level, partly sloping site with young trees and bushes, set in fell meadowland. Off A592 3m N of Windermere. 15acres 345pitches 20static
Apr–Oct booking advisable peak periods last arrival 22.30hrs last departure 13.00hrs 7 individual pitches 110wc lit all night 2cdp 170washbasins hc 1central hot water 40hc 40⊙ warden (2wash, 2dry) 3iron games room CTV cold storage calor gas cafe restaurant licensed bar ☎ ⊞ children's playground & licensed club stables cinema launderette pub
195£2–£3.76 or 195£2–£3.76 345▲£2–£3.76 (awnings)

►►► Braithwaite Fold Touring Caravan Park *(SD400961)* Glebe Rd, Bowness-on-Windermere. Apply to: South Lakeland District Council, Tourism & Recreation Dept, Ashleigh, Windermere, Cumbria
1 ❷ ⚠ signposted
Level, grass site with trees and bushes set in urban area adjacent to lake and ferry. Site is situated ½m S of town of Bowness.

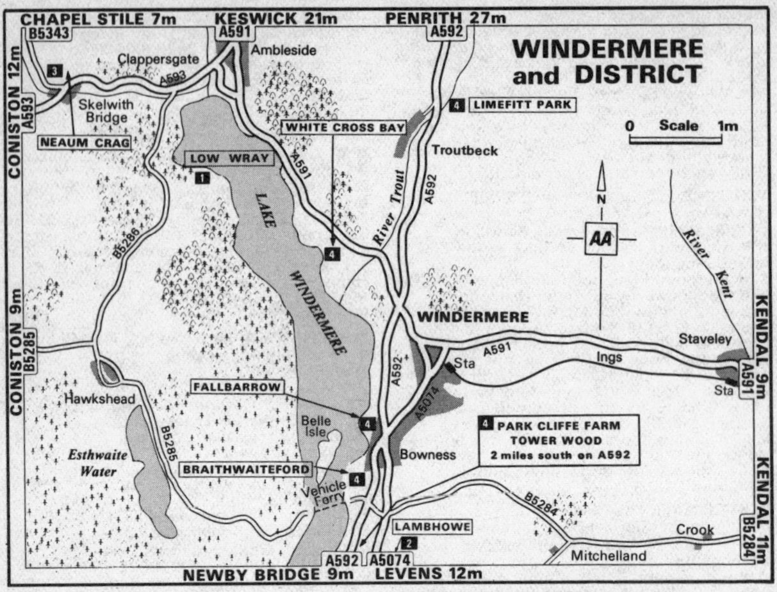

Sites listed under: **1** Ambleside **2** Crosthwaite **3** Skelwith Bridge **4** Windermere

No cycling or skateboards 60pitches Etr–mid Oct booking advisable last arrival 22.00hrs last departure 12.00hrs 4 individual pitches 8wc lit all night 1cdp 10washbasins hc 4🚿hc 4⊙ warden cafe ⊞ stables cinema launderette pub 60🚐£2–£3.50 or 60🚐£2–£3.50 awnings

▶▶▶ Park Cliffe Farm Caravan & Camping Site *(SD391912)* Tower Wood ☎ Newby Bridge 344 (to be changed to Newby Bridge 31344)
1 ❶ ⚠ signposed
A hillside site on level and sloping ground with trees, bushes, rocks and a mountain stream. 4m S of Windermere off A592. 12acres 250pitches 50static
Etr–Oct booking advisable peak periods last departure 12.00hrs 7 Ⓐ wc lit all night 2cdp washbasins hc central hot water 🚿hc ⊙ warden calor gas camping gaz ☎ ⊞ 250▲£3–£3.60 (awnings)

▶▶▶ *White Cross Bay Caravan Site* *(NY397004)* Troutbeck Bridge ☎3937
2 ❶ ⚠
Level site with concrete standings, set in hilly moor and woodland country adjacent to lake. 2½m N of Windermere on A591. 8acres 125pitches 353static
Mar–Oct must book Public & school hols last arrival 23.00hrs last departure 12.00hrs 13 individual pitches wc lit all night 3cdp washbasins hc 🚿hc ⊙ warden swimming in lake games room CTV calor gas toilet fluid cafe restaurant licensed bar ☎ ⊞ stables cinema launderette pub 125🚐

WINKSLEY North Yorkshire Map 8 SE27
▶▶▶ Woodhouse Farm Caravan & Camping Park *(SE241715)*
☎Kirkby Malzeard 309
2 ❷ ⚠ signposted
Situated on sloping land in well wooded area amongst pleasant agricultural surroundings. 6m W of Ripon off B6265 Pateley Bridge road. 2½m from Fountains Abbey. 14acres 85pitches 15static
Apr–Oct must book peak periods last arrival 23.00hrs last departure 17.00hrs 9 Ⓐ late arrivals enclosure 17wc lit all night 1cdp 12washbasins hc (12central hot water, 4🚿hc) 4⊙ iron (games room) TV (2cold storage) calor gas camping gaz paraffin toilet fluid ☎ ⊞ children's playground, battery charger & touring service stables pub 30🚐£1.85 5🚐£1.85 50▲£1.85 (awnings)

WOLVEY Warwickshire Map 4 SP48
▶▶▶ Wolvey Villa Farm Caravan & Camping Site *(SP428869)* ☎Hinckley 220493
2 ❷ ⚠ signposted
Level, grassy site with mature trees and bushes set in meadowland. Drive south from Wolvey on what was once the A46. 6acres 140pitches
All year must book peak periods last arrival 23.15hrs last departure 12.00hrs 4 late arrivals enclosure 11wc lit all night 1cdp 6 washbasins hc (🚿hc) ⊙ warden (wash, spin, dry) TV cold storage calor gas camping gaz toilet fluid ☎ ⊞ putting green stables launderette pub 140🚐fr£1.20 or 140🚐fr£1.10 or 140▲fr£1.10 (awnings)

WOODBURY Devon Map 3 SY08
►►► Castle Brake Caravan Park
(SY029878) ☎32431
2 ❷ ⚠
Situated in a picturesque part of East Devon, the site lies on the edge of Woodbury Common in a secluded position. 1acre 24pitches 30static May–5 Oct must book peak periods last arrival 22.00hrs last departure 10.00hrs 2 individual pitches 5wc lit all night 1cdp 5washbasins hc (4hc) 1 warden (spin, dry, iron) games room TV cold storage calor gas camping gaz cafe licensed bar ☎ ⊞ children's playground & (licensed club) stables cinema launderette pub
12£2.10 or 12£2.10 12▲£1.80 (awnings)

WOOKEY HOLE Somerset Map 3 ST54
See Cheddar sketch map.
►►► Homestead Caravan & Camping Park ☎Wells (Som) 73022
2 ❶ ⚠
Grass site with mature trees, set in hilly woodland and meadowland, with access to river and Wookey Hole. 1½m off A371 Wells–Cheddar road. 2acres 60pitches 33static Etr–Oct no bookings last arrival 22.00hrs last departure 12.00hrs 3 13wc lit all night 1cdp (8washbasins hc) (1hc) (2hc) 2 warden (wash, dry) iron cold storage calor gas camping gaz licensed bar ☎ ⊞ stables cinema launderette
60 or 60 or 60▲ (awnings)

WOOLACOMBE Devon Map 2 SS44
See Ilfracombe sketch map.
►►►► Golden Coast Holiday Village
(SS482436) Station Rd ☎418
2 ❸ ⚠
This holiday village includes villas and static caravans as well as the camping site. Woolacombe is surrounded by National Trust land. 1½m from beach at Woolacombe. no pets 9½acres 231pitches Etr–Sep must book last arrival 22.00hrs last departure 10.00hrs 26 individual pitches wc lit all night cdp washbasins hc central hot water hc warden (wash, spin, dry) iron (games room) calor gas camping gaz toilet fluid restaurant licensed bar ☎ ⊞ children's playground, licensed club & entertainment in season stables launderette .pub
231£1.75–£4.90 or 231£1.75–£4.90 or 231▲£1.95–£4.50 awnings

Woolacombe Bay Caravan Park
(SS468442) ☎221
2 2 ⚠
Sloping, grass site in meadowland overlooking sea and sands. 10acres 230pitches 175static 17 May–19 Sep rs29 Mar–16 May & 20 Sep–Oct must book last arrival 19.00hrs last departure 10.00hrs 15 individual pitches for caravans 75wc lit all night 35washbasins hc (16hc) 5 (2wash, 2spin, 2dry, 1iron) games room calor gas camping gaz toilet fluid cafe ☎ ⊞ children's playground licensed club & entertainment stables cinema launderette pub 50£2–£3.25 180£1.50–£2.75 or 180▲£1.50–£2.75 (awnings) ltr

WOOLER Northumberland Map 12 NT92
Bridge End Caravan Site *(NT998277)*
Bridge End ☎447
1 1 ⚠
A level, grassy site with trees and bushes set in woodland and moorland near river. ¼m S of Wooler on A697. 3acres 55pitches 100static Mar–Oct must book peak periods last arrival 20.00hrs last departure 12.00hrs 14 individual pitches 25wc lit all night 2cdp 16washbasins hc (2central hot water) (10hc) 5 (3wash, 2spin) 2dry (cold storage) calor gas camping gaz toilet fluid dry cleaning pony trekking ☎ ⊞ stables launderette pub 25 or 25 30▲ (awnings) ltr

WORSBROUGH South Yorkshire
Map 8 SE30
Greensprings Holiday Park *(SE330020)*
Rockley Ln ☎Barnsley 88298
1 1 ⚠ signposted
Part level, part sloping, grass site with young trees and bushes, set in wood and meadowland with access to river. From exit 36 off M1 turn along A61 to Barnsley, then signposted. 4acres 73pitches Apr–Oct 8 individual pitches 12wc lit all night 2cdp 12washbasins hc 6central hot water (10hc) 2 calor gas camping gaz toilet fluid ⊞ stables cinema launderette pub 73£1.50 or 73£1.50 or 73▲£1.50 (awnings) ltr

WORTWELL Norfolk Map 5 TM28
Little Lakeland Caravan Park *(TM287857)*
☎Homersfield 646 (Harleston 852423 out of season)
3 2 ⚠ signposted
Level grass site with bushes and trees set in meadowland with direct access to river and lake 2m from Harleston town centre. 4acres 10pitches 20static 20 Mar–Oct must book public hols 14 individual pitches wc 1cdp hc calor gas camping gaz toilet fluid children's playground & fishing pub 10£2 or 10£2 3▲£2 awnings

Lone Pine Camping Site *(TM274843)*
Low Rd ☎Homersfield 646 (Harleston 852423 out of season)
2 2 ⚠ signposted
A mainly level, grassy site with saplings and bushes set in downland and meadowland. 2acres 25pitches May–Oct 1 individual pitches 4wc (hc) calor gas camping gaz toilet fluid pub 25£1.70 or 25▲£1.70

WOTTON UNDER EDGE Gloucestershire
Map 3 ST79
Cotswold Gate Caravan Park
☎3128
2 2 ⚠ signposted
Level, grassy site with mature trees and bushes. 1m NW of town. 4m E of Exit 14 (M5) by B4509. 6acres 60pitches Mar–Oct booking advisable peak periods last arrival 21.00hrs last departure 12.00hrs 8 late arrivals enclosure 6wc lit all night 4cdp 6washbasins hc (2central hot water, 2hc) 2 warden (iron) (cold storage) calor gas camping gaz licensed bar ⊞ licensed club & children's playground launderette pub 60£2.70 or 60£2.70 30▲£2.70 (awnings)

WROXALL Isle of Wight Map 4 SZ57
See Shanklin & district sketch map.
Appuldurcombe Caravan Park
(SZ542805) Appuldurcombe Rd
☎Ventnor 852597
2 2 ⚠
An attractive, secluded site – with a small stream running through, situated a few miles from Ventnor. 5½acres 100pitches 40static May Sep rsMar & Apr, Oct & Nov must book peak periods last arrivals 23.00hrs last departure 23.00hrs 6 individual pitches late arrivals enclosure 14wc lit all night 1cdp washbasins hc central hot water (hc) warden (wash, spin, dry) iron CTV cold storage calor gas camping gaz paraffin toilet fluid licensed bar ☎ ⊞ banking service battery charging stables cinema launderette pub 20 or 20 80▲

WYKEHAM North Yorkshire Map 8 SE98
St Helens Caravan Park
(SE967836) ☎Scarborough 862771
2 3 ⚠ signposted
Part level, part sloping, grass site with young and bushes in the Rye Valley. On the north side of A170 E of village. 11acres 250pitches Mar–Oct must book peak periods last departure 12.00hrs late arrivals enclosure wc lit all night 4cdp washbasins hc hc warden (wash, spin, dry, iron) cold storage calor gas camping gaz toilet fluid ☎ ⊞ children's playground stables cinema launderette pub 250£2.50 or 250£2.50 20▲£2.50 (awnings)

YARMOUTH (GREAT) Norfolk Map 5 TG50
See sketch map.
Vauxhall Holiday Park
(TG520083) ☎57231
2 3 ⚠ signposted
Level grass site with trees and bushes, set in urban area with access to sea, beach, river, estuary, lake and main road (A47). 435pitches 605static 21 May–24 Sep no bookings last departure 12.00hrs 14 individual pitches late arrivals enclosure 80wc lit all night 4cdp 46washbasins hc 40hc 16 warden (wash, spin, dry, iron) CTV cold storage calor gas camping gaz cafe licensed bar ☎ ⊞ stables cinema launderette 230 or 230 205▲

YORK North Yorkshire Map 8 SE65
►► *Caravan Club Site* *(SE604507)*
Terry Av ☎58997
2 ❷ ⚠ signposted
A level, grassy site with mature trees and bushes, near river. 3acres 90pitches
Apr–Sep must book last arrival 22.00hrs last departure 12.00hrs 3 individual pitches late arrivals enclosure 10wc lit all night 2cdp 12washbasins hc 8hc 5 warden calor gas camping gaz toilet fluid ⊞ stables cinema launderette
70 or 70 20▲ (awnings)

CHANNEL ISLANDS

GUERNSEY (No map)

CÂTEL (FAUXQUETS VALLEY)
► Fauxquets Valley Farm Camp Site
Fauxquets Valley Farm ☎Guernsey 55460
2 ❸ ⚠ signposted
Level grass site with bushes in hilly woodland; access to sea and beach at Cobo and Vazon Bays. 3acres 90pitches
May–Sep rsApr must book 4 7wc lit all night 15washbasins hc 6hc 1 1iron games room TV (cold storage) calor gas camping gaz paraffin ☎ ⊞ children's playground stables cinema launderette pub
90£3 or 90▲£3

JERSEY (No map)

ST BRELADE
►►► Quennevais Camping Site
Les Ormes Farm ☎ Jersey 42436
1 ❶ ⚠ signposted
Partly level and gently sloping grass and sand site with trees and bushes set in hilly woodland country. Near airport on road B43. 15acres 250pitches
Jun–Sep rsMar–May must book peak periods last arrival 22.00hrs last departure 12.00hrs 5 28wc lit all night 64washbasins hc 20hc 13 warden (1dry, 3iron) games room CTV (cold storage) calor gas camping gaz paraffin cafe restaurant ☎ ⊞ children's playground stables launderette pub
250▲£4.90

►► *Rose Farm* Route des Genets
☎Jersey 41231
1 ❶ ⚠
Sloping grassy site with mature trees. 1m W of St Aubins village on A13. 3acres 100pitches
Apr–Sep must book peak periods last arrival 20.00hrs 3 wc lit all night washbasins hc hc TV calor gas paraffin ☎ ⊞ stables
100▲

ST MARTIN
►►► Beuvelande Camping Site
☎Jersey 53575
2 ❷ ⚠ signposted
Level grass site with mature trees and bushes, set in rural area 1m from beach. A3 from St Helier then on A6. 3acres 80pitches

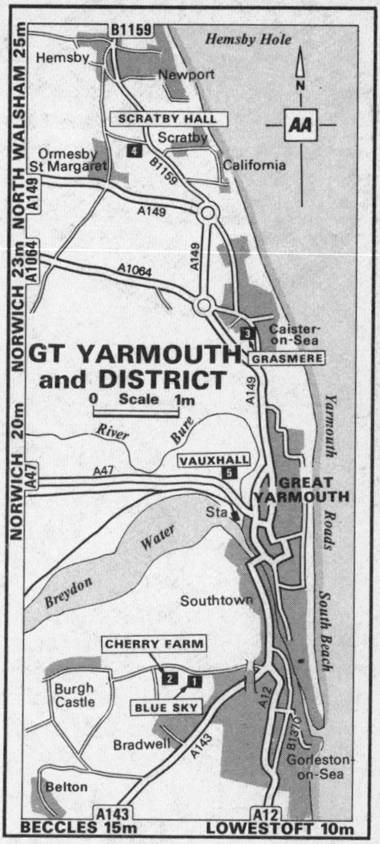

Sites listed under:
1 Bradwell **2** Burgh Castle **3** Caister-on-Sea
4 Scratby **5** Yarmouth (Great)

Etr–Oct must book last arrival 22.00hrs last departure 20.00hrs 4 10wc lit all night 24washbasins hc central hot water (10hc) 4 (1wash, 1spin, 1dry, 1iron) games room CTV cold storage calor gas camping gaz paraffin toilet fluid ☎ ⊞ children's playground stables launderette pub
80▲ no awnings

►►► Rozel Camping Park
Summerville Farm ☎Jersey 51989
2 3 △
Level grass site surrounded by tall trees. From St Helier follow Bagatelle Road (A6) or St Saviour's Road (A7). Last arrival and departure time as soon as possible after car ferry docks. 3acres 70pitches 15static Apr–Sep must book peak periods last arrival & last departure see description 2 individual pitches 9wc lit all night 20washbasins hc 10hc (2) warden 1spin 2iron games room CTV cold storage calor gas camping gaz paraffin ☎ ⊞ children's playground stables pub
70▲£1–£1.60

ISLE OF MAN

HILLBERRY Nr Douglas Map 6 SC37
►► Glendhoe International Farm Camping Site *(SC383796)* ☎ Douglas 21254
1 1 △ signposted
A simple camping site, situated in a sheltered wooded valley 2½m from Douglas. Entrance to site is 100yd from Hillberry Corner, on the mountain road, and TT course. 12acres 140pitches
20 May–20 Sep rsApr–19 May, 21–30 Sep must book early Jun last arrival 23.00hrs 4 individual pitches 10wc lit all night 1cdp (10washbasins hc, 6hc) 2 warden (1spin, 1dry) games room cold storage calor gas camping gaz ☎ ⊞ stables cinema launderette pub
40£2.92 100▲£2.92 awnings

LAXEY Map 6 SC48
► Laxey Commissioners Campsite *(SC438841)* ☎781241
1 1 △
Level grass site set in hilly country with access to sea, beach and hills. 1½acres 40pitches Apr–Sep must book 3 5wc lit all night (central hot water) (hc,) pub
40£1.35 or 40▲£1.35 awnings

WALES

WALES

ABERCRAVE Powys Map 3 SN81
►► Dan-Yr-Ogof Caves Caravan Park
(SN841160) ☎284
2 ⚠ signposted
A part level grassy site with mature trees. Hardstandings for caravans. Set in mountainous country near a river. 3m N of village on A4067 Sennybridge road. Follow signs for 'Dan-Yr-Ogof Caves'. 7acres 60pitches
Etr–Oct no bookings last arrival 20.00hrs last departure 11.00hrs 5 shower Ⓐ no cars by tents 9wc lit all night 1cdp 9washbasins hc 6 shower hc 2⊙ ⊖ stables ↬ launderette pub
30 caravan £1.50 or 30 motorvan £1.50 30▲£1.50 awnings

ABERMULE Powys Map 6 SO19
►► Ye Olde-Smithy Caravan Park
Dolforwyn ☎657
1 ❶ ⚠
A mainly level grassy site with trees and bushes set in meadowland near river and main road.
2acres 20pitches 52static
Apr–Sep must book peak periods 2 shower wc lit all night 7washbasins hc (2 shower hc) 2⊙ calor gas camping gaz ☎ ⊞ launderette ⊖ ♿ cinema ↬ launderette pub
20 caravan £2 or 20 motorvan £2 or 20▲£2 (awnings) ltr

ABERSOCH Gwynedd Map 6 SH32
►► Haulfryn Camping Site *(SH318307)*
The Warren ☎2045/2047
1 ❷ ⚠ signposted
Slightly sloping site overlooking Cardigan Bay. Off A499 1¾m E of Abersoch. ✈ 2½acres 75pitches
Mar–Oct must book last arrival 18.00hrs last departure 10.00hrs shower Ⓐ 8wc lit all night 1cdp 8washbasins hc central hot water (6 shower hc, 5⊙) warden ☎ ⊞ ⊖ stables ♿ ✈ cinema ↬ launderette pub
45▲£2–£3

► Pant-Gwyn Cottage Sarn Bâch ☎2268
1 ❶
Gently sloping site in quiet elevated position near to Abersoch, on the Lleyn Peninsula.
5acres 62pitches
Spring Bank Hol–Sep rsEtr must book peak periods for tents last arrival 22.00hrs 4 shower 9wc lit all night (shower hc) ⊙ warden (cold storage) calor gas camping gaz ⊞ launderette ⊖ stables ♿ ✈ ↬ launderette pub
62 motorvan fr£1.50 or 62▲fr£1.50 awnings ltr

ABERYSTWYTH Dyfed Map 6 SN58
► 'U' Tow Caravans Aberystwyth Holiday Village *(SN536809)* ☎4211
1 ❶ ⚠ signposted
A sloping, hilly site set on a roadside about 1m from town centre off A487 Aberaeron road.
no motorbikes 33acres 300pitches 173static
Apr–Oct no bookings last departure 10.30hrs 14 shower late arrivals enclosure no cars by caravans/tents wc 1cdp 18washbasins hc 1central hot water 22 shower hc 5⊙ warden (4wash, 1spin, 2dry) 2iron (iron) games room CTV (cold storage) calor gas camping gaz paraffin toilet fluid cafe restaurant ☎ ⊞ (licensed club) children's playground & fishing launderette ⊖ stables ♿ ✈ cinema launderette pub
50 caravan £2.60 50 motorvan £2.60 50▲£2.60 (awnings) ltr

BALA Gwynedd Map 6 SH93
See sketch map.
►► Penybont Touring Park *(SH931350)*
Llangynog Rd ☎520549
2 ❶ ⚠
Part level, part sloping, grass and gravel site with trees and bushes set in mountainous woodland country, adjacent to River Dee and Bala Lake. ½m from Bala on side of B4391. 7½acres

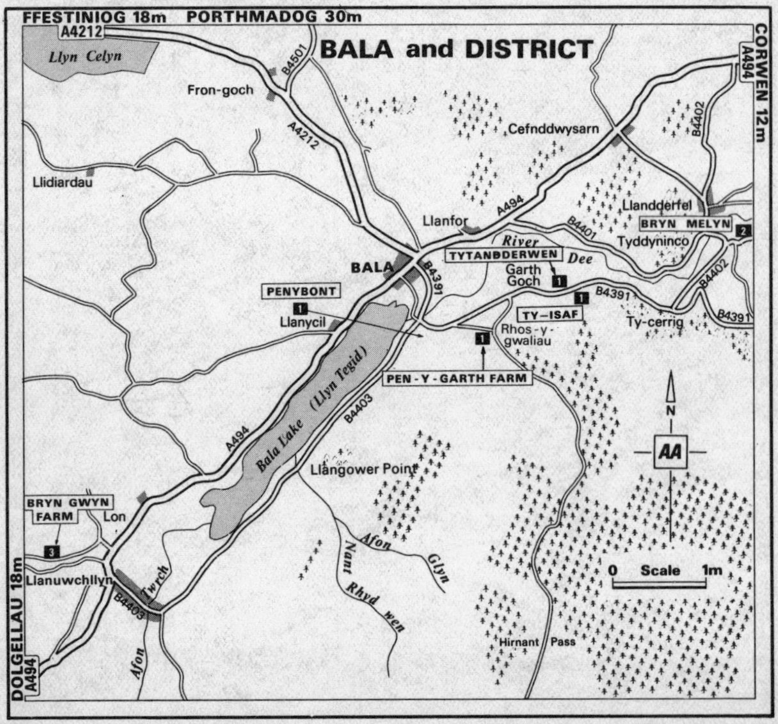

Sites listed under: **1** Bala **2** Llandderfel **3** Llanuwchllyn

75pitches
Apr–Sep must book peak periods last departure 14.00hrs 5 individual pitches 9wc lit all night 1cdp (11washbasins hc, 2hc) 2 warden (cold storage) calor gas camping gaz stables launderette pub
25£2 or 25£2 50£1.60 (awnings)

Pen-y-Garth Farm *(SH940349)*
Rhos-y-Gwalia 520485
2 signposted
A level site with well laid-out pitches for tourers, amidst attractive scenery. 3acres 48pitches 45static
Mar–Sep must book last arrival 21.00hrs last departure 12.00hrs 7 late arrivals enclosure 12wc lit all night 1cdp (10washbasins hc, 4hc) 3 (2spin, 1iron) calor gas camping gaz children's playground batteries charged stables cinema launderette pub
20£2 or 20£2 28£1.75 (awnings)

Ty Isaf Caravan & Camping Park
(SH960354) 520574
2 signposted
A level and grassy attractive farm site.
2acres 30pitches
Apr–Oct must book last arrival 22.00hrs last departure 12.00hrs 2 6wc lit all night 1cdp (washbasins hc, hc) (1dry) (cold storage) calor gas camping gaz cinema launderette pub
30£1.50 or 25£1.30 or 25£1.40 awnings

Tytandderwen Caravan Site
(SH955363) 520273
3 signposted
Grassy, level, touring and camping site with fine mountain views, well maintained.
3acres 10pitches
Etr–Oct must book peak periods last departure 12.00hrs 2 10wc 1cdp (4washbasins hc) (2hc) (2) calor gas camping gaz stables cinema launderette pub
10 or 10 or 10 (awnings)

BEDDGELERT Gwynedd Map 6 SH54
Snowdonia Forest Park Camping Ground 288
3 signposted
Part level, part sloping grass and gravel site amidst trees and bushes. Set in mountainous woodland country near to river and main road.
14acres 280pitches
Apr–Oct rsNov–Mar no bookings last arrival 22.00hrs last departure 14.00hrs 8 27wc lit all night 2cdp washbasins hc hc wash dry TV calor gas camping gaz cafe restaurant children's playground stables launderette pub
140£2.10 or 140£2.10 140£2.10 awnings

BETHESDA Gwynedd Map 6 SH66
Ogwen Bank Caravan Park
(SH626656) 600486
2 signposted
Part level, part sloping, grass and gravel site with mature trees and bushes set in mountainous country adjacent to river. On A5 between Betws-y-Coed and Bangor. 5acres 30pitches 100static
14 Mar–Oct must book peak periods last arrival 22.30hrs last departure 12.00hrs 13 individual pitches late arrivals enclosure 17wc lit all night 1cdp 8washbasins hc central hot water hc warden (wash, spin, dry, iron) calor gas camping gaz toilet fluid cafe restaurant (licensed club) stables launderette pub
30£2.37–£3.24 or 30£2.37–£3.24 (awnings)

BETTWS EVAN Dyfed Map 2 SN34
Pilbach Caravan Park
Rhydlewis 434
3 signposted
An exceptionally well-run small site set in secluded countryside. 3m N of Newcastle Emlyn and 7m E of Cardigan. 3acres 40pitches 55static
Mar–Oct must book peak periods last arrival 22.00hrs last departure 12.00hrs 6 late arrivals enclosure 11wc lit all night 1cdp (washbasins hc, central hot water, hc) warden (wash, spin, dry, iron, cold storage) calor gas toilet fluid (licensed club) children's playground stables pub
40£2.25 or 40£2.25 or 40£2.25 (awnings)

BETWS GARMON Gwynedd Map 6 SH55
See Caernarfon sketch map.
Bryn Gloch Farm Caravan & Camping Park *(SH575534)* Waunfawr 216
2 signposted
A well-maintained site with a sloping grassy surface, situated close to the main road with good country views. 6acres 80pitches 15static
Mar–Oct must book 5 late arrivals enclosure wc lit all night 9washbasins hc central hot water (4hc) 4 (1spin, dry) cold storage calor gas camping gaz toilet fluid cafe restaurant children's playground stables pub
20£2.40 20£2.20 60£2.20 (awnings)

BROAD HAVEN Dyfed Map 2 SM81
Rosehill Country Hotel Caravan Park
(SM892151) Portfield Gate 304
2
Small, secluded touring site in sheltered situation amidst trees. 1¼acres 20pitches
Etr–Oct 2 4wc 1cdp 4washbasins hc 2hc 2 warden CTV restaurant licensed bar
20

BROADMOOR Dyfed Map 2 SN10
See Tenby sketch map.
Cross Park Caravan Site
Saundersfoot 813205
1
Landscaped grass site adjacent to A477 Carmarthen–Pembroke road. 3½acres 15pitches 85static
Etr–15 Oct must book peak periods last arrival 22.30hrs last departure 10.00hrs 8 6wc lit all night cdp washbasins hc central hot water 3hc warden 3wash 2dry
15 or 15 or 30 (awnings)

BRONLLYS Powys Map 3 SO13
Anchorage Caravan Park *(SO142351)*
Talgarth 246
2 signposted
Touring pitches are on grassy slopes with good mountain views of the Brecon Beacons. 8m NE of Brecon. 7acres 110pitches 101static
All year must book public hols last arrival 23.00hrs 8 25wc lit all night 1cdp washbasins hc (13hc) 4 (4wash, 1spin, 2dry, 1iron) CTV calor gas camping gaz paraffin toilet fluid children's playground stables launderette pub
60£2 10£2 40£2 awnings ltr

BRYNSIENCYN Gwynedd Map 6 SH46
Fron Farm 310
2 signposted
Well facilitated, small farm site in convenient situation for touring North Wales. Off A4080 Llanfair PG–Newborough road. 5acres 79pitches 1static
Apr–Sep must book peak periods last arrival 23.00hrs last departure 12.00hrs 4 individual pitches late arrivals enclosure 8wc lit all night 1cdp (washbasins hc, central hot water, hc) warden (cold storage) calor gas camping gaz paraffin toilet fluid children's playground stables pub
39£1.75 40£1.50 or 40£1.50 (awnings)

BRYNTEG Gwynedd Map 6 SH48
Tyddyn Llwyd Caravan Site
Tynygongl 2334/2378
2 signposted
Secluded country site within easy reach of the coast. From Benllech take B5108 for 1m.
6acres 150pitches 95static
Mar–Oct booking advisable peak periods –

Caernarfon

min 1wk last departure 12.00hrs 6⛭ ⊚ 22wc lit all night 1cdp 18washbasins hc (6🚿hc) 2⊙ warden calor gas camping gaz toilet fluid ☎ ⊞ children's playground ⛳ ⊖ stables ✈ cinema ↬ launderette pub
50🚐£1.50–£1.75 20🚌£1.25 80▲£1.25 awnings

►► Nant Newydd Caravan Park
(SH480825) ☎ Tynygongl 2842
[1] ❶ △
Gently sloping grass site with mature trees and bushes; set in meadowland adjacent to main road, 3m from Benllech off A5025.
2acres 45pitches 80static
May–Sep rsMar–Apr & Oct must book Jul & Aug last arrival 22.00hrs last departure 12.00hrs 10⛭ 16wc lit all night 2cdp 8washbasins hc 2central hot water (6🚿hc) 3⊙ (1wash, iron) calor gas toilet fluid ⊞ ⛳ ⊖ stables ✈ ↬ launderette
15🚐 or 15🚌 30▲ (awnings)

► Garnedd Touring Site *(SH495818)*
Garnedd ☎ Tynygongl 3240
[1] ❶ △
Mainly level grass site set in meadowland close to sea, beach and main road. Off A5025 Menai Bridge–Amlwch road. 5½acres 120pitches 1static
15 Mar–Oct must book for caravans last arrival 23.00hrs last departure 12.00hrs 4⛭ individual pitches ⊚ 8wc lit all night 2cdp (3washbasins hc, 2🚿hc) 1⊙ warden cold storage ⛳ ⊖ stables ✈ cinema ↬ launderette pub
20🚐£1.80 50🚌£1.80 or 50▲£1.50 (awnings)

CAERNARFON Gwynedd Map 6 SH46
See sketch map.

►► Cadnant Valley Camping Park
(SH487628) Llanberis Rd ☎3196
[2] ❷ △ signposted
Situated close to main Caernarfon–Llanberis road and conveniently near the town; yet with benefit of level, terraced pitches in a secluded landscaped wooded valley. Some camping pitches near the stream. 5acres 70pitches
Etr–Oct must book peak periods last arrival 22.00hrs last departure 11.00hrs 4⛭ individual pitches ⊚ 17wc lit all night 1cdp ⊕ (4washbasins hc, 2central hot water, 3🚿hc) 2⊙ warden (1iron) (cold storage) calor gas camping gaz paraffin toilet fluid ⊞ children's playground ⛳ ⊖ stables ƃ ✈ cinema ↬ launderette pub
20🚐£2 10🚌£2 40▲£2 (awnings) ltr

CENARTH Dyfed Map 2 SN24

►► Aberdwylan Caravan Park
Abercych ☎ Boncath 476
[3] ❸ △ signposted
On banks of River Cych, 1¾m SW of Cenarth on B4322. 1acre 16pitches 54static
Mar–Oct booking advisable peak periods last arrival 23.00hrs 3⛭ 8wc lit all night 1cdp 8washbasins hc (1central hot water, 4🚿hc) 2⊙ warden (1wash, 1spin, 1dry) 1iron calor gas ⊞ children's playground ⊖ stables ↬ pub
16🚐£1.50 or 16🚌£1.50 awnings ltr

CHEPSTOW Gwent Map 3 ST59

►►► Trax Campsite *(ST522951)*
Chepstow Racecourse, St Arvans
[1] ❶ △ signposted
Level grass site near river Wye, the hills of the Forest of Dean and Severn Estuary. 1m N of town off A466. 4acres 75pitches
3 Apr–27 Sep no bookings last arrival 22.30hrs last departure 15.00hrs 2⛭ 48wc lit all night 3cdp washbasins hc 4central hot water 6🚿hc 11⊙ warden (2wash, 2spin) 1iron CTV calor gas camping gaz ☎ ⊞ free racing for campers 7 & 8 Apr, 26 & 27 May, 28 Jun, 8 Jul, 25 & 26 Aug, 13 Sep games area ⛳ ⊖ stables ƃ ✈ cinema ↬ launderette pub
75🚐£2–£2.75 or 75🚌£2–£2.75 or 75▲£2–£2.75

CHURCH STOKE Powys Map 7 SO29

► Mellington Hall Caravan Park
(SO258920) ☎456
[2] ❷ △ signposted
Well-maintained site with level pitches, in the grounds of a gracious country house. Magnificent views of the Welsh Border Counties. 4m SE of Montgomery on B4385.
4acres 20pitches 140static
Mar–Oct must book public hols last arrival 22.00hrs last departure 18.00hrs 16⛭ individual pitches 16wc lit all night 1cdp (4🚿hc) 2⊙ (1wash, 1dry) iron TV calor gas toilet fluid restaurant licensed bar ☎ ⊞ take away food ⛳ ⊖ stables ↬ launderette pub
10🚐£2 10🚌£2 awnings ltr

CLYNDERWEN Dyfed Map 2 SN11

► Derwenlas Caravan Park Derwenlas ☎324
[1] ❶ △ signposted
A small touring site on level grassy field. N of village on A478 Cardigan Road.
2acres 20pitches 10static
Mar–Nov must book peak periods

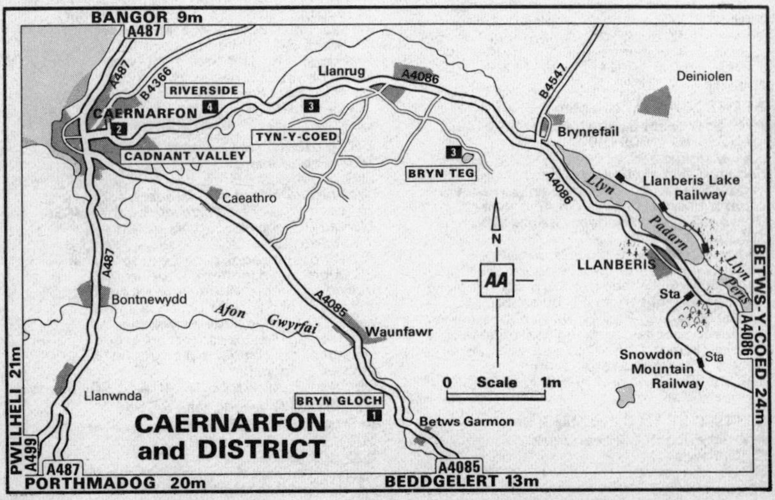

Sites listed under: **1** Betws Garmon **2** Caernarfon **3** Llanrug **4** Pont-Rug last arrival 23.00hrs last departure 13.00hrs 4 5wc lit all night 1cdp 5washbasins hc 2central hot water (2hc) 1⊙ (1iron) (cold storage) calor gas ⊞ children's playground launderette pub 20£1.50 or 20£1.30 or 20▲£1.10 (awnings) ltr

CLYRO nr Hay-on-Wye, Powys Map 3 SO24
Fforest Cwm Caravan Site *(SO198438)*
☎ Hay-on-Wye 820649
1 signposted
Small site set above the Wye Valley, with marvellous views. 6acres 35pitches 20static 15 Mar–Oct must book peak periods last arrival 22.30hrs 4 5wc 1cdp (hc) ⊙ calor gas camping gaz stables launderette pub 12 70p 3 70p 20▲70p (awnings)

CREUDDYN BRIDGE nr Lampeter, Dyfed Map 2 SN55
Bertheos Caravan Park ☎ Aeron 438
2 signposted
Small touring site situated in elevated position with fine mountain views. On the main A482 Lampeter–Aberaeron road. 1acre 8pitches 12static
Mar–Oct must book peak periods last arrival 20.00hrs last departure 11.00hrs 1 3wc 1cdp washbasins hc (hc) ⊙ calor gas ⊞ stables pub 8£1.50 3£1.50 (awnings)

CRICCIETH Gwynedd Map 6 SH43
See sketch map.
Cae-Canol Caravan & Camping Site
☎2351
2 2
A level grassy site with trees set in meadowland 2m from Criccieth on the B4411. 2acres 50pitches 20static
Apr–Oct 6 6wc lit all night 1cdp (washbasins hc, hc) ⊙ (cold storage) calor gas camping gaz stables launderette pub 8fr£1 8fr£1 40▲fr£1 (awnings)

Tyddyn Morthwyl ☎2115
2
Site has good level grass pitches, sheltered by trees, and is conveniently situated for touring the Snowdon National Park and the many narrow gauge railways in the area. 8acres 50pitches 22static
Mar–Oct must book for caravans last departure 12.00hrs 3 8wc lit all night 1cdp (central hot water, hc) ⊙ calor gas camping gaz ⊞ stables launderette pub 10£1.40 or 10£1.10 40▲£1.10 (awnings)

Eisteddfa Campsite Pentrefelin ☎2104
1 signposted
Part level, part sloping, site set in hilly countryside. At Pentrefelin 1½m NE on A497. 15acres 150pitches
Etr–Oct no bookings 7 20wc lit all night 2cdp 20washbasins hc central hot water 6hc 4⊙ (1wash, 1dry, 2iron) games room CTV cold storage calor gas camping gaz paraffin ☎ ⊞ stables cinema launderette pub 150▲£1.60

Llwyn-Bugeilydd Farm *(SH498398)*
Llwyn-Bugeilydd ☎2235
1 signposted
Situated 1m N of Criccieth on the B4411. First site on right. 5acres 10pitches
Apr–Oct must book peak periods last departure 11.00hrs 4 individual pitches 5wc lit all night 1cdp (4washbasins hc, 1central hot water, 2hc) 2⊙ 1iron cold storage calor gas ⊞ stables cinema launderette pub 10fr£1 or 10fr£1 or 10▲fr£1 (awnings)

CROESGOCH Dyfed Map 2 SM83
Torbant Caravan Park *(SM844308)*
☎261
2 signposted
Part sloping grass site, 6m N of St David's on A487. 5acres 65pitches 55static
Spring Bank Hol–Oct rsEtr–May booking advisable peak periods last arrival 23.30hrs last departure 13.00hrs 6 individual pitches 17wc lit all night 1cdp 17washbasins hc (4hc) 3⊙ 1spin (1dry) iron games room CTV (cold storage) calor gas camping gaz toilet fluid ⊞ children's playground pub 35£1.50–£2.70 or 35£1.50–£2.70 30▲£1.50–£2.70 (awnings)

CROSSGATES Powys Map 3 SO06
Park Caravan & Camping Site *(SO081651)* Rhayader Rd ☎ Penybont 201
1
A peaceful and quiet site set in beautiful countryside. 1acre 10pitches 15static
Etr–Oct must book public hols last arrival 22.00hrs last departure 22.00hrs 3 individual pitches late arrivals enclosure 7wc lit all night 1cdp 4washbasins hc 1central hot water 2hc 1⊙ calor gas cafe

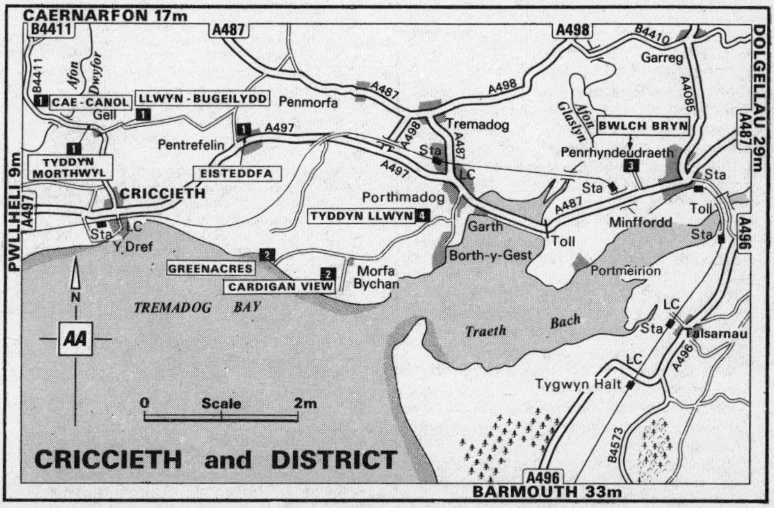

Sites listed under: **1** Criccieth **2** Morfa Bychan **3** Penrhyndeudraeth **4** Porthmadog

restaurant licensed bar ☎ ⊞ children's playground & take-away fish bar ⛵ ⊖ ♘ ✈ ⛳ launderette pub
10🚐£2.50 or 10🚗£2.50 or 10▲£2.50 awnings ltr

DINAS CROSS Dyfed Map 2 SN03
►►► *Fishguard Bay Caravan & Camping Site* *(SN005395)* ☎285
② ❶ ⚠
Partly level and sloping grass site with bushes, near the sea. 1m N of A487. 2½acres 50pitches 50static
Etr& Spring Bank Hol—Aug rsEtr–Spring Bank Hol & Sep–6 Oct booking advisable school hols 10♨ ⊛ 17wc lit all night 1cdp washbasins hc (2🛁hc) (🚿hc) 2⊙ (1wash, 1spin, 1dry, 1iron) TV (cold storage) calor gas camping gaz paraffin toilet fluid ☎ ⊞ ⛵ ⊖ ✈ cinema ⛳ launderette pub
🚐 🚗 30▲ (awnings)

EYTON Clwyd Map 7 SJ34
►►► Plassey Touring Caravan Park
☎Bangor-on-Dee 780277
③ ❸ ⚠ signposted
A mainly level, grassy site with trees situated amidst woodland and meadowland off the B5426. 3acres 60pitches
Apr–Oct must book last arrival 22.30hrs last departure 12.00hrs 3♨ individual pitches 13wc lit all night 1cdp washbasins hc (🚿hc) ⊙ warden (wash) spin (dry) iron (▭) games room (cold storage) calor gas camping gaz toilet fluid ☎ ⊞ (licensed club) children's playground badminton courts & boating ⛵ ⊖ stables ⛳ launderette pub
40🚐£1.25–£2.25 10🚗£1.25–£2.25 10▲£1.25–£2.25 (awnings) ltr

FAIRWOOD West Glamorgan Map 2 SS59
► Blackhills Caravan Park *(SS581915)*
Blackhills Rd, Fairwood Common
☎Swansea 27065
② ❷ ⚠ signposted
Mainly level grass site set in meadowland. 6m SW of Swansea along A4118 then unclassified road for 1m. Signposted at junction of A4118 and unclassified road.
13acres 300pitches 120static
Apr–Oct must book peak periods last arrival 21.00hrs last departure 12.00hrs 9♨ ⊛ late arrivals enclosure 50wc 3cdp central hot water 🚿hc ⊙ calor gas camping gaz ☎ ⊞ children's playground ⛵ ⊖ stables ♘ launderette pub
100🚐£2 200🚗£1.50 or 200▲£1.50 (awnings)

FORESTRY COMMISSION CARAVAN AND CAMPSITES
Only those Forestry Commission sites which come within the scope of the Automobile Association's Caravan and Campsite classification scheme are listed in this guide. There are others which are deliberately maintained as minimum-facility sites and are suitable for the camper or caravanner who prefers to be completely self-sufficient and carries his own chemical toilet.
FREE PAMPHLETS The following give details of all recreational facilities in forests:
See Your Forests – Northern England
See Your Forests – Southern England
See Your Forests – Wales
See Your Forests – Scotland
Forestry Commission Cabins and Holiday Houses
Single copies will be sent on application to the Forestry Commission, 231 Corstorphine Road, Edinburgh EH12 7AT.

GARTHMYL Powys Map 7 SO19
►►► Argae Hall *(SO192989)*
☎Berriew 216
② ❶ ⚠ signposted
Slightly sloping, grass and sand site with trees and bushes, set in hilly woodland, adjacent to river, Shropshire Union Canal, lake and main road. 6m W of Welshpool. 1acre 12pitches 75static
All year must book peak periods 6♨ 18wc lit all night 12washbasins hc central hot water (🛁hc, 🚿hc) ⊙ games room TV cold storage calor gas ☎ ⊞ licensed club & children's playground ⊖ stables ♘ ⛳ pub
12🚐£2 or 12🚗£2 no awnings ltr

GLAN-YR-AFON Clwyd Map 6 SJ04
►► Llawrbetws Farm Caravan & Camping Park ☎Maerdy (Clwyd) 224
① ❶ ⚠ signposted
Mainly level site with grass and mature trees. 3m W of Corwen off A494 Bala road.
5acres 65pitches 72static
Mar–Oct must book peak periods last arrival 21.00hrs last departure 12.00hrs 12♨ ⊛ late arrivals enclosure 14wc lit all night 1cdp ⛟ washbasins hc central hot water (🚿hc) ⊙ warden wash (games room) (cold storage) calor gas camping gaz paraffin toilet fluid ⊞ children's playground ⛵ ⊖ stables ♘ cinema ⛳ launderette pub
35🚐£2 10🚗£1.50 30▲£2 (awnings)

GLYN CEIRIOG Clwyd Map 7 SJ23
► Glan Llyn Caravan Park Glan Llyn ☎320
① ❶
Level, grass and gravel site with trees and bushes, set in hilly wood and meadowland country, adjacent to river. Off B4500. 1acre 7pitches 5static
Etr–Sep booking advisable peak periods last arrival 22.00hrs last departure 12.00hrs 2♨ 4wc lit all night 1cdp (1🚿hc) ⊙ calor gas camping gaz ⊞ ⊖ stables ⛳ ⛵ pub
7🚐£1.40 or 7🚗£1.40 or 7▲£1.40 (awnings)

HASGUARD CROSS Dyfed Map 2 SM80
►►► Hasguard Cross Caravan Park *(SM850108)* ☎Broad Haven 443
② ❷ ⚠ signposted
Pleasantly situated, screened by trees and shrubs with views of surrounding hills. In Pembrokeshire National Park. 1½m from sea and beach at Little Haven. 1½acres 25pitches 35static
All year must book last arrival 23.59hrs last departure 12.00hrs 6♨ individual pitches late arrivals enclosure wc lit all night 1cdp 10washbasins hc central hot water (🚿hc) 2⊙ warden (2spin) 1iron calor gas paraffin ☎ ⊞ (licensed club) & children's playground ⛵ ⊖ stables ✈ ⛳ pub
25🚐£2–£3 or 25🚗£2–£3 (awnings)

►►► Redlands Touring Caravan Site *(SM851109)* ☎Broad Haven 301
② ❷ ⚠
Level grass site with young conifers set in meadowland. In Pembrokeshire National Park, 1½m from the sea and beach at Little Haven.
5acres 60pitches
Apr–Sep must book peak periods last departure 12.00hrs 4♨ individual pitches 12wc lit all night 1cdp 2⛟ 8washbasins hc (4🚿hc) 2⊙ 1spin (1dry) 2iron cold storage ⊞ ⊖ stables ✈ ⛳ ⛵
60🚐£1.50–£2 or 60🚗£1.50–£2 awnings

HAY-ON-WYE Powys Map 3 SO24
► Hollybush Inn ☎Glasbury 371
① ❶ signposted
A small, level grass site in pleasant surroundings at the roadside, and 2m from Hay-on-Wye. 2acres 17pitches 5static
Etr–Oct must book public hols last arrival 23.59hrs last departure 14.00hrs 3♨ 3wc lit all night washbasins ⊙ calor gas camping gaz restaurant licensed bar ⊖ stables ✈ ⛳ pub
17🚐£1.50 or 17🚗£1.30 or 17▲£1.60 awnings ltr

HOWEY Powys Map 3 SO05
► ***Dalmore Camping Site*** *(SO045568)*
☎ Llandrindod Wells 2483
[1] ❶ signposted
Small touring site on A483 but screened from road and traffic noise by hedgerow. 1½m S of village. ½acre 6pitches 12static
All year must book peak periods last arrival 23.00hrs last departure 12.00hrs 2 individual pitches 4wc lit all night 2cdp (hc) ⊙ warden cold storage calor gas ⊞ pub
4 2 or 6▲ (awnings) ltr

LANDSHIPPING Dyfed Map 2 SN01
►►► **New Park Caravan Site** *(SN026111)*
☎ Martletwy 284
[1] ❶ ⚠
Sloping grass site with trees. 7m W of Narberth. 2acres 15pitches 30static
Spring Bank Hol–Sep must book peak periods last arrival 20.00hrs last departure 12.00hrs 2 10wc lit all night 1cdp 8washbasins hc (1central hot water, 6hc) 3⊙ (1wash, 1dry, cold storage) calor gas camping gaz paraffin toilet fluid cafe ⊞ post office stables launderette pub
5fr£1.50 or 5fr£1.50 10▲fr£1.50 (awnings) ltr

LAUGHARNE Dyfed Map 2 SN31
►►► **Ants Hill Caravan Park** *(SN299118)*
☎ 293
[2] ❷ ⚠ signposted
A small touring site on sloping grassy ground, located near to the village of Laugharne on the Taff estuary. 5acres 60pitches 60static
May–Sep must book peak periods last arrival 23.30hrs last departure 10.30hrs 4 individual pitches 20wc lit all night 1cdp 12washbasins hc central hot water (8hc) 3⊙ games room calor gas camping gaz ⊞ licensed club & children's playground stables pub
60£1.50–£2.50 or 60£1.50–£2.50 or 60▲£1.50–£2.50 awnings

LITTLE HAVEN Dyfed Map 2 SM81
For details of sites see Hasguard Cross

LLANBEDROG Gwynedd Map 6 SH33
►► **Crugan Caravan Site**
☎ Abersoch 2045
[1] ❶ ⚠ signposted
Mainly level site with slight gradient with grass surface and trees and bushes. Set in meadowland in urban area overlooking Llanbedrog Bay. Off A499 ½m E of town. 1acre 20pitches 90static
Mar–Oct must book last arrival 18.00hrs last departure 10.00hrs 9wc 1cdp (11washbasins hc, central hot water, 8hc) 2⊙ warden (1wash, 1spin) ☎ ⊞ stables launderette pub
20£2–£3.50 awnings

LLANDDERFEL Gwynedd Map 6 SH93
See Bala sketch map.
►► **Bryn Melyn Caravan Site**
☎ Llandderfel 212
[3] ❷ ⚠ signposted
A mainly level grassy site with saplings and bushes set in wooded hilly country above River Dee. 2m SE on B4401. 8acres 40pitches 75static
Etr–Oct must book public hols last arrival 22.00hrs last departure 12.00hrs 12 22wc 1cdp (12washbasins hc, 6hc) 3⊙ games room cold storage calor gas camping gaz ☎ ⊞ shooting stables pub
10£1 590p 25▲£1 (awnings)

LLANDRE Dyfed Map 6 SN68
►►► ***Riverside Park*** ☎ Bow Street 682
[1] ❶
Level, grass site with trees and bushes set in woodland and meadowland with access to River Leri. On A487 4m from Aberystwyth take B4353 and turn right at second turning. 6acres
Etr & Jun–Sep rsMar–May last departure 12.00hrs 4 late arrivals enclosure 4wc lit all night 2cdp 10washbasins hc (4central hot water) (8hc) 2⊙ warden (2wash, dry, iron) calor gas toilet fluid ☎ ⊞ launderette
▲ (awnings)

LLANDRILLO Clwyd Map 6 SJ03
►► **Hendwr Farm Site** ☎ 210
[2] ❶
Level grass site with mature trees near river, hills, woodland and moorland. 4m SW of Corwen A5, then left onto B4401. 4acres 60pitches 80static
Apr–Oct rsNov–Mar must book peak periods last arrival 22.00hrs last departure 16.00hrs 6 individual pitches 12wc lit all night 2cdp (14washbasins hc, 1central hot water, 8hc) 5⊙ (wash dry iron cold storage) calor gas camping gaz toilet fluid ☎ ⊞ pub
20£2 or 20£2 40▲£1.50 awnings

LLANDUDNO JUNCTION Gwynedd Map 6 SH87
► ***Glan Morfa Farm*** Queens Rd
☎ Deganwy 81111
[1] ❶
Small residential site with level, grassy field for touring caravans. Overlooks Conwy Estuary and mountains. 1acre 20pitches 20static
All year last arrival 23.00hrs last departure 12.00hrs 3 individual pitches 3wc 1cdp (washbasins hc) (hc, hc) ⊙ calor gas ⊞ stables cinema launderette pub
20 or 20 (awnings) ltr

LLANDWROG Gwynedd Map 6 SH45
► **White Tower Caravan Park**
☎ Llanwnda 830649
[1] ❷
Grass site with young trees, set in mountainous country close to Caernarfon Bay. Views to Snowdon. Off A499 Caernarfon–Pwllheli road. ½acre 12pitches 52static
20 May–25 Sep rsMar–19 May & 26 Sep–Oct must book peak periods last departure 12.00hrs 6 individual pitches 12wc lit all night (hc, ⊙) warden cold storage calor gas ☎ ⊞ children's playground stables cinema launderette
12£2 or 12£2 awnings ltr

LLANGOLLEN Clwyd Map 7 SJ24
►►► Ty-Ucha Farm Maesmawr Rd
☎860677
③ ❷ ⚠ signposted
Small, neat touring site in a quiet position yet conveniently placed close to A5. Ideal for country and mountain walking, with small stream traversing its south boundary. 4acres 40pitches
Etr–Oct must book peak periods last arrival 22.00hrs last departure 14.00hrs 4 individual pitches 6wc lit all night 1cdp 6washbasins hc (4 hc) 1 warden (games room) (cold storage) calor gas camping gaz toilet fluid ⊞ children's play area stables launderette pub
30 £1.50 10 £1.50 (awnings)

LLANGRANOG Dyfed Map 2 SN35
►►► *Gilfach Farm Caravan Site* ☎250
① ❶ ⚠
A static and touring site set in open countryside within 2m of the sea. 5acres 70pitches 150static
Etr–Oct 12 30wc 1cdp washbasins hc central hot water (hc) (wash) (dry) games room cold storage calor gas camping gaz licensed bar ☎ ⊞ stables launderette pub
30 10 30▲ (awnings)

LLANGYNIEW Powys Map 6 SJ10
►►► Henllan Caravan Park *(SJ136088)*
☎ Llanfair Caereinion 343
③ ❷ ⚠ signposted
Level, grassy site near river. Good centre for exploring the Border Counties. ½acre 10pitches 57static
Mar–Oct must book peak periods last arrival 22.00hrs last departure 12.00hrs 6 individual pitches 4wc lit all night 1cdp 4washbasins hc 1central hot water (hc) (1wash, 1dry, 1iron) games room TV cold storage calor gas camping gaz ☎ ⊞ (licensed club) children's playground & fishing stables launderette pub
10 £2 or 10 £1.50 or 10▲£1.50 (awnings) ltr

LLANON Dyfed Map 6 SN56
►►► Woodlands Caravan Park ☎342
② ❷ ⚠ signposted
Level, grass site with trees and bushes, set in hilly wood and meadowland, adjacent to sea, beach and river. 11m from Aberystwyth on A487. 4acres 40pitches 60static
Apr–Oct rsMar must book peak periods last arrival 22.30hrs last departure 12.00hrs 3 individual pitches 13wc lit all night 1cdp (washbasins hc, 6 hc) 3 (dry) calor gas camping gaz toilet fluid ☎ ⊞ pub
40 £1.80 or 40 £1.60 or 40▲£1.80 (awnings) ltr

LLANRHYSTUD Dyfed Map 6 SN56
►►► *Pengarreg Caravan Park*
☎ Llanon 247
② ❶ ⚠ signposted
Level, stony and grass site near sea and river. On A487 Aberystwyth 9m, Aberaeron 7m. 5acres 75pitches 150static
Mar–Oct must book 20 late arrivals enclosure 48wc lit all night 6cdp (27washbasins hc) (central hot water) (hc) ( ) warden calor gas camping gaz toilet fluid ☎ ⊞ laundry room children's play area stables launderette
25 25 25▲ (awnings)

LLANRUG Gwynedd Map 6 SH56
See Caernarfon sketch map.
►► *Tyn-Y-Coed Camping Site* *(SH543624)* ☎ Caernarfon 3565
① ❶ ⚠ signposted
Part sloping, part level site set in hilly country. 2acres 20pitches 40static
May–Sep rsMar–Apr & Oct must book Jul & Aug last arrival 23.59hrs last departure 12.00hrs 3 12wc lit all night 1cdp 8washbasins hc

4⛆hc 1⊙ calor gas ⊞ ⊖ stables ♘ ✈ cinema ⊳ launderette ♨ pub
10🚐 10🚗 40▲ ltr

►*Bryn Teg Caravan Park* *(SH524636)*
☎ Llanberis 542
2 ❷ ⚠ signposted
Level, grass site with mature trees, set in mountainous wooded meadowland country adjacent to lake. 3m from Llanberis on A4086. 5acres 68pitches 286static
Etr–Sep rsMar & Oct must book Bank Hols last arrival 22.00hrs last departure 12.00hrs 10♿ ⊗ 30wc 2cdp (1central hot water) (12⛆hc) 7⊙ (☐) games room TV calor gas camping gaz toilet fluid private lake children's playground licensed bar ☎ ♨ ⊖ stables ♘ ✈ cinema ⊳ launderette
68🚐 or 68🚗 ▲ (awnings)

LLANRWST Gwynedd Map 6 SH86
►►Bodnant Caravan Site *(SH805609)*
Nebo Rd ☎640248
2 ❷ signposted
Small, well-maintained, level touring site. S of village off A470. 3acres 30pitches
14 Mar–Oct must book last arrival 22.00hrs last departure 11.00hrs 4♿ individual pitches 9wc lit all night 1cdp (washbasins hc, central hot water, ⛆hc) ⊙ warden calor gas ⊞ children's playground ♨ ⊖ stables ♘ ⊳ pub
30🚐£2 4🚗£1.90 (awnings)

►Kerry's Orchard Site *(SH802615)*
School Bank Rd ☎640248
2 ❶ signposted
Grass and gravel site, level pitches adjacent to River Conwy. 2acres 24pitches 2static
Etr–Sep no bookings last arrival 22.00hrs last departure 12.00hrs 3♿ ⊗ 7wc lit all night (washbasins hc, central hot water) ⊙ calor gas ⊞ ♨ ⊖ stables ♘ ⊳ pub
4🚗£1.40 24▲£1.05 (awnings)

LLANUWCHLLYN Gwynedd Map 6 SH82
See Bala sketch map.
►*Bryn Gwyn Farm Caravan Park*
(SH867306) ☎272
2 ❶ signposted
Satisfactory, small site with open grassy ground in sheltered area. 10pitches 30static
Etr–Oct must book peak periods last arrival 19.00hrs last departure 10.00hrs 3♿ ⊗ 6wc lit all night 1cdp (2⛆hc) 1⊙ calor gas ♨ ⊖ ✈ cinema ⊳ launderette pub
10🚐 or 5🚗 or 15▲ (awnings) ltr

LLANWRDA Dyfed Map 3 SN73
►*Feathers Inn Petrol Station* Lampeter Rd
☎ Llangadog 491
1 ❶ signposted
Level, grass site with bushes, near river and mountains. W of Llandovery on A482. 2acres 40pitches
Apr–Oct rsMar & Nov 1♿ 4wc 1cdp ⊙ warden calor gas camping gaz toilet fluid cafe restaurant licensed bar ☎ ⊞ ♨
40🚐 or 12🚗 or 40▲ (awnings) ltr

LLWYNGWRIL Gwynedd Map 6 SH50
►►*Gwril Caravan Site* ☎ Fairbourne 431
1 ❶ ⚠
A flat site with grass and gravel surface set near to roadside and facing the sea. 2acres 40pitches 264static
Etr–Sep 16♿ wc lit all night (washbasins hc) (3⛆hc) ⊙ calor gas ☎ ⊞ ⊖ stables ⊳
40🚐 or 40🚗

LLYSFAEN Clwyd Map 6 SH87
►Westwood Caravan Park
☎ Colwyn Bay 57410
1 ❶ signposted
Small touring site in elevated position overlooking the sea. 6¾acres 43pitches 45static
Apr–Oct must book last arrival 19.00hrs last departure 12.00hrs 2♿ individual pitches 9wc lit all night 1cdp washbasins hc central hot water (⛆hc) ⊙ calor gas ⊞ ♨ ⊖ stables ♘ cinema pub
43🚐£1.75 or 43🚗£1.75 (awnings) ltr

LUDCHURCH Dyfed Map 2 SN11
See Tenby sketch map.
►►►Woodland Vale Caravan Park
(SN139107) ☎ Llanteg 319
1 ❶ ⚠
Grass and gravel site set in rural surroundings. 3m to beach at Amroth. 4acres 45pitches 60static
23 May–6 Sep rsEtr & Oct must book last arrival 22.00hrs last departure 12.00hrs 7♿ late arrivals enclosure 24wc lit all night 1cdp washbasins hc central hot water (⛆hc) ⊙ warden (wash, spin, iron) calor gas ☎ ⊞ (licensed club) & children's playground ♨ ⊖ stables ✈ ⊳ pub
45🚐£1.25–£2.50 or 45🚗£1.25–£2.50 (awnings)

►►Little Kings Caravan Site *(SN149085)*
☎ Llanteg 340
3 ❸ ⚠
Level hedged site set in rolling downland. 2m N of the beach at Amroth. 4acres 60pitches 20static
Etr–Oct rsMar & Apr must book last departure 12.00hrs 4♿ individual pitches ⊗ 10wc lit all night 1cdp 10washbasins hc (4⛆hc) ⊙ warden wash (spin) dry iron ⛱ games room cold storage calor gas camping gaz ☎ ⊞ children's playground ⊖ stables ✈ ⊳ launderette ♨ pub
20🚐 20🚗 20▲ awnings

MIDDLETOWN Powys Map 7 SJ31
►►Bank Farm Caravan Park *(SJ293123)*
☎ Trewern 260
2 ❶ ⚠
Part level, part sloping grass site near hills, mountains and woodland. 3acres 20pitches
Apr–Oct must book public hols last arrival 21.00hrs 6♿ wc lit all night 1cdp washbasins hc (2⛆hc) ⊙ warden (iron) calor gas ⊞ hairdryer ⊖ ⊳ pub
20🚐£1.25 or 20🚗£1.25 or 20▲£1.25 (awnings) ltr

MITCHEL TROY Gwent Map 3 SO41
►►Glen Trothy Caravan & Camping Site
(SO495106) ☎ Monmouth 2295
2 ❶ ⚠ signposted
Level, grass site with trees, set in meadowland amid hills and adjacent to river. 7acres 76pitches
Apr–Oct must book public hols last arrival 19.00hrs last departure 16.00hrs 3♿ individual pitches ⊗ late arrivals enclosure wc lit all night 2cdp 14washbasins hc (6⛆hc) 6⊙ (1wash, 1spin, iron) cold storage calor gas camping gaz toilet fluid ⊞ children's playground ♨ ⊖ stables ♘ ✈ cinema ⊳ launderette pub
76🚐£1.85 or 76🚗£1.85 or 76▲£1.85 awnings

MORFA BYCHAN Gwynedd Map 6 SH53
See Criccieth sketch map.
►►►Cardigan View Caravan Park
☎ Porthmadog 2032
1 ❶ ⚠ signposted
Level, grassy site, well-maintained; shale and concrete standings for tourers. 2½m SW of Porthmadog. ⚠ 2acres 40pitches 192static
May–Oct rsMar & Apr must book May–Sep last departure 12.00hrs 6♿ individual pitches late arrivals enclosure 20wc lit all night 2cdp washbasins hc central hot water ⛆hc ⊙ warden (wash, spin, dry, iron) calor gas ☎ ⊞ children's playground & private beach ♨ ⊖ ♘ ✈ cinema ⊳ launderette pub
40🚐£2 or 40🚗£2 (awnings)

►►►Greenacres Caravan Site
☎ Porthmadog 2781
2 ❷ ⚠ signposted
Level grassy site with trees set in mountainous country near main road. ⚠ May–Sep 130pitches 800static
May–Sep rsMar, Apr & Oct must book peak periods last arrival 21.00hrs last departure 11.30hrs ♿ wc lit all night 4cdp washbasins hc ⛆hc ⊙ wash spin calor gas ☎ ⊞ licensed club children's playground private beach & take away food ♨ ⊖ stables ♘ cinema ⊳

launderette pub
130🚐£1.50–£3 or 130🚌£1.50–£3
awnings ltr

NARBERTH Dyfed Map 2 SN11
►►► Redford Caravan Park *(SN135134)*
Princes Gate ☎860251
② ❷ ⚠
Sloping grass site with mature trees, just off A40. 5acres 50pitches 55static
25 May–7 Oct rsApr–24 May must book peak periods last arrival 23.30hrs last departure 12.00hrs 5♨ individual pitches ⊛ 20wc lit all night 2cdp (washbasins hc, ⩎hc) ⊙ (spin) (⌂) games room TV calor gas camping gaz toilet fluid ☎ ⊞ licensed club & children's playground ⛀ ⊖ stables ⊃ launderette pub
50🚐90p–£2 or 50🚌90p–£2 or 50▲90p–£2 (awnings) ltr

► Dyrham Caravan Site ☎860367
① ❶ ⚠ signposted
A small site in an elevated position offering open views, set close to the A40. A short drive and grassy banks give shelter from the road and traffic noise. 2acres 20pitches 10static
May–Sep booking advisable Jul & Aug
last arrival 23.59hrs last departure 12.00hrs 2♨ individual pitches ⊛ late arrivals enclosure 4wc lit all night 1cdp (⩎hc) ⊙ warden cold storage calor gas camping gaz paraffin toilet fluid ☎ ⊞ children's playground ⛀ ⊖ stables ⊃ launderette pub
20🚐£1.50 or 20🚌£1.25 or 20▲£1 (awnings)

► Noble Court Caravan Site *(SN111158)*
Redstone Rd ☎860213
① ❶ ⚠ signposted
A small, well-maintained site on sloping ground, with fine open country views, and situated 7m from coastal resorts. Situated on B4313, ½m S of A40 and ½m N of Narberth. 2acres 40pitches 60static
Mar–Oct must book peak periods last departure 12.00hrs 5♨ 12wc lit all night 1cdp (4washbasins hc, 4⩎hc) 4⊙ calor gas ☎ ⊞ (licensed club) children's playground ⊖ ⊃ launderette ⛀ pub
40🚐£1.50 or 40🚌£1.50 or 40▲£1.50 (awnings) ltr

NEWCASTLE EMLYN Dyfed Map 2 SN34
► Dolbryn Farm Capel Ifan Rd ☎710683
② ❶ ⚠ signposted
A simple farm site in an area of great natural beauty. S of town across river bridge; entrance road opposite cattle market on A484 Cardigan Road. 2acres 25pitches
Jul–Sep last arrival 23.00hrs last departure 12.00hrs 1♨ 4wc lit all night (2⩎hc) 1⊙ 1spin dry games room cold storage ⊞ licensed club ⛀ ⊖ stables ⊃ launderette pub
25🚐£2 or 25🚌£2 or 25▲£2 (awnings)

PENMAENMAWR Gwynedd Map 6 SH77
►►► Gardens Caravan Park Glanyrafon Rd ☎2334 (to be changed to 622334)
① ❶ ⚠ signposted
Level, grass site with mature trees, set in meadowland with access to sea, beach, river and hills. 3m W of Conwy on A55. 2½acres 12pitches 40static
Etr–Sep must book last arrival 23.00hrs last departure 10.00hrs 7♨ individual pitches late arrivals enclosure wc lit all night 1cdp 8washbasins hc 1central hot water (2⩎hc) ⊙ warden (iron) cold storage calor gas camping gaz paraffin toilet fluid ⊞ children's playground ⛀ ⊖ stables ♂ ✈ cinema ⊃ launderette pub
6🚐£2 6🚌£2 (awnings)

PENRHYNDEUDRAETH Gwynedd Map 6 SH63
See Criccieth sketch map.
► Bwlch Bryn Caravan Park
☎Porthmadog 365
① ❶ signposted
A sloping, stony and grass site set in hills close to the Festiniog Railway. ½acre 10pitches 40static
Mar–Oct must book peak periods last arrival 18.00hrs last departure 12.00hrs 8♨ 12wc lit all night 1cdp (⩎hc, ⊙) calor gas toilet fluid ⊞ ⛀ ⊖ ♂ ✈ cinema ⊃ launderette
10🚐 or 10🚌 no awnings

PENTRAETH Gwynedd Map 6 SH57
► Rhos Caravan Park ☎214
① ❶ ⚠ signposted
Clean, well-maintained site on level, grassy ground situated off main road to Amlwch. 10acres 100pitches 60static
Mar–Oct must book peak periods 10♨ ⊛ 22wc lit all night (4washbasins hc, 2central hot water, 6⩎hc) 4⊙ cold storage calor gas camping gaz toilet fluid ☎ ⊞ ⛀ ⊖ stables ⊃ launderette pub
52🚐£2 8🚌£1 50▲£1.20 (awnings)

PENTREBEIRDD Powys Map 7 SJ11
►►► *Valley View Caravan Park* *(SJ192144)* ☎Meifod 265
③ ❸ ⚠
Elevated terraced site overlooking countryside east of Meifod Valley. 5m out of Welshpool on A490. 1½acres 14pitches 54static
Mar–Oct must book Bank Holidays last arrival 20.30hrs last departure 12.00hrs 5♨ 6wc lit all night 1cdp 2washbasins hc (2central hot water) (3⩎hc) 2⊙ warden (1spin, 1dry, 1iron) games room TV calor gas camping gaz licensed bar ☎ ⊞ ⊖ ♂ cinema ⊃
14🚐 or 14🚌 (awnings) ltr

PENYBONTFAWR Powys Map 6 SJ02
►► *Park Farm* *(SJ092245)* ☎Pennant 212
② ❷
Quiet site in beautiful surroundings beside river. 1acre 15pitches 65static
Etr–Oct must book peak periods last departure 12.00hrs 2♨ 12wc lit all night 1cdp 10washbasins hc 4⩎hc 2⊙ warden calor gas ☎ ⊞ ⛀ ⊖ stables ⊃
15🚐 (awnings) ltr

PONT-RUG Gwynedd Map 6 SH56
See Caernarfon sketch map.
► Riverside Camping *(SH505630)*
Caer Glyddyn ☎Caernarfon 2524
② ❶
Simple, level grassy site with pleasant camping area 2m E of Caernarfon on A4086.
4½acres 60pitches
Mar–Oct no bookings last departure 17.00hrs 1♨ 6wc lit all night 1cdp washbasins hc (⩎hc) ⊙ ⊖ stables ♂ ✈ cinema ⊃ launderette ⛀ pub
20🚐£1.50 or 20🚌£1.50 40▲£1.20 (awnings)

PORTHCAWL Mid Glamorgan Map 3 SS87
► Broadawell Campsite *(SS817790)*
Moor Ln ☎3231
① ❶ signposted
A level, grassy touring and camping site positioned in quiet surroundings within 1½m of the seaside resort. 4acres 85pitches
Spring Bank Hol–Aug no bookings
last arrival 23.00hrs last departure 12.00hrs 3♨ 10wc lit all night 1cdp (1central hot water, 2⩎hc, 1⊙) (cold storage) calor gas camping gaz ☎ ⊞ children's playground ⛀ ⊖ stables ♂ ✈ cinema ⊃ launderette pub
20🚐fr£1.50 5🚌fr£1.50 60▲fr£1.50 (awnings) ltr

PORTHMADOG Gwynedd Map 6 SH54
See Criccieth sketch map.
► Tyddyn Llwyn Caravan Site Black Rock Rd ☎2205
② ❶ ⚠ signposted
Site set amidst mountains and meadowland. 30acres 237pitches
Mar–Oct must book peak periods 12♨ 30wc lit all night 1cdp washbasins hc ⩎hc ⊙ (wash, spin, dry, iron) calor gas camping gaz cafe restaurant ☎ ⊞ licensed club ⛀ ⊖ stables ♂ cinema ⊃ launderette pub
7🚐£2.30 or 7🚌£2.30 230▲£1.73 (awnings)

PRESTATYN Clwyd Map SJ08
►►►► ***Presthaven Sands Caravan Park***
☎3353
2 ❶ ⚠ signposted
A large, level commercial holiday site situated behind sand dunes on beach and near railway. Hillside country views form a pleasant background. 8acres 136pitches 800static Etr–Oct rsMar–Etr last departure 12.00hrs 47 late arrivals enclosure 40wc lit all night 4cdp washbasins hc central hot water (hc) ⊙ (3wash, 3dry, 2iron) calor gas camping gaz children's playground disco sauna bath toilet fluid cafe restaurant licensed bar ☎ ⊞ cinema launderette pub
136 or 136 (awnings)

PRESTEIGNE Powys Map 3 SO36
► **Rock Bridge Caravan & Camping Site**
☎Whitton 300
2 ❷ ⚠
Part level, part sloping, grass site with trees and bushes, set in hilly wood and meadowland country with access to River Luga. 1m W of Presteigne off B4356. 2½acres 35pitches 35static
Apr–Oct no bookings last arrival 23.00hrs last departure 12.00hrs 2 5wc lit all night 1cdp 4washbasins hc (2hc) 2⊙ warden cold storage calor gas camping gaz ⊞ stables launderette pub
35£2 or 35£1.90 or 35▲£2 (awnings) ltr

PWLLHELI Gwynedd Map 6 SH33
►►►► **Gimblet Rock Caravan Park**
South Beach ☎Abersoch 2045
2 ❶ ⚠ signposted
Level, grass, gravel and sand site with direct access to sea, beach and harbour. A497 to Pwllheli, ¾m from Station Square. 2acres 26pitches 111static
Mar–Oct must book last arrival 18.00hrs last departure 10.00hrs 7 individual pitches 12wc 1cdp 9washbasins hc central hot water (hc) ⊙ warden (2wash, 2dry) calor gas toilet fluid ☎ ⊞ (licensed club) stables cinema launderette pub
26£2–£3.50 awnings

REYNALTON Dyfed Map 2 SN00
See Tenby sketch map.
►►► **Croft Caravan Park** *(SN092094)*
☎Narberth 860315
2 ❷ ⚠
Set in meadowland, this site has level grassy pitches. 85pitches 60static
Etr & Spring Bank Hol–14 Oct rsmid Apr–mid May must book last departure 12.00hrs 6 individual pitches 21wc lit all night 1cdp 12washbasins hc 2central hot water (4hc) 3⊙ (iron) games room cold storage calor gas camping gaz paraffin toilet fluid ⊞ licensed club & children's playground stables pub
65£1.90 or 65£1.90 20▲£1.90 awnings

RHOSNEIGR Gwynedd Map 6 SH37
► **Bodfan Farm** ☎810563
1 ❶
A farm site on gentle sloping ground with sea and country views. Within walking distance of sea. 15acres 96pitches
Apr–Sep must book for caravans last arrival 12.00hrs last departure 12.00hrs 5 16wc 1cdp washbasins hc (central hot water, hc) ⊙ warden (spin, dry) cold storage calor gas camping gaz stables pub
6 30 60▲ rates on application awnings

RHYDCYMERAU Dyfed Map 2 SN53
►► **Rhydcymerau Camping & Caravan Site**
(SN577389) ☎Talley 409
2 ❶ ⚠

A pleasant, secluded grassy site, slightly sloping at near, set amidst wooded surroundings.
11acres 26pitches 6static
Etr–Sep no bookings last arrival 22.00hrs last departure 12.00hrs 2 wc lit all night 1cdp 6washbasins hc 3central hot water (4hc) 1 warden iron (cold storage) calor gas camping gaz paraffin stables pub
26£1.80 or 26£1.50 or 26▲£1.80 awnings

RUABON Clwyd Map 7 SJ34
▶▶ James Farm ☎820148
2 ❷ △
Small secluded site in the heart of the Welsh countryside. Within easy walking distance of leisure centre in nearby village. 3acres 20pitches
Apr–Oct must book peak periods last arrival 20.00hrs last departure 10.30hrs 3 4wc lit all night 1cdp washbasins hc central hot water hc warden ☎ stables launderette pub
20£1.50 or 20£1.50 10▲£1.50 (awnings)

ST DAVID'S Dyfed Map 2 SM72
▶▶ *Caerfai Bay Caravan Camping Park*
(SM759244) ☎274
2 ❶ △
Grassy site with bushes set in meadowland, with magnificent coastal scenery – bathing beach 300yd from park entrance. Off A487, end of unclassified road to Caerfai Bay. 10acres 84pitches 30static
27 May–14 Sep rsmid Apr–26 May & 15 Sep–1 Oct last arrival 21.00hrs last departure 12.00hrs 10 individual pitches 21wc lit all night 2cdp (10washbasins hc) (8hc) 5 calor gas camping gaz toilet fluid launderette
30 15 39▲ (awnings)

▶▶ Hendre Eynon Site *(SM773280)*
☎474
2 ❷ △
Mainly level grassy site in farmland. 2m NE of St David's on unclassified road. 6½acres 80pitches 10static
May–Sep must book peak periods last arrival 23.00hrs last departure 11.00hrs 7 late arrivals enclosure 12wc lit all night 1cdp 2 12washbasins hc (central hot water) (4hc) 6 (1wash) 1spin 1dry 1iron cold storage calor gas ☎ children's playground stables launderette pub
40£1.50–£2.10 5£1–£1.50 30▲£1.50–£1.75 awnings

ST FLORENCE Dyfed Map 2 SN10
▶▶▶ New Minerton Caravan Park
(SN093027) Devonshire Dr ☎Carew 461
2 △
Level grass site with bushes and trees. W of village on B4318. 10acres 100pitches 120static
Spring Bank Hol–30 Sep rsMay must book last arrival 21.00hrs last departure 12.00hrs 7 wc lit all night washbasins hc (hc) (wash, dry, iron) games room (cold storage) calor gas camping gaz ☎ (licensed club) & children's playground stables launderette pub
100£2.16–£3.24 or 100▲£1.62–£2.70

SARNAU Dyfed Map 2 SN35
▶ Brynawelon Caravan Park
☎Llangranog 584
2 ❷
Mainly level grassy site within 2m of beach. 400yds from A487 along unclassified road opposite Sarnau Chapel. 1acre 20pitches
Apr–Oct booking advisable peak periods last arrival 22.30hrs last departure 12.00hrs 4 indivdual pitches late arrivals enclosure 8wc lit all night 1cdp (1central hot water, 4hc) 1 calor gas children's playground stables
20£1.30–£1.60 or 20£1.30–£1.60 awnings

SAUNDERSFOOT Dyfed Map 2 SN10
See Tenby sketch map.
▶▶▶ Saundersvale Caravan Park
(SN118055) Valley Rd ☎812310
2 ❷ △ signposted
Part level, part sloping grass site with bushes, set in meadowland. 3m N of Tenby.
2acres 25pitches 60static
Mar–Oct must book peak periods last arrival 20.00hrs 2 6wc lit all night 1cdp 4washbasins hc 1central hot water 4hc 2 (2wash, 2dry) 2iron games room TV calor gas camping gaz toilet fluid cafe restaurant ☎ licensed club & children's playground stables cinema launderette pub
5fr£2.50 25▲fr£2.50 ltr

TALGARTH Powys Map 3 SO13
▶▶▶▶ Riverside Caravan Park
(SO148346) ☎320
3 △ signposted
Well-appointed touring site with pitches available on riverside. Elevated position with magnificent views of the Black Mountains.
6½acres 85pitches 5static
Apr–Oct no bookings last arrival 22.00hrs last departure 12.00hrs 12 individual pitches late arrivals enclosure 12wc lit all night 1cdp 50 (17washbasins hc) 1central hot water (1hc, 5hc) 3 warden (1wash, 1dry) 1iron games room calor gas camping gaz paraffin toilet fluid ☎ fishing & wash up sinks stables launderette pub
59£2.20 10£2.20 100▲£2.20 (awnings)

TAL-Y-BONT nr Barmouth, Gwynedd
Map 6 SH52
▶▶▶ *Islaw R'ffordd Caravan Site*
☎Dyffryn 269
1 ❶ △ signposted
Level, grass site set in meadowland adjacent to sea and beach, amid Snowdonia National Park scenery. 4m N of Barmouth. 11acres 425pitches 200static
Etr–Oct no bookings last arrival 22.00hrs

last departure 22.00hrs 10 ⓐ 55wc lit all night 1cdp (2washbasins hc) (8hc) 3⊙ (2wash, 1dry) 1iron (1cold storage) calor gas camping gaz toilet fluid cafe licensed bar ☎ ⊞ stables launderette pub
25 or 25 400▲

TENBY Dyfed Map 2 SN10
See sketch map.
►►►►► **Kiln Park Caravan Park** *(SN119002)* Kiln Park ☎4121
2 ❷ ⚠ signposted
A large, commercial touring, camping and static holiday site, situated on level ground on the town's outskirts. A short walk through sand dunes leads to the sandy south beach with Caldey Island in the background.
mid Jun–Aug 20acres 240pitches 550static
Mid May–Sep rsEtr–mid May must book last arrival 21.00hrs last departure 10.00hrs 42 ⓐ late arrivals enclosure 120wc lit all night 2cdp washbasins hc (hc, hc) ⊙ warden (wash, spin, dry) iron () games room CTV cold storage calor gas camping gaz paraffin toilet fluid cafe restaurant ☎ ⊞ (licensed club) children's playground, amusement arcade & take away food stables cinema launderette pub
60£10–£24 per wk or 60£10–£24 per wk 180▲£8–£17 per wk awnings

►►► **Well Park Caravan & Camping Site** *(SN125020)* New Hedges ☎2179
1 ❶ ⚠ signposted
Slightly sloping and level grass site with trees and bushes. 1½m N of Tenby off A478 New Hedges by-pass. 4½acres 90pitches 42static
Spring Bank Hol–Aug rsApr, May & Sep must book peak periods last arrival 23.00hrs last departure 12.00hrs 7 individual pitches for caravans ⓐ 20wc lit all night 1cdp (washbasins hc, central hot water, hc) ⊙ warden (spin, dry, iron) (cold storage) calor gas camping gaz ☎ ⊞ children's playground stables cinema launderette pub
10fr£3 10fr£2 70▲fr£2 awnings

►►► **Wood Park Caravans** *(SN128021)* New Hedges ☎3414
2 ❷ ⚠ signposted
Slightly sloping and level, grass site with trees and bushes. 1½m N of Tenby off A478 New Hedges by-pass. mid Jul–Sep 3acres 60pitches 90static
Spring Bank Hol–Sep rsEtr–mid May must book last arrival 21.00hrs last departure 10.00hrs 5 individual pitches for caravans 25wc lit all night 1cdp (washbasins hc, hc) ⊙ (wash, spin, dry, iron) (cold storage) calor gas camping gaz ☎ ⊞ (licensed club) & children's playground stables cinema launderette pub
20£3 or 20£3 40▲£2 (awnings)

► ***Lodge Farm Caravan Site*** *(SN131029)* New Hedges ☎2468
1 ❶ signposted
This site is set in level grassy ground 1½m from Tenby. 25acres 50pitches 40static
Etr–Sep must book Mar last departure 12.00hrs 6 individual pitches ⓐ 20wc lit all night 1cdp (washbasins hc) (hc) (⊙) warden calor gas ⊞ stables cinema launderette pub
10 or 10 40▲

TREFRIW Gwynedd Map 6 SH76
►► **Plas Meirion Caravan Park** Gower Rd ☎Llanrwst 640247
3 ❷
A level site with mature trees set in the Conwy Valley. Off B5106 Conwy–Betws-y-Coed road. 2½acres 10pitches 21static
Etr–Sep must book peak periods last arrival 22.00hrs last departure 10.30hrs 4 individual pitches 6wc lit all night 1cdp 8washbasins hc central hot water (1hc,

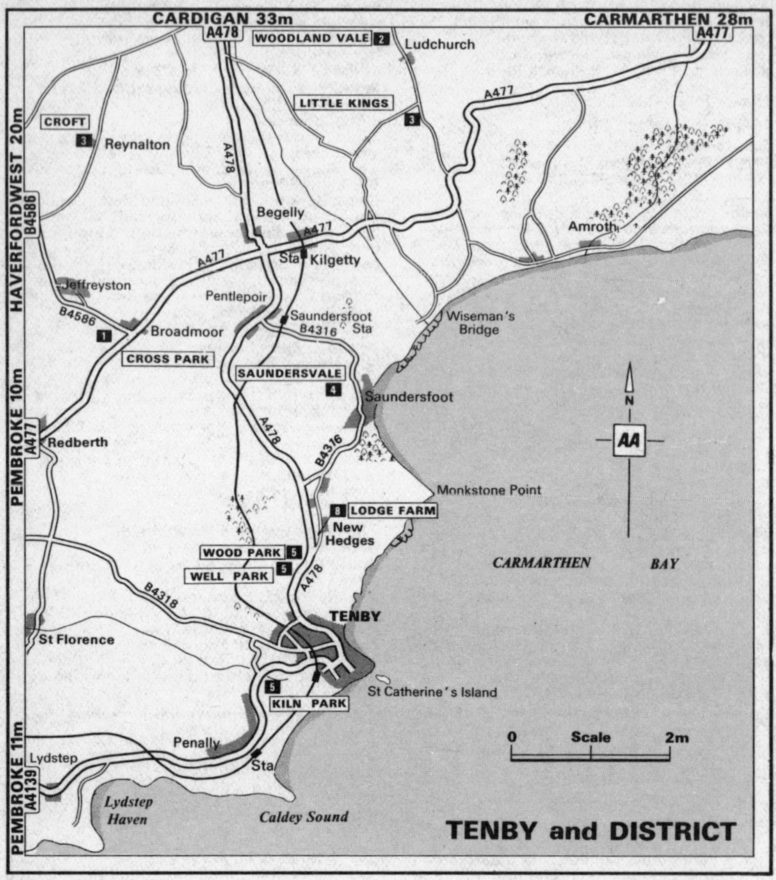

Sites listed under: **1** Broadmoor **2** Ludchurch **3** Reynalton **4** Saundersfoot **5** Tenby

2 hc) 1 warden (1dry) iron cold storage calor gas paraffin ⊞ children's playground stables pub
10 £2 or 10 £1.80 no awnings

TRESAITH Dyfed Map 2 SN25
►► **Gwalia Falls Caravan Park** *(SN279517)*
☎Aberporth 810361
3 2

Well-situated in its own valley and within easy reach of beach. 5acres 58pitches 40static Apr–Sep must book Aug last arrial 20.00hrs last departure 10.30hrs 6 individual pitches late arrivals enclosure 9wc lit all night 1cdp (washbasins hc, central hot water, hc) warden iron calor gas camping gaz ⊞ children's playground stables launderette pub
58 £1.75 or 58 £1.75 no awnings

TYWYN Gwynedd Map 6 SH50
►►► ***Woodlands Holiday Park***
(SH618035) Bryncrug (2m NE) ☎710471
③ ❶ ⚠ signposted
Attractive, well laid-out, static holiday site, situated on terraced wooded hillside affording lovely country views. 20pitches 121static
2 Apr–Oct must book at all times last departure 11.30hrs 2✿ individual pitches late arrivals enclosure 5wc lit all night 1cdp (4washbasins hc) (2central hot water) (2⛆hc) (1⊙) warden (1wash, spin) ⌂ games room CTV cold storage calor gas camping gaz toilet fluid restaurant licensed bar ☎ ⊞ children's play area ⛪ ⊖ stables ✈ cinema ⛳ launderette
20⛟ or 20⛟

►► ***Ynysymaengwyn Caravan Park***
(SH599024) Apply to: Meirionnydd District Council Offices, Neptune Road, Tywyn, Gwynedd ☎710684
① ❶ ⚠ signposted
A level grass site with mature trees, situated on A493 Dolgellau road 1½m N of town centre. The Talyllyn narrow gauge railway runs near the site.
10½acres 175pitches
Etr–Sep must book peak periods last arrival 22.00hrs 8✿ Ⓐ wc lit all night cdp washbasins hc ⛆hc ⊙ ☎ ⊞ ⊖ cinema ⛳
20⛟ or 20⛟ 135▲ (awnings) ltr

►► **Ysguboriau Caravan Site** *(SH604023)*
☎710321
② ❷ signposted
Mainly level site 1m inland from Tywyn on A493 Dolgellau road. The Talyllyn narrow gauge railway runs near the site. 11acres 30pitches 145static
Apr–Oct must book peak periods 12✿ 33wc 2cdp (24washbasins hc, 12⛆hc) 3⊙ ⊖ stables ♁ ✈ cinema ⛳ launderette ⛪ pub
30⛟£1.50 or 30⛟£1.50 (awnings)

SCOTLAND

SCOTLAND

Details for islands off the mainland of Scotland are shown under individual placenames. A useful first point of reference is to consult the location maps which show where sites are situated.

ABERCHIRDER Grampian *Banffshire*
Map 15 NJ65
▶ ***McRobert Park*** *(NJ624527)*
☎ Macduff 32861
[1] ❷ signposted
1acre 12pitches 3static
May–Sep 3🚿 3wc lit all night 4washbasins hc 🚿hc 1⊙ paraffin 🏪 ⊖ ♨
10🚐 or 10🚌 2▲

ABERDEEN Grampian *Aberdeenshire*
Map 15 NJ90
▶▶▶ **Hazelhead Caravan & Tent Site** *(NJ893057)* Groats Rd. Apply to: Aberdeen City District Council, St Nicholas Ho, Aberdeen AB1 1XJ ☎23456 ext 475
[2] ❷ ⚠ signposted
A level grass site with mature trees, set in woodland countryside. 3m W of Aberdeen on A944. 6acres 165pitches 35static
Apr–Sep must book 5🚿 individual pitches 36wc lit all night 6cdp washbasins hc central hot water 🚿hc ⊙ (wash, iron) calor gas ⊞ 🏪 ⊖ stables ♁ cinema launderette
165🚐£1.50–£2 or 165🚌£1.50–£2 or 165▲£1.50–£2 awnings

ABERFELDY Tayside *Perthshire* Map 14 NN84
▶▶ **Municipal Caravan Site** *(NN858495)*
Dunkeld Rd ☎662
[1] ❷ ⚠ signposted
A level, grass site with a perimeter of mature trees, situated at the eastern end of the town and lying between main road and banks of the River Tay. Good views, from site, of surrounding tree-clad Perthshire hills. 5acres 120pitches 30static
28 Mar–Oct no bookings last arrival 21.00hrs last departure 12.00hrs 3🚿 individual pitches for caravans Ⓐ 27wc lit all night 1cdp washbasins hc (🚿hc) ⊙ ☎ ⊞ children's playground 🏪 ⊖ ♁ cinema ♨ pub
80🚐£1.50 or 80🚌£1.50 40▲60p–£1 (awnings)

ABERLOUR Grampian *Banffshire*
Map 15 NJ24
▶▶ **Aberlour Gardens Caravan Park** *(NJ282432)* Aberlour Gardens ☎586
[2] ❷ ⚠ signposted
Site within the beautiful setting of the Old Aberlour Estate with its walled gardens. 3acres 35pitches 17static
Apr–Oct last arrival 22.00hrs last departure 12.00hrs 4🚿 individual pitches Ⓐ 7wc lit all night 1cdp washbasins hc central hot water 🛁hc (🚿hc) ⊙ warden (wash, spin) iron calor gas camping gaz ☎ ⊞ children's playground mobile shop ⊖ ♁ ♨ 🏪 pub
18🚐£2 7🚌£2 20▲£1.89 awnings ltr

ABOYNE Grampian *Aberdeenshire*
Map 15 NO59
▶▶▶ **Aboyne Loch Caravan Park** *(NO538998)* ☎2244
[3] ❸ ⚠ signposted
Attractively sited caravan park set amidst woodland beside Aboyne Loch in scenic Deeside. 65pitches 55static
Apr–Sep no bookings last arrival 20.00hrs last departure 12.00hrs 10🚿 individual pitches 23wc lit all night 1cdp ⊕ 23washbasins hc 8🚿hc 6⊙ warden (spin, iron) calor gas camping gaz ☎ ⊞ 🏪 ⊖ stables ♁ ♨ 🏪 pub
70🚐£1.95 3🚌£1.95 (awnings)

ACHNAMARA Strathclyde *Argyll*
Map 10 NR78
▶ **Castle Sween Bay Holidays** *(NR770858)*
☎223
[2] ❶ ⚠ signposted
Predominantly static site, laid out in terraces on a hillside above Loch Sween. Beautiful setting. A restaurant and bar are at present being built.
20pitches 200static
Etr–Sep last arrival 21.30hrs 6🚿 individual pitches Ⓐ 12wc lit all night 2cdp (🚿hc) ⊙ warden (wash, spin) iron calor gas cafe 🏪 ⊖ ♨
10🚐£2 or 10🚌£2 10▲£1 awnings ltr

ALFORD Grampian *Aberdeenshire*
Map 15 NJ51
▶▶▶▶ **Haughton House Caravan Site** *(NJ583169)* ☎2107
[3] ❸ ⚠ signposted
This impressive site with central mansion house dating back to 1800, is part of an estate set amongst woodland and beside the river Don. Approx ½m NW of Alford. Situated within country park. 10acres 70pitches 20static
Etr–early Oct must book peak periods last arrival 18.00hrs last departure 12.00hrs 7🚿 individual pitches Ⓐ wc lit all night 7cdp 20washbasins hc (10🚿hc, 6⊙) (2wash, 1dry, 1iron) (games room) TV calor gas toilet fluid ☎ ⊞ children's playgrounds putting green bird aviary & nature trails 🏪 ⊖ stables ♨ launderette
70🚐£2.30 or 70🚌£2.30 or 70▲£2.30 (awnings) ltr

ALVES Grampian *Moray* Map 15 NJ16
▶▶▶▶ **North Alves Caravan Park** *(NJ122633)* ☎223
[3] ❸ ⚠ signposted
A pleasant, quiet, grassy site with views over farmland. 7acres 50pitches 25static
Apr–Oct booking advisable peak periods last arrival 22.00hrs last departure 12.00hrs 6🚿 late arrivals enclosure 9wc lit all night 1cdp 9washbasins hc central hot water 4🚿hc 4⊙ warden 1wash 1spin 2iron games room TV cold storage calor gas camping gaz paraffin toilet fluid ☎ ⊞ children's playground & licensed shop 🏪 ⊖ stables ♁ ✈ 🏪
45🚐fr£2.20 or 45🚌fr£2.20 or 45▲fr£2.20 (Jun–Aug 75🚐 or 75🚌 or 75▲) awnings

AMISFIELD Dumfries & Galloway *Dumfriesshire* Map 11 NY08
▶▶ **Glen Clova Caravan Park** *(NY003831)*
Glen Clova ☎447
[2] ❸ ⚠ signposted
Adjacent to the busy A701, Moffat to Dumfries road. A level grassy site bordered by trees and on the edge of the village. 1¾acres 30pitches
Mar–Oct must book peak periods last arrival 22.00hrs 4🚿 8wc lit all night 1cdp washbasins hc central hot water 🚿hc ⊙ cold storage calor gas ⊞ dishwashing facilities ⊖ stables ♨ launderette
30🚐£2.20 or 30🚌£2.20 or 30▲£2.20 (awnings)

APPLECROSS Highland *Ross & Cromarty*
Map 13 NG74
▶ **Applecross Campsite** *(NG714443)*
☎268
[2] ❷ ⚠ signposted
Level, grass site with trees and bushes, set amidst mountains and moorlands, and adjacent to sea and beach. Caravans should approach via Shieldaig. 6acres 90pitches 6static
May–Sep no bookings last arrival 20.00hrs last departure 12.00hrs 7🚿 16wc lit all night 16washbasins hc (8🚿hc) 3⊙ (1wash, 1spin, 1dry) (cold storage) calor gas camping gaz ☎ ⊞ children's playground 🏪 ⊖ stables ✈ ♨ launderette pub
30🚐£1.55 30🚌£1.55 30▲£1.55 awnings ltr

ARDGARTAN Strathclyde *Argyll* Map 10 NN20
▶▶▶ **Ardgartan Campsite** *(NN275030)*
☎ Arrochar 293
[2] ❶ ⚠ signposted
Level, grass and gravel site with trees, set in hilly woodland country, adjacent to sea, beach, Loch Long and river. 3m SW of Arrochar on A83. 10acres 220pitches
Mid Mar–Oct last arrival 20.00hrs last departure 12.00hrs 12🚿 individual pitches late arrivals enclosure 22wc lit all night 1cdp 32washbasins hc 4central hot water 8🚿hc 8⊙ warden (20dry) (games room) calor gas

camping gaz toilet fluid ☎ ⊞ private beach & fishing 🏊 ⊖ ✈ pub
220🚐£1.35–£2 or 220🚗£1.35–£2 or 220▲£1.35–£2 awnings

ARDMAIR Highland *Ross & Cromarty*
Map 14 NH19

►►Ardmair Point Campsite *(NH108983)*
☎ Ullapool 2054
[2] ❸ ⚠
Small, well-maintained grass site 3½m N of Ullapool on A835, with unspoilt views from Ardmair. 3½acres 45pitches 1static
Etr–Sep must book peak periods, no booking for tents last arrival 23.00hrs last departure 12.00hrs 3🚿 individual pitches 9wc lit all night 1cdp 3🚐 washbasins hc central hot water (🚿hc) ⊙ (1spin, 1iron) cold storage calor gas ☎ ⊞ boats for hire ⊖ stables ⌒ launderette 🏊 pub
45🚐fr£1.60 or 45🚗fr£1.60 or 45▲fr£1.60 (awnings)

AUCHENBOWIE Central *Stirlingshire*
Map 11 NS78

►►Auchenbowie Caravan & Camping Site
(NS795880) ☎ Denny 822142
[2] ❶ ⚠ signposted
A partly level and sloping grassy site. ½m S of M80 Snabhead Interchange on A872. 3acres
Apr–Oct must book peak periods 3🚿 8wc lit all night 1cdp 11washbasins hc 2central hot water 4🚿hc 2⊙ calor gas camping gaz paraffin toilet fluid ☎ ⊖ stables cinema launderette
60🚐 or 60🚗 or 60▲ (awnings) ltr

AUCHENMALG Dumfries & Galloway
Wigtownshire Map 10 NX25

►►►Cock Inn Caravan Park *(NX238518)*
☎227
[2] ❷ ⚠ signposted
Part level, part sloping, grass site set in meadowland, close to sea, beach and main road; A747 Glenluce to Fort William road. Overlooks Luce Bay. no ball games 3acres 75pitches 45static
Mar–Oct must book peak periods last arrival 22.00hrs last departure 12.00hrs 4🚿 individual pitches 30wc lit all night 2cdp 🚐 washbasins hc (central hot water) (🚿hc) ⊙ (wash, spin, iron) games room cold storage calor gas camping gaz toilet fluid licensed bar ☎ ⊞ 🏊 ⊖ stables ⛳ ✈ ⌒ launderette
75🚐£2.10 or 75🚗£2.10 5▲£1.85 (awnings)

AVIEMORE Highland *Inverness-shire*
Map 14 NH81

►►►Aviemore Centre Caravan Park
(NH894120) ☎810751
[1] ❶ ⚠ signposted
Set amongst pine trees, adjacent to the Aviemore Centre where caravanners can make full use of the facilities. 6acres 90pitches
Closed Nov must book peak periods last arrival 18.00hrs last departure 12.00hrs 8🚿 individual pitches 18wc lit all night 1cdp 12washbasins hc central hot water (4🚿hc) 2⊙ (wash, spin, iron) (📺) games room calor gas camping gaz toilet fluid cafe restaurant licensed bar ☎ ⊞ children's playground 🏊 ⊖ stables ⛳ ✈ cinema ⌒ launderette
90🚐£1.90–£2.40 or 90🚗£1.90–£2.40 (awnings)

►►►Dalraddy Caravan Park *(NH859083)*
☎810330
[2] ❶ ⚠ signposted
A well-secluded site situated off the A9, 4m S of Aviemore, set amidst heather and young birch trees, looking towards the Cairngorm mountains. 20acres 230pitches 40static
Closed Nov must book peak periods last arrival 19.00hrs last departure 12.00hrs 24🚿 individual pitches for caravans ⊗ 32wc lit all night 1cdp washbasins hc central hot water (🚿hc) ⊙ (wash, dry) calor gas camping gaz toilet fluid ☎ ⊞ children's playground 🏊 ⊖ ✈ ⌒ launderette pub
80🚐£1.70 or 80🚗£1.70 150▲£1.20 awnings

►►► **Speyside Caravan Park** *(NH895115)*
☎810236
[1] ❶ △ signposted
Level, grass and gravel site with trees and bushes, set in hilly country and woodland, adjacent to River Spey. Immediately S of Aviemore close to junction of A9 and A951.
10acres 104pitches
1–15 Apr, 23 Jun–Aug rs16 Dec–Mar, 16 Apr–22 Jun, Sep & Oct no bookings last arrival 20.00hrs last departure 12.00hrs 8 individual pitches late arrivals enclosure 21wc lit all night 1cdp washbasins 2central hot water 6 (1wash, 1spin, 1dry, 1iron) calor gas ☎ cinema launderette
104£1.60–£2.10 or 104£1.60–£2.10 (awnings)

►► **Glen More Forest Park** *(NH975097)*
[2] ❸ △
Level, grass and gravel site with young trees and bushes set in mountainous moorland and woodland, adjacent to Loch Morlich. From Aviemore follow A951 for 7m. 20acres 221pitches
All year no bookings last arrival 21.00hrs last departure 12.00hrs 12 individual pitches wc lit all night 40washbasins hc (12hc) calor gas camping gaz paraffin toilet fluid cafe licensed bar ☎ ⊞ private beach
70£1.90 or 70£1.90 151▲£1.90 awnings

AYR Strathclyde *Ayrshire* Map 10 NS32
►►► **Trax Campsite** *(NS348224)*
Ayr Racecourse, Whitletts Rd
[1] ❷ △ signposted
A level grassy site near sea. Off A719 Mauchline road. 12acres 250pitches
3–8 Apr & 23 May–13 Sep except 10–12 Jul, 18–22 Jul & 4–6 Aug no bookings last arrival 22.30hrs last departure 15.00hrs 10 individual pitches 62wc lit all night 2cdp 30washbasins hc central hot water 12hc 8 warden (1wash, 1spin, 1dry) TV calor gas camping gaz restaurant licensed bar ☎ ⊞ free racing for campers 31 May, 20 & 21 Jun children's playground & games area stables cinema launderette pub
250£2–£2.75 or 250£2–£2.75 250▲£2–£2.75

BALLATER Grampian *Aberdeenshire*
Map 15 NO39
►► ***Ballater Caravan & Camping Site***
(NO371955) Braichlie Rd Apply to: Kincardine & Deeside District Council, Environmental Health Dept, Viewmount, Stonehaven, Kincardineshire
[1] ❷ △ signposted
A level, grassy site near the river, set in hilly country with nearby woodland and moorland. ½m on A93. 5acres 18pitches 72static
Apr–Oct must book peak periods last arrival 21.00hrs last departure 10.30hrs 3 18wc lit all night 1cdp 18washbasins hc (8hc) 6 calor gas camping gaz toilet fluid ⊞ stables cinema
18 or 18 ltr no awnings

BALLOCH Strathclyde *Dunbartonshire*
Map 10 NS38
►►► **Tullichewan Caravan Park**
(NS381816) Old Luss Rd ☎ Alexandria 59475
[2] ❸ △ signposted
A quiet and pleasant rural site near Loch Lomond, surrounded by woodland and hills. Close to the A82. 15acres 200pitches
17 Mar–Oct must book peak periods last departure 12.00hrs 7 individual pitches late arrivals enclosure 40wc lit all night 3cdp washbasins hc central hot water hc warden (wash, dry, iron) (cold storage) calor gas camping gaz toilet fluid ☎ ⊞ children's playground & wash up sinks stables launderette pub
170£2.60–£3.20 or 170£2.60–£3.20 30▲£2.60–£3.20 (awnings) ltr

BALMACARA Highland *Ross and Cromarty*
Map 14 NG82
►► **Reraig Caravan Site** *(NG815272)*
☎285
[2] ❷ △ signposted
Set on level, grassy ground surrounded by trees, the site looks S towards Loch Alsh and Skye.
2¼acres 40pitches
May–Sep no bookings last arrival 22.00hrs last departure 12.00hrs 2 individual pitches 7wc lit all night 1cdp 8washbasins hc (2hc) warden restaurant licensed bar pub
40£1.75 or 40£1.75 (awnings)

BALMAHA Central *Stirlingshire* Map 10 NS49
►► ***Cashell Caravan & Camping Site***
(NS396939) ☎234
[2] ❷ △
An attractive and well-wooded site, lying on the eastern shores of Loch Lomond within the Queen Elizabeth Forest Park, offering seclusion to campers and splendid views over the loch.
12acres 180pitches 10static
Mid Mar–mid Oct last arrival 22.00hrs last departure 12.00hrs 8 individual pitches late arrivals enclosure 24wc lit all night 1cdp 30washbasins hc (10hc) 12 warden (1wash, 2spin) calor gas camping gaz ☎ ⊞
180 or 180 or 180▲

BALMINNOCH Dumfries & Galloway *Wigtownshire* Map 10 NX26
►►►► **Three Lochs Caravan Park**
(NX272655) ☎Kirkcowan 304
[3] ❷ △ signposted
Level, grass and sand site with trees and bushes set in meadowland and woodland with access to river and lake. 5m N of Kirkcowan off A75. 15acres 80pitches 140static
Etr–Sep rsOct last arrival 23.00hrs last departure 12.00hrs 12 individual pitches 18wc lit all night 2cdp 10 washbasins hc central hot water (hc) warden (wash, dry, iron) games room TV (cold storage) calor gas camping gaz toilet fluid cafe ☎ ⊞ pitch & putt fishing & off licence
80£2 or 80£2 or 80▲£2 awnings ltr

BANFF Grampian *Banffshire* Map 15 NJ66
►►► **Banff Links Caravan Site** *(NJ672646)*
Apply to: Banff & Buchan District Council, Director of Leisure & Recreation, 1 Church St, Macduff, Banffshire AB4 1UF (pre season bookings) ☎Macduff 32861
2 ❸ ⚠ signposted
Mainly static site set right on sea front, bordered by fine beach, and with golf links to one side. Situated off A98, 1m W of Banff. 42pitches 95static
May–Sep must book 5 individual pitches 14wc lit all night 10washbasins hc central hot water 6hc (2wash, 2dry) calor gas camping gaz paraffin toilet fluid cafe restaurant ☎ ⊞ children's playground launderette pub
37£1.40 or 37£1.20 5▲85p (awnings)

BARCALDINE Strathclyde *Argyll* Map 10 NM94
►►► **Barcaldine Garden Caravan Park** *(NM955415)* ☎Ledaig 348
2 ❸ ⚠ signposted
Mainly level grass site with young trees and bushes. Set in mountainous woodland country with a lake nearby. 4acres 75pitches
Jun–Oct rsApr & May booking advisable peak periods last arrival 22.00hrs last departure 12.00hrs 4 late arrivals enclosure 17wc lit all night 1cdp 16washbasins hc (4hc) 1dry (1iron) (cold storage) calor gas toilet fluid ☎ ⊞ private beach, boats for hire & battery charging
70fr£1.80 5fr£1.80 (awnings)

BEAULY Highland *Inverness-shire* Map 14 NH54
►►► **Cruivend Caravan & Camping Site** *(NH516446)* ☎2367
2 ❷ ⚠ signposted
Level, grassy site situated off A9 and 1m S of Beauly. 2acres 30pitches 4static
Apr–Sep must book peak periods last arrival 23.00hrs last departure 12.00hrs 2 individual pitches 8wc lit all night 1cdp (8washbasins hc, 2hc) 2 cold storage calor gas camping gaz paraffin ☎ ⊞ children's playground stables pub
10£1.60 10£1.60 10▲£1.60 (awnings) ltr

►► **Lovat Bridge Caravan & Camping Site** *(NH517451)* ☎2374
2 ❶ ⚠ signposted
Mainly level, grass site with trees; direct access to river and main road. 6acres 140pitches 4static
Apr–Sep last arrival 20.00hrs last departure 12.00hrs 6 late arrivals enclosure 15wc lit all night 3cdp washbasins hc 4hc 3 warden ⊞ children's playground & (fishing) stables pub
75£1.50 or 75£1.50 65▲£1.50 (awnings)

BENDERLOCH Strathclyde *Argyll* Map 10 NM93
►►► **Tralee Bay Caravan Park** *(NM896393)* ☎Ledaig 255
2 ❶ ⚠ signposted
Attractive site on level ground, sloping gently towards the sea. Outstanding views over Ardmuckmish Bay, towards Oban. A 16th-century castle lies N of the site on the same peninsula. 4½acres 80pitches
Apr–Oct no bookings last arrival 21.00hrs last departure 14.00hrs 6 no cars by tents 31wc lit all night 1cdp 27washbasins hc (20central hot water, 8hc) 8 (1wash, 1spin, 1dry) 1iron calor gas camping gaz toilet fluid ☎ ⊞ private beach & children's play area stables pub
40£1.70 or 40£1.40 40▲£1.70 (awnings)

BIRNAM Tayside *Perthshire* Map 11 NO04
►►►► **Erigmore House Caravan Park** *(NO036416)* ☎Dunkeld 236
2 ❸ ⚠ signposted
A predominantly touring site in the tree-studded grounds of 18th-century Erigmore House which offers a wide variety of unusual trees including Japanese maple and cherry. Site well-secluded from the main road and a considerable degree of privacy can be found. Situated on B898 just off A9 through Birnam village. 13acres 188pitches 12static
Apr–Sep no bookings last arrival 21.00hrs last departure 12.00hrs 15 individual pitches 36wc lit all night 1cdp 51washbasins hc (1hc, 10hc) warden (2wash, 2spin, 2iron) games room calor gas camping gaz toilet fluid restaurant licensed bar ☎ ⊞ stables launderette
168£1.75–£2.25 or 168£1.35–£1.60 20▲£1–£2.25 (awnings)

BLAIR ATHOLL Tayside *Perthshire* Map 14 NN86
See Pitlochry sketch map.
►►►► **Blair Castle Caravan Site** *(NN874656)* ☎263
3 ❸ ⚠
This is a predominantly touring site set in tree-studded land within the grounds of Blair Castle and bordered on one side by the River Tilt. Although situated near to the main road there is ample screening by trees to provide seclusion. 30acres 325pitches 50static
Etr–Sep must book peak periods last arrival 22.00hrs last departure 12.00hrs 20 individual pitches late arrivals enclosure 84wc lit all night 2cdp 110washbasins hc 26hc 12 (4wash, 2spin, 2iron) calor gas camping gaz toilet fluid ☎ ⊞ children's playground stables launderette pub
325fr£2 or 325fr£2 or 325▲fr£2 (awnings)

►►► **River Tilt Caravan Site** *(NN875653)* ☎333
1 ❷ ⚠ signposted
Level, grass site with trees and bushes set in hilly woodland country with access to River Garry. 7m N of Pitlochry on A9. 4acres 60pitches 40static
All year no bookings last arrival 20.00hrs last departure 12.00hrs 15 20wc lit all night 1cdp washbasins hc central hot water hc warden wash spin dry iron games room TV cold storage calor gas camping gaz toilet fluid cafe restaurant ☎ ⊞ licensed club fishing & shooting stables launderette pub
50£2 or 50£2 10▲£2 (awnings)

BLAIRLOGIE Central *Stirlingshire* Map 11 NS89
►► **Witches Craig Farm Caravan & Camping Park** *(NS823967)* ☎Stirling 4947
1 ❶ ⚠
A small, predominantly residential site on the main road, with tree-studded hills to the rear. Separate area for touring caravans and tents. 3m from town centre on A91. 3½acres 60pitches 8static
Apr–Sep no bookings last arrival 20.00hrs last departure 12.00hrs 4 5wc lit all night 1cdp washbasins hc central hot water (hc) warden (wash, spin) (cold storage) calor gas camping gaz paraffin ☎ ⊞ children's playground stables cinema launderette pub
60£1.80 or 60£1.60 or 60▲£1.80 (awnings)

BLAIRMORE Strathclyde *Argyll* Map 10 NS18
►► **Gairletter Caravan Park** *(NS193844)* ☎Ardentinny 208
3 ❷ ⚠ signposted
On the W shore of Loch Long, south of Ardentinny this site gives outstanding views of mountains and loch. 3acres 4pitches 16static
Apr–Oct must book 2 individual pitches no cars by caravans 5wc lit all night 1cdp washbasins hc (hc) warden (wash, spin, dry, iron) cold storage calor gas paraffin toilet fluid ☎ ⊞ children's playground private beach & library mobile shop stables pub
4£2.25 or 4£2.25 no awnings

BOAT OF GARTEN Highland *Inverness-shire*
Map 14 NH91
►►► Boat of Garten Camping & Caravanning Park *(NH939191)*
[2] ❶ ⚠ signposted
Level, grass site with young trees and bushes set in mountainous woodland in the village itself, near the River Spey and Loch Garten. Off A95. 4acres 50pitches 55static
Closed Nov no bookings last departure 12.00hrs 8⛐ individual pitches Ⓐ late arrivals enclosure 20wc lit all night 1cdp ⛐ 24washbasins hc 2central hot water (6⛆hc) 3⊙ warden (2wash, 1dry, 1iron) games room TV cold storage calor gas camping gaz paraffin toilet fluid cafe ☎ ⊞ children's playground & bicycle hire ⛐ ⊖ stables ♪ ✈ ⛐
50⛟fr£1.95 or 50⛟fr£1.95 or 50▲fr£1.95 awnings ltr

BOTHWELL Strathclyde *Lanarkshire*
Map 11 NS75
►►► Strathclyde Park Caravan Site *(NS715585)* Bothwellhaugh Rd
☎Motherwell 66155 ext 55
[2] ❸ ⚠ signposted
A mainly level grass site with saplings and bushes situated amidst woodland and meadowland. 20acres 100pitches
All year booking advisable peak periods last departure 12.00hrs 4⛐ individual pitches Ⓐ late arrivals enclosure 32wc lit all night 4cdp washbasins hc central hot water ⛆hc ⊙ warden (wash, spin, dry) ⛐ calor gas camping gaz paraffin toilet fluid cafe restaurant licensed bar ☎ ⊞ children's playground private beach sailing boating & putting ⛐ ⊖ stables ♪ ✈ cinema ⛐ launderette pub
100⛟£1.50 or 100⛟£1.50 50▲£1.25 (awnings)

BRIDGE OF ALLAN Central *Stirlingshire*
Map 11 NS79
►►► Allanwater Caravan Site *(NS787981)*
Blairforkie Dr ☎832254
[3] ❷ ⚠ signposted
This is a secluded and well-maintained static and touring site set on level grass on the banks of the River Allan. It is surrounded by wooded hills. The site is positioned north of the small town and access is good. 5acres 50pitches 40static
Apr–Sep no bookings last departure 14.00hrs 6⛐ 10wc lit all night washbasins hc (⛆hc) ⊙ (wash, dry) iron calor gas ☎ ⊞ ⛐ ⊖ stables ♪ cinema ⛐ launderette pub
50⛟£2 or 50⛟£2 no awnings

BRIDGE OF CALLY Tayside *Perthshire*
Map 15 NO15
► *Middleton Farm Caravan & Camping Site* *(NO135585)* ☎Blacklunans 226
[1] ❶ ⚠
A level site in hilly and mountainous country near river. 11m N of Blairgowrie on A93. 30static
Etr–Oct 6⛐ 6wc lit all night washbasins hc ⊙ ⊖ stables ⛐
⛟ ⛟ ▲ (awnings)

BRIGHOUSE BAY Dumfries & Galloway *Kirkcudbrightshire* Map 11 NX64
See Gatehouse of Fleet sketch map
►►► Brighouse Bay Holiday Park *(NX628458)* ☎Borgue 267
[3] ❸ ⚠ signposted
Part level, part sloping grass site with mature trees and bushes set in downland, wood and meadow country adjacent to sea and wide sandy beach. 12acres 190pitches 120static
Apr–Oct bookings advisable for caravans peak periods last arrival 21.30hrs last departure 11.30hrs 10⛐ individual pitches for caravans Ⓐ late arrivals enclosure 24wc lit all night 1cdp ⛐ 32washbasins hc central hot water (2⛆hc) 8⛆hc 8⊙ warden (wash, spin, 1dry, 2iron) (cold storage) calor gas camping gaz paraffin toilet fluid ☎ ⊞ children's

playground bicycles & boats for hire fishing slipway sauna & solarium 🏊 ⊖ pub 120🚃£2.40 or 120🚐£2.40 70▲£2.40 (awnings)

BRODIE Grampian *Moray* Map 14 NH95
►►► Old Mill Inn *(NH980570)* ☎244
[2] ❷ ⚠ signposted
Level, grassy site, bordered by trees, with a small river on W side. Well-screened from main road.
5acres 70pitches 40static
Apr–Oct booking advisable last arrival 22.00hrs last departure 12.00hrs 4✿ ⓐ 14wc lit all night cdp 16washbasins hc 8⋒hc 2⊙ calor gas restaurant ☎ ⊞ licensed club children's playground 🏊 ⊖ stables ♿ ✈ cinema ⛵ launderette pub
70🚃 or 70🚐 or 70▲ (awnings)

BRORA Highland *Sutherland* Map 14 NC90
► Riverside Caravan Site *(NC888036)*
Stonehouse Doll ☎353
[2] ❷ ⚠ signposted
Part level, part sloping grass site with meadowland, adjacent to River Brora.
500yd W of A9. 2acres 21pitches 2static
May–Sep last arrival 22.00hrs 2✿ 4wc lit all night 1cdp washbasins hc central hot water ⋒hc ⊙ calor gas camping gaz ☎ ⊞ children's playground ⊖ ♿ ✈ ⛵ 🏊
6🚃£1 15🚐90p or 15▲80p awnings ltr

BUCKIE Grampian *Banffshire* Map 15 NJ46
► *Strathlene Caravan Site* *(NJ446668)*
[1] ❶ ⚠ signposted
Level, stony and grassy site situated 2m from town on A942. 57pitches 40static
9 Apr–Sep 4✿ individual pitches ⓐ 16wc lit all night 3cdp washbasins hc ⋒hc ⊙ (wash, dry) ⊞ 🏊 ⊖ ♿ ✈ ⛵ launderette pub
45🚃 or 45🚐 .12▲ rates on application ltr

CAIRN RYAN Dumfries & Galloway *Wigtownshire* Map 10 NX06
►►► Cairn Ryan Caravan & Chalet Park *(NX075673)* ☎231
[1] ❷ ⚠ signposted
Neatly laid-out site, standing on sloping ground exposed to Loch Ryan. 1acre 20pitches 105static
Jun–Aug rsApr, May & Oct must book last arrival 22.00hrs last departure 12.00hrs 5✿ individual pitches 32wc lit all night 1cdp 40washbasins hc 2central hot water 8⋒hc 6⊙ (2wash, 2spin, 2iron) ⛴ games room CTV calor gas cafe licensed bar ☎ ⊞ children's playground 🏊
20🚃£3–£4 or 20🚐£3–£4 awnings ltr

CALLANDER Central *Perthshire* Map 11 NN60
►►► Callander Holiday Park *(NN615074)*
Invertrossachs Rd ☎30265
[3] ❷ ⚠ signposted
This is an attractive, terraced site situated in a tree-studded estate to the NW of Callander with splendid views over the surrounding countryside. The site is well laid-out with mature trees and shrubs providing screening and seclusion. 2acres 60pitches 120static
15 Mar–Oct bookings accepted day before arrival last arrival 21.30hrs last departure 10.30hrs 12✿ individual pitches wc lit all night 2cdp 17washbasins hc 6⋒hc 3⊙ (2wash, 1spin) iron calor gas toilet fluid ☎ ⊞ ⊖ ♿ ⛵ launderette 🏊 pub
50🚃£2.16 10🚐£2.16 no awnings

►►► Gart Estate Caravan Park *(NN643070)* The Gart ☎30002
[2] ❷ ⚠
A well developed, mainly level grass site lying back from the main road and screened by shrubs and trees. 1m E of Callander on A84.
8acres 112pitches 42static
Apr–mid Oct must book peak periods last departure 12.00hrs 10✿ individual pitches late arrivals enclosure 15wc lit all night 3cdp (washbasins hc) ⋒hc ⊙ (wash, spin, dry) iron cold storage calor gas camping gaz toilet fluid cafe ⊞ children's playground 🏊 ⊖ ♿ ⛵ launderette pub
75🚃£2 or 75🚐£2 awnings

CAMUSTIANAVAIG Isle of Skye, Highland *Inverness-shire* Map 13 NG53
► *Braes Campsite* *(NG501390)*
☎Sligachan 248
[1] ❶ ⚠ signposted
Part level, part sloping, grass and gravel site with mature trees, set in mountainous, hilly country, with access to sea, beach and loch.
4½m SE of Portree on B883. 2acres 8pitches 6static
15 Apr–15 Oct must book July & Aug last arrival 22.00hrs last departure 12.00hrs 3✿ individual pitches 4wc lit all night 1cdp 4washbasins hc (2⋒hc) 1⊙ calor gas toilet fluid ⊞
8🚃 or 8🚐 (awnings)

CARGILL Tayside *Perthshire* Map 11 NO13
►► Beech Hedge Restaurant & Caravan Park *(NO165374)* ☎Meikleour 249
[2] ❷ ⚠ signposted
Part level, part sloping grass and gravel site, set in hilly woodland area, close to the River Tay and A93 Perth–Blairgowrie road. ¾acre 8pitches 9static
All year must book peak periods last arrival 23.00hrs last departure 12.00hrs 2✿ individual pitches 6wc 1cdp ⊕ washbasins hc ⋒hc ⊙ calor gas toilet fluid cafe restaurant licensed bar ☎ ⊞ children's playground 🏊 ⊖ ⛵ pub
8🚃£2.50 or 8🚐£2.50 3▲£2.50 (awnings)

CARRADALE Strathclyde *Argyll* Map 10 NR83
►► Carradale Bay Caravan Site *(NR815385)*
The Steading ☎665
[2] ❷ ⚠
Rolling grass site near beach. Views over Killbrannan Sound to Isle of Arran.
Approach from north is via Tarbert. Leave Tarbert by A83 Campbeltown road; within 5m turn on to B842 Carradale road. This is a 20 mile single track road with passing places. In Carradale take road to the pier, site is ½m distant. 9acres 60pitches
Etr–Sep booking advisable 5✿ individual pitches ⓐ late arrivals enclosure 16wc lit all night 2cdp 16washbasins hc (central hot water) 4⋒hc 2⊙ (1spin, 1dry) ⊞ ⊖ ♿ ✈ ⛵ 🏊 pub
50🚃£3.40 or 50🚐£3.40 10▲£3.40 (awnings) ltr

CASTLE DOUGLAS Dumfries & Galloway *Kirkcudbrightshire* Map 11 NX76
►► Lochside Park *(NX764619)*
[2] ❷ ⚠ signposted
Municipal touring site incorporating park with recreational facilities, situated on southern edge of town in attractive setting adjacent to Carlingwark Loch. The site has two types of standings, asphalted areas with marked pitches and more informal grassed areas. 5acres 148pitches
Etr–Sep rsOct–Mar no bookings last arrival 20.00hrs last departure 12.00hrs 7✿ individual pitches ⓐ 28wc lit all night 3cdp washbasins hc central hot water ⋒hc ⊙ (⚘) ☎ ⊞ children's playground mobile shop ⊖ ✈ cinema ⛵ launderette
95🚃£1.50 or 95🚐£1.50 53▲£1.50 awnings ltr

COCKBURNSPATH Borders *Berwickshire* Map 12 NT77
►► Chesterfield Caravan Park *(NT772701)*
The Neuk ☎226
[2] ❷ ⚠ signposted
Grass site set in secluded rolling Border Hill country, bordered by hills and screened by gorse-covered hills. It is about ½m from the village and within 3m of the sea. 4acres 72pitches 12static
Apr–Sep last arrival 22.00hrs last departure 12.00hrs 6✿ individual pitches late arrivals enclosure 19wc lit all night 1cdp ⊕ 22washbasins hc 10⋒hc 2⊙ warden cold storage calor gas ☎ ⊞ ⊖ stables ✈ ⛵ 🏊 pub
72🚃£1.50 or 72🚐£1.50 or 72▲£1.50 (awnings)

COLDINGHAM Borders *Berwickshire*
Map 12 NT96
▶▶ ***Scoutscroft Camping Site*** *(NT908661)*
☎338
1 1 signposted
Part level, part sloping grass site with saplings and bushes. Set in border country adjacent to sea and beach. 3m E of A1 at Reston. 3acres 60pitches 110static
Jul–Aug rsMar–Jun & Sep–Oct must book peak periods last departure 12.00hrs
8 30wc lit all night 1cdp washbasins hc (6hc) 4 warden (2wash) spin, iron (games room) TV (cold storage) calor gas camping gaz paraffin toilet fluid cafe restaurant licensed bar ☎ sub aqua diving centre stables cinema launderette
10 10 40▲

COLL SANDS Lewis, Western Isles
Ross and Cromarty Map 13 NB43
▶ **Broad Bay Caravan Site** *(NB462383)*
☎Stornoway 2053
1 2 signposted
A sandy site near the beach and sea, situated on the coast road between Tong and Upper Coll. ½acre 20pitches 12static
Apr–Oct must book 2 wc lit all night 1cdp washbasins hc (hc) calor gas ☎ private beach
6£1.25 6£1.25 10▲£1 awnings ltr

COMRIE Tayside *Perthshire* Map 11 NN72
▶▶▶ **Twenty Shilling Wood Caravan Site** *(NN763221)* ☎411
2 2 signposted
This secluded site of level pitches on gravel bases is set in tree-studded hill country lying to the west of the picturesque village off A85.
4acres 30pitches 30static
5 Apr–Sep no bookings last arrival 22.00hrs 7 14wc lit all night 1cdp 16washbasins hc (4hc) 3 (1wash, 1spin, 2dry, 2iron) games room CTV cold storage calor gas toilet fluid ☎ stables pub
30£2 or 30£2 (awnings)

▶▶ **West Lodge Caravan Site** *(NN785225)*
Lawers ☎354
2 2 signposted
A sloping, grass site set amidst wooded hillside in rolling Perthshire scenery. The site is adjacent to main road but screened by wall and hedge. ½acre 25pitches 35static
Apr–Oct must book last arrival 21.00hrs last departure 11.00hrs 6 13wc lit all night 1cdp washbasins hc central hot water (hc) calor gas
25£1.80 or 25£1.80 or 25▲£1.50 (awnings)

CONNEL Strathclyde *Argyll* Map 10 NM93
▶▶▶ **North Ledaig Caravan Site** *(NM907368)*
2 2
Spacious touring site, adjacent to main road and offering fine views out across the bay.
4acres 60pitches
Etr–Sep must book peak periods last arrival 20.00hrs last departure 12.00hrs 5 late arrivals enclosure 12wc lit all night 3cdp washbasins hc (central hot water, hc) warden dry calor gas camping gaz paraffin toilet fluid cafe ☎ private beach
60 (awnings)

CORPACH Highland *Inverness-shire*
Map 14 NN07
▶▶▶▶ **Linnhe Caravan Park** *(NN074771)*
3 2 signposted
Situated 1m W of Corpach on A830, overlooking Loch Eil, with Ben Nevis to the E and mountains of Sunart to the W. Although site is predominantly static, caravans are accommodated on landscaped terracing with uninterrupted views of surrounding countryside.
8acres 90pitches 100static
Etr–Sep no bookings last departure 12.00hrs 9 30wc lit all night 1cdp (24washbasins hc, 9hc, 12) (spin, dry, iron) calor gas ☎ children's playground, private beach & slipway stables launderette pub
90£1.60–£2 or 90£1.60–£2 (awnings)

CRAIL Fife Map 12 NO60
▶▶ **Balcomie Links Caravan Park** *(NO605084)* Balcomie Rd ☎383
1 1
Slightly sloping, grass site with young trees and bushes, set in downland and meadowland adjacent to sea and sandy beach – within the urban area. Junction of A917 and A918.
3acres 6pitches 75static
Apr–Sep must book peak periods last departure 12.00hrs 5 16wc lit all night washbasins hc (7hc) (wash) spin (dry) iron calor gas camping gaz ☎ launderette pub
6£1.50 or 6£1.50 no awnings

▶▶ **Sauchope Caravan Site** *(NO623078)*
Apply to: North East Fife District Council, Dept of Recreation, Cairngreen, by Cupar, Fife ☎460 (Cupar 4941 out of season)
1 2
This is a sloping grassy site comprising a large stretch of land bordering rocky foreshore on Fife coast. Secluded but somewhat exposed to sea breezes, with panoramic views over the Fife estuary, to the Island of Moy, Basc Rock and Berwick Law. 12acres 150pitches
26 Mar–Sep must book last arrival 20.00hrs 10 individual pitches 31wc lit all night 1cdp 28washbasins hc 16hc 8 2wash 1dry ☎ launderette pub
25£1.75 or 25£1.75 or 25▲90p–£1.75 (awnings)

CREETOWN Dumfries & Galloway
Kirkcudbrightshire Map 11 NX45
▶▶ **Cassencarie Holiday Park** *(NX475576)*
☎264
3 2 signposted
A mainly level, grassy site with trees and bushes set in woodland and meadowland just off A75, ½m from Creetown. 3½acres 60pitches
Mar–Sep must book peak periods last arrival 22.00hrs last departure 12.00hrs 4 late arrivals enclosure 12wc lit all night 1cdp 16washbasins hc 2central hot water 4hc 2 spin games room TV calor gas camping gaz toilet fluid children's playground putting green & slipway pub
60£2 or 60£2 or 60▲£2 (awnings)

CRIEFF Tayside *Perthshire* Map 11 NN82
▶▶▶ **Crieff Holiday Village** *(NN857225)*
☎3513
3 2 signposted
Level, gravel site with trees and bushes set in woodland within the urban area and with access to river. 1m W of Crieff on A85. 1½acres 38pitches 40static
Mar–Dec must book peak periods last arrival 23.59hrs last departure 10.30hrs 4 individual pitches 16wc lit all night 2cdp washbasins hc central hot water hc (wash, spin, dry, iron) (cold storage) calor gas camping gaz toilet fluid restaurant ☎ children's playground & off licence stables cinema launderette pub
28£2.70 or 28£2.70 10▲£2.70 awnings

CROCKETFORD Dumfries & Galloway
Kirkcudbrightshire Map 11 NX87
▶▶▶▶ **Brandedleys Carafarm** *(NX830725)*
☎250
3 3 signposted
Grass and gravel, part level, part sloping site with trees and bushes, set in hilly meadowland country adjacent to lake. 4acres 45pitches 20static
May–Sep rsMar, Apr & Oct must book last arrival 22.00hrs last departure 12.00hrs 3 late arrivals enclosure 9wc lit all night 1cdp 15washbasins hc (1hc) 4hc 2 (1wash, 1spin, 1iron) games room TV (cold storage) calor gas camping gaz toilet fluid cafe ☎ children's playground badminton area off-licence bicycles for hire pub
45£2.60–£3 or 45£2.60–£3 or 45▲£2.60–£3 (awnings)

►► **Galloway Arms Hotel** *(NX831728)*
☎240
[1] ❸ ⚠ signposted
Level, grass site with trees and bushes set in downland, woodland and meadowland within the urban area. 9m W of Dumfries at junction A712 and A75. 6acres 60pitches
Mar–Sep must book peak periods last arrival 22.00hrs last departure 12.00hrs 3 Ⓐ 10wc lit all night 1cdp washbasins hc hc ⊙ 1wash 1spin iron cold storage calor gas cafe restaurant licensed bar ☎ ⊞ pub
30£2.30–£2.40 or 30£2.30–£2.40 30▲£2.30–£2.40 awnings ltr

CROMARTY Highland *Ross and Cromarty* Map 14 NH76
►► **Shore Mill** *(NH749658)*
☎Poyntzfield 216
[2] ❷ ⚠
Part level, part sloping grass site set in meadowland, with access to sea and beach. 2m W of Cromarty on B9163. 2½acres 11pitches 4static
Apr–Sep must book peak periods last arrival 22.00hrs last departure 12.00hrs 2 3wc lit all night 1cdp 4washbasins hc 2hc 1⊙ warden ⊞ pub
11£1.50 or 11£1.50 or 11▲£1.50 awnings

CROOK OF DEVON Tayside *Kinross-shire* Map 11 NO00
► **Drum Caravans & Filling Station** *(NO044006)* Fossoway ☎Fossoway 246
[1] ❶ ⚠
This is a small touring site offering 1½acres of level grass bordered by trees with pleasant views. 4½m W of Kinross on A977. 15pitches
All year no bookings last arrival 22.00hrs 1 Ⓐ 4wc lit all night washbasins hc hc ⊙ warden calor gas camping gaz paraffin toilet fluid ⊞ launderette pub
15£1.62 or 15£1.62 10▲£1.08 awnings

CULLEN Grampian *Banffshire* Map 15 NJ56
►► ***Logie Camping & Caravan Site*** *(NJ516674)* ☎40766
[1] ❷ ⚠ signposted
Part level and sloping grassy site near sea and beach. ¼m E of A98. 72pitches 40static
9 Apr–29 Sep 5 individual pitches Ⓐ 16wc lit all night cdp washbasins hc central hot water (hc) ⊙ (wash, dry) ☎ ⊞ launderette pub
60 or 60 12▲ ltr

CUMINESTOWN Grampian *Aberdeenshire* Map 15 NJ85
► **A B Caravans** *(NJ842516)* ☎261
[2] ❶ ⚠ signposted
Mainly grass site set in agricultural land, 3m NE off B9027 for East Balthangie. 3acres 6pitches 12static
Jun–Oct rsMay must book peak periods last arrival 22.00hrs last departure 12.00hrs 1 Ⓐ 6wc lit all night 1cdp washbasins hc (central hot water, hc) ⊙ wash spin iron games room TV cold storage calor gas camping gaz toilet fluid cafe ☎ ⊞ stables launderette pub
6£1.50 or 6£1 or 6▲£1 (awnings) ltr

DALRYMPLE Strathclyde *Ayrshire* Map 10 NS31
►► **Doon Valley Caravan Park** *(NS365145)*
☎242
[2] ❷ ⚠
Part level, part sloping grass site with trees and bushes, set in downland and meadowland, with access to main road. 5m SE of Ayr off B742. 3acres 9pitches 90static
Jun–Sep rsOct–May must book peak periods last arrival 18.00hrs last departure 12.00hrs 6 individual pitches wc lit all night 1cdp 12washbasins hc 2central hot water 6hc 1⊙ warden (5wash, 1dry, 1iron) games room CTV cold storage calor gas camping gaz toilet fluid ☎ ⊞ children's playground pub
9£2.50 or 9£2.50 awnings ltr

DORNOCH Highland *Sutherland* Map 14 NH78
►►►► **Grannie's Heilan Hame** *(NH818924)* ☎260
[2] ❶ ⚠ signposted
This site is in a coastal setting amidst grass and sand dunes. 40acres 325pitches 75static
Jun–Aug rsSep–May no bookings last arrival 22.00hrs last departure 18.00hrs 20 Ⓐ late arrivals enclosure 56wc lit all night 1cdp 65washbasins hc central hot water (25hc) 14⊙ (5wash, 1spin, 4dry, 3iron) games room TV (cold storage) calor gas camping gaz toilet fluid cafe restaurant ☎ ⊞ licensed club children's playground private beach & take away food stables launderette pub
225£1.30–£2.50 or 225£1.30–£2.50 100▲£1.30–£2.50 awnings ltr

►►► **Royal Dornoch Links Caravan & Camping Site** *(NH804888)*
☎423 (Golspie 392 Nov–Mar)
[1] ❶ ⚠ signposted
A level, grass and sand site near the sea and beach, set in hilly woodland and moorland. 2m off A9 on E side of town. 10acres 160pitches 40static
Apr–23 Oct booking advisable peak periods last arrival 22.00hrs last departure 12.00hrs 15 44wc lit all night 2cdp washbasins hc (hc) ⊙ (wash, dry, iron) (games room) TV cafe ☎ ⊞ children's playground & putting green stables pub
160£1.60 or 160£1.60 or 160▲£1.60 (awnings) ltr

DRINNISHADDER Harris, Western Isles *Inverness-shire* Map 13 NG19
► **Laig House Caravan Site** *(NG171951)*
☎207
[1] ❶ ⚠ signposted
Part level, part sloping, sand-surfaced site with mature trees set in mountainous and hilly country with access to sea and beach. 4½m S of Tarbert. 2acres 18pitches 5static

May–Oct must book peak periods last arrival 23.59hrs 2⛺ individual pitches Ⓐ 5wc lit all night ⚇ washbasins hc ⊙ warden iron cold storage calor gas ⊞ children's playground private beach & fishing ⛳ ⊖ ✈ ⊳ 6🚐£1.50 or 6🚙£1.25 or 6▲90p (awnings) ltr

DUMFRIES Dumfries & Galloway *Dumfriesshire* Map 11 NX97
►► Newbridge Caravan Park *(NX952787)*
Glasgow Rd ☎ Newbridge 249
1 ❷ ⚠ signposted
Level, grassy site on outskirts of busy town. Long and narrow site with central hard core road. 2m N on A76. ⚘ 35pitches 90static
Mar–Oct no bookings last arrival 23.00hrs 2⛺ individual pitches 6wc lit all night 1cdp washbasins hc central hot water ⛾hc ⛆hc ⊙ warden games room calor gas camping gaz paraffin ☎ ⊞ children's playground ⛳ ⊖ stables ♿ cinema ⊳ launderette
18🚐£1.70 17🚙£1.70 awnings

DUNBAR Lothian *East Lothian* Map 12 NT67
►► Kirk Park Caravan Site *(NT667789)*
2 ❶ ⚠
Part level, part sloping site, in meadowland adjacent to A1 off A1087. 3½acres 21pitches 100static
15 Mar–Oct no bookings last departure 10.30hrs 3⛺ individual pitches 14wc lit all night 2cdp 16washbasins hc (6⛆hc, 4⊙) calor gas camping gaz toilet fluid ☎ ⊞ ⛳ ⊖ stables ♿ ✈ ⊳ launderette pub
21🚐£1.50–£1.80 or 21🚙£1.50–£1.80 or 21▲£1.50–£1.80 (awnings) ltr

►► Winterfield Caravan Site *(NT673793)*
West Prom
1 ❶ ⚠
Level, grassy site with access to the sea and beach. Situated on the corner of Back Road and Knockenhair Road. 19pitches 70static
Apr–Sep no bookings last departure 10.30hrs 3⛺ individual pitches 16wc lit all night 3cdp 12washbasins hc 8⛆hc 6⊙ calor gas camping gaz ☎ ⊞ ⛳ ⊖ stables ♿ ✈ ⊳ launderette pub
19🚐£1.50–£1.80 or 19🚙£1.50–£1.80 or 19▲£1.50–£1.80 (awnings) ltr

DUNDEE Tayside *Angus* Map 11 NO33
►► Camperdown Caravan Site *(NO361325)*
Camperdown Park, Liff Rd. Apply to: General Manager of Parks, Parks Dept, Dundee District Council, 17 King St, Dundee DD1 1LD
☎645626 (or 23141 ext 413)
2 ❷ signposted
Modern neatly laid out touring site adjacent to municipal park, just off Dundee by-pass at its western end. Degree of seclusion despite close proximity of industrial estate.
90pitches
Mar–Sep must book peak periods last arrival 21.00hrs last departure 12.00hrs 4⛺ individual pitches 36wc lit all night 2cdp washbasins hc central hot water ⛆hc ⊙ wash (spin) iron cafe restaurant ☎ ⊞ ⛳ ⊖ stables ♿ launderette
90🚐£1.20–£1.40 or 90🚙£1.20–£1.40 or 90▲£1.20–£1.40 awnings

► South Baldovan Caravan Site *(NO389345)*
Baldovan Rd, Downfield ☎88962
1 ❶ ⚠ signposted
Slightly sloping grass and gravel site set in urban area, adjacent to Dighty Water. In northern outskirts of city about 2m from city centre. 1acre 20pitches 7static
Apr–Oct must book peak periods last arrival 22.00hrs last departure 12.00hrs 1⛺ individual pitches 5wc lit all night washbasins hc central hot water ⛆hc ⊙ warden iron ⊞ ⊖ stables ♿ ✈ cinema ⊳ launderette ⛳ pub
20🚐£1.20 or 20🚙£1.20 or 20▲£1.20 awnings ltr

DUNKELD Tayside *Perthshire* Map 11 NO04
► Inver Mill Caravan Site *(NO015422)*
2 ❷ ⚠ signposted
A level and grassy site with mature trees and bushes set in hilly country with nearby moorland, woodland and river. 2acres 50pitches
Apr–Oct last arrival 22.00hrs last departure 12.00hrs 8⛺ 14wc lit all night washbasins hc central hot water ⛆hc ⊙ calor gas ☎ ⊞ mobile⛳ ⊖ stables ♿ ⊳ ⛳ pub
50🚐 or 50🚙 (awnings)

DUNNET Highland *Caithness* Map 15 ND27
►► Dunnet Bay Caravan Site *(ND219703)*
Apply to: Highland Regional Council, Leisure & Recreation Dept, Glenurquart Rd, Inverness
☎Inverness 34121 ext535
1 ❶ ⚠ signposted
This is a mainly level grassy site with gravel driveways, set alongside 3 miles of white shell sands. Access is directly onto A836 approx 8m E of Thurso, immediately W of the village of Dunnet. 5acres 45pitches
May–Sep last arrival 21.00hrs 8⛺ wc lit all night 1cdp 14washbasins hc (4⛆hc) 3⊙ (2wash, 1dry) calor gas camping gaz cafe ☎ ⊞ ⛳ ⊖ ✈ ⊳ pub
45🚐£1.30 or 45🚙£1.30 or 45▲£1.30 awnings ltr

DUNVEGAN Isle of Skye, Highland *Inverness-shire* Map 13 NG24
►► Dunvegan Caravan Park *(NG260477)*
☎336
1 ❷ ⚠ signposted
A mainly level site set in hilly moorland.
28pitches 5static
Apr–15 Oct must book Jul & Aug last departure 12.00hrs 4⛺ individual pitches 12wc lit all night 1cdp washbasins hc ⛆hc ⊙ (wash, dry) ⊖ ✈ ⊳ launderette
28🚐 or 28🚙 ltr

DURNESS Highland *Sutherland* Map 14 NC36
►► Sango Sands Caravan Site *(NC406678)*
Sangomore (1m E) ☎262
1 ❷ ⚠ signposted
On the outskirts of Durness on A838 this open cliff-top site overlooks Sango Bay, and is mainly grass and sand. 9½acres 75pitches
May–Aug rsApr & Sep no bookings last departure 12.00hrs 6⛺ Ⓐ 22wc lit all night 2cdp 18washbasins hc (2⛆hc) 3⊙ warden calor gas camping gaz paraffin cafe restaurant licensed bar ☎ ⊞ ⛳ ⊖ stables ✈ ⊳ pub
75🚐£1.50–£2 or 75🚙£1.50–£2 or 75▲£1.50–£2 awnings ltr

EAST LINTON Lothian *E Lothian* Map 12 NT57
►► Monksmuir Caravan Park *(NT548756)*
☎340
2 ❶ ⚠ signposted
Mainly level site with trees and bushes set in meadowland. Off A1 Edinburgh–Dunbar road. 4acres 43pitches 7static
Apr–Sep rsOct–Mar no bookings last arrival 23.59hrs last departure 12.00hrs 4⛺ 14wc lit all night 2cdp ⚇ 4washbasins hc (central hot water, ⛆hc) 2⊙ warden calor gas camping gaz cafe ☎ ⊞ ⛳ ⊖ stables ♿ ⊳ launderette pub
23🚐£1.55–£1.95 or 23🚙£1.55–£1.95 20▲£1.50–£1.85 (awnings) ltr

EASTRIGGS Dumfries & Galloway *Dumfriesshire* Map 11 NY26
► Gemmel Caravan Site *(NY245666)*
Central Rd ☎304
1 ❶ ⚠ signposted
Part level, part sloping, grass site set in meadowland and adjacent to sea and river. 4m N of Gretna off A75. 1acre 30pitches 6static
Apr–Sep must book peak periods last arrival 23.30hrs last departure 11.30hrs 1⛺ Ⓐ 4wc lit all night ⊙ calor gas ⊞ ⛳ ⊖ cinema ⊳ launderette
10🚐£1.30 10🚙£1.30 10▲£1.30 (awnings)

ECCLEFECHAN Dumfries & Galloway *Dumfriesshire* Map 11 NY17
►►►► Hoddom Castle Caravan Park *(NY154729)* Hoddom ☎251
3 ❸ ⚠ signposted
Predominantly touring site created within the grounds of Hoddom Castle with the keep and outhouses now housing the site amenities. The

site lies 2m SW of Hoddom Bridge which carries the B725 over the River Annan. 24acres 170pitches 30static
Apr–Sep rsOct must book peak periods last departure 10.00hrs 24 individual pitches late arrivals enclosure 48wc lit all night 1cdp 10washbasins hc (15 hc) 10 (2wash, 1dry, 2iron) games room TV cold storage calor gas camping gaz toilet fluid cafe restaurant licensed bar ☎ ⊞ children's playground stables launderette pub 150£2.25–£2.50 or 150£2–£2.25 50▲£1.75–£2.50 (awnings) ltr

EDINBURGH Lothian *Midlothian* Map 11 NT27
►►►► Morton Hall Caravan Park *(NT265680)* 30 Frogston Road East ☎031-664 1533
3 ❸ ⚠ signposted
Located on the S side of Edinburgh within 20 minutes' walk of the city centre, this site is part of a 200-acre estate surrounding the 18th-C Morton Hall mansion designed by Robert Adam.
15acres 250pitches
23 Mar–Oct must book peak periods last departure 12.00hrs 8 individual pitches late arrivals enclosure 45wc lit all night 2cdp 49washbasins hc 18 hc 21 warden (2wash, 1spin, 2dry) 2iron games room CTV (cold storage) calor gas camping gaz toilet fluid restaurant (licensed bar) ☎ ⊞ children's playground & battery charging stables cinema launderette
250£2.10–£3.20 or 250£2.10–£3.20 or 250▲£2.10–£3.20 (awnings)

ELGIN Grampian *Moray* Map 15 NJ26
►►► Riverside Caravan Park *(NJ197627)*
West Rd ☎2813
2 ❶ ⚠
Pleasant grassy site on banks of River Lossie, partly surrounded by trees. Situated ½m W of Elgin on A96. 2acres 42pitches 10static
Apr–Oct must book peak periods last departure 12.00hrs 5 individual pitches for caravans 11wc lit all night 1cdp 2 11washbasins hc central hot water (2 hc, 2 hc) 2 2wash 2spin 1iron games room cold storage calor gas camping gaz paraffin toilet fluid ☎ ⊞ children's playground & hairdryers cinema launderette pub
42£1.75 or 42£1.75 30▲£1.75 awnings ltr

► Spynie Hall Caravan Site *(NJ182641)*
Spynie ☎45344
2 ❶ ⚠ signposted
A simple site in attractive position on hillside overlooking Moray Firth. 2acres 12pitches
Apr–Sep no bookings last arrival 20.00hrs 1 4wc lit all night washbasins hc ⊞ stables cinema launderette
6£1 or 6£1 6▲£1 awnings ltr

FINDHORN Grampian *Moray* Map 14 NJ06
►►►► Findhorn Bay Caravan Park *(NJ048637)*
1 ❷ ⚠ signposted
A level, grass and sand site near sea and beach. 4m E of Forres on B9011. 10acres 130pitches 175static
Jul–Sep rsOct–Jun no bookings last arrival 20.00hrs last departure 12.00hrs 4 38wc lit all night 2cdp 45washbasins hc (4central hot water) (13 hc) 4 (2wash, 1dry, iron) calor gas camping gaz toilet fluid ☎ ⊞ theatre/cinema stables cinema launderette
130 or 130 or 130▲ (awnings)

►► Findhorn Sands Caravan Park *(NJ040647)* ☎324 (to be changed to 2324)
2 ❷ ⚠ signposted
Mainly level site with bushes set in moorland. Facing Moray Firth. 4m N of Forres.
50pitches 150static
Apr–Oct must book last arrival 19.00hrs 2 8wc lit all night 1cdp washbasins hc central hot water (hc) (2wash, dry) iron calor gas cafe licensed bar stables
30£2.16 or 30£2.16 or 30▲£2.16 awnings

FINDOCHTY Grampian *Banffshire* Map 15 NJ46
► Findochty Caravan Site *(NJ458679)*
2 ❷ ⚠ signposted
A neat towing site set on sea front overlooking rocky bay, on the edge of a quaint fishing village.
3acres 30pitches 10static
Etr–Sep must book peak periods last arrival 17.00hrs last departure 10.00hrs 2 individual pitches 8wc lit all night 1cdp washbasins hc central hot water (hc) (wash, spin) ⊞ children's playground
24£1.50 or 24£1.50 6▲50p–£1 (awnings) ltr

FOCHABERS Grampian *Moray* Map 15 NJ35
►►► **Burnside Caravan Site** *(NJ350580)*
Keith Rd ☎820362
2 ❷ ⚠ signposted
This site is on level ground amidst natural landscaping with a burn flowing through.
11acres 140pitches 40static
Apr–Oct must book peak periods last departure 12.00hrs 8 ⓐ 24wc lit all night 2cdp 24washbasins hc 4hc 8⊙ warden (1wash, 1spin, 1iron,) games room TV ☎ ⊞ children's playground & table tennis
pub
60£2 or 60£1.75 50▲£1.50–£2 awnings

FORESTRY COMMISSION CARAVAN AND CAMPSITES

Only those Forestry Commission sites which come within the scope of the Automobile Association's Caravan and Campsite classification scheme are listed in this guide. There are others which are deliberately maintained as minimum-facility sites and are suitable for the camper or caravanner who prefers to be completely self-sufficient and carries his own chemical toilet.

FREE PAMPHLETS The following give details of all recreational facilities in forests:
See Your Forests – Northern England
See Your Forests – Southern England
See Your Forests – Wales
See Your Forests – Scotland
Forestry Commission Cabins and Holiday Houses
Single copies will be sent on application to the Forestry Commission, 231 Corstorphine Road, Edinburgh EH12 7AT

FORFAR Tayside *Angus* Map 15 NO45
►► ***Lochside Caravan Park*** *(NO450505)*
☎2528
2 ❷ ⚠ signposted
Mainly level, grassy site in meadowland adjacent to loch and main road. 4acres 48pitches
Apr–Oct must book peak periods last arrival 21.00hrs last departure 12.00hrs 4 individual pitches 11wc lit all night 1cdp 10washbasins hc (4hc) 2⊙ 1wash (1spin) toilet fluid ⊞ mobile cinema launderette leisure centre
48 or 48 ltr

FORTROSE Highland *Ross and Cromarty*
Map 14 NH75
►► ***Fortrose Site*** *(NH736563)*
1 ❷ ⚠ signposted
A level, grassy site near sea and beach. ½m S of Fortrose on A832. 4½acres 70pitches
May–Sep no bookings 6 individual pitches 12wc lit all night (17washbasins hc) (4hc) 4⊙ calor gas ⊞
70 or 70 or 70▲

FORT WILLIAM Highland *Inverness-shire*
Map 14 NN17
►►► **Glen Nevis Caravan & Camping Park** *(NN124722)* Glen Nevis ☎2191
3 ❸ ⚠ signposted
At the foot of Ben Nevis, bordered by rugged pine-covered forests, the site is 2m from Fort William, in this most impressive glen. The River Nevis runs through the tree lined banks.
19acres 350pitches 30static
31 Mar–3 Oct no bookings last arrival 22.00hrs last departure 12.00hrs 13 ⓐ no cars by tents 58wc lit all night 1cdp 42washbasins hc (1central hot water, 15hc) 17⊙ (4wash, 1spin, 4dry, 2iron) calor gas camping gaz toilet fluid ☎ ⊞ children's playground stables pub
120£1.60–£2 or 120£1.40–£1.80
230▲£1.40–£1.80 (awnings)

FRASERBURGH Grampian *Aberdeenshire*
Map 15 NJ96
►► Kessock Road Caravan Site
(NJ999661) Esplanade, Kessock Rd.
Apply to: Banff & Buchan District Council, Leisure & Recreation Dept, 1 Church St, Macduff, Banffshire AB4 1UF ☎ Macduff 32861
1 ❷ ⚠ signposted
A level and grassy site near the sea and beach. 100yds off A92 on Kessock Road. 3acres 120pitches
Apr–Sep must book 3♨ 12wc lit all night 1cdp 16washbasins hc central hot water (6⚿hc) 8⊙ (1wash, iron) calor gas camping gaz paraffin toilet fluid ☎ ⊞ children's playground ⛫ ⊖ ♂ ↝ ⇜ launderette pub
30🚃£1.40 30🚐£1.20 40▲85p (awnings)
► Esplanade Caravan Site *(NK000662)*
Harbour Rd. Apply to: Banff & Buchan District Council, Leisure & Recreation Dept, 1 Church St, Macduff, Banffshire AB4 1UF ☎ Macduff 32861
1 ❷ ⚠ signposted
Mainly level, grass and sand site, in urban area, near sea, beach and main road. 1acre 53pitches
May–Sep must book 2♨ 6wc lit all night 12washbasins hc (2⚿hc) 6⊙ iron ⊞ children's playground ⛫ ⊖ ♂ ↝ ⇜ launderette pub
20🚃£1.40 33🚐£1.20 (awnings)

GAIRLOCH Highland *Ross and Cromarty*
Map 14 NG87
►► Sands Holiday Centre *(NG758784)*
☎2152
2 ❷ ⚠ signposted
Part level site set in moorland, 3m W of Gairloch on A832. 55acres 360pitches 4static
Mid May–Sep rsApr–mid May must book peak periods last arrival 22.00hrs last departure 22.00hrs 10♨ Ⓐ 56wc lit all night 1cdp 67washbasins hc (22⚿hc) 22⊙ (3wash, 1spin, 4dry, 3iron) calor gas camping gaz toilet fluid ☎ ⊞ private beach ⛫ ⊖ ↝ ⇜ launderette
170🚃£1.90 or 170🚐£1.70 200▲£1.90 (awnings)

GAIRLOCHY Highland *Inverness-shire*
Map 14 NN18
► Gairlochy Caravan Park *(NN187835)*
☎229
1 ❷ ⚠ signposted
Site set near river, lake and canal. 2m on B8004 off A82. 1acre 20pitches 2static
Apr–Sep must book last departure 11.00hrs 1♨ individual pitches 4wc lit all night 1cdp washbasins hc (⚿hc) ⊙ calor gas ⊞ ⊖ ♂ ↝ ⇜ ⛫ pub
20🚃£1.30 or 20🚐£1.30 or 20▲£1.30 (awnings)

GARTMORE Central *Perthshire* Map 11 NS59
► *Cobeland Campsite* *(NS531989)*
☎ Aberfoyle 392
2 ❶ ⚠ signposted
Set within the Queen Elizabeth Forest Park, this grass and tree-studded site offers seclusion, views, forest walks, and free fishing on the River Forth which borders the camping area.
5acres 100static 5static
15 Mar–Sep no bookings last arrival 20.00hrs last departure 12.00hrs 5♨ 14wc lit all night 1cdp 18washbasins hc central hot water (⚿hc) 2⊙ calor gas ☎ ⊞ ⛫ ⊖ stables ♂ ⇜
100🚃 or 100🚐 or 100▲

GARVE Highland *Ross and Cromarty*
Map 14 NH36
► Garve Caravan Park *(NH393619)*
Garve Hotel ☎205
2 ❶ signposted
A large touring site comprising four acres of level grassland bordered on one side by the main road and on the other by the River Blackwater. The site lies on sheltered ground to the S side of the Garve Hotel and secluded on all sides by mature trees. Site facilities are basic but there is plenty of space on the site which is pleasantly situated amid highland scenery. 4acres 60pitches
Apr–Oct must book peak periods last arrival 23.00hrs 3♨ Ⓐ 6wc lit all night 1cdp washbasins hc central hot water ⚿hc ⊙ calor gas camping gaz paraffin cafe restaurant licensed bar ☎ ⊞ ⛫ ⊖ ↝ ⇜ pub
60🚃£1.50 or 60🚐£1.50 or 60▲£1 awnings

GATEHOUSE OF FLEET Dumfries & Galloway *Kirkcudbrightshire* Map 11 NX65
See sketch map.
►► Anwoth Caravan & Camping Site
(NX595563) ☎ Gatehouse 333
2 ❶ ⚠ signposted
Compact touring site situated on southern edge of small holiday town. Although the site lies just off the main road behind garage and filling station, trees surrounding most sides still manage to create a degree of seclusion.
4acres 45pitches 20static
Etr–mid Oct rs1–3 Apr & end Oct must book peak periods last arrival 22.00hrs last departure 12.00hrs 8♨ individual pitches Ⓐ 14wc lit all night 1cdp ⊕ 14washbasins hc 2central hot water 6⚿hc 4⊙ (1wash, 1spin, 1dry, 1iron) games room (cold storage) calor gas camping gaz toilet fluid ☎ ⊞ children's playground ⛫ ⊖ stables ♂ ⇜ launderette pub
35🚃£2–£2.50 10🚐£2–£2.50 30▲£2–£2.50 (awnings)
►► Cardoness Caravan Site *(NX564534)*
Cardoness Estate ☎ Mossyard 288
2 ❷ ⚠ signposted
Beautifully situated park created out of the woodland and coastline of the Cardoness Estate, 3m SW of Gatehouse of Fleet. The natural environment has been utilised to every advantage whilst still retaining the unspoilt character.
8acres 24pitches 188static
Apr–Oct must book peak periods last arrival 21.00hrs last departure 11.30hrs 5♨ individual pitches 8wc lit all night 4cdp 8washbasins hc 2central hot water (2⚿hc) 2⊙ (1wash, 1dry) calor gas toilet fluid ☎ ⊞ ⛫ ⊖ stables ♂ ⇜ launderette pub
24🚃£2 or 24🚐£2 (awnings)

GLENCOE Highland *Argyllshire* Map 14 NN15
►►► Glencoe Campsite *(NN111578)*
☎ Ballachulish 397
2 ❷ ⚠ signposted
Part level, part sloping, grass, gravel and sand site with young trees and bushes, set in mountainous woodland with direct access to river and main road (A82). no caravans over 5 metres 22acres 218pitches
Mid Dec–Sep last arrival 23.00hrs last departure 12.00hrs 6♨ individual pitches for caravans Ⓐ late arrivals enclosure 16wc lit all night 1cdp washbasins hc (6⚿hc) 4⊙ warden (dry) calor gas camping gaz ☎ ⊞ ⛫ ⊖ stables ↝ ⇜ pub
110🚃£1.20–£2 or 110🚐£1.20–£2 108▲£1.20–£2 awnings
►► Invercoe Caravan Site *(NN098594)*
☎ Ballachulish 210
2 ❶ ⚠ signposted
Level, grass site set in mountains with access to sea, beach and river. On A82 from Fort William, turn left to Kinlochleven. 5acres 100pitches 6static
Etr–Oct no bookings last departure 11.00hrs 5♨ wc lit all night 1cdp washbasins hc (⚿hc) ⊙ (2wash, 2dry) calor gas camping gaz ☎ ⊞ ⛫ ⊖ ↝ ⇜ launderette pub
60🚃£1.60 or 60🚐£1.60 40▲£1.60 awnings

GLENDARUEL Strathclyde *Argyll*
Map 10 NR98
► Glendaruel Caravan Park *(NS005865)*
☎267
2 ❷ ⚠ signposted
Mainly level grass site in valley adjacent to river and main road. ⛒ 3acres 40pitches 30static
Apr-Oct bookings advisable peak periods last arrival 22.00hrs last departure 12.00hrs 3♨ individual pitches Ⓐ late arrivals enclosure 10wc lit all night 1cdp washbasins hc (⚿hc) ⊙ (spin, dry, iron) games room (cold storage) calor gas camping gaz toilet fluid ⊞ children's playground & fishing ⛫ ⊖ ⇜ launderette pub
30🚃£2 or 30🚐£2 10▲£2 (awnings) ltr

Glengoulandie

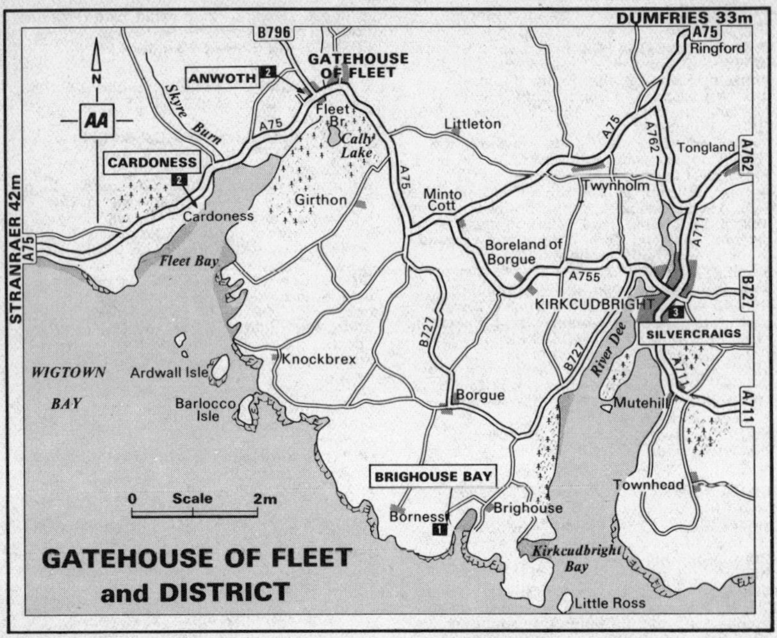

Sites listed under: **1** Brighouse Bay **2** Gatehouse of Fleet **3** Kirkcudbright

GLENGOULANDIE Tayside *Perthshire*
Map 14 NN75
►►► ***Glengoulandie Farm Site***
(NN766525) ☎ Kenmore 306
[1] ❶ ⚠
Level, grass site situated at the foot of rugged hills and with small burn through grounds. Small deer park is situated on the lower slopes from site. 3acres 30pitches 10static
Jun–Sep rsApr, May & Oct last arrival 22.00hrs
2 9wc lit all night 10washbasins hc
central hot water 2hc 2⊙ warden calor gas
fishing wild life park ⊞ ⊖ pub
30 or 30 or 30▲ (awnings) ltr

GLENLUCE Dumfries & Galloway
Wigtownshire Map 10 NX25
►►► **Glenluce Caravan Site** *(NX201576)*
☎Stranraer 2447
[2] ❷ ⚠ signposted
Partly level site in sylvan surroundings off A75 Stranraer road. Concealed entrance at telephone kiosk in centre of main street. 2½acres
40pitches 25static
Apr–mid Oct must book peak periods
last arrival 22.00hrs last departure 12.00hrs
4 Ⓐ 12wc lit all night 1cdp washbasins hc
(central hot water, hc) ⊙ (wash, spin, iron)
children's playground ⊖ stables
launderette pub
20fr£1.70 5fr£1.60 20▲fr£1.70
(awnings)

GLEN TROOL Dumfries & Galloway
Kirkcudbrightshire Map 10 NX47
►►► **Caldons Caravan & Camping Ground**
(NX400790) Apply to: Recreation Forester, Forest Office, Glen Trool, Newton Stewart, Wigtownshire D68 6SZ ☎Bargrennan 200
[3] ❶ ⚠ signposted
Level, grass site with trees and bushes, set in hilly, wooded moorland country, with access to river and Loch Trool. 7m N of Newton Stewart on A714. 8acres 240pitches 25static
Apr–Sep must book last arrival 20.00hrs
13 27wc lit all night 2cdp 30washbasins hc
10hc 6⊙ 4dry calor gas camping gaz ☎ ⊞
⊖
240£1.55–£2 or 240£1.55–£2 or
240▲£1.55–£2 awnings
►► **Merrick Caravan Park** *(NX354775)*
☎Bargrennan 280
[2] ❷ ⚠ signposted
Part level, part sloping, gravel and sand site with trees and bushes, set in mountainous moor and woodland, adjacent to river estuary and lake in the heart of Galloway National Forest Park. Off A714 from Girvan. 2acres 11pitches
29static
Mar–Oct must book peak periods last arrival
23.59hrs last departure 12.00hrs 3
individual pitches 12wc lit all night 1cdp
12washbasins hc (4hc) 2⊙ warden
cold storage calor gas camping gaz ⊖
pub
11£1.75–£2 or 11£1.75–£2 (awnings)

GRANTOWN-ON-SPEY Highland *Moray* Map 14 NJ02
▶▶▶ Municipal Caravan Site *(NJ028283)*
Seafield Av
2 ❷ ⚠ signposted
Part level and sloping, grass site with mature trees and bushes, near river and set amidst hills, mountains, moorland and woodland. ½m from town centre on A939. no motorcycles
20acres 360pitches 50static
Etr–Sep no bookings last departure 12.00hrs 13 individual pitches Ⓐ 32wc lit all night 3cdp 39washbasins hc central hot water 5hc 11hc 25⊙ 2spin (1dry) 2iron calor gas camping gaz toilet fluid ☎ ⊞ children's playground putting green stables pub
180£3.20 or 180£3.20 180▲£2.90 (awnings)

GREENLAW Borders *Berwicks* Map 12 NT74
▶▶▶ Greenlaw Caravan Park *(NT709461)*
Bank St ☎341
2 ❷ ⚠ signposted
Part level, part sloping, grass site amidst various trees and bushes; set in meadowland, adjacent to main A6105 road with direct access to river. 2½acres 35pitches 45static
Etr–Oct must book peak periods last arrival 22.00hrs last departure 12.00hrs 5 individual pitches 8wc lit all night 1cdp 8washbasins hc 6hc 3⊙ (1wash, 1dry) cold storage calor gas camping gaz toilet fluid ⊞ fishing stables pub
35£1.75 or 35£1.75 or 35▲£1.75 (awnings) ltr

GRETNA Dumfries & Galloway *Dumfriesshire* Map 11 NY36
▶ Braids Caravan Site *(NY314675)*
The Braids ☎409
1 ❶ ⚠
Small, peaceful touring site bordered by fields on N side of B721 1m W of the village of Gretna. 1½acres 30pitches
Apr–1 Nov must book peak periods last arrival 23.00hrs last departure 12.00hrs 2 individual pitches late arrivals enclosure 4wc lit all night washbasins hc (hc) ⊙ cold storage calor gas camping gaz toilet fluid ⊞ stables cinema launderette pub
30£1.65 or 30£1.50 or 30▲£1.50 (awnings) ltr

GRETNA GREEN (A74 Service Area, northbound) Dumfries & Galloway *Dumfriesshire* Map 11 NY36
▶▶ Canny Scots Caravan Park *(NY306688)*
Northbound Service Area ☎Gretna 598
1 ❸ ⚠ signposted
Part level, part sloping, mainly grass site with saplings, overlooking the Solway Firth. 1m N of English/Scottish border on A74. 8acres 90pitches
Mar–Oct last departure 12.00hrs 5 15wc lit all night 1cdp washbasins hc central hot water hc ⊙ cold storage camping gaz cafe restaurant ☎ ⊞ children's playground stables launderette pub
45£1.50 or 45£1.50 45▲£1.50 awnings ltr

GUARDBRIDGE Fife Map 12 NO41
▶▶▶▶ Clayton Milk Bar & Caravan Park *(NO432182)* ☎Balmullo 242
2 ❷ ⚠ signposted
This is a level tree-studded grassy site adjoining farm, in gently rolling hill land. 5acres 75pitches 200static
Mar–Oct must book peak periods last arrival 21.00hrs last departure 13.00hrs 8 individual pitches Ⓐ late arrivals enclosure 16wc lit all night 1cdp washbasins hc central hot water (1hc, hc) ⊙ (wash, spin, dry) iron games room CTV cold storage calor gas camping gaz toilet fluid cafe restaurant ☎ ⊞ licensed club children's playground fishing putting launderette pub
40fr£1.89 or 40fr£1.89 35▲fr£1.89 awnings

HARRIS, (ISLE OF) Western Isles *Inverness-shire* Map 13 NG
See Drinnishadder

HAWICK Borders *Roxburghshire* Map 12 NT51
▶▶▶ Riverside Caravan Park *(NT537169)*
☎3785
2 ❷ ⚠ signposted
A level and grassy site near A698 Hawick–Kelso road 2½m E of Hawick. Located on the banks of the River Teviot. 2½acres 50pitches 25static
Apr–Oct last arrival 23.00hrs last departure 12.00hrs 7 individual pitches Ⓐ 15wc lit all night 1cdp 21washbasins hc (2central hot water, 4hc) 2⊙ warden wash spin (cold storage) calor gas camping gaz ⊞ children's playground stables cinema launderette pub
50£2.75 or 50£2.75 or 50▲£2.75 (awnings)

HOLLYBUSH Strathclyde *Ayrshire* Map 10 NS31
▶▶ Skeldon Caravans *(NS389144)*
☎Dalrymple 202
2 ❶ ⚠ signposted
A small, secluded touring site on the banks of the River Doon. 2m from Dalrymple on B7034.
3acres 30pitches 12static
Apr–Sep must book peak periods last arrival 18.00hrs last departure 10.00hrs 5 7wc lit all night 12washbasins hc 1central hot water (2hc) 2⊙ warden iron calor gas camping gaz ⊞ children's playground fishing pub
30£1.90 or 30£1.90 or 30▲£1.90 (awnings)

HOPEMAN Grampian *Moray* Map 15 NJ16
▶▶ *Ashgate Caravan Park* *(NJ145698)*
☎409
1 ❷ ⚠
Level grass and gravel site near sea, beach and main road. Off B9102 Lossiemouth–Forres road. ¾acre 12pitches 8static
Etr–Oct must book Jul & Aug last departure 12.00hrs 2 individual pitches 6wc lit all night 6washbasins hc (2hc) 1⊙ warden calor gas ⊞ stables pub
12 or 12 (awnings)

INCHTURE Tayside *Perthshire* Map 11 NO22
▶ Inchmartine Nurseries *(NO263277)*
Carse of Gowrie ☎251
2 ❷ ⚠
A level and grassy site with mature trees and bushes, set amidst hills, mountains, moorland, woodland and downs. Near to A85 Perth–Dundee road. 3acres 45pitches
15 Mar–Oct last departure 12.00hrs 3 late arrivals enclosure 9wc lit all night 1cdp washbasins hc central hot water hc ⊙ warden ⊞ children's playground stables pub
45£1.50 or 45£1.50 (awnings) ltr

INNERLEITHEN Borders *Peeblesshire* Map 11 NT33
▶ Tweedside Caravan Site *(NT338367)*
☎Galashiels 830260
1 ❶ ⚠
A spacious site standing on perimiter of village, in a relatively secluded and sheltered position, offering panoramic views of the Tweed Valley and surrounding hills. 4acres 50pitches 110static
Apr–Oct no bookings last arrival 20.00hrs last departure 20.00hrs 3 15wc lit all night 1cdp washbasins hc central hot water (hc) ⊙ calor gas ⊞ children's playground
40£1.75 or 40£1.75 10▲£1.75 no awnings ltr

INVERARAY Strathclyde *Argyllshire* Map 10 NN00
▶▶▶ Battlefield Caravan Park *(NN075055)*
☎2285
2 ❷ ⚠ signposted
Level site with mainly grass and stoney surface set among wooded hills. Overlooks Loch Fyne. 35acres 260pitches 170static

Inverchapel

Apr–Oct must book peak periods last departure 12.00hrs 9 individual pitches for caravans late arrivals enclosure 24wc lit all night 5cdp washbasins hc central hot water hc warden iron (games room) calor gas camping gaz toilet fluid licensed bar children's playground, squash court, boat hire, bar snacks
60£1.60 or 60£1.60 200▲£1.30 (awnings) ltr

INVERCHAPEL Strathclyde *Argyllshire*
Map 10 NS18
►►► **Stratheck Caravan Site** *(NS144865)*
Kilmun 472
2 2 ⚠ signposted
Part level, part sloping, grass site amidst mature trees and bushes, set in mountainous woodland country close to river, loch and main road. 13acres 100pitches 50static
Apr–Oct must book peak periods last arrival 21.00hrs 3 18wc lit all night cdp washbasins hc (hc) (wash, spin) iron calor gas camping gaz toilet fluid children's playground, putting, boat for hire & fishing launderette
100£2.42 or 100£2.42 or 100▲£1.88 (awnings) ltr

INVERMORISTON Highland *Inverness-shire*
Map 14 NH41
►► **Lochness Camping Site** *(NH424150)*
1 3 ⚠ signposted
Part level, part sloping, grass and gravel site amid mountains and wooded hill country, with access to Loch Ness. 5m N of Fort Augustus.
85pitches 6static
25 Mar–14 Oct no bookings last arrival 10.30hrs last departure 13.00hrs 10 15wc lit all night 3cdp 19washbasins hc 6hc 3 warden (1wash, 1dry, 1iron) calor gas camping gaz launderette pub
40£2 10£2 35▲£2 (awnings) ltr

INVERNESS Highland *Inverness-shire*
Map 14 NH64
See sketch map.
►►► **Bught Caravan & Camping Site** *(NH658438)*
2 2 ⚠ signposted
Level and grassy site with mature trees and bushes near canal and river, set among hills and mountains. 1m W of Inverness on A82.
5acres 245pitches
Etr–Oct no bookings last arrival 22.00hrs last departure 12.00hrs 6 individual pitches 36wc lit all night 6cdp 36washbasins hc 36central hot water hc dry iron cafe restaurant children's playground invalid toilets stables cinema launderette pub
245£1.50 or 245£1.50 or 245▲£1.50 awnings

►► **Dochfour Site** *(NH616404)*
Dochgarroch
2 1 ⚠ signposted
A level, grassy site near the canal and 4m from Inverness on A82. 3½acres 190pitches 12static
Etr–Sep no bookings last arrival 19.00hrs last departure 12.00hrs 6 wc lit all night 1cdp washbasins hc central hot water hc calor gas camping gaz paraffin
100£1.40–£1.80 or 100£1.40–£1.80 90▲£1.35–£1.50 (awnings) ltr

INVERUGLAS Strathclyde *Dunbartonshire*
Map 10 NN30
►► **Loch Lomond Caravan Park** *(NN320092)*
224
2 1 ⚠
Level site with mature trees and bushes. On A82 between Inverbeg and Ardlui. 1acre 6pitches 54static
Apr–Oct no bookings last arrival 22.00hrs 4 wc lit all night 2cdp 10washbasins hc 2central hot water 2hc 2 calor gas toilet fluid pub
6£2 or 6£2 awnings ltr

ISLE OF WHITHORN Dumfries & Galloway *Wigtownshire* Map 11 NX43
►►►► **Burrow Head Holiday Farm**

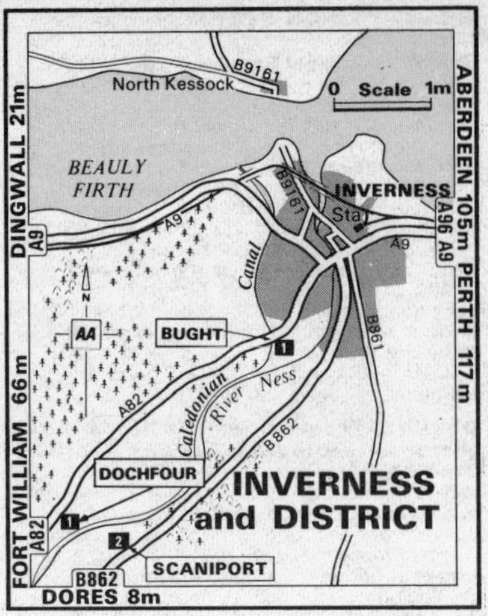

Sites listed under: **1** Inverness **2** Scaniport

(NX450346) Whithorn 252
2 2 ⚠ signposted
Part level, part sloping grass site with bushes set in hilly moorland country on cliff edge with access to sea for fishing only. 2m W of Isle of Whithorn. 260pitches 300static
Etr–Sep rsMar Bar & shop closed last arrival 21.00hrs last departure 14.00hrs 10 wc lit all night 1cdp washbasins hc central hot water (hc) (wash, dry) (games room, cold storage) calor gas camping gaz toilet fluid cafe restaurant licensed club children's playground stables cinema launderette pub
260£2 or 260£2 or 260▲£2 awnings ltr

JEDBURGH Borders *Roxburghs* Map 12 NT62
►►►► **Lilliardsedge Park** *(NT620267)*
Ancrum Ancrum 271
2 3 ⚠ signposted
A part level, part sloping, stony and grassy site with mature trees and bushes set amid woodland, moorland and downs. 6m NW on A68. 23acres 190pitches 30static
23 May–26 Aug rsEtr–22 May & 27 Aug–Oct must book peak periods last arrival 22.00hrs last departure 12.00hrs 18 49wc lit all night 4cdp 49washbasins hc (hc) warden (1wash, 1spin, 1dry, iron) TV calor gas camping gaz paraffin toilet fluid licensed bar children's playground take away meals skateboarding stables launderette
190£2–£2.50 or 190£2–£2.50 or 190▲£2–£2.50 (awnings) ltr

JOHN O'GROATS Highland *Caithness*
Map 15 ND37
► **Stroma View Site** *(ND373782)* Huna 313
1 1 ⚠ signposted
Slightly sloping, grass site set in downland with cliff scenery and access to sea and beach. 1½m W of John O'Groats on A836. ½acre 15pitches
Apr–Oct must book peak periods last arrival 23.00hrs last departure 11.00hrs 2 wc 1cdp washbasins hc (hc) camping gaz restaurant licensed bar children's playground stables cinema launderette pub
15£1.50 or 15£1.50 or 15▲85p (awnings) ltr

KEITH Grampian *Banffshire* Map 15 NJ45
►► **Keith Caravan Site** *(NJ435501)*
1 3 ⚠ signposted
A compact, newly developed site, located on the southern edge of town off the A96. Adjacent to housing estate. 3½acres 33pitches 4static
Etr–Sep must book peak periods last arrival

17.00hrs last departure 10.00hrs 3⛭ individual pitches Ⓐ 8wc lit all night 2cdp washbasins hc central hot water (⋒hc) ⊙ (wash, spin) iron ⊞ ⊖ ♁ cinema ⌒ launderette ⛭ pub 23 £1.50 or 23 £1.50 10▲50p–£1.50 (awnings) ltr

KELSO Borders *Roxburghshire* Map 12 NT73
▶▶▶ **Springwood Caravan Park**
(NT720334) ☎2596
3 ❷ ⚠ signposted
The site is located in a secluded position close to the tree-lined River Teviot about 1m W of the town. 30pitches 230static
Apr–Sep must book peak periods last arrival 22.00hrs 14⛭ 18wc lit all night 1cdp washbasins hc ⋒hc ⊙ (wash, iron) (cold storage) calor gas camping gaz ☎ ⊞ (bowling alley) table tennis & children's playground ⛭ ⊖ ♁ cinema ⌒ launderette 30 £2–£2.40 or 30 £2–£2.40 (awnings) ltr

KENMORE Tayside *Perthshire* Map 11 NN74
▶▶▶ **Kenmore Caravan Site** *(NN772458)*
☎226
2 ❷ ⚠ signposted
Part level, part sloping, grass site with trees, set in mountains, woods and meadowland, adjacent to River Tay. W of Aberfeldy on A827. 10acres 150pitches 70static
Apr–10 Oct rs11Oct–1 Nov must book peak periods last arrival 21.00hrs last departure 12.00hrs 12⛭ individual pitches for caravans Ⓐ late arrivals enclosure 35wc lit all night 2cdp washbasins hc ⋒hc ⊙ (spin, dry, iron) (cold storage) calor gas camping gaz toilet fluid ☎ ⊞ children's playground, football pitch ⛭ ⊖ stables ♁ ✈ ⌒ pub 50 £1.84 10 £1.40 100▲£1.40 (awnings)

KILBERRY Strathclyde *Argyllshire* Map 10 NR76
▶▶ **Port Ban Park** *(NR710655)*
☎Ormsary 224
1 ❶ ⚠
Secluded site, set on sea-front, with uninterrupted views of Islay and Jura. ✂Jul & Aug 2acres 20pitches 40static
Apr–30 Oct must book peak periods last arrival 22.00hrs 3⛭ individual pitches 9wc 1cdp washbasins hc ⋒hc (⊙) calor gas camping gaz toilet fluid ☎ ⊞ children's playground private beach putting crazy golf boats for hire ⊖ ⌒ ⛭ 20 £1.45–£2.15 or 20 £1.45–£2.15 or 20▲£1.45–£2.15 (awnings) ltr

KILMARNOCK Strathclyde *Ayrshire* Map 10 NS43
▶ **Cunningham Head Estate Caravan Park** *(NS370418)* ☎Torranyard 238
1 ❶ ⚠ signposted
Compact site within the grounds of a farmland estate. 3m NE of Irvine. 4acres 80pitches 100static
Apr–Sep no bookings last arrival 22.00hrs last departure 14.00hrs 6⛭ Ⓐ 22wc lit all night 1cdp central hot water (⋒hc) ⊙ (wash, spin, dry) (cold storage) camping gaz toilet fluid ☎ ⊞ children's playground ⛭ ⊖ stables ♁ ✈ cinema ⌒ launderette pub 40 £2.20 10 £2.20 40▲£2.20 (awnings)

KINGHORN Fife Map 11 NT28
▶▶▶▶ **Pettycur Bay Caravan Park** *(NT259865)* ☎890321
1 ❶ ⚠ signposted
This sloping, hillside, terraced site has splendid views of Edinburgh across the River Forth. 4acres 50pitches 350static
Last wk Mar–1st wk Oct must book for caravans peak periods. No booking for tents last arrival 22.00hrs last departure 12.00hrs 17⛭ individual pitches Ⓐ late arrivals enclosure 60wc lit all night 5cdp washbasins hc (⇌hc) ⋒hc ⊙ warden (wash, spin, dry) iron CTV calor gas toilet fluid cafe ☎ ⊞ children's playground ⛭ ⊖ ♁ ⌒ launderette pub 25 £2.50 5 £2 20▲£2.60 (awnings)

KINROSS Tayside *Kinross* Map 11 NO10
▶▶▶ **Loch Leven Caravan Site** *(NO123019)* Sandport ☎63560
2 ❷ ⚠ signposted
This level, grassy site is situated behind the town and on the shores of Loch Leven with good views of loch and surrounding countryside. The location is relatively secluded being off the main road. 1½acres 36pitches 38static
Apr–Sep must book peak periods last arrival 23.30hrs last departure 12.00hrs 5⛭ 15wc lit all night 1cdp 14washbasins hc (central hot water, 4⋒hc) 5⊙ (2wash, 2dry, 1iron) games room CTV (cold storage) calor gas camping gaz ☎ ⊞ ⛭ ⊖ ♁ cinema ⌒ launderette 36 fr£1.70 or 36 fr£1.60 or 36▲fr£1.70 (awnings)

▶▶▶ **Turfhills Tourist Centre** *(NT124892)* ☎63123
1 ❸ ⚠ signposted
Mainly level, grass and gravel site amidst young trees and bushes. Set in hilly country, adjacent to main road. 3acres 40pitches 20static
All year last arrival 22.00hrs last departure 17.00hrs 4⛭ individual pitches Ⓐ late arrivals enclosure 20wc lit all night 1cdp ⊕ 16washbasins hc 6central hot water 8⋒hc 3⊙ warden (1wash, 1spin, 1dry, 1iron) calor gas camping gaz toilet fluid cafe restaurant licensed bar ☎ ⊞ children's playground go-kart track ⛭ ⊖ stables ♁ ✈ ⌒ launderette pub 40 fr£1.25 or 40 fr£1.25 or 40▲fr£1.25 awnings

▶ **Milk Bar** *(NT129985)* Hatchbank ☎62436
1 ❶ ⚠ signposted
Level, grassy site in hilly country near lake. 1m S of Kinross and ½m N of Junction 5 of M90. 1acre 30pitches 5static
Apr–Oct rsNov–Mar no bookings 1⛭ 10wc lit all night 1cdp washbasins hc central hot water ⋒hc ⊙ wash calor gas

Kippford

camping gaz cafe restaurant licensed bar ☎ licensed club children's playground 🏊 ⊖ stables ♂ ✈ cinema ↪ launderette pub 30🚐£1.20 or 30🚗£1.20 or 30▲£1.20 (awnings) ltr

KIPPFORD Dumfries & Galloway *Kirkcudbrightshire* Map 11 NX85
▶▶ Kippford Caravan Site *(NX844564)* ☎636
② ❷ ⚠ signposted
Part level, part sloping grass site with bushes, set in hilly country adjacent to Urr Water estuary, main road and stony beach.
5acres 45pitches 70static
Mar–Oct no bookings 5🚿 12wc 1cdp washbasins hc central hot water 🚿hc ⊙ warden spin iron calor gas ⊞ children's playground 🏊 ⊖ stables ♂ ✈ ↪ pub 45🚐£2–£2.50 or 45🚗£2–£2.50 or 45▲£2–£2.50 awnings

KIRKCALDY Fife Map 11 NT29
▶▶▶ Dunnikier Caravan Site *(NT285942)* Dunnikier Rd ☎67563
② ❸ ⚠ signposted
Level, grass site with trees and bushes. Within the urban area on B926. 3acres 97pitches
Apr–1 Oct must book peak periods last arrival 20.00hrs last departure 12.00hrs 10🚿 individual pitches Ⓐ late arrivals enclosure wc lit all night 1cdp 6⊕ washbasins hc central hot water 🚿hc ⊙ (wash, dry, iron) cold storage calor gas camping gaz ☎ ⊞ 🏊 ⊖ stables ♂ ✈ cinema ↪ launderette pub 72🚐£1.65 or 72🚗£1.65 25▲£1 (awnings) ltr

KIRKCUDBRIGHT Dumfries & Galloway *Kirkcudbrightshire* Map 11 NX65
See Gatehouse of Fleet sketch map.
▶ Silvercraigs Caravan & Camping Site *(NX686508)* Silvercraigs Rd ☎30291
① ❶ ⚠ signposted
Touring site in pleasant elevated location, behind and overlooking the town. Famed for its Artists' Colony. 6acres 50pitches
Etr–Sep no bookings last departure 12.00hrs 5🚿 individual pitches Ⓐ 10wc lit all night 2cdp 8washbasins hc 4🚿hc ⊙ calor gas camping gaz children's playground 🏊 ⊖ stables ♂ ✈ ↪ 37🚐£1.50 or 37🚗£1.50 13▲£1.50 awnings

KIRKFIELDBANK Strathclyde *Lanarkshire* Map 11 NS84
▶▶ *Clyde Valley Caravan Park* *(NS868441)* ☎Lanark 3951
② ❷ ⚠
Level, grass site with trees and bushes set in mountains and hilly country with access to river.
4acres 50pitches 100static
Apr–Sep rsOct–Mar last arrival 22.00hrs last departure 14.00hrs 6🚿 individual pitches Ⓐ 11wc 1cdp washbasins hc ⇐hc (🚿hc) ⊙ warden (wash, spin) calor gas camping gaz fishing ⊞ 🏊 ⊖ stables ♂ launderette pub 50🚐 or 50🚗 or 50▲ (awnings)

KIRKGUNZEON Dumfries & Galloway *Dumfriesshire* Map 11 NX86
▶▶▶ Mossband Caravan Park *(NX873664)* ☎280
① ❷ ⚠ signposted
Level park on site of old railway station in hilly country with trees and bushes; adjacent to main road, A711 to Dalbeattie. 4acres 37pitches 3static
Mar–Oct must book peak periods last arrival 22.00hrs last departure 12.00hrs 6🚿 late arrivals enclosure 8wc lit all night 1cdp ⊕ washbasins hc central hot water 🚿hc ⊙ spin ⇐ ⊷ cold storage calor gas paraffin toilet fluid cafe restaurant ⊞ children's playground 🏊 ⊖ ↪ pub 27🚐£1.80 10🚗£1.80 (awnings) ltr

KIRKPATRICK FLEMING Dumfries & Galloway *Dumfriesshire* Map 11 NY27
▶▶ Bruce's Cave & Caravan Site *(NY266705)* (formerly Cove Estate) ☎285
① ❶ ⚠ signposted
Part level, part sloping, grass, gravel and sand site with trees and bushes, set in wooded country and meadowland, with direct access to the river. Off A74 at Kirkpatrick. 80acres 75pitches 25static
Mar–Oct rsNov–Feb must book peak periods last arrival 23.00hrs last departure 12.00hrs 8🚿 individual pitches 15wc lit all night 1cdp ⊕ washbasins hc central hot water ⇐hc 🚿hc ⊙ (wash, dry) iron cold storage calor gas camping gaz ☎ ⊞ free fishing 🏊 ⊖ stables ♂ ✈ cinema launderette pub 45🚐£1 15🚗£1 15▲£1 (awnings)
▶▶ Greenfield Caravan Park *(NY275706)* ☎237
① ❶ ⚠
A mainly level, grass and gravel site with young trees and bushes set within the urban area with direct access to main road and river.
2acres 40pitches 20static
All year must book 3🚿 Ⓐ 6wc lit all night 1cdp ⊕ washbasins hc central hot water (🚿hc) ⊙ (wash) spin dry iron calor gas ⊞ children's playground 🏊 ⊖ stables cinema ↪ launderette pub 10🚐£1.50 or 10🚗£1.50 30▲£1 awnings ltr

KIRRIEMUIR Tayside *Angus* Map 15 NO35
▶▶▶ Drumshademuir Caravan Park *(NO381509)* Roundyhill ☎3284
② ❸ ⚠
Mainly level, part sloping, grass site with saplings and bushes. Set in a valley in hilly country adjacent to main road (A928).
5½acres 82pitches 28static
Apr–Oct rsNov–Mar must book peak periods 7🚿 individual pitches 15wc lit all night 2cdp ⊕ 17washbasins hc 🚿hc 4⊙ (1wash, 1spin, 1dry, 1iron) (cold storage) calor gas camping gaz paraffin toilet fluid ☎ ⊞ children's playground 🏊 ⊖ ♂ ↪ pub 82🚐£2 or 82🚗£2 or 82▲£2 (awnings) ltr
▶ Thrums Caravan Site *(NO394533)* Maryton ☎2436
① ❶
Level grassy site just outside town, backed by fruit trees on the B926 to Forfar. No football 2acres 30pitches
Apr–Sep no bookings 2🚿 1wc ⊕ (washbasins hc, central hot water) ⊙ calor gas camping gaz toilet fluid ☎ ⊖ ♂ ✈ ↪ 🏊 pub 30🚐 or 30🚗 or 30▲ (awnings)

LAGGANMORE Strathclyde *Argyllshire* Map 10 NM82
▶▶ Glen Gallain Caravan Park *(NM843196)* Kilninver
② ❶ ⚠ signposted
Part level, part sloping, grass and gravel site with young trees, set in mountainous wooded hill country adjacent to River Euchar. 4acres 60pitches
Etr–Sep no bookings last departure 12.00hrs 2🚿 individual pitches for caravans wc lit all night 1cdp 4washbasins hc (2central hot water, 2🚿hc) 2⊙ 1dry calor gas camping gaz ⊞ children's swings 🏊 35🚐£1.70 or 35🚗£1.50 25▲£1.30 (awnings) ltr

LAIRG Highland *Sutherland* Map 14 NC50
▶ *Woodend Caravan & Camping Site* *(NC551127)* ☎2248
① ❶ ⚠
Part level, part sloping, grass site set in hilly moorland and woodland country with access to sea, beach, river and Loch Shin off A836 to Tongue. 4acres 45pitches 6static
May–Sep rsApr last arrival 23.00hrs 3🚿 11wc lit all night 1cdp 14washbasins hc 4🚿hc ⊙ (wash) cold storage ☎ ⊞ 🏊 ⊖ ✈ ↪ 45🚐 or 45🚗 or 45▲

LAUDER Borders *Berwickshire* Map 12 NT54
▶▶ Thirlestane Castle Caravan Site *(NT536473)* Thirlestane Castle ☎542
② ❷ ⚠ signposted
Mainly level grass site set in the grounds of the impressive Thirlstane Castle. The site is situated off the A697. 2½acres 60pitches

Mid Apr–mid Oct must book peak periods 4⛺ individual pitches Ⓐ 12wc lit all night 1cdp 10washbasins hc (6🚿hc) 2⊙ ☎ ⊖ stables δ ↬ 🏊 pub
50🚐£2.25 or 50🚙£2.25 10▲£1.75 (awnings)

LETHAM FEUS Fife Map 11 NO30
►►► **Letham Feus Caravan Park**
(NO369084) ☎Kennoway 350323
② ❷ ⚠ signposted
This is a 5-acre grassy site near to a forest. Good southern views are obtained over the River Forth and to the Bass Rock. 1acre 11pitches 100static
Apr–Sep no bookings for tents must book peak periods for caravans last arrival 22.00hrs last departure 12.00hrs 7⛺ late arrivals enclosure wc lit all night 1cdp ⊕ 18washbasins hc 6🚿hc 5⊙ 1wash 1dry 1iron games room CTV cold storage calor gas toilet fluid ☎ ⊞ children's playground 🏊 ⊖ δ ↝ cinema ↬ launderette pub
11🚐£2 or 11🚙£2 or 11▲£1.50 awnings ltr

LEWIS, ISLE OF Western Isles *Ross and Cromarty* Map 13 NB
See Coll Sands.

LOCHGILPHEAD Strathclyde *Argyllshire* Map 10 NR88
►► **Lochgilphead Caravan Site** *(NR859881)* ☎2939
① ❷ ⚠
Mainly level grassy site set in the most beautiful mountain and loch scenery in Argyll. Fishing and sailing available on the loch. 3acres 30pitches 30static
Apr–Oct must book peak periods last arrival 22.00hrs last departure 12.00hrs 3⛺ late arrivals enclosure 18wc lit all night 1cdp 18washbasins hc central hot water 4🚿hc 2⊙ warden calor gas camping gaz toilet fluid ⊞ 🏊 ⊖ stables δ ↝ cinema ↬ pub
30🚐£1.50 or 30🚙£1.50 (awnings) ltr

LOCHGOILHEAD Strathclyde *Argyllshire* Map 10 NN20
►► **Lochgoilhead Caravan Site** *(NN192013)* ☎312
③ ❶ ⚠ signposted
A partly level and sloping grass and stony site with mature trees and bushes set in hills, and near river, lake, sea and beach. B828 and B839 to Lochgoilhead then ½m on Carrick Castle road. ½acre 10pitches 160static
Apr–Oct must book peak periods 1⛺ wc lit all night washbasins hc 🚿hc ⊙ warden (wash, spin, dry, iron) calor gas ☎ ⊞ 🏊 ⊖ stables ↝ ↬ launderette
10🚐£2 or 10🚙£2 no awnings

LOCHMABEN Dumfries & Galloway *Dumfriesshire* Map 11 NY08
►► **Halleaths Caravan Site** *(NY098818)* ☎321
① ❸ ⚠ signposted
Level, grassy site with hard standing. Situated within an estate in a sheltered position with a wood on one side and a high hedge on the other. 3acres 80pitches
Apr–Sep last arrival 22.00hrs 5⛺ individual pitches Ⓐ late arrivals enclosure 12wc lit all night ⊕ (washbasins hc, central hot water, 🚿hc, ⊙) calor gas camping gaz ⊞ children's playground 🏊 ⊖ δ ↝ cinema ↬ launderette
40🚐£1.50 20🚙£1.50 20▲£1.25 (awnings)

►► **Kirloch Brae Caravan Site** *(NY082825)*
② ❷ ⚠ signposted
Mainly level, grass site with mature trees set in meadowland, adjacent to loch and main road. 1¼acres 30pitches
Etr–Oct no bookings 1⛺ wc lit all night 1cdp 8washbasins hc 4🚿hc 4⊙ ⊞ children's playground laundry room 🏊 ⊖ δ ↬ pub
30🚐£1.25 or 30🚙£1.25 no awnings ltr

LOCHNAW Dumfries & Galloway *Wigtownshire* Map 10 NX96
►►► **Drumlochart Caravan Park**
(NX997634) ☎ Leswalt 232
② ❷ ⚠ signposted
Part level, part sloping, grass site with trees and bushes set in hilly woodland – adjacent to Loch Ryan and Luce Bay. 5m SW of Stranraer on A7043. 24pitches 78static
Spring Bank Hol–Oct rsMar & Apr – shop open 1hr daily & pool not heated must book peak periods last arrival 21.00hrs last departure 16.00hrs 8⛺ 13wc lit all night 1cdp 18washbasins hc 1central hot water 4🚿hc 3⊙ (1wash, dry, iron) ⛵ games room (cold storage) calor gas camping gaz toilet fluid licensed bar ☎ ⊞ licensed club children's playground fishing boating 🏊 ⊖ stables δ launderette pub
24🚐£1.70 or 24🚙£1.70 or 24▲£1.70 (awnings)

LOCKERBIE Dumfries & Galloway *Dumfriesshire* Map 11 NY18
►► **Glasgow Road Caravan Site**
(NY133823)
① ❶ ⚠ signposted
Level, grass site set in an urban area. Close to A74 on outskirts of town. 55pitches 15static
Etr–Oct no bookings 2⛺ 11wc lit all night 1cdp washbasins hc (🚿hc) warden ⊞ ⊖ δ cinema ↬ 🏊 pub
35🚐£1.25 or 35🚙£1.25 20▲£1.25 awnings ltr

LUIB Central *Perthshire* Map 11 NN42
► ***Glen Dochart Caravan & Camping Park***
(NN472268) ☎ Killin 538
① ❶ ⚠
Mainly level, part sloping, gravel and sand with trees and bushes set in mountainous country adjacent to main road (A85). 7½acres 125pitches 49static
Etr–mid Oct no bookings last arrival 21.00hrs last departure 12.00hrs 5⛺ Ⓐ late arrivals enclosure 26wc lit all night 1cdp 25washbasins hc central hot water (🚿hc) ⊙ (wash, spin, dry, iron) TV (cold storage) calor gas camping gaz toilet fluid hot drinks vending machine ☎ ⊞ 🏊 ⊖ ↬ launderette
76🚐 or 76🚙 50▲ (awnings)

LUNDIN LINKS Fife Map 12 NO40
►► **Woodlands Gardens** *(NO418031)*
Blindwell Rd ☎ Upper Largo 319
② ❸ ⚠ signposted
A predominantly touring site situated in hilly country at the foot of Largo Law and about ½m from Lundin Links. It has level grass areas and is bordered by well-established trees and shrubs which give seclusion and shelter. ½acre
Mar–Oct no bookings last arrival 22.30hrs last departure 12.00hrs 2⛺ 7wc lit all night 1cdp 8washbasins hc central hot water 2🚿hc 2⊙ warden iron games room CTV cold storage ☎ ⊞ children's playground & wash up area 🏊 ⊖ δ ↬ pub
🚐£2.70 🚙£2.70 ▲£2.70 (awnings)

MACDUFF Grampian *Banffshire* Map 15 NJ76
►►► **Myrus Caravan Site** *(NJ710634)*
☎ Banff 2845
② ❸ ⚠ signposted
Part level, part sloping, grass site with trees and bushes, set in meadowland. On Main A947. 2½acres 40pitches 20static
Jun–Aug rsApr, May, Sep & Oct must book peak periods last departure 12.00hrs 8⛺ Ⓐ 21wc lit all night 1cdp washbasins hc central hot water (🚿hc) ⊙ (wash, spin, dry, iron) games room with CTV (cold storage) calor gas camping gaz toilet fluid ☎ ⊞ children's playground wash up sinks & bicycle hire 🏊 ⊖ δ ↬ launderette pub
30🚐£1.50 or 30🚙£1.50 10▲£1.50 (awnings) ltr

MAIDENS Strathclyde *Ayrshire* Map 10 NS20
►► **Sandy Beach Caravan Park** *(NS215082)*
☎ Turnberry 456
① ❶ ⚠
This is a mainly level, grass site near to the sea and beach. 5pitches 40static
Apr–Sep must book peak periods last arrival 19.00hrs last departure 12.00hrs 3⛺

individual pitches 9wc lit all night 1cdp washbasins hc central hot water ⋒hc ⊙ (wash, spin, dry) games room TV paraffin toilet fluid cafe ☎ ⊞ ⛫ ⊖ stables ♘ ✈ ⛳ launderette pub
5🚐£2 or 5🚌£2 no awnings

MARYCULTER Grampian *Aberdeenshire* Map 15 NO89
►► Lower Deeside Caravan Park *(NJ855001)* ☎ Aberdeen 733860
1 ❶ ⚠ signposted
A level and grassy site with mature trees, near river. 5m SW of Aberdeen. 3acres 45pitches 60static
Apr–Sep must book peak periods last arrival 22.00hrs last departure 10.00hrs 3⛬ ⊛ wc lit all night 1cdp ⛭ washbasins hc central hot water ⋒hc ⊙ (wash, spin, dry) iron games room TV calor gas camping gaz toilet fluid ☎ ⊞ children's playground ⛫ ⊖ ⛳ launderette
15🚐£2 or 15🚌£1.50 30▲£1.50 (awnings) ltr

MELROSE Borders *Roxburghshire* Map 12 NT53
►► Gibson Park Caravan Site *(NT545341)*
Apply to: Ettrick/Lauderdale District Council, Council Chambers, Paton St, Galashiels TD1 3AS ☎ Galashiels 4751 ext 47
1 ❷ ⚠ signposted
A secluded, sloping grass site partially screened by mature trees, with views of Elidon Hills. The site adjoins a recreation park and is situated a short distance from the small Border town shopping centre. 2½acres 50pitches
Apr–Sep must book peak periods last arrival 21.00hrs last departure 12.00hrs 3⛬ individual pitches ⊛ 10wc lit all night 1cdp washbasins hc central hot water ⋒hc ⊙ ⛭ games room ⊞ children's playground recreation area & putting green ⛫ ⊖ stables ♘ cinema ⛳ launderette pub
50🚐£1.60–£2 or 50🚌£1.60–£2 30▲£1.60–£2 (awnings) ltr

MEMUS Grampian *Angus* Map 15 NO45
►► Glens Caravan Site *(NO426592)*
☎ Foreside 258
3 ❷ signposted
Level, grass site with young trees and bushes set in mountainous meadowland. 5m off A94. 2acres 9pitches 12static
Apr–Oct must book peak periods last arrival 22.00hrs last departure 13.00hrs 1⛬ individual pitches ⊛ late arrivals enclosure 5wc lit all night washbasins hc (⋒hc) ⊙ warden calor gas camping gaz paraffin toilet fluid ☎ ⊞ ⛫ ⊖ stables ♘ ⛳
9🚐£1.40 or 9🚌£1.40 4▲£1.40 (awnings) ltr

MONIFIETH Tayside *Angus* Map 12 NO43
►►► Riverview Caravan Park *(NO502322)*
Apply to: General Manager of Parks, Parks Dept, Dundee District Council, 17 King Street, Dundee DD1 1LD ☎2837 (or Dundee 23141 ext 413)
1 ❶ ⚠ signposted
A level and grassy site near sea and beach. 400yds S of A930. 6acres 180pitches 180static
Apr–Oct must book peak periods last arrival 21.00hrs last departure 12.00hrs 4⛬ individual pitches 36wc lit all night 2cdp washbasins hc central hot water ⋒hc ⊙ (wash, spin) iron (⛭) ☎ ⊞ children's playground mobile shop ⊖ stables ♘ launderette ⛫ pub
180🚐£1.20–£1.40 or 180🚌£1.20–£1.40 or 180▲£1.20–£1.40 awnings

MONTROSE Tayside *Angus* Map 15 NO75
►► South Links Site *(NO725575)*
Traill Dr. Apply to: Angus District Council, South Links Site, c/o Director of Parks and Cemeteries, Town House, Montrose DD10 8QW ☎2044
1 ❷ ⚠ signposted
A grassy, sloping site near the sea and beach. 6acres 48pitches 68static
14 Apr–26 Oct must book peak periods late arrival 21.00hrs last departure 12.00hrs 6⛬ individual pitches 21wc lit all night 2cdp washbasins hc central hot water ⋒hc ⊙ (1wash, 1spin) ⊞ children's playground ⛫ ⊖ ♘ cinema ⛳ launderette
48🚐£1.50 or 48🚌£1.50 (awnings)

MORENISH Central *Perthshire* Map 11 NN53
►► High Creagan *(NN594352)* ☎ Killin 449
2 ❷ ⚠
Level, grass and gravel site with trees, set in mountainous moorland country adjacent to river and loch. 1acre 22pitches 8static
Etr–Oct must book peak periods last arrival 21.30hrs last departure 12.00hrs 4⛬ individual pitches late arrivals enclosure 4wc lit all night 1cdp washbasins hc central hot water ⋒hc ⊙ calor gas toilet fluid ⊞ ⛫ ⊖ stables ♘ ✈ ⛳ pub
22🚐£1.50 or 22🚌£1.50 awnings

MOUSWALD Dumfries & Galloway *Dumfriesshire* Map 11 NY07
►► Mouswald Caravan Park *(NY060740)* ☎218
2 ❷ ⚠ signposted
Level, grass site with mature trees and bushes. Off A75 Dumfries–Annan road. 3½acres 35pitches 15static
Mar–Oct must book peak periods last arrival 23.00hrs 2⛬ 10wc lit all night 1cdp 11washbasins hc (6⋒hc) ⊙ warden (1wash, 1spin, iron) cold storage calor gas toilet fluid ☎ ⊞ ⊖ ♘ cinema ⛳ ⛫ pub
35🚐£1.75 or 35🚌£1.75 6▲£1.75 (awnings)

NAIRN Highland *Nairnshire* Map 14 NH85
► *Househill Site* *(NH887553)* ☎53241
1 ❶
Part level, part sloping, grass site set in mountainous woodland and meadowland adjacent to Moray Firth. 1m S of Nairn off A939. 15pitches 15static
Apr–Sep must book Jul & Aug last arrival 21.00hrs last departure 11.30hrs 8⛬ individual pitches 5wc lit all night 5washbasins hc central hot water 2⋒hc 1⊙ warden calor gas ⊞ ⊖ ♘ ✈ cinema ⛳ launderette
15🚐 or 15🚌 15▲

NEWTON STEWART Dumfries & Galloway *Wigtownshire* Map 10 NX46
►►► Creebridge Caravan Park *(NX415656)* ☎2432
1 ❶ ⚠ signposted
Level, grass and gravel site with trees set in urban areas. ¼m E of Newton Stewart on A75. 3½acres 46pitches 40static
Apr–Oct must book peak periods last departure 12.00hrs 12⛬ 24wc lit all night 1cdp washbasins hc central hot water ⋒hc ⊙ warden (wash) spin dry iron calor gas camping gaz toilet fluid ☎ ⊞ children's playground ⛫ ⊖ cinema ⛳ launderette pub
26🚐£1.65 10🚌£1.65 10▲£1.65 (awnings)

NORTH BERWICK Lothian *East Lothian* Map 12 NT58
►► Rhodes Caravan Site *(NT566850)*
2 ❷ ⚠
Level grass site in meadowland in the urban area with direct access to sea and beach. 10acres 350pitches
22 Mar–24 Sep no bookings last departure 12.00hrs 17⛬ ⊛ 68wc lit all night 8cdp 54washbasins hc (24⋒hc) ⊙ (1wash) iron calor gas camping gaz toilet fluid ☎ ⊞ ⛫ ⊖ stables ♘ cinema ⛳ pub
350🚐£1.50–£1.80 or 350🚌£1.50–£1.80 or 350▲£1.50–£1.80 (awnings) ltr

PARTON Dumfries & Galloway *Kirkcudbrightshire* Map 11 NX67
►►► Loch Ken Holiday Centre *(NX687702)* ☎282
2 ❸ ⚠ signposted
A compact touring site on the eastern shores of Loch Ken. 4acres 31pitches 26static
Etr–Oct rsMar must book peak periods last arrival 22.00hrs last departure 12.00hrs 7⛬ individual pitches for caravans ⊛ 10wc

washbasins hc central hot water (🚿hc, ⊙) (wash, spin, dry, iron) (cold storage) calor gas camping gaz toilet fluid ☎ ⊞ children's playground fishing boat & bicycle hire 🏊 ⊖ stables launderette pub
31🚐£2.16 or 31🚙£2.16 or 31▲£2.16 (awnings)

PEEBLES Borders *Peeblesshire* Map 11 NT24
►►►► *Rosetta Caravan & Camping Park* *(NT245415)* ☎20623
2 ❷ ⚠ signposted
Part level, part sloping, grass site with mature trees and bushes, set in hilly woodland country. ½m from town centre off A72. 40acres 130pitches Apr–Oct must book peak periods last arrival 23.00hrs last departure 12.00hrs 6⛟ individual pitches Ⓐ 24wc lit all night 2cdp washbasins hc 🚿hc ⊙ (wash, spin, dry) iron games room TV calor gas camping gaz toilet fluid licensed bar ☎ ⊞ 🏊 ⊖ stables ♪ ✈ ⛳ launderette
100🚐 or 100🚙 30▲ (awnings)

►►► Crossburn Caravan Park *(NT248417)*
Edinburgh Rd ☎20501
2 ❷ ⚠
A gently sloping, grassy site, in a peaceful and relatively quiet location, despite the proximity of the main road which partly borders the site, as does the Eddleston Water. Natural screening by mature and young trees all add to the feeling of seclusion. 2acres 25pitches 95static Apr–14 Oct must book peak periods last arrival 23.00hrs last departure 12.00hrs 11⛟ individual pitches 17wc lit all night 2cdp ⊡ 18washbasins hc (7🚿hc) 4⊙ (1wash, 1spin, 2iron) calor gas camping gaz toilet fluid ⊞ children's playground 🏊 ⊖ stables ♪ ✈ ⛳ launderette pub
25🚐£2.20 or 25🚙£2.20 or 25▲£2.20 (awnings)

PERTH Tayside *Perthshire* Map 11 NO12
►► Cleeve Caravan Park *(NO095228)*
Glasgow Rd ☎25662
2 ❷ ⚠ signposted
Level grass site with young trees and bushes. 60pitches
Etr–Oct last arrival 18.00hrs last departure 16.00hrs 5⛟ individual pitches wc lit all night washbasins hc central hot water 🚿hc ⊙ ☎ ⊞ children's playground 🏊 ⊖ stables ♪ ✈ cinema ⛳ launderette pub
60🚐£1.50 or 60🚙£1.50 awnings ltr

►► Windsor Caravan Park *(NO110225)*
Windsor Ter ☎23721
2 ❷ ⚠ signposted
A small, sloping, grass site situated within residential area of the city but with a pleasant rural atmosphere owing to effective screening by bushes and mature trees. An attractive feature is the waterfall tumbling over a natural rocky outcrop at one end of the park. 7pitches 16static Apr–14 Oct must book – min booking 1wk Jul & Aug – last departure 11.00hrs 1⛟ individual pitches 6wc 1cdp washbasins hc central hot water 🚿hc ⊙ calor gas ⊞ 🏊 ⊖ stables ♪ ✈ cinema ⛳ launderette
7🚐£1.50 or 7🚙£1.50 no awnings

PITLOCHRY Tayside *Perthshire* Map 14 NN95
See sketch map.

►►► Faskally Home Farm *(NN916603)*
☎2007
1 ❷ ⚠ signposted

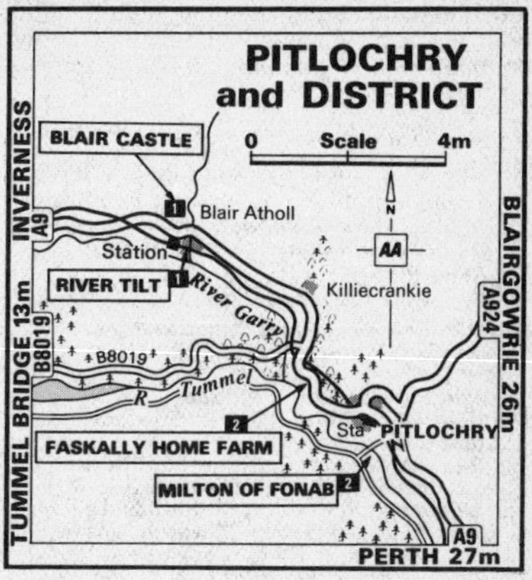

Sites listed under:
1 Blair Atholl **2** Pitlochry

This site is situated outside the town and on the banks of the River Gary. Although bordered on one side by the main road, most of the site is on gently sloping grassland dotted with trees. Splendid views. 20acres 400pitches 50static Etr–Oct booking advisable peak periods 20⛟ Ⓐ 104wc 1cdp ⊡ 104washbasins hc (18🚿hc) 26⊙ (4wash, 2dry, 2iron) cold storage calor gas camping gaz toilet fluid ☎ ⊞ children's playground 🏊 ⊖ stables ♪ ✈ cinema ⛳ launderette pub
250🚐fr£1.80 or 250🚙fr£1.70 150▲fr£1.60 (awnings) ltr

►►► *Milton of Fonab Caravan Site* *(NN945573)* ☎2882
2 ❸ ⚠ signposted
Level, grass site with mature trees. Access to River Tummel. ½m S of town. no motorcycles no hikers 8acres 145pitches 45static End Mar–early Oct must book Jun–Aug last arrival 20.00hrs last departure 13.00hrs 16⛟ individual pitches Ⓐ 42wc lit all night 1cdp 50washbasins hc (4🛁hc) (6🚿hc) 16⊙ (wash) spin (dry) iron cold storage calor gas camping gaz toilet fluid ☎ ⊞ 🏊 ⊖ stables ♪ ✈ cinema ⛳ launderette pub
90🚐 10🚙 40▲ (awnings)

POOLEWE Highland *Ross and Cromarty* Map 14 NG88
►►► *Inverewe Stage House* *(NG861811)* ☎249
2 ❸ ⚠ signposted
Level, grass and sand site with trees and bushes, set in mountainous moorland and hills, with access to sea and beach. 4½acres 50pitches Apr–Sep must book Jul–Aug last arrival 20.00hrs last departure 12.00hrs 4⛟ individual pitches late arrivals enclosure 10wc lit all night 1cdp washbasins hc central hot water (🚿hc) ⊙ (wash, spin, dry) paraffin cafe restaurant licensed bar ☎ ⊞ 🏊 ⊖ stables ♪ cinema launderette pub
45🚐 or 45🚙 5▲ (awnings)

PORTKNOCKIE Grampian *Banffshire*
Map 15 NJ46
► ***Macleod Park Camping Site*** *(NJ494684)*
☎ Cullen 40270
1 ❶ signposted
A level and grassy site near to the sea and beach.
30pitches 5static
9 Apr–Sep individual pitches 6wc
lit all night washbasins hc (hc) (wash, dry)
⊞ launderette pub
20 or 20 10▲ rates on application ltr

PORTPATRICK Dumfries & Galloway
Wigtownshire Map 10 NX05
►►► ***Galloway Point Caravan Park***
(NX005538) Portree Farm ☎367
2 ❷ ⚠
A sloping, grass site near the sea. ½m S of Portpatrick on A7042. 10acres 90pitches
60static
Etr–Sep rsMar–Etr & Oct must book peak periods mid Jul–mid Aug last arrival 23.00hrs
last departure 13.30hrs 12 individual pitches
20wc lit all night 1cdp 20washbasins hc
(7hc) 4 (2wash, 2dry, 1iron) games room
calor gas camping gaz toilet fluid restaurant
licensed bar ☎ ⊞ launderette
pub
40 or 40 40▲

PORTSOY Grampian *Banffshire* Map 15 NJ56
► **Portsoy Links Site** *(NJ592662)* Apply to:
Director of Leisure & Recreation, Banff & Buchan District Council, 1 Church St, Macduff
AB4 2UF ☎ Macduff 32861
2 ❷ signposted
Local authority run site, in pleasant position on seafront giving unrestricted views over Moray Firth. 8m NW of Banff. 82pitches
Apr–Sep must book 2 individual pitches
10wc lit all night 13washbasins hc 4hc
(wash, dry) calor gas camping gaz ⊞
children's playground mobile shop stables
pub
35£1.20 35£1 10▲60p (awnings)

POWFOOT Dumfries & Galloway *Dumfriesshire*
Map 11 NY16
►►► **Queensberry Bay Caravan Park**
(NY140654) ☎ Cummertrees 205
2 ❷ ⚠ signposted
Touring and static site in quiet location on Solway Estuary adjacent to golf course. 25pitches
Apr–Oct must book peak periods 3 13wc
lit all night 1cdp washbasins hc 8hc 4
warden 1spin 1iron calor gas camping gaz
toilet fluid ☎ ⊞ children's playground
stables cinema launderette pub
25£1.50–£2 or 25£1.50–£2 or
25▲£1.50–£2 awnings ltr

RAVENSTRUTHER Strathclyde *Lanarkshire*
Map 11 NS94
►► **Newhouse Farm** *(NS926456)*
☎ Carstairs 228
2 ❷ ⚠ signposted
Level grass and gravel site, with young trees and bushes. Situated on A70, Ayr–Edinburgh road 3m E of Lanark. 2acres 10pitches
30 Mar–30 Oct must book peak periods
last departure 12.00hrs 1 4wc lit all night
1cdp washbasins hc central hot water hc
calor gas camping gaz ⊞ children's
playground stables launderette
pub
10£1.50 or 10£1.50 or 10▲£1.50
awnings ltr

REAY Highland *Caithness* Map 14 NC96
► **Dunvegan Euro-Camp Site** *(NC960644)*
2 ❷ ⚠ signposted
Level and grassy site with slight gradients, young trees and bushes, set in meadowland and in urban area with access to sea and beach. 12m W of Thurso. 1acre 15pitches
31 May–Oct last arrival 21.00hrs last departure
12.00hrs 1 4wc lit all night (washbasin
hc, central hot water, hc) warden ☎ ⊞
stables
10fr£1.70 5fr£1.70 6▲fr£1.70
(awnings) ltr

RESIPOL (Loch Sunart) Highland *Argyllshire*
Map 13 NM76
► **Resipole Farm** *(NM725639)* ☎ Salen 235
2 ❷ ⚠
A spacious and grassy site in isolated roadside position overlooking Loch Sunart. 8acres
160pitches 4static
Jun–Oct rsApr & May no bookings last arrival
23.00hrs last departure 11.00hrs 6 16wc
lit all night 1cdp 8washbasins hc 4hc 4
cold storage calor gas camping gaz paraffin
toilet fluid ⊞ private beach fishing pony
trekking & boat for hire pub
50£1.60–£2 10£1.60–£2 100▲£1.60–£2
(awnings)

ROSEHEARTY Grampian *Aberdeenshire*
Map 15 NJ96
► **Rosehearty Caravan Site** *(NJ935675)*
Apply to: Director of Leisure & Recreation,
Banff & Buchan District Council, 1 Church St,
Macduff AB4 1UF ☎ Macduff 32861
1 ❶ ⚠
A level, grass site near the sea and beach. 4m W of Fraserburgh on B9031. 40pitches
May–Sep must book 2 9wc lit all night 1cdp
12washbasins hc central hot water 6hc 2
(1wash, 1dry) iron ⊞ children's playground
mobile shop pub
30£1.20 or 30£1 10▲60p (awnings)

ROSEMARKIE Highland *Ross and Cromarty*
Map 14 NH75
►► ***Rosemarkie Site*** *(NH739570)*
1 ❷ ⚠ signposted
A level and grassy site near sea and beach. ½m E of Fortrose on A832. 6acres
May–Sep no bookings 6 individual pitches
14wc lit all night (18washbasins hc) (4hc)
4 ⊞
70 or 70 or 70▲

ROY BRIDGE Highland *Inverness-shire*
Map 14 NN28
► **Bunroy Caravan Park** *(NN273806)*
☎ Spean Bridge 332
3 ❷ ⚠ signposted

Level, grass site sheltered by mature trees and bordered by River Spean, set in mountainous country. 300yds off A86. 2acres 30pitches 1static
Apr–Sep no bookings last arrival 21.00hrs last departure 12.00hrs 3 wc lit all night (6washbasins hc, central hot water, 2 hc) 2 warden pub
30 £1.60 or 30 £1.60 or 30▲£1.60 (awnings)

►**Stronreigh** *(NN258812)* ☎ Spean Bridge 275
1 ❶ ⚠ signposted
Part level, part sloping, grass and gravel site with trees and bushes, set in meadowland, adjacent to River Spean. ½acre 8pitches 20static
Apr–Oct last departure 12.00hrs 3 4wc lit all night (washbasins hc, central hot water, hc) spin calor gas ☎
8 £1 or 8 £1 or 8▲£1 awnings

ST ANDREWS Fife Map 12 NO51
►►►►►**Craigtown Meadows Holiday Park** *(NO483153)* Mount Melville ☎75959
3 ❸ ⚠ signposted
Set in downland with mixed woodland and pasture, 2m from sea and sandy beaches. 2m from St Andrews on the Craigtown road.
8acres 90pitches 135static
Mar–Oct booking advisable peak periods last arrival 21.00hrs last departure 12.00hrs
40 individual pitches late arrivals enclosure 19wc lit all night 2cdp 15washbasins hc 20central hot water 8 hc 7 warden (2wash, 1spin, 1dry) 3iron games room CTV cold storage calor gas camping gaz toilet fluid cafe restaurant ☎ ⊞ children's playground stables cinema launderette pub
90 £2–£3 or 90 £2–£3 or 90▲£2–£3 (awnings)

ST FILLANS Tayside *Perthshire* Map 11 NN72
►►►**Lochearn Caravan Park** *(NN680239)* South Shore Rd ☎270
2 ❸ ⚠
Part level, part sloping and gravel site, with young trees and bushes, set in mountainous country adjacent to lake. 6m W of Comrie on A85. 4acres 40pitches 200static
Apr–14 Oct no bookings last arrival 22.00hrs last departure 12.00hrs 12 32wc lit all night 32washbasins hc (1central hot water, 12 hc) 4 warden (2wash, 2dry, 2iron) (cold storage) calor gas toilet fluid ☎ ⊞ private beach launderette pub
40 £2.10 or 40 £2.10 (awnings)

SANDBANK Strathclyde *Argyllshire* Map 10 NS18
►***Cot House Garage*** *(NS154831)* Cot House ☎ Kilmun 351
1 ❶ ⚠

This level grass and gravel site with trees and bushes, is set in mountains in the urban area, adjacent to sea, beach and river. 5m NE Dunoon on A815. 1½acres 12static
Apr–Oct no bookings last arrival 21.00hrs last departure 12.00hrs 2 ⓐ no cars by tents 6wc lit all night (6central hot water) (1hc) 1⊙ camping gaz paraffin cafe licensed bar ⊞
15 or 15 or 30▲

SANQUHAR Dumfries & Galloway *Dumfriesshire* Map 11 NS70
►►Castle View Caravan Park *(NS786095)* ☎291
1 ❶ ⚠ signposted
Small site set behind filling station and general store on edge of village in Upper Nithsdale.
1acre 10pitches 20static
Mar–Oct no bookings last arrival 22.00hrs last departure 12.00hrs 1 ⓐ late arrivals enclosure 4wc lit all night 1cdp washbasins hc central hot water (hc) ⊙ (wash, spin) cold storage calor gas camping gaz paraffin ⊞ children's playground stables pub
10£1.60 or 10£1.60 or 10▲£1.60 (awnings)

SCANIPORT Highland *Inverness-shire* Map 14 NH63
See Inverness sketch map.
►Scaniport Caravan Site *(NH628398)*
2 ❶ ⚠
A level and grassy site with mature trees and bushes, set in hills, woodland, moorland and near canal. 2acres 25pitches
Etr–Sep no bookings last arrival 19.00hrs last departure 12.00hrs 1 ⓐ wc lit all night (washbasins hc, central hot water, hc) calor gas camping gaz ☎ stables
15fr£1.25 or 15fr£1.25 10▲fr£1.15 (awnings) ltr

SCOURIE Highland *Sutherland* Map 14 NC14
►►Scourie Caravan & Camping Site *(NC153446)* ☎2217
2 ❷ ⚠ signposted
Mainly level site adjacent to beach and sea. In centre of village off the Kylesku–Laxford road A894. 4acres 60pitches
Apr–Oct no bookings last arrival 22.00hrs last departure 12.00hrs 2 10wc lit all night 1cdp 16washbasins hc (2hc) 2⊙ 1spin 1iron ⊞ pub
45£1.40 or 45£1.40 15▲£1.40 (awnings)

SHIEL BRIDGE Highland *Ross and Cromarty* Map 14 NG91
►*Glenshiel Site* *(NG938185)* ☎ Glenshiel 221
1 ❶ ⚠
Level, grass and sand site set in mountainous country with access to sea, beach at head of Loch Duich, and river estuary. 15m from Kyle of Lochalsh. 2acres 44pitches
Etr–Oct last arrival 20.00hrs last departure 13.00hrs 4 ⓐ 5wc lit all night (4washbasins hc) 1⊙ calor gas paraffin toilet fluid cafe restaurant ☎ ⊞ stables
32 or 32 12▲ (awnings)

SKYE, ISLE OF Highland *Inverness-shire* Map 13 NG
See Camustianavaig, Dunvegan and Staffin

SOUTHERNESS Dumfries & Galloway *Dumfriesshire* Map 11 NX95
►►►Southerness Holiday Village *(NX976545)* ☎ Kirkbean 256
2 ⚠ signposted
A large campsite situated in close proximity to sandy beach. 8½acres 210pitches 35static
Mar–Oct rsNov–Feb must book peak periods last departure 12.00hrs 25 individual pitches ⓐ late arrivals enclosure 46wc lit all night cdp washbasins hc central hot water hc ⊙ warden (wash, spin, dry) cold storage calor gas camping gaz toilet fluid ☎ ⊞ children's playground private beach paddling pool & boating pool launderette pub
170£1.50–£2.25 or 170£1.50–£2.25 40▲£1.50–£2.25 awnings

STAFFIN Isle of Skye, Highland *Inverness-shire* Map 13 NG46
►►Staffin Caravan & Camping Site *(NG496668)* ☎213
2 ❷ ⚠ signposted
Level and gently sloping, gravel, grass and sand site with young trees and bushes, set in hilly downland and meadowland, adjacent to sea, beach and river. 16m N of Portree on A855.
2½acres 78pitches 4static
Apr–Sep must book peak periods last arrival 23.00hrs last departure 11.00hrs 5 individual pitches ⓐ late arrivals enclosure 8wc lit all night 1cdp 4washbasins hc 1hc 1⊙ warden calor gas camping gaz ⊞ children's playground launderette
23£1.80 10£1.80 45▲£1.80 (awnings) ltr

STIRLING Central *Stirlingshire* Map 11 NS79
►Cornton Caravan Park *(NS786952)* ☎4503
1 ❶ ⚠ signposted
This is a level, grass site situated on the outskirts of the town and near to the main road. Some nearby housing development is apparent but splendid views are obtained of both Stirling and the Wallace monument. 2acres 80pitches 21static
Jun–Oct rsMar–May must book peak periods last arrival 20.00hrs last departure 14.00hrs 3 individual pitches ⓐ 12wc lit all night 1cdp washbasins hc hc ⊙ iron cold storage calor gas camping gaz ⊞ children's playground cinema launderette pub
22£1.80–£2.40 8£1.80–£2.40 30▲£1.80–£2.40 (awnings)

STONEHAVEN Grampian *Kincardineshire* Map 15 NO88
►►►*Queen Elizabeth Caravan Site* *(NO875866)* Apply to: Kincardine & Deeside District Council, Environmental Health Dept, View Mount, Stonehaven, Kincardineshire
1 ❸ ⚠
A gently sloping grass site offering a good range of recreational facilities, situated between a main road and seafront adjoining a public park.
70pitches 50static
Apr–Oct must book Jun–Aug last arrival 20.00hrs last departure 10.30hrs 4 individual pitches 24wc lit all night 4cdp 24washbasins hc central hot water (hc) ⊙ (2wash, spin) dry, iron ☎ ⊞ stables cinema launderette
70 ltr

STRACHAN Grampian *Kincardineshire* Map 15 NO69
►►Feughside Caravan Site *(NO642926)* ☎ Feughside 669
2 ❷ ⚠
Level, grass site with young trees and bushes, set in hilly moorland and woodland country, adjacent to Water of Feugh. ½acre 8pitches 40static
Apr–mid Oct must book peak periods last arrival 22.00hrs 5 individual pitches 9wc lit all night 1cdp washbasins hc hc ⊙ (1wash, 1spin, 1dry) 1iron games room cold storage calor gas ⊞ children's playground pub
8£1.80 or 8£1.60 (awnings) ltr

STRACHUR Strathclyde *Argyll* Map 10 NN00
►►Strathlachlan Caravan Park *(NN013953)* ☎300
2 ❶ ⚠ signposted
Mainly level grass site screened by mature trees on edge of river. Views of Loch Fyne. 2acres 20pitches 75static
Apr–Oct must book peak periods last arrival 22.00hrs 5 individual pitches 9wc lit all night 2cdp 12washbasins hc 4hc 1⊙ (2wash, 2spin, 2dry) calor gas camping gaz ⊞ launderette pub
20£2 or 20£2 no awnings ltr

STRANRAER Dumfries & Galloway *Wigtownshire* Map 10 NX06

►►► **Aird Donald Caravan Park** *(NX075605)* ☎2025
[2] ❶ △ signposted
Level, grass and sand site with trees and bushes. Set in woodland and meadowland within the urban area. There is a tarmac hard standing for 25 caravans. 12acres 175pitches 200static
All year no bookings last arrival 22.00hrs last departure 16.00hrs 9♣ Ⓐ 28wc lit all night 2cdp washbasins hc central hot water (⋒hc) ⊙ (spin, iron) (cold storage) calor gas camping gaz ☎ ⊞ children's playground ♨ ⊖ stables ♁ ⇝ ⇜ launderette pub
175 £2.20 or 175 £2.20 or 175▲£2.20 (awnings) ltr

STRATHAVEN Strathclyde *Lanarkshire* Map 11 NS74
►► **Gallowhill Caravan Park** *(NS708440)* Lesmahagow Rd ☎21267
[1] ❸ △ signposted
Level grass site with young trees, set in meadowland, adjacent to river. On A726 ½m S of Strathaven. 2acres 30pitches
Apr–Sep must book peak periods last arrival 23.00hrs last departure 13.00hrs 2♣ individual pitches wc lit all night 1cdp 8washbasins hc (2⋒hc) 2⊙ (1wash, 1spin, 1dry) calor gas camping gaz paraffin toilet fluid ⊞ ⊖ ♁ ⇜ ♨
30 £1.75 or 30 £1.75 or 30▲£1.50 (awnings)

STRONTIAN Highland *Argyllshire* Map 14 NM86
►►► ***Strontian Caravan Site*** *(NM817618)*
Apply to: Messrs A Munro & Sons, Strontian Acharacle, Argyll ☎2268
[2] ❶ △
A level, grass site with young trees and bushes; adjacent to Loch Sunart. 2acres 24pitches
Apr–Oct must book Jul & Aug last arrival 21.00hrs last departure 12.00hrs 2♣ individual pitches Ⓐ 8wc lit all night 1cdp (6washbasins hc) (2⋒hc) 2⊙ calor gas camping gaz paraffin toilet fluid cafe restaurant, licensed bar ☎ ⊞ laundry ♨ ⊖ ⇜
24 or 24 15▲ (awnings) ltr

TARLAND Grampian *Aberdeenshire* Map 15 NJ40
►►► **Drummie Hill Caravan Park** *(NJ478045)* ☎388
[2] ❸ △
Landscaped site set on edge of village amidst hill and farmland, five miles north of Deeside. 5acres 20pitches 40static
Apr–mid Oct must book last arrival 23.00hrs last departure 12.00hrs 6♣ individual pitches late arrivals enclosure 12wc 1cdp washbasins hc central hot water ⋒hc ⊙ warden (spin, dry, iron) cold storage calor gas ☎ ⊞ ♨ ⊖ stables ♁ ⇜ launderette pub
20 £1.50 or 20 £1.50 (awnings) ltr

TAYPORT Fife Map 12 NO42
►► **East Common Site** *(NO465283)*
Apply to: North East Fife District Council, Dept of Recreation, Cairngreen, Cupar, Fife (out of season) ☎2334 (Cupar 4941 during closed season)
[2] ❸ △ signposted
Level, grass site set in meadowland, adjacent to River Tay. 4acres 100pitches
26 Mar–Sep must book last arrival 20.00hrs last departure 20.00hrs 4♣ individual pitches 13wc lit all night 1cdp 16washbasins hc (6⋒hc) 4⊙ (1wash) 1spin (1dry) 1iron games room TV ☎ ⊞ ⊖ ♁ ⇜ launderette ♨ pub
20 £1.75 or 20 £1.75 or 20▲90p–£1.75 (awnings)

THURSO Highland *Caithness* Map 15 ND16
►► ***Thurso Burgh Caravan Site*** *(ND111688)* Scrabster Rd
[2] ❷ △ signposted
A level and grassy site near the sea and beach. ½m from Post Office on A882. 4acres 60pitches 10static
May–Sep last arrival 21.00hrs 2♣ individual pitches Ⓐ wc lit all night washbasins hc (⋒hc) ⊙ (wash, spin) iron TV calor gas camping gaz cafe restaurant ☎ ⊞ ♨ ⊖ ♁ ⇝ cinema ⇜ launderette
60 or 60 25▲ (awnings)

TUMMEL BRIDGE Tayside *Perthshire* Map 14 NN75
►►► **Riverside Caravan Park** *(NN765591)* ☎221
[2] ❷ △
Part level, part sloping site with mature trees and bushes, set in hilly, wood and meadowland country, adjacent to River Tummel in Grampian hill scenery. 20acres 110pitches 100static
Spring Bank Hol–Sep rs late Mar, Apr & Oct no bookings last arrival 23.00hrs last departure 22.00hrs 20♣ individual pitches late arrivals enclosure 40wc lit all night 4cdp 50washbasins hc 4central hot water 14⋒hc 20⊙ (2wash, 1spin) 2iron games room TV calor gas camping gaz toilet fluid cafe restaurant ☎ ⊞ licensed club children's playground ♨ ⊖ stables ⇝ ⇜ launderette pub
110 £1.95 or 110 £1.95 or 110▲ (awnings)

TURRIFF Grampian *Aberdeenshire* Map 15 NJ75
► **Kinnaird House** *(NJ733506)* Banff Rd ☎2550
[1] ❷ signposted
Mainly level grass site with mature trees and bushes, set in woodland adjacent to the A947 road. ¼acre 6pitches 2static
Apr–Oct last arrival 23.00hrs 1♣ individual pitches 2wc lit all night 4washbasins hc 1central hot water 2⋒hc 3⊙ 1wash 1spin 1iron cold storage calor gas ☎ ⊞ children's playground ⊖ stables ♁ ⇝ ⇜ ♨ pub
6 £1.75 or 6 £1.50 awnings ltr

TUSHIELAW Borders *Selkirkshire* Map 11 NT31
► **Honey Cottage Caravan Site** *(NT295164)* Ettrick Valley ☎ Ettrick Valley 246
[2] ❶ △
Pleasantly situated near River Ettrick in quiet

Ettrick Valley. 30pitches 45static
Apr–Sep must book 6⛟ Ⓐ 16wc lit all night (washbasins hc) ⋔hc ⊙ games room TV cold storage calor gas camping gaz paraffin toilet fluid ☎ ⊞ children's playground ⛀ ⊖ stables ⟲ pub
30🚐£2 or 30🚙£1.50 or 30▲£1.50 (awnings)

WATERBECK Dumfries & Galloway *Dumfriesshire* Map 11 NY27
►► Fallford Lodge Caravan Site
(NY268807) ☎275
2 ❶ ⚠
A quiet, country site, picturesquely situated in a fold of the hills beside the Kirtle Water.
no motorcycles 1½acres 15pitches 15static Etr–mid Oct must book peak periods last arrival 22.00hrs last departure 13.00hrs 4⛟ 4wc lit all night 2cdp washbasins hc central hot water ⊙ cold storage calor gas paraffin toilet fluid ⊞ ⊖ launderette
15🚐£2.25 or 15🚙£2.25 or 15▲£2.25 (awnings) ltr

YETHOLM Borders *Roxburghshire*
Map 12 NT82
►► Kirkfield Caravan & Camping Site
(NT821281) ☎346
3 ❷ ⚠ signposted
Part level, part sloping, grass site with trees and bushes, set in hilly moorland country adjacent to river. 7m S of Kelso on B6352. 1acre 34pitches 15static
Apr–Oct must book peak periods last arrival 21.00hrs last departure 13.00hrs 3⛟ individual pitches Ⓐ 12wc lit all night washbasins hc ⋔hc ⊙ warden calor gas camping gaz paraffin ⊞ ⛀ ⊖ ⟲ pub
34🚐£2.10 or 34🚙£2.10 or 34▲£2.10 (awnings)

DOGS-WARNING

Visitors should not bring pets of any kind with them to Britain unless they are prepared for the animals to go into lengthy quarantine. Owing to the continuing threat of rabies, penalties for ignoring the regulations are extremely severe.

Countryside information

Country Parks

ENGLAND

AVON
Ashton Court Estate Map 3 ST57
(OS172 550725) 1m W of Bristol on A369 and A370. 60 acres. Nature trail, putting.
Management: Bristol District Council.
Doddington House Map 3 ST77
(OS172 755795) 200 yds N M4 junction 8 A46. Near Chipping Sodbury. 700 acres. Landscaped and natural parkland with house, carriage museum and various features. Inclusive admission fee to most amenities.
Management: General Manager Dodington Chipping Sodbury.

BEDFORDSHIRE
Stewartby Lake Map 4 TL04
(OS153 008423) 5m SW of Bedford on A5140. 290 acres. Watersports.
Management: Bedfordshire County Council.
Stockgrove Country Park, Heath and Reach Map 4 SP92
(OS165 918293) 2½m N of Leighton Buzzard. 75 acres. Woodland and Parkland with lake. Fishing, picnicking.
Management: Bedfordshire County Council.

BERKSHIRE
Snelsmore Common Map 4 SU47
(OS174 461711) 3m N of Newbury on B4494. 145 acres woodland and heath. Riding, picnicking.
Management: Newbury District Council.

BUCKINGHAMSHIRE
Black Park Map 4 TQ08
(OS176 0058339) Access via Black Park Road (unclassified) N from A412 3m NE of Slough. 550 acres attractive woodland surrounding a lake, fishing, swimming, pleasant walks, picnicking. Parking 350.
Management: Buckinghamshire County Council.
Emberton Country Park Map 4 SP85
(OS152 887502) On W side of A509 at Emberton 1m S of Olney. Signposted in advance and at entrance. 175 acres. Riverside and lakeland setting. Boating, fishing, children's playground, first aid post, picnicking. Parking 200.
Management: Milton Keynes District Council.
Langley Country Park Map 4 TQ08
(OS176 009817) Access via Billet Lane (unclassified) S from A412 3m N of Slough. 110 acres. Large woodland park with secluded gardens. Nature trail, forest walks, rhododendron gardens, picnicking. Parking 100.
Management: Buckinghamshire County Council.

CAMBRIDGESHIRE
Burghley Park Map 4 TF00
(OS141 032065) SE of Stamford.
Elton Park (private country park) Map 4 TL09
(OS142 089934) A505 5m NE of Oundle.
Ferry Meadows Map 4 TL19
(OS142 145975) 2m W of Peterborough City Centre on A605 and A57. 500 acres of grassland and lakes. Within an area which is under development as the Nene Valley Regional Park. Adjacent to the Nene Valley footpath and the restored Nene Valley railway. Own miniature steam railway, Roman remains, picnic sites, natural history information centre. Facilities for angling, boating, sailing, wind surfing, model boating, riding and walking. Parking 1000.
Management: Peterborough Development Corporation.
Thorney Map 4 TF20
(OS142 288043) A47 7m NE of Peterborough.
Wandlebury Estate Map 5 TL45
(OS154 494536) Cambridge 5m S of City off A604. Management: Cambridge Preservation Society.

CHESHIRE
Eastham Country Park Map 7 SJ38
(OS108 363816) Near junction of M53 and A41 S of Eastham from the centre of which it is signposted. 71 acres. Attractive woodland and grassland beside the River Mersey and entrance to the Manchester Ship Canal. Nature trail, playground.
Management: Bebington Metropolitan District Council.
Little Budworth Common Map 7 SJ56
(OS117 587657) W of Winsford. 90 acres. Heath, woodland, moorland. Riding, picnicking.
Management: Cheshire County Council.
Lyme Park Map 7 SJ98
(OS109 965820) Near Disley, SE of Stockport. 1320 acres. Parkland and moorland. Stately home, children's playground, walking, nature trail, putting, winter sports, riding.
Management: Stockport Metropolitan District Council.
Marbury Park Map 7 SJ67
(OS118 653762) 2m N of Northwich. 190 acres. Woodland and pasture. Arboretum, lake, waterbus, picnicking.
Management: Cheshire County Council.
Styal Country Park Map 7 SJ88
(OS109 835833) From Wilmslow B5166 to Styal Village. 80 acres. Wooded river valley, Quarry Bank Cotton Mill 18th-C and Styal model village with many unusual buildings.
Management: National Trust.
Teggs Nose Map 7 SJ97
(OS109 948724) N of Langley, 2m E of Macclesfield off A537. 135 acres. Foothill of the Pennines with woodlands, grass and heath. Rugged summit formerly quarried. Viewpoint, nature trail, picnicking, riding.
Management: Cheshire County Council.
Wirral Countryside Park – see Merseyside.

CORNWALL
Mount Edgcumbe House and Country Park Map 2 SX45
(OS201 455533) Off B3247 to Cremyll. Parkland and formal gardens under restoration. Tudor mansion open 1 May–30 Sep 2pm–6pm (fee). Deer park, play area, footpaths, bridleways, Warden service.
Management: City of Plymouth and Cornwall County Councils.

CUMBRIA
Bardsea Country Park Map 7 SD27
(OS96 299740) Morecambe Bay. 2m S of Ulverston on A5087. Woodland and shingle beach. Nature trail.
Management: Cumbria County Council.
Fell Foot Map 7 SD38
(OS96 381869) Near Newby Bridge on E shore of Lake Windermere. 18 acres. Wood and grassland by lake shore, swimming, sailing, canoeing, fishing.
Management: National Trust.

Country Parks

Lowther Wildlife Park Map 12 NY52
(OS90 536236) Access near Lowther Village. Off A6 5m S of Penrith.
Talkin Tarn Map 12 NY55
(OS86 545588) 11m S of Brampton E of Carlisle on B6413. 151 acres. Woodland and pasture, lake, rowing, sailing, swimming, fishing, riding.
Management: Cumbria County Council.

DERBYSHIRE
Elvaston Castle Map 8 SK43
(OS128 406327) 6m SE of Derby off B5010. 200 acres. Woodland, parkland with gardens and castle, lake, canoeing, fishing, nature trail, children's playground.
Management: Elvaston Castle Joint Management Committee (Derbyshire County Council and Derby District Council).
Hardwick Hall Map 8 SK46
(OS120 463368) Doe Lea, 6½m SE of Chesterfield. Hall and parkland, lakes, canoeing, fishing, nature trail within the Peak National Park.
Management: National Trust.
Longshaw Estate Map 8 SK27
(OS119 260795) 4m NW of Mansfield 9m SW Sheffield in Peak National Park. Meadows and woodland, walks, nature trail, rock climbing, nature reserve.
Management: National Trust.
Pools Cavern Map 8 SK07
(OS119 048726) Green lane off A515 Buxton, tree planted limestone quarry. Show cave, woodland walks, nature trail.
Management: Buxton and District Civic Association.
Shipley Map 8 SK44
(OS129 433440) 8m NE Derby. Off A608 at Heanor. 324 acres. Wood and meadowland, reservoir, zoo, museum, water sports, nature trail, picnicking.
Management: Derbyshire County Council.

DEVON
Berry Head Map 3 SX95
(OS202 941565) E of Brixham. 100 acres. Within area of outstanding natural beauty. High limestone headland with lighthouse, Napoleonic fortifications and linked to a long distance footpath system. Nature reserve, nature trails, warden, leaflets available on site, café, car park.
Management: Torbay District Council.
Farway Countryside Park Map 3 SY19
(OS192 187932) Holnest Farm 4m S of Honiton. 70 acres woodland, heath and pasture, farm animals, donkeys and ponies.
Management: Mrs J M Forbes, Holnest Farm, Farway, Devon.
Grand Western Canal Country Park
Map 3 ST91
(OS181 963123) Tiverton Basin car park A373 Tiverton. 11½m of restored canal and towpath with open views, deep cuttings and wooded banks running NE from Tiverton and linking a number of quaint villages. Access parking difficult except at Tiverton Basin from which a horsedrawn barge provides excursions and boats may be hired; non-powered boats may be licensed by written application to the County Estates Surveyor. Fishing permits available at local tackle shops. Toilets at Tiverton Basin.
Management: Devon County Council.
River Dart Country Park SX Map 3 SX77
(OS202 733702) 1m from Ashburton on B3357. 80 acres in South Dartmoor, moorland and riverside walks, boating lake, licensed restaurant, heated swimming pool, adventure playground, nature trail, fishing, picnic site. Entrance fee. Parking 200.
Management: Dartmoor National Parks Committee.

DORSET
Durleston Map 4 SZ07
(OS195 034773) 1½m S of Swanage on road to Anvil Point Lighthouse. 261 acres of natural coastland within the Dorset area of outstanding natural beauty and a designated part of the Heritage Coastline forming the SE corner of the Isle of Purbeck. Designated area of scientific interest for geological features and wildlife. Cliffs with seabird colonies, mixed shrubs, trees and grassland. Tilly Whim Caves, 19th-C castle, path to lighthouse, guided walks, picnic areas. Information Centre, Warden service, ample centralised car parking.
Management: Dorset County Council.
Upton Park Map 3 SY99
(OS195 992933) S side of A35. 1m W Fleetbridge intersection entrance off slip road to Upton. Extensive parkland beside Holes Bay, interesting collection of shrubs and trees, nature trail, picnic area, warden service at weekends.
Management: Borough of Poole.

DURHAM
Derwent Walk Map 12 NZ16-15
(OS88 197619-101524) Access point from B6310 (NZ 104535). Derwent Valley between Swadwell and Consett 10½m footpath, bridleway and cycle track following an old railway track through a wooded valley connecting various features converted to picnic sites including Shotley Bridge. Information centre at Ebchester Station B6309 (NZ 107449).
Management: Durham County Council and Tyne & Wear Metropolitan County Council.
Hardwick Hall Map 12 NZ32
(OS93 346289) Sedgefield 10m S of Durham on A177. 40 acres reclaimed from remains of the former Hardwick Park and Gardens. Serpentine lake partly restored with the remainder containing a 5 acre fen traversed by a nature trail raised upon a board walk. Fishing, picnicking, access from A177.
Management: Durham County Council and Sedgefield DC.
Pow Hill Map 12 NZ05
(OS87 011518) Between Derwent Reservoir and B6306 Edmundbyers/Blanchland. Laid out with picnic areas, extensive tree planting, footpaths on upper slopes overlooking sailing activities. 45 acres. Fishing, birdwatching.
Management: Durham County Council.
Waldridge Fell Map 12 NZ24
1m SW of Chester Le Street OS88 250497. Moorland.
Management: Durham County Council.

ESSEX
Cudmore Grove Map 5 TM01
(OS168 070150) East Mersea, Mersea Island approached from Bromans Lane. 35 acres of coastal land with access to beach. Warden Service. Parking fee.
Management: Essex County Council.
Danbury Park Map 5 TL70
(OS167 768048) 5m E of Chelmsford approached from the A414 on A130 through Sanden Village or Well Lane, Danbury. Developed from the lakeside gardens of Danbury Palace and adjoining woodland and parkland. Day permits for fishing available from the water bailiffs.
Management: Essex County Council.
Hatfield Forest Map 5 TL52
(OS167 537201) On A120 4m E of Bishops Stortford. 1010 acres of woodland with lake. Boating, fishing.
Management: National Trust.
Langdon Hills West Map 5 TQ68
(OS177 683865) S of Basildon. 200 acres of woodland and grassland on one of the highest points in Essex. Car parks signposted off Dry Street and near the Crown Hotel.
Management: Essex County Council.
Upper Mardyke Valley Map 5 TQ68
(OS177 610815) E of S Ockenden between Mollands Lane, Buckles Lane and the Mardyke River. 64 acres under development but open for general use; sailing, water-ski-ing, sub-aqua diving at Grangewater Water Recreation Centre.
Management: Thurrock Borough Council.
Thorndon Park Map 5 TQ69
(OS177 630900) Brentwood. Off A128 or B186. Two separate areas approx 2 acres each. Lion Lodge TQ630900: area of woodland with wide paths and picnic area. Parking off main carriageway through Lion Gates. Southern Section TQ615913: off A128 1m N of Halfway House Roundabout. 50 acres open grassland 150 acres woodland with rides and open glades.
Management: Essex County Council.

Weald Park Map 5 TQ59
(OS177 570945) 2m NW of Brentwood.
428 acres of park and woodland. Horse riding permitted on 56 acres. Parking off Weald Road and Lincolns Lane.
Management: Essex County Council.
Westley Heights Map 5 TQ68
(OS177 681863) 1m S of Basildon off B1007.
Park and Woodland, Nature trails.
Management: Essex County Council.

GLOUCESTERSHIRE
Keynes Park (Cotswold Water Park)
Map 4 SU09
(OS163 028957) Ashton Keynes. 4m S of Cirencester. Access (a) off A419 2½m NW of Cricklade (b) off A417 1m E of Fairford 3m W of Lechlade. 100 acres. Reclaimed gravel workings forming a series of lagoons which attract a diversity of waterfowl and other wildlife, picnicking areas, fishing by day permit, also sailing subject to evidence of boat insurance, launching facilities, dinghy park, sailing club, warden service. No bathing.
Management: Gloucestershire and Wiltshire County Councils and Local Councils through Joint Committee.
Robinswood Hill Map 3 SO81
(OS162 835150) 2m S of Gloucester, via Reservoir Road off The Ring Road. 97 acres, a conical wooded hill, formerly source of Gloucester's Water supply. Well House and Well Cross, footpaths, nature trails, riding, information centre in season. AA Viewpoint.
Management: Gloucester District Council.

HAMPSHIRE
Farley Mount Map 4 SU42
(OS185 420294) W of Winchester on unclassified road. 265 acres. Woodland and downland with earthworks and Roman road.
Management: Hampshire County Council.
Lepe and Calshot Foreshores Map 4 SZ49
(OS196 461986) 2m S of Fawley on Solent. 122 acres. An open grassed recreational area narrowing to a long strip of grass and woodland beside the foreshore, access to beach, picnicking, barbecue site, fishing, swimming.
Management: Hampshire County Council.
Queen Elizabeth Park Map 4 SU71
(OS197 722190) Butser, Nr Petersfield (access from A3). 10m N Portsmouth. Open downland and forest. Within the boundary, Butser Hill is a centre for grass skiing, hang-gliding and flying radio-controlled gliders. Picnic areas, bridle paths, waymarked trails, warden service, forestry demonstrations, information centre with bookstall and exhibition. Charges for parking, access to iron age farm demonstration area.
Joint Management: County Council, Forestry Commission.
Wellington Country Park Map 4 SU76
(OS175 717610) Stratfield Saye Estate, Heckfield. 8m NE of Basingstoke at junction of A33 and A32. 605 acres. Woodland, heath, lake and meadowland. Riding, fishing, boating, nature trails, playground, picnicking.
Management: The Duke of Wellington.
Yateley Common Map 4 SU85
(OS175 686591) N of A30 to W of Blackwater. 493 acres. Heathland with ponds, riding, fishing.
Management: Hampshire County Council.

HEREFORD AND WORCESTER
Broadway Tower Map 7 SP13
(OS150 113360) 2m S of Broadway. 35 acres. Grassland and woodland, nature trail.
Management: Batsford Estate Co.
Clent Hills Map 7 SO97
(OS139 928798). South of Halesowen. 8m W of Birmingham off A456, 364 acres.
Management: Hereford & Worcester County Council.
Kingsford Map 7 SO88
(OS138 828818) 3m N of Kidderminster, W of A449. 216 acres.
Management: Hereford & Worcester County Council.
Lickey Hills Map 7 SO97
(OS139 998754) B4096 2½m NE of Bromsgrove 8m S of Birmingham. 525 acres. Woodland, heath and meadowland, bird sanctuary, riding, boating.
Management: City of Birmingham.
Windmill and Waseley Hills Map 7 SO97
(OS139 973777) SW of Birmingham, 2m NW of Rubery. 131 acres. Elevated grassland. Riding, nature trails, AA Viewpoint.
Management: Hereford & Worcester County Council.

HERTFORDSHIRE
Aldenham Reservoir Map 4 TQ19
(OS166 169957) Off A1 NW of Elstree. 185 acres. Meadowland beside reservoir. Fishing, sailing.
Management: Hertfordshire County Council.
Great Wood Northaw Map 4 TL20
(OS166 284042) 4m SE of Hatfield on B157. 247 acres of woodland. Riding, marked walks.
Management: Welwyn & Hatfield District Council.
Knebworth Map 4 TL22
(OS166 228210) 1½m SW of Stevenage W of A1 (M). 190 acres. Parkland, house with gardens, riding.
Management: Lytton Enterprises Ltd.

HUMBERSIDE
Burton Constable Map 8 TA13
(OS107 184362) Sproatley, 8m NE of Hull. 200 acres. Parkland with stately home. Fishing, boating, swimming, birdwatching, nature trail, museum, animals.
Management: Mr Chichester-Constable.
Normanby Hall Map 8 SE81
(OS112 892162) 2m N of Scunthorpe. 170 acres. Park and stately home including 40 acres of pleasure grounds. Play area, lido, deer park, fishing lake, nature trail, riding school, model railway.
Management: Scunthorpe District Council.

ISLE OF WIGHT
Fort Victoria Map 4 SZ38
(OS196 335895) West of Yarmouth. 50 acres. Woodland with access to beach and fort, picnicking.
Management: Isle of Wight County Council.
Robin Hill Map 4 SZ36
(OS196 536878) 2m E of Newport. 80 acres. Woodland and farmland. Roman remains, nature trail, animals, playground, picnicking.
Management: Dowend Enterprises.

KENT
Camer Park Meopham Map 5 TQ66
(OS177 635670) Between Sole Street and Meopham. 45 acres of wood and grassland within an area of outstanding natural beauty.
Management: Gravesham District Council.
Eastcourt Meadows Map 6 TQ86
(OS178 806684) Lower Rainham Road, Gillingham. Grassland on bank of River Medway. Fishing, sailing, canoeing.
Management: Gillingham Borough Council.
Manor Park Map 5 TQ65
(OS188 678573) E of A228 (St Leonards St) S of West Malling, signposted. 52 acres, open parkland with lake fishing, playground.
Management: Kent County Council.
Trosley Towers Map 5 TQ66
(OS188 635611) Off and E of A227 S of Vigo Village. N of Wrotham. Signposted. 120 acres. Extensive areas of woodland on top of the Downs with scrub and grassland on a steep slope within an area of outstanding natural beauty. Walking, picnicking.
Management: Kent County Council.

LANCASHIRE
Beacon Fell Map 7 SD54
(OS102 568428) 8m N of Preston, 3m E of M6. 185 acres of conifer woods and moorland in the Forest of Bowland. Picnic area, information centre, nature trail, viewpoint.
Management: Lancashire County Council.
Witton Park Map 7 SD62
(OS102 656277) On Western outskirts of Blackburn. Woodland and heath. Riding, nature trails, picnicking.
Management: Blackburn District Council.
Wycoller Map 7 SD93
(OS103 935396) SE of Colne, 363 acres of heath, moor and grassland around the Hamlet

of Wycoller, a designated conservation area. Footpaths and access to public rights of way, riding, nature trail. Ranger service at weekends.
Management: Lancashire County Council.

LEICESTERSHIRE
Bradgate Park and Swithland Woods Map 8 SK51
(OS129 533111) 5m NW of Leicester. 1223 acres of woods and parkland in Charnwood Forest. Ruins, riding, nature trail.
Management: Bradgate Park Management Committee.
Wanlip Park Map 8 SK61
(OS129 606104) 5m NE of Leicester. 49 acres. Farmland with restored gravel pits. Boating, fishing.
Management: Wanlip Countryside Club Ltd.

LINCOLNSHIRE
Hartesholme
(OS121 945688) 2m SW Lincoln. A lake bordered by parkland leading to grassland and woodland. 85 acres. Footpaths, fishing, picnic facilities, warden service.
Management: Lincoln City Council.

LONDON (GREATER)
Bayhurst Wood Map 4 TQ08
(OS176 068889) In Colne Valley, 2m N of Uxbridge, 1m W of Ruislip Lido. 98 acres of woodland. Barbecue sites, picnicking.
Management: London Borough of Hillingdon.
Hainault Forest Map 5 TQ49
(OS177 474935) E of Chigwell. 960 acres. Well wooded part of the ancient forest of Essex, golf course, pleasant walks, horse riding, fishing, picnic areas. Parking.
Management: Greater London Council.
Trent Park Map 4 TQ29
(OS176 282973) West of Enfield. 412 acres. Nature trail, woodland trail for the blind, fishing, riding, picnic areas. Parking.
Management: Greater London Council.

MANCHESTER (GREATER)
Chadkirk Map 7 SJ99
(OS109 940900) S of Romily on A627. 70 acres. Wood and farmland. Riding, canoeing, fishing, picnicking.
Management: Stockport Metropolitan District Council.
Daisy Nook Map 7 SD90
(OS109 923009) 3m S Oldham. Wooded parkland with canal and lake.
Management: Oldham MBC/Greater Manchester MBC.
Etherow Park Map 7 SJ99
(OS109 973918) Off B6104 at Compstall. 165 acres, mixed woodland, open countryside, marshland and fishponds next to River Etherow. Nature Reserve, fishing, sailing, rowing, canoeing, nature trail.
Management: Stockport Metropolitan District Council.
Haigh Hall
(OS108 595079) 2m NE Wigan. Woods and heathland, lake, fishing, nature trail, arboreta.
Management: Wigan Metropolitan Borough Council.
Hollingworth Lake
(OS109 940154) 3m NE of Rochdale on B6225. Woods and grassland with lake, sailing, boating, fishing, nature reserve.
Management: Rochdale Metropolitan Borough Council.
Jumbles Reservoir Map 7 SD71
(OS109 734144) 4m N of Bolton. 255 acres. Reservoir with woods and meadows. Riding, boating, fishing.
Management: Blackburn District Council.
Tandle Hill Map 7 SD90
(OS109 906088) Off A627 at Royton, 140 acres.
Management: Oldham District Council.

MERSEYSIDE
Croxteth Park Map 7 SJ49
(OS108 409944) 6m NE of Liverpool, park and woodlands with walled garden.
Management: Merseyside County Council.
Eastham Woods Map 7 SJ38
(OS108 363816) Off A41 at Eastham. Woodland and grassland beside River Mersey, nature trail, playground.
Management: Wirral Metropolitan Borough Council.
The Wirral Map 7 SJ28
(OS108 215869) Between West Kirby and Parkgate, near Dee estuary. Access from A540 Chester to Hoylake road at Croft Drive, Caldy; Station Road, Thurstaston; Parkgate Baths, The Parade, Parkgate; Hadlow Road, Willaston. 105 acres developed from 12m length of disused railway line; picnicking, riding, fishing. Information centres at Thurstaston, Caldy and Heswell.
Management: Cheshire and Merseyside County Councils.

NORFOLK
Fritton Lake Map 5 TQ40
(OS134 476001) Off A143 Fritton—Great Yarmouth road. 170-acre lake edged with reeds, gardens and woodland with grassed areas. Fishing, boat hire, picnic areas, gift and tackle shop, children's assault course and play area. Parking free, entrance fee to park.
Management: Lord Somerleyton.
Sandringham Map 9 TF62
(OS132 679280) 8m NE of King's Lynn. 720 acres. Woodland and heath.
Management: Sandringham Estate.

NORTHAMPTONSHIRE
Barnwell Map 4 TL08
(OS141 035873) S of Oundle on Barnwell Road A605. Restored gravel pits on bank of the River Nene. Angling for disabled, riverside walk, warden service.
Management: Northamptonshire County Council.
Little Irchester Map 4 SP96
(OS152 913660) S of Wellingborough. 200 acres of forest. Nature trail, picnicking.
Management: Northamptonshire County Council.

NORTHUMBERLAND
Bolam Lake Map 12 NZ08
(OS81 080819) Belsey, Nr Morpeth. 90 acres of woodland, fishing, nature trail.
Management: Northumberland County Council.
Plessey Woods Map 12 NZ27
(OS88 240799) 1½m SW of Bedlington on A1068. 100 acres, grass and woodland with lake. Riding, fishing, nature trail, picnicking.
Management: Northumberland County Council.
Wansbeck Map 12 NZ28
(OS81 266862) ½m S Ashington. Grass and woodland river valley. Boating, picnic site.
Management: Wansbeck District Council.

NOTTINGHAMSHIRE
Burnstump Map 8 SK55
(OS120 578807) 3m N of Nottingham off A60. 61 acres. Woods and parkland. Nature trail, picnicking.
Management: Gedling District Council.
Colwick Map 8 SK63
(OS129 608395) 1½m E Nottingham. Woodlands and water. Fishing, nature trail.
Management: Nottingham City Council.
Clumber Park Map 8 SK67
(OS120 630750) 2½m SE of Worksop. 3784 acres. Woodland, farmland and grassland with lake. Fishing.
Management: Clumber Park Management Committee.
Holme Pierrepoint Map 8 SK63
(OS129 619394) 2m W of Radcliffe, N of A52. 239 acres. Restored gravel pits by River Trent. Mainly for water sports. Admission fee varies according to events.
Management: Nottinghamshire County Council.
Major Oak, Sherwood Forest Map 8 SK66
(OS120 623683) N of Edwinstowe off A614. 86 acres. Forest. Nature Reserve.
Management: Nottinghamshire County Council.
Rufford Park Map 8 SK66
(OS120 644650) 3m S of Ollerton on A614. 330 acres. Woodland and parkland with lake. Riding fishing, nature trail.
Management: Nottinghamshire County Council.

OXFORDSHIRE
Mapledurham Map 4 SU67
(OS175 669769) 3m NW of Reading, Berkshire. 24 acres of meadow beside river. Old Mill, picnicking.
Management: Oxfordshire County Council.

SOMERSET
Ham Hill Map 3 ST41
(OS193 478171) S of Stoke-sub-Hamdon, 6m W of Yeovil off A3088. 155 acres. Restored quarry of archaeological interest.
Management: Yeovil Borough Council.

STAFFORDSHIRE
Cannock Chase Map 4 SJ91
(OS127 987174) N of Hednesford. 2687 acres.
Management: Staffordshire County Council.
Central Forest Park Map 4 SJ84
(OS118 886485) Stoke on Trent. Part of reclamation scheme in city centre. AA Viewpoint. 80 acres.
Greenway Bank Map 4 SJ85
(OS118 893554) Knypersley off A527, 4m N Stoke on Trent. 121 acres. Wooded valley with lake and rocky features.
Management: Staffordshire County Council.
Highgate Common Map 7 SO89
(OS138 840900) S of Wolverhampton. 327 acres. Heath and woodland, riding.
Management: Staffordshire County Council.
Ilam Map 7 SK15
(OS119 135508) 6m NW of Ashbourne. 140 acres of parkland with woodland and river. Nature trail.
Management: National Trust.
Parkhall SJ94
(OS118 930450) Weston Coyne, E of Stoke. Heath and woodland, nature trail, fishing, model aircraft, flying, bridleways, information centre.
Management: Stoke District Council/ Staffordshire County Council.

SUFFOLK
Brandon Park Map 5 TL78
(OS144 758851) 1m S of Brandon on B1106. 32 acres. Landscaped grounds of Branden House in Thetford Forest, Nature trail, picnicking, riding.
Management: County Council.
Clare Castle and Bailey Map 5 TL74
(OS155 772452) Between Clare Village and River Stour. 18½ acres. Remains of Castle and Bailey with old railway station developed as a country park and picnic place by conservation corps volunteers.
Management: County Council.
Easton Farm Park Map 5 TM25
(OS156 275582) W of Easton. 32½ acres. Displays and demonstrations of both early and modern dairy farming, bee keeping, farm animals including rare breeds, pets' paddock, early agricultural machinery, nature trail, fishing, craft shop, tea room, facilities for disabled. Admission fee.
Management: Mr J M Kerr.
Knettishall Heath Map 5 TL87
(OS144 895780) 4m SE of Thetford, Norfolk (near Euston Park). 240 acres. Claimed to be the first country park developed under the National Parks Act. Wild breckland along the valley of the River Little Ouse. Traversed along the western boundary by the Peddars Way.
Management: Suffolk County Council.

SURREY
Box Hill Map 4 TQ15
(OS187 181519) 1½m NE of Dorking. 560 acres. Commonland with woods and downland.
Management: National Trust.
Frensham Common Map 4 SU84
(OS186 854407) 3m S of Farnham on A287. 778 acres. Commonland and heath, with pond. Boating and fishing.
Management: Waverley District Council.
Horton Map 4 TQ16
(OS187 190628) NW of Epsom. 205 acres. Farm and woodland. Nature trail, fishing.
Management: Epsom & Ewell District Councils.
Lightwater Map 4 SU96
(OS186 913619) W of Lightwater Village Inn S of Bagshot. 125 acres. Woodland and heath. Riding, fishing.
Management: Surrey Heath District Council.

SUSSEX (EAST)
Ditchling Common Map 4 TQ31
(OS196 334186) E of Burgess Hill, 2m N of Ditchling. Pastures and scrubland with ponds. Fishing, nature trail, riding.
Management: East Sussex County Council.
Forest Way Map 5 TQ43
(OS187 425335) 9-mile linear park along the route of the former railway line from Ashurst Junction to East Grinstead. Car park and main access from A22 at Forest Row, Foresters Arms. Walking, riding, cycling.
Management: East Sussex County Council.
Hastings Country Park Map 5 TQ81
(OS199 850103) Located between Hastings and Fairlight, access via entrance close to Fairlight Church. 260 acres. Meadowland with woods and heath. Fishing, boating and swimming.
Management: Hastings District Council
Seven Sisters Map 5 TV59
(OS199 529984) 5m W of Eastbourne between A259 and the coast. Downland and marshland. Nature trail, fishing. 700 acres.
Management: East Sussex County Council.

SUSSEX WEST
Goodwood Estate Map 4 SU81
(OS197 890111) 6m N of Chichester. 60 acres. Within area of outstanding natural beauty woods and downland, nature trail for the blind.
Management: Goodwood Terrana Ltd.
Weald and Downland Open Air Museum
Map 4 SU81
(OS197 873126) ¼m SW of Singleton. 35 acres. Lake with woodland and meadows within area of outstanding natural beauty. Museum and historic buildings.
Management: Weal and Downland Open Air Museum.

WARWICKSHIRE
Burton Dassett Hills Map 3 SO35
(OS151 396520) 4m NE of Kineton. 100 acres. Grassland and farmland. Footpath and bridleways.
Management: Warwickshire County Council.
Coombe Abbey Map 4 SP37
(OS140 395795) 4m E of Coventry City Centre on A427, 290 acres. Gardens and woodland with lake. Boating, fishing, nature trail.
Management: Coventry Metropolitan District Council.
Hartshill Hayes
(OS140 316947) 12m N of Coventry off A47. Wood and grassland.
Management: Warwickshire County Council.
Kingsbury Map 4 SP29
(OS139 209959) 12 NE of Birmingham W of town, 1050 acres. Lakes within reclaimed gravel pits. Fishing.
Management: Warwickshire County Council.

WEST MIDLANDS
Lickey Hills Map 7 SO97
(OS139 998754) 8m S of Birmingham. 530 acres. Meadows, woodland and heath. Riding, boating.
Management: Coventry County Borough.

WILTSHIRE
Barbury Castle Map 4 SU17
(OS173 157761) 5m S of Swindon, access from M4 (Junction 15) and Swindon via A345, or A361 then B4005 from Wroughton. 130 acres of downland incorporating an important iron age fort, 'Ridgeway Path', Long Distance Route 'The Ridgeway', public paths, walking and picnicking, information display, AA Viewpoint. Vehicles restricted to car park.
Management: Wiltshire County Council.
Barton Farm Map 3 ST86
(OS173 823605) Bradford on Avon access from A363 in town centre. 36 acres of pastureland fringed by woodland following the River Avon and enclosed to the south by the Kennet and Avon Canal, access to canal towpath,

information boards, fishing by day permit from Bradford on Avon and District Angling Association, boats may be launched subject to license from the Wessex Water Authority.
No vehicles; adjacent parking at town centre car park.
Management: Wiltshire County Council.
Highwood and Hazel Wood Woodland Park Map 3 ST55
(OS183 835524) Brokerswood nr Westbury. 120 acres of preserved woodland with a 120-acre lake stocked with waterfowl and fish. The Phillips Countryside Museum of Natural History and Forestry adjoins the lake. Picnicking, woodland walks, fishing charged by the day limited to four rods, moderate entrance fee, up to three children free.
Management: Private.

YORKSHIRE (NORTH)
Brimham Rocks Map 8 SE26
(OS99 206650) 3½m NW of Ripley off B165. Unusual rock forms on elevated moorland. Café and information centre under development in old shooting lodge. Parking fee.
Management: National Trust
Church Cliff Map 8 TA18
(OS101 121814) Filey.
Management: Scarborough Borough Council.

YORKSHIRE (SOUTH)
Cannon Hall Park Map 8 SE20
(OS110 247081) 4½m W of Barnsley. 70 acres. Hall with parkland, gardens and lake. Fishing, foothpath, picnicking.
Management: Barnsley Metropolitan District Council.
Cusworth Country Park Map 8 SE50
(OS111 546038) 2m W of Doncaster nr Sprotborough. 57 acres of woodland and gardens developed from parkland of Cusworth Hall which is now a museum. History trail, fishing.
Management: Doncaster District Council.
Howell Wood Map 8 SE40
(OS111 437092) 1½m SE of South Kirby. 115 acres of woodland under development as a country park, specimen trees, nature trails.
Management: North Yorkshire County Council.
Worsborough Mill Map 8 SE30
(OS111 346033) S of Worsborough off A61. 95 acres of woodland and farmland under development as a country park around a reservoir, mill pond and working corn mill restored as an industrial museum. Interpretative centre, fishing, sailing, nature trail.
Management: North Yorkshire County Council.

YORKSHIRE (WEST)
Penistone Hill Map 8 SE03
(OS104 022367) Keighley. Heathland, old quarry workings, railway, nature trail.
Management: West Yorkshire Metropolitan County Council.

WALES

CLWYD
Erddig Park Map 7 SJ34
(OS117 335486) 1m SW Wrexham. Parkland and woodland with river. Picnic site, industrial trail, agricultural museum.
Management: National Trust.
Loggerheads Map 6 SJ16
(OS116 198629) 2m W of Mold on A494, 65 acres. Woodland in river valley. Information centre, nature trail.
Management: Clwyd County Council.
Moel Arthur Map 6 SJ16
(OS116 151625) 5m equidistant from Mold, Ruthin, Denbigh and Holywell. Access road poor. 300 acres. Moorland. Hill fort, Offa's Dyke.
Management: Clwyd County Council.
Moel Famau Map 6 SJ16
(OS116 142671) 6m W of Mold, access roads poor. 1800 acres. Moorland. Reservoir, hill fort. Offa's Dyke.
Management: Clwyd County Council.
Waun-y-Llyn Map 7 SJ25
(OS117 284582) 6m N of Wrexham, difficult access roads. 74 acres. Moorland with lake.
Management: Clwyd County Council.

DYFED
Llys-y-Fran Map 2 SN02
(OS157 036250) 8m NW of Haverfordwest. 308 acres around the 7½ mile perimeter of Llys-y-Fran reservoir, picnic sites, slipway, boat pond, details of licences for boating and fishing from the park office, information board, warden service, nature trail.
Management: County Council and Welsh National Water Development Authority.
Scolton Manor Map 2 SM92
(OS157 989219) Parkland, picnic site, nature trail.
Management: Dyfed County Council.

GLAMORGAN (MID)
Dare Valley Map 3 SN90
(OS170 975025) (Prince of Wales Award 1972) W of Aberdare. Access from A4059 N of Trecynon, through Cwmdare or from B4277 at Highland Place in Aberdare. 400 acres reclaimed from derelict land forming lakes, pools and cascades, grassland and 25 acres of mixed tree planting. Nature and Industrial Archaeology trails, walks and access to public paths, fishing, warden service.
Management: Aberdare District Council.

GLAMORGAN (SOUTH)
Cefn Onn Map 3 ST18
(OS171 175845) 3m N of Cardiff. 135 acres of ponds, arboreta and gardens. Café.
Management: Cardiff City Council.
Comeston Map 3 ST16
(OS171 175845) 1m Penarth on B42167 to Barry. 10 acres of reclaimed land. Nature conservation area with observation points, signed walks, sailing, fishing, canoeing, model boating, sub aqua diving, picnic area.
Management: Vale of Glamorgan Borough Council.
Porthkerry Park Map 3 ST06
(OS171 092672) Between Barry and Rhoose. 225 acres. A wooded valley ending at the seashore, beach, nature reserve, pitch and putt, shop.
Management: Vale of Glamorgan District Council.

GLAMORGAN (WEST)
Afan Argoed Map 3 SS89
(OS170 817950) 5m NE of Port Talbot on A4107. 140 acres, forested valley with short forest walks and longer forest trails. Countryside Centre, Welsh Miners' Museum, disabled facilities including walks, access to Afan Valley scenic route, orienteering course.
Management: West Glamorgan County Council and Forestry Commission.
Margam Park Map 3 SS88
(OS170 813849) Access 2m NW of Pyle on A48. 800 acres. A leisure park. Park and ride buses, marked walks, parkland centre. Charge for parking.
Management: West Glamorgan County Council.

GWENT
Caldicot Castle Map 3 ST48
(OS171 486884) Near Caldicot town centre. 53 acres. Parkland around castle with wooded slopes and open meadowland.
Management: Gwent County Council and Monmouth District Council.
Pen-y-Fan Pond Map 3 SO00
(OS170 019006) Access via new industrial estate road off the B4251 Blackwood to Crumlin Road. Area around a canal feeder pond with access to many public paths and providing good walking terrain. Picnic area, rowing boats for hire, fishing by permit, model boating, refreshment kiosk. Warden Service.
Management: Gwent County Council.
Tredegar House Map 3 ST28
(OS171 289854) Off A48 ½m W of Newport. Signposted in advance and at entrance. 90 acres. Grounds of Tredegar House in the process of long-term restoration to show gardening styles of various periods. Access at moderate additional charge to the house, boating lake, children's farm with bird garden and aquarium. Donkey rides, fishing, picnic site, play area, café.
Management: Gwent County Council.

GWYNEDD
Llyn Padarn Map 6 SH56
(OS124 585602) E of Llanberis. 320 acres. Wood and heathland, disused quarry containing lake. Water sports, nature trail, industrial trail, woodland walks, descriptive leaflets on site.
Management: Gwynedd County Council.

POWYS
Craig-y-Nos Map 3 SN81
(OS160 845155) 6m N of Ystradgynlais on the A4067 Swansea–Sennybridge road, 40 acres of woodland and meadow with river and artificial lake, access by footpath to Dan-yr-Ogof caves, tickets and licenses available for fishing.
Management: Brecon Beacons National Park Authority.

SCOTLAND

FIFE
Craigtown Country Park Map 12 NO41
(OS59 477142) 2½m SW of St Andrews. Off unclassified road from B939 in St Andrews to Pitscottie. 50 acres.

GRAMPIAN
Haddo Country Park Map 15 NJ83
(OS30 NJ867346) 20m N Aberdeen on B9005. 180 acres of mature parkland with lake and mixed woodland supporting a variety of wildlife. Picnic sites, footpaths, information service, ranger service.
Management: Grampian Regional Council.

LOTHIAN
Almondell and Calderwood Country Park Map 11 NT06
(OS65 076676 & 092696) 10 W Edinburgh, 2m S Broxburn in Almond Valley, access from Mid and East Calder. Access signposted from A8 at Broxburn. Almondell between A98 and A71, Calderwood S of A71. Lies in a natural gorge featuring woodland and an artificial waterway. 240 acres. Nature trails, picnic areas, riverside and woodland walks, barbecue site, 90 acres. Calderwood has been left completely undeveloped, 130 acres, car parks, ranger service.
Management: Lothian County Council.
Beecraigs Country Park Map 11 NS97
(OS65 993742-998741) 2m S of Linlithgow. Mixed woodlands, grassland, loch and burns, 700 acres. Trout farm, deer farm, picnic and barbecue sites, orienteering course, daily permit fishing, ranger service.
Management: Lothian County Council.
John Muir Country Park Map 11 NT67
(OS67 678792) W of Dunbar access from A1087 via three car parks; Linkfield, Shore Road, Belhaven and Castle Park, Dunbar. Coastal area of great natural beauty offering marked walks, cliff top walk, barbecue area, ranger service.
Management: East Lothian District Council.

STRATHCLYDE
Culzean Maybole Map 10 NS21
(OS70 231102) Between Maidens and Dunure on A719. Castle and 531 acre estate with restored gardens, wooded walks, ponds, cliff walk, access to shore with dunes and rock pools, ranger naturalist service, park centre with exhibition and shop.
Management: National Trust for Scotland and Local Authorities.
Muirshiel Country Park Map 10 NS36
(OS63 318631) Signposted from Loch Winnoch, access by road through Calder Glen. High valley amidst moorland, mixed habitat of moor, woodland and river. Picnic sites, nature trail. Information Centre, ranger service.
Management: Strathclyde Regional Council.
Castle Semple Water Park Map 10 NS35
(OS63 362596) Signposted from Loch Winnoch. Large loch, launching facilities for sailing craft, rowing boats and canoes, hiring facilities for craft, angling facilities. Warden Service.
Management: Strathclyde Regional Council.
Cornalees Bridge Centre Map 10 NS27
(OS63 249724) Beside moorland road from Greenock to Inverkip at the head of Shielhill Glen. Moorland and wooded glen. Walking trail, Information Centre, ranger service.
Management: Strathclyde Regional Council.
Palacerigg Map 11 NS77
(OS64 788738) 2m SE of Cumbernauld. 614 acres.
Strathclyde Regional Park Map 11 NS75
(OS64 715586) N and S of M74 between Hamilton and Motherwell. Access from A725 at M74 Junction 5. Constructed by clearance and excavation of derelict land and diversion of the River Clyde. 2000 acres including 200 acre artificial loch. Picnic areas, nature reserves, areas of scientific interest, scheduled areas of historical interest, sailing, canoeing, fishing, national rowing centre, ranger service.
Management: Strathclyde Park Joint Committee.

Answers to quiz on page 246

A Red squirrels
B Grey squirrel
C Common toad
D Wood mice
E Magpie
F Great tit
G Wren
H Hedgehog
J Stoat
K Badger

Picnic Sites

All AA-listed picnic sites have been visited by an AA inspector and recommended as worthy of listing because they are sufficiently attractive and/or provide useful 'park and walk' access to the countryside.

A Transit Picnic Site may, though well equipped, be utilitarian in character but will be suitable for breaking long journeys for rest and refreshment.

ENGLAND

AVON

Crabtree Slipwood Map 3 ST57 ***(A4)*** 1m E of M5 junction at Avonmouth on A4. (OS172 542767). Signposted in advance and at entrance on undulating ground with access to river. 2 acres. Access to wooded area, furniture. Toilets. Parking 20.

Ashton Park Map 3 ST57 ***(Off A369)*** 1m W of Bristol centre off A369/A370 (OS172 550725). Well maintained, open parkland with wooded areas. 100 acres. Nature trail, deer park, putting course, drinking water. Toilets. Parking 100.

Tog Hill Map 3 ST77 ***(A420)*** 8m E of Bristol, ½m E of junction with A46 (OS172 734728). Signposted in advance and at entrance. Elevated site with spectacular views. 2 acres. Drinking water, furniture. Chemical toilets. Parking 80.

Chew Valley Lake Map 3 ST56 ***(Off B3114)*** 8m S of Bristol centre on NE side of lake, on unclassified road from B3114 (OS172 577613). Signposted in advance and at entrance. 4 acres attractively landscaped area of grassy mounds, shrubs and trees. Drinking water, furniture, toilet facilities for the disabled, local sailing and fishing. Cafeteria with outdoor seats or takeaway Apr–Oct each day Nov–Mar Sat and Sun only. Toilets. Parking 100.

BEDFORDSHIRE

In Stockgrove Country Park Map 4 SP92 ***(Off A418)*** On unclassified road ½m W of A418, 3m NW of Leighton Buzzard (OS165 917298). Signposted in advance and at entrance. Situated among hills and woodland. Drinking water, furniture, lake. Toilets.

Brogborough Hill Map 4 SP93 ***(A5140)*** On W side of A5140, 3½m NE of Woburn Sands (OS153 964386). Hilltop site. Drinking water, furniture. Toilets. Parking 50.

Totternhoe Knolls Map 4 SP92 ***(B489)*** 2m W of Dunstable, on E side of unclassified road off B489 (OS165 986216). Signposted in advance and at entrance. In village of Totternhoe. 3 acres. Good views, furniture, access to Norman Castle.

Whipsnade Heath and Green Map 4 TL01 ***(Off B4540)*** Off B4540 adjacent to Whipsnade Zoo (OS166 006178). Open grass area. 10 acres. Extensive parking. Toilets.

Dunstable Downs Map 4 TL02 ***(B4541)*** W side of B4541, 2m SW of Dunstable (OS166 007200). Signposted in advance and at entrance. Overlooking the Vale of Aylesbury. Information centre, refreshments, gliding activities.

BERKSHIRE

Childe Beale Trust Map 4 SU67 ***(A329)*** 2m NW of Pangbourne on A32 (OS175 626772). 15 acres. Panoramic view of Thames, peacock farm, ornamental stonework display. Parking 100.

Bracknell/Bagshot road Transit Picnic Site Map 4 SU96 ***(A332)*** ½m S of Hartford on S side of A556 (OS 186 904640). Toilets.

Alexandra Gardens Map 4 SU97 ***(Off A332 in Windsor)*** Access via car park in River Street or Barry Avenue on S side of Thames (OS175 962772). Riverside gardens. 8 acres. Drinking water, furniture. Toilets. Parking 200.

Windsor Great Park Map 4 SU97 ***(A332)*** Ascot road, 2m S of Windsor (OS175 960740). Signposted in advance and at entrance. Parking.

Marlow-Bisham by-pass (East) Map 4 SU88 ***(A404)*** On E side of Marlow-Bisham by-pass, 2½m S of Marlow (OS175 849843). Signposted in advance and at entrance. Parking 30.

Marlow-Bisham by-pass (West) Map 4 SU88 ***(A404)*** On W side of Marlow-Bisham by-pass, 3m S of Marlow (OS175 843828). Signposted in advance and at entrance. Parking 30.

Winter Hill, near Marlow Map 4 SU88 ***(Off A404)*** First turn left on S side of Marlow Bridge. After approx 2m on unclassified Marlow/Cookham road, fork left (OS175 875863). Grassy area with beech trees, high above River Thames. 3 acres. Furniture. Parking 50.

BUCKINGHAMSHIRE

Burnham Beeches Map 4 SU98 ***(Off A355)*** On unclassified road ½m W of A355 at Farnham Common (OS175 951851). Extensive site in forest setting. Woodland walks, shelters, first aid post, furniture, drinking water. Toilets. Large parking area.

Chilterns Picnic Place (Hodgemoor Wood) Map 4 SU99 ***(Off A355)*** ¼m E of A355 via Bottrells Lane; Amersham, Beaconsfield 3m (OS175 958942). Woodland setting in Chiltern Hills. Extensive area. Parking 200.

Wendover Forest Map 4 SP80 ***(Off A4011)*** SE of A4011 on unclassified road, signposted St Leonards, 2m NE of Wendover, 3m SW of Tring (OS165 889090). Signposted at entrance. An extensive and picturesque woodland site high in the Chilterns with excellent views from several vantage points. Walks and nature trails, information board and map, furniture. Toilets with provision for the disabled.

CAMBRIDGESHIRE

Grafham Water Map 4 TL16 ***(A1)*** 2m off A1 on B661, approx 2m from Buckden (OS153 170685). Signposted in advance and at entrance. Excellent views over Grafham Water. 3 acres. Toilets. Parking 600.

Brandon Creek Map 5 TL69 ***(A10)*** 2½m N of Littleport Bridge on A10 (OS143 608918). Signposted in advance and at entrance. Landscaped ground sloping to River Ouse. 4 acres. Drinking water, furniture, toilet with facilities for the disabled. Parking 100.

Eaton Ford Picnic Area Map 4 TL18 ***(A45)*** Western outskirts of St Neots (OS153 180600). Signposted at entrance. 3 acres, grassy tree-planted riverside site. Furniture. Toilets. Parking 60.

Houghton Mill Map 4 TL27 ***(A1123)*** 1¼m out of Wyton towards Houghton, in Mill Street (OS153 281720). A field sloping down to the River Ouse, subject to flooding. 10 acres. Toilets. Parking (fee).

CHESHIRE

Oulton Park Map 7 SJ56 ***(A49)*** Near Oulton Park, ½m from A49 (OS117 580640).

Overton Hill Map 7 SJ57 ***(Off A56)*** 2¼m from Helsby (OS117 517768).

Hartford Transit Picnic Site Map 7 SJ67 ***(A556)*** ½m S of Hartford on S side of A556 (OS118 640712). Toilets.

Lostock Transit Picnic Site Map 7 SJ67 ***(A556)*** ½m W of Lostock Green on N side A556 (OS117 691736). Toilets.

Delamere Forest Map 7 SJ57 ***(Off B5152)*** 1m N of Delamere off B5152 (OS117 555700). AA Viewpoint.

CORNWALL

Tregadillet Transit Picnic Site Map 2 SX38 ***(A30)*** 2m W of Launceston on A30 (OS201 305842). Toilets.

Treliever Map 2 SW73 ***(A394)*** 1½m W of Penryn (OS204 767350). Signposted in advance and at entrance. Tarmac parking area with grassed picnic section protected by 5ft banks. Drinking water, furniture. Toilets. Parking 25.

CUMBRIA

Brockhole Map 7 NY30 ***(A591)*** $2\frac{1}{2}$m N of Windermere, $2\frac{1}{2}$m S of Ambleside (OS90 391011). $\frac{1}{2}$ acre. Parking 20.

Waterhead Transit Picnic Site Map 7 NY30 ***(A5075/A591)*** $\frac{1}{2}$m SE of Ambleside (NY377032). Toilets.

Aira Force Map 11 NY32 ***(A5091/A592)*** 6m SW of Pooley Bridge (OS90 398201). Signposted at entrance. National Trust property. 50 acres. View of Ullswater and fells, waterfall and woodland walks, furniture, no caravans in car park, no camping. Parking 100.

Stock Lane Transit Picnic Site Map 7 NY30 ***(B5287)*** 300yds Grasmere Village (OS90 338074). Toilets.

Ouse Bridge Map 11 NY23 ***(Off B5291)*** 6m E of Cockermouth (OS90 200322). Signposted in advance and at entrance. $\frac{1}{2}$ acre. Footpath to Bassenthwaite. Parking 20.

Whinlatter Map 11 NY22 ***(B5292)*** 1m from Braithwaite (OS90 230237). Signposted in advance and at entrance. $\frac{1}{2}$ acre. Extensive view of valley and lake. Parking 20.

Allonby & Beckfoot Map 11 NY04 ***(B5300)*** On B5300, on the coast, within the parish of Allonby (OS85 080430). Signposted in advance and at entrance. View across Solway Firth. Furniture. Toilets. Parking 100.

DERBYSHIRE

White Lodge Map 7 SK17 ***(A6)*** On W side 4m W of Bakewell (OS119 165709). Signposted in advance and at entrance. 3 acres. Useful access point to Monsal Dale, information board giving details of local walks, furniture, portaloo. Parking 40.

Alsop en le Dale Station Map 7 SK15 ***(A515)*** On Ashbourne-Buxton road $5\frac{1}{2}$m N of Ashbourne (OS119 156549). Signposted entrance. On former station site lying on the line of the Buxton Ashbourne Railway now the Tissington Trail, furniture. Parking 60.

Hurdlow Map 7 SK16 ***(Off A515)*** $\frac{1}{4}$m W of A515, Monyash–Longnor road (OS119 127659). Signposted at entrance. Access to Tissington trail, furniture. Parking 50.

Parsley Hay Map 7 SK16 ***(Off A515)*** 200yds on W side of A515 $8\frac{1}{2}$m S of Buxton (OS119 147636). Signposted in advance and at entrance. 2 acres. Former railway station site on junction between Tissington and High Peak Trails. Cycles for hire April–October, drinking water, furniture. Toilets. Parking 60.

Tissington Map 7 SK15 ***(Off A515)*** SE Corner of Tissington Village $\frac{1}{2}$m E of A515 (OS119 177521). Signposted at entrance. 2 acres. Situated on the Tissington Trail, drinking water, furniture. Toilets. Parking 60.

Ashover (Eddlestow) Map 8 SK36 ***(Off A632)*** Off A632 (SP Uppertown) $2\frac{1}{2}$m NE of Matlock (OS119 324632). Signposted in advance and at entrance. 3 acres. Map of area, furniture. Parking 20.

Staunton Harrold Reservoir Map 8 SK32 ***(Off B587)*** 1m SW of Melbourne. Turn W off B587 along Calke Lane (OS128 379237). Lawns planted with young trees. 2 acres. Observation tower, drinking water. Toilets. Parking 70.

Middleton Top Map 8 SK25 ***(Off B5023)*** S of Rise End, W of B5023 via unclassified road under old railway bridge. 1m NW of Wirksworth (OS120 275551). 1 acre. Access to High Peak Trail, Middleton Top Power House, drinking water, furniture. Toilets. Parking 25.

Black Rocks Map 8 SK25 ***(Off B5036)*** E of B5036, $\frac{3}{4}$m S of Cromford (OS119 292557). 5 acres. Signposted in advance and at entrance. Extensive area. Access to High Peak Trail, drinking water, furniture. Toilets. Parking 25.

Hartington Map 7 SK16 ***(Off B5054)*** $1\frac{1}{2}$m NE of Hartington (OS119 150611). Signposted at entrance. $1\frac{1}{2}$ acres. On the site of old Moneystones Station on the Tissington Trail, drinking water, furniture. Toilets. Parking 60.

Ogston Reservoir (North) Map 8 SK36 ***(Off B6014)*** 2m SW of Clay Cross on N side of B6014, on unclassified road at Woolley (OS119 368613). Signposted, 'car park'. Grass area fenced from water. 5 acres. Drinking water. Toilets.

Ogston Reservoir (West) Map 8 SK36 ***(Off B6014)*** S side of B6014 at N end of reservoir (OS119 369608). Signposted at entrance. Grass area, $\frac{1}{2}$ acre. Drinking water. Toilets. Parking 25.

DEVON

Honiton Clyst Map 3 SX99 ***(A30)*** 1m E of Honiton Clyst (OS192 993941). Signposted in advance and at entrance. Adjacent to Exeter Airport. 1 acre. Furniture. Parking 30.

Tamar Bridge Transit Picnic Site Map 2 SX45 ***(A38)*** At E end of bridge on A38. (OS201 438587). Toilets. Parking 50.

Trimstone Cross Map 2 SS54 ***(Off A361)*** 1m SW of Mullacott Cross (OS180 501435). Advance signposting. Old road adjacent to grass area. $3\frac{1}{2}$ acres. Furniture. Parking 60.

Morwellham Map 2 SX46 ***(Off A390)*** In Tamar Valley 4m SW of Tavistock, 1m S of A390 (OS201 446695). Old iron-ore river port of historical interest. Drinking water, furniture. Toilets. Parking 100.

Stoke Woods Map 3 SX99 ***(Off A396)*** 3m N of Exeter (SX 928962). Signposted in advance and at entrance. Woodland, 113 acres. Woodland trails. Parking 30.

Bellever Map 2 SX67 ***(Off B3212)*** $1\frac{1}{4}$m S of B3212 at Postbridge (SX 654775). Moorland, 1 acre. Bridle paths. Toilets. Parking 100.

Newbridge, Holne Map 3 SX77 ***(B3357)*** 4m W of Ashburton (OS191 711709). Signposted in advance and at entrance. Moorland, woodland walks: 8 acres. Toilets. Parking 100.

Fernworthy Reservoir Map 2 SX68 ***(Unclassified Rd)*** Approach via unclassified rds 3.7m SW of Chagford (OS191 669838). Signposted at entrance. Near forest and reservoir. 1 acre. Forest trail, signed walks. Furniture. Toilets including facilities for disabled. Parking 50.

DORSET

Higher Kingston Transit Picnic Site Map 3 SY79 ***(A35)*** On A35 $2\frac{1}{4}$m E of Dorchester N side. Wide tarmacadam layby. (OS194 724929). Toilets. Parking 40.

Thorncombe Wood Map 3 SY79 ***(Off A35)*** $2\frac{1}{2}$m E of Dorchester on unclassified road signposted to Higher/Lower Bockhampton (OS194 728925). Signposted in advance and at entrance. Example of a neglected area being reinstated to attractive woodland 45 acres. Map display and leaflets, marked trails, furniture. Parking 30.

Bulbarrow Hill Map 3 ST70 ***(Off A354)*** 5m S Sturminster Newton on unclassified road off A354 signposted from Bulbarrow Crossroads (OS194 775055). Gravelled area on hill top with AA view point.

Matchams View Map 4 SX10 ***(A358)*** 7m NE Bournemouth on E side of unclassified road (OS195 134024). Signposted at entrance. Peaceful wooded area on plateau with winding river, approach through heathland. 30 acres. Parking 40.

Bishops Lime Kiln Map 3 ST72 ***(B3157)*** $\frac{1}{2}$m from Abbotsbury off B3157 on narrow steep unclassified road from centre of Abbotsbury. 1 acre. (OS194 754215). Signposted at entrance. Remote rural setting with well-preserved remains of lime kiln. Explanatory metal tablet, panoramic views to Chesil Beach. Furniture. Parking 12.

Ibberton Hill Map 3 ST70 ***(Unclassified Rd)*** 5m S of Sturminster Newton/Blandford A357 on unclassified road through Okeford Fitzpaine. (OS194 784071). Signposted at entrance. Elevated grassy slopes overlooking rural Dorset. 10 acres. Parking 100.

DURHAM

Middleton-One-Row Map 8 NX31 ***(Off A67)*** 5m SE of Darlington off A67 (OS93 350125). Signposted in advance. River, trees and views of Cleveland Hills, deep riverbank with paths. Furniture. Toilets. Parking at roadside.

Picnic Sites

Whorlton Map 12 NZ11 ***(Off A67)***
3½m SE Barnard Castle off A67
(OS92 108146). Advance signposting to village only. 10 acres field beside a river. Drinking water. Toilets. Parking 100 (fee).
Collier Wood Map 12 NZ13 ***(A68)***
½m N of junction with A689 midway between Crook and Tow Law (OS92 128364). Signposted in advance and at entrance. Mixed woodland area. 8 acres, nature trail, information boards, drinking water, furniture. Toilets. Parking 40.
Swan House Map 8 NZ22 ***(A68)***
At junction with A6072 4m NW of Darlington on A68 (OS93 252200). 1½ acres.
Park Wall Map 12 NZ13 ***(Off A68)***
1m S of Tow Law (OS92 131379). 11 acres.
Witton le Wear Map 12 NZ13 ***(A68)***
E of A68, ½m S of Witton le Wear (OS92 147307). 15 acres. Castle, paddling pool, snack bar, drinking water, furniture. Toilets.
Witton le Wear Lido Map 12 NZ13 ***(A68)***
½m S of Witton le Wear (OS92 148307). Riverside area suitable for children. 2 acres. Drinking water. Toilets. Unlimited parking (fee).
Finchale Priory Map 12 NZ24 ***(A167)***
2½m N of Durham. Turn right on to unclassified road at Pity Me and continue for 1¾m (OS88 296472). Wooded priory grounds with river. 10 acres. Drinking water, furniture. Toilets. Unlimited parking.
Holmland Park Transit Picnic Site
Map 12 NZ25 ***(A167)*** ½m from Chester-Le-Street on A167 (OS88 270535).
Crimdon Park Map 8 NZ43 ***(A1086)***
A1086 4m N of Hartlepool (OS88 483370). Signposted in advance. 25 acres. Beach bathing, day chalets, first aid box, furniture. Toilets. Parking 560.
Carricks Picnic Area Map 12 NZ95 ***(B6278)***
1½m E of Blanchland 5m W of Consett, N of B6278, adjacent to Derwent Reservoir and the River Derwent (OS87 976505). Large grassed area. 3 acres.
Cowhill Map 12 NZ05 ***(B6306)***
SE side of Derwent Reservoir on B6306 (OS87 010520).
Shotley Bridge Map 12 NZ15 ***(B6310)***
At Shotley Bridge, 1m N of Consett on A694, take B6310 for ¾m (OS88 104535). Former station yard with access to Derwent Walk. 3 acres.
Hamsterley Forest
Map 12 NZ03 ***(Unclassified road)***
Hamsterley is signposted from Witton le Wear off A68 (OS92 073305). Extensive area of wooded hills. Drinking water, furniture, swimming pool. toilets. Unlimited parking (fee).

ESSEX

One Tree Hill Map 5 TQ68 ***(A13/B1420)***
2m SW of Basildon, N of A13 near junction with B1420 (OS177 695860). Good views of surrounding area. 6 acres. Toilets. Parking 350.
Weald Park Map 5 TQ59 ***(Off A28)***
On unclassified road off A28 at Pilgrims Hatch. 2m NW of Brentwood (OS177 570945). Signposted at entrance. Extensive area. Drinking water. Parking 200.
In Thorndon Country Park (North)
Map 5 TQ69 ***(A128)*** Off 'The Avenue', A128, 1m SE of Brentwood (OS177 605915). Densely wooded with bracken and grass. 100 acres.
In Thorndon Country Park (South)
Map 5 TQ69 ***(A128)*** At E Hordon on W side of A128, ½m N of junction with A127 (OS177 631900). Furniture. Parking 200.
Naze Point Map 5 TM22 ***(Off A136)***
N of Walton-on-the-Naze. E side of Old Hall Lane via Esplanade and Naze Park Road. (OS169 264234). Grassy clifftop area. Nature trail. No caravans or tents. Toilets. Parking 300.
Danbury Park Lake Map 5 TL70 ***(Off A414)***
Adjoins Well Lane SW side of Danbury Bridge, off A414 (OS167 765048). Advance signposting. Shrubs and grass areas amidst woods and parkland centred on well maintained lake. furniture. Toilets. Parking 80.

GLOUCESTERSHIRE

Peters Cross Transit Picnic Site
Map 3 ST59 ***(A48)*** On the Lydney to Chepstow section of the A48 1m SW of Alvington (OS 162 589993). Signposted at entrance. Toilets.
Edge End Map 3 SO51 ***(A4136)***
On A4136, 2½m E of Coleford (OS162 595135). Signposted in advance and at entrance. On the edge of the Forest of Dean. 1 acre. Signed forest walks, drinking water, furniture. Toilets closed in winter. Parking 50.
Coaley Peak Picnic Site
Map 3 SO70 ***(Off B4066)*** 2½m N of Ilney (OS162 795014). Signposted in advance and at entrance. A superb viewpoint near a gliding centre. Furniture. Toilets. Ample parking.
Beechenhurst Map 3 SO61 ***(B4226)***
2¾m W of Cinderford ½m W of Speech House. (OS 162 603119). Forestry Commission sign at entrance. 5 acres in Forest of Dean. Drinking water, furniture. Toilets closed in winter. Parking 150.
Cannop Ponds Map 3 SO61 ***(B4226)***
3¼m W of Cinderford 1m W of Speech House (OS 162 609106). Signposted in advance and at entrance. Around two small lakes in secluded area of Forest of Dean. 2 acres. Signed forest trails. Parking 15.
Speech House Map 3 SO61 ***(B4226)***
3m W of Cinderford on outskirts of Speech House Village (OS 162 622125). Forestry Commission sign at entrance. Attractive easily-accessible site in Forest of Dean.
4 acres. Signed forest walks, aboretum, drinking water, refreshment kiosk, furniture. Toilets. Parking 50.
Lambsquay Map 3 SO50 ***(B4228)***
1m S of Coleford (OS 162 582089). Signposted at entrance, screened parking areas planted with young trees. Furniture. Toilets. Parking 120.
Robinswood Hill Map 3 SO81 ***(Gloucester)***
2m S of City Centre, enter from Reservoir Road, off Ring Road (OS162 835150). Signposted at entrance. In Country park. 30 acres. Furniture, snack bar, toilets for disabled, toilets closed weekdays. Parking 60.

HAMPSHIRE

Danebury Ring Map 4 SU33 ***(Off A30)***
2½m NW of Stockbridge on unclassified road (OS185 328378). Site of AA tree planting scheme. Iron-age hill fort. Nature trail, drinking water. Toilets. Parking 80.
Hawley Common Map 4 SU85 ***(A30)***
On S side of A30, 4m SW of Camberley (OS175 845575). 5 acres. Small lake, drinking water, furniture. Signposted in advance and at entrance. Toilets. Parking 200.
Picnic Site (Bolderwood Ornamental Drive)
Map 4 SU20 ***(A31)*** 3m NW of Emery Down on the Ornamental Drive between the A31 and A35 (OS195 242087). Signposted in advance and at entrance. Gravelled clearing in the forest giving access to a number of picnic areas. Marked walks, deer sanctuary, descriptive leaflets, furniture, Chemical toilets. Parking 100.
Stoney Cross Map 4 SU21 ***(A31)***
In New Forest 2m W of Cadnam off A31 (OS195 248128). 2 acres.
Old Winchester Hill Map 4 SU62 ***(Off A32)***
From Warnford or West Meon (OS185 648212). Signposted in advance and at entrance. Nature reserve. 149 acres. Walks, furniture. Parking 150 (on lay-bys).
Southampton Common Map 4 SU41 ***(A33)***
On A33 London road, 1½m from city centre (OS196 415145). Open commonland with some wooded areas. 328 acres. Paddling pool, model boating lake, drinking water, furniture. Toilets. Extensive parking on access roads only.
Beacon Hill Transit Picnic Site
Map 4 SU45 ***(A34)*** 2½m N of Litchfield (OS174 460573). Toilets.
The Bench Map 4 SU30 ***(A35)***
On A35 on E side of Lyndhurst (OS196 305081). 50 acres area in New Forest. Furniture. Parking 70.
Rhinefield, Putter Bridge, Whitfield Moor
Map 4 SU20 ***(A35)*** 2m W of Brockenhurst on unclassified road adjacent to A35 (OS195 272030). Signposted in advance and at entrance. Leaflets on walks and facilities at Whitfield House at entrance. Toilets. Parking 500.

Portsdown Map 4 SU60 ***(A333)*** Near Portsmouth (OS196 662063). AA Viewpoint used as picnic site with good view of Portsmouth Harbour. 150 acres. Unlimited parking.
Crab Wood Map 4 SU42 ***(Off A3090)*** 2½m W of Winchester on unclassified road off A3090 (OS185 432293). Thickly wooded area. 197½ acres. Unlimited parking.
Abbotstone Down Map 4 SU53 ***(B3046)*** On the B3046 2m N of Alresford (OS185 585362). Signposted at entrance. Extensive area of grass clearing in wood and scrubland. Signed footpaths to Aylesford, Itchen Abbas, Winchester, Micheldever and Preston Candover. Furniture. Toilets May–Sep. Parking 350.
Avington Park Map 4 SU53 ***(Off B3047)*** 1m S of Itchen Abbas next to Avington House (OS185 533322). No toilets. Parking 300.
Mayflower Park Map 4 SU41 ***(Southampton)*** At Royal Pier (OS196 416111). Signposted at entrance. Overlooking Southampton Water and new docks. 10 acres.

HEREFORD and WORCESTER
Ross Spur Service Station Transit Picnic Site Map 3 SO62 ***(M50)*** ½m N of Ross-on-Wye on M50 (OS162 613257). Toilets.
Fish Hill Map 4 SP13 ***(A44)*** 1m S Broadway (OS150 117370). Signposted in advance and at entrance. 2 acres. Summit of Fish Hill planted with trees and shrubs. Drinking water, furniture. Toilets. Unlimited parking.
Goodrich Castle Map 3 SO52 ***(A40)*** Ross to Monmouth road 3½m Ross (OS162 577200). Signposted in advance and at entrance. 3½ acres. Near entrance to a ruined castle in woods and farmland. Drinking water, furniture. Disabled toilet. Parking 300.
Symonds Yat West Garders Restaurant Map 3 SO51 ***(Off A40)*** 6m Ross on B4164 off A40 (OS162 558158). Signposted at entrance. 4 acres open grassed area with footpath to River Wye, hire boats and small fairground. Drinking water, furniture. Parking 300 (fee).
Symonds Yat Rock East Map 3 SO51 ***(Off A40)*** 5½m Ross (OS162 564161). Signposted at entrance 4½ acres. Large woodland area in the Forest of Dean. Access to extensive walk, cafe, information bureau, furniture. Toilets. Parking 100.
Bromyard Downs Map 3 SO65 ***(Off A44)*** Between A44 and B4203 NE of Bromyard (OS149 673555). Large area of common land with spectacular views overlooking Bromyard and surrounding area. Furniture. Parking unlimited grassed pull-ins off minor roads.
Dinmore Hill Map 3 SO55 ***(A49)*** At Queens Wood on Leominster/Hereford road (OS149 507516). 500 acres of woodland. Cafe. Parking 500.
Riverside Map 3 SO62 ***(Off A49)*** Ross-on-Wye (OS162 607246). 10 acres, grassed area planted with shrubs on bank of the River Wye. Furniture. Toilets. Parking 100.
Riverside Evesham Map 4 SP04 ***(A435)*** Abbey Road, Evesham (OS150 035433). 20 acres meadowland adjacent to tree lined banks of River Avon. Drinking water, furniture. Toilets. Parking 250. Fee.
Lower Malvern Common Map 3 SO74 ***(A449)*** Situated N of road entering from Worcester (OS150 778470). 4 acres of common land with various parking areas. Furniture. Parking 60 (fee).
Riverside, Stourport on Severn Map 7 SO87 ***(Off A451)*** Off A451 ½m W of Stourport town centre (OS138 805713). Signposted in advance, 'Riverside Car Park'. 80 acres tree-planted, grassed and landscaped area. Steamer trips, motor boat hire, children's playground, paddling pool, access to riverside fairground, furniture, drinking water. Disabled toilets. Parking extensive (fee).
Wyre Forest Map 7 SO77 ***(A456)*** 2½m from Bewdley to Leominster (OS138 750739). Signposted at entrance. Extensive area in coniferous forest, numerous walks, information centre, furniture, drinking water. Disabled toilets. Parking 50.
Walton Hill Map 7 SO98 ***(Off A456)*** On unclassified road 2m SSW of Halesowen. Off A456 signposted Kidderminster (OS139 944805). Extensive area. Hill adjacent to Clent Country Park. Panoramic view from summit approached by steep path from the car park. Parking 100.
Ross Spur Service Area Eastbound and Westbound (Transit Picnic Site) Map 3 SO62 ***(A449)*** Nr junction with M50. 1m Ross-on-Wye (OS162 613235). Signposted in advance and at entrance. Situated at rear and side of garage. Toilets. Parking 50 per side.
Clent Hills Map 7 SO97 ***(A491)*** On unclassified road off A491 SW of Hagley (OS139 933795). Signposted in advance and at entrance. 2,000 acres. Parking 150.
Hartlebury Common Map 7 SO87 ***(A4025)*** Access from either A4025 or B4193 (OS138 825705). Signposted at entrance. 15 acres. Area of commonland with trees and gorse. Footpaths. Parking unlimited.
Avoncroft Museum of Buildings Picnic Site Map 3 SO96 ***(off A4024)*** Just off the A4024, 2m S of Bromsgrove (OS139 955685). Signposted in advance and at entrance. Close-cropped grass under trees. 3½ acres. Drinking water, refreshment facilities. Toilets. Parking 160.
Beacon Hill Map 7 SO97 ***(B4096)*** Monument lane off B4096 4m NE of Bromsgrove (OS139 995758). Signposted at entrance. 523 acres. Viewpoint with pedestal-mounted map and telescope on Beacon Hill, drinking water, furniture. Parking 200.
Hartlebury Castle Map 7 SO87 ***(B4193)*** Near Hartlebury Village (OS138 840713). Grass picnic area 60yds from car park in castle grounds. Furniture. Parking 60.
Castlemorton Common Map 3 SO73 ***(B4208)*** On B4208, Malvern–Gloucester Road, 1m S of Welland (OS150 785392). Signposted in advance and at entrance. 50 acres open common land. Unlimited parking.
Wyche Cutting Map 3 SO74 ***(B4232)*** 3m SW of Great Malvern on B4232 (OS150 768435). Signposted 'The Wyche' in advance. Good views of Malverns and surrounding countryside. Toilets. Parking 30.
Malvern Hills Map 3 SO74 ***(B4232)*** On B4232 between A449 and A4105 (OS150 769435). Signposted in advance. Extensive open area piped with spring water. Drinking water. Furniture. Parking 1000 (fee).
Old Hills Map 3 SO84 ***(B4424)*** 1m S of Callow End on B4424 (OS150 829487) Commonland with views of Malverns. Numerous entrances, furniture.
Waseley Hill Map 7 SO97 ***(B4551)*** 3m S of Halesowen on unclassified road off B4551 (OS196 976779). Signposted in advance and at entrance. 130 acres, elevated open grassland. Furniture. Parking 100.
Ravenshill Nature Reserve and Picnic Site Map 3 SO75 ***(Unclassified road)*** 1m N of Alfrick (OS150 738537). Signposted in advance and at entrance. 10 acres in woodland, natural history museum, drinking water, furniture. Toilets. Parking 15.

HERTFORDSHIRE
Aldenham Reservoir Map 4 TQ19 ***(A411)*** Entrance on unclassified road running N from A411, ¼m W of Elstree (OS176 172953). Signposted from A5 and A41 in advance and at entrance. Excellently laid out site overlooking reservoir. Drinking water. Toilets.
Stanborough Park Map 4 TL21 ***(Off A6129)*** Off A6129 E of junction with A1 at Welwyn Garden City (OS166 220110). Signposted in advance and at entrance. Lakeside setting. 20 acres. Additional charges for use of heated open-air swimming pool, boating and sailing facilities, furniture. Toilets. Parking 250 (fee).
Great Wood Map 4 TL20 ***(B157)*** On N side of B157, 1¼m W of Cuffley (OS166 285038). Signposted in advance and at entrance. Clearings in extensive forested area. Well marked paths, furniture. Toilets. Parking 50 (fee at peak periods).

Picnic Sites

HUMBERSIDE
Raventhorpe Farm Map 8 SE90 ***(A18)*** N side of junction with B1398, access for Eastbound traffic (OS112 937075). Old road screened by hedgerow. 2 acres.

ISLE OF WIGHT
Parkhurst Forest Map 8 SZ49 ***(A3054)*** 1m W of Newport (OS196 479903). Signposted at entrance. 1000-acre forest. Nature trails, furniture. Parking 30.
Afton Down Map 4 SZ38 ***(A3055)*** On A3055, $\frac{1}{2}$m E of Freshwater Bay (OS196 353855). Signposted in advance and at entrance. National Trust land overlooking Freshwater Bay. 1 acre. Parking 30.
Brading Down Map 4 SZ58 ***(Off A3055)*** (OS196 590870). Overlooking Sandown and Shanklin. 10 acres. Parking 100.
Blackgang Viewpoint Map 4 SZ47 ***(A3055)*** 1m W of Niton (OS196 488768). Signposted in advance and at entrance. National Trust area overlooking SW coast of the island. 1 acre. Furniture. Parking 30.
Bembridge Down Map 4 SZ68 ***(Off B3395)*** On unclassified road off B3395, $2\frac{1}{2}$m W of Bembridge (OS196 627859). National Trust property and AA Viewpoint overlooking coast. 5 acres. Parking 100.
Brightstone Forest Map 4 SZ48 ***(Off B3401)*** On unclassified road between Calbourne and Brightstone (OS196 420847). Signposted at entrance. National Trust. 400 acres. Nature trails to the forest. Parking 60.

KENT
Shepherds Gate Transit Picnic Site Map 5 TQ66 ***(A2)*** At B2009 interchange, $3\frac{1}{2}$m W of Rochester (OS177 680695). Toilets.
Hothfield Common Transit Picnic Site Map 5 TQ94 ***(A20)*** Both sides of A20. Ashford 4m. Chaving $3\frac{1}{2}$m (OS189 971460). Toilets.
Groveferry, Upstreet Map 5 TR26 ***(Off A28)*** S side of railway level crossing along Grove Ferry Road, $\frac{1}{4}$m SE of its junction with the A28 (OS179 235632). Signposted in advance. Grassed area with shrubs, along River Stour. Boat moorings, fishing by permit. Toilets. Parking 20.
Dryhill Quarry Transit Picnic Site Map 5 TQ45 ***(off A25)*** E side of Dryhill Lane 3/10m S A25 (W side A25/A21 interchange) SE of Sundridge. (OS188 497552). Toilets.
Camer Park Map 5 TQ66 ***(Off A227)*** S side of Green Lane (B2009) off A227 $\frac{1}{2}$m N of Meopham (OS177 655669). Signposted in advance from both directions, and at entrance for southbound traffic. Headroom 7ft 6in. Extensive area of well-kept grass under trees. Drinking water, furniture. Toilets. Parking 25.
Langdon Cliff Map 5 TR35 ***(Off A258)*** At bend on unclassified Dover/St Margaret's at Cliff road, 1m E of junction with A258 at Dover Castle (OS179 335422). Signposted Langdon Cliff, St Margaret's Bay for NE traffic only. Signposted at entrance. Grassed area with shrubs, on clifftop overlooking Straits of Dover and Dover Harbour. Toilets. Parking 150.
Bedgebury Pinetum Map 5 TQ73 ***(B2079)*** E side of B2079, 2m S of Goudhurst (OS188 715336). Signposted in advance and at entrance. Drinking water, furniture. Toilets. Parking 300 (fee).

LEICESTERSHIRE
Burbage Common Map 7 SP49 ***(A47)*** Between A47 and A5070, 1m W of Hinckley (OS140 447953). Signposted at entrance. 3 acres. Access to 29 acres of woodland, controlled sections for flying model aircraft. Parking 50.
Bosworth Park Map 8 SK40 ***(B585)*** On B585, $\frac{1}{4}$m from centre of Market Bosworth (OS140 412032). Signposted at entrance. Open area sloping to lake shore. 30 acres. Furniture. Toilets. Parking 50 (fee at peak periods).
Beacon Hill Map 7 SK51 ***(B591)*** $1\frac{1}{2}$m W of Woodhouse Eaves, N side of B591 (OS129 510149). AA Viewpoint. 10 acres. Drinking water, furniture. Toilets. Parking 50.
Nanpantan Outwoods Map 7 SK51 ***(Off B591)*** Turn off B591 on to unclassified Woodhouse Eaves/Nanpantan road, $1\frac{1}{2}$m from Woodhouse Eaves (OS129 515159). Wooded hillside. 54 acres. Woodland walks. Parking 60.
Old John Tower within Bradgate Country Park Map 7 SK51 ***(B5327)*** 7m NW of Leicester, on B5327 at Newton Linford (OS129 523117). 6 acres. Drinking water. Toilets. Parking 400.

LINCOLNSHIRE
Cater Plot Transit Picnic Site Map 8 TF14 ***(A17)*** $1\frac{3}{4}$m E Heckington S side A17 (OS130 168441). Toilets.
Chapel Point Map 9 TF57 ***(Off A52)*** 1m N of Chapel St Leonards (OS122 563732). 10 acres. Drinking water. Toilets. Parking 150.
Huttoft Bank Map 9 TF57 ***(A52)*** E of A52, 3m S of Sutton-on-Sea (OS122 541780). Signposted at entrance. On Lincolnshire coast. 10 acres. Toilets. Parking 400.
Newton-on-Trent Map 8 SK87 ***(A57)*** $\frac{3}{4}$m E of Newton-on-Trent, $9\frac{1}{4}$m W of Lincoln (OS129 861742). Signposted in advance and at entrance. Old road screened by newly planted trees. $\frac{1}{2}$ acre. Parking 15.
Hubbard's Hill Map 8 TF38 ***(Off A153)*** $\frac{1}{4}$m W of A153. $1\frac{1}{2}$m SW Louth (OS122 317861). Signposted in advance. 5 acres. Furniture. Toilets. Parking 30.
Tattershall Map 8 TF25 ***(A153)*** On NW side of A153, $\frac{3}{4}$m SW of Tattershall (OS122 203572). Signposted in advance and at entrance. Between A153 and Horncastle Canal on line of disused railway. Site of interest in rural area. $4\frac{1}{2}$ acres. Drinking water, furniture, plan of area displayed. Toilets. Parking 100.
North Reston Map 8 TF38 ***(A157)*** W side of A157, 1m SE of Legbourne (OS122 384837). Signposted in advance and at entrance. Open grass area 20ft from road. $\frac{1}{2}$ acre. Furniture. Parking 10.
Seaview Farm Map 9 TF56 ***(A158)*** N side of A158, $1\frac{1}{2}$m W of Skegness (OS122 545648). Signposted at entrance on W side only. Old road screened by trees. 1 acre. Parking 20.
Woodhall Spa Map 8 TF16 ***(Off B1191)*** $\frac{1}{2}$m from centre of Woodhall Spa off Stixwould road (OS122 191635). Signposted at entrance. Local authority park. 5 acres. Cricket ground, swimming pool, gardens, furniture. Toilets. Parking 100.

LONDON (GREATER)
Richmond Park Map 4 TQ27 ***(A3/A308)*** (OS176 200720). Parking 500.
Farthing Downs Map 4 TQ35 ***(A23/B2030)*** Adjacent to unclassified Coulsdon/Chaldon road, $1\frac{1}{2}$m S of junction of A23/B2030 (OS187 300570). Signposted in advance. On North Downs approx 600ft above sea level. 121 acres. Nature trail, furniture. Toilets. Parking 600.
Trent Park Map 4 TQ29 ***(Off A111)*** $\frac{1}{2}$m N of Cockfosters, 3m S of Potters Bar (OS176 280970). Signposted at entrance. In country park. 330 acres. Nature trail, fishing, riding, furniture. Toilets. Parking 200.
Addington Park Map 4 TQ36 ***(A212/B268)*** $\frac{1}{2}$m W of Addington village (OS177 368638). Signposted at entrance. Pleasant sloping woodland adjacent to Addington Palace, formerly residence of Archbishop of Canterbury. 70 acres. Small children's playground. Parking 100.
North Cray Transit Picnic Site Map 5 TQ47 ***(A223)*** A223 North Cray Road. 1m N of Ruxley Corner (A20). $1\frac{1}{2}$m S Bexley. (OS177 484718). Toilets.
Bushey Park Map 4 TQ16 ***(Off A308)*** $\frac{1}{2}$m W of Kingston-upon-Thames (OS176 155693). Parking 120.
Hainault Forest Map 5 TQ49 ***(A1112)*** E and SE of Chigwell Row (OS177 475935). Sigposted in advance and at entrance. Well-wooded part of the ancient forest of Essex. 1,100 acres. Golf course, pleasant walks, horse riding, fishing, drinking water, furniture. Toilets. Parking 100.
Mad Bess Wood Map 4 TQ08 ***(B455)*** Adjacent to Ruislip/Northwood road, $1\frac{1}{2}$m N of

Ruislip (OS176 080895). Signposted at entrance. Pleasant woodland, part of which is a bird sanctuary. 186 acres.
Bayhurst Wood Map 4 TQ08 ***(Off B455)*** On unclassified Harefield/Ruislip road, off B455 (OS176 068890). Pleasant woodlands surrounded by quiet countryside. 98 acres. Furniture. Toilets. Parking 100.
Coulsdon Common Map 4 TQ35 ***(B2030)*** 1¼m NW of Caterham, on North Downs approx 600ft above sea level (OS187 320570). Signposted in advance and at entrance. 130 acres. Nature trail.

MIDLANDS (WEST)
Sandwell Valley Map 7 SP09 ***(off A41)*** Park lane (between A41 and A4041) West Bromwich 1¾m ENE opposite football ground (OS139 025923). Signposted at entrance. Open land with picnic site, located on the edge of a large lake, sailing, nature trail, play area, miniature golf course. Furniture. Drinking water. Toilets. Parking 100.
Sutton Park Map 7 SP19 ***(A453)*** 1m from centre of Sutton Coldfield (OS139 130975). Signposted in advance and at entrance. Large natural park with lake and woodlands, surrounded by urban development. Drinking water, furniture. Toilets. Extensive parking.
Shenstone Woods Map 7 SO98 ***(A458)*** ¾m NE Halesowen (OS139 975838). 3½ acres. Grassed hill, small lake and woods, children's playground. Furniture. Parking 100.
Recreation Park Lickey Hills Map 7 SO97 ***(B4096)*** 4½m NE Bromsgrove NW side B4096 (OS139 996759). Signposted at entrance. 7 acres picturesque park, pools, gardens, children's playground. Furniture, drinking water. Toilets. Parking 120.
Cofton Common Map 7 SP07 ***(B4096)*** Lowhill Lane, Rednal. 3m NE Bromsgrove. (OS139 005764). Signposted at entrance. 130 acres. Public park. Drinking water. Furniture. Parking 60.
Warren Lane Lickey Hills Map 7 SO97 ***(B4096)*** 4¼m NE of Bromsgrove on E side B4096 (OS139 995755). Area bordered by small wall, café, children's playground. Parking 200.

NORFOLK
Lynford Map 5 TL89 ***(A134)*** 1m SE of Mundford (OS144 813917). Signposted at entrance. 60 acres. Level grassland in Thetford Forest. Drinking water and nature trails, children's play area. Toilets. Parking.
Grimes Graves Map 5 TL89 ***(A134)*** On the Thetford/Mundford road, 6m from Thetford (OS144 815918). Signposted in advance. Access through forest to open grass area surrounded by trees in Thetford Chase. 5 acres. Ancient monument nearby, Grimes Graves and Weeting Castle. Parking 50 (fee).
Two Mile Bottom Map 5 TL88 ***(A134)*** 3m NW of Thetford (OS144 845878). Signposted in advance and at entrance. 25 acres. Open woodland by roadside, extending back to pine wood walks. Extensive parking.
Emily's Wood Map 5 TL78 ***(A1065)*** On the Mundford/Brandon road, 2m S of Mundford (OS144 797895). Open area of several hundred yards, backed by forest. 40 acres.
Hockham Map 5 TL99 ***(A1075)*** 1m W of Great Hockham (OS144 938919). Signposted at entrance. Rough grassland adjacent to pine woods. 2½ acres. Walks. Parking 40.
Punchbowl Map 5 TL88 ***(Unclassified road)*** 3½m N of Thetford on unclassified road (1m N of Croxton) (OS144 877893). Signposted at entrance. 10 acres. Toilets. Parking 50.

NORTHAMPTONSHIRE
Wakerley Great Wood Map 4 SP99 ***(Off A43)*** Unclassified road off A43. 2½m SW of Duddington, (OS141 967984). Wooded area. Toilets with provision for disabled. Parking 100.
Harlestone Heath Map 4 SP76 ***(A428)*** 1m SE of Harlestone, A428 Northampton/Rugby road (OS152 712637). Large lay-by set in woodland. 100 acres. Walks. Parking 40.
Pitsford Reservoir Map 4 SP76 ***(Off A508)*** On unclassified road, ½m E of A508 5½m N of Northampton (OS152 758686). Signposted in advance and at entrance. Parking 100.
Barnwell Map 4 TL08 ***(A605)*** ½m S of Oundle, W side of A605 (OS141 035873). 30 acres. Toilets.
Salcey Forest Map 4 SP75 ***(Off B526)*** On unclassified Quinton/Hartwell road, off B526 1m from Hartwell (OS152 793518). Signposted in advance. 6 acres Crown Land. Walk through Salcey Forest game reserve. Dogs must be on lead. Toilets.

NORTHUMBERLAND
Breamish Valley Map 12 NU01 ***(A697)*** 8½m S of Wooler, following signs to Ingram (OS81 020160). Signposted in advance and at entrance. Grass valley following River Breamish into the Cheviot foothills. 50 acres. Toilets. Parking 1,000.
Blanchland Map 12 NY95 ***(B6306)*** In the village (OS87 950520). Signposted in advance. Picnic area by river and woods near Derwent Reservoir. Parking 100 (fee).
Brocolita Map 12 NY87 ***(B6318)*** 3m NW of Chollerford (OS87 878725). 30 acres. Parking 40.
Housesteads Map 12 NY76 ***(B6318)*** 9m E of Greenhead (OS87 790687). Signposted in advance. 30 acres. Museum on site. Parking 60.
Once Brewed Car Park Transit Picnic Site Map 12 NY76 ***(B6318)*** 11m W of Chollerford. (OS87 741669). Parking.
Winshields Crag Map 12 NY76 ***(B6318)*** 5m E of Greenhead (OS87 755681). Signposted in advance. Near Roman Wall. 50 acres. Parking 40.

NOTTINGHAMSHIRE
Newstead Abbey Gardens Map 7 SK55 ***(Off A60)*** 4½m S of Mansfield and W of A60 (OS129 541537). Cultivated gardens set in Abbey grounds. 70 acres. Parking 1,000.
Clumber Park Map 8 SK67 ***(A6005)*** 5m SE of Worksop. Access off A6005 Worksop/Ollerton road (OS120 627746). Signposted at entrance. A wooded site situated on N side of Sherwood Forest. Extensive area. Fishing facilities by permit from Clumber Estate Office. Toilets. Parking unlimited.

OXFORDSHIRE
Cowleaze Wood Map 4 SU79 ***(Off A40)*** On unclassified road at Christmas Common off A40, 2m W of Stokenchurch, 4m SE of Watlington (OS165 726956). Woodlands on the edge of the Chiltern escarpment. Forest walks, drinking water. Toilets. Parking 100.
Oxford Transit Picnic Site Map 4 SP50 ***(A40)*** 1½m SE of Ring Road (OS164 575075). Toilets.
Abbey Meadow Map 4 SU59 ***(Off A415)*** Adjacent to Abingdon town centre (OS164 500970). Signposted 'car park at Abbey Hall'. Alongside River Thames adjacent to Abbey Gardens. 5 acres. Swimming pool, tennis courts, pitch and putt. Toilets.
Sinodun Hills (Wittenham Clumps) Map 4 SU59 ***(Off 4130)*** On unclassified road between Brightwell and Little Wittenham, 4m NW of Wallingford (OS164 566924). Wooded hilltop with pleasant views. 5 acres. Parking 30.
White Horse Hill Nr Uffington Map 4 SU38 ***(Off B4507)*** Off B4507 3m E of Ashbury (OS174 302866). Signposted in advance. Overgrown castle ruins. 10 acres. Parking 40.

SALOP
Ercall Wood Map 7 SJ60 ***(Off A5)*** 1m SSW of Wellington off unclassified road from Haygate on A5(T) to Shrewsbury (OS127 643097). 5 acres. Wooded area on hillside with footpaths to summit. Furniture. Parking 30.
Colemere Map 7 SJ43 ***(Off A5)*** Off A5 to Colemere Village then follow sign to Lyneal for ½m (OS126 434328). Signposted at entrance. 7 acre grassed area surrounded by trees overlooking mere. Fishing, furniture, drinking water. Toilets. Parking 30.

Picnic Sites

Whitlington Castle Map 7 SJ33 ***(A5)***
Just N of Whitlington (OS126 325312). Signposted at entrance. 20 acres within castle ruins, landscaped area of grass on banks of moat. Furniture, playground. Parking 70.
Brown Moss Map 7 SJ53 ***(Off A41)***
1½m SE of Whitchurch (OS126 562395). Signposted in advance and at entrance. 80 acres of common land crossed by open tracks and footpaths, areas of bracken and open grazing, woodland and a number of pools, fishing, warden. Furniture. Parking 100.
Corbett Wood Map 7 SJ52 ***(Off A49)***
3m S of Wem (OS126 518238). Signposted in advance and at entrance. 23 acres of mixed woodland on Grinshill, footpaths, good views, drinking water. Parking 30.
Long Mynd Map 7 SO49 ***(Off A49)***
Unclassified road 2m from Church Stretton (OS137 420945). Signposted in advance and at entrance. Extensive area of gorse and grass-covered undulating ground rising to 1,666ft traversed by rough tracks, hazardous for vehicles in places. Hang-gliding. Parking unlimited.
Whitcliffe Common Map 7 SO57 ***(Off A49)***
On unclassified road off A49, 2m W of Ludlow (OS137 505743). Signposted in advance and at entrance. Small picnic areas surrounded by scrub and gorse on common land. 20 acres. Parking 50.
Severn Park, Bridgnorth Map 7 SO79 ***(A442)***
Edge of Bridgnorth Low Town, alongside A442 Bridgnorth–Telford road (OS138 723934). Signposted at entrance. 30 acres. Riverside Park. Pitch and putt, putting. Parking unlimited.
The Mere, Ellesmere Map 7 SJ43 ***(A495)***
On A495 SE of town, ½m from town centre (OS126 405347). Signposted in advance. Partly a bird sanctuary. 171 acres. Drinking water, furniture, warden during season. Toilets. Parking (fee).
Swimming Pool Map 7 SJ63 ***(Off A529)***
Off A529 to Hinstock approximately 400yds from town centre (OS127 676346). 1½ acres. Pleasant grassed site on bank separated from car park by a small stream, flower borders, shrubs, trees. No dogs. Furniture, drinking water. Parking 100.
Cleehill Map 7 SO57 ***(A4117)***
At Cleehill between Ludlow and Cleobury Mortimer (OS138 594754). Signposted in advance. Grass common and numerous quarries adjacent to road. 2,000 acres. Panoramic views. Toilets. Parking 1,000.
Cardingmill Valley Map 7 SO49 ***(Off B4270)***
On edge of Church Stretton Village (OS137 445946). Signposted in advance and at entrance. Small attractive river valley 250 acres. Hill walking, drinking water, furniture. Parking 700 (fee).
Old Racecourse, Oswestry
Map 7 SJ23 ***(B4580)*** 2m NW of Oswestry on B4580 (OS126 258310). Commonland with gorse and trees. 50 acres. Panoramic views. Toilets. Parking 40.

SOMERSET

Brent Knoll (East & West) Transit Picnic Sites
Map 3 ST35 ***(M5)*** North and Southbound carriageways 2m N of junction 22, 5m S of junction 21 (OS182 358526). Signposted in advance and at entrance. Public telephone, snacks, shop. Toilets. Parking 200 (fee) after 2 hours, overnight caravan parking.
County Gate Map 3 SS74 ***(A39)***
5m S of Lynton (OS180 793487). Signposted in advance and at entrance. Natural wooded site. 1 acre. Furniture. Toilets. Parking 100.
Pittcombe Head Map 3 SS84 ***(Off A39)***
1½m W of Porlock (OS181 839464). At junction with Porlock Hill Toll Road, access requires caution. Signposted at entrance. 2 acres. Situated in woodland, good access point for Exmoor walks. No toilets. Parking 50. (Parking lanes cut in small woods).

STAFFORDSHIRE

Froghall Map 7 SK04 ***(Off A52)***
On edge of Froghall Village (OS128 025470). Elevated position adjacent to disused lime kilns.
Highgate Common Map 7 SO88 ***(Off A458)***
Off unclassified roads and adjacent to Enville Gold Course, 2m N of Enville (OS138 838896). Signposted in advance. Commonland, furniture. Toilets. Parking 1,000.
Cannock Chase Map 7 SJ92 ***(A513)***
4m ESE of Stafford at Milford village adjacent to common (OS127 974214). Signposted in advance. 3,000 acres. Area for flying model aircraft. German war cemetery. Toilets.
Hanchurch Hills Map 7 SJ83 ***(Off A519)***
3m S of Newcastle-under-Lyme (OS127 840399). Portion of hilltop with fine turf and gorse. 80 acres. No caravans allowed. Parking 200.
Churnet Picnic Area Map 7 SK04 ***(B5417)***
Cheadle Road, Oakamoor 3m E of Cheadle (OS128 053446). 16 acres. Signposting at entrance. Village picnic site on the River Churnet. Drinking water, furniture. Toilets. Parking 30.

SUFFOLK

Haughley Map 5 TL96 ***(A45)***
4m NW of Stowmarket (OS155 995615). Signposted in advance and at entrance. Sharply sloping grassland with young trees. 5 acres. Drinking water. Toilets. Parking 80.
Mildenhall Woods Transit Picnic Site
Map 5 TL77 ***(A1065/A11)*** Barton Mills roundabout E side of A1065 ¾m N Barton Mills (OS143 728744). Signposted in advance and at entrance. 5 acres of grassland backed by pinewoods. Furniture. Toilets. Parking 50.
Knettishall Map 5 TL98 ***(Off A1088)***
On unclassified road from Euston, 3m from Hopton (OS144 950805). Signposted in advance and at entrance. 10 acres. Heathland with trees and bracken. Parking 200.
The King's Picnic Place Map 5 TL87 ***(B1106)***
E side of B1106, 7m N of Bury St Edmunds (OS144 826740). Signposted at entrance. Areas of grass between trees. 7 acres. Furniture. Parking 150.

SURREY

Gibbet Hill Devil's Punch Bowl
Map 4 SU83 ***(A3)*** ½m N of junction with A287 at Hindhead (OS186 896358). Signposted at entrance. 2 acres. Nature trail, drinking water, furniture. Toilets. Parking 180.
Tilburstow Hill Viewpoint
Map 4 TQ35 ***(Off A22)*** 1½m S of Godstone (OS187 345501). Viewpoint commanding wide areas of surrounding countryside. Parking 65.
Box Hill Map 4 TQ15 ***(Off A24)*** On unclassified road 1m NE of Dorking, 1m E of A24 (OS187 173516). Signposted at road and at entrance. 50 acres. Drinking water, furniture. Toilets. Parking 150.
Leith Hill Map 4 TQ14 ***(Off A25)***
5m SW of Dorking on unclassified road off A25 (OS187 135433). Highest point in Surrey (National Trust property). Furniture. Parking 60.
Newlands Corner Map 4 TQ04 ***(A25)***
On A25 at its junction with A247 3m E of Gomshall (OS186 042492). Signposted in advance and at entrance. Furniture. Toilets. Parking 200.
Ranmore Common Map 4 TQ15 ***(Off A25)***
Unclassified road off A25, 2m NW of Dorking (OS187 133504). Signposted at entrance. National Trust property which gives access to good walking area. Parking 250.
Virginia Water Map 4 SU96 ***(A30)***
On A30, 2m NE of Sunningdale (OS175 977687). Large lake surrounded by parkland (Part of Windsor Great Park). Toilets.
Hogs Back Transit Picnic Site Map 4 SU94 ***(A31)***
On A31 S side. ½m W of B3000. Farnham 5m (OS186 930484). Toilets.
Puttenham Common Map 4 SU94 ***(Off A31)***
1½m SW of Puttenham (OS186 915465). Grassy slopes with wide views of surrounding countryside. Parking 3,000.
Frensham Ponds Map 4 SU84 ***(A287)***
4m S of Farnham (OS186 849401). Signposted at entrance. Large open area. 3 acres. Boating facilities. Toilets. Parking 250.
Epsom Downs Map 4 TQ25 ***(B290)***
1½m SE of Epsom (OS187 218575). Extensive area crossed by minor roads.

SUSSEX (EAST)

Ashdown Forest (Brick Kiln Farm) Map 5 TQ43 ***(A22/A275)*** N side of unclassified Wych Cross/Coleman's Hatch road, 1m E of Wych Cross (OS187 437324). Signposted at entrance for eastbound traffic. Grassy area with trees, gorse and fern. $\frac{3}{4}$ acre. No camping or caravanning, furniture.
Wych Cross (Ashdown Forest) Map 5 TQ43 ***(A22/A275)*** S side of unclassified Sharpthorne/Wych Cross road, 1m W of Wych Cross (OS187 404323). Signposted at entrance for westbound traffic. No camping or caravanning. Parking 300.
In Hastings Country Park Map 5 TQ81 ***(Off A259)*** Two picnic areas. N side of Fairlight $\frac{3}{4}$ and $\frac{1}{2}$m E of A259 (OS199 850123). Signposted at entrance. Rugged cliffs, ferns, woodland and heath. 508 acres. Nature trails, furniture. Toilets. Parking 220.
Vine Hall Forest Trail Map 5 TQ72 ***(B2089)*** S side of B2089 between A21 and A229, 3m SE of Robertsbridge (OS199 764203). Signposted in advance. 'Car-Park' for westbound traffic and at entrance. 'Forestry Commission Vine Hall Forest'. Extensive forest area. Access to pleasant walks, furniture. Parking 35.
Piltdown Pond Map 5 TQ42 ***(B2102)*** 4m from Uckfield via A22 and B2102 (OS198 444223). Natural site overlooking 4 acre pond. $\frac{1}{4}$ acre. Parking 45.
Beachy Head Map 5 TV59 ***(Off B2103)*** 3m SW of Eastbourne (OS199 595955). Signposted in advance. Clifftop affording excellent views of sea, coastline and lighthouse. Furniture. Toilets. Parking 300.
Ditchling Beacon Map 4 TQ31 ***(Off B2112)*** On unclassified road between Brighton (6m) and Ditchling (2m) (OS198 332131). Signposted in advance. Access to South Downs Way. Parking 100.

SUSSEX (WEST)

Devil's Dyke Map 4 TQ21 ***(A23/A281)*** $5\frac{1}{2}$m NW of Brighton (OS198 259108). 5 acres. Refreshment facilities, coin-operated telescope viewpoint, furniture. Toilets. Parking 90.
Fairmile Bottom Transit Picnic Site Map 4 TQ01 ***(A29)*** $\frac{1}{4}$m NE Whiteways Lodge. NW of Arundel. (OS167 002111). Toilets.
Whiteways Lodge Map 4 TQ01 ***(A29)*** A29 at its junction with A284 3m N of Arundel (OS197 003108). Signposted in advance and at entrance. 3 acres. Nature trail, drinking water, furniture. Toilets. Parking 80.
Cowdray Hill (Benbow Pond) Map 4 SU92 ***(Off A272)*** Situated N side of A272 at east end of Cowdray Park, Midhurst 2m, Petworth $4\frac{3}{4}$m (OS197 915223). Signposted in advance. Pleasant woodland with pond. 2 acres. Parking 65.
Duncton Hill Map 4 SU91 ***(A285)*** 1m S of Duncton (OS197 955162). Signposted at entrance. 1/3 acre. Nature trail, AA viewpoint. Parking 15.
Finch's Field Map 5 TQ33 ***(Off B2028)*** West Hoathly (OS187 365325). 2 acres. Parking 40.
Marden Forest Map 4 SU81 ***(Off B2146)*** On unclassified road 1m NE of Stoughton (OS197 814126). Signposted 'Marden Forest' in advance and at entrance. Forest area. 5 acres. Marked walks. Parking 150.

WARWICKSHIRE

Burton Hills Map 4 SP35 ***(Off A41)*** 1m from A41 near Avon Dassett approx 8m N of Banbury (OS151 398518). On high ground. 20 acres. Furniture. Parking 200.
Burton Dassett Map 4 SP35 ***(Off A41)*** $9\frac{3}{4}$m Banbury (OS151 398519). Signposted in advance and at entrance. 100 acres. Open sheep-grazed grass land approached by tarmac roads and very safe for children. Toilets. Unlimited parking, ticket meter.
Yarningdale Common Map 4 SP16 ***(B4095)*** $\frac{1}{2}$m NW of Claverdon unclassified road off B4095 5m W Warwick (OS151 190660). Signposted in advance. 20 acres grass and gorseland. Parking 50.

WILTSHIRE

Savernake Forest Map 4 SU26 ***(Off A4)*** $1\frac{1}{2}$m SE of Marlborough. Signposted in advance 'Savernake Forest'. Extensive natural wooded area with many access roads and parking areas. Parking unlimited.
Pepperbox Hill Map 4 SU22 ***(A36)*** On NE side of A36 5m SE of Salisbury, 7/10m NW of AA box (OS184 215247). National Trust site on pleasant hill top with extensive views. Site of ornamental tower which is a local landmark, grassland shrubs and trees.
Norridge Common Transit Picnic Site Map 3 ST97 ***(A36)*** 2m NW of Warminster (OS184 855480). Toilets.
Inglesham/Lechlade Map 4 SU29 ***(Off A361)*** $\frac{1}{4}$m S of Lechlade off A361 on W side adjoining Lechlade bridge. (OS 163 212993). Signposted, 'Riverside Park' in advance and at entrance. 20 acres. Large fenced meadow adjacent to river and moorings planted with shrubs and trees. Drinking water, furniture. Toilets. Extensive parking.
Kingston Langley Transit Picnic Site Map 3 ST97 ***(A429)*** 2m N of Chippenham (OS173 912763). Both sides of carriageway screened from traffic. Toilets.
Stourhead Map 3 ST73 ***(Off B3092)*** $3\frac{1}{2}$m NW of Mere in Stourton village (OS183 780345). Signposted in advance and at entrance. In extensive and elaborately-landscaped grounds of house of historic interest owned by National Trust. 2 acres. Ideal for children, wooded walks, lakes, follies and miniature architectural reproductions, furniture, drinking water, refreshment facilities near house. Toilets. Parking free, house and landscaped grounds not included.
King Alfred's Tower Map 3 ST73 ***(off B3092)*** $2\frac{1}{2}$m NW of Stourton $2\frac{1}{2}$m SW of Kilmington on unclassified road off B3092 (OS183 755351). Signposted in advance and at entrance. Meadowland in extensive wooded natural area centered around a brick tower circa 1271. Forest walks. Parking 150. (Fee.)

YORKSHIRE (NORTH)

Sheep Wash Map 8 SE48 ***(Off A19)*** On unclassified road, signposted Osmotherly and Swainby, off A19 11m N of Thirsk (OS100 460985). Reservoir and streams set in picturesque surroundings. $2\frac{1}{2}$ acres. Parking 50.
Staxton Hill Map 8 TA07 ***(A64)*** 1m from junction $1\frac{1}{2}$m from Staxton village (OS101 012784). Signposted in advance and at entrance. Sloping tree-planted grass area adjoining separate car park. 3 acres. Panoramic moorland views, furniture, drinking water, disabled toilets. Parking 40.
Sil Howe Map 8 NZ80 ***(Off A169)*** Off A169 7m S of Whitby (OS94 853028). Elevated moorland area. Parking 6.
Cockmoor Hill Troutsdale Map 8 SE98 ***(Off A170)*** On unclassified Snainton/Hackness road. Snainton 3m (OS101 915868). Signposted at entrance. Commonland surrounded by woods. $\frac{1}{2}$ acre. Parking 15.
Sutton Bank Map 8 SE58 ***(A170)*** A170 6m E of Thirsk (OS100 514827). Signposted at entrance. AA Viewpoint. 4 acres. Parking 220.
Bickley Gate Map 8 SE99 ***(Off A171)*** On unclassified road 6m W of A171 at Scalby (OS101 913912). Signposted at entrance. Natural site on hilltop above village. 1/3 acre. Furniture. Parking 10.
Reasty Hill Top Map 8 SE99 ***(Off A171)*** On unclassified road to Harwood Dale 4m W of A171 at Scalby (OS101 966944). Signposted at entrance. On brow of steep hill with narrow, steeply ascended approach for cars. $\frac{1}{8}$acre. Furniture. Parking 10.
Skelder Top Map 8 NZ80 ***(A171)*** S side of A171 4m W of Whitby (OS94 841080). 948ft above sea level on E side of N Yorkshire moors. $\frac{1}{2}$ acre. Parking 100.
Sledgates Fylingdales Map 8 NZ90 ***(Off A171)*** $\frac{1}{2}$m along unclassified road off A171 signposted Fyling Thorpe (OS94 931020). Signposted at

entrance under brow of steep hill. ⅛ acre. Parking 50.
Hardrow Scaur Map 7 SD89 ***(Off A684)*** 2m N of A684 from Hawes on unclassified road to Hardrow (OS98 870915). Signposted in advance and at entrance. Natural site with a waterfall reputed to be the longest in England. Admission charge with access from Green Dragon Inn. Drinking water, furniture. Toilets. Parking 50.
River Swale Map 8 NZ10 ***(A6108)*** 1m W of Richmond (OS92 147005). 135 acres.
Clay Bank Map 8 NZ50 ***(B1257)*** 3m S of Broughton (OS93 572040). 842ft above sea level. Parking 50.
Ingleby Bank Map 8 NZ50 ***(Off B1257)*** ½m E of Ingleby Greenhow on unclassified road from Broughton (OS93 580062). Signposted in advance. In Forestry Commission and National Parkland. Parking 30.
Falling Foss Map 8 NZ80 ***(Off B1416)*** Off unclassified road to Ruswarp off B1416 (OS94 889038). Signposted in advance and at entrance. ¾ acre. Parking 30.
Bolton Abbey (Cavendish Pavilion) Map 8 SE05 ***(Off B6160)*** On unclassified road 1m W of Bolton Abbey (OS104 055540). 9 acres.
Brimham Rocks Map 8 SE26 ***(B6165)*** In Country Park 3m E of Pateley Bridge N of B6165 and S of B6265, signed from both. (OS99 212650). Signposted in advance and at entrance. Elevated local beauty spot which is a prominent geological formation. Drinking water. Toilets. Parking 150.

YORKSHIRE (SOUTH)
Cannon Hall Map 8 SE20 ***(Off A635)*** In Country park off A635, 4½m NW of Barnsley ½m N of Cawthorne (OS104 272085). Parking 150.

WALES

CLWYD
Moel Famau Map 7 SJ16 ***(A494)*** Off Mold/Ruthin road on unclassified road ¾m N of Llanferres (OS116 172611). 1 acre. Parking 30.
Bod Petrual Map 6 SJ03 ***(B5105)*** In Clocaenog Forest on B5105, Llanfihangel Glyn Myfyr 3½m (OS116 037512). Open area among trees with small lake. 1½ acres. Furniture. Parking 20.

DYFED
Fishguard Harbour Transit Picnic Site Map 2 SN93 ***(A40)*** Between Fishguard and Goodwick 1m from Fishguard town centre (OS160 952377). 1 acre. Signposted at entrance. Purpose built terrace overlooking the harbour. Furniture. Toilets. Parking 14.
Coed Deufor Map 2 SN24 ***(A474)*** S side A474 ¾m W Cenarth (OS145 255422). Signposted at entrance. 1 acre rising wooded land. Walk, furniture. Parking 20.
Black Mountains Map 3 SN71 ***(A4069)*** 4m N of Brynamman (OS160 732189). A small site provided as part of the National Park amenities. 1 acre. Furniture. Parking 20.
Carew Mill Map 2 SN00 ***(Off A4075)*** On unclassified road 400yds from A4075 at Carew (OS158 045040). Signposted in advance at entrance. Pleasant open grass area overlooking estuary and Carew Mill. 1 acre. Furniture. Parking 25.
Abergorlech Map 2 SN53 ***(B4310)*** At Abergorlech Village 12m N of Llandeilo between Brechfa and Llansawel (OS146 587336). Signposted in advance and at entrance. Small attractive site bordering a small stream, grassy banks and young trees. 1 acre. Forest walks, furniture. Parking 20.
Ffynnon Byrgwm Brechfa Map 2 SN53 ***(B4310)*** Between Brechfaad and Abergoroch, 2m NE Brechfa. (OS146 544315). Signposted in advance and at entrance. Set among mature trees on elevated position with extensive views. 1 acre. Forest walks, furniture, ample parking.
Unnamed Map 3 SN51 ***(B4300)*** 1m E of junction with B4310 6m E of Carmarthen (OS 159 501199). Signposted in advance and at entrance. Screened by trees overlooking River Towy. 1 acre. Furniture. Disabled toilets. Parking 16.
Coed-Craig-yr-Ogof Map 6 SN67 ***(Off B4340)*** ½m E of B4340 on unclassified road from Llanafan Bridge to Pontrhydygroes (OS135 695717). Signposted in advance and at entrance. On riverside in wooded area. 1 acre. Forest walk, furniture. Parking 10.
Pwllpeiran Map 6 SN77 ***(Off B4574)*** On unclassified road off B4574 2½m SE of Devil's Bridge (OS135 774748). 1 acre. Parking 10.
The Arch Map 6 SN77 ***(B4974)*** 2m S of Devil's Bridge (OS135 765735). Forestry Commission signpost at entrance. 1½ acres. Furniture, chemical toilets. Parking 30.
Llyn Brianne Dam Map 2 SN74 ***(Unclassified road)*** Access N from A40 at Llandovery via 12 miles of well-signed unclassified roads (OS1460 794482). Exclusive area overlooking reservoir. Portaloo.

GWENT
Mitchell Troy Transit Area Transit Picnic Site Map 3 SO51 ***(A40)*** On trunk road linking M4/M5 1m S of Monmouth on N carriageway (OS162 500113). Toilets.
Nine Wells Map 3 ST49 ***(Off A48)*** 6m SE of Usk on unclassified road between A449 and A48 in Wentwood Forest (OS171 426943). Forestry Commission sign at entrance. Attractive sheltered area. 2 acres. Forest walks, furniture. Parking 25.
Cadira Beeches Map 3 ST49 ***(A48)*** 5m SE of Usk on unclassified road between A449 and A48 (OS171 423948). Forestry Commission sign at entrance. Natural forest site. 2 acres. Viewpoint, forest walks, furniture. Parking 50.
Llandegfedd Reservoir Map 3 ST39 ***(Off A449/A4042)*** 8m N of Newport signed off A449 and A4042, 2m E of New Inn which is 1½m S of Portybra. (OS171 329984). Signposted in advance and at entrance. A developed site which has retained its natural beauty overlooking the reservoir. 9 acres, furniture. Toilets closed in winter. Extensive parking.
Whitehall Picnic Area Transit Picnic Site Map 3 ST39 ***(A449)*** Both sides A449 Coldra Usk Road 3m North of M4 junction 24. (OS171 389934). Signposted in advance and at entrance. Toilets for disabled.
Tintern Railway Station Picnic Area Map 3 ST50 ***(A466)*** A seasonal site open 10.30am–6pm. Right-hand side of road N from Tintern (OS162 538008). Signposted in advance and at entrance. Furniture, drinking water, guided walks, railway exhibition, warden, information service, on route of 16m Wye Valley Walk. Toilets. Parking 50 (fee).
Sor Brook Map 3 ST39 ***(Off A4042)*** S end of Llandegfedd Reservoir approximately 8m N of Newport on unclassified road between Coed y Paen and Cwymbran 3m W of A4042 (OS171 324978). Signposted in advance and at entrance Sheltered area 1.4 km walk from reservoir. 18 acres. Signed walks with guide leaflets available. Furniture. Parking 30.
Prysgau Bach Map 3 ST49 ***(B4235)*** 3m W of Chepstow (OS162 494943). Signposted in advance. On edge of forest overlooking valley. ½ acre, furniture. Parking 20.
Barnets Woods Map 3 ST59 ***(B4235)*** 2m W of Chepstow (OS162 502942). Signposted at entrance. Simple site on the edge of Great Barnets Woods. 1 acre. Horse riding trail, signposted forest walks. Parking 20.
Wentwood Reservoir Map 3 ST49 ***(Unclassified road)*** 6m Usk 9m Chepstow. On unclassified road between A48 and A449 (OS171 429939). Signposted 'Wentwood' at entrance. Quiet area with excellent views on elevated position overlooking reservoir. 10 acres. Drinking water, furniture. Toilet facilities for disabled. Parking 50.
Whitestone Map 3 SO50 ***(Unclassified road)*** 1½m Llandogo 2¼m Trelleck on unclassified

road between A466 and B4293 (OS162 524030). Signposted at entrance. Attractive wooded site in elevated position. 2 acres. Barbecue facilities, signed forest walks, furniture. Portaloos. Parking 40.

GWYNEDD

Cae'n-y-Coed Map 6 SH75 ***(A5)*** 1½m N of Betws-y-Coed (OS115 767575). Signposted in advance and at entrance. 1 acre. Forest walks, furniture, aboretum. Toilets. Parking 30.

Aberangell Map 6 SH81 ***(A470)*** Cwm-Du Aberangell on A470 2m S of Mallwyd (OS125 833105). ½ acre. Parking 10.

Aberhirnant Valley Map 6 SH72 ***(Off A470)*** Along unclassified road approx 1m S of Ganllwyd (OS124 727232). ¼ acre. Parking 12.

Bont Newydd Map 6 SH74 ***(A470)*** 1m SE of Ffestiniog (OS124 713408). Signposted at entrance. Grassy riverbank with young trees. 2 acres. Parking 6.

Dolgyfeiliau Bridge Map 6 SH72 ***(Off A487)*** Alongside River Eden approx 1½m N of Ganllwyd (OS124 722269). Signposted in advance and at entrance. ½ acre. Furniture. Chemical toilets. Parking 18.

Tyn-y-Groes Transit Picnic Site Map 6 SH72 ***(Off A487)*** Alongside river Mawddach off A470 1m S of Ganllwyd (OS124 737225). Signposted in advance and at entrance. ¼ acre. Forest trail, furniture. Chemical toilets. Parking 20 (fee).

Crogenan Lakes Map 6 SH61 ***(Off A493)*** In Snowdonia Forest Park 6m SW of Dolgellau. 5 gates along approach (OS124 658146). Unsuitable for large vehicles and caravans. 1 acre. Parking 60.

Pont-Caer Gors Map 6 SH55 ***(A4085)*** 2m N of Beddgelert (OS115 576509). Signposted at entrance. 1 acre. Furniture. Toilets. Parking 30.

Bala Lake Foreshore Map 6 SH93 ***(B4403)*** Alongside B4403 approx 3½m W of Bala near Llangower (OS125 905327). ½ acre. Access to Lake, furniture. Parking 15.

POWYS

Grwyne Fawr Valley Map 3 SO22 ***(Off A40 & A465)*** In Mynydd Dhu Forest on unclassified road to Grwyne Fawr Reservoir from Abergavenny via unclassified roads from A40 and A465 (OS161 266252). Signposted at entrance. Flat grassy riverside area. 1 acre. Furniture. Parking 20.

Ffawydday Map 3 SO23 ***(Off A40 & A465)*** At head of Grwyne Fawr Valley approx 11m N of Abergavenny via unclassified roads from A40 and A465. (OS161 241328). Signposted at entrance. Flat grassy area by river running through forest. 2 acres, furniture. Parking 20.

Hafren Road Map 6 SN88 ***(Off A470)*** 7m from Llanidloes off A470 (OS135 865868). Signposted in advance and at entrance by Forestry Commission sign. Open ground in wooded valley overlooking stream. Cautious approach advised on narrow road with bends. Furniture, children's climbing frame.

Brecon Beacons Map 3 SN92 ***(Off A4215)*** Off A4215 6m SW of Brecon (OS160 977262). Signposted in advance and at entrance. Within national park. Drinking water, furniture, preparation and washing up facilities for disabled, cafeteria daily closing 5–8pm according to season. Toilets. Parking 85.

Llyn Clywedog Map 6 SN98 ***(B4518)*** On B4518 4m NW of Llanidloes (OS147 905885). Signposted 'Parking Area' at entrance. Three parking areas beside lake. ½ acre. Toilets. Parking 50.

SCOTLAND

BORDERS

Teviothead Map 12 NT40 ***(A7)*** W side of A7 1m S of Teviothead Post Office (OS79 404038). Signposted in advance. Grassy riverside site with tarred parking area. 10 acres. Drinking water, furniture. Toilets. Parking 12.

Cambridge Picnic Site Map 12 NT54 ***(A697)*** A697 Lauder 3½m, at junction with unclassified road to Spottiswoode (OS74 585482). Signposted in advance and at entrance. Converted lay-by with grassed picnic areas. ½ acre, furniture. 'Portaloo'. Parking 20.

Rosetta Map 11 NT24 ***(Off A703)*** On Northern outskirts of Peebles ½m from town centre (OS73 244415). Signposted in advance. Tree studded grass slope in Rosetta Park. 2 acres. park walks, walled gardens, licensed bar, furniture. Toilets.

St Mary's Loch Map 11 NT22 ***(A708)*** Midway between Selkirk and Moffat (OS73 238205). Grass on shingle between two lochs. 3 acres. Yacht Club. Toilets. Parking 200.

Glenmayne Haugh Map 12 NT53 ***(Off A6091)*** 2m S of Galashiels on unclassified road between A6091 and A7 (OS73 504537). On south bank of River Tweed. 4 acres. Fishing, drinking water, furniture. Toilets. Parking 120.

Rankleburn Map 11 NT31 ***(Off B709)*** ¾m SE of Tushielaw on B711 off B709. (OS79 310169). Parking 100.

CENTRAL

Strathyre Map 11 NN51 ***(A84)*** Outside Strathyre village (OS57 562165). Signposted in advance and at entrance. Large grassy area beside river. 10 acres. Toilets. Parking 50.

Queens View Map 11 NS58 ***(A809)*** On A809 4m S of Drymen (OS64 500830). Signposted at entrance. On the edge of moorland. 1 acre. AA Viewpoint. Access to hill walking. Parking 60.

David Marshall Lodge (Carneigie Building) Map 11 NN50 ***(A821)*** ¾m E of Aberfoyle (OS57 520014). Signposted in advance and at entrance. Extensive area of tree- and bracken-studded forestry land with parking bays and adjacent grassed picnic areas grouped around central lake. Furniture, drinking water, restaurant, information centre, static displays and maps of local features, waterfall trail, AA viewpoint, disabled toilets. Parking 50.

Kincardine Bridge Map 11 NS98 ***(A876)*** Near S access to bridge on A876. (OS65 912863). Signposted at entrance. Toilets. Parking 50.

Gallochy Map 10 NS39 ***(Continuation of B837)*** On unclassified road approx 2½m S of Rowardennan (OS56 390950). Woodland site on shore of Loch Lomond.

Mealldhuinne Map 11 NS39 ***(Continuation of B837)*** On unclassified road approx 1m S of Rowardennan on E side of Loch (OS56 365974). Signposted in advance and at entrance. Natural woodland site with stream. 3 acres. Parking 70.

Milarrochy Map 10 NS49 ***(B837)*** 1m N of Balmaha (OS56 408928). Natural woodland on Loch shore. 2 acres.

Rowardennan Map 10 NS39 ***(Continuation of B837)*** On unclassified road adjacent to village (OS56 365985). On hillside adjacent to right of way to Ben Lomond. 3 acres. Access to hill walking. Parking 150.

DUMFRIES AND GALLOWAY

Opposite Glenairlie Bridge Map 11 NS80 ***(A76)*** On W side 4½m S of Sanquhar (OS71 835056). Signposted in advance and at entrance. Attractive riverside environment fenced from road. Furniture. Toilets. Parking 20.

Portpatrick Harbour Map 10 NW95 ***(A77)*** A77, N side of Harbour (OS82 999541). Safe bathing, drinking water. Toilets. Parking 100.

Grey Mare's Tail Map 11 NT11 ***(A708)*** 10m NE of Moffat (OS79 187147). Signposted at entrance. By large waterfall. Access to bridle path. Parking 30.

Sandhead Beach Map 10 NX15 ***(A715/A716)*** Junction A715/A716 (OS82 100510). Overlooking Luce Bay. Safe bathing, drinking water.

Craignarget Shore Map 10 NX25 ***(A747)*** Between Glenluce and Port William (OS82 255514). Overlooking Luce Bay, rocky coastline. Safe bathing. Parking 100.

St Medan, Monreith Map 10 NX34 ***(A747)*** 1m SE of Monreith village (OS83 380402). On

Picnic Sites

shoreline. Rock fishing, safe bathing. Parking 100.
Port Logan Shore Map 10 NX14 ***(B7065)***
At Port Logan (OS82 100410). Fishpond. Drinking water, furniture. Toilets.

GRAMPIAN
Speymouth Forest Map 15 NJ35 ***(A96)***
½m E of Fochabers (OS28 358587). Signposted in advance and at entrance. On forest road in woodland area. 5 acres. Forest walks, viewpoint. Parking 30.
Unnamed Map 15 NJ41 ***(A97)***
1m N Kildrummy Castle (OS37 465175). Signposted at entrance. Simple grassed site planted with young trees. ½ acre. Furniture. Parking 10.
Well of Lecht Map 15 NJ21 ***(A939)***
5m SE of Tomintoul (OS36 235153). Signposted in advance and at entrance. Mountain streams, footpaths to old ironstone mine, drinking water. Parking 10.

HIGHLAND
Glen Finnan Transit Picnic Site
Map 14 NM98 ***(A830)*** At the head of Loch Shiel between Fort William and Mallaig (OS40 905808). Toilets.
Loch Maree Map 14 NH06 ***(A832)***
2½m NW of Kinlochewe (OS19 004647). Signposted at entrance. Sheltered sites on loch shore. Nature reserve, walks, furniture.
Coldbackie Sands Map 14 NC66 ***(A836)***
3m NE of Tongue (OS10 612600). 200yd from sheltered sandy bay with steep approach. Parking 8.
Sangomore Map 14 NC46 ***(A838)***
At Durness (OS9 406675). Sandy Bays. Near Smoo Cave. Parking 20.

LOTHIAN
Pencraig Picnic Place Map 12 NT57 ***(A1)***
N side of A1 4m E Middleton 1m East Linton (OS67 573765). Signposted at entrance. On high ground within wooded area. 1 acre. Tourist Information Centre, drinking water, furniture. Toilets. Parking 20.

STRATHCLYDE
Cauldshore Map 10 NX19 ***(A77)***
At Girvan (OS76 181980). Signposted in advance and at entrance. On sandy foreshore. 1½ acres, toilets, furniture.
Finnarts Bay Map 11 NX02 ***(A77)***
3m N of Cairnryan (OS76 052757). Signposted at entrance. Parking 100.
Duck Bay Map 10 NS38 ***(A82)***
1m N of Balloch (OS56 380823). Signposted in advance and at entrance. Grassed area overlooking Loch Lomond. 1½ acres. Drinking water, furniture. Toilets.
Maidens Map 10 NS20 ***(A719)***
In village of Maidens (OS76 213079). Signposted in advance and at entrance. Furniture. Toilets. Parking 100.
Garelochhead Map 11 NS29 ***(A814)***
1m N of Garelochhead (OS56 236916). Signposted at entrance. Small trees on heather slopes. 10 acres. No overnight parking, drinking water, furniture. Toilets. Parking 20.
St Columb's Bay Map 11 NM94 ***(A828)***
10m NE of Oban (OS49 945413). Signposted at entrance. Cleared forest area. 10 acres. Furniture. Parking 100.
Jubilee Picnic Site Map 10 NS07 ***(A8003)***
2m N of Tighnabruaich (OS63 000760). Signposted in advance and at entrance. Steep hillside with bays carved into thick undergrowth, cooking area in rocks. 2 acres. Pay telescope, drinking water, furniture. Parking 30.

TAYSIDE
Tummel Forest—Faskally Walk
Map 14 NN95 ***(A9)*** 2m N Pitlochry (OS53 0588). Signposted in advance and at entrance. 10 acres. Forest walks, play area, wildlife hide, drinking water, furniture. Toilets. Ample parking (ticket machine).
East Haven Beach Map 12 NO53 ***(Off A92)***
1½m SE of Muirdrum (OS54 591362). Grass area beside small beach. 3 acres. Parking 50.
Montrose Links Map 15 NO75 ***(Off A92)***
1m off A92 E of Montrose (OS54 726582). Parking 200.
Victoria Park Map 12 NO64 ***(Off A92)***
¾m E of Arbroath (OS54 653412). Public park bordering promenade. Drinking water, furniture. Toilets. Parking 200.
Birks O'Aberfeldy Map 14 NN85 ***(A826)***
At Aberfeldy (OS52 855485). Furniture.
Dalerb Map 11 NN74 ***(A827)***
On N shore at East end of Loch Tay ¾m from Kenmore (OS52 761452). Signposted at entrance. Landscaped field with access to rocky shore. Bathing dangerous. Furniture, drinking water, disabled toilets. Parking 50.
Allean-Tummel Forest Map 14 NN86 ***(B8019)***
7m NW of Pitlochry ½m W Queens View (OS43 852602). Signposted in advance and at entrance. 2 acres. Hillside site with part-excavated ring fort, forest walks. Drinking water, furniture. Disabled toilet. Parking 20.
Queens View Tourist Park
Map 14 NN85 ***(B8019)***
A. On B8019 (OS52 859600). Signposted in advance and at entrance. Forest walks, furniture. Parking 40.
B. 500yds W of above. Signposted in advance and at entrance. Extensive tree-studded area. AA Viewpoint. Forestry Commission Tourist Information Centre. Parking 100.
Findatie Picnic Area Map 11 NT19 ***(B9097)***
In national nature reserve 1½m N of Ballingry S side of Loch Leven (OS58 160990). Signposted at entrance. Extensive grass- and gorse-clad slopes bordering and overlooking loch. Parking 175.

Forest Parks

Six-figure map references have not been provided because of the large areas involved.
Border Forest Park Map 11 NY68/69 (OS79, 80 and 86) 145,000 acres of woodland hills and farms in Northumberland and Cumbria in England, Dumfries and Galloway and Borders in Scotland. The route of the Pennine Way long-distance walk crosses the park.
Campsite: See gazetteer under Hexham.
Dean Forest Park Map 3 SO50/60 (OS162) Covering 35,000 acres in Gloucestershire, Hereford and Worcester in England, and Gwent in Wales, including thirty miles of signposted walking routes, five nature trails, and a scenic motor drive.
Snowdonia Forest Park Map 6 SH65 (OS115, 116, 124, 125 and 135) 23,400 acres of woodland, moorland and lakes in NW Wales.
Campsite: See Gazetteer under Beddgelert (Wales).
Argyll Forest Park Map 10 NS18/19 (OS56) Over 60,000 acres of rugged hills and lochs extending to Loch Goil and the Holy Loch near Dunoon.
Campsite: See Gazetteer under Ardgartan, Argyll (Scotland).

Galloway Forest Park Map 11 NX47 (OS76 and 77) 150,000 acres in the Galloway Highlands including Loch Trool and much of the Rhinns of Kells.
Campsite: See Gazetteer under Glen Trool, Kirkcudbrightshire (Scotland).

Glenmore Forest Park Map 14 NH90 (OS36) 12,500 acres in the Cairngorms, including some of Scotland's best ski-ing grounds, and Loch Morlich with its sandy shores and pine trees.
Campsite: See Gazetteer under Aviemore, Inverness-shire (Scotland).

Queen Elizabeth Forest Park Map 10 NS49 (OS56) Over 40,000 acres of mountain, loch, moor and forest scenery. Over 60m of signposted walking routes.
Campsites: See Gazetteer, under Gartmore and Balmaha (Scotland).

National Parks

Details of National Parks Information Centres are given in the text. Most information centres are only open during the summer season (normally Easter to October) so it is advisable to telephone first before making a special journey. *Correspondence should only be sent to those places marked with an asterisk.

ENGLAND

DARTMOOR

945 square kilometres (365 square miles) of high moorland. Includes nature reserves. Details from *Information Officer 'Parke', Haytor Road, Bovey Tracey, Newton Abbot ☎ Bovey Tracey 832093, or Information Centres at:
Newbridge (Caravan).
Postbridge Steps Bridge.
Tavistock Bedford Square.

EXMOOR

686 square kilometres (265 square miles) of heather-clad moorland plateau, down to coast. Details from Information Officer, Exmoor National Park Department. *Exmoor House, Dulverton, Somerset. ☎ Dulverton 23665/6, or Information Centres at:
Combe Martin (Caravan) Beach Car Park ☎3319.
County Gate A39 between Porlock and Lynmouth ☎ Brendon 321.
Lynmouth Parish Hall, Watersmeet Road ☎ Lynton 2509.
Minehead Market House, The Parade ☎2984.

LAKE DISTRICT

2,243 square kilometres (866 square miles) of mountain and lake scenery, including England's three highest mountains and largest lake. Details from *Information Officer, National Park Offices, Busher Walk, Kendal, Cumbria ☎24555 or Information Centres at:
Ambleside Old Court House, Church Street ☎3084 (Closed Nov–Mar).
Bowness Bowness Bay, Glebe Road ☎ Windermere 2895 (Closed Jan–Mar).
Coniston (Caravan) Village Car Park ☎533.
Glenridding (Caravan) Car Park ☎414.
Hawkshead (Caravan) Car Park ☎525.
Keswick Moot Hall ☎72803.
Pooley Bridge (Caravan) Car Park ☎530.
Seatoller adjacent village Car Park ☎ Borrowdale 294.
Waterhead (Caravan) Car Park, at head of Lake Windermere, National Park Centre, Brockhole ☎2231.
Caravan Advisory Service ☎ Windermere 555/5515.
Weather Information Service ☎ Windermere 5151/2/3/4.

NORTHUMBERLAND

1,031 square kilometres (398 square miles) of hills and moorland. Stretches from Hadrian's Wall in the south to the Cheviot Hills on the Scottish border. Details from *Information Officer, Northumberland National Park, Eastburn, South Park, Hexham, ☎5555, or Information Centres at:
Byrness 9 Otterburn Green ☎ Otterburn 20622.
Ingram Old School House ☎ Powburn 248.
Once Brewed Military Road, Hexham ☎ Bardon Mill 396.
Rothbury Church House, Church Street ☎20887.

NORTH YORK MOORS

1,432 square kilometres (553 square miles) of hills, moors and coast. Details from *Information Officer, North York Moors National Park, North Yorkshire County Council, The Old Vicarage, Bondgate, Helmsley, North Yorkshire YO6 5BP. ☎04392 657/658, or Information Centres at:
Danby National Park Centre, Danby Lodge, near Whitby. ☎ Castleton 654.
Pickering Station ☎73791.
Sutton Bank Information Centre, top of Sutton Bank by the A170, personal callers only. ☎ Sutton 426.

PEAK DISTRICT

1,404 square kilometres (542 square miles) of country varying from limestone uplands in the south and east, to wild moorland in the north. Details from *Information Officer, Peak District National Park, Aldern House, Baslow Road, Bakewell, Derbyshire, DE4 1AE. ☎2881 (closed weekends) or Information Centres at:
Bakewell Market Hall, Bridge Street ☎3227 (closed Wednesday and Thursday in winter).
Castleton Castle Street ☎ Hope Valley 20679 (closed Monday, Tuesday, Thursday and Friday in winter).
Dovestones Dovestones Reservoir, near Greenfield, Sundays only.
Edale Field Head ☎ Hope Valley 70207/70216.
Goyt Valley Derbyshire Bridge, Sundays only.
Hartington Old Station, Saturdays and Sundays only.
Tideswell Dale Car Park, Sundays only.

YORKSHIRE DALES

1,761 square kilometres (680 square miles) of wide, sweeping upland moors and deep pastoral valleys. Details from *Information Officer, Yorkshire Dales National Park, 'Colvend', Hebden Road, Grassington ☎752748.
Aysgarth Falls Car Park ☎ Aysgarth 424.
Clapham Reading Room ☎419.
Hawes (Caravan) Station Yard ☎450.
Malham Car Park ☎ Airton 363.
Sedbergh 72 Main Street ☎20125.
Settle Town Hall ☎3617.
Weather Information Service ☎ Horton-in-Ribblesdale 333 (weekends only).

WALES

BRECON BEACONS

1,344 square kilometres (519 square miles) of mountain moorland including three nature reserves. Details from *Information Officer, Brecon Beacons National Park, Glamorgan Street, Brecon, Powys LD3 7DW. ☎2763. Open Easter–October, closed Sundays.
Abergavenny Monk Street ☎3254 closed Sundays.
Libanus Mountain Centre ☎ Brecon 3366.
Llandovery 8 Broad Street ☎20693.

PEMBROKESHIRE COAST

583 square kilometres (225 square miles) of spectacular cliffs, secluded bays, and sandy coves. Details from *Information Officer, Pembrokeshire Coast National Park, Dyfed County Council, County Offices, Haverfordwest ☎3131, or Information Centres at:
Broad Haven Pembrokeshire Countryside Unit, Car Park ☎412.
Fishguard Town Hall ☎873484.
Haverfordwest 40 High Street ☎66161.
Kilgetty Kingsmoor Common ☎ Saundersfoot 813672/3.
Pembroke Castle Terrace ☎2148.
St David's City Hall ☎392.
Tenby The Norton ☎3510.

SNOWDONIA

2,171 square kilometres (838 square miles) of mountains and woodlands in North Wales including the Snowdonia Forest Park. Details from National Park Officer, Yr Hen Ysgol, Maentwrog ☎274, or Information Centres at:
Aberdovey The Wharf ☎321.
Bala Old British High School, High Street ☎367.
Blaenau Ffestiniog Caerblaidd Office, Queen's Bridge ☎360.
Conwy Castle Street ☎2248.
Dolgellau Beechwood House ☎422888.
Harlech Gwyddfor House, High Street ☎658.
Llanberis Community Centre ☎765.
Llanrwst Glan-y-Borth ☎640604 (closed Thursday pm and weekends in winter).
Plas Tan y bwlch (Caravan).

SCOTLAND

The Countryside Commission for Scotland has for various reasons not deemed it necessary to develop National Parks in Scotland, as has been implemented in England and Wales, but several large tracts of land have been identified as areas where National Parks could be created should circumstances arise. See Forest Parks page 232.

Long-distance footpaths

ENGLAND

CLEVELAND WAY
93 miles (150 kilometres). Open throughout length. Route entirely in North Yorkshire, from Helmsley to a point near Filey.

NORTH DOWNS WAY
141 miles (227 kilometres). The route is open, with temporary links in some sections, between Farnham and Dover and follows the crest of the North Downs; in a few places coinciding with the medieval Pilgrims' Way. The main route skirts Folkestone, but there is an alternative link from Boughton Lees (north east of Ashford, Kent), via Canterbury to Dover. Proposals are under consideration to extend the path to Winchester.

PENNINE WAY
250 miles (402 kilometres). Open throughout length. Strenuous route from Edale, Derbyshire to Kirk Yetholm in Scotland.

RIDGEWAY PATH
85 miles (137 kilometres). Open throughout length. Route is from Overton Hill near Avebury, Wiltshire to Ivinghoe Beacon in Buckinghamshire.

SOUTH DOWNS WAY
80 miles (129 kilometres). Open throughout length. Bridleway from outskirts of Eastbourne to Harting. A 26 mile extension from Harting to the outskirts of Winchester is proposed.

SOUTH WEST PENINSULA COAST PATH
Someset and North Devon 82 miles (132 kilometres). Cornwall 268 miles (431 kilometres). South Devon 93 miles (150 kilometres). Dorset 72 miles (116 kilometres). No rights of way in some sections. The route, totalling some 515 miles, extends from Minehead to Studland, near Poole.

WOLDS WAY
72 miles (115 kilometres). The latest long distance footpath to be approved, work has commenced on its implementation but it will be some time before it can be officially opened. This path will eventually extend from near Hull to Filey and will link with Cleveland Way.

WALES

OFFA'S DYKE PATH
168 miles (270 kilometres). Open throughout length. Route runs north to south the entire length of Wales, from Prestatyn to Chepstow.

PEMBROKESHIRE COAST PATH
167 miles (269 kilometres). Open throughout length. Route follows the coastline from Amroth to St Dogmaels.

SCOTLAND

No long distance paths have yet been established, but some proposals are under consideration. A drawback is that provision could unwisely encourage use by people who are unprepared for the severe rigours of the Scottish climate.

Bridges, tunnels and ferries in Great Britain

The map reference given in the text refer to the atlas section at the end of this book. No details of prices are given, but when a free service operates it is stated.

Principal bridges and tunnels in Great Britain
Special regulations apply to the Erskine, Forth (No breakdown charges), Severn, Tamar (driver responsible for obtaining assistance), and Tay toll bridges and to the Clyde, Dartford, Mersey and Tyne Tunnels. Brief details are given below.

Stopping is not allowed. In some cases, parking facilities are provided at one end of the bridge. Toll booths are situated at one end only. The correct money should be held ready – in some cases there are automatic collection facilities. Charges normally cover driver and passengers.

In the event of a breakdown (including wheel changes the driver and passengers should remain with the vehicle, which will be removed by the bridge or tunnel authority breakdown service.

In some cases traffic is observed by the control room or patrol car and in others breakdown telephones are provided along the carriageway. A charge is made for the removal of any vehicle; the minimum charge is usually £1.50, but can be as much as £10 per hour (£4 for lack of petrol).

In tunnels, overtaking is prohibited and maximum and minimum speeds are specified. Stopping is not permitted unless directed. Vehicles carrying goods of a dangerous nature, such as inflammable or corrosive substances, are subject to certain restrictions. Vehicles carrying no more than two cylinders of hydrocarbon gas (e.g. butane, Calor Gas) for leisure purposes are usually permitted without escort, but the Authority have the right to impose restrictions, or require an inspection, at any time. It is prohibited to refuel a vehicle in the tunnel.

PRINCIPAL BRIDGES
(Toll, or limited by service conditions)

Batheaston Map 3ST76.
Near Bath, off A4.
Limit weight 4 tons.
Cleddau Map 2SM90
A477 Pembroke–Haverfordwest.
Limited restrictions on high vehicles when wind speed exceeds 45mph.
Clifton Map 3ST57
Bristol B3124 W of city.
Limit weight 4 tons.
Mechanical system of toll collection.
Dunham Map 8SK87
A57 Lincoln–Worksop 12m W of Lincoln.
Erskine Map 11NS47
10m NW of Glasgow ☎ Bishopton 2022.
Forth Map 11NT17
10m W of Edinburgh ☎031-331 1699.
Humber Map 8TA02
Approximately 5m upstream from Hull.
Under construction, expected to open Spring 1980.
Itchen Map 4SU41
A3025 Woolston–Southampton.
Toll free between Midnight and 06.00 hours (09.00 Sun).
Vehicles over 3 tons banned during these hours.
Middlesbrough (Cleveland Transit) Map 8NZ42
A178 N of town.
Service frequent 05.00–23.00 (14.00–23.00 Sun).
Limit weight 3 tons, length 40ft.
☎ Middlesbrough 248411.
Newport, Gwent Map 3ST38
Transporter Bridge, B4327 across R Usk
6 cars free.
Limit weight 13 tons, length 30ft, width 15ft.
Service frequent 05.30–22.52 (Sun 05.30–08.00 then 13.00–22.52) (22.15 winter).
☎ Newport 64580.
Penrhyndeudraeth (Briwet Bridge) Map 6SH63
Unclassified road between A496 and A487
3½m E of Porthmadog (saves 6½m on road to Barmouth).
Limit weight 2 tons.
Caravans not permitted.
Porthmadog Map 6SH53
A487 E of town.
Selby Map 8SE63
A19 E of town.

Severn Map 3ST59
M4 3m SE of Chepstow between A38 and A48.
☎ Pilning 2436.
Shard Map 7SD34
A588 Blackpool–Lancaster.
Limit weight 12 tons.
Swinford Map 4SP40
B4044 Oxford–Witney 5½m W of Oxford.
Tamar Map 2SX45
A38 Plymouth–Liskeard ☎ Plymouth 361577.
Tay Map 12NO42
Newport–Dundee ☎ Dundee 21881/2.
Warburton Map 7SJ68
B5159 6m E of Warrington across Manchester Ship Canal.
Limit weight 5 tons.
Whithchurch Map 4SU67
B471 Pangbourne–Whitchurch.
Whitney Map 3SO24
B4350 Hereford–Hay-on-Wye.

Principal Tunnels

(Toll, or limited by service conditions)

Blackwall Map 5TQ37
River Thames 3m E of Tower Bridge. Twin tunnels. Free. Open always. Limit, height northbound 13ft 4in, southbound 15ft 6in, width 9ft 6in. Conveyance of gas cylinders restricted.
Clyde Map 11NS56
River Clyde W side of Glasgow at Whiteinch. Free. Open always. Caravans restricted to carrying 2 cylinders of gas of 10lb capacity.
☎041-339 2236.
Dartford Map 5TQ57
River Thames 15m E of Tower Bridge.
Open always.
☎ Dartford 21222.
From mid July to end of August/early September. Traffic delays Sat mornings, Sun evenings. Conveyance of gas cylinders restricted to 2 containers of 34lb capacity.
Mersey Map 7SJ39
River Mersey between Liverpool and Birkenhead and Liverpool and Wallasey. Open always.
Queensway tunnel ☎051-647 8814.
Kingsway tunnel ☎051-638 9441.
Conveyance of gas cylinders is limited to 2 cylinders not exceeding 10lbs capacity for each cylinder. In excess of this, or in cases of doubt drivers *must* report to police control before proceeding.
Rotherhithe Map 5TG38
River Thames 1m E of Tower Bridge. Free.
Open always.
Conveyance of gas cylinders restricted.
Tyne Map 12NZ36
River Tyne 5m E of Newcastle.
Open always.
Conveyance of gas cylinders restricted to 2 x 36lb (16 kilos) cylinders.
☎ Wallsend 624451.

Ferries

Ferries are listed below in alphabetical order; England, mainland Ferries (including Isle of Wight) shown first, followed by Scotland, mainland ferries (including islands where site facilities are available). More detailed information is given in the booklets 'Bridges, tunnels and Ferries in Great Britain' HR54 and 'Scottish Islands' HR98, available free of charge to members on request from any AA Office. The information given is: name and map reference, vehicle carrying capacity, frequency of service and daily period of operation, and telephone number. Services are described as frequent if they operate every 30 minutes or less. Services may be altered at Christmas and bank holidays, and are operated subject to tide, weather, and other conditions. Journeys are undertaken at the vehicle owner's risk. On ferries where passengers are allowed to remain in their vehicles, enough room must be left between to allow doors to be opened in an emergency.

GAS CYLINDERS
The carriage or shipment of inflammable materials is subject to regulations, but the interpretation or implementation is a matter for the company concerned. In practice, providing no more than two cylinders of hydrocarbon gas (e.g. butane, Calor Gas) are carried, there is usually no formality, but the operating company has the right to impose restrictions, or require an inspection, at any time. Pierced cartridges or cylinders cannot be carried aboard under any circumstances.

ENGLAND MAINLAND FERRIES
Bodinnick–Fowey Map 3SX15.
6–8 cars limit weight 3 tons.
Service according to demand
07.00 (08.00 Sun)–20.45 (or dusk whichever later).
Not Christmas or Boxing Day.
☎ Polruan 232.
Approaches are narrow and steep.
Not advised for caravans.
Dartmouth Higher Map 4SX85
18 cars, Service frequent 06.30 (09.00 Sun)–22.50 (Christmas Day 09.00–12.00 then 15.00–18.30).
☎ Dartmouth 3351.
Dartmouth Lower Map 4SX85
8 cars, Service frequent 07.00 (08.00 Sun)–22.45. Christmas Day no service. Boxing Day and New Year's Day 10.00–12.00; 17.00–19.00. Good Fri as Sun. Other Bank Holidays, normal service.
☎ Kingswear 342.
Humber (Hull–New Holland) Map 8TA02
20–40 cars limit weight unladen 2 tons.
Service 17–18 sailings 06.30–21.15 (6–9 sailings Sun 07.55–19.40). ☎ Hull 28613.
For details see BR Eastern and North Eastern Region timetables.
Vehicles must be at the pier 10 mins before departure (30 mins at peak periods). The Ferry service will be withdrawn when Humber Bridge (toll) is available.
Anticipated opening date, Spring 1980.

ISLE OF WIGHT
From the Mainland
Services from the mainland operate between the following places. **On these services it is advisable to make advance reservations for all sailings, and essential for travel at summer weekends.** For travel on Sat end May – early Sep arrangements must be made at least six weeks before date of travel. (Advance reservations are not accepted for solo motor cycles or scooters as they are conveyed as space permits). Full details and booking forms are available from the AA, or the operating company.
Lymington–Yarmouth Map 4SZ38
Operator: Sealink Car-Ferry Services.
For travel on a Fri, Sat or Sun between late May and early Sep see Portsmouth address below. On other days throughout the year: Sealink Car-Ferry Booking Office, Lymington Pier, Lymington, Hants SO4 8ZE
☎ Lymington 73301.
Portsmouth–Fishbourne Map 4SZ59
Operator: Sealink Car-Ferry Services.
Bookings: Sealink Central Reservation Office, Isle of Wight Car-Ferry Services, Portsmouth Harbour Station, Portsmouth, Hants PO1 3EU
☎ Portsmouth 27744.
Southampton–Cowes and East Cowes
Map 4SZ49/59
Operator: Red Funnel Services, 12 Bugle Street, Southampton SO9 4LJ.
☎ Southampton 26211 or Cowes (IoW) 2101.
Written applications for booking at Summer weekends.

ON THE ISLAND
Cowes–East Cowes Isle of Wight
Map 4SZ49
12 cars.
Service frequent 05.30 (Sun 07.00)–23.00.
☎ Cowes (IoW) 3041.

Bridges, tunnels and ferries

King Harry–Philliegh Map 2SW83
28–30 cars.
Service F Summer: 08.00–20.00 mid May–early Jul (21.00 early Jul–beginning Sep; 20.00 Sep) (Sun 10.00–18.00 late Mar–early May) (20.00 mid May–early Jul; 21.00 early Jul–late Aug; 20.00 Sep) Winter 08.00–18.00 Oct–mid May (Sun no service Oct–late Mar). No service Christmas Day and Boxing Day. Other Bank Holidays as Sun.
☎ Truro 862312.
Reedham Map 5TG40
2–3 cars.
Service according to demand 08.00–22.00.
☎ Freethorpe 429.
Limit max length 30ft. Approach roads not advised for caravans.
Sandbanks–Shell Bay Map 4SZ08
28 cars.
Service frequent Summer: (1st Mon May–1st Sun Oct): 07.00–22.00 (23.00 Fri, Sat, Sun and Bank Holidays. Also daily from last Mon in May–2nd Sun Sep). Winter: (1st Mon Oct–1st Sun May) 07.00 (08.00 Sun)–21.00 (23.00 Fri, Sat, Sun and Bank Holidays, excluding Christmas Day and New Year's Day).
☎ Studland 216.
Torpoint–Devonport Map 2SX45
32 cars.
Service frequent day and night.
☎ Plymouth 812233.
Alternative route via Tamar (toll) bridge always open.
Windermere Map 7SD39
10 cars.
Service according to demand Easter–Sep 06.50–21.50 (09.50–21.50 Sun); Mid Sep–Sun before Easter 06.50–20.50 (Sun 09.50–20.50).
Woolwich–North Woolwich Map 5TQ47
45–50 cars all vehicles free.
Service frequent 06.00–22.15 (Sun 07.40–21.45)
☎01-854 3488.
Alternative routes via Blackwall Tunnel (free) or Dartford Tunnel (toll).

SCOTLAND

Ferries and services to selected islands

MAINLAND

Corran–Ardgour Map 14NN06
9 cars.
Service frequent Easter to 30 Sep 07.45 (Sun 09.00)–21.00. Remainder of year 07.45 (Sun 10.00)–18.30 (Sun 16.30) or dusk, whichever later. No service 25, 26 Dec and 1, 2 Jan. Normal Service other Bank Holidays.
☎ Ardgour 243. Slight delays at low tide.
Dunoon–Gourock Map 10NS17
40 cars.
Service frequent 06.45–20.45 (20.00 winter); Sun 08.45–20.00 (19.45 winter).
Operator: Caledonian MacBrayne Ltd.
☎ Gourock 34567.
Dunoon (Hunters Quay)**–Gourock** (McInroy's Point) Map 10NS17
18–26 cars.
Service frequent hourly throughout year Mon–Thu 07.00–22.30 Fri, Sat, Sun 07.00–midnight.
☎041-332 9766.
Kessock (Beauly Firth) Map 15NH64
22 cars.
Service frequent 07.15–22.45 (09.45–18.00 Sun).
☎ Inverness 33270.
Kylesku (Loch Cairnbawn) Map 14NC23
16 cars.
Service frequent 09.00–21.00 or dusk, whichever earlier. Signs erected at Laxford Bridge and Skiag Bridge giving warning if ferry is inoperative for any lengthy period.
☎ Kylesku 222.
Renfrew–Yoker Map 13NS56
15 cars.
Service continuous day and night.
☎041-221 8733.

ISLANDS

This is not a comprehensive list of services to all the Scottish islands; only those islands where site facilities are available are included.
Harris: Uig (Skye)–Tarbert (and via Lochmaddy, North Uist) Map 13NB10 1–2 services daily. Winter: 3 sailings weekly: Tue, Thu, Sat. Spring and Autumn: 1 service daily (1 extra Tues via Lochmaddy). No Sun service. Advance reservations: Caledonian MacBrayne Ltd, The Pier, Gourock, Renfrewshire PA19 1QP.
☎ Gourock 33755 (general enquiries).
Lewis; Ullapool–Stornoway Map 60NB43
2 sailings daily.
Late May–end Sep (1 winter: 2 sailings Tue, Thu, April–late May and Oct). No Sun service. Advance reservations: details as for Harris, Uig.
Skye; Kyle of Lochalsh–Kyleakin
Map 13NG72
Frequent daily service, approx hourly service Sun. Operator as for Harris, Uig.
Skye; Mallaig–Armadale Map 13NM69
Service 4–5 sailings daily. No winter service or Sun service. Operator as above.

SITES OPEN ALL YEAR

The following are open all year (some with restricted services) according to information supplied by the proprietors before going to press *(July 1979)*.
For the current conditions it is advised that you check with your chosen site in advance, especially during the winter months.

England

ALCESTER Warwicks Hoo Mill (rs Nov-Feb)
ASHBURTON Devon Ashburton Caravan Park
BATH Avon Newbridge Caravan Park
BIDDENDEN Kent Woodlands Park (rs Nov-Feb)
BOURNEMOUTH Dorset Cara Caravan Park
BRIDLINGTON Humberside Poplars Caravan Site (rs Dec-Feb)
CHRISTCHURCH Dorset Hoburne Farm Caravan Park (rs Nov-Feb)
CHUDLEIGH KNIGHTON Devon Ford Farm (rs Nov-Feb)
DERBY Derbys Alvaston Mobile Home Park (rs Nov-Mar)
GRAFHAM Cambs Old Manor Caravan Park
HARROGATE N Yorks Shaws Trailer Park
HATFIELD S Yorks Hatfield Marina
HEDGE END Hants Grange Caravan Park
HELSTON Cornwall Glenhaven Touring Park
HEMINGFORD ABBOTS Cambs Heming Abbots Caravan Park (rs Nov-Mar)
HUNTINGDON Cambs Anchor Cottage Riverside Caravan & Camping Site
KEMPSEY Heref & Worcs Court Meadow Caravan Park
LONDON (Abbey Wood) Co-operative Woods Camping & Caravan Site
MORECAMBE Lancs Municipal Caravan Park (rs Nov-Feb)
MORECAMBE Lancs Encee Caravan Park
NEWQUAY Cornwall Trevelgue Caravan Park (rs Nov-Mar)
NORTH KILWORTH Leics Kilworth Caravan Park (rs Jan-Mar)
NOTTER BRIDGE Cornwall Notter Bridge Caravan & Camping Park (rs Oct-Mar)
NOTTINGHAM Notts Surprise View Trailer Park (rs Oct-Mar)

Sites open all year

OLNEY Bucks Emberton Park (rs Nov-Mar)
ORMSKIRK Lancs Abbey Farm Caravan Site
PAIGNTON Devon Blagdon Park Camping Site (rs Oct-Etr)
PATHFINDER VILLAGE Devon Pathfinder Touring Caravan Park
PENZANCE Cornwall Mount's Bay Holiday Centre (rs Nov-Mar)
PERRANARWORTHAL Cornwall Cosawes Caravan Park
PLYMOUTH Devon Riverside Caravan Park
PRAA SANDS Cornwall Pengersick Caravan & Camping Site
ST AUSTELL Cornwall Trewhiddle Caravan & Camping Park (rs Oct-26May)
ST HILARY Cornwall Wayfarers Camping Site
SHEPTON MALLET Somerset Manleaze Caravan Park
SHRAWLEY Heref & Worcs Lenchford Hotel (rs Nov-Feb)
SKIPTON N Yorks Overdale Trailer Park
SLIMBRIDGE Glos Tuder Arms Caravan Site
SOUTHWATER W Sussex Raylands Park (rs Nov-Feb)
STANTON Suffolk Shepherds Grove Park
TAUNTON Somerset St Quintin Hotel Caravan & Camping Park
TAVISTOCK Devon Higher Longford Farm Caravan Site (rs Oct-mid May)
UPLYME Devon Hook Farm Camping & Caravan Park (rs Nov-14Mar)
WEST BRIDGFORD Notts Green Acres
WEST DRAYTON Gt London Riverside Caravans
WESTON-SUPER-MARE Avon Weston Gateway Caravan Site (rs Oct-May)
WHALEY BRIDGE Derbys Happy Vans Caravan Site
WHATSTANDWELL Derbys Haytop Farm Caravanserai
WHATSTANDWELL Derbys Mere Brook Caravan & Camping Park
WILSHAMSTEAD Beds Briar Bank Park
WOLVEY Warwicks Wolvey Villa Farm Caravan & Camping Site

Wales

BRONLLYS Powys Anchorage Caravan Park
GARTHMYL Powys Argae Hall
HASGUARD CROSS Dyfed Hasguard Cross Caravan Park
HOWEY Powys Dalmore Camping Site
LLANDRILLO Clwyd Hendwr Farm Site (rs Nov-Mar)
LLANDUDNO JUNCTION Gwynedd Glan Morfa Farm

Scotland

AVIEMORE Highland Glen More Forest Park
BLAIR ATHOLL Tayside River Tilt Caravan Site
BOTHWELL Strathclyde Strathclyde Park Caravan Site
CARGILL Tayside Beech Hedge Restaurant & Caravan Park
CASTLE DOUGLAS Dumfries & Galloway Lochside Park (rs Oct-Mar)
CROOK OF DEVON Tayside Drum Caravans & Filling Station
DALRYMPLE Strathclyde Doon Valley Caravan Park (rs Oct-May)
DORNOCH Highland Grannie's Heilan Hame (rs Sep-May)
EAST LINTON Lothian Monksmuir Caravan Park (rs Oct-Mar)
FINDHORN Grampian Findhorn Bay Caravan Park (rs Oct-Jun)
KINROSS Tayside Turfhills Tourist Centre
KINROSS Tayside Milk Bar (rs Nov-Mar)
KIRKPATRICK FLEMING Dumfries & Galloway Bruce's Cave & Caravan Site (rs Nov–Feb)
KIRKPATRICK FLEMING Dumfies & Galloway Greenfield Caravan Park
KIRRIEMUIR Tayside Drumshademuir Caravan Park (rs Nov-Mar)
SOUTHERNESS Dumfries & Galloway Southerness Holiday Village (rs Nov-Feb)
STRANRAER Dumfries & Galloway Aird Donald Caravan Park

SITES WITH STATIC CARAVANS

The following list of sites with static holiday and/or residential caravans is taken from information supplied by the proprietors. Static vans are not inspected by the AA and this list is for information only. The number of static vans is shown in brackets following the site name but not all are available for letting to the public. Further information can be obtained from the gazetteer entry and by direct application to the site operator.

ENGLAND

AVON
Bleadon Purn Farm (80)
Clevedon Colehouse Farm (41)
Corston Bury View Farm (6)
Severn Beach Villa Caravan Park (75)
Severn Beach Salthouse Farm (90)
Sidcot Netherdale Camping Ground (37)
Weston-Super-Mare Manor Farm (35)
Weston-Super-Mare Ardnave Park (105)

BEDFORDSHIRE
Wilshamstead Briar Bank Park (150)

BUCKINGHAMSHIRE
Olney Emberton Park (114)

CAMBRIDGESHIRE
Grafham Old Manor Caravan Park (4)
Hemingford Abbots Heming Abbots Caravan Park (40)
Huntingdon Anchor Cottage Riverside Site (15)

CHESHIRE
Acton Bridge Woodbine Cottage (30)

CORNWALL
Ashton Boscreage Park (23)
Blackwater Trewarth Farm (61)
Boswinger Seaview International (59)
Bude Bude Holiday Park (150)
Bude Wooda Farm (25)
Camelford Juliot's Well (32)
Carleen Poldown Park (5)
Carlyon Bay Bethesda Site (2)
Carnon Downs Ringwell Park (25)
Chacewater Chacewater Caravan Park (15)
Chapel Porth Chapel Porth Caravan Park (16)
Crackington Haven Hentervene Farm (21)
Crantock Treago Farm (7)
Crantock Quarryfield Caravan Park (31)
Cubert Treworgans Farm (20)
Delabole Planet Park (40)
Edgcumbe Retanna Country Park (26)
Falmouth Maen Valley Caravan Park (138)
Falmouth Golden Bank Caravans (72)
Goonhavern Silverbow Park (13)
Grampound Lynwood Caravan Park (3)
Gunnislake Honicombe Holiday Centre (100)
Hayle St Ives Bay Park (200)
Hewas Water Trencreek Farm (37)
Kennack Sands Sea Acres (94)
Kennack Sands Silver Sands (30)
Kennack Sands Kennack Sands Caravan Park (46)
Lanlivery Powderham Castle Caravan Park (34)
Launceston Travadlock Hall (28)
Leedstown Calloose Farm (12)
Lelant Downs Sunny Meadow (6)
London Apprentice Molingey Campsite (40)
Looe 'Treble B' Holiday Centre (30)
Looe Polborder House (3)
Looe Tencreek Caravan Park (42)
Looe Tregoad Caravan Park (2)
Lostwithiel Downend Camp Site (3)
Mawgan Porth Gluvian Caravan Site (36)

Sites with static caravans

Mullion Mullion Cove Holiday Park (245)
Mullion Criggan Mill Caravans (33)
Mullion Teneriffe Farm Caravan Site (5)
Newquay Newquay Tourist Park (47)
Newquay Gannel View Holiday Park (45)
Newquay Trenance Caravan Park (214)
Newquay Trevelgue Caravan Park (132)
Notter Bridge Notter Bridge Caravan Park (17)
Padstow Penjoly Caravan Park (70)
Par Mount Holiday Park (60)
Par Par Beach Caravan Park (215)
Pelynt Trelawne Holiday Estate (200)
Pelynt Trelay Farm (20)
Pendeen Levant House (1)
Pentewan Pentewan Sands Caravan Ground (53)
Pentewan Sun Valley Caravan Park (60)
Penzance Mount's Bay Holiday Centre (150)
Perranarworthal Cosawes Caravan Park (85)
Perranporth Perran Beach Camping Park (307)
Perranporth Perranporth Camping Site (10)
Poundstock Middle Penlean (3)
Praa Sands Pengersick Caravan Site (86)
Praa Sands Two Chimneys Park (30)
Redruth Lanyon Farm Caravan Park (49)
Rejerrah New Braefel Tourist Park (2)
Rosudgeon Joyces Farm (9)
Rumford Music Water Touring Site (3)
Ruthernbridge Ruthern Valley Holidays (18)
St Agnes Presingoll Farm (2)
St Austell Trewhiddle Caravan Park (109)
St Buryan Lower Treave Caravan Park (5)
St Buryan Tower Farm Caravan Park (6)
St Clether Ta-Mill (3)
St Columb Major Tregatillian Caravan Park (85)
St Day Tresaddern Caravan Park (12)
St Hilary Wayfarers Camping Site (6)
St Ives Ayr Holiday Park (60)
St Just Kelynack Caravan Park (10)
St Mabyn Glenmorris Caravan Park (22)
St Minver St Minver House Estate (130)
Sennen Sea View Caravan Park (75)
Sticker Glenleigh Caravan Park (40)
Tintagel Ocean Cove Caravan Park (159)
Tintagel Headland Caravan Site (25)
Truro Leverton Place (30)
Wall Parbola Caravan Park (12)
Whitecross White Acres Holiday Park (81)
Whitstone Keywood Caravan Park (50)

CUMBRIA
Appleby Wild Rose Park (184)
Ayside Oak Head Caravan Park (71)
Beckfoot Abbey Holme Caravan Park (25)
Blackford Dandy Dinmont Caravan Site (15)
Bouth Black Beck Caravan Park (220)
Braithwaite Scotgate Caravan Site (35)
Brampton Irthing Vale Park (20)
Cark-in-Cartmel Old Park Wood Site (292)
Cockermouth Violet Bank Site (40)
Cockermouth Wyndham Hall (80)
Crosthwaite Lambhowe Caravan Park (110)
Cumwhitton Cairndale Caravan Park (10)
Eamont Bridge Lowther Caravan Park (375)
Greystoke Whit Barrow Hall (140)
Hale Fell End Caravan Park (215)
Hale Hallmore Farm (56)
Haverthwaite Bigland Hall (39)
Kirkby Thore Low Moor Caravan Site (25)
Knock Silver Band Caravan Park (1)
Levens Sampool Caravan Site (195)
Mealsgate Larches Caravan Park (177)
Penruddock Beckses Caravan Site (18)
Plumpton Greenacres Caravan Park (30)
Pooley Bridge Hillcroft Caravan Site (200)
Preston Patrick Milness Hill Site (17)
Silecroft Silecroft Caravan Site (128)
Silloth Tanglewood Caravan Park (41)
Skelwith Bridge Neaum Crag Caravan Site (38)
Sunderland Skiddaw View Caravan Park (60)
Troutbeck Hutton Moor End (15)
Watermillock Ullswater Caravan Site (55)
Westward Clea Hall Holiday Park (85)
Windermere Fallbarrow Caravan Park (267)
Windermere Limefitt Park (20)
Windermere Park Cliffe Farm (50)
Windermere White Cross Bay Site (15)

DERBYSHIRE
Ashford in the Water Greenhills Park (60)
Buxton Dukes Drive Caravan Site (25)
Derby Alvaston Mobile Home Park (137)
Hope Laneside Caravan Park (22)
Newhaven Newhaven Holiday Park (70)
Whaley Bridge Happy Vans Caravan Site (14)
Whaley Bridge Ringstones Caravan Park (36)
Whatstandwell Mere Brook Caravan Park (116)

DEVON
Ashburton Ashburton Caravan Park (40)
Barnstaple Midland Caravan Park (63)
Berrynarbor Sandaway Holiday Park (69)
Berrynarbor Berrynarbor Caravan Park (51)
Bickington Lemonford Holidays (20)
Chillington Union Inn Caravan Site (4)
Chudleigh Knighton Ford Farm (2)
Cove Orchard Caravan Park (2)
Croyde Bay Ruda Holiday Parks (200)
Dalwood Andrewshayes Caravan Park (80)
East Worlington Yeatheridge Farm (5)
Highampton South Trew Farm (6)
Horns Cross Steart Farm (9)
Instow Lagoon View Caravan Park (200)
Ladram Bay Ladram Bay Caravan Site (398)
Little Torrington Smytham Caravan Site (25)
Lynton Sunny Lyn Caravan Site (31)
Malborough Alston Farm Caravanning Site (40)
Modbury California Caravan Park (1)
Modbury Pennymoor Caravan Park (70)
Modbury South Leigh Caravan Park (67)
Mortehoe Twitchen House and Mortehoe (295)
Mortehoe North Morte Farm (73)
Mullacott Cross Mullacott Cross Caravan Park (150)
Paignton Beverley Parks Caravan Site (300)
Paignton Grange Court Holiday Centre (589)
Paignton Lower Yalberton Caravan Park (8)
Paignton Whitehill Farm Caravan Site (66)
Rattery Edeswell Caravan Site (27)
St Giles on the Heath Chapmanswell Park (20)
Salcombe Regis Salcombe Regis Caravan Site (10)
Starcross Crofton Farm (60)
Sticklepath Coombe Head Farm (20)
Sticklepath Olditch Farm (6)
Stoke Fleming Deer Park Holiday Estate (32)
Tavistock Harford Bridge Park (60)
Tavistock Higher Longford Farm (24)
Tavistock Langstone Manor Caravan Park (20)
Tedburn St Mary Woodlands Park (20)
Torrington (Great) Greenways Valley (18)
Uplyme Hook Farm Caravan Park (15)
Woodbury Castle Brake Caravan Park (30)
Woolacombe Woolacombe Bay Caravan Park (175)

DORSET
Bournemouth Cara Caravan Park (90)
Bridestowe Bridestowe Caravan Park (12)
Charmouth Newlands Caravan Park (220)
Christchurch Grove Farm Meadow Park (200)
Christchurch Hoburne Farm Caravan Park (298)
Christchurch Haven Caravan Park (58)
Eype Highlands End Farm (160)
Holton Heath Sandford Park Caravans (150)
Osmington Mills Osmington Mills Holidays (100)
Owermoigne Sandy Holme Caravan Park (35)
St Leonards Oakdene Holiday Park (200)
Weymouth Gloucester Farm (44)
Weymouth Littlesea Holiday Park (680)
Wimborne Minster Wilksworth Farm (60)

CO DURHAM
Castleside Allensford Park Caravan Site (48)

ESSEX
St Osyth Hutleys Caravan Park (740)

GLOUCESTERSHIRE
Perrott's Brook Mayfield Park (44)
Rodborough Rodborough Fort Caravanning Centre (27)
South Cerney Cotswold Leisure Centre (79)

HAMPSHIRE
Hayling Island Lower Tye Farm (72)
Hedge End Grange Caravan Park (155)
New Milton Bashley Park (380)
Ower Green Pasturers Farm (2)
Warsash Dibles Park (41)

HEREFORD and WORCESTER
Bromyard Bromyard Caravan Park (140)
Harvington Carr's Caravan's Ltd (100)

Sites with static caravans

Honeybourne Ranch Caravan Park (160)
Peterchurch Poston Caravan Park (13)
Ross-on-Wye Cottage Caravan Park (32)
Shrawley Lenchford Hotel (60)
Sledge Green Three Counties Caravan Park (92)

HUMBERSIDE
Skipsea Low Skirlington Caravan Site (386)
Skipsea Skipsea Sands Caravan Park (748)
Stamford Bridge Weir Caravan Park (98)

KENT
Biddenden Woodlands Park (205)
Birchington Quex Caravan Park (58)
Dover Plough Inn (20)
Folkestone Little Switzerland Caravanning Site (24)
Herne Bay Hillborough Park (395)
Kingsnorth Broad Hembury Farm (25)
Martin Mill Hawthorn Caravan Site (130)
Minster Wayside Caravan Park (54)
Sutton Sutton Vale Caravan Park (114)
Warden Point Warden Spring Caravan Park (250)
Whitstable Blue Waters Touring Harbour (452)

LANCASHIRE
Blackpool Marton Mere Leisure Centre (800)
Bolton-le-Sands Sandside Caravan Site (35)
Bolton-le-Sands Bolton Holmes Farm (40)
Bolton-le-Sands Detron Gate Farm (52)
Carnforth Netherbeck Caravans (32)
Caton Crook O'Lune Caravan Park (138)
Eccleston (Great) Meadowcroft (40)
Fleetwood Broadwater Holiday Centre (405)
Gisburn Todber Caravan Park (200)
Lytham St Annes Eastham Hall Caravan Site (175)
Morecambe Municipal Caravan Park (300)
Morecambe Regent Caravan Park (324)
Morecambe Encee Caravan Park (16)
Ormskirk Abbey Farm Caravan Site (40)
Scorton Six Arches Caravan Site (290)
Silverdale Holgates Caravan Park (350)
Thornton Cleveleys Kneps Farm (100)

LEICESTERSHIRE
Casterton (Great) Casterton Motel (12)
North Kilworth Kilworth Caravan Park (50)

LINCOLNSHIRE
Chapel Hill Orchards Caravans (48)
Hubbert's Bridge Orchards Caravan Park (100)
Mablethorpe Golden Sands Estates (1,750)
Skegness Richmond Drive Carapark (740)

NORFOLK
Bradwell Blue Sky Caravan Park (133)
Burgh Castle Cherry Farm (212)
Caister-on-Sea Grasmere Caravan Park (74)
Cawston Haveringland Hall Caravan Park (65)
East Runton Woodhill Camping Site (115)
Hunstanton Searles Camping Ground (575)
Potter Heigham Homestead Site (81)
Weybourne Kelling Heath Caravan Site (385)
Wortwell Little Lakeland Caravan Park (20)
Yarmouth (Great) Vauxhall Holiday Park (605)

NORTHAMPTONSHIRE
Thrapston Mill Marina Caravan Park (5)

NORTHUMBERLAND
Bamburgh Glororum Caravan Park (125)
Beadnell Beadnell Links (140)
Belford Waren Caravan Site (240)
Berwick-upon-Tweed Ord House Caravan Park (206)
Haltwhistle Yont The Cleugh (40)
Hexham Causey Hill Caravan Park (75)
Hexham Lowgate Caravan Site (65)
Rothbury Coquetdale Caravan Park (154)
Wooler Bridge End Caravan Site (100)

NOTTINGHAMSHIRE
Nottingham Surprise View Park (225)
Old Clipstone Sherwood Forest Site (4)
Stragglethorpe Thorntons Holt Site (1)
Tuxford Greenacres (9)
West Bridgford Green Acres (85)

OXFORDSHIRE
Cassington Cassington Mill (50)
Standlake Standlake Caravans (2)

SALOP
Hughley Mill Farm (49)
Lyneal Fernwood Caravan Park (150)
Wentnor Green Caravanning Site (12)

SOMERSET
Berrow Unity Farm (180)
Blue Anchor Beeches Holiday Site (130)
Blue Anchor Blue Anchor Bay Caravan Park (475)
Brean Northam Farm Caravan Site (90)
Cheddar Broadway House Caravan Park (38)
Cheddar Froglands Farm (60)
Emborough Old Down House Camping Site (20)
Exford Westermill (3)
Porlock Porlock Caravan Park (56)
Priddy Mendip Heights Caravan Park (2)
Rodney Stoke Bucklegrove Caravan Park (123)
Shepton Mallet Manleaze Caravan Park (6)
Taunton St Quintin Hotel Caravan Park (24)
Thorn Falcon Ashe Caravan Site (8)
Watchet Doniford Holiday Village (240)
Watchet Warren Bay Caravan Park (155)
Watchet Sunny Bank Camp (30)
West Coker Partway Lane Caravan Park (11)
Wookey Hole Homestead Caravan Park (33)

STAFFORDSHIRE
Fazeley Drayton Manor Park (75)
Rugeley Silver Trees Caravan Park (57)

SUFFOLK
East Bergholt Grange Caravan Park (52)
Kessingland Kessingland Beach Camp (100)
Kessingland Denes Holiday Village (200)
Kessingland Heathland Caravan Park (180)
Leiston King George's Caravan Park (24)
Stanton Shepherds Grove Park (120)
Waldringfield Moon & Sixpence (160)

EAST SUSSEX
Ewhurst Lordine Court Caravan Park (150)
Hastings and St Leonards Holiday Homes (44)
Heathfield Greenview Caravan Fields (51)
Pevensey Bay Castle View Caravan Site (37)

WEST SUSSEX
Bolney Alder House Caravan Site (50)
Selsey West Sands Caravan Park (1,400)
Southwater Raylands Park (3)

TYNE and WEAR
Southshields Lizard Lane Caravan Site (65)

WARWICKSHIRE
Alcester Hoo Mill (60)
Aston Cantlow Island Meadow Caravan Park (55)

ISLE OF WIGHT
Cowes Thorness Bay Village (327)
Newbridge Orchards Holiday Park (60)
St Helens Nodes Point Holiday Village (243)
Whitecliffe Bay Caravan Site (300)
Wroxall Appuldurcombe Caravan Park (40)

WILTSHIRE
Rowde Lakeside (3)

WORCESTERSHIRE
Far Forest Acre Farm Caravan Park (85)

NORTH YORKSHIRE
Acaster Malbis Chestnut Farm Caravans (45)
Acaster Malbis Mount Pleasant Caravan Village (200)
Acaster Malbis Moor End Farm (5)
Allerton Park Allerton Park (80)
Grewelthorpe Newholme Caravan Site (20)
Gristhorpe Bay Blue Dolphin Holiday Park (307)
Harrogate Shaws Trailer Park (146)
High Bentham Riverside Caravan Park (150)
Leyburn Yorkshire Dales Caravan Park (140)
Lothersdale Springs Caravan Park (7)
Nawton Wrens of Ryedale Caravan Site (15)
Osmotherley Cote Ghyll Caravan Park (18)
Patrick Brompton Akebar Park (80)
Richmond Swale View Caravan Site (100)
Skipton Overdale Trailer Park (174)
Stainforth Knight Stainforth Caravan Site (60)
Threshfield Long Ashes Caravan Park (300)
Warsill Warren House Caravan Site (70)
Winksley Woodhouse Farm (15)

CHANNEL ISLANDS
Jersey – St Martin Rozel Camping Park (15)

Sites with static caravans

WALES

CLWYD
Glan-Yr-Afon Llawrbetws Farm (72)
Glyn Ceiriog Glan Llyn Caravan Park (5)
Llandrillo Hendwr Farm Site (80)
Llysfaen Westwood Caravan Park (45)
Prestatyn Presthaven Sands Caravan Park (800)

DYFED
Aberystwyth 'U' Tow Caravans (173)
Bettws Evan Pilbach Caravan Park (55)
Broadmoor Cross Park Caravan Site (85)
Cenarth Aberdwylan Caravan Park (54)
Clynderwen Derwenlas Caravan Park (10)
Creuddyn Bridge Bertheos Caravan Park (12)
Croesgoch Torbant Caravan Park (55)
Dinas Cross Fishguard Bay Caravan Site (50)
Hasguard Cross Hasguard Cross Caravan Park (35)
Landshipping New Park Caravan Site (30)
Laugharne Ants Hill Caravan Park (60)
Llangranog Gilfach Farm Caravan Site (150)
Llanon Woodlands Caravan Park (60)
Llanrhystud Pengarreg Caravan Park (150)
Ludchurch Woodland Vale Caravan Park (60)
Ludchurch Little Kings Caravan Site (20)
Narberth Redford Caravan Park (55)
Narberth Dyrham Caravan Site (10)
Narberth Noble Court Caravan Site (60)
Reynalton Croft Caravan Park (60)
Rhydcymerau Rhydcymerau Caravan Site (6)
St Davids Caerfai Bay Caravan Park (30)
St Davids Hendre Eynon Site (10)
St Florence New Minerton Caravan Park (120)
Saundersfoot Saundersvale Caravan Park (60)
Tenby Kiln Park Caravan Park (550)
Tenby Well Park Caravan Site (42)
Tenby Wood Park Caravans (90)
Tenby Lodge Farm Caravan Site (40)
Tresaith Gwalia Falls Caravan Park (40)

WEST GLAMORGAN
Fairwood Blackhills Caravan Park (120)

GWYNEDD
Bala Pen-y-Garth Farm (45)
Bethesda Ogwen Bank Caravan Park (100)
Betws Garmon Bryn Gloch Farm (15)
Brynsiencyn Fron Farm (1)
Brynteg Tyddyn Llwyd Caravan Site (95)
Brynteg Nant Newydd Caravan Park (80)
Brynteg Garnedd Touring Site (1)
Criccieth Cae-Canol Caravan Site (20)
Criccieth Tyddyn Morthwyl (22)
Llanbedrog Crugan Caravan Site (90)
Llandderfel Bryn Melyn Caravan Site (75)
Llandudno Junction Glan Morfa Farm (20)
Llandwrog White Tower Caravan Park (52)
Llanrug Tyn-Y-Coed Camping Site (40)
Llanrug Bryn Teg Caravan Park (286)
Llanrwst Kerry's Orchard Site (2)
Llanuwchllyn Bryn Gwyn Farm (30)
Llwyngwril Gwril Caravan Site (264)
Morfa Bychan Cardigan View Caravan Park (192)
Morfa Bychan Greenacres Caravan Site (800)
Penmaenmawr Gardens Caravan Park (40)
Penrhyndeudraeth Bwlch Bryn Caravan Park (40)
Pentraeth Rhos Caravan Park (60)
Pwllheli Gimblet Rock Caravan Park (111)
Tal-Y-Bont Islaw R'ffordd Caravan Site (200)
Trefriw Plas Meirion Caravan Park (21)
Tywyn Woodlands Holiday Park (121)
Tywyn Ysguboriau Caravan Site (145)

POWYS
Abermule Ye Old Smithy Caravan Park (52)
Bronllys Anchorage Caravan Park (101)
Church Stoke Mellington Hall (140)
Clyro Fforest Cwm Caravan Site (20)
Crossgates Park Caravan Site (15)
Garthmyl Argae Hall (75)
Hay-on-Wye Hollybush Inn (5)
Howey Dalmore Camping Site (12)
Llangyniew Henllan Caravan Park (57)
Pentrebeirdd Valley View Caravan Park (54)
Penybontfawr Park Farm (65)
Presteigne Rock Bridge Caravan Site (35)
Talgarth Riverside Caravan Park (5)

SCOTLAND

BORDERS
Cockburnspath Chesterfield Park (12)
Coldingham Scoutscroft Camping Site (110)
Greenlaw Greenlaw Caravan Park (45)
Hawick Riverside Caravan Park (8)
Innerleithen Tweedside Caravan Site (110)
Jedburgh Lilliardsedge Park (30)
Kelso Springwood Caravan Park (230)
Peebles Crossburn Caravan Park (95)

CENTRAL
Balmaha Cashell Caravan Site (10)
Blairlogie Witches Craig Farm (8)
Bridge of Allan Allanwater Caravan Site (40)
Callander Callander Holiday Park (120)
Callander Gart Estate Caravan Park (42)
Gartmore Cobeland Campsite (5)
Luib Glen Dochart Caravan Park (49)
Morenish High Creagan (8)
Stirling Cornton Caravan Park (21)
Tushielaw Honey Cottage Caravan Site (45)
Yetholm Kirkfield Caravan Site (15)

DUMFRIES AND GALLOWAY
Auchenmalg Cock Inn Caravan Park (45)
Balminnoch Three Lochs Caravan Park (140)
Brighouse Bay Brighouse Bay Holiday Park (120)
Cairn Ryan Cairn Ryan Caravan Park (105)
Crocketford Brandedleys Carafarm (20)
Dumfries Newbridge Caravan Park (90)
Eastriggs Gemmel Caravan Site (6)
Ecclefechan Hoddom Castle (30)
Gatehouse of Fleet Anwoth Caravan Site (20)
Gatehouse of Fleet Cardoness Site (188)
Glenluce Glenluce Caravan Site (25)
Glen Trool Caldons Caravan Ground (25)
Glen Trool Merrick Caravan Park (29)
Isle of Whithorn Burrow Head Farm (300)
Kippford Kippford Caravan Site (70)
Kirkgunzeon Mossband Caravan Park (3)
Lochnaw Drumlochart Caravan Park (78)
Mouswald Mouswald Caravan Park (15)
Newton Stewart Creebridge Caravan Park (40)
Portpatrick Galloway Point Caravan Park (60)
Sanquhar Castle View Caravan Park (20)
Stranraer Aird Donald Caravan Park (200)
Waterbeck Fallford Lodge Caravan Site (15)

FIFE
Crail Balcomie Links Caravan Park (75)
Guardbridge Clayton Caravan Park (200)
Kinghorn Pettycur Bay Caravan Park (350)
Letham Feus Letham Feus Caravan Park (100)
St Andrews Craigtoun Meadows Holiday Park (135)

GRAMPIAN
Aberchirder McRobert Park (3)
Aberdeen Hazelhead Caravan Site (35)
Aberlour Aberlour Gardens Caravan Park (17)
Aboyne Aboyne Loch Caravan Park (55)
Alford Haughton House Caravan Site (20)
Alves North Alves Caravan Park (25)
Ballater Ballater Caravan Site (72)
Banff Banff Links Caravan Site (95)
Brodie Old Mill Inn (40)
Buckie Strathlene Caravan Site (40)
Cullen Logie Caravan Site (40)
Cuminestown A B Caravans (12)
Elgin Riverside Caravan Park (10)
Findhorn Findhorn Bay Park (175)
Findhorn Findhorn Sands Park (150)
Findochty Findochty Caravan Site (10)
Fochabers Burnside Caravan Site (40)
Hopeman Ashgate Caravan Park (8)
Keith Keith Caravan Site (4)
Macduff Myrus Caravan Site (20)
Maryculter Lower Deeside Park (60)
Memus Glens Caravan Site (12)
Portnockie Macleod Park (5)
Stonehaven Queen Elizabeth Site (50)
Strachan Feughside Caravan Site (40)
Tarland Drummie Hill Caravan Park (40)
Turriff Kinnaird House (2)

HIGHLAND
Applecross Applecross Campsite (6)
Ardmair Ardmair Point Campsite (1)
Aviemore Dalraddy Caravan Park (40)

Beauly Cruivend Caravan Site (4)
Beauly Lovat Bridge Caravan Site (4)
Boat of Garten Boat of Garten Caravanning Park (55)
Brora Riverside Caravan Site (2)
Camustianavaig (Isle of Skye) Braes Camp (6)
Corpach Linnhe Caravan Park (100)
Cromarty Shore Mill (4)
Dornoch Grannie's Heilan Hame (75)
Dornoch Royal Dornoch Links Caravan Site (40)
Dunvegan (Isle of Skye) Dunvegan Caravan Park (5)
Fort William Glen Nevis Caravan Park (30)
Gairloch Sands Holiday Centre (4)
Gairlochy Gairlochy Caravan Park (2)
Glencoe Invercoe Caravan Site (6)
Grantown-on-Spey Municipal Site (50)
Invermoriston Lochness Camping Site (6)
Inverness Dochfour Site (12)
Lairg Woodend Caravan Site (6)
Nairn Househill Site (15)
Resipol Resipole Farm (4)
Roy Bridge Bunroy Caravan Park (1)
Roy Bridge Stronreigh (20)
Staffin (Isle of Skye) Staffin Caravan Site (4)
Thurso Thurso Burgh Caravan Site (10)

LOTHIAN
Dunbar Kirk Park Caravan Site (100)
Dunbar Winterfield Caravan Site (70)
East Linton Monksmuir Caravan Park (7)

STRATHCLYDE
Achnamara Castle Sween Bay Holidays (200)
Blairmore Gairletter Caravan Park (16)
Dalrymple Doon Valley Caravan Park (90)
Glendaruel Glendaruel Caravan Park (30)
Hollybush Skeldon Caravans (12)
Inveraray Battlefield Caravan Park (170)
Inverchapel Stratheck Caravan Site (50)
Inveruglas Loch Lomond Caravan Park (54)
Kilberry Port Ban Park (40)
Kilmarnock Cunningham Head Estate (100)
Kirkfieldbank Clyde Valley Caravan Park (100)
Lochgilphead Lochgilphead Caravan Site (30)
Lochgoilhead Lochgoilhead Caravan Site (160)
Maidens Sandy Beach Caravan Park (40)
Sandbank Cot House Garage (12)
Strachur Strathlachlan Caravan Park (75)

TAYSIDE
Aberfeldy Municipal Caravan Site (30)
Birnam Erigmore House Caravan Park (12)
Blair Atholl Blair Castle Caravan Site (50)
Blair Atholl River Tilt Caravan Site (40)
Bridge of Cally Middleton Farm (30)
Cargill Beech Hedge Caravan Park (9)
Comrie Twenty Shilling Wood Site (30)
Comrie West Lodge Caravan Site (35)
Crieff Crieff Holiday Village (40)
Dundee South Baldovan Caravan Site (7)
Kenmore Kenmore Caravan Site (70)
Kinross Loch Leven Caravan Site (38)
Kinross Turfhills Tourist Centre (20)
Kinross Milk Bar (5)
Kirriemuir Drumshademuir Caravan Park (28)
Monifieth Riverview Caravan Park (180)
Montrose South Links Site (68)
Perth Windsor Caravan Park (16)
Pitlochry Faskally Home Farm (50)
Pitlochry Milton of Fonab Caravan Site (45)
St Fillans Lochearn Caravan Park (200)
Tummel Bridge Riverside Caravan Park (100)

WESTERN ISLES
Coll Sands (Lewis) Broad Bay Caravan Site (12)
Drinnishadder (Harris) Laig House (5)

COUNTY LIST

Places appearing in the gazetteer are here arranged in County order (Regional order in Scotland). Look for the County in which you wish to stay to find the names of places where AA-recommended sites are situated; these placenames appear alphabetically within the gazetteer.

ENGLAND

Avon
Bath
Bleadon
Clevedon
Corston
Locking
Redhill
Severn Beach
Sidcot
Weston-super-Mare
Bedfordshire
Wilshamstead
Buckinghamshire
Olney
Cambridgeshire
Comberton
Grafham
Hemingford Abbots
Huntingdon
Cheshire
Acton Bridge
Chester
Lower Kelsall
Cornwall
Ashton
Blackwater
Bodmin
Bolventor
Boswinger
Bude
Camborne
Camelford
Carleen
Carlyon Bay
Carnon Downs
Chacewater
Chapel Porth
Crackington Haven
Crantock
Cubert
Delabole
Edgcumbe
Falmouth
Fowey
Goonhavern
Gorran
Grampound
Gunnislake
Gwithian
Hayle
Helston
Hewas Water
Kennack Sands
Kilkhampton
Lamorna
Landrake
Lanlivery
Launceston
Leedstown
Lelant Downs
London Apprentice
Long Downs
Looe
Lostwithiel
Mawgan Porth
Mullion
Newquay
Notter Bridge
Padstow
Par
Pelynt
Pendeen
Pentewan
Penzance
Perranarworthal
Perranporth
Poundstock
Praa Sands
Redruth
Rejerrah
Relubbus
Rosudgeon
Rumford
Ruthernbridge
St Agnes
St Austell
St Buryan
St Clether
St Columb Major
St Day
St Ewe
St Hilary
St Ives
St Just
St Just-in-Roseland
St Mabyn
St Merryn
St Minver
Sennen
Sticker
Tintagel
Truro
Veryan
Wall
Whitecross
Whitstone
Cumbria
Ambleside
Appleby
Ayside
Barrow-in-Furness
Bassenthwaite
Beckfoot
Bewaldeth
Blackford
Bouth
Braithwaite
Brampton

County list

Cark-in-Cartmel
Cartmel
Cockermouth
Crosthwaite
Cumwhitton
Dalston
Eamont Bridge
Greystoke
Hale
Haverthwaite
High Hesket
Kendal
Kirkby-in-Furness
Kirkby Thore
Knock
Levens
Mealsgate
Penrith
Penruddock
Plumpton
Pooley Bridge
Preston Patrick
Ravenglass
Sedgwick
Silecroft
Silloth
Skelwith Bridge
Sunderland
Troutbeck
Watermillock
Westward
Windermere

Derbyshire
Ashbourne
Ashford in the Water
Buxton
Derby
Elvaston
Fenny Bentley
Hartington
Hope
Matlock
Newhaven
Whaley Bridge
Whatstandwell

Devon
Ashburton
Barnstaple
Berrynarbor
Bickington
Bridestowe
Brixham
Buckfastleigh
Chillington
Chudleigh Knighton
Clifford Bridge
Cove
Croyde Bay
Dalwood
Dawlish
Dunkeswell
East Anstey
East Worlington
Haldon Racecourse
Hawkchurch
Highampton
Honiton
Horns Cross
Ilfracombe
Instow
Kennford
Ladram Bay
Little Torrington
Lydford
Lynton
Malborough
Modbury
Molland
Mortehoe
Mullacott Cross
Newton Abbot
Okehampton
Paignton
Pathfinder Village
Plymouth
Rattery
Rockbeare
Rousdon
St Giles on the Heath
Salcombe Regis
Sampford Courtenay
Sourton Down
Starcross
Sticklepath
Stoke Fleming
Tavistock
Tedburn St Mary
Torrington (Great)
Umberleigh
Uplyme
Waterloo Cross
Weston
Whiddon Down
Woodbury
Woolacombe

Dorset
Bournemouth
Cerne Abbas
Charmouth
Christchurch
Corfe Castle
Crossways
Evershot
Eype
Fleet
Holton Heath
Lytchett Minster
Organford
Osmington Mills
Owermoigne
St Leonards
Weymouth
Wimbourne Minster

Co Durham
Castleside
Sedgefield

Essex
Chigwell
St Osyth

Gloucestershire
Cheltenham
Perrott's Brook
Rodbourgh
Slimbridge
South Cerney
Wotton under Edge

Hampshire
Ashurst
Bransgore
Brockenhurst
Hayling Island
Hedge End
Holmsley
New Milton
Ower
Warsash
Winchester

Hereford & Worcester
Bromyard
Harvington
Hawford
Hereford
Honeybourne
Kempsey
Peterchurch
Ross-on-Wye
Shrawley
Sledge Green

Humberside
Bridlington
Broughton
Skipsea
Stamford Bridge

Isle of Wight
Cowes
Newbridge
St Helens
Shanklin
Whitecliffe Bay
Wroxall

Kent
Biddenden
Birchington
Canterbury
Dover
Folkestone
Herne Bay
Kingsnorth
Martin Mill
Minster
St Nicholas at Wade
Sutton
Warden Point
Westenhanger
Whitstable

Lancashire
Blackpool
Bolton-le-Sands
Carnforth
Caton
Eccleston (Great)
Fleetwood
Gisburn
Lytham St Annes
Middleton
Morecambe
Ormskirk
Scorton
Silverdale
Thornton Cleveleys
Weeton

Leicestershire
Casterton (Great)
North Kilworth

Lincolnshire
Chapel Hill
Hubberts Bridge
Mablethorpe
Market Rasen
North Somercotes
Skegness

London (Greater)
Abbey Wood (SE2)
Edmonton (N9)
West Drayton

Norfolk
Bradwell
Burgh Castle
Caister-on-Sea
Cawston
Clippesby
East Runton
Fakenham
Hunstanton
Narborough
Potter Heigham
Scratby
Trimingham
Weybourne
Wortwell
Yarmouth (Great)

Northamptonshire
Thrapston

Northumberland
Bamburgh
Beadnell
Belford
Berwick upon Tweed
Haltwhistle
Hexham
Rothbury
Wooler

Nottinghamshire
Nottingham
Old Clipstone
Rolleston
Stragglethorpe
Tuxford
West Bridgford

Oxfordshire
Cassington
Standlake
Wallingford

Salop
Hughley
Kinnerley
Lyneal
Wem
Wentnor

Somerset
Berrow
Blue Anchor
Brean
Cheddar
Emborough
Exford
Highbridge

Porlock
Priddy
Rodney Stoke
Shepton Mallet
Taunton
Thorn Falcon
Watchet
West Coker
Wincanton
Wookey Hole
Staffordshire
Fazeley
Rugeley
Trentham
Uttoxeter
Suffolk
East Bergholt
Gisleham
Kessingland
Leiston
Lowestoft
Newmarket
Shottisham
Stanton
Waldringfield
Surrey
Churt
Laleham
East Sussex
Ewhurst
Hastings & St Leonards
Heathfield
Pevensey Bay
Plumpton Racecourse
Three Oaks
Westham
West Sussex
Billingshurst
Bolney
Chichester
Fontwell
Goodwood
Selsey
Southwater
Tyne & Wear
Newcastle upon Tyne
South Shields
Warwickshire
Alcester
Aston Cantlow
Tiddington
Warwick
Wolvey
Wiltshire
Potterne
Rowde
Worcestershire
Far Forest
North Yorkshire
Acaster Malbis
Allerton Park
Brompton-on-Swale
Coneysthorpe
Constable Burton
Filey
Fylingdales
Grewelthorpe
Gristhorpe Bay
Harome
Harrogate
High Bentham
Lebberston
Leyburn
Lothersdale
Nawton
North Stainley
Osmotherly
Patrick Brompton
Redmire
Richmond
Ripon
Scarborough
Skipton
Snainton
Stainforth
Swainby
Thirsk
Threshfield
Ugthorpe
Warsill
Winksley
Wykeham
York
South Yorkshire
Doncaster
Hatfield
Worsbrough
West Yorkshire
Wetherby
Channel Islands
Guernsey:
Câtel (Fauxquets Valley)
Jersey:
St Brelade
St Martin
Isle of Man
Hillberry
Laxey

WALES

Clwyd
Eyton
Glan-yr-Afon
Glyn Ceiriog
Llandrillo
Llangollen
Llysfaen
Prestatyn
Ruabon
Dyfed
Aberystwyth
Bettws Evan
Broad Haven
Broadmoor
Cenarth
Clynderwen
Creuddyn Bridge
Croesgoch
Dinas Cross
Hasgaurd Cross
Landshipping
Laugharne
Llandre
Llangranog
Llanon
Llanrhystud
Llanwrda
Ludchurch
Narberth
Newcastle Emlyn
Reynalton
Rhydcymerau
St David's
St Florence
Sarnau
Saundersfoot
Tenby
Tresaith
Mid-Glamorgan
Porthcawl
West Glamorgan
Fairwood
Gwent
Chepstow
Mitchel Troy
Gwynedd
Abersoch
Bala
Beddgelert
Bethesda
Betws Garmon
Brynsiencyn
Brynteg
Caernarfon
Criccieth
Llanbedrog
Llandderfel
Llandudno Junction
Llandwrog
Llanrug
Llanrwst
Llanuwchllyn
Llwyngwril
Morfa Bychan
Penmaenmawr
Penrhyndeudraeth
Pentraeth
Pont-Rug
Porthmadog
Pwllheli
Rhosneigr
Tal-y-Bont
Trefriw
Tywyn
Powys
Abercrave
Abermule
Bronllys
Church Stoke
Clyro
Crossgates
Garthmyl
Hay-on-Wye
Howey
Llangyniew
Middletown
Pentrebeirdd
Penybontfawr
Presteigne
Talgarth

SCOTLAND

Borders
Cockburnspath
Coldingham
Greenlaw
Hawick
Innerleithen
Jedburgh
Kelso
Lauder
Melrose
Peebles
Tushielaw
Yetholm
Central
Auchenbowie
Balmaha
Blairlogie
Bridge of Allan
Callander
Gartmore
Luib
Morenish
Stirling
Dumfries & Galloway
Amisfield
Auchenmalg
Balminnoch
Brighouse Bay
Cairn Ryan
Castle Douglas
Creetown
Crocketford
Dumfries
Eastriggs
Ecclefechan
Gatehouse of Fleet
Glenluce
Glen Trool
Gretna
Gretna Green
Isle of Whithorn
Kippford
Kirkcudbright
Kirkgunzeon
Kirkpatrick Fleming
Lochmaben
Lochnaw
Lockerbie
Mouswald
Newton Stewart
Parton
Port Patrick
Powfoot
Sanquhar
Southerness
Stranraer
Waterbeck
Fife
Crail
Guardbridge
Kinghorn
Kirkcaldy
Letham Feus
Lundin Links
St Andrews
Tayport
Grampian
Aberchirder
Aberdeen
Aberlour

County list

Aboyne
Alford
Alves
Ballater
Banff
Brodie
Buckie
Cullen
Cuminestown
Elgin
Findhorn
Findochty
Fochabers
Fraserburgh
Hopeman
Keith
Macduff
Maryculter
Memus
Portnockie
Portsoy
Rosehearty
Stonehaven
Strachan
Tarland
Turriff

Highland
Applecross
Ardmair
Aviemore
Balmacara
Beauly
Boat of Garten
Brora
Camustianavaig (Isle of Skye)
Corpach
Cromarty
Dornoch
Dunnet
Dunvegan (Isle of Skye)
Durness
Fortrose
Fort William
Gairloch
Gairlochy
Garve
Glencoe
Grantown-on-Spey
Invermoriston
Inverness
John O'Groats
Lairg
Nairn
Poolewe
Reay
Resipol
Rosemarkie
Roy Bridge
Scaniport
Scourie
Shiel Bridge
Staffin (Isle of Skye)
Strontian
Thurso

Lothian
Dunbar
East Linton
Edinburgh
North Berwick

Strathclyde
Achnamara
Ardgartan
Ayr
Balloch
Barcaldine
Benderloch
Blairmore
Bothwell
Carradale
Connel
Dalrymple
Glendaruel
Hollybush
Inveraray
Inverchapel
Inveruglas
Kilberry
Kilmarnock
Kirkfieldbank
Lagganmore
Lochgilphead
Lochgoilhead
Maidens
Ravenstruther
Sandbank
Strachur
Strathaven

Tayside
Aberfeldy
Birnam
Blair Atholl
Bridge of Cally
Cargill
Comrie
Crieff
Crook of Devon
Dundee
Dunkeld
Forfar
Glengoulandie
Inchture
Kenmore
Kinross
Kirriemuir
Monifieth
Montrose
Perth
Pitlochry
St Fillans
Tummel Bridge

Western Isles
Coll Sands (Lewis)
Drinnishadder (Harris)

Follow the Country Code

Guard against all risk of fire

Leave all gates as you find them (which usually means fastening them)

Keep dogs under proper control

Keep to the paths across farm land

Avoid damaging fences, hedges and walls

Leave no litter

Safeguard water supplies

Protect and do not disturb wild life

Protect wild plants and trees (do not take specimens)

Go carefully on country roads

Respect the life of the countryside

NATURE TRAILS

Birds, animals, insects, trees, wild flowers ...

There is so much to see and hear as you walk through the wild places of Britain — if you know how to look and listen.

Nature Trails are arranged to please and instruct, covering distances from under a mile to three miles or so, in locations from sand-dunes to deep forests.

The AA is preparing a booklet giving full details of Nature Trails throughout Great Britain. It will be available free to AA members from early in 1980.

Know these creatures?

Answers on page 221

HIRE FIRM GAZETTEER

Listed below is a selection of firms hiring out camping and caravanning equipment. They are not necessarily recommended by the AA. The list is in alphabetical order under administrative counties, towns and the firms' names. Postal addresses may differ slightly as far as the counties are concerned. Telephone exchanges are as the town heading unless otherwise indicated.
What each firm hires out is indicated in the left-hand column.

KEY

▲	Tents/equipment
🚋	Touring caravans
🚐	Motor caravans
C	Available for Continental use
(NCC)	National Caravan Council Member

ENGLAND

AVON
▲C **Bristol** Blacks Camping and Leisure Ltd, 41a Colston Street. ☎298178.

BEDFORDSHIRE
🚋C **Bedford** Courtesy Caravans, Bedford Road A6, Haynes West End. ☎740934.

▲C **Bedford** Jeans Mountain Shops, 40 Allhallows. ☎62115.

BERKSHIRE
▲ **Reading** Carter & Son (Thatcham) Ltd., 99 Caversham Road, RG1 8AN. ☎55589.

▲C **Reading** Blacks Camping and Leisure Ltd., St Mary's Butts, RG1 2LN. ☎595150.

🚋 **Reading** Colins Caravans of Berkshire Ltd., Bath Road, Aldermaston, RG3 2HH. ☎Woolhampton 07352.

BUCKINGHAMSHIRE
🚐C **Beaconsfield** Old Beaconsfield Camper Vans, 68 London Road, HP9 2JD. ☎77573.

🚋C **High Wycombe** Gailey Caravan Co. Ltd., London Road. ☎28577.

CAMBRIDGESHIRE
🚋🚐 **Cambridge** Associated British Caravan Ltd., 264 Newmarket Road, CB5 8JR. ☎61431.

▲C **Cambridge** The Cambridge Outdoor Centre, 7 Bridge St., CB2 1UA. ☎53956.

🚋 **Elsworth** Courtesy Caravans, The Drift. ☎Elsworth 280.

🚋🚐C **Peterborough** Whiteley Caravans (NCC), 1270 Lincoln Road, Werrington, PE4 6LG. ☎71666.

CHESHIRE
🚐 **Altrincham** NADAS Ltd., Forest Edge, Charcoal Rd., Bowdon. ☎061 928 7430.

🚐C **Frodsham** Peter Crooks Enterprises, The Mews, Vicarage Lane. ☎33520.

CLEVELAND
▲C **Middlesbrough** Blacks Camping and Leisure Ltd., 107 Linthorpe Road. ☎242052.

CORNWALL
🚋 **Redruth** GB Caravans (NCC), Scorrier. ☎St Day 820254.

🚋 **St Austell** Mount Caravans Ltd. (NCC), The Caravan and Camping Centre, Holmbush. ☎5056.

CUMBRIA
🚐 **Whitehaven** SMT Sales Service Co. Ltd., High St. ☎2697/8.

DERBYSHIRE
🚐 **Castle Donington** Wilsons Motor Caravan Centre, Station Road, DE7 2NJ. ☎0332 810085.

🚋C **Derby** Spondon Caravan Centre (NCC), Nottingham Road, Spondon DE2 7NJ. ☎0332 662727.

DEVON
🚋C **Ashburton** Ashburn Caravans (NCC), Chuley Road. ☎52377.

🚐C **Newton Abbot** Eggintons Self Drive Hire Ltd., Bank Street. ☎4422.

▲C **Plymouth** Blacks Camping and Leisure Ltd., 109 New George Street, PL1 1RG. ☎29551.

▲C **Plymouth** West Country Camping and Leisure Centres, 192/194 Keyham Road. ☎57219 and 21883.

DORSET
🚐C **Bournemouth** Amble Motor Caravan Hire, 1 Seafield Drive, Southbourne, BH6 5LZ. ☎Daytime 522028. Evenings/Weekends 424560.

🚐 **Bournemouth** Carefree Caravans International, 9 Wycliffe Road, BH9 1JP. ☎510386.

🚋C **Christchurch** Green Pennant Caravans (NCC), 123 Somerford Road. ☎3657.

DURHAM
🚋C **Bishop Auckland** Gailey Caravans Ltd. (NCC), St Helens. ☎Auckland 603003.

ESSEX
🚐C **Epping** Godfrey Davis Caravan Hire Ltd. (NCC), High Street. ☎73281.

🚐C **Hornchurch** Hireway (Sales and Service) Ltd., Motor Caravan Specialists, King House, Elm Park Avenue, RM12 4RS. ☎43782/44791.

GLOUCESTERSHIRE
🚋C **Gloucester** Aldington Caravans (NCC), Minsterworth. ☎75353.

HAMPSHIRE
🚐C **Eastleigh** Martins Self Drive Service Ltd., Winchester House School Lane, Chandlers Ford, SO5 3YL. ☎04215 68386. (3 weeks minimum hire.)

▲ **Fareham** Continental Tent Hire and Sales Service Ltd., 137 Gosport Road, PO16 2QA. ☎0329 280697/235303.

🚋C **Hartley Wintney** John Adams Caravan Centre (NCC), A30 Road, Murrell Green. ☎Hook 2576.

🚋 **Portsmouth** Gailey Caravan Ltd. (NCC), Portsmouth Sales Centre, London Road, Purbrook. ☎070 18 74921.

▲ **Ringwood** Forsyth Bunch Camping Hire, 133 Southampton Road. ☎04254 4239.

▲ **Southampton** Fairfield Caravans, Southampton Road, Hythe, SO4 5ZA. ☎0703 552421. *Small ridge and frame only.*

Hire firm gazetteer

HEREFORD AND WORCESTER

C **Stourport on Severn** Stourport Caravans (NCC), Vale Road. ☎0299 32341.

C **Wythall** Birches Caravans (NCC), 423 Alcester Road, Birmingham, B47 6JL, West Midlands. ☎0564 826931.

HERTFORDSHIRE

C **Broxbourne** Manor Caravans (Wormley) Ltd. (NCC), 74 High Road, Wormley. ☎099-24 41616/9.

C **Elstree** Godfrey Davis Caravans Ltd. (NCC), Stirling Corner (A1/A411). ☎01 207 2020.

AC **Watford** Culverhouse, 73 Gammons Lane. ☎44100.

HUMBERSIDE

C **Barton on Humber** Sally Onion Motor Caravan Hire, 20 Whitecross St. ☎32134.

AC **Hull** Blacks Camping and Leisure Ltd., 21 King Edward St., HU2 2RL. ☎223851.

KENT

C **Ashford** The Aldington Caravan Group (NCC), Aldington. ☎Aldington 462/3.

C **Herne Bay** Arthur Fitt Caravans (NCC), Sweechbridge Road, Hillborough. ☎3848.

C **Margate** Margate Motor Caravan Centre, Addiscombe Road. ☎0843 291456.

Stanford nr Ashford TK Caravans, Stone St., ☎ Sellindge 2052.

C **Ramsgate** STS Transport, 84-96 Hereson Road, CT11 7DU. ☎582235.

C **Tunbridge Wells** Fernden Caravans (NCC), Frant Station, TN3 9BL. ☎Frant 456.

Tunbridge Wells Tolhurst Service Garage Ltd., 69 Calverley Road. ☎25671.

LANCASHIRE

AC **Burnley** H Fitzpatrick Co. Ltd., 150-154 St James St. ☎23096.

Burnley Whitfords Caravan Centre (NCC), off Marlborough St., Healeywood Industrial Estate. ☎20029.

C **Oldham** Mayfair Caravans Ltd. (NCC), Manchester Road. ☎061 624 9331.

C **Preston** Preston Caravans, Croston Road, Lostock Hall, PR5 3JY. ☎35093.

C **Todmorden** MG Caravan Co. Ltd., Burnley Road. ☎2832.

LEICESTERSHIRE

C **Leicester** AP Hire, 2 High St., Whetstone. ☎863063.

AC **Leicester** Blacks Camping and Leisure Ltd., 121 Granby St., LE1 6EX. ☎20145.

C **Leicester** Gailey Caravans Ltd. (NCC), 479-489 Aylestone Road, Aylestone, ☎832342.

C **Loughborough** Times Caravans Ltd. (NCC), 26 The Rushes. ☎66341.

LINCOLNSHIRE

A **Lincoln** Lincoln Sports and Camping Co. Ltd., The Quarry, Grantham Road, Waddington LN5 9PQ. ☎720792.

LONDON (GREATER)

C Airport Vehicle Hire Ltd., Biggin Hill Airport, Biggin Hill, Kent. ☎095 94 72279.

AC W Birchall, 185 Old Oak Road, East Acton W3. ☎01-743 2503.

AC Blacks Camping and Leisure Ltd., 53/54 Rathbone Place, W1P 1AN. ☎01-636 6645/6.

AC Blacks Camping and Leisure Ltd., 10/11 The Broadway, Catford, SE6. ☎01-690 6364.

AC Blacks Camping and Leisure Ltd., 146 Holborn, London, EC1 2NJ. ☎01-405 4426.

AC Blacks Camping and Leisure Ltd., 146/8 The Grove, Stratford, E15 1NS. ☎01-534 6547.

AC Blacks Camping and Leisure Ltd., 100 Haydons Road, Wimbledon, SW19 1AW. ☎01-542 1088.

C Car Hire International Ltd., 23 Swallow St., Piccadilly, W1R 7HD. ☎01-734 7661. Telex 23761.

AC Crystal Palace Camping, 5-11 Church Road, Upper Norwood, SE19 2TF. ☎01-653 6890.

AC Eatons Outdoor Centre, 100 Haydons Road, Wimbledon, SW19. ☎01-542 1088.

C Hammerton Caravans (NCC), Gallows Corner, Romford. ☎040 23 41017/41597/70353.

AC Greenwood and Sons, 179-180 Forest Lane, Forest Gate, E7 9BB. ☎01-534 1918.

C Morleys of Kingston Ltd., 64/74 Cambridge Road, Kingston upon Thames, KT1 3LB. ☎01-549 1351.

C The Motorhome Centre Ltd., 21 Elborough Road, South Norwood, SE25. ☎01-654 1168.

C Stevens Travel Ltd., 94 High Street, Hampton Hill, Middlesex, TW12 1PA. ☎01-977 2117.

C Owners Club Hire, Elwood Street, Highbury, London, N5. ☎01-226 3181.

C Turners (Motor Caravan Hire) Ltd., 11a Barry Road, East Dulwich, SE22 0HX. ☎01-693 1132.

MANCHESTER (GREATER)

AC **Ashton-under-Lyne** Millin Camping Services, 292 Oldham Road, OL7 9BA. ☎061-330 3807.

C **Ashton-under-Lyne** Shipleys, Dale Street. ☎061-330 2054 and 4790.

AC 1020 **Manchester** Blacks Camping and Leisure Ltd., 200 Deansgate, M3 3NN. ☎061-833 0349.

AC **Bolton** Howards (Bolton) Ltd., 235 Blackburn Road. ☎0204 28729 and 34379.

Cheadle Hulme Northern Caravans (NCC), Earl Road, Cheadle, SK8 6QE. ☎061-485 8611. Telex 669740.

MERSEYSIDE

AC **Liverpool** Blacks Camping and Leisure Ltd., 54 Hanover St., L1 4AF. ☎051-709 1023.

Liverpool Liverpool Caravans Ltd. (NCC), Chester High Road, Heswall, Wirral, L60 3SQ. ☎051-342 3759.

AC **Liverpool** Roberts Motor Caravans, Pier Head 3. ☎051-227 3841.

MIDLANDS (WEST)

AC **Birmingham** Blacks Camping and Outdoor Leisure Ltd., 34 Edgbaston Shopping Centre, B16 8SJ. ☎021 454 8771.

C **Coventry** F. Pedley and Sons, Lockhurst Lane. ☎82221.

See also Hereford and Worcestershire, Wythall.

NORFOLK

C **Kings Lynn** Peter Guest Ltd., Horsley's Fields. ☎62011.

C **Kings Lynn** H. John Mallet Ltd. (NCC), Caravan Centre, Hardwick Road, PE30 4HT. ☎3876.

C **Norwich** Norwich Caravans (NCC), H. J. Mallet (Norwich) Ltd., Norfolk Caravan Centre, Showground Garage, Dereham Road, Costessey, NOR 45J. ☎742317.

C **Norwich** Whiteley Caravans, Bishopbridge Road, Ketts Hill, NR1 4ES. ☎0603 21640.

C **Great Yarmouth** J. S. Carter Vehicle Hire, 2 Long Lane, off Beccles Road, Bradwell, NR31 8PR. ☎61702.

Hire firm gazetteer

NORTHUMBERLAND

Berwick upon Tweed G & E Marshall (Caravans), (NCC), Ord House, Caravan Park, East Ord. ☎5288.

Morpeth George Hartley Caravans (NCC), West Moor, Felton. ☎ Felton 367 and 437.

NOTTINGHAMSHIRE

C **Nottingham** Gailey Caravans Ltd. (NCC), Nottingham Road, Stapleford. ☎ Sandacre 397657.

▲C **Nottingham** Blacks Camping and Leisure Ltd., Shakespeare St., NG1 4FD. ☎43165.

Nottingham Midland Counties Caravans Ltd. (NCC), Colwick Road, Colwick. ☎247246/7.

OXFORDSHIRE

C **Oxford** Humphris (Oxford) Ltd., 72 Rose Hill. ☎774696.

Tiddington Gailey Caravan Co. Ltd., Oxford Road, OX9 2LL. ☎Ickford 566.

C **Witney** Sound Service (Oxford) Ltd., 55 West End. ☎Daytime 04981/5362. Evening/Weekend, Sandlake 287.

SOMERSET

Bridgewater Lakeside Caravans (NFSO), 121 Taunton Road. ☎3352.

Taunton Walford Caravan Distributors Ltd. (NCC), Walford Cross. ☎ West Monkton 412616/7.

STAFFORDSHIRE

Gailey Gailey Caravan Co. (NCC), Gailey Sales Centre, Nr Stafford, ST19 5PP. ☎790246.

▲C **Stoke** Blacks Camping and Leisure Ltd., 42 Marsh Street, Hanley. ☎22870.

SURREY

C **Egham** Godfrey Davis Caravans Ltd. (NCC), Station Road. ☎2207/8/9.

C **Epsom** Wilsons Motor Caravan Centre, Nonsuch Estate, East Street, KT17 1EH. ☎037 27 28391. Telex 8812150.

Gomshall McAllisters Caravan Sales Ltd. (NCC), Station Approach. ☎048 641 2016.

▲ **Reigate** HSS Hire Group Ltd., Warenne House, 31 London Road. ☎49441.

▲C **Sutton** Blacks Camping and Leisure Ltd., 250 High St., SM1 1PA. ☎01 642 8655.

SUSSEX (EAST)

Brighton Autohomes, 69 Upland Road, Hollingdean, BN1 7FA. ☎552998.

C **Eastbourne** Car Comfort Hire Ltd., Marine Road. ☎30636. Telex 877152.

▲C **Hove** Hove Surplus Stores, 12 Boundary Road. ☎417455.

C **St Leonards on Sea** Channel Hire, 241 Wishing Tree Road. ☎Hastings 420777.

C **Uckfield** The Aldington Caravan Group (NCC), London Road. ☎4151/2.

C **Warninglid** Godfrey Davis Caravan Hire (NCC), Brighton Road. ☎317/8/9.

SUSSEX (WEST)

C **Chichester** The Aldington Caravan Group (NCC), A27, Nutbourne. ☎Emsworth 2925.

C **Haywards Heath** Caraventure, Teagues Farm, Scaynes Hill. ☎Scaynes Hill 330.

TYNE AND WEAR

▲C **Newcastle upon Tyne** Blacks Camping and Leisure Ltd., 48/52 Grainger St. ☎0632 23132.

Newcastle upon Tyne Gosforth Motor Co. Ltd., off Hawthorn Road, High Street, Gosford, NE3 4DF. ☎ Gosford 858173.

C **Newcastle upon Tyne** United British Caravans (Northumbrian) Ltd. (NCC), Sandy Lane, Wideopen, NE3 5HE. ☎089-426 3156.

WARWICKSHIRE

Meriden Gailey Caravan Company (NCC), Meriden Sales Centre, CV7 7JS. ☎22292.

YORKSHIRE (NORTH)

▲ **Richmond** Teesside Caravans (NCC), Station Display Ground, Catterick Bridge. ☎818391.

C **York** H. C. Fawcett, Caravan Centre, 201 Acomb Road, Acomb. ☎798321.

YORKSHIRE (SOUTH)

Barnsley P and S Caravan Centres (Barnsley) Ltd., Old Mill Lane, S71 1LS. ☎5838.

▲C **Sheffield** Blacks Camping and Leisure Ltd., 1 Earl St., S1 4PY. ☎23878.

C **Sheffield** Gailey Caravan Co. Ltd. (NCC), 326 Middlewood Road, S6 1TF. ☎344597.

YORKSHIRE (WEST)

C **Bradford 4** Quigley's Hire, 9 Tyersal Close. ☎662321 & 35369.

Huddersfield Stafford and Co. (Caravans Ltd.) (NCC), Kirkheaton, HD5 0PQ. ☎23857/26190.

▲ **Leeds** Blacks Camping and Leisure Ltd., 21/22 Grand Arcade. ☎458634.

Leeds Magnetic Caravans, Water Lane, LS11 5PR. ☎30901/2.

▲C **Leeds** Skitts Euro Camping, 90 Kirkstall Road, LS3 1LT. ☎452021.

C **Pudsey** Four Seasons (Leisure) Ltd., Springfield, Bagley Lane, Farsley. ☎564373/4.

DOGS-WARNING

Visitors should not bring pets of any kind with them to Britain unless they are prepared for the animals to go into lengthy quarantine. Owing to the continuing threat of rabies, penalties for ignoring the regulations are extremely severe.

Clubs and organisations

Wales

GLAMORGAN (SOUTH)

Bridgend Caravan Care, Kenfig Hill. ☎742506.

C **Cardiff** Blacks Camping and Leisure Ltd., 17/19 Castle Street, CF1 2BT. ☎44034.

GLAMORGAN (WEST)

C **Cardiff** Gailey Caravan Company Ltd., Cowbridge Road West, Culverhouse Cross. ☎593276.

Scotland

CENTRAL

Stirling Borestone Caravans Ltd. (NCC), 96 Glasgow Road, FK7 0PQ. ☎811767.

DUMFRIES AND GALLOWAY

Dumfries Cumbria Leisure, Brasswell, Annan Road. ☎Dumfries 2917/3399.

C **Gretna** The Braids Caravans, Annan Road, CA6 4DQ. ☎409

GRAMPIAN

Aberdeen Milletts Stores Ltd., 44 Union Street, AB1 1BD. ☎23175.

LOTHIAN

Dalkeith Scott's Touring Caravans (NCC), Mayfield. ☎031-663 1471.

Edinburgh Blacks Camping and Leisure Ltd., 13-14 Elm Row, EH7 4AA. ☎031-556 3491.

Stoneyburn Knowe Park Caravans (NCC), Main St., By Bathgate. ☎259.

STRATHCYLDE

Glasgow Andersons Ltd., Newton Mearns, 268 Ayr Rd., G77 6AF. ☎041-639 2271.

C **Glasgow** Blacks Camping and Leisure Ltd., 132 St Vincent St., G2 5HF. ☎041-248 3979.

Glasgow Glen Caravan Co. (Glasgow) Ltd. (NCC), 1920 London Road, Shettleston. ☎041-778 5212.

C **Glasgow** Halley Caravans Ltd. (NCC), Glasgow Road, Milngavie. ☎041-956 1088.

Glasgow Millar, 11 Hayston Road, Kirkintilloch, G66 1BP. ☎041-776 2807.

Milngavie T and S Liddell Ltd., Fairview Garage, G62 6BY. ☎041-956 2255.

C **Dundee** Blacks Camping and Leisure Ltd., 93/117 Princess St., DD4 6DA. ☎43766.

TAYSIDE

C **Perth** Gloabtrotter Caravans, 166 Glasgow Road. ☎26415.

C **Scone** Cameron Motors (Scone) Ltd., 58/60 Perth Road. ☎Perth 51276/9.

SOURCES OF FURTHER INFORMATION

Clubs and Organisations

The Caravan Club, East Grinstead House, East Grinstead, West Sussex RH19 1UA.
Motor Caravanner's Club, 52 Wolseley Road, London N8 8RP.
The Camping Club, 11 Lower Grosvenor Place, London SW1W 0EY.
The National Caravan Council Ltd, 43 High Street, Weybridge, Surrey KT13 8BT.

Further information can also be obtained from any AA Regional Office at the addresses given below: they will deal with most aspects and will put you directly in touch with specialist departments if necessary.

SOUTH-EAST REGION
AA Regional Headquarters
Fanum House, 7 High Street, **Teddington**, Middlesex TW11 8EQ. 01-977 3200.

MIDLANDS REGION
AA Regional Headquarters
Fanum House, Dogkennel Lane, **Halesowen**, W Midlands B63 3BT. 021-550 4721.

NORTH REGION
AA Regional Headquarters
Fanum House, Station Road, Cheadle Hulme, **Cheadle**, Cheshire SK8 7BS. 061-485 6188.

WEST AND WALES REGION
AA Regional Headquarters
Fanum House, Park Row, **Bristol** BS1 5LY. Bristol 297272.

SCOTLAND AND NORTHERN IRELAND REGION
AA Regional Headquarters
Fanum House, Erskine Harbour, **Erskine**, Renfrewshire PA8 6AT. 041-812 0144.

Ask the AA 1980

Let the AA take the effort out of holiday route-planning. For the best routes to anywhere in the British Isles, complete the form below, and send to your nearest regional headquarters (for regional addresses, see *Members' Handbook*).

BLOCK CAPITALS PLEASE

Name

Address (to which route should be posted)

AA Membership No.

Telephone exchange and number (home) (work)

Routes

Unless otherwise requested, the *quickest* route will be provided. When appropriate, this will be in the form of a throughroute map.

From **To** (place and **County**)

Day, date, and time of travelling

Mark X if a caravan is being towed

State type of route (scenic, most direct, touring)

State any other special requirements

The above details may affect the route provided

Confidential report form 1980

The purpose of this form is for readers to voice their complaints – if they feel that a campsite they have visited does not come up to standard.
The form should be completed in conjunction with the list on page 255.

Please send to:
The Automobile Association
Hotel and Information Services Department
Fanum House
Basingstoke Hants RG21 2EA

BLOCK CAPITALS PLEASE

Name of site

Address of site

Arrival date

Length of stay

I do/do not agree to my name being used in the event of any correspondence with the site concerned.

Your name

Your address

Membership No.

Do you agree with the pennant classification? Yes ☐ No ☐

What is your qualitative assessment if different from that given? (For details see page 75). □ ○ △

Did you speak to the site warden about any complaint? Yes ☐ No ☐

Comments

Site questionnaire 1980

Please complete the questionnaire below and send off with the report form.
Tick for yes and cross for no.

Name of site

▶

- Any restrictions on entry ☐
- Pitches available as indicated in the guide ☐
- Spacing satisfactory ☐
- Drinking water supply satisfactory ☐
- Waste water disposal arrangements satisfactory ☐
- Site clean and tidy ☐
- Lavatories satisfactory ☐
- Reasonable provision of garbage bins ☐
- Garbage bins cleaned out regularly ☐
- Satisfactory access roads and entrances ☐
- Ground drainage seemed satisfactory ☐
- Condition of pitches satisfactory ☐
- Satisfactory fire precautions apparent ☐
- Presence of first-aid facilities and emergency telephone numbers signposted ☐

▶▶

- Wash rooms open ☐
- Wash rooms clean ☐
- Chemical closet disposal point with rinsing tap available ☐
- Wash hand basins with satisfactory hot water supply ☐
- Warden available at certain times ☐

▶▶▶

- Shower/baths with satisfactory hot water supply ☐
- Deep sinks for clothes washing ☐
- Electric shaver points and mirrors available ☐
- Toilet block lit throughout night ☐
- Daily facilities for purchase of food, camping requisites, etc (off-site facilities within 100yd included) ☐
- Warden available during day/on call during night ☐

▶▶▶▶

- Permanent shop open daily (if licensed for 7 days) ☐
- Signposted reception area ☐
- Signposted late arrivals enclosure ☐
- First-aid facilities ☐
- Fenced children's playground ☐
- Evidence of site landscaping ☐

▶▶▶▶▶

- 24hr supervision by wardens ☐
- Café or restaurant available ☐
- Satisfactory automated laundry ☐
- Public telephone ☐
- Indoor recreation for children ☐
- Separate car park ☐
- Heated wash room on a site open between November and March ☐
- Recreational amenities of acceptable standard ☐

The site we should see 1980

If you are a camper and/or caravanner and you know of a site which you think should be in this guide, and which we have not listed, please complete the form below, and send to:

The Automobile Association
Hotel and Information Services Department
Fanum House
Basingstoke Hants RG21 2EA

BLOCK CAPITALS PLEASE

Name of site

Address

Your name

Your address

What you like about the site

If you know a picnic site, nature trail, etc., which may be of interest please give details.

If you are a site owner or warden, your site is not listed in this guide and you would like it to be next year, please complete the form below and send to the address as above.

Name of site owner

Your name (if different from above)

Name of site

Address of site

Location of site

Has your site ever been inspected by an AA Inspector Yes ☐ No ☐

How long has the site been open years months

Are there at least six pitches available for the touring camper/caravanner on your site Yes ☐ No ☐

Comments (cont)

Please complete questionnaire opposite

For office use only

Head office action

Regional office action

Acknowledged

Recorded

Action

Date